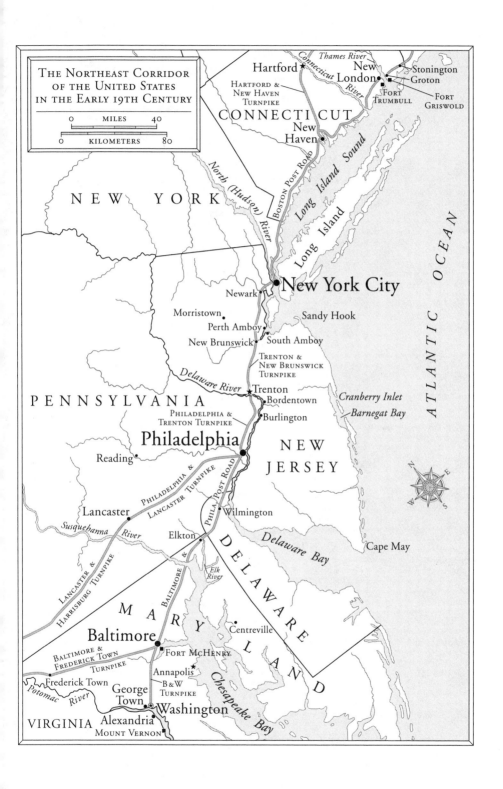

THE NORTHEAST CORRIDOR
OF THE UNITED STATES
IN THE EARLY 19TH CENTURY

MILES 0 — 40

KILOMETERS 0 — 80

Thames River

Hartford ★

New London
Stonington
Groton
Fort Griswold
Fort Trumbull

Connecticut River

HARTFORD &
NEW HAVEN
TURNPIKE

CONNECTICUT

New Haven ●

NEW YORK

North (Hudson) River

Boston Post Road

Long Island Sound

Long Island

New York City ●

ATLANTIC OCEAN

Newark ●

Sandy Hook

Morristown ●

Perth Amboy ●

New Brunswick ●
South Amboy

TRENTON &
NEW BRUNSWICK
TURNPIKE

Delaware River

Trenton ★
Bordentown ●

Cranberry Inlet

Barnegat Bay

PENNSYLVANIA

PHILADELPHIA &
TRENTON TURNPIKE

Burlington ●

Philadelphia ●

NEW
JERSEY

Reading ●

PHILADELPHIA &
LANCASTER TURNPIKE

Phila. Post Road

Lancaster ●

Wilmington ●

Susquehanna River

Elkton ●

Delaware Bay

Cape May

LANCASTER &
HARRISBURG TURNPIKE

BALTIMORE &

Elk River

DELAWARE

MARYLAND

Centreville ●

Baltimore ●
Fort McHenry ■

BALTIMORE &
FREDERICK TOWN
TURNPIKE

Annapolis ★

B & W
TURNPIKE

Chesapeake Bay

Frederick Town ●

Potomac River

George
Town ✦
Washington

VIRGINIA

Alexandria ●

MOUNT VERNON ■

A Long Time Ago

In a Young Country

Called

The United States of America

There was a Man

Who had a Dream

The Fulfillment of Which

Would Change the World

Forever

STEAM COFFIN

Captain Moses Rogers
and
The Steamship *Savannah*
Break the Barrier

JOHN LAURENCE BUSCH

Hodos Historia

Published by Hodos Historia LLC.
Manufactured in the United States of America.

LIBRARY OF CONGRESS
CATALOGING-IN-PUBLICATION DATA

Busch, John Laurence
Steam Coffin: Captain Moses Rogers and The Steamship *Savannah*
Break the Barrier / John Laurence Busch
p.   cm.
Includes bibliographical references and index.
1. Rogers, Moses, 1779–1821   2. *Savannah* (Steamship)
3. United States—Maritime History—19th century
4. United States—Technological History—19th century
I. Title.
Library of Congress Control Number: 2009942158.

ISBN-13: 978-1-893616-00-4.
ISBN-10: 1-893-616-00-2.

Front Dust Jacket Art: *Searching For Ireland,*
by Samuel Conlogue, Copyright © 2010 Hodos Historia LLC.
Back Dust Jacket Portrait: Captain Moses Rogers,
by an unknown artist, circa 1820.

All maps by David Lindroth, Copyright © 2010 Hodos Historia LLC.
Contemporary drawings of the *Savannah* by Jean Baptiste Marestier.

NOV 29 2010

FOR MY PARENTS,
Caroline Billhime Busch
and
Laurence Edward Busch Jr.

CONTENTS

All distances noted throughout the book are in statute miles.

All quotations retain their original spelling and punctuation, unless indicated in the Source Notes.

CHAPTER ONE

FIRST, YET AGAIN

THERE WERE at least four kinds of people looking at the strange vessel tied up along Charleston's Cooper River that Wednesday morning—

First, there were the prospective passengers, who knew full-well they were about to participate in something that would have been thought impossible little more than a decade before;

Second, there were the passengers' families and friends, who came down to see them off, probably wondering whether or not their loved ones would arrive at their destination as planned;

Third were the shareholders of the Charleston Steam Boat Company, which had built this floating contraption, the recently-christened Steam Boat *Charleston*;

And finally were the many onlookers, who had come down to the wharves that December 10th in the year 1817 to see the *Charleston* do something never before attempted, and that was introduce the first steamboat passenger service between Charleston, South Carolina and Savannah, Georgia.

The Charleston Steam Boat Company had been formed the previous year to do just that. Some enterprising investors from Philadelphia had organized the venture, offering to provide at least one-half of the $25,000 in capital necessary, plus some experienced workmen to help build the steamboat. The Philadelphians also would supply the steam engine.

This had been too good an offer to pass up. These new steamboats, already operating successfully up North and out West for several years, had proven their worth to both the traveling public and investors alike. By predictably pushing their way through waters that previously could be traversed only with the aid of oars or sails, steamboats were accomplishing things never before possible in the history of the maritime world—

They could leave on schedule;

They could arrive on schedule;

Put plainly, these steamboats could place a person at a specific location at a given time with a degree of certainty that was virtually unknown in the human experience. The potential effects of such predictability on people's lives could be enormous, and the Charlestonians wanted to be a part of it.

* * *

When the sign-up books for investing in the Charleston Steam Boat Company were opened, back in June of 1816, the shares allotted for sale at Charleston had been immediately taken up.

Soon thereafter, construction began on the hull of the Company's first steamboat, at a Cooper River shipyard near Harleston's Green. By December of that same year, the 20-horsepower steam engine, built at Philadelphia by engine-maker Daniel Large, had arrived by ship from that city, much of it carefully stowed in 21 boxes, 3 barrels, and 10 packages, the whole of which weighed some ten tons. The entire apparatus had been manufactured specifically for installation in the hull under construction, because, at that time, virtually every steamboat built was unique. This new means of transport remained so new that its promoters were constantly taking lessons learned from their last steamboat and applying them to the new one on the drawing boards.

The ensuing winter of 1817 had been spent finishing the wooden hull. By early March, it was ready to be launched, at which time the vessel gained its name, being christened the *Charleston*. It took most of the spring to install the machinery. By early June, the *Charleston* was complete, just one year after the money had been raised.

The summer and most of the autumn of 1817 had been spent testing the steamboat on short ferry runs between Charleston and Sullivan's Island, at the mouth of Charleston Bay. With the success of these trials, and the end of the hot weather season, this new craft was ready for a new challenge.

* * *

The steamboat *Charleston* floating before the crowd that December 10th was a most impressive sight. She measured some 98 feet in *length* upon the deck, and 20 feet in *breadth* from side to side, excluding the paddlewheels. Her *depth*, or *draft* (which is the measure of how deep the water has to be for the hull to float), was only 6 feet, 2 inches. This last measure was the most important of all, for it would allow the *Charleston* to easily navigate through the shallow waters she would encounter along the coast.

Starting at the front (or *bow*) of the vessel, one could see some sort of bird-like figurehead, pointing the way forward.

Midway back along the hull were *paddlewheels*, jutting out from both sides. The upper half of each wheel was covered by a *paddlebox*, which was a semi-circular wooden housing that kept any kicked-up water created by the wheels' movement from splashing onto the deck.

Rising out of the middle of the deck itself was a tall, black tubular stack, puffing dark-gray smoke.

Also hard-fastened to the deck was a single wooden sailing mast, with canvas sails wrapped (or *furled*) around it. If the new technology broke down, the crew could revert to the old method for power.

Finally, at the rear (or *stern*) of the deck was the *tiller*, a long, horizontal wooden pole connected to the *Charleston's rudder*, which steered the steamboat as it moved through the water.

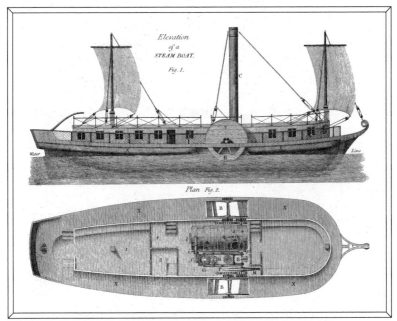

An Early Steamboat.

Since the *Charleston* would be exposed to salt water on the run to Savannah, her promoters had decided that she needed to be built of the best materials. Her hull was made of *live oak*, a wood which came from trees of the same name that were native to South Carolina and Georgia. Oak of any kind was considered excellent for building the hulls of vessels. This is because oak is a very dense wood, and the denser the wood, the harder it is for water to penetrate it. Live oak was considered the best of all, simply because it is the densest within the oak family. Much of the rest of the *Charleston*'s exterior was made from cedar, another wood well-known for its resistance to the ravages of rot.

In addition, the lower part of the steamboat's outer hull was covered with a thin copper plating. Using this virtually rust-free metal served several purposes. First, it kept pesky little water worms—called *teredos*—from boring into the wooden hull. Second, the copper's smooth surface improved the speed of the vessel as it slid through the water. And third, it made scraping barnacles off the hull a much easier task.

While final preparations for the *Charleston*'s departure were proceeding above deck, down below, several crewmen were busy "getting steam up." This was done by tossing split logs of yellow pinewood onto the fires at the bottom of the steam engine's copper *boilers*. Sitting above these fires, in separate compartments of each boiler, was water. As the fires below heated these compartments, the water inside them began to boil, creating steam. This steam could escape through piping at the top of the boilers, except when the valves built into them were closed, as they were at that point. With the valves shut, the boilers were, in effect, giant plugged tea kettles, the steam pressure in them slowly building. When called for, the crew would open these valves, and turn this trapped steam into the new motive power.

Once the baggage and packets of mail had been loaded, the *Charleston*'s bell rang out to signal her imminent departure. Those willing to risk the inaugural journey to Savannah stepped aboard, including a man named Crocker.

This was probably Doddridge Crocker, a 48-year-old native of Connecticut who was one of the steamboat's shareholders. His office, or *counting house*, served as the focal point for the Company's activities. Just about everything—from the trading of Company shares, to the receipt of contract proposals for the *Charleston*'s fuel supply, to the purchase of passenger tickets—took place at Crocker's counting house. His presence on this maiden trip to Savannah sent an important message: if an owner trusted the steamboat to make a safe journey, so too could the public.

There to see him off must have been a number of his fellow shareholders, including John Haslett, a 43-year-old native of Ireland who had made good as a merchant in his adopted city. With a residence on the prestigious East Bay and a seat on the city council, Haslett was one of the most prominent owners of the *Charleston*.

A second clanging of the bell signaled the final call for all aboard. Any remaining customers crossed over from the wharf, and joined those already on deck. The total passenger count was one dozen, supported by a crew of eight or so.

At ten minutes past 8 o'clock, the captain ordered the deckhands to cast off. Then, he ordered the engine into action.

Down below, the steamboat's engineer opened the boiler valves, allowing the trapped steam to be released through narrow piping that led to a large iron *cylinder*, which looked like a tall drum. Inside this hollow cylinder was a *piston*, which was a disk that fit snugly around the sides of the drum-shaped interior, and acted like an internal lid. When enough steam from the boilers entered the top end of the cylinder, that expansive pressure pushed the piston to the bottom end; then the steam at the top was released, and new steam from the boilers was channeled into the lower end of the cylinder, pushing the piston back up to the top. By this repeated action, the piston was moved up and down within the cylinder.

Attached to the top of the piston was a long vertical rod, the next link in the power train. As the piston moved up and down within the cylinder, this *piston rod* moved with it. The rod passed through a small airtight opening in the top of the cylinder. At its far end outside the cylinder, the piston rod was attached to an additional mechanism, and while this varied depending upon the design, it was usually a *crank* or a series of *gears*, which were turned as the rod moved up and down. The gears' motion then turned the steamboat's long horizontal *axle*, and the large *paddlewheels* mounted on either end of it, just outside the hull. As the paddlewheels turned, the individual blades of the wheels (or *paddleboards*) sequentially pushed the steamboat through the water.

That the entire apparatus worked to such positive effect was—to this first generation who saw it—simply incredible.

As the clanking engine came to life, the grayish smoke puffing from the stack suddenly poured out in torrents, and the paddlewheels slowly began to turn, churning water up into the paddleboxes. Slowly, the spinning wheels pushed the steamboat away from the crowded wharf.

Once clear of the pier, the *Charleston* was turned southward, down the blue Cooper River. Off her right (or *starboard*) side, the passengers took in a splendid view of the city's wharves, houses, and church steeples. These structures soon gave way to the Battery, a V-shaped stone fort at the southern tip of Charleston. After the steamboat had pushed past that bastion, the passengers could look northward, up the Ashley River, and at the swampy, undeveloped western side of this city on a peninsula.

Directly ahead, to the south, lay the broad waters of Charleston Bay. It was traveling across this body that the steamboat had spent the summer and autumn, ferrying passengers the 4 miles to Sullivan's Island, right at the mouth of the Bay. Local residents' desire to escape the city's heat, and take in the cool sea breezes of Sullivan's, had kept the *Charleston* very busy.

Charleston Bay.

But serving as a summer ferry to Sullivan's Island was only half of this steamboat's purpose. With the hot weather over, and her worthiness proven, the *Charleston* was switching to her intended winter route. The voyage all the way down to Savannah, at about 100 miles, was a far longer and more dangerous trip.

In anticipation of the risks involved, the Charleston Steam Boat Company had seen fit to hire a new captain for its vessel midway through the ferry season. The shareholders had done so because they recognized that the upcoming service to Savannah would require a commander with special skills.

Such a captain was anything but ordinary. After all, it had been only 10 years since Robert Fulton and his *North River Steam Boat* proved that steam-powered vessels could not just work, but operate consistently and profitably. And by 1817, there were still but a handful of men who could claim any substantial experience operating these novelties.

The *Charleston's* newly-hired captain was one of those few.

Back in the summer of 1807, while the master of a coastal sailing sloop, he had witnessed the first runs of Fulton's *North River Steam Boat*, from New York City up to Albany, New York. That cathartic experience had given him the fever—*steamboat fever.*

By 1809, he had abandoned the age of sail, never to return, assuming command of the first viable all-American-made steamboat, called the *Phoenix.* He had then taken that vessel from New York out onto the Atlantic Ocean, carefully maneuvering it down the coast to Philadelphia, thereby completing the first ocean voyage by a steamboat in history. Based in the "City of Brotherly Love," he had run the *Phoenix* as the first successful steamboat service ever seen on the Delaware River.

In 1815, he had challenged the sea again, taking another steamboat, the *Eagle,* from Philadelphia down to the Chesapeake Bay, becoming only the second captain to bring such a vessel into Norfolk, Virginia. Shortly thereafter, he became the very first to ascend the James River in a steamboat, making it all the way to Richmond.

In 1816, he had dared the waves once again, maneuvering yet another steamer, the *New Jersey,* from the shipyards of Philadelphia down to the Chesapeake, successfully completing his third ocean voyage in a steamboat.

Through his own initiative, hard work and determination, this 38-year-old son of a Connecticut mariner and lumberyard owner had become not just one of the most experienced steamboat captains in the world, but a trailblazer in this new motive power.

His name was Moses Rogers.

Moses Rogers.

On this early December morning in 1817, he was doing it yet again, initiating the first steamboat service ever between Charleston and Savannah. The protected inland route that Moses planned to take would require him to snake his way through a number of shallow waterways, and across several ocean inlets, until he reached the Savannah River. The dangers would include snags, sandbars, and unpredictable conditions on the wide open bays exposed to the sea.

Beyond managing these hazards, it was also his obligation as captain to play host to the passengers. Moses had to make sure they were comfortable, and answer any questions they might have about the machinery, be it the paddlewheels, or the steam engine, or the boilers—*especially the boilers.* The fact that the traveling party on board was only twelve-strong spoke volumes. Most folks didn't want to risk their necks on any maiden voyage to Savannah. That this daring dozen probably had some questions about their safety, however carefully masked, would not be unusual.

Any concerns aside, there was plenty of pleasant scenery for the travelers to behold, as the steamboat pushed its way through waters

surrounded by lush, swampy flatlands, which were occasionally interrupted by large plantation fields of cotton and rice.

If the passengers tired of the view, they could go below deck to the
main cabin. There, a bartender was on duty to make them a drink;
they could take a seat, relax, and engage in the art of conversation.
Beyond talk of the steamboat's journey, discussions amongst the passengers and their host invariably turned to the state of the markets,
prices, and the promising future they saw for their young country.

* * *

Depending upon how one chose to count, 1817 was either the 41st
or 42nd year of independence for the United States of America. Since
its birth in 1776, the new American experiment had been forced to
confront obstacle after challenge after threat—

The Revolutionary War itself;

The difficult process of creating a country beyond a loose confed-
eration of States;

A "quasi-war" with France;

Friction with the native Indian tribes;

And most recently, a second nasty, divisive war with Britain, which
had ended just a few years earlier, in 1815.

It was only after the end of that second conflict with the Mother
Country that Americans finally got what they had been craving for
years: an economic boom. By 1817, just about every part and parcel
of the United States was experiencing unprecedented growth.

This boom was possible because the products that America had to
offer the world—the bounty of the land—were in great demand. The
country's ports were teeming with activity, as shiploads of wheat, corn,
rice, and tobacco were loaded for transport to Europe, the Caribbean,
and beyond. For the first time in more than two decades, the Europeans were at peace, and that continent's pent-up appetite for American crops seemed insatiable, driving their prices further and further
upward, to levels never seen before.

In addition to these tillable consumables, there was yet one other
relatively new member of the family of exportable crops which also
benefited from high demand, and that was cotton. The burgeoning
textile mills of Britain and France, combined with American Eli
Whitney's innovative cotton gin (which easily separated the seeds
from the fiber), made cotton farming a growth business. As the public

demand for cheaper, uniformly-made textiles grew, so too did the industrial demand for cotton.

As a result, once peace was restored on the oceans in 1815, the starved textile mills of Middle England and Upper France couldn't get enough of the stuff. The price for a pound of Upland Cotton had steadily increased, from about 15 cents at war's end to around 33 cents by December of 1817. The more prized Sea Island variety, which produced thinner, longer fiber strands for finer yarn, was fetching upwards of 50 cents per pound. Never before had cotton been worth so much, and never before had the American South been so prosperous.

As powerful as the boom was down South, it was only a part of the American promise just beginning to unfold.

Up North, major cities and towns continued to expand, and were seeing the erection of the first small wave of labor-saving factories and mills.

Out West, settlers were pushing further into the wilderness, invigorating a renewed expansion of America's political footprint, previously frozen by the late war. Indiana had become a State in 1816 (being the first admitted since Louisiana in 1812), and on the very day the steamboat *Charleston* was making her inaugural departure for Savannah—December 10th, 1817—the United States Senate was busy approving the admission of Mississippi as the 20th State to enter the Union. Still other federal territories had their own petitions before Congress, asking for Statehood.

The imperative for better communications with these lands in the West, as well as with the interiors of existing States, had become overwhelming. Part of the solution lay in a broad array of transportation projects, both public and private, to improve the flow of people and goods. Foremost among these efforts was the extension and improvement of the National Road, a federally-funded turnpike running from eastern Maryland through western Virginia to the Ohio River. Further north, the Pennsylvanians had nearly completed their own series of turnpikes to the Ohio, running from Philadelphia to Pittsburgh. Even more ambitious was the groundbreaking in upper New York earlier that summer for a State-financed canal of unprecedented length, intended to link the Hudson River with Lake Erie in the West.

Yet while the National Road, Pennsylvania's turnpikes, and the barely-begun Erie Canal were seen as valuable answers to the country's hunger for better transportation, there was another, entirely novel means of moving people and goods and mail that also held great promise. In fact, its promoters said that this *new mode of transport* held such incredible potential that it would not only change the country's relationship with the interior, but alter the entire national dynamic in ways never before imagined. And all that was needed to impress this point upon anyone at the time was to mention just one solitary new word—

"*Steam*boats."

* * *

By early afternoon, the *Charleston* had made it through the winding Dawhow ("Dáw-hoo") River, and entered the Pon Pon River, some 30 miles southwest of her home port. There, at eight minutes past 2 o'clock, Moses ordered the engine stopped and the anchor dropped, just off a swampy bend in the river called Block Island.

The reason for the pause was simple enough: the river level had fallen so low with the outgoing tide that proceeding any further was too dangerous. While the *Charleston*'s first voyage to Savannah benefited from the perceived safety of the inland river route, the steamboat still had to contend with sandbars and snags, made all the more perilous at low tide. Even though Captain Rogers was one of the leading and most aggressive proponents of these new steamboats, he was not reckless. The most important goal of this first trip to Savannah was to get there *safely*.

By the time the tide had turned sufficiently—around 6 o'clock that evening—it was too dark to proceed. All that those onboard could do was wait.

With the arrival of Thursday morning, and another rising tide, Moses ordered the anchor pulled up, and the paddlewheels set in motion. The *Charleston* pushed onward, down the twisting Pon Pon River, until she reached St. Helena Sound. Despite being exposed directly to the sea, the steamboat crossed the Sound without difficulty, and headed northwest and inland, into the Coosaw River. A few miles upstream, the *Charleston* was turned southwest, into a narrow, shallow creek, which separated Port Royal Island from Ladies Island.

After spending the late morning steaming past fields of orange and lemon trees, the *Charleston* and her passengers came upon the little town of Beaufort ("Byóo-fert"). Situated along a shallow coastal river some 10 miles from the ocean, Beaufort usually didn't receive

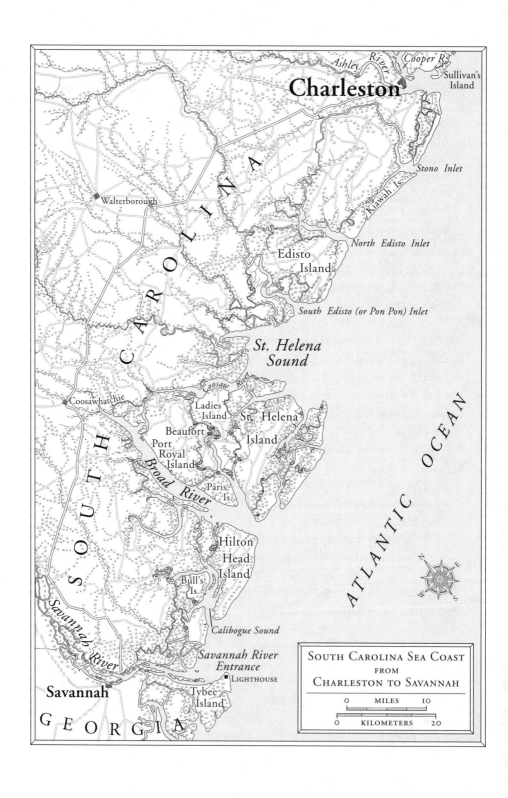

Ashley River
Cooper R.
Sullivan's Island
Charleston

Stono Inlet

Walterborough

Kiawah Is.

North Edisto Inlet

Edisto Island

CAROLINA

South Edisto (or Pon Pon) Inlet

St. Helena Sound

Coosaw River

Coosawhatchie

Ladies Island

St. Helena Island

Beaufort

Port Royal Island

Broad River

Paris Is.

SOUTH

Hilton Head Island

Bull's Is.

ATLANTIC OCEAN

N
E
W
S

Savannah River

Calibogue Sound

Savannah River Entrance
LIGHTHOUSE

Savannah

Tybee Island

GEORGIA

SOUTH CAROLINA SEA COAST
FROM
CHARLESTON TO SAVANNAH

0   MILES   10

0   KILOMETERS   20

waterborne visitors any larger than single-masted sailing sloops, or double-masted schooners. The only prior experience the townspeople had ever had with steamboats was back in 1816, when they had welcomed the Savannah-built *Enterprize*, as she passed through the area. Beyond that, the small port had not seen a steamboat since, and certainly not one promising to keep coming back.

So naturally enough, as the *Charleston* approached, a crowd of curious locals quickly gathered along Beaufort's waterfront. Once the steamboat had eased up to the public wharf, the engine was stopped, and the deckhands secured the vessel. The time was 1 o'clock in the afternoon, nearly 29 hours after the *Charleston's* departure from her home port.

This one and only intended stop was a perfect opportunity for Moses to show the people of Beaufort just what a steamboat could do. As soon as some additional passengers, their baggage, and the mail had come aboard, Captain Rogers ordered the crew to cast off, and the engine into action. Just 15 minutes after tying up, the *Charleston* was on her way. No master of a sailing vessel could ever guarantee such a swift turnaround.

For the next four hours and forty-five minutes, the *Charleston* churned further south, down the Port Royal River, across the Broad River, and then into a creek that separated Hilton Head Island from the mainland. A little further to the southwest, this creek emptied into a broader body of water, called Calibogue Sound.

It was at this point that the steamboat encountered what one observer described as "thick weather." Fog along the coastline, even on a late afternoon in December, was not unusual, and it must have been heavy enough to justify a pause. At 5 o'clock, Captain Rogers ordered the crew to stop the engine, and drop anchor.

The cautiousness Moses exhibited that second day, just as he had on the first, was not out of timidity. Rather, it was founded upon years of experience working with the earliest of successful steamboats, as well as contending with the public's perception of these new-fangled machines. It would be far better for the *Charleston* to arrive at her destination later than expected than not at all. Such knowledge was a result of the life Moses Rogers had chosen to lead, when, just a decade before, he had been present at the creation.

* * *

Born in New London, Connecticut back in 1779, Moses was the first child of Amos and Sarah Phillips Rogers, and as such, represented the beginning of a sixth generation of Americans in his family. He was descended from James Rogers, who had emigrated from England in 1635, and settled in New London. By the time Moses made his appearance nearly a century and a half later, the roots of the Rogers clan in southeastern Connecticut were both broad and deep.

When Moses was a young boy, his father purchased some land in the town of Groton ("Gráw-tun"), which was on the east side of the Thames ("Thaymz") River, directly across from New London. It was in Groton that Amos and Sarah Rogers settled, and raised their growing family. About four years after Moses was born, he gained a brother, Amos Junior, who was followed in turn by Sarah, Gilbert, Daniel, Mary, and finally Ebenezer, who was born in 1800. Father Amos, like so many others in the extended family, initially made his living by the sea, as a coastal sailing captain. Once firmly established in Groton, he opened a brick and lumberyard, located in a part of town called Poquonnock Bridge.

Precisely what kind of education Moses received as a boy is not known. Judging from his few surviving letters, either the schooling was good, the pupil learned well, or both. In an era when spelling was still a creative practice for many, the words Moses wrote were easily legible and usually spelled correctly. His grammar, usage and style had the air of someone who, having been exposed to the ways of others, knew how to adapt.

From a young age, Moses took to the sea, like his father. By age 21, according to his family, Moses was master of his own small sailing vessel. This was soon followed by command of a single-masted sloop called *Two Brothers*, which he captained until April of 1802.

It was at that time that his father, Amos Senior, purchased an eleven-year-old sloop named *Industry*. This 45-foot-long craft would serve as a family vessel, with his eldest son, Moses, taking immediate command. Eventually, the same privilege would be given to younger sons Amos Junior and Gilbert.

Over the next several years, Moses and the *Industry* made their way through the coastal waters in and around Connecticut, from New Bedford, Massachusetts in the east, to New York City in the west. His sailing times varied, of course, depending upon conditions, but a good sloop captain could make the trip between New London and New

York in a day, and sometimes as little as 16 hours. It was the loading
and unloading, and procurement of new cargoes, that took so much
time, and patience, and savvy. With the help of one crewman—often
his younger brother Amos Junior—Moses could lug whatever goods
the markets required: clay (probably for his father's brickyard), flour,
molasses, rum, beef, pork, cheese, potatoes, mast hoops, and once even
a marble tombstone.

While the mind of Moses paid attention to the cargo-hauling business, his heart soon became focused on something entirely more
appropriate, that being a mariner's daughter by the name of Adelia
Smith. Living in nearby Stonington, Adelia was six years younger
than Moses, and had to know that if she married him, she would also
marry the sea. The experience of growing up with her father, Captain
Nathan Smith, could not have left much doubt about what a life with
Moses would be like.

Whatever the sacrifices considered, love overcame them. In the
middle of February 1804, when trade was slow and the *Industry* lay
tied up to the wharves, Moses and Adelia were married. Either later
that same year or early the next, she gave birth to their first child, a
son who was named after his grandpa Smith. A few months after
young Master Nathan's arrival, Moses found himself brought further
into the Smith family fold, when he and his father-in-law registered
themselves as joint owners of a 5-year-old sloop named *Liberty*.

Moses immediately took command of her. Over the next year, he
continued trading with New York City, and made at least one trip up
the Connecticut River to the capital of Hartford, which, despite its
distance from the coast, was a port in its own right. While "catch as
catch can" was a captain's usual method for filling the hold, by this
time Moses was blessed with enough experience and the right contacts to procure single-item cargoes. To Hartford he took 950 bushels
of salt, and the *Liberty* was completely filled with sugar on two different trips to New York.

By 1806, Moses saw a new opportunity within his reach. Two
prominent Stonington merchants, William Williams and Coddington
Billings, had just taken delivery of a brand new schooner, and they
needed a captain.

A schooner represented entry into a new realm. The one-masted
sloops that Moses had commanded to date seldom made long voyages
out on the open ocean, since most owners and captains preferred to

keep them close to shore. Their single mast and small size left them vulnerable to unfriendly seas. Schooners, by contrast, could do much more. With two masts and a larger hull, they could be sailed down to the Caribbean, or even across the Atlantic.

A Sloop.   *A Schooner.*

It was a logical next step for Moses, and he took it. In early May of 1806, he became the captain of the schooner *Experiment*, based out of Stonington.

The summer fishing season having just begun, the *Experiment's* owners decided to put captain and craft to work on the cod harvest. With a federal fishing license procured, Moses took the new schooner out toward the Grand Bank, off the coast of Newfoundland. There, he and his crew of about a half-dozen men spent the summer and early autumn catching as much cod as they could.

Once they returned to Stonington in October, Moses received a new assignment from the *Experiment's* owners. With the fishing season over, the schooner was to switch to the cargo trade.

Moses took the *Experiment* to New York, and after filling the hold with cargo, departed for the warm waters of the Caribbean, and the island of Cuba.

After landing his cargo at the Spanish colonial port of Santiago de Cuba, he then loaded the schooner's hold with coffee, cocoa, and logwood (which was used for making dyes). After a return voyage of 30 days, Moses sailed the *Experiment* back into New York harbor at the beginning of February 1807.

Upper New York Bay, and New York City.

While the schooner's cargo was being unloaded, it would have been natural enough for Moses to ask the locals what had been going on since his departure the previous November. Beyond the latest news on markets and prices, there was also talk along the waterfront of a newcomer who was proclaiming his intention to do something that sounded impossible.

This new arrival was an American expatriate by the name of Robert Fulton. Having spent nearly two decades living and working abroad, mostly in Britain and France, Fulton had landed at New York back in December. Thanks to connections with the prominent and powerful Livingston family, he quickly gained entry into the upper echelons of the city's society. Fulton soon made it known that he and his financial partner, Robert Livingston, were planning to build a new kind of vessel, with a steam engine and paddlewheels. The power created by the engine would be used to turn the paddlewheels, supposedly pushing the boat through the water, without the aid of wind, and even against the current.

This was not a new idea. People had been proposing and building experimental "steamboats" for a generation or more, in both Europe and America. A man named John Fitch had actually run such a vessel on the Delaware River way back in the summer of 1790, but the effort had failed to attract enough ridership or additional capital to justify making improvements, and keep the boat running. Others had tried since then, but no one could make any of these "steamboats" work beyond a few limited experiments.

And therein lay the rub. Fulton was expressly promising to run his proposed "steamboat" from New York City up the North (or Hudson) River to the state capital of Albany and back, not just once, but repeatedly. It would be a regular passenger service, competing with the sailboats that provided the most comfortable, if unpredictable, means of transport between the two cities. Once the North River service was established, these steam-powered vessels would be introduced on other rivers, providing a new kind of transportation on water.

The skeptics were more than many. Nearly everyone who heard about this venture thought it was simply crazy. Indeed, Robert Fulton himself acknowledged that he had built a "steamboat" before, in France, and it hadn't really worked to anyone's satisfaction. He also had tried to generate interest in that country and Britain for some of his other ideas, including "torpedoes" (or sea mines) and "submersible boats," but his experiments for those ideas had generated only derision. That this creative-thinking American had returned to his home country to try his inventions made no difference. In some circles, the ridicule soon ran thick.

About six weeks after Fulton's arrival in New York, two aspiring writers named Washington Irving and James K. Paulding began publishing a satirical magazine called *Salmagundi*. In it, the writers created a fictional New York called "Gotham," so named to commemorate the town in England whose inhabitants were famed for doing ridiculous things. (Little could the magazine's creators know that their new name for New York City would live on—*for centuries*.)

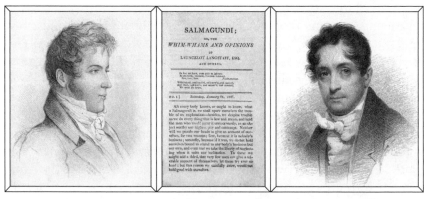

Washington Irving.   *The First Issue of*   *James K. Paulding.*
                             Salmagundi.

As readers of the very first issue of *Salmagundi* quickly discovered, some of the characters in this pretend city of Gotham bore an uncanny resemblance to real New Yorkers. One of them was a "drama critic" by the name of "William Wizard":

> ...Though Will has not had the advantage of an education at Oxford or Cambridge, or even at Edinburgh, or Aberdeen, and though he is but little versed in Hebrew, ... He has improved his taste by a long residence abroad, particularly at Canton, Calcutta, and the gay and polished court of Hayti...

This first issue of *Salmagundi* (which was only ten days old by the time Moses and the *Experiment* arrived) led readers to wonder about the true identity of Will Wizard. Some people thought that Wizard was a parody of the newly-arrived, Pennsylvania-born Robert Fulton. Speculation on the subject became so widespread that *Salmagundi*'s creators felt it necessary to respond in their second issue, which was published just after Moses and the *Experiment* had arrived at New York:

> ... Will Wizard was not a little chagrined at having been mistaken for a gentleman, "who is no more like me," said Will, "than I am like Hercules..."

It was a most curious reference. Hercules, in addition to being considered by the ancient Greeks as the strongest man in the world, also participated in the voyage of Jason and the Argonauts.

At one point in that epic saga, Hercules challenged the crew of their vessel, the *Argo*, to engage in a contest to see who could row the longest. Everyone rowed for many hours before admitting defeat, with only Jason and Hercules remaining in the competition, pushing the *Argo* forward. After much further exertion, Jason suddenly fainted, and almost simultaneously, the oar of Hercules snapped, much to his chagrin.

It was a story that many people in early 19th century America would have known. Astute readers inevitably made the logical comparison: the challenge of Hercules was to the promise of Fulton, as Hercules' broken oar would be to busted paddlewheels on Fulton's proposed steamboat. But the *Salmagundians* tried to put the matter to rest, assuring the public that William Wizard was just a fictional character, and begging to hear "no more conjectures on the subject."

Nevertheless, there remained plenty of conjecture in New York about Robert Fulton and his plans for a "steamboat." Driving the gossip was a steam engine, imported by Fulton from the firm of Boulton, Watt & Company, of Birmingham, England. Since the British placed strict controls on the export of their most advanced technologies, the very appearance of one of their steam engines at an American port could only serve to boost the ongoing rumors and speculation.

Just as Moses was preparing the *Experiment* for a return to Stonington, the third issue of *Salmagundi* came out. This time, the magazine's creators left out Will Wizard, but nevertheless offered their opinion of Fulton's plans:

> ...we pledge ourselves to the public in general, and the Albany skippers in particular, that the North-river shall not be set on fire this winter at least, for we shall give the authors of that nefarious scheme, ample employment for some time to come...

Just how much of this jabbering and joking over Fulton's "nefarious scheme" Moses was exposed to is impossible to say. Having spent two full weeks at newly-named Gotham in that winter of 1807, he surely must have heard about it. In any event, by mid-February, Moses had unloaded the *Experiment's* cargo and departed, sailing up the East River and into Long Island Sound for the trip home.

Upon his arrival at Stonington on February 20th, Moses dutifully submitted a cargo manifest to the local customs official. Normally, that would have signified the end of the voyage—only it didn't.

Four days later, a customs official came to visit the *Experiment,* and in the course of his inspection, he found three bags of cocoa hidden on board. This was a problem. The manifest submitted by Captain Rogers, duly certified by the New York Custom House, indicated that the *Experiment* was returning to Stonington with only "sea stores" for the crew, her entire cargo from Cuba having been disgorged at New York. Since the cocoa was a foreign item, an import tax, or *duty*, had to be paid on it.

But no one claimed ownership of this illegal cargo, so it was seized by the New London Custom House, and the case of the *United States vs. Three Bags of Cocoa* was initiated by the U.S. District Attorney. Such lawsuits, while sounding silly on their face, were actually quite common at the time. If undeclared cargo was found, the authorities would seize it, and take the legal steps necessary to confiscate it, in lieu of the duties owed.

Whether Moses was aware of the bags of cocoa is unknown, but in the end, it really didn't matter. As master of the schooner, he was responsible. Considering this was his first commercial voyage to a foreign land in the largest vessel he had ever commanded, it was a rather embarrassing state of affairs.

With one year at the helm of the *Experiment* under his belt, and the accounts for the trip to Cuba settled, Moses and his employers took stock. Succeeding as a merchant or a captain in the risky world of trade was never guaranteed—it required the right judgment combined with proper action, which, for most, only came with experience, accumulated over time. While the discussions between Moses and Messrs. Williams and Billings were a private affair, the subsequent actions of the *Experiment's* owners seemed to betray some degree of discord—perhaps over the cocoa incident, or the voyage's profitability, or something else.

On March 9th, owner William Williams gave Moses a *promissory note* (or IOU) for $64.20, that being the balance of his wages due. Fellow owner Coddington Billings then promptly honored the note, by paying Moses off.

Ten days later, Williams walked into the Custom House in New London to re-register the schooner *Experiment*, which was required whenever the ownership or captainship of a vessel changed. The schooner's new enrollment showed that Moses Rogers was no longer the captain of the *Experiment*. Furthermore, it indicated that an error had been made in listing the ownership. The form originally stated that William Williams "together with Moses Rogers + Coddington Billings" were the owners of the schooner. This had been corrected by drawing a single line through the name of Moses Rogers. While it may have been just an innocent mistake, the inclusion of his name as a new partial owner, then crossed out, was somewhat unusual. Since all custom house records were public documents, the deletion probably generated at least a few questions and commentary along the waterfront over what had transpired between the owners and their ex-captain.

In any event, the end of the relationship caught Moses flat-footed. Without a new command lined up, he was compelled to hit the wharves and counting houses, looking for a new employer. Moses might have considered going back to his old position at the helm of the family sloop, the *Industry*, but to do so would have been complicated. Amos Junior then had command of her, so Moses would not only have to ask father for his old job back, but demote his own brother in the process. Such a move was probably too much pride for an eldest son to swallow, and too strong a shove for a big brother to impose.

Fortunately, the search for new employment didn't take long. By mid-April, about one month after leaving the *Experiment*, Moses was hired by a New London merchant named Isaac Treby, who gave him the captaincy of a sloop named *Lydia*. Clearly, this was a come-down from being the master of a schooner. If there was any consolation, it was that this was the largest sloop Moses had ever commanded, measuring nearly 50 feet in length, and having a carrying capacity, or *burthen*, of more than 45 tons.

Moses quickly returned to the familiar ways of a coastal sloop captain, spending the rest of the spring and early summer of 1807 hauling cargo up to Hartford, as well as down to New York. By the end of July, having filled the *Lydia*'s hold with barrels of sugar, he set sail once again, this time for Gotham.

Upon their arrival in the East River, Moses and the *Lydia* passed, as usual, a part of Manhattan called Corlear's Hook. This area, located about two miles above the island's southern tip, was where all the major shipbuilders had their construction yards. Tied up to a dock at one of these yards was a strange-looking vessel, with a big metal smokestack rising from its deck, and what looked like large, wooden watermill wheels attached to either side of its hull. This was, of course, Robert Fulton's newly-built steamboat, or as the skeptics called it, "Fulton's Folly."

Egging on the disbelievers through the spring and summer had been the writers of *Salmagundi*. While the satirists were still trying to mask the true identities of their fictional characters, the ongoing descriptions of William Wizard made it obvious that they were jabbing their pens at Fulton. In early March, they had written of Wizard's uncertain social ways, noting "that he generally prefers smoking his segar, and telling his story among cronies of his own gender:—and thundering long stories they are, let me tell you." For Wizard, they explained, this was far more preferable than going to a party, which "he considered . . . as equivalent to being stuck up for three hours in a steam-engine."

Smoking "segars," "thundering" long stories, and steam engines were all obvious references to Fulton's Folly, yet these allusions were only the beginning. By the end of June, the *Salmagundians* were at it again, sneering at Wizard for frequenting the estate of "old Cockloft's, where he never fails to receive the freedom of the house," and "a pinch from his gold box."

"Old Cockloft" was, in full, "Christopher Cockloft," or *Salmagundi's* thinly-veiled version of Fulton's partner, Robert Livingston, who lived in the family manor at Clermont, which was situated along the North River. Without "pinches" from Livingston's "gold box," Fulton never would have been able to build his steamboat in the first place.

Robert Fulton,
also known as
"Will Wizard."

Robert R. Livingston,
also known as
"Christopher Cockloft."

Fulton's further dependence upon an English mechanic, who, according to the *Salmagundians*, "had just arrived in an importation of hardware, fresh from the city of Birmingham," provided still more ammunition for their broadsides.

Despite such public lampooning, Fulton pressed on.

By mid-July, work on the steamboat had progressed far enough to allow Fulton to make limited tests of the boilers and paddlewheels.

By the beginning of August, as Moses and the *Lydia* sailed past this odd-looking vessel, Fulton was preparing for his creation's first trial run.

Once the *Lydia* was tied up to the wharves along South Street, the process of unloading the barrels of sugar began. It took Moses a little over a week to disgorge his cargo and find a new one for the return trip to New London. By Sunday, August 9th, he was ready to go.

So was Robert Fulton. With spectators lining the waterfront along Corlear's Hook, Fulton and a small crew got steam up in the boilers of his experimental craft, and then put the paddlewheels in motion. A set of auxiliary sails, installed for back-up power should the engine break down, were left furled around their masts.

At around noon, the long, thin steamboat pushed away from the wharf, and turned upriver. Since the tide was going out at that moment, Fulton was attempting to overcome the strongest current the East River could deliver.

He was not alone. Fulton soon found himself in the company of a number of sailing vessels also trying to push their way upriver, toward Long Island Sound.

Even though the paddlewheels had only a partial complement of boards, the steamboat still managed 3 miles per hour, and that was better than anything else afloat at that moment. As Fulton later wrote to his partner Robert Livingston, "I beat all the sloops that were endeavoring to stem the tide with the slight breeze which they had; had I hoisted my sails, I consequently should have had all their means added to my own."

Once he had steamed upriver for about one mile, outrunning the sloops in the process, Fulton ordered the anchor dropped. He had the crew double the size of the paddleboards, by adding identical boards to those already in place. Then he proceeded back downriver, going 4 miles per hour, this time benefiting from the outgoing tide, and returned to the wharf where he had begun.

This first trial of Fulton's steamboat had gone remarkably well. While adjustments still needed to be made to get the most out of the machinery, Fulton nevertheless felt the vessel was nearly ready for a full test-run up the North River.

Exactly where Moses Rogers was when all this happened is not absolutely clear. He may have been watching from shore, along with the multitudes who wanted to see if this invention really worked. But under the circumstances, it seems just as likely that one of the sailing sloops that Robert Fulton's steamboat overtook on the East River that Sunday afternoon was the *Lydia*. Wherever Moses had been, his actions and behavior in the months to come revealed a certain new sense of purpose that is impossible to dismiss.

Arriving back in New London the day after Fulton's river test, Moses set to work turning his *Lydia* around as quickly as possible. Just four days later, on Friday, August 14th, he went into the Custom House and submitted a cargo manifest for departure, destination New York. The *Lydia*'s cargo was, once again, sugar, but her hold was not even close to full this time. Apparently, it didn't matter—the objective was New York, as soon as possible.

Back in Gotham that same day, the creators of *Salmagundi* were advancing their own objective like never before. Issue number XIII of their magazine appeared, and from its first words, the *Salmagundians'* intent was clear:

> I was not a little perplexed, a short time since, by the eccentric conduct of my knowing coadjutor Will Wizard. For two or three days, he was completely in a quandary. He would come into old Cockloft's parlour ten times a day, swinging his ponderous legs along, with his usual vast strides, clap his hands into his sides, contemplate the little shepherdesses on the mantelpiece for a few minutes, whistling all the while, and then sally out full sweep, without uttering a word. To be sure a pish, or a pshaw occasionally escaped him; and he was observed once to pull out his enormous tobacco-box, drum for a moment upon its lid with his knuckles, and then return it into his pocket without taking a quid:—'twas evident Will was full of some mighty idea:—not that his restlessness was any way uncommon; for I have often seen Will throw himself almost into a fever of heat and fatigue—doing nothing. . .

That Washington Irving and James K. Paulding were depicting Fulton, pretending to be his own steamboat at the Livingston's manor, was obvious enough to *Salmagundi*'s readers. So too, for that matter, was Irving and Paulding's opinion on the outcome of Fulton's impending experiment. Yet they were hardly finished:

"I wonder what can be the matter with Mr. Wizard?" asked Mrs. Cockloft.

"Nothing," replied Christopher Cockloft, "only we shall have an eruption soon."

On and on the *Salmagundians* went, devoting much of that Friday's installment of their magazine to roasting Will Wizard and his mad ideas, as well as the Cocklofts and their eccentric ways.

It was not until Sunday, August 16th, that the winds off New London were able to send the *Lydia* and her master on their way.

While Moses was sailing his sloop westward through Long Island Sound that day, Robert Fulton was getting ready. He carefully maneuvered his steamboat down the East River, around the Battery at the southern tip of Manhattan, and into the North River, where it was tied up to a dock near the State Prison at Greenwich Village. The steamboat's movement that day, past hundreds of New Yorkers performing the Sabbath ritual of a walk along the Battery, served as a very public notice that the real test—all the way to Albany—was imminent.

Moses and the *Lydia* were set to arrive in New York the following day. It would prove to be one of the most extraordinary Mondays in the history of Gotham. Robert Fulton's steamboat, newly-tied up to a wharf by the State Prison, looked very much like the experiment that it still was. Certain aspects of the vessel remained incomplete, including holes in the decking over parts of the engine, which Fulton deliberately left as they were, so that he could more easily monitor the machinery from above.

The newspapers of New York were almost universally oblivious to the moment; only a single, brief article in one of them that Monday morning alerted the city that judgment day had arrived. But even this solitary notice was unnecessary—many Gothamites already knew what was about to transpire, and hundreds of them streamed northward to Greenwich Village, in order to witness Fulton's Folly.

With all this *Salmagundian* ridicule and public skepticism heaped upon him, Fulton must have felt the weight of the world upon his shoulders as he made his final preparations to depart. Standing by him on the steamboat's deck were some 40 or so passengers, all either friends of Fulton or members of the extended Livingston clan. In turn surrounding them was a huge mass of spectators on the adjoining wharves.

At about 1 o'clock on that Monday, August 17th, 1807, Fulton gave the order for departure. As the steamboat was untied from the wharf, Fulton himself "heard a number of sarcastic remarks" from those watching on shore. He later described what happened next:

The moment arrived in which the word was to be given for the boat to move. My friends were in groups on the deck. There was anxiety mixed with fear among them. They were silent, sad and weary. I read in their looks nothing but disaster, and almost repented of my efforts. The signal was given and the boat moved on a short distance and then stopped and became immovable. To the silence of the preceding moment, now succeeded murmurs of discontent, and agitations, and whispers and shrugs. I could hear distinctively repeated— "I told you it was so; it is a foolish scheme: I wish we were well out of it."

I elevated myself upon a platform and addressed the assembly. I stated that I knew not what was the matter, but if they would be quiet and indulge me for half an hour, I would either go on or abandon the voyage for that time. This short respite was conceded without objection. I went below and examined the machinery, and discovered that the cause was a slight maladjustment of some of the work. In a short time it was obviated. The boat was again put in motion. She continued to move on. All were still incredulous. None seemed willing to trust the evidence of their own senses. . .

The steamboat slowly moved northward, up the wide river, overtaking sloops and schooners as it went. In time, it disappeared from sight.

Robert Fulton's North River Steam Boat.

Four days later, on Friday, August 21st, Fulton's Folly re-appeared at Gotham, splashing downriver and tying up to the wharf at 4 o'clock in the afternoon.

In the years to come, many people would step forward to claim that they had been on this, the first experimental trip of Fulton's steamboat to Albany, yet only a few of their stories would ring true. With no surviving passenger list, it is impossible to know the names of all of the participants. Even so, for every true passenger on this inaugural voyage, there were countless others who witnessed it from shore, or nearby boats.

At least as far as Moses Rogers was concerned, one thing is absolutely clear: he was still in New York on Friday, when the steamboat returned. Having unloaded the *Lydia's* partial cargo of sugar in the interim, Moses waited until Saturday before setting sail for home.

Arriving in New London on Sunday, Moses wasted no time. Once again, he filled the *Lydia's* hold with another partial shipment of sugar, and hurried back to New York just four days later, on August 27th.

Moses made it to Gotham in plenty of time for the first advertised commercial run of Fulton's newly-registered *North River Steam Boat*. That the inventor would give his creation such a name was hardly presumptuous—there was no other vessel like it on that river, or for that matter, anywhere in the world.

For the next three weeks, the *Lydia* remained tied up at New York. Considering how quickly Moses had been moving for the past month, it seems odd that he idled his sloop for so long. But in this same span of time, Robert Fulton's steamboat made its first three commercial runs up to Albany and back.

As with the first experimental voyage, no passenger lists have survived for these first commercial trips of the *North River Steam Boat*. Nevertheless, many years later, Moses Rogers would be described as having been "actively and usefully engaged on the North River in the earliest experiments" of Robert Fulton.

This vague statement subsequently led some to expand its meaning, making Moses a member of Fulton's steamboat crew, or even the engineer, or captain. Regardless of such speculations, what the movements of the sloop *Lydia* in the summer of 1807 *do* make absolutely clear is that Moses was present in New York when the *North River* made her first epochal strides, and very likely traveled on her. Based upon his subsequent life, it also seems quite clear that having been present at the creation, Moses Rogers caught the fever. He would never be the same again.

* * *

Not until the early morning light of December 12th, 1817 was the passage into Calibogue Sound finally clear. Having waited 12½ hours for the fog to dissipate, Captain Rogers gave the order to weigh anchor, and the *Charleston* got under way. Pushing southwest, between Bull's Island and Hilton Head Island, the steamboat and its reinforced complement of 25 passengers headed toward the broad ocean entrance to the Savannah River. Unfortunately, the coastal pilot hired as a guide proved to have an imperfect knowledge of the area, which, combined with some lingering mist, forced Captain Rogers to drop anchor again, and wait for an hour and a half. Only when the fog lifted, and the pilot found his confidence, did Moses allow the *Charleston* to proceed.

At mid-morning, as the steamboat reached the lower end of Calibogue Sound, those on deck could see in the distance, to their south, a tall, thin figure upon the sandy coast. This was Tybee lighthouse, the sentinel marking the entrance to the Savannah River.

As the steamboat churned closer, a series of buoys became visible in the waters directly ahead. These marked the safe route over the enormous sandbar created by the Savannah River's outflow. Even with the buoys as guides, crossing over the sandbar and entering the river could be accomplished only at high tide.

Once the *Charleston* pushed over the bar and entered the Savannah River proper, the pilot and crew had to be even more vigilant. There were many muddy shallows hidden along the banks, and a vessel charging ahead at 5 or 6 miles per hour could easily get stuck along the way.

Steaming upriver in a northwesterly direction, the *Charleston*'s passengers had a view to their right of South Carolina; to their left was the State of Georgia; and some 12 miles ahead lay the city of Savannah. The landscape along both sides of the dark river was mostly flat, marshy and wild, the haven of beavers, partridges, quail, and alligators. There was very little in the way of riverfront development, aside from some rice fields tucked in amongst the clusters of tall reeds, high grass, and shrubs. The only trees to be seen were so far off in the distance that they appeared to be nothing more than a thick black line along the horizon.

After several hours of steaming upriver, the city of Savannah slowly came into view, perched on a high sandy bluff on the south bank.

First to be seen was the outline of Fort Wayne, a curved stone fortification at the southern edge of the bluff, standing ready to challenge any traffic from the sea.

Immediately beyond Fort Wayne was the city proper, a mass of structures and steeples sitting some 50 to 70 feet above the water, and extending for one mile upriver.

Readily visible atop the bluff, set back from the edge, was a line of mostly wooden, multi-story buildings facing the river. These were the counting houses, warehouses and stores of the city's most prominent merchants.

Overshadowing them all was a four-story brick building with a tall white steeple, sitting alone and much nearer the bluff's edge. This was the Exchange, where much of the city's commercial trading took place. Its spire was manned by a lookout, charged with signaling the approach of any vessels, either from upriver or the sea.

Below the Exchange, at the bottom of the bluff, and seemingly growing out of the river, lay a forest of masts. Sailing vessels of every size and profile, from single-masted sloops, to two-masted schooners and brigs, to three-masted ships, were tied up to the wharves and to each other. There were only a dozen or so places in the whole country where such a large collection of craft bunched together like this could be seen, and Savannah was one of them. It was the third most active port in the Deep South (after New Orleans and Charleston), and boasted a population of about 7,500.

As the pilot guided the steamboat *Charleston* along the waterfront, all on board could see that the Exchange's lookout had done his duty, and done it well. The riverbank, the wharves and the shipping were all packed with people, who had scurried down the sandy bluff to greet the new arrival.

Once the *Charleston* neared Exchange Wharf, Moses ordered the steam engine to a halt, and the crew to *make fast* (i.e., tie her up to the pier). The time was, according to one observer, ten minutes before noon. The entire voyage had taken 2 days, 4 hours and 40 minutes, with about 24 hours of that time spent at anchor.

Off went the passengers into the waiting crowd. This was followed by the baggage. Then, finally, the packets of mail, which provided part of the name by which the *Charleston*'s business would be known: *steam packet service.*

Among the first Savannahans to approach Captain Rogers were the Howard brothers, Samuel and Charles. These transplanted Massachusetts natives had put down roots in Savannah around the turn of the century, and prospered. Samuel Howard had managed to gain the exclusive right to run steamboats on the Savannah River from both the Georgia and South Carolina legislatures, and was in the process of fashioning the business into a new entity called "The Steam Boat Company of Georgia." Because of Sam Howard's exclusive steamboating franchise, the *Charleston* could not operate on the Savannah River without some kind of approval from him. This he had granted, and as part of the arrangement, his brother Charles had been made the *Charleston's* booking agent in Savannah.

Also present were correspondents from the local newspapers, who took the measure of the scene before them, and by the next day, had put ink to press:

> We had the pleasure of witnessing the arrival yesterday of the new and elegant Steam-boat *Charleston*, intended to ply between this City and Charleston. Her grand appearance, and the handsome style in which she entered our waters, attracted the attention of numerous spectators, who bore testimony to the perfection of her machinery, and the elegance of her construction. The interior accommodations for passengers, are really elegant, and superior to any thing of the kind ever before offered to this public.

Another witness scribbled off a letter to a friend in the *Charleston's* home port:

> *... She came up to town in very handsome style, and I am happy to say that her movements met with general approbation. She was detained some time in Calaboga Sound by thick weather which, with the inexperience of the pilot, prevented her being here yesterday. The expedition made on this trip, under all the disadvantages of a first attempt, is a very favorable evidence of her future success.... Captain Rogers appears to be extremely well calculated for the business.*

Despite the length of the journey, the *Charleston's* first trip as a steam packet to Savannah had been a success. Most people applauded what this new service could mean for communications between the two cities. After all, it promised a predictability for water travel that was absolutely unheard of in the annals of human experience.

But not everyone viewed the new arrival so positively. There were some men who had no cause to cheer Moses Rogers and his steamboat, and those were the captains of the sailing packets.

* * *

Anyone visiting Savannah at the end of 1817 would have found a city that was not just vibrant, but flourishing.

As Georgia's oldest port, Savannah had always been a focal point for trade. Because of this, the city was often measured against its immediate rival to the north, Charleston. Such a comparison almost always had been to Charleston's advantage, since it enjoyed a broad, deep-water harbor. Savannah, on the other hand, had to contend with a narrow, tide-driven river for its port. This difference was reflected in the two rivals' early growth. By 1817, Charleston's population of more than 24,000 was three times that of Savannah.

More recently, however, this comparative dynamic had changed. Since the end of the war with Britain in 1815, the voracious appetite of British and French textile mills had unleashed an unprecedented cotton boom. While all American ports which served as transit points for the white fiber were growing, Savannah found itself with a particular advantage over Charleston in the years after the war. This advantage, ironically enough, was based upon the feature that previously had been a hindrance.

The Savannah River, while still naturally subject to tides, shallows and narrows, nevertheless had been made navigable all the way up to the city of Augusta, some 130 miles from the sea. This meant that all of the crops grown on both the Georgia and the South Carolina sides could be readily transported downriver, to the port of Savannah.

And the crop of choice along much of the river had become, not surprisingly, the one in greatest demand. Ever since Whitney's cotton gin had made it profitable to grow short-staple cotton in the "uplands," just about any acreage within a short wagon trip of any navigable river could be used to grow that variety.

The result in the years after the war was an agricultural bonanza all along the Savannah River, up to Augusta and beyond. Water transport was far and away the cheapest mode of moving cargoes, and the obstruction-free river quickly became an internal highway for cotton and foodstuffs. Once the white fiber in the uplands had been harvested and baled, it was piled high onto flatboats, and sent floating downriver to Savannah for export.

Compounding Savannah's advantage over its South Carolina rival was the steamboat angle. By December of 1817, Samuel Howard's steamboat, the *Enterprize*, had been successfully operating between Savannah and Augusta for a year, and two more nearly-completed steamers, the *Carolina* and the *Georgia*, would soon be towing even more cargo barges up and down the river, swiftly and dependably. These steamboats did not just support the flow of commerce—they made it move *faster*.

The result of these twin features—a plentiful supply of cotton, coupled with the ability to deliver it quickly—was a prosperity that could be seen all over Savannah in 1817. New construction was everywhere. Residences, stores and warehouses were being built at a brisk pace, putting the number of buildings in the city at over one thousand. While most new structures were still being built with wood, at least a few Savannahans had done so well from the boom as to be able to afford construction with more expensive brick and stone.

Getting a feel for Savannah's layout was best accomplished by standing at the Exchange, on Bay Street, and facing northeast, toward the river. There, a visitor would first note just how high the city was above the water. The tops of virtually all of the masts of the shipping tied up along the river would be below them. The most direct means of reaching the wharves was by one of six wide ramps cut straight down through the sandy bluff. Across the river lay Hutchinson's Island, a low, swampy place the city had purchased and drained, in the hope of making the port area healthier. Just beyond that was more swampland, and the beginning of South Carolina territory.

Turning directly around and facing inland, the city's immediate panorama was filled with counting houses and stores, along the south side of Bay Street. Beyond were still more shops and houses lining the city's streets, which were laid out in a grid-like pattern. Interrupting this grid at regular intervals were fifteen public squares, a distinctive feature for an American city that was noted by domestic and foreign visitors alike.

Savannah's unique personality, however, went well beyond the squares. Almost none of the city's streets were paved, consisting instead of the bluff's native sand. This meant that pedestrians crossing

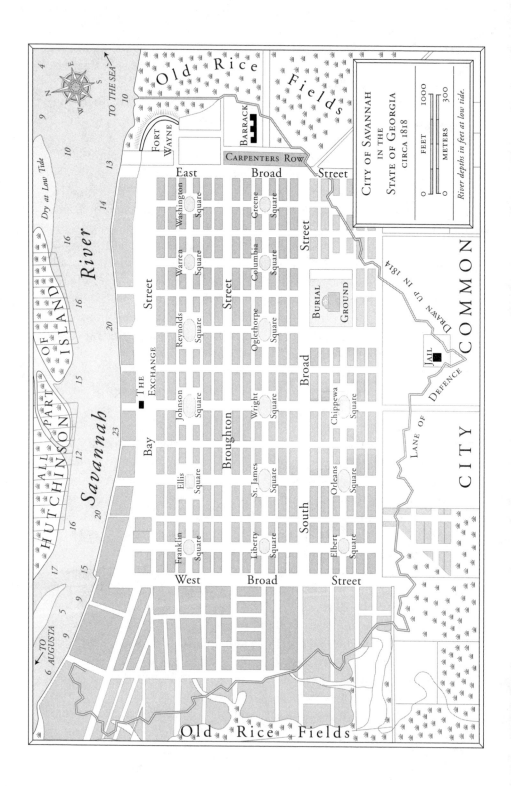

the street often sank in up to their ankles, and walking the sands on a hot sunny day could be a particularly uncomfortable experience. If there was one great consolation to having sandy streets, it was that wagons and carriages trundling about the city barely made a sound.

The many varieties of trees which thrived in the warm, humid climate also gave the "Sand Hill," as some residents called Savannah, a very distinctive feel. The city boasted not only the massive live oaks used for shipbuilding, but also the beautiful, exotic Pride of India, as well as evergreen pines and palm trees.

Perched in some of these trees was another local peculiarity, that being turkey vultures. These creatures were attracted to Savannah by the never-ending piles of garbage, deposited wherever the prior owners saw fit to dump them. Since residents viewed turkey vultures as very useful street cleaners, the city protected them, levying a fine of five dollars against any perpetrator who dared to kill one.

The human inhabitants of Savannah, on the other hand, were a very diverse lot, full of both contrasts and contradictions. In the coming 1820 census, the city would register a population of 7,523, of whom 3,866 were free white residents, and 3,075 were slaves. But those simplistic categories did not begin to describe the complexities of the city.

The total black population of Savannah actually would be recorded as 3,657, the additional 582 being black citizens who had their liberty, subject to certain restrictions. These "free people of color," as they were called, held all sorts of jobs—from seamstress, to carpenter, to pastry cook, to barber—and some were themselves slave-owners.

The much larger slave population also held a variety of occupations, and experienced very different treatment, depending upon their circumstances. For the men who worked down on the wharves— loading and unloading barrels and the enormously heavy cotton bales—the workday was incredibly long, difficult, and exhausting. For the rest of the slaves in Savannah, both place and purpose depended upon the demands of their owners and the needs of the city. While some lived and worked in their owner's household, many others who had skills were sent outside, to live and ply in whatever trades the market would bear. In return, these slaves had to pay their master a part of their earnings.

Telling who was enslaved was not always an easy thing. Many of Savannah's slaves were well-dressed, and in the eyes of some visitors, seemingly content. This sometimes led those who did not venture out to the plantations to develop a skewed view of the American version of slavery. Further still, since intimate relationships between masters and slaves were not uncommon, Savannah had, as one observer put it, a populace whose skin colors included "every variety of shade" imaginable.

The free white population was not monolithic, either. There were certainly many families who could trace their lineage back to Savannah's founding generation, which settled the bluff as an English colony back in 1733. But many others had come later, including northerners who saw commercial opportunities in the growing South, and immigrants from the British Isles and elsewhere, seeking a new start, as well. One of the more unusual groups of new Savannahans was made up of French merchants and their families, who had fled the colony of Saint-Domingue (Haiti) after a slave rebellion there at the turn of the century.

On top of this potpourri of residents, black and white, free and slave, native and immigrant, were the men who came tumbling off the many vessels which sailed into port. It would not be unusual for anyone walking the wharves to hear some combination of the English, French, Dutch, Swedish, German, Spanish and Portuguese languages being spoken. While the merchant seamen came and went, sometimes never to return, they nevertheless added yet another dimension to life in the city.

These many traits of the place and the people gave Savannah not just a unique personality, but a sense of purpose. Whatever the faults or contradictions, seen or unseen, this city by the river near the sea in the year 1817 exuded a belief in itself which reflected not just its own perspective, but that of the entire American nation. This faith had many pillars, from the political, to the religious, to the economic, all standing in concert to support an ever-growing optimism.

But for anyone who thought about it, there were other, newer reasons for the country's confidence in the future. It was based upon the growing sense that anything was possible, any dream could be achieved. And there was no better example of this new American sense of potential than that strange-looking vessel tied up to the wharf below the Savannah Exchange.

* * *

Once Captain Moses Rogers had brought the *Charleston* safely to Savannah, the next objective was to turn the steamboat around, and head back home as quickly as possible. By so doing, he would demonstrate to the public the promise of predictability, which was a concept simply unheard of in the sailing realm. The skippers of the sloops that regularly sailed between Savannah and Charleston could never guarantee when they would leave port, or when they would arrive at their destination. Furthermore, since carrying passengers was viewed as bonus revenue, over and above the money made hauling cargo, many sailing packet captains cared little if passengers had to wait until the vessel's hold was full. Under the circumstances, all a passenger could do was sit and stew, until departure.

Moses was about to change all that. On the very day of his steamboat's arrival at the Sand Hill, Charles Howard placed an advertisement in a local newspaper, the *Savannah Republican*:

For Charleston

The Steam Boat CHARLESTON will start ToMORROW, (Saturday) at 1 o'clock, P.M. precisely—the accommodations for passengers are elegant. Light freight can be taken for Beaufort.—Apply for passage or freight to captain Rogers on board, at the Exchange wharf, or to

Charles Howard

The next morning, a similar ad was placed in the competing *Columbian Museum*. True to promise, Moses managed to get the *Charleston* off at about twenty minutes past 1 o'clock that afternoon.

This goal accomplished, the secondary mission of Moses and his crew was to improve on the steamboat's transit time. Unfortunately, a miscalculation of the tide delayed the *Charleston*'s crossing over the sandbar off Tybee lighthouse, putting them behind schedule. Moses pushed through the inland passage as quickly as prudence allowed, arriving at Charleston early in the morning on December 15th.

This return trip had taken about 1½ days. While better than the voyage down, it still was not as fast as some of the sailing packets, which, under ideal conditions, could make the trip in 24 hours.

Nevertheless, the Charleston newspapers quickly rewarded Moses for his mission accomplished. One praised his "judicious management" of the *Charleston*. Another expressed confidence that communication between Charleston, Beaufort and Savannah would double, at the least.

But one round-trip did not make a packet service—the real proof would come in making the voyage again, soon, and faster.

After several days spent checking the machinery and replenishing the supply of pine wood fuel, the steamboat was advertised to leave on Thursday, December 18th.

On the morning of departure, the effect of the first voyage's success was amply verified. More than 30 passengers came aboard, and the *Charleston* left the wharf just twenty minutes past her appointed departure time of 11 o'clock.

* * *

What Moses Rogers and the steamboat *Charleston* were bringing to these two southern cities had already made its mark on rivers, lakes and bays in the North. Since the successful introduction of steamboat travel by Robert Fulton back in 1807, people had seen just how reliable these vessels could be. This reliability eventually encouraged some open-minded men to think about how they could adopt what the steamboats had wrought.

In the last several months of 1817, these same men began making their plans public. Newspapers coming south from New York City had carried their advertisements, which were so unusual that they generated news stories in their own right. This was because these paid advertisements contained a very unique proposition:

LINE OF AMERICAN PACKETS
BETWEEN N. YORK & LIVERPOOL

IN order to furnish frequent and regular conveyance for GOODS and PASSENGERS, the subscribers have undertaken to establish a line of vessels between NEW-YORK and LIVERPOOL, to sail from each place on a certain day in every month throughout the year...

The commanders of them are all men of great experience and activity; and they will do all in their power to render these Packets eligible conveyances for passengers. It is also thought, that the regularity of their times of sailing, and the excellent condition in which they deliver their cargoes, will make them very desirable opportunities for the conveyance of goods.

It is intended that this establishment shall commence by the departure of the JAMES MONROE, from NEW-YORK on the 5th, and the COURIER from LIVERPOOL on the 1st, of First Month (January) next; and one of the vessels will sail at the same periods from each place in every succeeding month.

> ISAAC WRIGHT & SON,
> FRANCIS THOMPSON,
> BENJAMIN MARSHALL,
> JEREMIAH THOMPSON.

What these New York merchants were proposing had never been tried before. To depart on a predetermined date far in the future risked sailing without a full hold. This was, to the conventional mind of a captain or owner, cargo revenue foolishly forsaken. In addition, since the weather never could be predicted, a sailing vessel could waste days, or even weeks, if it tried to leave port when the winds were unfavorable.

But these New York merchants were thinking differently.

What if people knew that a vessel was leaving for Liverpool on a specific date, every month?

Could they begin to plan their lives, and their businesses, based upon such a schedule?

In time, would this not provide some degree of predictability, benefiting passengers who needed to leave, or merchants who needed goods sent, by a date certain?

These questions, and their anticipated answers, represented the gamble that the five merchants listed in the advertisement were willing to make. Such a calculated risk was based upon a number of factors, but the primary source of their radical and revolutionary idea could be readily seen in the waters off Manhattan in 1817. The steamboats moving all around that island were allowing people to be at a given place at a given time with a certainty never known before.

And these five New York merchants, with their public declaration, made it clear that they wanted to apply some of that same predictability to sailing ships.

CHAPTER TWO

―――――

NEW PLAN

IN THE EARLY 19th century, the sailing schedule for vessels engaged in the North Atlantic trade was founded in the seasons. Typically, any craft large enough to make such a voyage—be it a schooner, or a brig, or a ship—would leave home port in the springtime. Arriving at its destination on the other side of the Atlantic in early summer, the vessel would unload its cargo, bring on a new one for the return trip, and sail back home by early autumn.

Then the first half of the procedure might be repeated, if possible, leaving the vessel in a foreign port as winter set in. Crossing the Atlantic Ocean in the winter months was generally considered imprudent, since the storms of that season could easily wreck even the stoutest of ships. Once the worst of winter was past, back home the vessel would go with another cargo. This could be especially profitable for American vessels delivering British manufactured goods to the United States just in time for the spring buying season.

If a captain was agile enough, he might get in two round-trip sailings in a calendar year, but this would be unusual. The unpredictable amount of time needed to procure, load and unload a hold full of barrels, bales and boxes simply prevented making any more voyages in the normal trade season.

It was these elemental characteristics of the North Atlantic cargo route between the United States and Britain that the five New Yorkers were challenging when they announced their set-departure, sailing packet service. Even if no one could predict when their new service's vessel would arrive at its destination, knowing with absolute certainty when it planned to sail would produce a number of benefits.

Among these would be a change in the treatment of goods. With the departure date known well in advance, merchants would be able to plan and prioritize their shipments like never before. Also, their new ability to send cargo in the slow winter months would introduce a continuity of trade never offered by seasonal vessels.

Of equal if not greater importance would be a change in the treatment of passengers. As the New Yorkers' advertisement made plain, this unprecedented service was for the conveyance of goods *and* passengers. No more waiting for the captain to finish filling the hold. By promising to leave on a predetermined date, this new trans-Atlantic packet service implicitly promised to respect the value of a passenger's time. The only other vessels which did the same, of course, were the New Yorkers' most immediate inspiration: the steamboats.

This newfound respect for a person's time meant that as far as the trans-Atlantic passenger trade was concerned, the New Yorkers' new service would have no direct competition. They did, however, have indirect competition, and that came from their oceanic inspiration: the mail brigs of the British Post Office.

Intent on moving the mails as regularly as possible despite the vagaries of the ocean, the British Post Office had its own fleet of small brigs. These were two-masted, *square-rigged* vessels, meaning the masts had horizontal poles (or *yards*) lashed to them at right angles to the keel. The British mail brigs left Falmouth (on the southwestern tip of England) once a month and headed for New York, offering passage to anyone willing to go.

There were a few catches, however.

First, the mail brigs left Britain from a remote port, and made a stop in each direction. In the warm weather months, the port of call was Halifax, Nova Scotia. In the winter, it was Bermuda. This obviously prolonged the passage for anyone wishing to go to New York direct.

Second, the accommodations on the mail brigs were both limited and Spartan. About a half-dozen passengers per sailing was all that a mail brig could take. (They furthermore refused all cargo beyond the mail itself.)

Third, the British mail brigs had something of a reputation for being dangerous. This was in part because their skippers sailed aggressively, trying to get across quickly, but also because they were forced to sail straight through the winter months.

The five enterprising New Yorkers had an answer for each of these shortfalls.

First, they would sail between New York and Liverpool directly, with no stops.

Second, the vessels that would make up this new scheduled packet service were not two-masted brigs, but *three*-masted, square-rigged ships. With their greater hull size, and more comprehensive complement of masts, rigging and sails, these vessels were better able to both accommodate passengers in comfort and contend with whatever the Atlantic threw at them.

And third, the specific mention in the advertisement that the new service's captains were "of great experience and activity," who would be "doing all in their power to render the Packets eligible conveyances for passengers," was a subtle message that safety would be of the greatest importance.

The one thing these five New Yorkers could not do was predict when their packet ships would arrive. This was why they needed four of them to maintain a monthly schedule. While two of their ships were crossing the Atlantic in opposite directions, the other two would be in New York and Liverpool, preparing for the next set of departures.

Putting something like this together took some planning. Just exactly when these New Yorkers first had the idea of trying to run merchant sailing ships on a set-departure schedule is not known, but it was at least as early as the spring of 1816. At that time, a writer to one of the New York newspapers described seeing in the shipyard of Adam Brown the "hull of a ship intended for a packet to England to sail with the regularity of a stage." This was the ship *James Monroe*, then under construction in Brown's yard.

Both interesting and telling is the correspondent's use of stage-coaches for his comparison. While some steamboats had been able to complete single voyages on the ocean, transferring from one port to another, the idea that they could maintain a regular service at sea was—in the spring of 1816—simply beyond the bounds of common belief.

Nevertheless, steamboats already had made their mark in protected waters, especially in New York City. Less than a decade after Fulton's triumph, there were at least a dozen steamboats operating around Manhattan. From taking people up the North River to Albany; to ferrying them across that same river to different ports in New Jersey; to taking increasing numbers of workers on their daily commutations between Brooklyn and Manhattan; to transporting passengers through Long Island Sound to ports in Connecticut; the steamboats' presence in and effect upon New York had become so common and so obvious as to be somewhat ordinary, except for the visitor unaccustomed to this new way of life.

Since the United States and Britain were the only countries yet to adopt these new inventions in force, and Gotham was both their birthplace and earliest adopter, it's not too surprising that the attempt to adapt steamboats' predictability to sailing vessels originated with a group of New York merchants, three of whom were British immigrants.

Isaac Wright and his son William were the only native-born Americans in the venture. Very active in shipping circles, the Wrights did business with many New York merchants, but were especially close to their fellow Quakers, Francis Thompson and his nephew Jeremiah. Born in Yorkshire, England, the Thompsons had immigrated to New York to import textiles made by their family's woolen mills. The fifth partner brought into the venture was Benjamin Marshall, also originally from Yorkshire.

The new service they were organizing was not a company, per se. Rather, it was an agreement to pool their four ships, each of which was owned in differing fractions by the partners. Once the *James Monroe* was launched as the fourth vessel in the fleet, they were ready to begin.

Jeremiah Thompson took the lead in organizing the effort. Just before the advertisements ran in the New York papers, he had written to his Liverpool agent, laying out what was expected of the ships and the people involved:

> ... Each vessel will be required to complete a voyage in four months...

Given that Atlantic crossings between New York and Liverpool usually took from 25 to 35 days eastbound (with the Gulf Stream), and 30 to 45 days westbound, the crews would have only a few weeks in each port to unload cargo, re-load, and prepare for departure. The schedule was a tight one.

> ... each of the Owners will direct all their own Goods to be shipped in these Vessels; they will not have a single package in any other conveyance...

The intended message was obvious: the owners were putting their cargoes where their mouths were. If *they* were depending on their packet ships to leave by a date certain, so could other merchants and the traveling public.

> ... It is our intention that these Ships shall leave New York, full or not full, on the 5th, and Liverpool on the 1st, of every Month throughout the year:—and if it be necessary to employ a Steam Boat to tow them out of the River we wish it to be done...

By being so precise, Thompson and his partners signaled how important it was to honor the only time-promise of the voyage they believed they could keep, and that was when the ships departed. If they had to use steam power to accomplish this, so be it.

> ... with the general circulation of a Knowledge of this establishment, both in England and in this Country, together with the Vessels themselves being really of a Superior Class, and the Captains experienced and active, we think there can be but little doubt of the success of the undertaking. ..

Such confidence could only breed still more.

With planning and preparations in hand, attention turned to the first scheduled departure from New York, on January 5th, 1818. This was less than one month after Moses had taken the steamboat *Charleston* down to Savannah for the first time.

On that Monday morning, the weather in Gotham could not have been much worse. It was bone-chillingly cold and snowing hard, as the crew prepared the *James Monroe* for departure. A crowd had gathered at the South Street wharf where the ship was tied up. Beyond mere curiosity, they wanted to see if the captain, James Watkinson, was really going to leave port in such conditions, or whether he would find some excuse to delay his departure, as skippers often did, when Nature was disobliging.

If things had gone according to plan on the other side of the Atlantic, the ship *Courier* already had left Liverpool four days before. Jeremiah Thompson had written previously to her captain, giving him very specific instructions, which Thompson no doubt repeated to Captain Watkinson:

... Thou must put thy Ship in the very best Condition...

As the 10 o'clock departure time approached, eight passengers came aboard the *James Monroe*, each of them having paid about $200 for the trip to Liverpool. They joined a cargo of apples, cranberries, flour, ashes, cotton, wool, and turpentine, which filled much, but not all, of the hold. Also on board was a small shipment of *specie*—that being gold or silver, the ultimate international currency—which was probably being sent to pay off some paper-money debt. Finally came the last-minute mail packet, delivered from the nearby Tontine Coffee House.

... I hope thou will be exactly punctual in sailing at the time prescribed...

At precisely 10 o'clock, with heavy snow continuing to blanket all in sight, Captain Watkinson ordered the crew to cast off. Slowly, the *James Monroe* moved out into the East River, and then turned south, toward New York Bay and the path to the sea.

... after beginning on the New Plan, there will not be much rest for you...

As the crew unfurled the sails from their yards, the canvas in the middle of the foremast (or *fore-topsail*) revealed that it had been specially marked. Upon it was a very large, solid-black circle, which was the signal used by port authorities to denote the approach of a square-rigged vessel. In seaman's slang, it was a *black ball*.

The unrelenting snowstorm made traversing the Bay very slow and difficult. Not until 4 o'clock that afternoon did the *James Monroe* finally make it to Sandy Hook, the lighthouse-topped spit of land that marked the exit to the sea.

With the ship's departure into the Atlantic, the "New Plan" had begun. Yet this great step was only part of an even greater vision brewing in the minds of a bold few—a new thinking that would eventually change the world, and the human race's relationship with it, forever.

CHAPTER THREE

NEW THINKING,
EVEN THE CHIMERICAL

NEAR AUTUMN'S END in 1807, Robert Fulton took his *North River Steam Boat* upriver to Clermont, the country estate of his partner, Robert R. Livingston. Running the *Steam Boat* during the winter months was out of the question. Ice floes in the North River were simply too dangerous for the wooden paddlewheels. Besides, the only commercially operating steamboat in the world needed to be repaired, and improved.

While Fulton oversaw what amounted to a virtual reconstruction of the *North River*, one of Robert Livingston's relatives was busily preparing to build his own steamboat. Colonel John Stevens, a veteran of the Revolution and Livingston's brother-in-law, had been working on steamboat designs and experiments since the late 1780s, after becoming familiar with the efforts of inventors John Fitch and James Rumsey. Indeed, John Stevens and Robert Livingston had been partners in seeking a workable steamboat, but parted ways after disagreeing about how to proceed.

Once Fulton returned from Europe at the end of 1806, he had suggested to his partner that Colonel Stevens be included in their enterprise, but Livingston demurred. Nevertheless, Fulton gave Colonel Stevens an open ticket to inspect the *North River*, as she was being built during the spring and summer of 1807. That he was unafraid of what knowledge Colonel Stevens might gain from such visits was a testament to Fulton's confidence in his own design (as well as his desire to gain whatever allies he could find).

Colonel Stevens believed his own ideas for steamboats, nearly two decades in the making, were as good as Fulton's, if not better. Once he saw the *North River* successfully make runs to Albany through the autumn of 1807, Colonel Stevens prepared to challenge. In January of 1808, while Fulton was rebuilding the *North River*, the Colonel signed a contract with a shipbuilder for a steamboat hull. It was expected to be some 100 feet long (or about two-thirds the length of Fulton's), and perhaps 16 feet wide. Construction would take place directly across the North River from Manhattan, at a New Jersey island called Hoboken, where the Colonel had a large estate.

The first head-to-head steamboat duel in history was about to begin.

* * *

The confrontation which soon followed—with Fulton and Livingston on one side, and Colonel John Stevens along with many additional actors on the other—became a part of one of the great debates in the early United States: how could inventors protect the fruits of their labor, and reap the rewards of bringing a new device into use, without others simply copying it?

The old-fashioned way was the monopoly. Used in Europe for hundreds of years, a monopoly right was intended to provide entrepreneurs with the chance—and that's all it was—to make an acceptable return on the risk they took in creating something in the first place.

The precise definition of that risk depended upon the objective.

Sometimes the objective was commerce, and a king or queen would grant a monopoly right to trade with a certain far-flung colony, or nation. The risk of losing ships, men and cargoes to prove such trade was achievable would be countered by the possibility of profits without competition.

Other times the objective was the introduction of some new invention. In this case, the sovereign would grant the inventors a monopoly right to build and apply their creation within a certain geographic area for a certain period of time. The risk of failure, and ridicule, was offset by the knowledge that if the invention worked and was found useful, then the creators alone would receive the financial benefit, provided they managed their business well.

In time, this tradition of monopoly grants was exported from Britain to the American colonies. It was still in use by the individual States of the newly-formed United States when the Constitution was ratified in 1788.

The adoption of that document, however, changed everything.

Included in its final form was a section giving the U.S. Congress the ability "to promote the Progress of Science and useful Arts, by securing for limited Times to Authors and Inventors the exclusive Right to their respective Writings and Discoveries."

With this power duly authorized, and thanks to prodding by various inventors such as Colonel John Stevens, the First Congress set about debating and eventually passing the Patent Act of 1790. This law created a system for registering inventions with a U.S. Patent Office.

A federally-issued patent was in many ways the same as a State-sponsored monopoly. The key difference was geography, with significant consequences: the new federal law offered inventors a monopoly that was national in scope, and further decreed that individual States could no longer create monopolies to encourage inventions within their own borders. A federal patent for an invention—approved as being unique by a committee made up of the Secretary of State, Secretary of War and Attorney General—would supersede the authority of the States in this area.

But there remained one very significant problem: many people simply did not agree with this interpretation of the Constitution and the new patent law. They believed that any powers not expressly granted to the federal government were reserved for the States, as the Constitution clearly declared. This included a State's power to encourage development within its own borders. Congress and its new Patent Act had no authority to nullify this right, and so, State monopolies for inventions still could be granted.

Subsequent actions by Congress made such arguments sound even more attractive.

Once the Patent Act of 1790 was passed, the three Cabinet officers charged with approving patents soon found themselves overwhelmed with applications. Determining whether an applicant truly had invented something unique was an incredibly time-consuming task. The three Cabinet officers, led by Secretary of State Thomas Jefferson, pleaded for relief.

Also at issue was the Patent Act's questionable treatment of pre-existing State monopolies.

In response, the Second Congress duly passed a revised Patent Act of 1793. This new law eliminated the requirement that the Patent Office certify an invention as unique before issuing a patent, thereby

relieving the three Cabinet officers of their most burdensome obligation. All that was required of an applicant was a written description
of the invention, a model or drawings, and the payment of a $30 fee.
As long as the applicant also declared a belief that the invention was
unique, then the patent would be automatically granted.

The new law further stipulated that upon being granted a federal
patent, the inventor automatically relinquished any "exclusive rights"
to the invention granted at the State level. This would hopefully
sweep any remaining State monopolies into the federal patent system,
thereby eliminating them.

Unfortunately, the Patent Act of 1793 did not work. By relieving the
three Cabinet officers of their primary burden, the revised law placed
a virtually indefensible one upon the inventor. If someone violated their
patent, inventors had to prove not only that the violator was guilty, but
also that their patented invention truly was unique in the first place.
In point of practice, Congress had simply transferred the originality
judgment from the Patent Office to the federal courts. That meant
inventors would have to spend a lot of money on lawyers to defend
their federal patents, something that most of them were in no position
to do. To some skeptics of this new patent law, State monopolies looked
more enforceable, in addition to being still perfectly permissible.

Robert Livingston was among these skeptics. His training as a
lawyer, and position as Chancellor of the State of New York, which
oversaw the Court of Chancery, gave him a certain credibility on the
subject. Further underpinning came from his active involvement in
the country's founding. Livingston had been one of the Committee
of Five responsible for drafting the Declaration of Independence. He
also had served as a delegate to the New York State convention which
ratified the Constitution. Based upon his own legal knowledge as a
member of the founding generation, Livingston believed that States
still retained the power to grant monopolies.

Among those monopolies granted by the State of New York was
one for steamboats, given to pioneer John Fitch. But when Fitch failed
to make any use of his monopoly, Chancellor Livingston stepped forward. He petitioned the New York Legislature to transfer Fitch's
exclusive steamboat franchise to him. To activate this privilege, Livingston would have to make such a vessel go 4 miles per hour.

The Chancellor's request was met with open ridicule. At that point,
in early 1798, the word "steamboat" was readily believed to be a

synonym for "fantasy," or "failure." Members of the Legislature in Albany accordingly dubbed Chancellor Livingston's proposal the "hot water bill," and laughed at him some more. But they passed it, nevertheless.

Livingston immediately formed a steamboat partnership with his brother-in-law, Colonel John Stevens, and a promising mechanic named Nicholas Roosevelt. Their attempts to build a working steamboat ended—as all efforts before them—in dispute and defeat.

Livingston's subsequent 1801 appointment as the American minister to France interrupted his steamboat quest, but only temporarily. Upon meeting Robert Fulton in Paris, Livingston determined to make the young man his new partner, and try again.

When Fulton actually succeeded in creating a working steamboat in 1807, thereby meeting the conditions set for activating Livingston's exclusive franchise, the stage was set for a gargantuan struggle.

On the one side were Robert Livingston and Robert Fulton, arguing that their State monopoly was legal, and Fulton's steamboat design was unique.

On the other side was John Stevens, along with many others, who believed State monopolies were clearly contrary to the Constitution, and that Fulton's design, while ingenious, could not be patented as original.

The battle that ensued would last for years to come.

* * *

Through the winter of 1808, Robert Fulton engrossed himself in the re-building of his *North River Steam Boat*, near Clermont, New York.

At the same time, further to the south, at the island of Hoboken, New Jersey, Colonel John Stevens was hard at work overseeing the construction of the hull for his own rival steamboat.

All the while, Colonel Stevens also continued negotiating with his brother-in-law Robert Livingston, as well as Robert Fulton, over the future of this new technology. The two sides alternately argued, cajoled, threatened, placated, cursed and flattered each other, in an effort to determine whether they would join forces, or fight.

As all this activity and agitation was transpiring along the North River, Moses Rogers, captain and by then part-owner of the sloop *Lydia*, continued to sail for profit. He spent a good part of the winter of 1808 on a voyage down to Wilmington, North Carolina, hauling an incredible potpourri of goods, from "cyder," to hats, to hazelnuts, shoes, and whale oil. Upon his return to the North in late March, Moses made a point of putting in to New York City for a spell. This brief stop in Gotham seems to have served more than the usual purposes of trade. It allowed Moses to get his bearings, learn the latest, and prepare his next steps. Those tasks accomplished, he and the *Lydia* set sail for New London.

Just a few weeks later, in April of 1808, both sides in the steamboat race took big steps forward.

In New York City, the re-built and re-named *North River Steam Boat of Clermont* was ready for a second season. The simple fact that Fulton and Livingston were resuming their runs to Albany served as proof positive that the previous year's trips had been no fluke.

Meanwhile, on the opposite side of the North River, at Hoboken, Colonel John Stevens was celebrating the launch of his own steamboat's hull. Before him lay months of additional work, including the installation of a home-made steam engine, paddlewheels, and a back-up mast and sails, but the Colonel was clearly making rapid progress.

A few weeks after that, in early May, Captain Moses Rogers and the sloop *Lydia* were ready to set sail again from New London. Their new destination was Perth Amboy, in New Jersey. This small port was situated on the southwestern coast of Lower New York Bay, at the entrance to the Raritan River.

Once they arrived at Perth Amboy, Moses, in his capacity as half-owner, sold the *Lydia* to a local merchant, and relinquished his position as her master. Having done all this, it would have made sense for Moses to return home to New London, and seek the captaincy of another vessel.

But he didn't do that. Instead, he stayed.

In short order, Moses arranged to take command of a much smaller sloop, called the *Hope*. Her home port was South Amboy, which was situated just across the Raritan River.

And South Amboy it would remain. For the first time in his career, Moses was trading from a base outside his native Connecticut. On the surface, his choice appeared to make little sense. Perth Amboy and South Amboy served as feeder ports for New York City. To their docks came the produce of New Jersey farmers, much of it headed for Gotham, and in return came all sorts of manufactured goods, mostly imported from Europe. If being in the Amboys did anything for

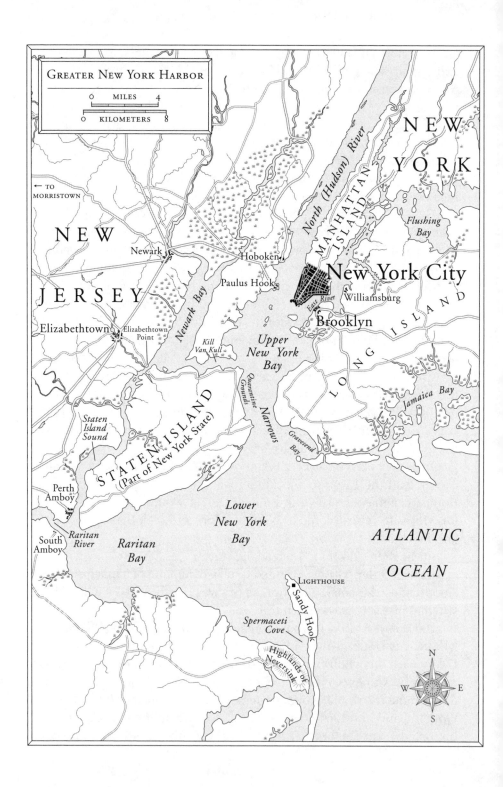

Moses, it got him closer to the action in New York, and in time would give him even more intimate knowledge of the waters around it.

That, apparently, was precisely what he wanted.

*   *   *

Through the late spring and summer of 1808, Moses and the *Hope* coasted back and forth within New York Bay, sometimes carrying little more than a few boxes of cargo.

During those same months, the *North River Steam Boat of Clermont* also made trip after trip, from Manhattan to Albany, and back. Gotham's press finally gave Fulton's Folly its due, printing story after story of the *Steam Boat's* increasing passenger counts, and usually decreasing transit times. By late summer, 100 customers per trip was not unusual, and there were reports that Fulton was forging ahead with plans to build a second steam vessel.

It was then, as the summer was drawing to a close, that the Amboys began receiving a very unusual visitor. Churning and smoking its way between Staten Island and the coast of New Jersey came the completed steamboat of Colonel John Stevens, making a series of test runs. The Colonel made sure his still-unnamed craft stayed as close as possible to the New Jersey coast, lest he unduly antagonize Livingston and Fulton. On one of these experimental runs, the Colonel's steamboat achieved a speed of more than 5½ miles per hour, making it as fast as Fulton's *North River*.

In the midst of these tests, on September 14th, Moses walked into the Custom House at Perth Amboy and removed his name from the captaincy of the *Hope*. In her place, he assumed command of a larger sloop, the *Lady Washington*, with their home port remaining South Amboy. Moses wasn't going anywhere.

And for good reason. Two weeks later, at the very same Custom House where Moses had been recording his vessel-jumping over the past four months, Colonel Stevens officially enrolled his steamboat. Ever-conscious of his cross-river rivals, the Colonel gave his creation a name worthy of his come-from-behind effort. This newest steamboat, all of it made in America, was to be called the *Phoenix*, after the mythical bird destroyed by fire, only to be reborn from its own ashes.

Also enrolled with the *Phoenix* was her first master, Captain Arthur Roorbach. While the new steamboat and its master still required additional testing, Colonel Stevens made it clear he intended to defy Livingston and Fulton by running his *Phoenix* from New York City to New Brunswick, New Jersey. For this planned trespass into New York State waters, and other perceived insults, the battle between the two sides intensified.

In the following month of October, Fulton contracted to build his second steamboat. This one was to be called the *Car of Neptune*, and was intended to complement the *North River* on her runs to Albany.

But the challenge of Colonel Stevens had not been forgotten. At that same time, John R. Livingston, younger brother of the Chancellor, began construction on yet another steamboat. Based upon a license granted to him by the New York franchise, he was to run this third vessel between Gotham and any port on the western side of New York Bay. The destination John Livingston publicly chose was New Brunswick. No matter where Colonel Stevens planned to run his *Phoenix*, the Livingstons and Fulton would be there to counter-challenge him— unless he agreed to their terms.

Through the course of the ongoing negotiations, which continued to alternate between cordial and confrontational, the idea of creating a larger system of steamboat lines was broached. If the Colonel would not agree to procure a license from the New York franchise, why not start a complementary steamboat service on the Delaware River, between Trenton, New Jersey and Philadelphia? With stagecoach lines running across New Jersey, linking with steamboats at either end, travel between the two largest cities in the country could be made far more expeditiously. This was clearly the logical next step in expanding steamboat service from New York City.

Colonel Stevens took this idea to heart, and in that same month of October, he publicly announced his proposal for a line of steamboats linking New York and Philadelphia. The only catch was he refused to concede the New York-to-New Brunswick leg. He still intended to run his steamboat all the way to Manhattan, in defiance of the Livingstons and Fulton. Yet in spite of the Colonel's belligerence, the rival parties continued debating and negotiating with each other into the winter months of early 1809.

At some point during this period, John Stevens was introduced to sloop captain Moses Rogers. While the details of their first meeting are unknown, the personal circumstances of these two men yield important clues as to how they must have reacted to one another.

On one side of this encounter was John Stevens, then 59 years of age. Standing 5 feet, 7 inches in height, of middling build, and with short grey hair that barely masked his increasingly bald head, Stevens was the grandson of an indentured servant, and the son of a successful ship-owning merchant. He had graduated from King's College (which became Columbia University) in 1768, along with Robert Livingston (the future Chancellor). The two men became brothers-in-law three years later, when Robert married John's sister, Mary Stevens. During the Revolution, John Stevens split with his many Tory friends, and joined the fight for independence. He received a commission in the Continental Army, attaining the rank of colonel, which, by tradition, he could use as a title for the rest of his life, if he chose.

John Stevens.

His interest in steam engines as a means of propelling boats had been born in the 1780s, thanks to the experiments of pioneers John Fitch and James Rumsey. Ever since, Colonel Stevens had been trying to develop a practical steamboat.

With Fulton's undeniable success in 1807 and 1808, the Colonel was facing critical decisions on how to proceed with the quest that had been the passion of his life for two decades. Stevens, Livingston and Fulton, after months of wrangling, were at an impasse. The pressure was building. As soon as the winter of 1809 was over, and the ice was gone, the steamboat duels would begin. It must have become apparent that Captain Roorbach did not fit the bill for what lay ahead. A new master was needed for the *Phoenix*—the only question was ... *who?*

Colonel Stevens' eldest son, Robert Livingston Stevens (so named after his uncle, the Chancellor) was one possibility. Robert was a first-class mechanic; the Colonel had seen to that personally, by placing tools in his son's little hands when he was a baby. And Robert knew the steam apparatus installed on the *Phoenix* better than anyone, save the Colonel himself. But at only 21 years of age, Robert Stevens' experience on the water was limited. It made far more sense to focus his talents on maintaining and improving the steam engine and paddlewheels.

On the other side of this encounter was another possibility: Captain Moses Rogers of Connecticut. He stood stout and tall, with a strong face crowned by a full head of curly black hair, and equally black side-whiskers. At that point, he was just about 30 years old, making him half the age of the Colonel. Nevertheless, Captain Rogers already had nearly a decade of sailing experience to his credit. He knew Long Island Sound like the back of his hand, and had been to New York City so many times that he could claim its harbor as part of his intimate knowledge. Having traded out of the Amboys since the previous spring, he also knew the narrow waters leading around Staten Island, and into the Raritan River.

But there were plenty of sloop captains with this kind of experience. If there was one thing that made Captain Rogers stand out, it surely must have been his abiding interest in Fulton's first experiments, back in 1807.

That alone, however, would not have been enough. John Stevens was no pushover. There must have been something else about this particular sloop captain that made him appealing to so disciplined a taskmaster as the Colonel. Given the challenges to be faced, Stevens must have taken the measure of the young man before him and come to a critical conclusion—

Captain Moses Rogers had fire in his belly.

* * *

Determined to begin running his steamboat in challenge to Livingston and Fulton, Colonel Stevens hired Moses Rogers to serve as captain of the *Phoenix* by the early spring of 1809.

At the beginning of May, the Colonel advertised his new service. Rather than give the New York authorities ample opportunity to seize the *Phoenix*, if Livingston and Fulton demanded it, Colonel Stevens planned to minimize the risk. The *Phoenix* would start from White-hall Street Wharf, in Lower Manhattan, cross the North River to the New Jersey side, steam down to the entrance to the Raritan River, and then proceed upriver to New Brunswick. That way, Colonel Stevens' "New Brunswick Steamboat," as he advertised it, would spend most of its transit near the Jersey shore.

But Fulton and Livingston quickly countered. The Chancellor's brother, John R. Livingston, informed Colonel Stevens that he would carry through on his previous threat, and run the third franchise steamboat, the recently-completed *Rariton*, to New Brunswick, as well . . . . . . at the same departure times as the *Phoenix* . . . . . . for one-third the fare the Colonel was charging.

This was, in fact, a charitable act. Rather than try to seize Colonel Stevens' steamboat and sue him for trespass, the New York franchise had decided to out-compete him.

Colonel Stevens got the message, and accepted that he had to give up the fight, at least temporarily. Before the *Rariton* even began the competition, the Colonel made plans to flee. The logical place to take his steamboat was down to the Delaware River, where it could run unmolested.

There was, however, one very dangerous problem: to get there, the *Phoenix* would have to venture out onto the open ocean.

This had never been done before. Whether a vessel with a heavy engine in its hold, fire in its boilers and heavy paddlewheels sticking out its sides could accomplish such a voyage safely was the subject of deep skepticism in New York.

Perhaps part of the reason Colonel Stevens hired Moses in the first place was because he thought he might have to attempt such a feat, and wanted an experienced mariner in command for the trip. Given fuel limitations, the *Phoenix* could not steam all the way down the New Jersey coast—she would have to employ her auxiliary sails for much of the journey, and Captain Rogers would know just how and when to use them.

On June 7th, 1809, the plan was set in motion. Moses went into the Custom House in New York City, and cleared the steamboat *Phoenix* for her journey to Philadelphia. He filled out a cargo manifest show-ing that he would be transporting nothing but a few sea stores—and ballast, of course, to keep the steamboat right-side-up. Three days later, Moses, as captain, and 21-year-old Robert Stevens, as engineer, were ready to go.

* * *

At 11 o'clock on the morning of Saturday, June 10th, Moses ordered the crew to cast off from the wharf in Lower Manhattan. By noon, Robert judged the steam pressure in the boilers sufficient to start the engine. Soon thereafter, the paddlewheels were set in motion, and the *Phoenix* began pushing her way south, into Upper New York Bay. Tagging along was an escort vessel*, just in case. Despite headwinds and fog, the steamboat was able to reach the Quarantine Grounds off Staten Island in one hour. Once there, the engine was stopped, and Moses ordered the crew to drop anchor.

While the final decision to proceed no further that day was in the hands of Moses as the captain, Robert Stevens, as engineer and son of the owner, was the equivalent of a first mate. If the steamboat was to reach its destination safely, the two of them had to work together, and agree on the best course of action.

The second day dawned the same as the first: foggy, with light breezes from the south. This meant the *Phoenix* would have to proceed blindly into a headwind if she tried to push her way through the Narrows, which led into Lower New York Bay. It also would be difficult for the sailing escort to keep up in such conditions, so Moses and Robert decided to wait.

On the third day, the winds had shifted to strong northerlies, and the fog had lifted, as well. It was time to proceed. Once through the Narrows, Moses pointed the *Phoenix* toward Sandy Hook lighthouse, and the passage to the sea. But as the steamboat bounced over the rough waves in the Lower Bay, some of the boards on the right (or *starboard*) paddlewheel gave way. Rather than risk further injury by continuing out onto the ocean, Moses and Robert took the *Phoenix* down to the very bottom of the Bay, to a place called Spermaceti Cove. There, they anchored for the evening, while the paddlewheel was repaired.

Very early on the fourth day, they set off again, passing Sandy Hook lighthouse, and moving out onto the open sea.

The *Phoenix* made good progress down the coast, leaving her

---

* Probably a small sailing sloop.

sailing escort far behind. But this advantage soon turned to disadvantage, when, later that afternoon, as Moses was guiding the steamboat into Cranberry Inlet for the night, the left (or *larboard**) paddlewheel gave way.

The fifth day was spent fixing the boards on the broken paddlewheel, and waiting, since the escort vessel was still nowhere in sight.

The sixth day delivered lightning storms and rain, but no escort. All Moses and Robert could do was wait within the protection of the inlet, and send the jolly boat over to the town of Tom's River, for more supplies.

Finally, on the seventh day, the escort vessel arrived at Cranberry Inlet. Steam was raised for a departure, but the swells at sea appeared so large that Moses and Robert decided to wait.

Early on the eighth day, the *Phoenix* and her escort ventured back out to sea. Before long, the weather turned "very doubtful," in Robert's words, and the decision was made to put in to Barnegat Bay, by Waretown. Once again, the escort vessel was nowhere in sight.

For the next three days, the *Phoenix* and her crew lay hunkered down in Barnegat Bay, as the Jersey coast was wracked by heavy gales, rough seas, and rain. On the night of June 18th, the crew watched helplessly as a schooner caught in the storm was driven ashore.

It was not until the 20th that the escort vessel finally caught up. As Moses and Robert prepared to make another foray out to sea, one of the crew decided he had had enough, and left the *Phoenix* for good.

At first light on the twelfth day, June 21st, the steamboat left the protection of Barnegat Bay, and headed southwest down the coast. A heavy fog rolled in by late afternoon, making it impossible to safely put in to any of the nearby bays. So Moses and Robert decided to push on to Cape May, at the southern tip of New Jersey, where they spent the night anchored over a shoal called Five Fathom Water.

The next morning, despite the fog, they got under way, rounded the Cape, and moved into Delaware Bay. The weather turned ominous yet again, but Moses and Robert determined that they should press on, through pelting rain, thundering skies, and streaks of lightning. It was well-past dark by the time they came to anchor at the mouth of the Delaware River.

On the fourteenth day, June 23rd, the *Phoenix* entered the Delaware

---

* The nautical term *port* (for left) was not yet in use.

River proper, and the approach to Philadelphia. Unfortunately, using the new mode of power was no longer an option—Robert found the boilers to be "very foul," and decided not to get steam up. Drifting upriver with the tide, the *Phoenix* finally reached Market Wharf at 9 o'clock that evening.

The transfer of the *Phoenix* had taken nearly two weeks, most of it spent sheltered from an angry sea. The superstitious could be excused for wondering whether Nature had been deliberately fighting this unnatural craft, as it had dodged and weaved its way down the storm-wracked Jersey coast. There certainly was plenty about the experience to give anyone pause. The frailty of the *Phoenix*—in particular, her paddlewheels, and her boilers—could not be denied.

For Captain Moses Rogers, though, the important thing was that he made it. In so doing, he had accomplished the first ocean voyage by a steam-powered vessel in history. He also had learned lessons that, in time, would prove invaluable for endeavors yet to come.

* * *

Colonel John Stevens' plan was straightforward: with his creation safely transferred to friendlier waters, he was going to run the *Phoenix* as a passenger vessel on the Delaware River, from Philadelphia to Trenton, the capital of New Jersey. At the latter place, passengers could transfer to stagecoaches, which would take them across the midsection of that State, to New Brunswick. Once there, they could transfer to John Livingston's new steamboat, the *Rariton*, and proceed to New York City. In this way, the Colonel could cooperate with Fulton and the Livingstons while continuing to challenge them elsewhere.

Captain Moses Rogers' instructions were equally clear: having safely maneuvered the *Phoenix* down to the Delaware River, he then had to make the "steam-boat" work—as a business. His experience doing so was still very limited, but so was everyone else's, since the world had only a tiny handful of commercially operating steamboats, all of them in the northeastern United States. At least the Delaware River had no competitors. It was a wide-open market, and an ideal place to learn how to adapt this new mode of transport to the needs of a traveling public.

With Robert Stevens initially serving as engineer, Moses started running the *Phoenix* up to Trenton within one month of their arrival. It didn't take long for many travelers to conclude that it was worth it to pay one dollar for the certainty of being 30 miles upriver, or down-river, in some 6 or 7 hours.

The Steamboat Phoenix, under the command of Captain Moses Rogers.

In the process of creating the first successful steamboat packet on the Delaware, Moses received both accolades and suggestions. At one point during his captaincy, a passenger wrote to one of the Philadelphia newspapers, commending "the gentlemanly conduct of Captain ROGERS, and the accommodating disposition of the men, who are in his service," which the writer said "merit, and have received applause." But at the same time, the passenger continued, many people thought the means of embarking and disembarking at the wharf in Philadelphia was "very unsafe," and needed to be remedied.

Such were the details of this brand new business, which had to be worked out, bit by bit, until the *Phoenix* ran as efficiently as possible. There was no denying that at its heart, this steamboating business was a "service." Making sure that the customers were not just comfortable with riding on a floating steam kettle, but happy with how they were treated, was critical to success.

Beyond playing host to loads of passengers, Moses also had to learn the peculiarities of both the Delaware River and the local officials in each of the towns where he stopped. Just as importantly, he had to learn from Robert Stevens all the ins and outs of the steam apparatus.

On the personal front, Moses and Adelia had to decide where to settle, and, it seems, keep within a budget. Philadelphia was an expensive city in which to live, and raise first-born Nathan and second-born Sarah (who came into this world while Moses was captain of the *Experiment*). So instead, they chose Bordentown, New Jersey, a bucolic village on the Delaware just below Trenton.

For Moses, seeing Adelia and the children during the steamboat season was a sporadic affair, since Bordentown was often only a brief stop on the way to and from Trenton. But during the winter, when ice on the river prevented the *Phoenix* from running, Moses had a lot more time to tend to his family.

For Adelia, being the wife of one of the first steamboat captains was something like that of a mariner's spouse, only the absences were much shorter. She pitched in to help when called for, periodically doing the steamboat's laundry (for which she charged 53 cents per dozen pieces washed).

Together, Moses and Adelia grew their brood on a regular basis. In the next five years, joining Master Nathan and Miss Sarah were George Washington, Daniel Moses and Delia Antoinette.

Back on the business side, Moses had to keep Colonel Stevens apprised of any and all issues affecting the steamboat, from bad weather, to breakdowns, to steaming times, to customer complaints, to a litany of expenses.

On expenses in particular, Moses had to send his employer receipts for everything, from pine wood fuel (at $3.25 per cord), to a wide assortment of alcoholic beverages for the on-board bar (at a couple dollars per gallon, usually), to tabletop condiments such as mustard (at 12½ cents a bottle). The Colonel, in turn, kept close track of these expenses, down to the penny. As the bills piled up, the cost of maintaining this new technology exasperated the Colonel more than anything.

Compounding John Stevens' frustrations over expenses were the early accounts and receipts which Captain Rogers sent to him. They often didn't seem particularly well organized, and frequently the steamboat captain declared he was owed money for the many disbursements he had made.

In any event, since Colonel Stevens remained on his estate at Hoboken, or at his New York residence on Broadway, Moses became his intermediary for trying to build yet more steamboats in Philadelphia. As the *Phoenix's* captain and host, Moses also naturally met a lot of business travelers who wanted to bring steamboats to their own cities and rivers. He dutifully passed these propositions on to his employer.

Initially, however, Colonel Stevens remained fixated on his Gotham rivals. By the end of the 1809 steamboating season, the Colonel had come to a kind of accommodation with them.

First, rather than fight over originality, Stevens and Fulton agreed to share patent credit for their respective steamboat designs.

Second, rather than fight over territory, both sides provisionally agreed to carve it up. Livingston and Fulton would develop virtually all the steamboat markets from New York City northward, as well as the Ohio and Mississippi River systems. John Stevens' steam domain would encompass the Delaware River south to the Savannah River, plus the waterways of Connecticut and Rhode Island. Anyone else who dared to build steamboats and introduce them into any market within these territories would be resisted, using all legal means available.

* * *

By the spring of 1811, Moses had nearly two years as a steamboat captain under his belt. There were still only a handful of these vessels operating successfully in the United States, and the rest of the world, while intrigued by the news of them, still viewed this new mode of transport with skepticism.

Since the *Phoenix* remained the only steamer on the Delaware, Moses must have felt secure enough to branch out. That May, he announced in one of the Philadelphia newspapers that he had opened a boarding house at Bordentown. As both a favorite country escape for Philadelphians and a connection point for the stagecoaches to New Brunswick, Bordentown figured to be an ideal place for such an establishment. Most of the day-to-day management of the boarding house was probably in the hands of Adelia, while Moses contributed steamboat customers, as well as victuals from the Philadelphia markets.

At the same time, Moses found himself working with a new member of the extended Stevens family. The Colonel had seen fit to send one of his nephews, Francis Stockton, to act as purser and accountant for the *Phoenix*.

The reason why soon became apparent: Colonel Stevens was not happy with Captain Rogers' disorganized reports regarding the steamboat's revenues and expenses. The Colonel simply could not believe how much it cost to run and maintain the *Phoenix*, so from then on, he wanted his nephew to be in charge of the money.

Further complicating matters was the tardiness with which Colonel Stevens reimbursed Captain Rogers for monies owed to him. Moses appears to have compensated for this by taking advances against his salary. This practice Francis Stockton was instructed specifically to curtail. As the nephew himself wrote in confirmation to his uncle, "it is always better to keep <u>within</u> the month's pay for fear of any <u>possible</u> danger."

Moses was not pleased with the imposition of this additional layer of management, but there was nothing he could do about it except get along with the young man.

For his part, Francis Stockton reported to the Colonel that Captain Rogers "really seems to have the good of the Boat as much at heart as if it were his own." The devotion of Moses to the *Phoenix* even crossed into the surreal at one point, when Stockton informed his uncle that one night Captain Rogers had "dreamt . . . there was something trouble the matter with the engine." This led Rogers to hurry down to the steamboat early the next morning, and check over the machinery with a member of the crew. After a thorough examination, they tried to start the engine, only to discover that it wouldn't work.

Later that season, in August, Stockton was compelled to leave the *Phoenix* temporarily for a trip to Canada (to act as a *supercargo*, or agent for a merchant's cargo). This circumstance invited yet another indirect rebuke of Captain Rogers. With the nephew gone, Moses was ordered to give all of the steamboat's monies to the Colonel's Philadelphia lawyer, Horace Binney, who would act as purser until Stockton's return.

When the nephew made another trip later that autumn, to the West Indies, the same procedure was followed, only this time Moses took the opportunity to show the Colonel that he had learned from his prior sloppiness. In addition to his usual reports, Moses also provided

John Stevens with detailed accounts of receipts for the *Phoenix*, in the same style as the Colonel's nephew.

In spite of all the financial oversight, Moses nevertheless continued to act as a conduit between his employer and eager entrepreneurs trying to build steamboats in the Colonel's territories. There were men at both ends of the Delaware run who, by then, were willing to try their hands at steamboating, including a Philadelphia shipbuilder named Joseph Grice. Moses implored Colonel Stevens to come to Philadelphia and negotiate directly with Grice, which the Colonel did do, at his leisure. There were others—passengers on the *Phoenix*—who also approached her captain. One passenger from Charleston, South Carolina suggested that a steamboat could be run on an inland route between that city and Savannah; again, Moses duly passed on this inquiry to the Colonel. Still other budding entrepreneurs publicly claimed that Captain Rogers had endorsed their steamboat engine design for use on Long Island Sound, obliging Moses to deny to the Colonel that he had ever done so.

Once the *Phoenix* was laid up for the winter, at the end of 1811, Moses had to focus on repairs and renovations. The wooden paddle-wheels in particular always took a beating, and needed substantial work. Certain cast-iron engine parts also needed to be replaced.

The cost of running and maintaining this new technology continued to vex the Colonel. His frustration eventually reached the point that Robert Stevens felt compelled to set his father straight: there was a receipt for every expense incurred, and furthermore, Captain Rogers said he was still owed money from the previous season.

As the 1812 season began, the discreet pushing and pulling on the relationship between Moses and his employer only intensified. In March, Colonel Stevens ordered Captain Rogers to give up responsibility for making out the steamboat's *waybills* (or shipping manifests). Robert, the bearer of this news, could tell Moses was reluctant to accept this—it was, after all, one of the usual duties for the master of any vessel—but he agreed to do so, if the Colonel thought it best.

While Colonel Stevens continued to push Moses away, the attraction of other opportunities beckoned. Erstwhile competitors were building Delaware steamboats not only for the runs upriver, to connect with stagecoaches to New York, but downriver to Wilmington, Delaware, to connect with stagecoaches to Baltimore.

In response, Colonel Stevens ordered Captain Rogers to run the

Phoenix in both directions. The spring and early summer of 1812 were spent juggling upriver runs to Trenton during the week with downriver runs to Wilmington on Sundays. At the same time, Moses continued to try to negotiate with these prospective rivals, suggesting again that Colonel Stevens travel to Philadelphia to come to terms with them. But the Colonel proved intransigent, believing his federal patent put him in a strong legal position to prevent any competition.

Eventually, Robert Stevens began to take greater notice of Captain Rogers and his movements, and duly passed on such intelligence to his father. In May of 1812, he reported that Robert Fulton himself had ridden on the *Phoenix*. "I am sorry I did not see him," wrote Robert, "as the Captain told me he had been to see all the boats" being fitted with steam engines at Philadelphia. More tellingly, a month later, Robert informed his father that "Captain rogers was obliged to attend to some business of his own at Phila—which prevented him from coming up in the B.[oat] today."

Two months after that, in August, Robert reported that a Captain Elihu S. Bunker had come to see him. This man had run a steamboat on the North River—in defiance of the Livingston-Fulton franchise—until it was seized by the New York authorities. Having lost his vessel, Captain Bunker was in need of employment, and he wanted to alert Robert that he thought the command of the *Phoenix* would soon be available. According to Bunker, Captain Rogers was secretly working on a rival steamboat.

Bunker didn't get the job, but his intelligence turned out to be right, and it should not have been too surprising. After four seasons running the *Phoenix*, Moses surely recognized that he had little chance to advance beyond his current position. The inclusion of so many Stevens relatives in the business—sons Robert, Richard and Francis, plus nephew Francis Stockton—provided ample evidence that not being blood kin limited his potential. Furthermore, Colonel Stevens' inability to come to terms with the new mode's newest believers left Moses with an obvious opening. At the end of the 1812 season, he bolted.

Moses joined a group of entrepreneurs which included Philadelphia shipbuilder Joseph Grice, with whom he had been negotiating on the Colonel's behalf since late 1809. Since the Colonel had failed to reach an agreement with Grice, the shipbuilder offered Moses a new beginning, and he took it.

At Grice's shipyard in the Northern Liberties, just north of Philadelphia, sat a nearly-completed steamboat. Moses was to be its first captain. Measuring 108 feet long, nearly 30 feet wide, and 261 tons burthen, it was both broader and heavier than his old command.

Grice and his partners, which included English émigré steam engine builder Daniel Large, knew full-well they would be going head-to-head with John Stevens' *Phoenix*. In recognition, they openly embraced the competition to come by naming their new steamboat the *Eagle*.

Getting this rival into operation took time. The *Eagle* was not ready for service until mid-June of 1813, when she was officially registered at the Philadelphia Custom House. Direct competition with the *Phoenix* commenced soon thereafter. Each steamboat was scheduled to leave Philadelphia at 7 o'clock in the morning, on Mondays, Wednesdays, and Fridays.

Accordingly, passengers could choose the *Phoenix*, which would head upriver to Trenton, as usual. There, her passengers would board stagecoaches for New Brunswick, and then take John Livingston's steamer *Rariton* to New York City.

Or, they could board the *Eagle* at Philadelphia, which would take them to Bordentown, where they would connect with a rival line of stagecoaches to New Brunswick. Once at New Brunswick, however, the *Eagle's* passengers were encouraged to make their own choice: they could either board John Livingston's *Rariton* for New York, or they could take passage on an upstart competitor, the steamboat *Sea Horse*. This newer entrant was the creation of former New Jersey Governor Aaron Ogden, with the help of engine designer Daniel Dod. They intended to succeed where Colonel Stevens had failed, breaking the Livingston-Fulton hold over New York waters.

In offering his passengers a choice at New Brunswick, Moses Rogers placed himself squarely against the established powers. He was both competing with his old employer, John Stevens, *and* allying himself against the Livingstons and Fulton by supporting their rival, Aaron Ogden's *Sea Horse*.

Through the summer of 1813, the *Eagle* ran against the *Phoenix*, with Colonel Stevens anxiously keeping track of each steamboat's performance. He was pleased to learn that the *Phoenix* seemed to outperform her rival on a regular basis.

But that was not enough. The Colonel instructed his Philadelphia lawyer, Horace Binney, to sue Captain Rogers and the owners of the

Eagle for infringement of his and Robert Fulton's steamboat patents. Fulton's personal lawyer, a man named Cadwallader D. Colden, offered to provide whatever information he could to help Colonel Stevens press the lawsuit.

However, this second plan of attack immediately hit a snag. In early August, Horace Binney informed the Colonel that he needed specific details as to just how Captain Rogers had violated the Stevens and Fulton steamboat patents.

The problem implied went beyond the obvious. The steamboat patents of Stevens and Fulton had been issued under the revised Patent Act of 1793—without any determination as to whether their claimed inventions were original. Once in court, it would be up to Horace Binney to not only cite the specific violations of their steamboat patents, but also show that those patents were for original inventions. Without proving both violation *and* originality, John Stevens would have no case.

This legal dilemma left Colonel Stevens with only one viable alternative: open battle in the marketplace. In late August, the Colonel exhorted his son Robert to get the *Phoenix* into top shape, for a direct confrontation with Captain Rogers and the *Eagle*.

But the older steamboat, despite repeated refurbishments, needed a lot more maintenance. By late September, the *Eagle* was so consistently beating the *Phoenix* that most passengers going upriver chose to ride the newer steamboat.

Robert Stevens felt he had no choice but to lay up the *Phoenix* for quick repairs, only to have her engine seize up a few days later, while on the run upriver. With each breakdown of the *Phoenix*, Captain Rogers and his *Eagle* gained an even greater advantage, and the chance to solidify their reputation with the public.

Unfortunately, this advantage didn't last long. Colonel Stevens had not sat still while others had been building new steamboats to serve the Delaware market. Knowing his *Phoenix* was getting old and obsolete, the Colonel previously had ordered a second steamer to be built, which his son Robert was working feverishly to complete. By mid-October, this new steamboat—named *Philadelphia*—was ready, and began making runs to Trenton.

Once both the *Phoenix* and *Philadelphia* were operational, Robert Stevens laid plans to ambush the *Eagle*. For Monday morning, October 25th, he intended to have both the Stevens steamboats depart

Philadelphia at the same time as the *Eagle*, and race her up the Delaware.

But it all proved unnecessary. Captain Rogers, having run the *Eagle* hard throughout the competition with the *Phoenix*, could literally feel his steamboat vibrating itself to pieces beneath his feet.

Two days before the planned ambush, the *Eagle* shook so much on her downriver run that the *Phoenix's* captain, in passing her, perceived his competitor's deck to be moving with each stroke of the engine. By the time Captain Rogers reached Philadelphia, he had not only lost the race with the *Phoenix* that day, but crippled his own steamboat in the process.

Upon hearing the news from Robert, Colonel Stevens could not hold back:

> *... that the Eagle, whose rapid flight was to have out stript far away that of the old Phoenix— That this vaunted Eagle should be beaten so disgracefully by the Phoenix— That she should be totally disabled for the season at least, is a victory as glorious on the Delaware as was that of Com.[modore] Perry on Lake Erie. Yes my Dear Boy I now feel the fullest confidence that the victory you have so meritoriously obtained will prove complete— That the enemy will never again dare to unfurl his flag on the waters of the Delaware—*

The damage done to the *Eagle* was indeed serious. In the week that followed, several tons of broken cast-iron parts—the weakest components of the machinery—were taken out of her. This experience, and its implications, would not be lost upon Moses.

Casting new parts would take time. Luckily, the steamboating season was nearly over, giving Moses and his partners the ensuing winter to rebuild the *Eagle's* machinery.

This respite in the marketplace also allowed the Colonel's legal action to play out. In the wake of Robert Livingston's death earlier that year, Robert Fulton, along with Livingston's heirs, were trying desperately to keep their exclusive New York franchise intact. Aaron Ogden's steamboat *Sea Horse*, as well as antagonistic maneuverings in the New Jersey Legislature, had put them on the defensive. In reaction, Fulton asked Colonel Stevens to drop any lawsuits against his Delaware steamboat competitors, lest an unfavorable result alter the New York franchise's own standing.

From the Colonel's perspective, foregoing legal action on the Delaware didn't dramatically affect his position. His primary nemesis, the *Eagle*, was disabled, and according to his son Robert, the other newly-introduced steamboats either shook so much or broke down so often as to offer no serious competition.

This advantage lasted until April of 1814, when the *Eagle*, repaired and refurbished, returned to the fray.

But as Captain Rogers discovered, the prior accident had yet another lesson to teach. Gaining customers had become more difficult. The very public breakdown of the *Eagle*'s machinery the previous October had damaged her reputation to the point that many travelers were hesitant to book passage on her.

Moses was compelled to improvise as best he could, alternating between competition with the Colonel's vessels going upriver, and rival steamboats going downriver, to Wilmington. By September of 1814, business was terrible. The *Eagle* was "making out very poorly," according to James Stevens, yet another son of the Colonel.

If there was any consolation, by that time the Stevens steamboats were not doing so well, either. The dangers of the ongoing war with Britain, previously of little consequence on the inland waters of the country, finally had become unavoidable. Washington, D.C. had just been sacked, and Baltimore barely escaped the same fate. With Britain's Royal Navy seemingly unafraid to thrust itself into American bays and rivers, many people concluded that steamboat travel on the Delaware was tempting fate too far. Until the war was over, the business of steamboating anywhere near the sea would have to remain involuntarily restricted.

* * *

As much as some people took to using this new mode of transport, there were many others who would not.

The reason why was simple: they didn't trust steamboats. Initially, the idea of overcoming Nature in the way these vessels did was just too bizarre for the superstitious. However, once a few more steamboats were built and running, the primary argument against them changed, to become one of safety.

Would an injured paddlewheel damage the hull, and result in a leak?

Would the incredible vibrations from the motion of the piston within the cylinder weaken the timbers in the hull, causing the boat to sink?

Would the crew lose control of the flames in the boiler, and set the whole steamboat on fire?

Would the incredible heat radiating from the boilers so dry out the timbers in the hull's structure as to cause spontaneous combustion?

And most terrifying of all, would the pressure in the boilers be allowed to rise to such a level as to cause them to explode, blowing passengers and crew to kingdom come?

Such qualms led many to forego using the new mode, and stick with the familiar sailing packets, or the just-introduced *teamboats*, which used a team of animals to provide the power for turning the paddlewheels.

But for the very few who really knew, the inherent risks of steamboats could be managed, and minimized. With each new steam vessel came improvements, allowing it to achieve more, leading to still more improvements on the next one.

As the technology continued to advance, the imaginations of its leading proponents inevitably wandered further afield: if steamboats could be made to run on rivers, surely they could be made to operate on larger bodies of water, anywhere in the world.

For many observers, such ideas brought to mind the ancient Greek myth of the *chimera* ("khi-máir-uh"). This could not have been more appropriate. The chimera—composed of a lion's head, a goat's body and a serpent's tail—was a fire-breathing she-monster which bore more than a passing resemblance to steamboats.

More generally, the mythical chimera also had come to represent anything thought to be a figment of the imagination. To skeptics of the new mode of transport, this other definition was even more fitting, especially when applied to the proposition that steamboats could be employed beyond their current, limited uses in protected waters. To them, the whole idea that these fragile machines might be capable of operating out on the open ocean was simply an unrealistic fantasy— or, in a word, *chimerical.*

* * *

In the early months of 1812, while Moses was beginning his last season as captain of the *Phoenix*, Robert Fulton had received a proposition. It came from a man named Pavel Svin'in, who was a member of Russia's first diplomatic delegation to the United States.

Svin'in's official duty was to act as secretary to his country's mission at Philadelphia. But since he had some artistic talent, and Russia's rulers had little knowledge of what this new United States looked like, Svin'in also was instructed to travel around his new posting, and record, in words and watercolors, what he saw. In the course of his work, Svin'in had become infatuated with the one unique thing the Americans had, and that was steamboats.

Seeing their potential, the diplomat had decided to make a proposal to Fulton: introduce steamboats to Russia, and make Svin'in his partner in the venture.

In reply, Robert Fulton wrote to Svin'in in April of 1812. He informed the diplomat that the previous November he had written to the American minister to Russia, John Quincy Adams, requesting an exclusive steamboat franchise from the Russian government. Until Fulton heard back, he did not feel it necessary to make any deals.

A little more than a week later, Fulton wrote to Minister Adams in St. Petersburg. He asked Adams to apply to the Russian government on his behalf for an exclusive right to operate steam vessels in Russia, or alternately only on the route between St. Petersburg and the island port of Kronstadt. Fulton further stipulated that he would have the first steamboat operating within 3 years of the franchise's start date.

By the time this letter reached Russia, the United States had declared war against Britain, making such a Russian enterprise extremely difficult. Yet Adams made the inquiry anyway. He was told that the Russian emperor, Alexander (the First), was willing to grant an exclusive steamboat charter for a period of 15 years, activated only if Fulton could get a steamboat operating in Russian waters within 3 years. Fulton also would have to provide a complete set of drawings for his steamboat, in order to validate the charter.

Adams wrote back to Fulton in November of 1812, describing the terms that the Emperor had offered; the only remaining step was the issuance of an *ukaze* ("oo-káhz"), or imperial edict. Since the 3-year time limit would begin based upon the date of the ukaze, Adams suggested that it was in Fulton's interest to postpone the official signing of this edict until he was ready to build the vessel.

Since it usually took three or four months for a letter to make the journey between New York and St. Petersburg, Fulton and Adams spent most of 1813 confirming and solidifying the timing and terms of the charter. In the meantime, Robert Livingston died in February of that year, shattering Fulton, and forcing him to share the burden of maintaining the New York franchise with the Chancellor's heirs. Fulton pressed on, nevertheless.

On December 10th, 1813, the Emperor Alexander signed the ukaze granting Fulton an exclusive steamboat charter in Russia.

Once Fulton received news of the signing, in early 1814, he knew he had less than 3 years to get a steamboat operating in Russia, or the exclusive right would be lost. Going to St. Petersburg himself, while considered, was out of the question. Fulton had too much to manage at home, including the building of an enormous steam-powered war vessel for the U.S. Navy, intended to act as a floating battery to defend New York harbor from British attack. Besides, any journey to Russia risked capture by the Royal Navy blockading the American coast. The best course of action seemed to be waiting for peace to break out, and then organizing a construction team to be sent to Russia.

In the meantime, the New York franchise was busy building a new kind of steamboat. Unlike previous versions, which had relatively flat bottoms, this new one had a curved hull, like that of sea-going vessels. This deeper keel, it was argued, would allow it to steam a straight course through rougher, deeper waters.

The need for such a design was based upon the target market for this new steamboat, which was Long Island Sound. While the market-sharing agreement between Fulton, Livingston and Stevens had ceded the ports of Connecticut and Rhode Island to the Colonel, getting any vessels into operation there had proved impossible. This was because Colonel Stevens had been thwarted, he said, by "combined attacks of prejudice" against the very idea that steamboats could operate in such turbulent waters. With his failure to initiate service, the New York franchise stepped forward to meet the challenge.

When the newly-designed steamer was completed and ready for service in the autumn of 1813, Fulton pronounced himself very pleased with the result. In fact, he thought the design of this deep-keel steamboat, called the *Fulton*, was so good that he declared he would not be afraid to cross the ocean in it.

In such a radical thought lay the seed of an idea for fulfilling the Russian charter: instead of building a steam vessel in Russia, why not just send one across?

But at that moment, the *Fulton* could not even run on Long Island Sound. The risk of capture or destruction by the Royal Navy was just too great. So instead, this deep-water steamboat, under the command of Captain Elihu S. Bunker, was put on the North River route to Albany. The Russian market would have to wait until the end of the war.

* * *

On Saturday evening, February 11th, 1815, a Royal Navy sloop-of-war entered New York harbor. Flying from its mast was a flag of truce. On board was a British diplomat, as well as a member of the American peace delegation, which had been sent to Europe to negotiate with the British government.

The news these two men brought sent Gotham into delirious celebration: the United States and Great Britain had signed a peace treaty the previous December 24th, at the city of Ghent. The war was *over!*

While news of the peace treaty was being spread throughout the country in the days that followed, the Gothamites wasted little time, and got ready for business. With the oceans finally safe for trade, the city's merchants, mechanics and mariners began moving with renewed purpose.

But their absolute exuberance was short-lived.

Twelve days after the peace news, New York was rocked by the loss of its greatest adopted son. Robert Fulton was dead. Exhausted by efforts to defend his steamboat franchise in court, and exposed to the harsh winter while overseeing the outfitting of his steam battery for the Navy, Fulton had developed an infection. Unable to overcome it, he passed away on February 23rd.

New Yorkers fully appreciated what Fulton had done for them. It was thanks to him that their city had become the birthplace of the new mode of transport, and they responded accordingly. Gotham's newspapers framed their obituary articles and funeral coverage with a thick black line, something only done for heroes of great prominence. Organizations to which Fulton had belonged, such as the New York Historical Society and the Academy of Arts, instructed their members to wear black armbands in his honor. And on the day of his burial at Trinity Church, the whole of the funeral route along the Broadway was packed with mourners. No one better described the sentiment of the city in the wake of his death than the Society of Mechanics and Tradesmen, which called Fulton a "towering genius," and mourned "the loss which our country, and the civilized world have sustained."

* * *

Robert Fulton's death threw the Monopoly into a concealed panic. His wife, Harriet Livingston Fulton, and his executor, Harriet's brother-in-law William Cutting, wanted to preserve what value they could of what Robert Fulton had built. Once domestic issues were addressed, they turned their attention to the steamboat charter granted by Russia's emperor.

In the spring of 1815, William Cutting wrote to John Quincy Adams, who by then had become the U.S. minister to Britain. Cutting asked Adams, as the former minister to Russia, to intervene on Harriet Fulton's behalf, and confirm that the 1813 ukaze for her deceased husband remained in effect. Cutting promised that once a confirmation was received, Fulton's heirs would send a team of mechanics to Russia to build a steamboat within the 3-year limit, which would expire on December 10th, 1816. Once this inquiry had been sent, all the Monopoly could do was bide its time, and wait for an answer.

* * *

The end of the war did more than put American merchants and farmers back in business; it also gave a great boost to steamboat entrepreneurs. New markets for the new mode, effectively closed during the conflict, were suddenly wide open.

This was precisely what Moses Rogers and the *Eagle* needed. Their best opportunity lay not in continued competition with Colonel Stevens and the other, newer rivals on the Delaware River, but rather in satisfying the demand for steamboat service further to the south.

There was, for example, only one steamboat in all of the Chesapeake Bay. This vessel, the *Chesapeake*, had been clobbering her sailing packet competitors since 1813, running from Baltimore up to the top of the Bay, where she connected with the stagecoaches to Wilmington and Philadelphia.

Among those losing out to the *Chesapeake* were Baltimore sailing packet owners Samuel Briscoe and James Partridge. The only way for them to recover, they concluded, was to get their own steamboat, and match the competition. Under the circumstances, Captain Rogers and the *Eagle* looked like saviors. At the end of May 1815, Briscoe and Partridge bought out almost all the existing owners of the *Eagle*, while keeping Captain Rogers in command.

Two weeks later, Moses walked into the Philadelphia Custom House, and cleared the *Eagle* for departure. Immediately thereafter, he took the steamboat downriver, to Wilmington.

Then, once conditions looked favorable, Moses and the *Eagle* ventured out onto the Atlantic. Using a combination of steam and sail, he steered the *Eagle* southward, and into Chesapeake Bay.

Arriving safely at Norfolk, Virginia, Moses became only the second captain to bring a steamboat into that port. (The Monopoly's steamboat *Washington,* coming down from New York on its way to the Potomac River, had beat him for first place by less than a month.)

From Norfolk, Moses took the *Eagle* northward, to Baltimore. Once there, he set about running her regularly between Baltimore and Elkton, Maryland, at the top of Chesapeake Bay. He also made periodic forays to other ports along the Bay, including Annapolis and Norfolk on the western side, and Centreville on the eastern side. Moses even ascended the James River to Richmond, becoming the first to ever bring a steamboat to Virginia's capital city.

Beyond these accomplishments, though, the *Eagle*'s successful ocean transfer remained, in itself, the most unusual. Steamboat entrepreneurs strongly preferred to build these vessels in the market where they were going to operate, rather than chance even a one-time delivery by sea. The risk of calamity was just too great. That Moses Rogers could claim not one, but two ocean transfers to his credit by 1815 made him more than just an experienced steamboat captain—it made him extraordinary.

* * *

When the Russian government received word that Robert Fulton had died, it quickly came to realize that it was in a very difficult position.

After the Emperor Alexander had awarded a steamboat charter to Fulton in late 1813, a Scottish expatriate living in St. Petersburg had begun experimenting on his own with the new mode of transport. By the spring of 1815, this Charles Baird, who had produced iron and built steam engines in Russia for many years, proposed that the imperial government give *him* an exclusive steamboat charter. To back up his proposition, Baird built a small experimental steamboat, and ran it on St. Petersburg's Neva River.

The American chargé d'affaires at St. Petersburg, Levett Harris, immediately protested. Baird's activities were contrary to the steamboat franchise already issued in Robert Fulton's favor, Harris declared.

This diplomatic protest led to a great deal of discussion within the Russian government. In the end, it was confirmed that while the terms of the Fulton charter remained in force, it would not be officially recognized until a steamboat was in operation and drawings were submitted, as required.

Therefore, since Fulton's monopoly charter was not yet officially recognized, the Russian government also declared that Charles Baird could continue with his experiments. If Fulton's heirs did not have a steamboat operating in Russian waters by December 10th, 1816, then their charter would expire, and Baird could apply for his own. In this way, the Russians kept their promise to Fulton, without discouraging the efforts of an enterprising expatriate already on the scene.

Once the Monopoly learned that the Russian government had upheld the terms of Fulton's steamboat charter, they had to decide how to proceed. Sending engineers, mechanics and workmen all the way to Russia to build a steamboat from scratch must have seemed an intimidating proposition.

But there was another possibility. When the steamboat *Fulton* had been launched, Robert Fulton himself had declared that he was so confident of the design that he would not be afraid to take his name-sake across the ocean. Given how well the *Fulton* was performing on post-war runs through Long Island Sound, the Monopoly decided to act on their founder's idea.

At the dawn of 1816, construction began on a new Monopoly steamboat at the shipyard of Adam Brown, who, along with his brother Noah, had built the *Fulton*. The new vessel's dimensions and machinery were to be virtually identical to those of the Long Island steamer. Its intended purpose, however, would be entirely different, as the contemplated name made clear. This newest steam vessel was to be called the *Emperor of Russia*.

Just what the Monopoly was up to did not become public knowledge until August 1st, 1816, when several newspapers laid bare the plan. The particular article published by *The Evening Post* of New York was—all at once—short, stunning, and sarcastic:

Steam Boat up for Russia.—We hear that it is in contemplation to run a Steam Boat between this place and Russia and to start the 1st of September. We understand that great efforts will be made to engage if possible the seventh son, as *purser*.

As most Gothamites well-knew at the time, the "seventh son" referred to Daniel D. Tompkins, who was the seventh son of New York revolutionary Jonathan G. Tompkins.

But the personal history went far beyond that. Daniel D. Tompkins also was the sitting Governor of New York. He also was a candidate for the Vice-Presidency of the United States in the upcoming national election. And he also was one of the earliest investors in Robert Fulton's steamboats.

This last distinction made the Governor's supposed involvement in any steam-across-the-Atlantic scheme appear plausible—until one considered *The Evening Post*'s suggestion of Tompkins as the *"purser."* For if New York's most prominent politician had an Achilles' heel, it was his record of financial falsehoods, from the improper handling of State war loans, to padding his official salary as governor.

The underlying message of *The Evening Post*'s article was unmistakable: anyone foolish enough to fund an attempt to cross the Atlantic in a steamboat might as well just hand their money over to the "seventh son," and kiss it goodbye.

In direct contrast, another newspaper that same day, *The Columbian*, took a far more inspiring approach:

A NOBLE ENTERPRISE

It is reported and believed that a distinguished barrister of this city together with capt. Bunker of the steam-packet "Fulton," have resolved to cross the Atlantic to England, and proceed thence to Russia in the steam-boat above-mentioned. This grand undertaking, we understand, is in fulfillment or acceptance of a contract offered to Mr. Fulton by the emperor of Russia, allowing him the exclusive navigation of steam-boats in the Russian empire for 25 years. As the vessel is built as substantial and strong as a sloop of war, little or no doubt is entertained by naval men of the practicability of the attempt. We are delighted with the prospect of a steam-boat propelled across the Atlantic Ocean, by Americans "the first." There is no doubt of the expedition, it is determined; and, since the rumor is busy on the subject, we make free mention that Mr. Colden is the gentlemen alluded to.

"Mr. Colden" was none other than Cadwallader D. Colden, prominent New York lawyer, friend of Fulton, and investor in his steamboats.

With Fulton's death, Colden had assumed a greater role in the Monopoly's activities, and become a primary force behind meeting the terms of the Russian charter. Unbeknownst to the press, he was already in the process of trying to procure insurance for the undertaking, and would, the next day, gain approval from the New York Insurance Company for a $15,000 policy, although the premium to be paid had yet to be negotiated.

As word of the proposed Atlantic crossing spread up and down the coast of the United States, still more information came to light, which was dutifully reported by the newspapers, even though some of it proved very confusing.

—*It was not the Fulton, but rather a new steamboat under construction that would make the attempt.*

—*And Captain Elihu S. Bunker would not be in command. Instead, it was to be Captain Frank Ogden, who had successfully taken the steamboat Vesuvius from Pittsburgh all the way to New Orleans, back in 1814.*

—*On the contrary! Captain Samuel Reid, illustrious commander of the late privateer General Armstrong, would be making the crossing attempt with Mr. Colden.*

—*No, that wasn't entirely right, either. Navy war hero Captain Isaac Hull, prior commander of the completed steam battery Fulton, was the one rumored to be going, having volunteered to act as navigator.*

With all these speculations swirling around, the Monopoly realized it needed to get a better sense of just how the nearly-completed *Emperor of Russia* might perform on the unforgiving ocean. So on Thursday, August 8th, one week after the "steamboat to Russia" story first broke, the Monopoly placed an advertisement in *The Evening Post*:

> *Fishing Party.*—The Steam-Boat FULTON will leave New-York on Saturday morning, and proceed to the Sea Bass Banks, on an excursion of pleasure and fishing. Tickets to be had of Mott & Williams, corner of Beekman-slip and South-st.

It was a very unusual notice—the *Fulton* had never done such a thing before. The Sea Bass Banks, after all, were off the *south* shore of Long Island, in the Atlantic Ocean proper.

Yet the proposed excursion's purpose, beyond perhaps trying to create a new source of revenue, must have been clear to keen observers. Long Island Sound, where the *Fulton* normally plied, could get plenty rough, but it was still protected waters. Taking the *Emperor of Russia*'s closest relative out on the ocean would at least give the Monopoly some sense of what a steamboat would face trying to cross the width of the North Atlantic.

But this scheduled excursion, for Saturday, August 10th, does not appear to have come off as planned. Some of the reasons why were contained in *The Evening Post*'s Friday edition. Among the articles found there was news that one of the western steamboats, the *Despatch*, had sunk at Pittsburgh, while another, the *Vesuvius*, had caught fire and burnt on the Mississippi River, just north of New Orleans. Such stories were hardly encouraging for anyone thinking about going out to the Sea Bass Banks in the *Fulton*. Clearly, these steamboats were still dangerous conveyances.

The same advertisement for the same excursion was run again the following week, with the added courtesy of stating the exact hour of departure, that being 8 o'clock in the morning on Saturday, August 17th.

This time, the trip was made. The *Fulton* left with about 170 passengers at 9 o'clock, and returned over 12 hours later that evening. While there was not much fishing to be had, according to *The Evening Post*, the 80-mile trip out and back had been "a pleasant one."

No further excursions onto the ocean were advertised for the *Fulton*, and by late August of 1816, most of the Atlantic-crossing chatter in the New York newspapers had diminished into near silence.

The reason for the reticence was simple: the Monopoly was having second thoughts. One aspect of the *Fulton*'s test excursion to the Sea Bass Banks which gave pause was the issue of fuel. While steam engines in Britain ran mostly on coal, early American steamboat engines ran on wood, because it was plentiful and inexpensive. The problem was that compared to coal, wood produced far less heat for its bulk, and therefore had to be burned at a faster rate to run the boilers. While most observers realized that the *Emperor of Russia* could steam for only a fraction of the way across the Atlantic, having a fuel supply that would not give out quickly was still a factor to think over.

So the Monopoly tried a further experiment. At the very beginning of September, one of their North River steamboats, the *Car of Neptune*, departed on her normal run to Albany, but with one key difference: the fuel placed aboard to make her go was coal.

Her firemen, used to burning wood in the boilers, didn't think it could be done. The first attempt proved them right—the *Car* missed her departure time, not having a coal-based fire strong enough to work the engine. But a second try sent the steamboat on its way, and it reached Albany in the acceptable time of 35 hours.

Having proved that coal could be used, and would provide a longer-lasting fuel supply, the next step for an ocean crossing was simply to go. But the planned departure date of early September came, and went.

Beyond resolving the coal issue, one additional cause for delay may have been reports arriving from Europe that a "Mr. Baird" was already running a steamboat in Russia, from St. Petersburg to Kronstadt. Was the ukaze for Fulton still in effect, or not?

By mid-September, the silence of Gotham's press was deafening. The only way to learn what had happened was to read newspaper issues arriving from elsewhere, such as the *City Gazette* of Charleston:

> We understand that the attempt to send a Steam-Boat from New-York to Russia, has been abandoned, from a want of funds to carry the enterprise into effect. . .

That the Monopoly—of all the proponents of this new mode of transport—could not muster the money to push forward was a sobering admission. It showed all too clearly that beneath the outward confidence and fevered speculation of a month prior lay the most fundamental of human emotions.

And that this, the first effort to cross the Atlantic in a steam vessel, had succumbed as a result, surely dampened the hopes of the few who believed in the new mode's potential. It also must have fortified the perceptions of the many who did not.

* * *

By the autumn of 1816, a few months after the "steamboat to Russia" hubbub, Moses Rogers left the steamboat *Eagle* in the Chesapeake Bay, and headed north to Philadelphia.

There, a newly re-built steamer, the *New Jersey*, was ready for service. Samuel Briscoe and James Partridge wanted her to join the *Eagle*, so that their packet line would have two steamboats running between Baltimore and Elkton. But to put this plan into effect, someone had to take the *New Jersey* out onto the ocean, and bring her down to the

Chesapeake Bay before winter set in. For such a dangerous task, Briscoe & Partridge wanted Captain Rogers.

On November 16th, Moses went into the Philadelphia Custom House and filled out all the necessary paperwork, including a cargo manifest. As with his previous ocean journeys, he would make the voyage without any cargo in the hold.

On November 19th, he was ready to go. Proceeding out of Delaware Bay, Moses maneuvered the *New Jersey* down the coast and into the Chesapeake, arriving at Norfolk, Virginia in 36 hours, "safe and sound," as one local newspaper put it.

A few days later, Moses and the *New Jersey* continued on to Baltimore. By the first week of December 1816, they were able to make a few packet runs up to Elkton, before the waters froze over.

These initial packet trips, however, were really incidental. Far more important was the larger goal of getting the *New Jersey* in place, and ready for the start of the spring season of 1817. In the meantime, Captain Moses Rogers, having completed his third successful steamboat voyage on the Atlantic Ocean, could justifiably bask in his accomplishment, and look forward to whatever lay ahead.

* * *

With the collapse of its effort to send a steamboat to Russia, and the passage of the 3-year deadline on December 10th, 1816, the Monopoly resigned itself to losing the charter which the Emperor Alexander had granted to Robert Fulton.

The steam vessel originally contemplated as the *Emperor of Russia* instead became known as the steamboat *Connecticut*, Captain Elihu S. Bunker commanding, and was put on the New York-to-New Haven route.

Since the ability of steamboats to navigate Long Island Sound and the Chesapeake Bay was, by then, proven and accepted, the Monopoly turned its attention to the potential for coastal steamboat routes. Since the end of the war with Britain, a number of attempts had been made to raise money to start coastal steam packet companies.

In September of 1815, there had been moves afoot to raise money for a New York-to-Charleston service, but nothing came of the effort.

Another attempt for that same route was made six months later, in March of 1816. Subscription books were opened at Charleston, but again there were not enough takers.

Then, later that same year, in the wake of the aborted voyage to Russia, the Monopoly, which also had an exclusive franchise to run steamboats in the State of Louisiana, announced that a subscription book for a new company had been opened at New Orleans. The objective of this enterprise was to raise $125,000 for an "ocean steam boat," to run from New York to New Orleans, stopping at Havana along the way.

This was an enormous sum of money, and it clearly implied the Monopoly knew that to gain the public's confidence, a steam-powered vessel of unprecedented size and power would have to be built.

No matter—nothing came of this effort, either.

The simple fact was that steamboats on the rivers, lakes and bays of the country still suffered from plenty of accidents. As a result, there were just not enough investors willing to risk their money on running the new mode of transport at sea. Further fortifying such perceptions was the fact that some of the few ocean transfers being attempted from one port to another ended in near-disaster, or worse.

One such experience occurred in the late spring of 1817, when the steamboat *Massachusetts* was being taken from Philadelphia, where she was built, to her new owners in Salem, Massachusetts. In the course of the journey up the coast, the steam engine broke down, and the paddlewheels were badly damaged by rough seas. Without enough sail power to make headway, the steamboat had to be towed repeatedly by schooners in order to reach safety.

Eventually, though, the *Massachusetts* made it to Salem. After undergoing the necessary repairs, she took a few trial trips and excursions along the coast, down to Boston, and up to Portsmouth, New Hampshire. These test runs convinced the owners that their steamboat could never withstand repeated and extended exposure to the sea. So they decided to sell the *Massachusetts*, rather than risk sinking her.

In late November of 1817 (just as Moses was preparing the *Charleston* for her maiden trip to Savannah), a man by the name of Captain Charles Vanderford took possession of the *Massachusetts*. Vanderford's plan was to take the steamboat all the way to Mobile, Alabama, hop-scotching down the coast, stopping at ports along the way to refuel and seek protection from the sea, as needed. It was, as observers at the time noted, the longest steamboat ocean transfer yet attempted.

Unfortunately, they didn't make it. The *Massachusetts* ran aground near Little Egg Harbor, New Jersey in late December, and was soon given up for lost.

Such was the state of steamboats at the end of 1817. One-time, short-distance ocean transfers could be accomplished, but they were hardly guaranteed. Furthermore, no captain of this new mode of transport seemed both willing and able to challenge Nature by venturing a regular steam packet service out on the open ocean.

That, however, was about to change.

CHAPTER FOUR

FOUNDATION, AND FORMATION

A T 11:20 ON THE morning of December 18th, 1817, the order was given to cast off, as the steamboat *Charleston*, under the command of Captain Moses Rogers, began her second packet trip to Savannah. While the first voyage had encountered a lot of fog, the second trip experienced a different problem: the pilot at the tiller kept getting the steamboat stuck in the river shallows along the way. If reversing the paddlewheels didn't get the *Charleston* off, and the crew couldn't push her off using poles, then the only other solution was to wait for the rising tide.

* * *

Down in Savannah, Charles Howard already knew that the *Charleston* was coming. As the steamboat's agent, he ran a newspaper advertisement on Friday, December 19th, to alert the public. In it, he stated that the steamer "will probably be here this evening, or tomorrow morning.—She will return to Charleston immediately." The implied message was clear: the steamboat would achieve a quicker passage than before, as well as a quick turnaround.

But the *Charleston* didn't show. Howard ran the notice again, on Saturday.

Still the *Charleston* didn't show. Sunday came and went, and there was no sign of the steamboat. Howard ran the advertisement again, for Monday morning, December 22nd. Beyond that, he could do nothing more, but wait, and wonder.

* * *

As noon approached that Monday, there must have been sighs of relief as word came down from the Exchange lookout that the steamboat had been spotted, splashing its way up the Savannah River. By the time Captain Rogers got the *Charleston* to the wharves, it was 11:30 A.M. The steamboat's transit time had been 4 days and 10 minutes, nearly twice as long as the first trip down. Even worse, several of the regular sailing packets that had left Charleston along with the steamboat ended up arriving at Savannah much sooner.

It was, on the surface, an embarrassing state of affairs for Moses, but the *Charleston's* passengers, knowing the true story, came to his rescue. They gave the *Columbian Museum and Savannah Daily Gazette* a note for publication:

> The passengers in the steam boat Charleston, from Charleston to Savannah, having met with a considerable & unexpected detention by grounding the boat on the passage, and wishing the public not to misunderstand the cause, beg leave to state, that it was entirely owing, either to the ignorance, or wilful mismanagement of the Pilot. He was highly recommended to the inspectors of the boat as one who was qualified in every respect to conduct the navigation of the rivers: whereas he has proved himself to be the very reverse of the character which he was represented to sustain. We beg leave to bear our testimony to the excellence of the steam-boat, the skill, the vigilance, the careful, polite and gentlemanly deportment of captain Rogers—his attention to all of the interests committed to his care, to the comfort and convenience of his passengers, entitles him at once to their thanks, and to the perfect confidence of the public.

This unusual step by the passengers, and especially the content of their message, must have set tongues to-wagging in Savannah for days. While the pilot's own explanation for his conduct was not publicly reported, people could easily see the effect of it: the steamboat had been much slower than the sailing packets.

Whether the sailing packet masters themselves had a hand in the pilot's incompetence is also unknown, but certainly the old mode of transport had cause to fear this steamboat. The *Charleston* could injure their passenger trade, or maybe even kill it. In answer, the masters and owners of the sailing packets employed whatever strategies they could to compete.

One such tactic, subtle though it was, became apparent in the days that followed. Usually, the sailing sloops advertised their departures for Charleston in the local Savannah newspapers, on pages 2 or 3 of a normal four-page edition. But once advertisements for the steamboat *Charleston* began to run, always on the inside pages, the sailing packet departure notices began to dance. A number of sailing packet owners —like Scottish expatriate merchant John Bogue, who owned a packet sloop named *Valiant*—shifted their departure notices to the front page. Other vessels, such as the "fast sailing packet sloop" *Adeline*, had theirs strategically placed just below the *Charleston's* at first, only to decide later to have them moved to the front page, as well.

But beyond the distinctions of dancing newspaper ads and a slightly lower fare, the sailing captains still knew they would be hard-pressed to compete, unless ill-fortune or ill-repute tarnished the steamboat's image. To avoid that fate, Captain Rogers would simply have to persevere, carefully, regardless of the obstacles.

Leaving Savannah several days later, Moses managed to bring the *Charleston* back to her home port in 45 hours. While this was slower than the previous return trip, Moses nevertheless received praise from the passengers for his "skill and outgoing conduct."

At the end of December, the third trip down to Savannah was made in only 36 hours. This was a good transit time, but some sloops made the voyage in as little as one day. Moses would have to do better still.

Then, at the beginning of January 1818, as Moses prepared to depart on the fourth trip down to Savannah, he received a valuable endorsement for his steamboat. In addition to playing host to 21 passengers, he also was entrusted to carry what was arguably the most important freight available, and that was specie. While the American economy operated primarily on paper credit and paper currency issued by privately-run banks, the ultimate international money remained specie, meaning gold or silver, usually in the form of coins. The American dollar itself was based upon the ubiquitous eight-royals silver coin still being minted in the Spanish colonies of Mexico, Peru and Chile. That the *Charleston* had been hired to carry specie represented a subtle vote of confidence in her safety, and in Captain Rogers.

On the return trip, Moses brought the steamboat up to Beaufort by early evening, where he decided to stop for the night.

The next morning, he ordered the crew to push off from the Beaufort wharves promptly at half past 7 o'clock. The *Charleston* then proceeded, as usual, into St. Helena Sound.

Once there, however, Moses did something different. Instead of pointing the steamboat toward the swampy inland water route, he turned the vessel due east, and headed straight for the sea. Crossing over the sandbar at the Sound's entrance, the *Charleston* churned out onto the open ocean, skirting along the Carolina coast, toward her home port. In so doing, Moses was making a cautious, measured experiment.

As the *Charleston* passed the entrance to the North Édisto River, Captain Rogers and the crew spied a three-masted craft in the distance, rigged to carry swept-back, triangular lugger sails. Flying from one of its masts was a square white flag adorned with a solid-black circle. This flag's shape and scheme was the very specific signal for a vessel in distress. Soon the sound of two or three shots from its signal gun echoed across the waves, yet another indication that the lugger was in trouble.

The first instinct of Moses was the same as that of any mariner, which was to help. But to do so, he judged, would mean missing the high tide at Charleston's bar, and keeping the steamboat out at sea overnight. His first responsibility was to the safety of his passengers, which, on this trip, totaled 17 in all, including some children.

Rather than take such a risk, Moses decided to proceed on to port, and notify the authorities of the lugger in distress. The steamboat crossed over the sandbar at the entrance to Charleston Bay at half past 5 o'clock that afternoon, just as the sun was dropping below the Carolina horizon. By the time the steamboat reached the wharf, it was half past 6 o'clock, and dark.

Once news of what had transpired on this return trip spread, it must have been clear to Moses that he had broken through. The message sent to prospective passengers was both powerful and reassuring. On the one hand, he had completed the trip from Savannah in just 16½ hours running time, and 29½ hours in total, nearly equal to the best the sailing packets could ever hope to do. Yet on the other hand, he had shown the traveling public that it was perfectly alright to take the steamboat out on the ocean, and that no matter what the circumstances, he would never jeopardize their safety at sea.

From that point forward, Moses possessed a new power and responsibility. With each departure, he could choose to take the *Charleston* "inside" (through the coastal waterways) or "outside" (onto the open Atlantic). The determining factors would be conditions out on the ocean, and whether he thought the steamboat could make the passage safely.

The public's confidence in Captain Rogers' judgment, and the *Charleston's* strength, was reinforced by their performance later that January, when the steamboat made another trip on the outside, from Beaufort to Charleston. Despite encountering "a very rough sea," the steamboat arrived at her home port without suffering damage of any kind.

Once the *Charleston* had completed a number of round trips, and Moses cut the one-way transit time to as little as 24½ hours, he then felt comfortable committing to a weekly schedule. In late January, the steamboat was advertised to arrive in Savannah every Monday, and depart immediately for her home port the following day.

Then, at the beginning of February, some of the *Charleston's* departure notices dropped any invitation for freight, which previously had been accepted. This slight change helped Moses further differentiate his service from the cargo-first, passengers-second sailing packets. At the same time, it also helped him determine whether he could depend upon passenger traffic alone to sustain the steamboat.

Eventually, Moses pushed the limits of the oceanic route even further. On some trips, he took the *Charleston* as far as 10 miles from shore, nearly out-of-sight of the coast.

It was all part of the plan. Gradually, carefully, methodically, Moses improved the steamboat's performance, *and* built up the public's comfort with traveling in the new mode of transport upon the ocean.

Once the packet service achieved a degree of regularity, fares for passage could be more prominently advertised. Moses charged $15 for passage between Charleston and Savannah, $10 between Charleston and Beaufort, and $7.50 between Beaufort and Savannah. At these prices, the steamboat was generating anywhere from $500 to $1,000 in revenues per round trip.

Not surprisingly, Captain Rogers and the *Charleston* received a lot of attention from the press, in both their home port and Savannah. The steamboat captain's ability to consistently deliver news that was only one or two days old made him a great favorite among the newspaper editors. If Moses saw anything of interest in transit—incoming vessels, for example—he made sure to note it to the authorities and reporters upon arrival.

On at least one occasion, he did far more.

While the steamboat was crossing Calabogue Sound in early February, Moses saw a small coastal sloop stuck on a sand bar off Hilton Head Island. The sloop's name was *Morgiana*, and her occupants had disembarked onto the exposed sand bar, hardly a safe place for them once the tide rose. Moses promptly ordered the *Charleston*'s crew to *heave to* (meaning stop), and sent the jolly boat off to rescue the stranded souls. Once on board the steamboat, the *Morgiana*'s crew asked to be taken to Hilton Head, where they hoped to find help in getting the sloop off the bar. This, Moses obligingly did, before proceeding on to Charleston. The entire episode, so matter-of-factly reported by him to the local papers, represented one of the first rescues by a steam vessel in history.

A month later, in early March, the tables were turned. While heading back home on the ocean route, Moses and the *Charleston* found themselves being rocked and rolled off Édisto Island, by what the passengers described as "a very hard blow and high sea."

Suddenly, the tiller snapped. With no means to steer the rudder, the steamboat risked being turned and swamped by the oncoming waves. But before Nature could have its way, Moses and the pilot managed to regain control of the rudder, and carefully guide the *Charleston* back home. The passengers, who rightly believed their very lives had been at stake, provided one of the city's newspapers with a testimonial, praising Captain Rogers and the pilot for their "activity and skill" in bringing the injured steamboat to safety.

Such an accident as that could have literally doomed the *Charleston*, or at least her business. If people didn't think the situation had been handled well, travelers simply would have shunned the steamboat. The conduct of Moses on this occasion, as well as another one back in January, when the *Charleston* crossed St. Helena Sound in very bad weather, served to burnish his image. This newcomer to the South was receiving not just the public's admiration for his "skill and judicious management" of the steamboat, but applause for his "polite and gentlemanly treatment" of the passengers. He had gained the people's trust to a degree that few other steamboat captains could claim.

By early April of 1818, the newspapers of Charleston acknowledged this confidence in Captain Rogers in the most unique of ways. When the steamer left her home port, she did not take the "outside" route to Savannah, as the press had reported previously—instead, the newspapers stated that Captain Moses Rogers and the steam packet *Charleston* "went to sea."

* * *

In the course of his first months running the steamboat *Charleston* down to Savannah, Moses naturally met a lot of prominent people in Georgia's busiest port.

Among the first government officials he met was Archibald Stobo Bulloch, the U.S. Collector of Customs at Savannah. The second son of a Georgia revolutionary, Collector Bulloch had been in charge of the Custom House since his appointment in 1810 by President James Madison. This made Bulloch ultimately responsible for a wide variety of tasks, from collecting tariffs due on imported cargoes, to ensuring that maritime laws were followed by all vessels entering and leaving the port. Bulloch was the U.S. Navy Agent at Savannah, as well, which meant he handled the Navy's accounts and bill payments in Georgia. Moses also met a merchant named Isaac Minis ("Mý-nus"), who served as one of the port's Commissioners of Pilotage.

Beyond officialdom, Moses worked closely with the Charleston Steam Boat Company's agents in Savannah, Samuel and Charles Howard. Having moved to the South from their native Massachusetts at the end of the last century, the Howard brothers had put down permanent roots in Savannah, while still maintaining close ties to their relatives in the North. Both of them had married, started families, and established themselves as merchants in their adopted city. Once Robert Fulton had proved the practicability of steamboats, however, the lives of the Howard brothers quickly changed, turning them into some of the new mode of transport's first pioneers.

* * *

Among the many entrepreneurs who tried to find a way to use steamboats without incurring the New York Monopoly's wrath was a Massachusetts man named John L. Sullivan. An energetic engineer who was interested in making his native State's waterways more navigable, Sullivan had taken out a federal patent in 1814 for a method of towing cargo barges with steamboats. Using this federal patent as a basis, he then won approval from the legislatures of Massachusetts and New Hampshire for the exclusive right to use steamboats for towing cargoes on particular rivers in each State.

In this very clever way, Sullivan believed he was legally navigating the foggy relationship between federal power and patents on the one hand, and States' rights and monopolies on the other. He could argue that he had asked Massachusetts and New Hampshire only to regulate commerce within their own borders, which they had a right to do. Yet he also could say that he was respecting the federal Constitution's power to regulate coastal commerce, since his State monopoly charters did not extend to the tidewaters.

Furthermore, his federal patent was for a very limited use of steamboats—namely, towing barges—as opposed to the all-encompassing steamboat patent Robert Fulton had tried to claim.

If other inventors wanted to file their own federal patents for steam towing, they were naturally free to try, but they had better not attempt the concept on the Upper Connecticut or Upper Merrimack Rivers, where Sullivan had his exclusive rights.

And if others wanted to run *passenger* steamboats on those particular rivers, they were free to attempt it (although limited demand and Sullivan's competitive position would make it difficult for them to succeed).

It was arguably the most iron-clad, law-abiding, competition-killing steamboat monopoly possible at the time.

Massachusetts-transplant Samuel Howard, having worked previously on several early but unsuccessful steamboat ventures in Savannah, got wind of Sullivan's efforts, and procured from him a license for his steam towing patent. Howard then petitioned the Georgia Legislature to grant him a similar exclusive franchise as Sullivan had received up North, only with one significant difference: Howard wanted his franchise to cover all the rivers of his adopted State. Seeing the enormous potential for making Georgia's cluttered rivers more navigable for all, the Legislature granted Howard an exclusive 20-year charter for steam towing in late 1814.

There were, however, certain strict conditions to be met.

First, Howard's exclusive franchise would not go into effect on the Savannah River until the South Carolina Legislature approved, since the two States shared that waterway.

Second, Howard had to have a steamboat running within 3 years, or he would lose the grant.

And third, if Howard did not introduce steam towing on any river under State jurisdiction within 10 years, or discontinued steam towing for any 12-month period once it was started, he would lose his monopoly on that particular waterway.

The inherent message from Georgia's lawmakers could not have been clearer: either deliver on the promise, or step aside.

Once Samuel Howard received the South Carolina Legislature's approval for the Savannah River, he set about the task of building his first steamboat. This would be no easy thing—by late 1814, no one had yet built and operated a commercially successful steamboat anywhere in the Southeast. He had 3 years to try.

Despite the unprecedented nature of the effort, Howard was able to launch the steamboat *Enterprize* at Savannah in January of 1816. It was about 90 feet long and 20 feet wide, with a measured burthen of 152 tons. Three months later, he began running the new steamer up to Augusta, fulfilling the 3-year condition with 1½ years to spare. In so doing, Samuel Howard also became the father of the new mode of transport in Georgia.

Later that same year of 1816, Howard took the *Enterprize* through the protected coastal waterways to Charleston. His goal had been to capture the Sullivan Island ferry business before the Charleston Steam Boat Company could launch its own vessel (that being the *Charleston*, then under construction). Unfortunately, his initial success was undercut when the *Enterprize* met with an accident in Charleston Bay, and Captain Howard was forced to take the steamer back to Savannah for repairs. Since then, he had kept the *Enterprize* running on the Savannah River, towing barges filled mostly with cotton and tobacco.

With the successful establishment of the first steamboat in Georgia, Samuel Howard realized he needed more money to build still more steamboats. So in late 1817, he and 34 other investors petitioned the Georgia Legislature, asking them for an act to incorporate "The Steam Boat Company of Georgia."

It was not absolutely necessary for them to do this—most businesses at the time were run as partnerships, without any official sanction, and even corporations were not required to have government recognition—but getting an act of incorporation from the Legislature bestowed a certain legitimacy on a newly-formed venture.

Beyond this stamp of approval, Howard and his partners also wanted something else: an expansion of their exclusive franchise to include not just steam towing, but steamboating in all of its forms. Such a request was not without merit: ever since the *Enterprize* had been launched nearly two years prior, no one else had bothered to build a passenger steamboat anywhere in Georgia. Give this newly incorporated company a complete steamboat monopoly, Howard and his backers declared, and it would build plenty of steamers. (Perhaps they also were motivated by news that the *Charleston* would soon be coming to their waters.)

The Georgia Legislature agreed to all this in December of 1817, exactly one week after Captain Rogers and the *Charleston* arrived at Savannah for the first time. But there was a price to be paid: the legislators gave Howard and his partners only 7 years (instead of 10) to introduce steamboats on each river in Georgia, or else lose their exclusive right for that waterway. With this agreement in hand, all the Steam Boat Company had to do was raise a lot more money, very quickly.

* * *

The Howard brothers that Moses Rogers worked with going into early 1818 were men of considerable—though arguably different—reputations.

Samuel Howard, by persevering in his efforts to get a steamboat funded, built and operating where no one had before, demonstrated himself to be an aggressive and tough-minded man. He certainly had the personal reputation to prove it.

Back in 1803, when he was about 27 years old, Samuel had fought a duel in which he was gutshot, yet miraculously survived.

In 1811, he had been involved in the capture and burning of two French privateers, whose violent crews had overstayed their welcome in port.

In early 1813, he had been tried in Savannah's Chatham County Superior Court on a charge of rioting. The jury found him "Not Guilty."

Then in early 1814, Samuel was arrested for assault and battery, but the grand jury decided there was insufficient evidence to press charges.

Most people did not get themselves into this kind of trouble, regardless of the justification or outcome. Such a personal history clearly reflected Samuel Howard's unflinching willingness to accept risk.

Charles—who, at 32, was the younger of them by ten years—seems to have been something of a polar opposite. By the time he took up his duties as the steamboat *Charleston*'s agent at Savannah, Charles was already a successful merchant, largely in partnership with Samuel. But unlike his older brother, Charles largely steered clear of confrontations with others and the law. His health probably played no small role in his demeanor, since Charles had been suffering from heart complaints for some time.

Beyond the Howards, there were other investors in the Steam Boat Company of Georgia with whom Moses became familiar during his time in Savannah. First and foremost among them was the Company's president at the time, William Scarbrough.

* * *

Born to South Carolina in 1776, William Scarbrough had been exposed to the sea from childhood, since his father, also William, was a merchant and shipowner. His mother, Lucy Sawyer, was, by matter of interest, a descendent of Puritan clergyman John Cotton, who had fled religious persecution in England for the Massachusetts Bay Colony back in 1633.

William the Younger, as he was sometimes called, spent his childhood moving between Charleston, where his father was prominent in the foreign trade, and large inland plantations which his family owned further west, on Carolina lands near the Savannah River.

When William reached the proper age, he was sent to the Mother Country for schooling. First, he attended one of the privately-run "public" schools in Britain, and then went on to the University of Edinburgh. After spending a couple of years as a commercial apprentice in several European countries, including Denmark, Scarbrough returned to the United States, and set up shop as a merchant in Savannah. In 1802, the Danish government saw fit to name him as their vice-consul at Savannah, making Scarbrough the focal point for any local business with that country.

In 1805, he married Julia Bernard, a native of North Carolina who aspired by form and function to become a prominent member of Savannah society. Julia's parties (or "blowouts," as she called them) were famed for their lavishness in some circles, and her occasional singing at them the cause of distress in some others.

Through the mid-teens, William the Younger continued to build his business as a merchant, and widen his diplomatic and commercial contacts.

At the very beginning of 1818, Scarbrough resigned as Danish vice-consul, in order to assume temporarily the vice-consul positions at Savannah for both Russia and Sweden.

William Scarbrough.

And at the beginning of February of 1818, Scarbrough also signed on to a new trading partnership. This firm—created to take advantage of business relationships in the northern States, as well as Europe—included Scarbrough along with fellow merchants Joseph P. McKinne and John Nystrom. It would be known to the public by the name of "Scarbrough & McKinne."

* * *

In addition to Scarbrough, Captain Rogers also was introduced to other shareholders of the Steam Boat Company of Georgia. Among them was Robert Isaac, a Scottish immigrant who had married Scarbrough's sister, Lucy. Another was Sheldon C. Dunning, a former sailing captain who had become a major importer, auctioneer, and store owner in Savannah. Still other steamboat investors he met were part of the large McKinne clan of Augusta.

This collection of local Savannah contacts led Moses to even more introductions throughout the city, ranging from government officials, to merchants, to functionaries.

Southern hospitality aside, the best place for Captain Rogers to meet still more people was while playing host on the *Charleston*. In the early months of 1818, there were plenty of travelers who wanted to try out this new steam packet service. One of them was a New Jersey iron foundry owner named Stephen Vail, who had come down to Savannah to build a steam engine for the sawmill of Sheldon C. Dunning.

If Moses didn't know Vail previously, they certainly had at least one business contact in common, and that was New Jersey steam engine designer Daniel Dod. Moses knew Dod as the builder of Aaron Ogden's steamboat *Sea Horse*, which had been the anti-Monopoly partner of Moses and the *Eagle* on the New York-to-Philadelphia route back in 1813. Vail, for his part, had periodically ordered engine parts from Dod.

Upon meeting, Rogers and Vail immediately hit it off. In early March, after Vail traveled northward on the steamboat, they went together to see a play, *The Soldier's Daughter*, at Charleston's city theater. About a week later, Moses invited Vail on board the steamboat, and the two spent the afternoon polishing off a bottle of wine, and talking. Their friendship continued into the spring, with more meetings over a meal, be it breakfast aboard the *Charleston*, or afternoon tea, or dinner.

In the small diary Stephen Vail kept on his trip, he described his time with Captain Rogers as having been spent in a "Satisfactory and sociable manner." Precisely what they talked about he did not record, but undoubtedly their conversations centered around steam engines, and their applications. Captain Rogers' descriptions of his steamboat ocean voyages were probably what led Vail to write to Daniel Dod at the time, suggesting a purchase of the *Sea Horse*, and transfer from New Jersey down to the Savannah River. Given his experience, Captain Rogers was one of the few who could endorse such a long steamboat transfer with confidence.

Their conversations also must have touched upon an idea percolating between Captain Rogers and some of the shareholders of the Steam Boat Company of Georgia. The *Charleston's* voyages on the "outside" had shown that short packet trips by steamboats on the open sea could be accomplished in perfect safety. The next logical step was to show that steam vessels could make even longer voyages on the deep ocean, not only cutting the travel time between ports, but actually reducing the danger normally faced by sailing vessels.

At the same time Moses Rogers and Stephen Vail were busy socializing, the Steam Boat Company of Georgia was busy raising money. Its act of incorporation, passed by the Legislature the previous December, set the company's initial capital at $200,000, but also gave the shareholders the authority to raise as much as $600,000 more. This was a staggering sum of money, but given the new mode's potential, it reflected what resources Samuel Howard and William Scarbrough thought they would need to keep building steamboats.

So in mid-March, the Steam Boat Company announced that it would offer $400,000 in stock to the public, at a price of $500 per share. Financial statements were made available for inspection, and to give a sense of the profit potential, a first dividend on the outstanding shares of 25% was declared (this being based upon the company's past performance). For prospective investors, it was obvious that at $500 per share, the cost to participate was high, and so was the risk of set-back, given the dangers inherent in operating steamboats. But also obvious was the potential for high reward.

While the public offering of shares in the Steam Boat Company was underway in late April, so were private moves in Savannah to do something far more unusual, and daring. Planning for this new enterprise must have been several months in the making, but was carefully kept from the public eye until preparations were finalized.

Then, on Wednesday, May 6th, with the Steam Boat Company of Georgia's offering successfully completed, and Captain Rogers and the *Charleston* having just arrived at the Sand Hill, the decision was made to publicly announce this new endeavor. The *Savannah Republican*, an evening newspaper, was the first to break the story:

> A subscription will be opened for a Steam-Ship Packet to run from this port to Liverpool, under the superintendence, direction and navigation of captain ROGERS, at present of the Charleston steam boat. Further particulars will appear in the morning papers, as we have not time or room for their insertion to-day.

The article's initial declaration alone would have been enough to leave many readers incredulous.

The *Columbian Museum*, having the benefit of a whole night to set their type to press, provided details the next morning:

> *Savannah Steam Ship Company.*
> Capital $50,000, divided into 500 shares of 100 dollars each; ten per cent to be paid down at the time of subscription, and the remainder at the period designed by the committees appointed

for the preliminary arrangements for organizing the Company. No subscriber will be allowed in his own right or that of any other person to take more than ten shares, while the Bank is open during the day.

The plan proposed for carrying into effect the objects of the Company, is the purchase of a suitable ship of the first class, completely fitted and equipped in the ordinary manner—on board of which shall be placed a steam engine with the other necessary apparatus, upon the plan suggested by captain Rogers, who will take an interest in the concern—see that it is carried into effect in the best possible manner, and will afterwards take the charge of navigating the ship across the Atlantic.

If it were asked what are the advantages of the success of such a scheme? they are greater than may at first sight appear; and in the event of failure, which is not deemed probable, the loss sustained by the experiment would be nothing more than the expense of attaching the engine or machinery to the ship, as, in that event, the ship would be left nothing the worse—and the engine and machinery would be such, as to answer for any other purpose for which steam engines are generally applied. It is perhaps no disparagement to the claims of others to say that captain Rogers combines in himself more qualifications and requisites for the successful issue of such an experiment, than almost any person to be met with.

This more detailed explanation was, in a phrase, simply stunning. Never before had anyone actually attempted such a feat as crossing an ocean in a steam-powered vessel, or even been able to raise the money to try.

Later that Thursday morning, the steeple-topped Exchange became a bee-hive of activity.

The Building and Insurance Bank of Georgia, a brand new company aiming to provide loans for new construction and development all over the State, officially offered shares to the public.

Simultaneously, the innocuously-named Savannah River Navigation Company—which intended to compete against Samuel Howard's steamboat monopoly by employing animal-powered "teamboats"— also opened its own subscription books.

Finally, in a category by itself was the proposition of the Savannah

Steam Ship Company. By its description in the newspapers, this offering was an invitation to participate in an "experiment" more than it was to purchase shares in a business. After all, the very idea of just trying to cross the ocean in a steam vessel required a big enough leap of faith.

Since Captain Rogers was the only name publicly associated with the effort so far, and so much of the described plan rested on his abilities, he must have been at the Exchange that morning. Because the news articles also noted Moses would put his own money at risk, he was likely among the first to sign the subscription book.

So too must have John Haslett, one of the *Charleston*'s largest shareholders. He had come to Savannah, probably to be present for the offering, and his participation in the effort was a powerful sign of his confidence in Captain Rogers.

Within an hour of opening the subscription, fully 250 of the 500 shares offered in the Savannah Steam Ship Company had been taken up. "It was deemed proper to close the books for the day," reported *The Morning Chronicle*, "that the community generally, as well as the sister state of South Carolina, should have an opportunity" to invest in the undertaking.

With the initial offering complete, Moses took the *Charleston* out to sea the next day, heading back to home port. John Haslett was among his passengers, probably carrying copies of the new company's papers and subscription list, in order to drum up support for the plan in Charleston itself.

In time, the remaining shares of the Savannah Steam Ship Company were taken up, which was, in and of itself, an unprecedented accomplishment. The subscribers were a decidedly knowledgeable lot for their time, and their backgrounds make clear that they knew what they were getting themselves into.

First and foremost, there were the true steamboat pioneers. This included Moses Rogers and Samuel Howard. More than any others, they understood the technical challenges the effort would face.

Second were those who had previously invested in steamboats. This included Steam Boat Company of Georgia president William Scarbrough, who took the lead stake in the new venture. It also included fellow steamboat investors Charles Howard, Robert Isaac, and Sheldon C. Dunning, all of Savannah, as well as John Haslett of Charleston. By dint of having put their money into steamboats already, these men fully recognized just how pioneering this newest effort would be.

Third were investors who knew well the dangers of ocean travel, even by sail. This included merchants who sent ships, crews and cargoes between Savannah, the northern States, and Europe. Among them were Abraham B. Fannin, the firm of Andrew Low & Company, Isaac Minis, J. P. Henry, John Speakman, Robert Mitchell, the firm of Robert and Joseph Habersham, James S. Bulloch, and William S. Gillett. It also included John Bogue, the owner of the coastal packet sloop *Valiant*, which had tried to compete against the *Charleston*; and Archibald S. Bulloch, the Collector of Customs and a merchant in his own right.

While those who put their names to the subscription book were overwhelmingly from Savannah, five of the investors hailed from elsewhere. Besides John Haslett and Moses Rogers were ship chandler Samuel Yates of Charleston, and two New York-based merchants, Gideon Pott and Joseph P. McKinne, whose firm of Pott & McKinne served as the northern agents for the Savannah-based Scarbrough & McKinne.

Beyond their personal knowledge of the risks involved, this collection of participants also shared something else that was equally important, which was a bundle of intertwined relationships, blending family, religion, business, and civic service.

The familial links were many:

—Samuel and Charles Howard, as previously noted, were brothers;

—Joseph and Robert Habersham were also brothers;

—William Scarbrough and Robert Isaac were brothers-in-law;

—James Bulloch was the nephew of Archibald Bulloch;

—and William Gillett was the nephew of William Scarbrough.

The religious connections brought together a new set of matches, which shifted back and forth between Savannah's two most prominent denominations. Some of the Habershams and Bullochs, as well as John Speakman, were members of Christ Church, the first Anglican church established in Georgia, while the Howards, other parts of the Habersham clan, Archibald Bulloch and Robert Isaac were members of the Independent Presbyterian Church. Further links of faith existed between Jacob P. Henry and Isaac Minis, who were members of Savannah's longstanding Jewish community; and Charlestonians John Haslett and Samuel Yates were both Congregationalists.

Business relationships yielded another batch of combinations.

Steamboat activities aside, William Scarbrough alone was linked commercially to brother-in-law Robert Isaac and his partner Andrew Low, plus Joseph P. McKinne and Gideon Pott of New York. As a whole, most of the investors had shipped cargo in each other's vessels. Further still, some of the shareholders sat together on the boards of local banks and insurance companies, and many of them at one time or another had served the public on government boards or committees.

Far from being strangers to one another, these men knew not only the obstacles this unprecedented venture would face, but the minds of their fellow shareholders, as well. There could not have been much room for misunderstanding.

There was one additional factor which animated the relationship amongst this collection of risk-takers, and that was their sense of nation. They lived in a young country, founded upon new, enlightened ideals—and a country which willingly combined the firm roots of established families with the new blood of immigrants.

The Bulloch, Habersham and Minis families could all trace their Savannah lineage back several generations at least, to the city's earliest years as a colonial outpost. Still others, like Abraham Fannin and J. P. Henry, were also Georgia born and bred, although their families had settled in Savannah more recently.

Apart from these old-timers, however, there were plenty of newcomers. The Howard brothers and Moses Rogers were but a small sampling of the many New Englanders who had migrated to the South from the turn of the century onward, seeking new opportunities.

Beyond these native-born Americans were other shareholders who, while foreign to the land, had been welcomed into it, nevertheless. Robert Isaac, Robert Mitchell and Gideon Pott were all Scottish-born immigrants to the United States. Charleston-based John Haslett was himself originally from Ireland, having emigrated with his father while in his teens. Scotsman Andrew Low, while a naturalized American, was seldom in Savannah, spending much of his time in Liverpool, and Scotsman John Bogue was not even an American citizen, having retained his British citizenship while plying his trade in the former colony.

Far from being the uniform, provincial group that their new venture's name implied, these investors in the Savannah Steam Ship Company were, in fact, a worldly collection of savvy men. And they would need that knowledge, and whatever resources they could muster, if the effort was to succeed.

But for all of the shareholders' experience, the leadership necessary to put the Company's plan into effect rested primarily with just one of their number, and that was Captain Moses Rogers. Once the money was raised, his first order of business was to finish the *Charleston's* packet season, which would soon end with the arrival of the hot summer months. Only after that could he begin building a true ocean-*crossing* steam vessel, something the world had never seen before.

In the meantime, as word spread of the creation of the Savannah Steam Ship Company, newspapers all over the United States reported the story, and some editors felt compelled to wade into the ensuing debate.

CHAPTER FIVE

"Spirited"

I F THERE WAS one word which described the reaction of Savannah's newspapers to the creation of the Savannah Steam Ship Company, it was "spirited."

One fundamental fact of the United States in the early 19th century was that it remained a virtual wilderness. Cities and towns scattered along the eastern coast were connected to each other and the interior by the most rudimentary of roads, or rivers that just *might* be navigable, if conditions were right. Under the circumstances, anyone willing to risk their energy and resources on something that could improve people's lives, and help their community and country grow and prosper, was said to be acting in the "public spirit."

Steamboat promoters certainly fit that description. By providing a predictability to travel never before known, they were dramatically improving the country's transportation system. As a result, the word "spirited" was often used to describe their efforts. That a new group of entrepreneurs planned to build a steam vessel for use where no one had ever dared try—indeed, across the breadth of the Atlantic—certainly qualified for such an accolade.

As Savannah's newspapers spread the word of the Company's formation, fellow editors all over the country paid homage in the simplest and most powerful of ways: they reprinted the stories.

This in and of itself was no small thing. Most newspapers at that time were one large piece of printed paper, folded once to create a four-page broadsheet. The need for revenues led publishers to fill pages one, three and four with advertisements. Page two was usually reserved for the news, which sometimes ran over onto page three. Since most publishers didn't have the resources to do a lot of original reporting, they depended upon their peers to fill page two. This was easily done, given the incredibly large number of newspapers available in the United States.

The question for editors was one of selection. They could not possibly reprint everything they saw in other newspapers, so they had to pick and choose which stories to amplify. For a news story to be reprinted widely was a mark of its importance, at least as far as the country's newspaper editors were concerned.

Such was the case for the Savannah Steam Ship Company. From the District of Maine in the North to the State of Louisiana in the Southwest, the nation's newspapers saw fit to re-publish word of the Company's formation.

But some editors went further than just reprinting. Several Charleston newspapers published a private letter from a traveler, who noted what effect Savannah's gain would have on their own city:

> *Your losing a man of such consummate skill as Capt. ROGERS is much to be regretted; but I am happy to observe so able a substitute in Capt. BLACKMAN, who, from the experience he has had under Capt. R will, I have no doubt, do you and himself much credit.*

Some other newspapers, which had no direct knowledge of Moses Rogers but fully understood the dangers of the sea, felt compelled to opine on the endeavor's merits. Boston's *Columbian Centinel,* after noting that "a company is forming in Savannah, to build a steam-boat to run between Savannah and Liverpool," went on to declare that "navigators think the scheme dangerous if not impracticable."

The *Centinel*'s altering of the vessel type—from "steamship" to "steam-boat"—revealed a certain presumption that would have been all too natural for people to make at the time.

A *boat*, generally speaking, was a smaller vessel to be used on protected waters, or near the shore.

Since all operating examples of the new mode of transport up to that point were clearly intended for use on or near protected waters, they were logically referred to as "steamboats."

So when the Bostonians heard of this proposition to take a steam-powered vessel across the ocean, they presumed the attempt would be made by what was already known and accepted, namely, a "steamboat."

And trying to cross the Atlantic in such a craft as that, with limited sails and an unpredictable steam engine, was, to them, dangerous and foolhardy indeed.

The Bostonians were not the only ones who thought this way. Down in the nation's capital of Washington, a far more detailed opinion was published by the well-known *Daily National Intelligencer*, whose editors also fell back on the familiar term of "steamboat":

> A subscription has been opened at Savannah "for a steam-ship packet, to run from that port to Liverpool, under the superintendence, direction, and navigation of captain Rogers, at present of the Charleston steam-boat." This is a bold enterprize; and, if it succeeds, Atlantic steam-boats ought to be called *Savannahs*, in honor of the place whose public spirit introduced them; as the generic name of steam-boats ought to be *Fulton*. There is great doubt, however, we think, whether steam-boats can safely be employed in crossing the ocean. There are some dangers incident to sailing-vessels from which the former are exempt; but there are others, on the contrary, peculiar to them, such as fractures of the machinery, bursting of boilers, difficulty of managing fire and machinery in a gale of wind, or rough swell after a storm, hazard of paddles breaking, and rendering the vessel unmanageable, and of the wheels themselves being swept from the vessel. We shall be happy to find all these liabilities counteracted by a construction of the boat and machinery different from any we have yet seen.

Such a skeptical editorial from such an influential newspaper could hardly be ignored.

While a few fellow editors, such as those at *The Salem Gazette* and the *Independent Chronicle* (both of Massachusetts), reprinted only the first, positive part of the *Intelligencer's* editorial, other port-based newspapers reprinted the original opinion in full. To do so, especially without attribution to the original source, implied that those editors agreed with the *Intelligencer's* overall assessment.

Few were the newspapers who openly parried this widespread skepticism into hope for success. One that did was *The Genius of Liberty*, of Leesburg, Virginia, which also dared to recall the events of the summer of 1816:

A project is on foot in Savannah to navigate the Atlantic by a steam boat—Such a scheme was agitated some time ago in New-York; but from some cause or other was abandoned. It will be a poor compliment upon the enterprize of the New Yorkers should they succeed in Savannah. We hope however, let who will reap the honor of the enterprize, that the plan may succeed. The U.S. and the world will reap the benefits resulting.

Yet it was the *Intelligencer's* editorial, and "great doubt," which resonated the most. One additional voice from Virginia, the *Richmond Enquirer*, took the skeptics' arguments, considered them soberly, and carried the debate to a far more thoughtful level:

THE STEAM BOAT.

The Steam Boat has hitherto done no more, than the earliest essays of navigators, previous to the discovery of the mariner's compass, accomplished; going up and down the rivers, and coasting along the shores. The next step will be to launch it boldly upon the deep. A plan was in agitation some time ago to navigate a steam-boat from N. York to St. Petersburg; but for reasons not fully explained, it was abandoned. We are happy to see it revived to the South, under the auspices of the citizens of Savannah. . .

After describing the Savannah Steam Ship Company's plans, as well as the *Intelligencer's* "great doubt" about the safety of the undertaking, the *Enquirer* promptly waded in:

We agree with the Intelligencer, that in the infancy of steam navigation, this enterprize is a bold one; for that its difficulties are neither few nor trifling. No one who embarks in it, however great his enthusiasm may be, ought to despise them. The best way is to weigh them well, to anticipate all the dangers which may be expected to occur, to take time and employ every pains for overcoming them, to draw upon men of talent in all parts, for all the light they can shed upon this splendid enterprize, and not endanger the lives of the adventurers, or discourage future attempts by a premature experiment.

Then the *Enquirer*, its figurative mind racing faster than its prose,
provided one of the most detailed expositions of any newspaper on
the practicable means to the end:

> The plan, as far as it is developed, appears to us a wise one. The
> vessel which is to be launched, is not one of the common steam
> boats, but a sea vessel—calculated by her draft of water better
> to brave the storm. She is to take with her the usual masts, spars
> and sails of a sea vessel, that in case the steam machinery fails
> her, she may trust to the wind to bear her to her port; thus in
> all the cases mentioned, whether her paddles break in a storm,
> or her wheel is unshipped, her machinery breaks or her boiler
> bursts, she may still be, as other vessels, obedient to the wind.
> Without this double provision, both for *steam* and *wind*, we
> should think, in the present state of steam navigation, and at the
> first attempts to cross the sea, it would be very hazardous to
> tempt the dangers of the deep. All that we can safely attempt at
> present is, to call in the *aid* of the steam to expedite the motion
> of the ship, not to trust to it altogether; to attach the steam
> machinery to her, so as to do the least possible injury to the
> means at present adopted for moving her by the wind; and in
> case the machinery should fail of its purpose, to detach it from
> the ship with the greatest possible ease, so as to leave her free to
> the wind. Should the first experiment succeed, we may expect
> to witness a rapid course of improvement; the end is so brilliant
> a one, the saving of time and expense of transportation is so
> important, and so many will join in it! The effort will of course
> be, to use as much steam, and trust as little to the wind as pos-
> sible..., but though the improvements will approach this
> desideratum as rapidly as possible, yet they will never, perhaps,
> be able to dispense with the wind apparatus, if we may so call it,
> altogether; because of the dangers to which the steam fixtures
> are liable. A great field of improvement will of course be opened
> in the mode of attaching and detaching the machinery, of
> preparing and economizing the fuel so as to take up the least
> possible space in the ship, &c. &c.
>
> We confess there is no experiment, to whose result we look
> forward with more anxiety than the one before us. The Intelli-
> gencer proposes "if it succeeds," to call the "Atlantic steam boats

Savannahs, in honor of the place whose public spirit introduced them." We are willing to grant this or almost any other honor, which such a noble enterprize demands.—But we confess, we are so clannish or so patriotic, as to wish that this experiment may succeed first in the United States. America was first to give the steam-boat to the world. Let her also be the first to traverse the great deep by its assistance.

Should it succeed, the sea-boat would probably be put at first to the same use to which the steam-boat has been applied on our rivers. She will be used as a packet for passengers. As she will not have to keep in the course of the gulf stream or the winds, as much as the present ships do, she may take a more direct path and a shorter cut to her destined port. Her voyage may be shortened one fourth, or perhaps a half.—Intelligence may fly and passengers traverse from port to port in 12 or 15 days.— But all this is anticipation — let us make the attempt, first — before we dream more.

CHAPTER SIX

CHOICES

THE GREATEST OBSTACLE to building an ocean-going steam vessel in 1818 was overcoming the predominant doubt as to how such a craft could prevail against the incalculable, unpredictable powers of Nature at sea.

Sailing vessels themselves were hardly guaranteed to do so, but at least their designs and performance were well-known, the result of hundreds of years of trial, error, and experience. If someone went out on the ocean in a sailing vessel, they surely believed (or presumed) that the captain and crew would know precisely what to do in any given situation with the familiar equipment and tools at their disposal.

Not so with the new mode. Making an ocean crossing in a steam vessel had never before been attempted, let alone trying to maintain trans-oceanic steam packet service between two ports. Resistance to the idea of steamboats operating successfully and profitably on rivers, lakes and bays had only just been overcome in the previous decade. In the eyes of those who knew, the Atlantic Ocean represented a far, far more dangerous realm. Such knowledge naturally generated a wall of skepticism: how could a steam-powered vessel ever make it across?

The paddlewheels on a steamboat were the most obvious problem.

First of all, the fragility of the wooden wheels meant that the risk of damage or destruction from powerful waves was quite high.

Second, all that weight outside the hull led to fears that in heavy seas, a steamboat would roll over onto its side, or even capsize. While the Monopoly's deep-keeled steamboats *Fulton* and *Connecticut* had proved it was possible to successfully navigate a stormy Long Island Sound, suspicion over using such a design at sea remained strong. All it would take, many mariners believed, was for one of the heavy wooden paddlewheels, along with its enormous housing, to become immersed at the same time a wave or wind hit the opposite side of the vessel, and the steamboat would be pushed over in a violent ocean.

The third problem presented by the paddlewheels was drag. It was impossible to carry enough fuel to run these early steam engines for more than a fraction of a distant ocean voyage. This meant that for most of the journey, sails would have to be used. It also meant that while sailing, the wheels would be motionless, and the lower paddle-boards would drag in the water, slowing the vessel's movement to a crawl. Maneuvering would be more difficult, as well.

Furthermore, this acknowledgment that the old mode of power would play a key role in any steam-powered crossing led to yet another set of concerns regarding the sails. Almost all steamboats built up to that point included one or two small masts, along with auxiliary sails. If the steam engine broke down, or the paddlewheels were damaged beyond use, the old mode could be used as back-up power. Such minimal masts, sails and rigging were fine in the protected waters of the mainland, but they would never do out at sea.

The solution was to equip an ocean-going steam vessel with a bigger and stronger set of masts and sails. This would allow the traditional apparatus to both withstand more powerful winds and better propel a paddlewheel-dragging hull through the water.

But as with any traditional sailing vessel, the combination of masts, spars, rigging and sails would dramatically increase the amount of weight above the deck. Even with the sails furled, a strong enough gale hitting a vessel's masts and rigging could topple it over. Once all of that sailing apparatus hit the water, getting the hull righted again was virtually impossible. Add to that the stability fears created by the paddlewheels, and the whole idea of an ocean-traveling steamboat seemed very dangerous, if not untenable.

This circular set of worries only addressed what any person could see readily on the outside of such a contemplated vessel. The potential problems on the inside added still more.

The moving machinery of a steam engine was one such cause for concern. If it broke, flying or collapsing parts could damage the hull's supporting structure, or the hull itself. The powerful motion of the ocean, acting contrary to the designed movement of the engine, made this breakdown danger even more likely. The end result could be a crippled vessel with no steam power, a leak, and sluggish sailing abilities in the middle of a hostile sea.

It was also necessary to consider even the most unpredictable of dangers to the engine. Moses Rogers himself was familiar with at least one of them. Back in the spring of 1816, he had been taking the steamboat *Eagle* from Baltimore up into the Elk River, toward Elkton, Maryland, when suddenly the steam engine had stopped. After two hours of inspection, it was discovered that a small catfish had been drawn into the injection pipe, which supplied water to the boilers. The blockage had forced the engine to seize up. In the calm waters of the river, it was possible to remove the obstruction and proceed; trying to do so on the ocean could be another matter altogether.

Another more obvious risk of clogging the steam apparatus came from salt. When water was heated and converted to steam in the boilers, any evaporated salt from the water naturally solidified inside the bottom, sides and top of the boiler. Since most early steamboats operated on inland waters that had low salt content, the problem of salt build-up inside the boilers was a relatively minor one. Periodic cleaning would keep them operating safely.

But as steamboats began venturing into saltier waters, this problem became more pronounced. A sea-going steam vessel would have no choice but to draw water from the ocean, and salt build-up inside the boilers would be rapid. If the piping or valves connected to the boilers became clogged, the engine's efficiency would suffer, or even force a shut-down.

Salt deposits also created another kind of long-term risk. The accumulation of salt in the bottom of the boiler would create an additional layer between fire and water, thereby reducing the effective heating of the latter. This meant that the crew would need to build a fire far bigger and hotter than normal to heat the water and create the steam pressure desired. Repeated excessive heating of the boiler would eventually weaken its walls. Combining this hazard with the corrosive effects of salt, and it was clear to see that it would be only a matter of time before the boiler would give out.

The implications of such an accident as that got to the core of what really scared people the most about steamboats, and the idea of taking one out on the ocean. For those living in the early 19th century, there was practically no greater fear in their physical world than fire.

* * *

For the first generations of Americans, the kitchen represented one of the most potentially dangerous places in their lives. Most cooking, after all, was done in an open fireplace. It was for this reason that some early American homes were designed with the kitchen in a one-story shed attached to the back of the house. Should the cooking fire get out of hand, hopefully it would burn down only that small portion of the structure. If land and finances allowed, sometimes the kitchen was a completely separate building, linked to the house by a passage, or covered breezeway.

Open fireplaces also were needed to heat the home. Failure to carefully control any one of them could set the room ablaze. If the fire was not brought under control quickly, the only recourse for a farm family was to get out of the house, and helplessly watch it burn. The chance that far-flung neighbors could mount a defense fast enough was slim.

City dwellers didn't have it much better. While larger cities and towns could purchase horse-drawn engines which manually pumped water, firemen or volunteers armed with buckets remained the primary means for fighting fire. Given how tightly packed buildings often were, and how difficult it was to get the water to where it was needed, a city fire often destroyed not only the original source of the blaze, but several adjoining structures, as well.

This incredible vulnerability to a conflagration, and the limited ability to fight it, fed a very great fear of fire breaking out anywhere on land.

At sea, the anxiety was even greater. Sailing vessels were—obviously enough to anyone who dared to think about it—floating tinderboxes. With hulls made of wood, and masts adorned with ample canvas and miles of rigging, sailing craft both large and small were always at risk of being set ablaze.

The cargo being carried by a merchantman could also affect its fireworthiness. Anything such as cotton, tobacco, or lumber would make the vessel all the more vulnerable, should the fire reach below deck.

If a fire did break out on a vessel at sea, the crew and passengers would be struck, quite predictably, with sheer terror. The flames had to be brought under control very quickly, or else the occupants would be forced to make a grisly choice:

—death by fire, while ironically floating on the very substance that could extinguish it;

—death by drowning, in waters that were often so cold as to make the limbs go numb in a matter of minutes;

—or, likely death by starvation and exposure in a life boat, if it could be lowered in time.

It was stories of choices like these, imposed upon the unlucky victims, which made fire at sea the greatest nightmare of any mariner.

The simplest means of minimizing the risk of fire on board was to severely limit its use. The only place where a fire of any size was allowed was in the galley, and the cook was required to always have several buckets of water at the ready to douse the stove, if need be. Candles or lamps could be lit only under strict rules, to minimize the possibility of an accident. And smoking was often prohibited below deck, or even completely banned on board, making the chewing of tobacco the preferred method of enjoying the brown leaf among seamen.

The introduction of steamboats added an entirely new set of dangers.

First was simply having an enormous fire raging in the boilers, tucked far down in the hold. If the fire got too large, it could potentially leap from the open boiler doors to the surrounding wooden hull. Even more worrisome was the risk that the incredible heat given off by the boilers could cause the surrounding timbers to spontaneously combust. Steamboat builders had tried to prevent this possibility by placing brick floors underneath and behind the boilers. This helped diffuse the heat, just like in a fireplace. Even still, radiating heat from such a large fire remained a problem.

Second was the risk of explosion. If the steam pressure was allowed to rise too high within a boiler, the weakest part of the boiler wall could burst, usually along a riveted seam. Should this happen, the best outcome was a release of steam, hopefully with no crew or passengers standing nearby, lest they be scalded. The worst case was an explosion so powerful as to blast away a good part of the vessel, and very likely set the rest of it on fire.

This fear of exploding boilers was all the more pronounced in steamboats that had been fitted with controversial high-pressure steam engines. These designs, invented and largely promoted in the United States by Oliver Evans of Philadelphia, were intended to operate at a much higher pressure than traditional engines. The higher pressure meant more power for less fuel, and Evans was convinced that his invention represented the future of steam power.

Many others were far less sanguine. Even the widely-used, low-pressure engines could explode if the steam pressure produced in the boilers was allowed to rise above the normal 30 or 40 pounds per square inch. If such boilers had been in use for several years without major cleaning or refurbishment, then it was possible for them to fail at even lower pressures. By comparison, a high-pressure boiler operated at levels of anywhere from 100 to 150 pounds per square inch. Its failure could result in an explosion so destructive as to be catastrophic.

Some observers claimed that the risk of high-pressure engines was even more complex than the name implied. Since the safety valve on a "high steam" engine was set to trip at a much higher pressure, it would be unable to detect danger at far lower levels. A high-pressure boiler exploding at the normal operating level of a low-pressure boiler was hardly a comforting thought. Oliver Evans argued that his "high steam" boilers were far better built to withstand the pressure, but his detractors found this reply less than convincing.

There was yet one additional risk of fire on board a steam vessel, and that related to all the emissions inherent in burning wood, or coal, as fuel. The danger of sparks and cinders from the smokestack setting a steamboat's canvas sails on fire also had to be considered. This would be of even greater concern if an ocean-going steamer was to have a larger complement of sails.

Once this laundry list of fire hazards was added to the other worries over design, it is little wonder that many experienced mariners thought sending steamboats out onto the open ocean was a recipe for disaster.

As if this weren't enough, there were still other risks to be considered, ones completely beyond the control of a steamboat captain and his crew—the kind that a lawyer would refer to as *Acts of God.*

*　*　*

Back in the early summer of 1816, when Moses was still captain of the *Eagle* out of Baltimore, Samuel Howard had determined to bring his first steamboat, the *Enterprize,* from her home port of Savannah up to Charleston. His objective was to beat the newly-organized Charleston Steam Boat Company in its own market, before that venture's first vessel, the *Charleston,* could be completed.

This would be the first attempt to transfer a steamboat between these two cities. Perhaps to prove the point that his *Enterprize* was safe, Captain Howard brought his wife Rebecca and their children along on the adventure. Also on board was a willing U.S. Navy lieutenant named Thomas Paine.

Taking no chances, Howard guided the steamboat along the inland route, dropping anchor whenever he felt the tide or darkness prevented safe progress. After a three-day transit, the *Enterprize* entered Charleston Bay.

The effect of her arrival on the people of Charleston was electrifying. They certainly knew about steamboats, but never before had they seen one in their own waters. The Battery, at the southern tip of the city, was jammed with spectators as the *Enterprize* approached.

Once the steamboat had reached the wharves and tied up, Captain Howard invited over 120 passengers on board, and took them across the Bay, to the edge of Sullivan's Island. He then turned the *Enterprize* about, and returned to the city, steaming past cheering thousands, who packed the Battery and wharves along the Cooper River. On board the *Enterprize* herself, the passengers vented their own approval, by giving the steamboat and its captain three loud cheers before the assembled crowd. For Samuel Howard and the many who saw it, that day, June 23rd, 1816, was one to remember for the rest of their lives.

Within a few days, the *Enterprize* began taking hundreds of passengers out of the heat of the city, and delivering them into the cool sea breezes of Sullivan's Island. The steamboat was able to complete three scheduled round trips every day through the summer, making it a predictable fixture in Charleston Bay.

One Sunday near the end of that summer, Samuel Howard and the *Enterprize* were making the late afternoon trip to Sullivan's, when, upon reaching the middle of the Bay, they ran into a heavy rain squall. Since the Sabbath was often the busiest day of the week for early steamboats, Captain Howard knew there were many people on the island depending upon him to get them back to the city. So he pressed forward.

Despite the drenching rain, the *Enterprize* reached the cove on Sullivan's Island where the steamboat normally landed. After tying up, the crew took on a load of about 60 passengers for the return trip.

All the while, the storm grew worse. Heavy winds lashed the island, and lightning streaked across the sky. Captain Howard decided to wait.

By half past 5 o'clock, it was still raining, but the weather had improved enough to allow a departure. At 6 o'clock, Captain Howard ordered the crew to cast off. Since the tide was going out, the *Enterprize* was obliged to back out of the cove slowly, to avoid running aground.

In the course of doing so, six black men in a canoe came alongside the steamboat, and asked if they could be towed back to the city. Their request being granted, the canoe was tied to the steamboat, and the soggy canoers climbed aboard. They quickly joined a few other passengers who had gone below to the forward room—where the boilers were located—to dry off their wet clothes.

Before the *Enterprize* managed to clear the cove, she suddenly bumped to a halt. Her hull had become stuck on the muddy bottom, about 200 yards from shore. Given the angle of the incoming waves, water began to splash into several open portholes in the passenger cabin below deck. While Captain Howard went below to put covers (called *dead-lights*) on the portholes, the steamboat managed, with a little effort, to free itself, and begin moving again.

Just as the *Enterprize* was about to exit the cove, she was suddenly rocked by a short, sharp explosion. The front of the steamboat was immediately engulfed in smoke, and steam, and cries for help.

Captain Howard ran up on deck, and found the passengers in a state of complete panic. Some had already jumped overboard, and were swimming for their lives. Those remaining on board were wondering whether they should follow suit, since it looked like the entire vessel was about to disintegrate.

After ordering the furnace fires extinguished and the anchor dropped, Howard quickly examined the external damage. One of the portholes on the left (or *larboard*) side of the steamboat had been completely blown out, and one of the two iron smokestacks—also on the larboard side—had virtually disappeared. Only the lower section of that stack remained, jutting out of the deck, mangled and disfigured.

Concluding the danger was past, Howard went to the stern of the *Enterprize* to assure the petrified passengers crowded there that the situation was under control. Just then, the mate came up to the captain, and told him that a fire had broken out in the forecastle, at the very front of the steamboat.

Captain Howard ordered the crew to grab all the water buckets and axes on board, and move forward to attack the fire. The men quickly discovered the smoke pouring out of the bow was so thick that they could not reach the burning timbers. Realizing his passengers' safety was at risk, Howard called out for any boats nearby to help evacuate the *Enterprize*.

Soon after his distress call, the crew managed to reach the fire's source, and douse the flames. The passengers who had jumped overboard were soon hauled out of the water, while a few hundred yards away, a large crowd formed on shore, including soldiers from nearby Fort Moultrie, watching and helping as best they could.

Captain Howard and several crewmembers went below to search the forward boiler room. There, they found the larboard boiler had been blown wide open. Then they discovered a man—one of the passengers—lying in the wreckage, injured and burnt. He died moments later, right before their eyes. Scattered about the boiler room were the other passengers who had been drying their clothes. They were all either wounded by the explosion or scalded by the steam.

The injured were quickly moved to shore, but for some of them, it was only a matter of time. Within a few days, the death toll stood at 5 passengers, including two of the canoeing party who had come aboard just before the accident.

Not surprisingly, public speculation on the cause of the tragedy focused on too much pressure in the boilers.

But Samuel Howard was convinced that something else was to blame, and he had ample evidence to back up his claim.

First, the engine's safety valve read 5 pounds of pressure per square inch just before the accident—this was well below the normal level for a low-pressure engine. Since the firemen had gotten steam up just prior to departure, and Howard always told them not to apply too much steam to the engine before they left the cove, the safety valve's reading made sense.

Second, only the larboard boiler had blown. If too much pressure was to blame, then the right (or *starboard*) boiler should have exploded as well, since they were connected to each other.

Third, if the larboard boiler had exploded on its own, then the force of the blast should have torn the entire smokestack off at its base, where it connected to the boiler, and not at its midsection above deck, as it did.

Fourth, if the boiler had truly exploded from excessive pressure, it also should have blown the decking planks directly above it high into the air, which it did not.

Based upon these clues, Howard believed that the real culprit was lightning, which had struck the larboard smokestack. The electrical charge had then traveled down into the connecting boiler and out the bow of the *Enterprize*. This jolt, he speculated, probably popped the

rivets that held the boiler plates together, and may have simultaneously caused a surge in the "elasticity" of the steam inside. The result
was a low-pressure boiler subjected to the sudden shock of high pressure, and an immediate explosion.

It was truly an Act of God, completely beyond anyone's control.
Certainly the steamboat's equipment could not be directly blamed,
although Captain Howard's decision to run the steamboat in a storm
was open to question.

At the request of one of the Charleston newspapers, Captain
Howard wrote a long letter to the editor, explaining what he believed
had happened. The accident, and his letter, were picked up and
reprinted by newspapers all over the United States, so keen was interest in the disaster.

Regardless of what people thought elsewhere, in Charleston, the
psychological damage was done. Shortly after the accident, Samuel
Howard took the wounded *Enterprize* back to Savannah for repairs.
She would never return.

* * *

Given all the risks associated with steamboats, and the dangers
foreseen in trying to apply this new mode of transport to the ocean,
the organizers of the Savannah Steam Ship Company had a lot of
choices to make.

The very name they chose for their venture indicated that they
understood the importance of confronting the public's resistance to
the very idea of oceanic steam travel. It was not an ill-equipped steamboat that they proposed to take far out to sea, but rather a deep-water
vessel, or as it was sometimes generically called, a "ship."

The first choice to be made was whether to build from scratch, or
select a sailing vessel already under construction, and alter it as
needed to accept a steam engine and paddlewheels.

Captain Rogers' proposal seemed to allow for either. It stood to
reason that if a partially-built vessel could be found, then it should be
purchased, if possible, and the necessary modifications made. Otherwise, the Company would have to contract with a shipbuilder to begin
construction of a vessel from the keel up.

The next choice to be made was which type of engine to install.

A low-pressure design might not offer sufficient power to propel a
big vessel through the water, unless the engine was unusually large.

A high-pressure design, on the other hand, would provide a lot more power with less fuel expended. Additionally, since a high-pressure engine was smaller than its low-pressure counterpart, it would take up less space in the hold. This would make installation easier, and result in more room for fuel or cargo. The only major issue with high steam was safety, or the perception of it.

Another question that had to be answered was what material to use in constructing the boilers: copper, or iron?

Within the small but growing steamboat industry, the debate was far from over as to which one was the better metal.

Some early entrepreneurs thought that copper was clearly the preferable of the two. Robert Fulton fell solidly within this camp. Copper's primary benefit was that it was nearly impervious to corrosion from salt. While copper boiler interiors still had to be cleaned of salt on a periodic basis, the metal itself would hardly be damaged or affected by the deposits.

There were, however, some fundamental problems with using copper.

First, there was the cost. In the early 19th century, America had to import most of its copper, primarily from Britain. Given the repeated disruptions in trade between the two countries since 1807, supplies of copper had been unpredictable, and its market price during these disruptions was often outrageously high.

Even with the coming of peace, copper was still very expensive. Anyone looking at a price sheet for commodities could readily see that unlike other industrial metals, which were usually sold by the ton, the "red metal" continued to be quoted by the pound. A bolt of rolled copper cost around 34 cents per pound in 1818, equal to about $760 per (English long) ton. This meant that any steamboat entrepreneurs intending to build boilers with copper had to have very deep pockets.

Copper's second problem was the skill required to work with it. For those steamboat builders in the largest cities, it was possible to find coppersmiths to aid in the manufacture of something as specialized as a boiler. But for those entrepreneurs constructing steamboats in the smaller cities, or out on the frontier, acquiring the coppersmithing skills needed to build a large boiler was difficult at best.

These characteristics of copper encouraged many early steamboat promoters to form a different opinion. They thought iron was the right material to use in building the boilers. While iron clearly had the problem of rapid corrosion when exposed to salty water, it had advantages which contrasted dramatically with copper's disadvantages.

First, there was the cost. Iron bars, the refined form of the metal sold to manufacturers, traded for about $105 per ton in 1818, a fraction of copper's price. Considering how expensive and chancy steamboats were to begin with, the idea of limiting the cost of construction, however possible, was obviously an appealing one.

Second, there was the skill required to use it. While the knowledge needed to build a steam engine and boilers was very specialized, at least some parts of the manufacturing process could be taught readily to others who had basic metalworking skills. And the most numerous of all the metalworkers in the country were those who worked exclusively with the "black metal." Every city and town in the country had several blacksmiths, at least, and even many small villages had one. Given the greater availability of blacksmiths, it was only natural that many early steamboat builders decided to construct boilers of iron, instead of copper.

Third, the use of iron was supported by the innovation imperative. With the development of practical steamboats barely one decade old, the number of ideas swirling around for making better engines was dizzying. More than a few early steamboat investors wondered why they should spend so much money on a copper boiler that would quickly become obsolete. Surely an iron boiler would do, and when it gave out in a few years, it could be replaced with a more advanced version.

Beyond these design choices, the Savannah Steam Ship Company also had a major geographic decision to make, which was where to build.

Savannah itself was out of the question. The city's shipbuilding capabilities were limited, and its steam engine-making skills even more so.

Sister city and commercial rival Charleston, while three times larger, also did not have enough experience to carry out such an unprecedented effort.

Given the state of the American steamboat industry in 1818, there were three logical possibilities.

The first was Baltimore.

Having been little more than a regional port at the country's founding, Baltimore since then had catapulted into contention for the title of second largest city in America. That Baltimore's leading citizens wanted to compete with their rivals, the Philadelphians and the New Yorkers, was an obvious fact of the time.

The primary focus of that competition, unsurprisingly, was trade. Thousands of farmers along the Chesapeake Bay and the many rivers and streams that fed into it could most easily send their produce to Baltimore for sale. As a result, the city had become the largest exporter of two of the country's most important cash crops, wheat and tobacco. In return came manufactured goods from overseas, making Baltimore a primary distribution point for the country's midsection.

Further bolstering Baltimore's position was the building of the federally-funded National Road. Running from Cumberland, Maryland into the Appalachian Mountains, the National Road was slated to reach the Ohio River city of Wheeling, Virginia later that year. The amount of goods and people already traveling along it made Baltimore the most active, viable gateway to the West.

The city's rapid growth and prosperity were by no means purely a result of geography alone. Baltimore's civic and business community had developed a well-known reputation for being very aggressive.

There was no greater trumpet for this distinction than their promotion of privateering. During both the Revolution and the War of 1812, Baltimore distinguished itself by sending out scores of *privateers*, which were privately-owned merchant vessels armed for combat. This gave the city not only pride of place in volunteering so many resources for the fight, but also the financial benefit of any prizes taken.

The end of the second war with Britain hardly diminished Baltimore's privateering passion. The city's speculators were still sending out armed vessels, the only difference being that they flew the flags of the South American Patriots, fighting for independence from Spain.

The success of the city's privateers was based upon more than just the zeal of their owners and crews. It was also because of the superior qualities of the sailing vessels that were built at Baltimore's shipyards.

This was especially true of the two-masted schooner. The city's shipbuilders had refined the hull design, masts and rigging for this particular type of vessel to such a degree that it was said there was not a faster version in the world. Such a reputation justifiably led people at the time to crown Baltimore as America's schooner city.

Beyond shipbuilding, Baltimore also boasted several steam engine builders, as well as foundries. The city had been a bit late to the steam-boat party; its first vessel, the *Chesapeake*, had not been completed until 1813. However, once the war had ended, adoption and construction of steamboats there accelerated rapidly.

All this activity and energy on so many fronts was enough to qual-ify Baltimore as having the necessary capabilities, both physical and psychological, to construct an ocean-going steam vessel.

For Moses Rogers, on top of these vital elements was an equally important familiarity. Having run the steamboats *Eagle* and *New Jersey* out of Baltimore for more than two years, he knew both the identities and strengths of the major shipbuilders. He was also famil-iar with the proprietors of the steam engine factories in the area.

The open question was whether Baltimore's capabilities would be enough. Its steam engine manufacturers still had fairly limited expe-rience building and installing engines in vessels, and the one needed for an ocean steamer would have to be quite large, and unique.

There was also the question of what type of sailing apparatus the Company intended to employ for its trans-oceanic craft.

For this, there were three possibilities.

First was the schooner, which Baltimore's shipyards could obvi-ously deliver. With two masts rigged to carry sails *fore-and-aft*, mean-ing front to back (in line with the keel), a schooner would be ideal for maneuvering in difficult situations. Schooners also were known for their sleek hulls, which not only made them fast sailers, but potentially fast steamers. That Moses had once captained a schooner, the *Exper-iment*, probably fostered enough familiarity with the type to make its use a real possibility.

But the schooner had a number of drawbacks.

Because the sails were rigged fore-and-aft, where would the smoke-stack be placed? Even if it was installed off to one side on the deck, the cinders flying from a smokestack could still set the canvas afire.

Also, the hull of a schooner was not very wide or deep—fitting a large-enough steam engine into it would not be easy.

Finally, there was the issue of confidence in that particular craft, given its intended purpose. Merchant schooners usually didn't make trans-oceanic voyages, and trying to convince the public to take pas-sage on a "steam schooner" all the way across the Atlantic could prove difficult, if not impossible.

This left *square-rigged* vessels. These were designed to carry sails on horizontal poles (or *yards*) lashed to the masts. (Because the yards and sails were set at right angles to the keel line, these vessels were referred to as "square-rigged.")

There were, generally speaking, two types of square-rigged vessels. Those that had two masts were called *brigs*. Those that had three masts were called *ships*.

This latter name represented the very specific definition of that word at the time—"vessels" were any craft that sailed on the sea, and "ships" were the three-masted, square-rigged variety.

Both brigs and ships were used regularly to cross the ocean. They had bigger hulls, masts and sails to withstand conditions at sea, and the greater variety of sails deployable gave the crews more flexibility to contend with whatever Nature threw at them.

A Brig.

A Ship.

But Baltimore's dilemma in 1818 was that while brigs and ships were sometimes built there, they were not that city's particular specialty. Schooners were. Given the need for a large hull, and the relative inexperience of the local steam engine manufacturers, Baltimore would not have been the first choice to build such a revolutionary vessel.

The second possibility was Philadelphia.

One of the oldest and most storied ports in America, the City of Brotherly Love and its neighboring township, the Northern Liberties, had a long history of shipbuilding. What's more, the Philadelphians took second-place to no one when it came to pushing the new mode of transport. There were a number of first-class steam engine manufacturers in the city, and they were hardly content with serving only their own market.

Among the most active and prominent engine builders was British immigrant Daniel Large. Originally trained at the famed Boulton & Watt firm in England, Large had provided steam engines for three previous commands of Captain Rogers: the *Eagle*, the *New Jersey*, and the *Charleston*. All three of those engines had performed well in ocean conditions, as Moses could attest. Large was also in the process of building the engine for another steamboat that was to make a sea transfer, hopefully, all the way down to New Orleans. In Daniel Large could be seen not just the capability, but the confidence, to build steam engines that tested the limits. And on a personal level, Moses knew him very well.

There was also Oliver Evans, the American inventor of the high-pressure steam engine. His Mars Works, a combined iron foundry and steam engine factory, was well-known for the quality of its custom-made machinery. If the decision was made to use a smaller, more powerful high-pressure engine, then Oliver Evans was the only one who could execute such an order, and Philadelphia was the most logical place to build.

Having participated in several steamboat construction projects in Philadelphia, Captain Rogers had both the familiarity and the comfort to build the proposed vessel there. But like Baltimore, this candidate city had its own drawbacks.

First and foremost was the recent state of Philadelphia's shipyards. Since the end of the late war, the city's merchants had been hurt doubly, first by renewed competition with British merchant shipping, and then by their inability to trade large quantities of goods beyond their limited distribution network along the Delaware River. As a result, orders for new vessels had dropped accordingly. Since 1815, Philadelphia's shipyards had launched hardly any ocean-going vessels of size.

The second drawback centered on the best type of steam engine to use. Building this first ocean steamer with a high-pressure engine would be pure folly. The traveling public would never accept it. Whatever promise "high steam" might hold, employing it would have to wait until it was proven safe.

Since using a low-pressure design made the most sense, the next question was whether any Philadelphia foundry could cast an engine cylinder big enough to power a large vessel. While the city's steam entrepreneurs had proven very adept at exporting the new technology, in whole and in part, their capacity to "build big" remained limited. This circumscribed capability, combined with the dearth of new shipbuilding, meant Philadelphia probably was not the ideal place to go, either.

This left the third and final possibility: New York City.

As the birthplace of the first commercially successful steamboat, and the base of operations for the late Robert Fulton, Gotham had quickly become the capital of the new mode of transport. Even with Fulton's death and the spread of the technology elsewhere, many of the best and most experienced steam engine builders and designers were still in or near New York.

Among this select group was James P. Allaire, who had done some brass work on Fulton's first boats, and gradually became more interested in the steam machinery. Allaire had acquired the Fulton Iron Works after the inventor's death, and moved the facilities to the corner of Cherry and Corlear's Streets in Manhattan. There, just a few blocks away from the shipbuilding docks along the East River, the re-named Allaire Iron Works continued building some of the best and largest engines in the country.

Among Allaire's most recent accomplishments was the casting and construction of the steam engine for the Monopoly's *Chancellor Livingston*. This 486-ton behemoth, the largest steamboat in the world at its launching, also had the biggest steam engine ever installed in a vessel to date. Put on the New York-to-Albany route in 1817, the *Chancellor* quickly became a favorite with the traveling public.

Also in New York was Robert McQueen, whose Columbian Foundry and Steam Engine Manufactory was located on the west side of Manhattan. He had built the steam engines for two of Fulton's earliest Hudson River competitors, the *Hope* and *Perseverance* (which Fulton successfully defeated in court). McQueen also made engine parts for Colonel John Stevens. More recently, he had won the contract to build a steam engine for one of three new steam batteries to be constructed by the U.S. Navy.

And there were still other manufacturers, like the Steam Engine Manufactory of Elizabethtown, New Jersey, owned by former Governor Aaron Ogden and engine designer Daniel Dod. There was also Stephen Vail's Speedwell Iron Works, out in Morristown. All this talent concentrated in and around Manhattan offered a certain flexibility not available elsewhere.

New York City's other great advantage was the vitality of its ship-building industry. During the recent war with Britain, New York's shipbuilders had suffered greatly, like everyone else. But while orders for merchantmen had plummeted, the calls for help in fighting off the Royal Navy, wherever it appeared, had given the city's shipyards plenty to do.

When the battle for the Great Lakes demanded a fleet be built where none had existed before, it was the New Yorkers who rose to the challenge. Some of the city's most prominent shipbuilders, like Christian Bergh and Henry Eckford, gathered their artisans and tools, and traveled hundreds of miles upstate, to the shores of Lakes Erie and Ontario. There, they built an American Navy from scratch out of the wilderness, which went on to defeat the British, and gain control of the Lakes by war's end.

With the return of peace in 1815, the New York shipyards quickly became a focal point for new construction. Beyond the need to satisfy pent-up demand, the city's shipbuilders also held the advantage of working in the country's busiest port. The post-war decision by many British merchants to concentrate their shipments at New York meant that there were mountains of cargoes and monies coursing their way through the city in the years that followed. As trade skyrocketed, so too had the demand for new shipping of all sizes.

Further reinforcing New York's economic boom was the ground-breaking the previous summer for a 363-mile canal, which was to stretch from the upper Hudson River all the way to Lake Erie. While the rest of the country looked on with a mixture of doubt, curiosity and concern, the New Yorkers were confidently starting to chop and carve their way through the upstate wilderness, in pursuit of what would be the longest man-made canal yet built. If they succeeded, State and local leaders could see the bounty of the West—in Ohio, Indiana, and the Michigan Territory—flowing eastward to the port of New York, making it the unrivaled commercial center of the country for years to come.

It was this kind of optimistic, aggressive, progressive thinking that animated the city *Salmagundi* had nicknamed "Gotham." Combined with its leading position in both the old and new modes of transport, it stood to reason that New York City would be the ideal place to build the first ocean-crossing steam vessel the world had ever seen.

And Moses Rogers knew it well.

CHAPTER SEVEN

DIFFERENT FROM ANY
WE HAVE YET SEEN

WHEN THE Dutch colony of New Amsterdam was founded on Manhattan Island in 1626, the advantages were obvious. So many bodies of water connecting there made it a natural place for a trading outpost. This, in combination with the welcoming effects of Dutch tolerance, soon made the colony a magnet for all sorts of people looking to do all kinds of things, as long as they stood to profit.

When the British captured the city a little over a generation later, and re-named it New York, this original character of deal-making and risk-taking remained firmly entrenched.

More than a century after that, when New York became an American city at the close of the Revolution, it still possessed this same treasure trove of advantages: a central geographic position with deep-water outlets all around; extensive commercial contacts with many parts of the world; and a hunger to prosper.

These advantages soon showed like never before. By 1810, New York had become the largest city in the United States, with over 96,000 residents. Its emerging status as the primary emporium of the New World was bolstered even further by events in the years that followed.

After the second war with Britain ended in 1815, merchants on both sides of the Atlantic had warehouses full of produce and merchandise, ready to sell. Many British exporters, for their part, decided to send the bulk of their goods to New York. Their existing commercial contacts, combined with the knowledge that Gotham's distribution network was extensive enough to absorb a mountain of imports, made the decision a logical one. Their New York agents, in turn, would be able to provide British merchants with cargoes of American produce, be it cotton, tobacco, grains, or whatever else was in demand.

As a result, New York's lead over its nearest commercial rivals grew even more pronounced. By 1818, the city's population had ballooned to 120,000 residents. All the cargoes flowing both to and from foreign and American ports kept the city's wharves constantly busy. The digging of the great canal to Lake Erie was generating still more business, as supplies and manpower were sent north to join the effort. Raising the tempo even further was the predictable movement of steamboats to Williamsburgh, Brooklyn, Staten Island, New Jersey, Connecticut, and upstate New York.

The city capable of doing all this was located mostly on the southern quarter of Manhattan Island. On approach from the south, the first readily seen structure of New York was the West Battery, a large circular stone fortress that rose directly out of the water. Due east, on the southern tip of the island itself, was the far larger Battery, which previously had served as the primary fortification for the city, when the Dutch and British held sway. By 1818, the Battery was used largely as a promenade by the citizenry, who prized its frequent breezes and excellent view of the Upper Bay.

From the Battery, development along the western (or North River) side of Manhattan stretched for about 2½ miles of the island's 12-mile length. The heaviest concentration of wharves and shipping there stretched for about a dozen blocks, from Marketfield up to Murray Street, where Colonel Stevens' horse-powered "teamboat" ferry to Hoboken set off on a regular basis. Five blocks to the east of the Murray Street Wharf was Broadway, and the most prominent building in all of New York, the City Hall. Standing 2½ stories in height, its even taller central spire could be seen from just about any vantage point on the island or neighboring shores.

A dozen blocks to the south of City Hall, down Broadway, was the Battery once again. From there stretching up the East River, along South Street, were still more wharves. This was the main port area of the city. So concentrated was the shipping there that many visitors readily described it as a floating forest, thick with masts, furled sails, and rigging. Along this stretch were many of the most prominent wharves in the city: Old Slip, Coffee House Slip, Fly Market Slip, and at the foot of the recently-named Fulton Street was the slip for the Monopoly's steamboats to Brooklyn and Connecticut. Facing the wharves, on the inland side of South Street, were the counting houses and warehouses of many of the largest and most active merchants in Gotham.

But the piers did not stop at South Street. They continued north-ward, along Front Street, and then Water Street, going all the way up to Corlear's Hook, where most of the city's shipbuilders were located.

About a mile north of Corlear's Hook, the streets of Manhattan had been laid out, but the land was sparsely populated. Most blocks con-tained some combination of woods, vacant lots, and a few scattered dwellings.

Compared to other American cities, New York's fully developed sections possessed a number of noticeable differences.

First, there were few wooden buildings left, thanks to past fires and new city ordinances prohibiting their construction. Most buildings were made of brick, and the more prominent were constructed with stone. If the owners of a wooden house wished to replace it with brick, they sometimes arranged to have the older structure lifted up, put on wooden rollers, and moved to the suburbs north of Greenwich Village.

Second, while most of the streets were paved, New Yorkers seem-ingly had chosen the sharpest of stones to do the job. Such construc-tion often made it easy to tell who was who in the city. Newcomers inevitably would walk very gingerly across the stones, to avoid unnec-essary pain, while the native Gothamite simply waddled over the pavement, in the words of one English visitor, "like a parrot on a mahogany table."

All these cobble-stoned streets had one other significant conse-quence: wagons, carriages and carts rattling over them meant that noise was a constant in New York, from dawn to dusk. Even at night, when the trundling was done for the day, the city was still not quiet, since New York had an abundant population of cicadas and crickets, which took charge in the dark.

Besides the night bugs, there were also plenty of farm animals moving freely about the city, picking through piles of garbage left by residents along the curb. Pigs engaging in this ritual were a particular problem, since New Jersey and Long Island farmers were often sus-pected of bringing them in to roam and fatten up on garbage, before selling them at market. So aggressive were the pigs that an attempt had been made to ban the wandering swine, but the ordinance had been repealed before it went into effect. (Like the turkey vultures of Savan-nah, the pigs of New York actually performed a useful function.)

New York's human inhabitants were just as diverse as those found in any other major port city, if not more so. Mixing in with a local population of some 110,000 whites, 10,000 free people of color, and 500 slaves (whose numbers were rapidly dropping under the State's gradual emancipation law) came thousands more, in the form of immigrants, mariners, and travelers.

Feeding and supplying this mass of people required an infrastructure both large and varied. New York had five major public markets in 1818, the primary one being Fly Market, at the intersection of Maiden Lane and South Street. Just about anything edible could be purchased there, although the prices were steep. Beyond the open markets, the city also featured every variety of food shop, work shop, coffeehouse, boardinghouse, retailer, wholesaler, ship chandler, and any other business that any entrepreneur believed had a chance of turning a profit. One profession that seemed especially well-established was that of the lawyer—in the eyes of some observers, the city seemed to be crawling with them. If anyone had a dispute and needed representation, there were plenty of shingles from which to choose.

As the country's leading emporium, New York City also offered plenty of fashion, for those who could indulge in it. While it was not unusual to occasionally see old-time Dutchmen in their traditional dark suits and large-brimmed hats, most people dressed according to the current trends of London or Paris. While many of the clothing shops in the city were French, it was a well-known fact that most of the best textiles available came from the mills of Britain.

Fashionable gadgets were also of great interest to those residents who cared to notice. In 1818, the dandiest of New Yorkers were awaiting the arrival of London's latest, a new kind of personal transporter intended to replace the horse in certain circumstances. Comprising a slender metal frame mounting two wheels, one in front and one behind, riders were supposed to straddle the frame, pushing themselves along, and coasting on the wheels whenever the terrain allowed. The Latin name this device was given—*velocipede*—literally meant "swift foot."

Beyond fads, New York's public and press also had a fancy for the unexplained. In the late spring of that year, the city's newspapers were filled with stories of multiple sightings of "sea serpents" along the northeastern coast of the United States, primarily off Massachusetts. So many were the witnesses—from coastal fishermen to sea captains —and so detailed were the reports of what had been seen, that the press simply could not let go. They would continue printing accounts of attempts to capture the creatures through the summer, along with alternating doses of ridicule and insistent belief.

Such was the place the *Salmagundians* had first called "Gotham" just eleven years before.

From a more practical standpoint, anyone visiting New York City naturally had to address the issue of accommodations. Hotels were the obvious first option, but, like everything else, they were very expensive. The more economical choice for those staying more than a few days was the boardinghouse. Costing anywhere from $5 to $10 per week, most boardinghouses were run by women who could provide a guest with both a secure place to stay and plenty to eat—in effect, a home away from home.

For many families from the South who could afford it, the boardinghouses of New York and other northern cities provided just such a home during the hot, humid, and potentially disease-deadly summer months.

In late spring, the extended holiday would begin. Merchants and other professionals in the South would take passage to a northern city, with New York being the most popular choice. Along for the trip came their wives, their children, extended family members, and perhaps a servant. While the merchants conducted business, meeting with their New York agents or making new contacts, their families could enjoy the city's culture, or visit relatives and friends. Once the hot summer down South was over, these families would end their northern vacations, and return home.

As long as yellow fever and other tropical diseases were a risk, this annual migration from the southern States was a certainty. The summer of 1818 would be no different.

Yet for this particular season, the ritual *would* be different for some of the merchant families from Savannah who came to New York. There was, after all, a steamship to be built.

* * *

On May 23rd, Moses Rogers made his last run as captain of the steamboat *Charleston*. Shortly thereafter, he closed out his dealings with the Charleston Steam Boat Company, and headed north. By the latter part of June, Moses was among the thousands of anonymous travelers who disembarked at New York every month. Adelia and the children probably came to Gotham as well, and set up a temporary household, which was nothing new for this very mobile family.

Also joining Moses was his intended replacement as master of the *Charleston*, Mr. Blackman. Having served under Captain Rogers for some time, Mr. Blackman knew steam engines, steamboats, and ocean steaming like few others. There was arguably no better man to help Moses assemble the machinery for this new vessel, and serve as its engineer.

It stands to reason that once Moses had arrived at Gotham, knowledge of his presence spread quickly within the city's steamboating community. After all, news of the "steamship" effort, the successful raising of the money, and his active participation in the venture had preceded him to New York. There even had been a newspaper report that the French government had offered Captain Rogers the opportunity to push steam power at sea on their behalf. Such a collection of distinctions made him one of the most unusual practitioners of the new mode walking the streets of New York.

Once Moses was settled, he headed over to South Street, and the counting house of the two Company shareholders already waiting for him, the principals of Pott & McKinne.

* * *

Joseph P. McKinne was a South Carolina native whose family had deep roots in and around Augusta, Georgia. McKinne had moved to New York a decade earlier, and gone into business in 1810 with Scottish émigré Gideon Pott.

Their newly-styled partnership of Pott & McKinne acted as a broker, importer and exporter for all sorts of goods. McKinne could provide access to cotton and other crops for export through his extended family's plantations down South, and Pott had the contacts across the Atlantic to import British manufactured goods in return.

Gideon Pott himself was a Glasgow native who had arrived in America in 1805. Then only 19, he soon settled into the New York world of business. One month before he went into partnership with McKinne, he registered in court his intention to become an American citizen. About six months after that, in April of 1811, Pott married a Gotham girl by the name of Margaret Saidler, and started a family.

The outbreak of war in 1812 placed the partnership's very reason for being on hold. With trade at a near-standstill, Joseph P. McKinne and two other merchants turned partly to privateering, asking Secretary of State James Monroe for official approval to arm their brig, the

Regent, for service on the high seas. At least twice did this vessel manage to sneak past the Royal Navy blockade, bringing home valuable cargos from France.

By early 1813, the continuing war had forced the government to place restrictions on, or even deport, resident aliens like Gideon Pott. In response, he had written to Secretary of State Monroe in March of that year, asking for permission to stay. Since Pott's intention of becoming an American citizen was clear, the request was granted, and his partnership with McKinne waited out the war.

When peace came in 1815, it brought considerable prosperity to merchant houses like Pott & McKinne. The pent-up demand in Britain and France for cotton, and the American demand for manufactures, made the partnership's trading model the right one at the right time. With cotton prices reaching record highs by early 1818, Joseph P. McKinne had decided to expand, taking over the Savannah trading business of a relative, and inviting William Scarbrough into the partnership.

This new Savannah agency of Scarbrough & McKinne could then sell some of its cotton and other produce directly to Pott & McKinne of New York. The relationship was mutually beneficial. While the Savannah partnership would receive payment for its shipments a lot faster than if they were sent to Europe, the New York partnership would gain increased volumes to sell, and the bargaining leverage that came with it.

As for Gideon Pott, his immersion into the fabric of New York after the war had continued apace. In 1816, he was elected one of the managers of a prominent Scottish club, the St. Andrew's Society of New York (of which McKinne was also a member). With a home for his family at 26 Greenwich Street, just north of the Battery, Pott's short daily walk over to the partnership's office on South Street kept him in the thick of the city's commercial life. More recently, he had bought shares in one of Gotham's most closely-held commercial institutions, the Tontine Coffee House. Such a purchase was yet further evidence that as far as the old-line merchants of New York were concerned, Gideon Pott had truly arrived.

* * *

Joseph P. McKinne himself had been visiting Savannah at the time of the Steam Ship Company's offering, but once it was completed, he and his family returned to New York, arriving in late May on the brig *Amelia.*

The presence of both Pott and McKinne in New York was important. In addition to being shareholders, their firm would act as the Steam Ship Company's paying agent. Furthermore, their counting house, at 56 South Street, could serve as the base of operations for the construction effort.

While the shareholders recognized that New York was the most logical place to build their steamship, it was also one of the most expensive. Keeping costs under control would be of great importance, so it made sense for the organizers to use whatever contacts and resources they had at their disposal. To that end, a few days after McKinne's return to New York, the schooner *Antelope* arrived from Savannah, carrying anchors, cables, and rigging gear. This equipment was turned over to Pott & McKinne and J. & C. Bolton, another firm which did business with the partnership. Pott & McKinne also made arrangements to import some coal directly from Liverpool, rather than pay the marked-up price for it in New York.

Beyond the gathering of materials, the arrival of Captain Rogers served to energize the process of finding a suitable hull. Since the execution of marrying a steam engine and paddlewheels with a sailing vessel would rest with him, the selection of a hull had to meet with his approval. There were several factors that probably guided Moses in making his decision.

First, the hull had to be at the right stage of construction. If a candidate hull was too far along, altering it for the needed installation of the steam engine might be too difficult or expensive. If, on the other hand, the hull was not much beyond the keel laying, then Moses would have to wait months before he could begin his steam work.

Second, the candidate hull had to be available for purchase. Most shipbuilders did not lay a keel until they had a contract to build from a buyer. The amount of money required was usually too great for a shipbuilder to independently take on that kind of speculative risk. Since most vessels under construction in the New York shipyards were very likely already spoken for, the number of hulls available for consideration would have been fairly small.

Fortunately, there was a hull that fit these criteria. Earlier that spring, a local mercantile house with strong ties to the French market had floated the idea of mimicking the Black Ball sailing packets. But instead of going to Liverpool, this newest packet service was to start scheduled voyages to the port of Havre. Located near the mouth of the Seine River, Havre served as the cotton gateway to the largest concentration of French textile mills. It was also, by extension, the primary port of trade between America and France, and Pott & McKinne themselves were a regular player in that commerce.

This plan for a scheduled Havre packet line had fallen through recently, and one of the hulls originally under construction for it was available. The builders were a team of shipwrights from the District of Maine named Samuel Fickett and William Crockett.

Fickett previously had been one of the most prominent shipbuilders in Portland, but having outgrown his home market, decided to move to New York after the end of the war with Britain. He and Crockett, who were related by marriage, had set up their yard on Water Street, just below Corlear's Hook, where they began building vessels for the Atlantic trade.

The hull Fickett and Crockett had under construction was made of live oak, the strongest, most dense wood known to shipbuilding. Its burthen would be in excess of 300 tons, making it large enough to be rigged as a brig or a ship, and certainly big enough to cross the ocean. The hull would not be ready for launching until later that summer, which probably suited Moses just fine—until then, there was plenty of work to be done on the steam engine.

Before long, more shareholders began to arrive from Savannah. On June 29th, the newspapers announced the return of the brig *Amelia*, with Robert Habersham and his family on board. Just after Independence Day, the brig *Tybee* showed up, carrying William and Julia Scarbrough and their children, as well as Robert and Lucy Isaac and their family.

Considering the great effort these shareholders had come to oversee, some of the newspaper stories that greeted them upon arrival could hardly be seen as comforting. On June 22nd, the *Commercial Advertiser* reported that a Mississippi River steamboat named the *Pike* had struck a snag (or *sawyer*) just north of New Orleans, and immediately sunk. Luckily, everyone on board was saved, though some passengers were forced to swim to shore. Follow-up articles could not help but note that steamboats out on the Mississippi seemed to be sinking at an alarming rate. The steamers *Pike*, *Telegraph*, and *James Monroe* had all been lost within the previous five months alone.

The bad news didn't stop there. At the end of June, reports came in that a brand new steamboat, named the *Experiment*, also had run into trouble. While making an ocean transfer from Elizabethtown, New Jersey down to Philadelphia, she had sprung a leak off the Jersey coast. With water gushing in, the crew had little time to react beyond saving themselves, as the steamboat quickly sank.

Such a steady succession of accidents only served to reinforce in the public's mind what they had come to know over the past ten years: these steamboats were dangerous things. It made the task before the Savannah Steam Ship Company all that more of a challenge.

* * *

By early July, the venture's most important participants were in New York, and the outlines of their plan began to take shape.

First, the hull under construction at the yard of Fickett and Crockett had been secured. Other artisans and suppliers would be hired as needed, to complete the vessel and make it as comfortable and reassuring as possible.

Second, the means of manufacturing the new mode of power itself had been approved. The steam engine's construction was to be handled in great part by Stephen Vail and his Speedwell Iron Works, out in Morristown, New Jersey.

But Vail could not do it all alone. The casting of a steam cylinder big enough to propel such a large vessel was simply beyond his abilities. For this task, the Company would turn to James P. Allaire, and his Allaire Iron Works.

Vail also could not build the boilers and a few specialized parts. For this, the Company would turn to Daniel Dod and his Steam Engine Manufactory of Elizabethtown, New Jersey. Dod also would assist Captain Rogers with calculations and drawings for his design.

This collection of engine contractors offered both advantages and disadvantages.

Among the advantages was competence and cost.

Allaire had cast the largest cylinder ever put in a steam vessel to date. No one could do it better or cheaper.

Vail had impressed the Company with his work on shareholder Dunning's steam-powered saw mill. He also could build the engine for less at Speedwell than Allaire could in New York.

And Dod had a reputation for clever design work, and like Vail, enjoyed a cost advantage over New York.

The primary disadvantage was spreading the job among three contractors. Coordination would be the key.

Captain Rogers' familiarity with each of these men surely played an important part in the decision to build the apparatus in this way. So too did the potential benefit of having four active minds reviewing the proposed design, and checking and double-checking each other's work.

With the hull secured, and the engine contractors in place, the third and final consideration was the old mode of power. Since the vessel being purchased would need the same sails and rigging as any ocean-going craft, someone was needed to take charge of their production and installation. Captain Rogers, it turned out, knew just the man for the job.

Within the extended Rogers clan of greater New London was a 29-year-old mariner with a decade of sailing to his credit. He had served on all types of vessels—from sloops, to schooners, to brigs, to ships—and quickly worked his way up from novice seaman to first mate, the rank just below the captain. In between voyages, this distant relative had hired himself out to the sail-making shops found in any major port, and learned the skills of that trade, as well.

Such a candidate as this could not only make the sails at a good price, but also serve as the steam vessel's sailing master, and help Captain Rogers navigate across the Atlantic. For this latter task, he possessed the most powerful combination of traits that ever could be found in a first mate: wide-ranging experience at sea; physical strength set within a solid frame nearly six feet in height; and last, but certainly not least, an amiable disposition which served him well in the rough-and-tumble maritime world.

The name of this ideal candidate was Stevens Rogers.

Stevens Rogers.

Moses and Steve, as his familiars called him, were very distant cousins, each sharing as a great-great-great grandfather the original immigrant to New London, James Rogers.

However, this long-ago link was misleading, because their two immediate families were, in fact, much, much closer. Back in early March of 1807, just after Moses had returned from Cuba on the schooner *Experiment*, his brother Amos Junior had married Steve's older sister, Sarah. From that point on, Moses and Steve were brothers-in-law by affinity. Six years later, another brother of Moses, Gilbert Rogers, married one of Steve's younger sisters, Abigail.

Such unions between even first cousins were quite common at the time, so the marrying of distant relations was hardly remarkable. Yet it was still notable that these two separate households—one in Groton, one in New London—had been brought together in a way that simple kinship within the enormous Rogers family tree could never accomplish. As if two marriages were not enough, it must have been apparent to some family members by the summer of 1818 that Steve himself had eyes for Mary Rogers, a younger sister of Moses.

While selecting Stevens Rogers as the vessel's sailmaker was good, choosing him to be the sailing master was even better. For the shareholders of the Savannah Steam Ship Company, such strong blood ties between captain and first mate was precisely the kind of thing they would want to see.

* * *

The first New York newspaper willing to declare what was happening within their midst was the *Mercantile Advertiser*, which, less than a week after the arrival of William Scarbrough and Robert Isaac, broke the story:

> *Progress of Improvements.*—A ship of about 375 tons is now nearly ready to be launched, from one of our ship yards, which is actually to be fitted up with a steam engine and apparatus, as a *Steam Packet Ship* for crossing the Atlantic.

This rather awkward description of the new vessel was picked up by other newspapers in the days that followed. For the editor of the *New York Gazette*, however, the evolutionary leap implied by the name was too much, so his paper referred to the craft as a "Steam-Boat ship."

Yet other papers fell back on what was familiar and accepted, by calling the vessel under construction a "steamboat."

This descriptive disorder, which had begun immediately after the Company's announced formation, still remained very much intact.

Everyone knew what a "steamboat" was—

A "packet" was a vessel that traveled between two pre-determined ports—

A "steam packet" was just another name for a steamboat, operating on a regular route—

But a "ship" usually meant an ocean-crossing, three-masted, square-rigged sailing vessel.

What precisely was being built?

Clearing up this confusion, and reconciling these individually-known terms with the untested idea of oceanic steam travel, would have to wait for a more practical opportunity. At that moment, Moses Rogers had much more important things to do.

* * *

In the latter part of July, James P. Allaire received the final go-ahead to cast the huge iron cylinder at his Cherry Street facility. Because the engine would have only one cylinder (like most steam vessels at the time), the proper casting of it would be crucial. The intended dimensions of the cylinder appeared to be identical to those of the one Allaire already had cast for the Monopoly's *Chancellor Livingston.* All he had to do was reproduce it.

The process for casting such a piece required three steps: *model, mold,* and finally, *casting.*

First, the foundry had to create a model of the article to be cast. This model was usually made of wood, since that material could be cut and carved into just about any shape imaginable.

Second, a large two-piece rectangular casing had to be built. Into both sides of this casing would be placed a mixture of clay and sand. Then, the wooden model would be pressed into the soft mixture, and the two casing sides closed around it, and held shut. Any excess *molding sand* was pushed out through an opening built into the top of the closed casing. Once the mixture had hardened, the casing was opened, and the wooden model removed, leaving a finished mold.

Given the cylinder to be cast was identical in dimensions to the one put into the *Chancellor Livingston,* Allaire may have just re-used the mold he already had, or perhaps used the old wooden model to make a new mold.

In any event, once the mold was ready, the actual casting could begin.

In preparation, the mold had to be secured to the floor of the foundry. For smaller pieces, such as those to be made later at Speedwell or Elizabethtown, this was easy to do. But the cylinder was another matter. It was so big that the sheer weight of the iron, once poured inside the mold, could force the casing sides open, ruining the casting. The only way to avoid that was by partially burying the mold in the ground.

Once Allaire was ready to cast, his foundry workers dug a large hole next to the iron furnace. The cylinder's mold was then placed in the hole. Once it was determined that the two sides of the mold were securely fastened, the workers started shoveling. Dirt and sand were thrown into the hole around the cylinder mold, and packed down until only the top of the mold was showing. Then the casting could start.

Inside the foundry's furnace, sufficient iron was heated until it became liquid, or *molten*. For a large casting, this step alone could take several hours. Once ready, the molten iron was released from the furnace into an inclined trough. The orange-hot metal streamed down to the end of the conduit, and into the opening at the top of the buried mold.

Pouring the Cylinder.

As the molten iron was poured into the mold, brilliant sparks, flames and gases shot up into the air. If any gas bubbles developed inside the mold as it was filled, eventually they would be forced to the surface, often resulting in a small explosion of iron lava out the top. For those who witnessed it, this part of the process was one of the most dramatic man-made spectacles of their time.

The Explosion.

Once the molten iron had cooled and solidified, the workers took up their shovels again, and began digging out the mold. So much heat still remained in the dirt and sand surrounding the mold that the diggers soon found themselves enveloped by thick clouds of steam and vapor. It was a scene as surreal as the pouring was spectacular.

Digging Out the Cylinder.

Once the mold was uncovered and cool enough to handle, it was opened to reveal a solid-iron cylinder inside, about 6 feet in height and 3½ feet in diameter. A smaller air pump, which assisted the removal of spent steam from the cylinder, was also to be cast by Allaire, but this would be done later in the summer.

While the casting and cooling of the cylinder was in process at Cherry Street, the East River wharves further to the south welcomed still more shareholders. On July 20th, the newspapers announced the arrival of the brig *Speedy Peace* from Savannah, with Jacob P. Henry and his family, as well as bachelor Abraham B. Fannin. A few days after them came Robert Mitchell and his wife, on the ship *Rising States*.

With J. P. Henry's arrival, a task important to the completion of the hull could be set in motion. It had become customary for any well-built, ocean-going vessel to have its hull covered with a thin sheet of copper, which helped preserve the wood timbers and make cleaning easier.

Normally, the shipbuilder would be in charge of buying the copper. The metal's cost, plus any handling fees or builder's margin, would be charged to the vessel's buyer. Rather than leave this task, and profit, to Fickett and Crockett, the shareholders decided to purchase the copper themselves, and provide it to the shipbuilders.

J. P. Henry's presence in New York was helpful in this regard, since he was related to Harmon Hendricks, the most prominent copper merchant in the city.

Hendricks was the son of Uriah Hendricks, who had emigrated from London back in the 1750s, and opened an ironmongery and copper importing business in New York. Harmon joined the family trade as a teenager, and eventually took up the red metal as his specialty. Extensive contacts in London, Bristol, and elsewhere in Britain gave Harmon Hendricks access to what was then the best source of refined copper in the world. Even Paul Revere, still operating as Boston's most active copper seller, purchased much of his imported product through Hendricks.

When the practice of coppering ship hulls began to take hold, Hendricks naturally pitched for the business, winning many contracts from the U.S. Navy in the early years of the century.

When Robert Fulton began building steamboats, he turned to Hendricks for copper. Most of the Monopoly's steamboats had Hendricks copper either in them (the boilers) or on them (the hull sheathing), a testament to the quality of his product. Hendricks' brother-in-law and partner, Solomon Isaacs, became so identified with copper sales to the new mode of transport that he earned the nickname "Steamboat" Isaacs, and Hendricks himself had invested in the Monopoly's steamers.

On July 29th, with the Company's hull nearing completion, Hendricks sold $1,679.82 worth of copper to the account of Pott & McKinne, the first and largest of several purchases. This transaction, and the ones that followed, were all consummated at the prevailing market price of 32 to 33 cents per pound.

Back at Fickett and Crockett's shipyard, the men laboring to finish and sheath the hull found it to be very hot work. New York was experiencing a scorching summer, with temperatures regularly rising into the 90s, making the city intolerably torrid for both residents and visitors alike.

* * *

While the initial organizing of the Savannah Steam Ship Company had been under way in the spring of 1818, British newspapers began arriving in the United States with reports of another effort to construct an oceanic steam vessel—the only difference was that it was taking place over there:

> *The North Pole.*—It is said that Lord Cochrane has caused a steam boat to be built, in which he intends to make a voyage to the North Pole, and from thence to Behring's Strait. She is to be schooner rigged, and will be accompanied by some old collier, laden with coals, as far as Spitzbergen; here the coals will be taken into the schooner, and as the run is only five days to the pole, and from thence to Behring's Strait nine days, and as it is intended to make use of sails when the wind is fair, his Lordship is sanguine in the hope of being the first to accomplish the North West passage over the pole, and to get both the parliamentary rewards, amounting to £25,000.

Such a scheme was not as outlandish as it seemed, given the actor and the environment.

Lord Cochrane, the tenth Earl of Dundonald, was a Scottish nobleman who had distinguished himself in combat on the high seas against the French. A highly controversial figure in Britain because of his reform politics, this celebrity-warrior had recently taken an interest in steam propulsion.

The stated goal of trying to reach the North Pole, or being the first to make the Northwest Passage from the Atlantic to the Pacific, was based upon changing weather patterns which appeared to make such magnificent feats a real possibility. Great warming trends in the northern latitudes, and their dramatic effects, had been reported by mariners for a number of years. The higher temperatures had caused huge blocks of ice to break away from Greenland and the polar ice-cap, and slowly float away. Some of these icebergs, or "islands of ice" as they were sometimes called, were so large that they survived warmer temperatures far to the south. One had recently been spotted in the Atlantic at a latitude of 29 degrees, to the east of Spanish Florida.

The resulting break-up of the ice-covered waters north of British Canada had set many minds to wondering: *was there, in fact, a Northwest Passage, and could it be found?* If so, such a link to the Bering Strait, and the Northern Pacific Ocean, could dramatically shorten the voyage to Asia.

The British government had taken the lead in sending out vessels to determine if such a short-cut existed, and also had sent out expeditions to see if reaching the North Pole was achievable, as well. Britain's Parliament had added incentive to the effort, by promising healthy financial rewards for anyone who could achieve either goal.

That the British newspapers referred to Lord Cochrane's vessel as a "steam boat" was hardly surprising. Just like in the United States, calling it anything else would have been considered absurd. Combining this accepted description of the new mode of transport with the vessel's stated purpose, and the whole scheme sounded even crazier.

In any event, what to call Cochrane's creation was soon overwhelmed by confusion over its true purpose.

By June, there were conflicting reports that his steam vessel was either intended for an expedition to the Arctic, or instead was destined for waters far to the south, to aid the South American Patriots fighting for independence from Spain.

And by July, the story shifted once more, when a number of newspapers, including *The New-York Columbian*, reported that "Lord Cochrane is said to have altered his schemes again, and now contemplates exploring the river Congo in a steamboat."

This report was soon countered by several other Gotham newspapers, which tried to bring a new and distinctive clarity to the debate. Among them was *The National Advocate*, in its July 20th edition:

> By a gentleman arrived at Norfolk in the ship Averick, Captain Manlove, from London, we have been favored (says the Norfolk Herald) with a description of the new steam ship lately built for Lord Cochrane, and to be employed by him in the service of the republic of Buenos Ayres. It is understood that Lord Cochrane, on his arrival at Buenos Ayres will be invested with the supreme command of the naval forces of the patriots ... The steam ship is so constructed that she will be propelled at the rate of seven nots an hour, allowing for calms and stormy weather; and her passage across the Atlantic may be considered as forming a new era in navigation. Lord Cochrane was expected to proceed for South America about the 10th of June. We heartily wish success to him and every brave associate in so glorious a cause.

That Cochrane's vessel suddenly had become a "steam ship" in the space of a few months was no coincidence. In the wake of the Savannah Steam Ship Company's formation and first steps, cracks were beginning to appear in the conventional wisdom.

The obvious implication of Lord Cochrane's plan, if true, was not lost on some readers. One anonymous writer in Gotham, taking the name of "X Y Z," responded in a letter to *The National Advocate* the very next day:

> *SIR—In reading the account of Lord Cochrane's steamboat enterprize, and seeing it stated as likely "to form an era in navigation," I cannot repress [the] mortification I feel, that we, with all our enterprize, should not be the first to cross the Atlantic with steam, and that paltry feelings of pecuniary rapacity, "rigidly screwing up right into a wrong," should have blasted, as it did, the proud undertaking of one of our distinguished citizens, some time since set on foot. It is useless, however, to consume our feelings in vain regrets; and should Lord Cochrane succeed, as certainly we ought to wish he may, it will only remain for us to console ourselves with the reflection, that to us will still belong the merit of originating the first effective steamboat navigation!*

X Y Z's frustration at the failure of "distinguished citizen" Cadwallader D. Colden's effort to cross the Atlantic in the Monopoly's *Emperor of Russia* was palpable.

But *The National Advocate*'s editor was skeptical, and immediately followed X Y Z's letter with his own pointed opinion:

> *I doubt very much the possibility of carrying into successful operation the "steam ship" project of Lord Cochrane, with his vessel of only 200 tons. A voyage across the Atlantic, in a favourable season, might be prosecuted with a steamboat of proper dimensions and construction, but it is questionable whether it would ever overcome the well grounded fears of navigators of the multiplied dangers of the ocean.*

Beyond all this debate and skepticism over the feasibility of steam-powered ocean travel, Moses Rogers, William Scarbrough and their fellow shareholders must have wondered whether Lord Cochrane was going to beat them across. Yet at that point, there was nothing they could do but wait for more news, and press on with their own effort.

* * *

At the same time the Company was purchasing copper for the hull, the steam engine's cylinder was ready for delivery. Placed on a wagon, it was taken from the Allaire Iron Works to a nearby wharf. Once there, it was loaded onto a small vessel for transport to New Jersey.

Landing at Elizabethtown, the cylinder was picked up by a fellow named Enos Bonnel, who loaded it onto his own wagon. Bonnel then carted the cylinder about 16 miles inland, to the Speedwell Iron Works. Arriving there on August 1st, Bonnel turned his cargo over to Stephen Vail.

With the solid-iron cylinder delivered, the next step for Vail and his mechanics was to bore a shaft deep down into it. This would create the inner chamber, where the power of steam, in time, would work its magic.

* * *

As fabricating the new mode of power began to take shape in New Jersey, back in New York, attention turned to creating the old mode of power. The hull was nearing completion, and once it was launched, the installation of masts, rigging and sails could begin. As with the copper sheathing, directly purchasing materials for the sailing apparatus would be cheaper than letting Fickett and Crockett do it. So Moses set up an account with Francis H. Nicoll & Company, one of the city's largest ship chandlers, whose store was located on Front Street.

Since purchases from the ship chandler were but one of many parts of the effort to carry out this unique endeavor, the work of Captain Rogers and the Company must have been the talk of the waterfront that summer. It was in such an atmosphere that on Monday morning, August 10th, two men walked into the New York branch of the Bank of the United States, located on Broadway. Approaching one of the tellers, they presented a check for $600 that they wanted to cash. It had been issued by the firm of Pott & McKinne.

The bank employees did not like the looks of the check, or the two men who presented it. One of them claimed to be a crewman on the South American privateer *Curiaso*; the other was thought to be a German. While the two men were held, bank employees set about trying to verify the check's authenticity. They soon discovered that it was a counterfeit, and the suspects were immediately tossed into jail to await trial.

Such a charge of money forgery was very common in the early 19th century. Most transactions were concluded with some form of paper payment, whether checks, promissory notes, or bank-issued currency. All were susceptible to being faked, which meant that any individual on the receiving end had to make a judgment: *is it real, or not?*

Of course, anyone trying to pass counterfeit money had to believe they could succeed. That these two men apparently thought they would must have reflected the degree of hubbub created by Moses, the shareholders, and Pott & McKinne as they pushed forward. Careful as they were in trying to control costs, the Company was still spending a lot of money in a lot of different places, making the passing of a counterfeit Pott & McKinne check a very tempting proposition.

On August 12th, two days after the bogus check incident, the papers announced the arrival of still more of the venture's shareholders. On board the brig *Georgia* came Samuel and Rebecca Howard and their two children, as well as brother Charles, his wife Jane and their three children. Their appearance at New York was well-timed, since the launching of the hull was imminent.

* * *

The following Saturday, August 15th, in a dimly lit room in New London, a group of men gathered for a private meeting.

Among their number was Coddington Billings, the Stonington merchant who had been part-owner of the schooner *Experiment*, which Moses Rogers had captained back in 1807. Also present were Samuel Green, publisher of the local *Connecticut Gazette*, and Lyman Law, a New London lawyer and former legislator who had served in both the Connecticut and U.S. Houses of Representatives.

Once everyone was ready, the ceremony began. Into their presence walked a tall, robust man not yet 30 years of age, with curly dark hair and long side-whiskers—none other than Stevens Rogers.

If the ceremony unfolded as it should have, one of the leaders began reading out loud a Biblical passage from Paul's second letter to the Thessalonians:

> Now we command you, brethren, that ye withdraw yourselves from every brother that walketh disorderly, and not after the tradition which ye received of us...

So began the solemn rites which would lead Stevens Rogers to attain "the Most Excellent degree of Royal Arch Mason," the seventh level within the York Rite of Freemasonry.

That someone of Steve's place and profession had joined the Freemasons was not particularly unusual. In fact, in early 19th century America, it had become the very thing for aspiring men to do.

Believed to have originated in Britain many hundreds of years prior, Freemasonry was said to be founded upon the principles of the stonemasons of old. In building a structure, whether a castle, or a church, or a bridge, the stonemasons' work had to be "right and true," or else their effort would be for naught. Unlike nearly everyone else in Britain at that time, "right and true" stonemasons were not tied directly to the land upon which they were born. Therefore, they were considered to be "free." From these principles came their name: Freemasons.

Freemasons went wherever they were needed, living together at the construction site in temporary structures called *lodges*. So specialized were their skills, and so important was the need for accurate results in their work, that the Freemasons developed a firm system of moral beliefs, which tied the individual to his fellow masons. These loyalties, to both his beliefs and his brothers, were the guiding lights of the Freemason.

In the early 17th century, Freemasonry slowly began to change. Some lodges started to accept men who were not stonemasons, provided they abided by the fraternity's strict moral code. In time, this practice led to the formation of lodges without any stonemasons at all, but rather groups of men bound together by loyalty to their values and each other. By the early 19th century, this new kind of Freemasonry had spread over most of Europe, and traveled across oceans, to the Americas and beyond.

Underpinning Freemasonry's popularity in the United States was the very essence of its structure. American Freemasons, organized into lodges at the local level, were not only firmly rooted within their communities, but served to exemplify their young country's republican principle of limited central authority. Individual lodges ran their affairs as they saw fit—no one told them what to do.

Further supporting the surging membership of American Freemasonry was the knowledge that some of the country's most prominent revolutionaries—from Benjamin Franklin, to Robert Livingston, to George Washington—had been Freemasons. In the minds of those seeking admittance, to join this fraternity was to carry on the good works and goals of those founding fathers. The ongoing participation of the next generation—from Supreme Court Chief Justice John Marshall, to General Andrew Jackson, to New York Governor DeWitt Clinton, to President James Monroe himself—only reinforced that sentiment.

Wisdom, brotherhood, and charity to all mankind—these were the ideals which the Freemasons and Stevens Rogers, in identifying with them, were committed to uphold. There was perhaps no better, more poignant expression of these beliefs than the Biblical pronouncement of Isaiah, which every Royal Arch Mason, including Steve, had to know:

> *I will bring the blind by a way that they knew not; I will lead them in paths that they have not known; I will make the darkness light before them, and crooked things straight: These things will I do unto them, and will not forsake them.*

* * *

By the third week of August, Fickett and Crockett declared that they were ready. On Friday the 21st, a publicity notice was provided to several of the city's afternoon newspapers, in which the vessel's name was offered for the first time. In *The New-York Columbian*, the story ran as follows:

> *Launch.* To-morrow at 10 o'clock, will be launched from the ship-yard of Mess. Fivket & Crockett, the elegant STEAM-SHIP SAVANNAH, to be commanded by captain Moses Rogers, and intended as a regular trader between Savannah and Liverpool, principally for the accommodation of passengers. It is believed that this ship as to beauty of model and excellence of workmanship has not been surpassed by any ever built in this city, and will reflect great credit to the builders.
>
> P.

The same announcement also ran in the *New-York Evening Post* and the *Commercial Advertiser* that afternoon, only with one key difference: they each declared that the launch time would be *not* "10 o'clock," but "1 o'clock" the next day.

The discrepancy was most likely the result of uncertain handwriting, or rushed interpretation. Having received one of several distributed copies of the same press release, the *Columbian*'s typesetter must have misread some of the words, written as they were in cursive longhand. As a result, "Ficket" became "Fivket," and more importantly, the "o" in "o'clock" was mistaken for a zero, making the launch time, according to the *Columbian*, "10 o'clock."

Since newspaper editors often copied stories verbatim from their peers, once set in motion, this error regarding the launch hour was only perpetuated by the Saturday morning editions. While the *Mercantile Advertiser* and the *Daily Advertiser* said the correct time was 1 o'clock, the *New-York Gazette* and *The National Advocate* erroneously declared it to be 10 o'clock. The result that morning at Fickett and Crockett's shipyard must have been one of quiet confusion, as some people arrived at 10 o'clock for the launch, only to be told they were three hours early.

In any event, as the true launch time of 1 o'clock approached, people wedged themselves into and around the shipyard. The crowd must have been huge. The launching of any vessel, especially a large one, was among the few public spectacles open to all comers. It was also a perfectly good reason for a party, whether by the new owners, the builders, or anyone else who thought the occasion worthy of a drink.

This particular launching was even more noteworthy, since the press release had clarified, and amplified, just what observers would witness: the launching a "steam ship." In the literal sense of each word, that meant:

—a three-masted, square-rigged craft, or "ship"—the largest type that traveled the ocean—with the inherent message that it could withstand whatever Nature threw at it;

—a steam-powered craft that would be, like most of its steamboat sisters, "principally for the accommodation of passengers," which was in and of itself a novel idea for a sea vessel;

—a steamship that was intended to be used as a regular packet, just like the steamboats, only across the ocean;

—and finally, a vessel just like the newly-begun Black Ball ocean-sailing packets, only with the advantage of steam to propel it.

These features, in whole or in part, made the launch of this newly-named *Savannah* something that many port workers, mariners, and residents of New York would want to see. For the Company's shareholders and their families, the ceremony held the promise of being the highlight of their summer visit to Gotham. For the various contractors hired, the ritual represented either the end of a job well done, or the signal to commence their own work.

The vessel everyone saw sitting on the slip, angled toward the water stern-first, looked every bit the ship it was originally intended to be. The hull would be registered as being 98 feet, 6 inches in *length*, as measured on the deck, and 110 feet from bow to stern. The width (or *breadth*) amidship was 25 feet, 10 inches. The *depth* of water needed to make the hull float was calculated at 14 feet, 2 inches. The cargo capacity (or *burthen*) was 319 and $^{75}/_{95}$th tons, making the *Savannah* a typically-sized trans-Atlantic trader of the time.

The stern of the ship was squared, meaning flat with sharp 90° corners transitioning to the sides, as was the norm for most sea vessels. The bow carried the bust of a man as its figurehead. Set into the deck at nearly equal intervals were the bases for three masts, not yet fully installed. Their completion would come after the launch, when Fickett and Crockett could better determine the full masts' proper balance on the floating hull.

As for the revolutionary machinery—the steam engine, paddlewheels and funnel—nothing was yet in evidence. Like the old mode's equipment, installation of the new mode's mechanisms had to wait for the floating of the hull.

The rituals for launching a vessel in 1818 were based upon many traditions, some of which dated back centuries. A musical band was most likely hired to play during the festivities—this had been a common practice at major launchings for some time. The formal rites must have included a benediction or sermon, followed by a brief speech or two.

While the dignitaries moved closer to the moment of launch, Fickett and Crockett's yard workers saw to it that everything down below was ready. The wood blocks underneath the keel were slowly, methodically split and removed, leaving only a final few to be cleared when the signal was given. The wooden beams (called *shores*), which held the curved hull upright, were checked to make sure they could be pulled away with ease, once the ship began to slide into the water. And the slipway itself was heavily lathered with grease, to reduce both resistance as well as the friction that results from a wooden keel sliding down a wooden ramp.

> When we behold a vessel launched,
> for the first time, into the water,
> we know not what its future history may be...

Once the speeches were done, then came the blessing of the ship. The signal was given to knock away the remaining keel blocks near the stern, while a bottle of wine was swung and broken against the hull, as the vessel was christened "*Savannah.*"

> All we are sure of, is,
> that it will have to beat about the sea,
> to contend with storms and calms,
> to be endangered by currents and rocks and sands,
> to be in frequent peril from the breaking sea,
> the forked lightning...

If everything went according to plan, gravity and grease slowly eased the hissing, smoking hull down the slipway, as the shores were pulled away, and the creaks and groans of the timbers fused with the cheering of the crowd.

But how long it may float amidst these dangers,
and vicissitudes of evil, we know not...
It may founder soon after it leaves port;
it may be set on fire,
and consumed in the midst of the waters;
it may be torn, as it were, plank from plank
by its labouring and plunging
in a heavy and continued hurricane;
or it may be suddenly dashed to pieces
on some sunken rock...

With a great roaring splash, the hull plunged into the East River, and the steamship *Savannah* was born. The time was near half past 1 o'clock in the afternoon, on Saturday, August 22nd, 1818.

Or it may escape all these perils,
and, after weathering many storms,
and visiting many distant parts of the world,
it may return in peace,
and in its own port end its days;
full of credit,
and followed with many a long and kind remembrance
by those who had sailed on board.

* * *

With the launching successfully accomplished, there was still a tremendous amount of work to do. The masts and yards had to be erected. The rigging had to be set, and the sails made. The steam machinery had to be built, too, and then installed.

But before any of this could be started in earnest, a problem arose that had to be addressed. The following Monday, an article appeared in the *New-York Gazette*, which held the potential to create the worst impression:

On Saturday, about half past one o'clock, the Steam Ship was launched by her builders, Messrs. Fickett & Crockett. She belongs to a company at Savannah, and is to ply as a packet between that port and Liverpool. In a few days she will be taken to

Elizabethtown, N.J. where the ingeneous Mr. Dodd is to fix in her apparatus, according to the plan of the steam-boat Atalanta.

The *Gazette* did not reveal its source, but it was very likely the only person who received high praise in the article. The combination of inaccuracies and egotism on display called for corrective action; otherwise, the resulting ill-will might endanger the whole endeavor.

The very next day, the *Gazette* was compelled to re-print the story, which started precisely as before, only with the steam engine installation being "under the direction of Capt. Moses Rogers." Furthermore, the engine plan, rather than being based upon the Dod-designed steamboat *Atalanta*, was newly-described as being "different from any of those now in use." And finally, Stephen Vail received equal credit for making the engine along with Daniel Dod, whose intellect was no longer described in such a flattering light.

With the completion of this remedial chore, everyone could focus properly on the construction plan.

Stevens Rogers, for one, had to get to sailmaking.

The skills needed to do so were a natural extension of the mariner's ability to repair ripped sails and damaged rigging at sea. Once a seaman reached port, the easiest way to make some extra money was to hire himself out for work along the waterfront, and one consistent source of employment came from sailmakers. This was because sails were perishable items. The drubbing they took in use meant that a typical set of sails didn't last more than four or five years, so demand for replacements made the trade of sailmaking a steady, fairly dependable business.

For a mariner, the cost of entering the trade was relatively small. Sailmakers often provided the necessary tools, but a seaman could always buy them if he needed to, with just a little money. A *sail sewing needle* was not expensive; neither was a *palm* (which was a hardened piece of leather wrapped around the hand and used to push the needle through the canvas); and every seaman had a *knife*.

Steve, being both an able man and a quick learner, had readily picked up these skills of sailmaking. His proficiency undoubtedly played some part in his swift rise up the crew list, to the rank of mate, just a few years after he first went to sea.

The first thing a sailmaker needed was a work area, sheltered from the elements. The ideal work place was a *loft*, which was simply a large, open room on the second story of a building. There, a sailmaker would have all the space necessary to lay out the canvas and other materials.

Second came the extended tools of sailmaking, beyond the basic needle, knife and palm. For making holes in the sailcloth, there were *spikes*, *prickers*, *stabbers*, and *fids*; for smoothing out seams and pressing rope or twine into the canvas, there were *rubbers* and *serving mallets*; and for uniformity, there were *seam gauges*, *tape measures*, and *stencils*.

With the working space and tools in place, the third step was procuring the materials. Ship chandler Francis H. Nicoll & Company readily provided all that was required, which was *boltrope* and *duck*.

Boltrope was a loosely twisted, tarred rope made of hemp. It could be used to sew pieces of sailcloth together, or secure the edges of a sail to strengthen it.

Duck was the mariner's name for sailcloth (which came from *doek*, the Dutch word for cloth). Duck was weaved using a combination of hemp and flax plant fibers. The stronger the hemp, in particular, the stronger the duck. The sturdiest, most durable hemp in the world came from the lands of northern Europe, with the Russian variety considered the best of all.

Given the unprecedented nature of this steam-powered experiment, and the skepticism surrounding it, using the most reliable sail materials available made sense. So for the lower sails, 35 bolts of Russia Duck were purchased, at $22 per bolt. For the upper sails, a lighter-weight cloth would be needed, so 35 bolts of Ravens Duck were acquired, at $13 per bolt. With the help of some additional hands, Steve had everything he needed to get to work.

While creating the sailing apparatus was underway in New York, Stephen Vail and his mechanics in New Jersey were beginning to fabricate the steam engine. At the end of August, they took the solid-iron cylinder cast by Allaire and began boring a circular cavity into it. This would create the internal space where the steam would move the piston up and down.

The boring had to be both perfectly round and straight down. If the piston, once installed, did not fit snugly all the way around the curved interior wall of the cylinder, then the spaces above and below it would not be airtight. Without a tight seal, the steam-induced motion of the piston within the cylinder might be irregular, at best. Furthermore, if the boring was not precisely straight down into the cylinder, the movement of the piston, the piston rod, and any parts attached to it would be out of kilter; then the engine might break down prematurely, or not work at all. The only way to avoid these problems was to bore a chamber that was perfectly round, and straight down.

Once the excavation was complete, Stephen Vail inspected the resulting cavity in the cylinder. It measured 40 inches in diameter, and 5 feet, 5 inches deep.

Unfortunately, in Vail's opinion, this outcome "proved bad," as he dutifully recorded in his accounts. Without a boring that was straight and true, Stephen Vail realized he had no choice: he and his men would have to try again.

* * *

Back in New York, several matters that had been weighing on the Company's effort were soon clarified.

The *Mercantile Advertiser* reported on September 3rd that "Lord Cochrane, at the last accounts, was at Calais, on his way to Paris, his expedition to S. America being delayed by some defect in the machinery of his steam vessel." Subsequent reports confirmed that Cochrane's steamer was indeed intended as a man-of-war, to fight on behalf of the South American revolutionaries. But since this potential rival seemed to be having trouble with its machinery, Cochrane might not be able to attempt an Atlantic crossing for some time.

The following week, on September 9th, the matter of the check forgers finally reached the top of the court docket. In the early 19th century, the presiding judge for local criminal cases was often the mayor, who served not only as the municipality's chief executive, but the local magistrate, as well. So when the accused were brought to trial at City Hall that Wednesday, calling the court to order was none other than the new Mayor of New York, the Honorable Cadwallader D. Colden.

The grandson of a former New York colonial governor, Colden had only recently entered the world of politics. Having published a biography of his friend Robert Fulton in early 1817, Colden subsequently won election to the State Assembly, as part of Gotham's Tammany Hall political machine. Yet unlike the other "Tammany Men" in the Legislature—who were bitterly opposed to their fellow Democratic-Republican, Governor DeWitt Clinton—Assemblyman Colden refused to march in lock-step. Instead, he straddled the political divide, and his half-Tammany, half-Clintonian posture quickly paid off. In early 1818, the Clinton-led Council of Appointment readily approved Colden to become the new Mayor of New York City.

By late summer of that year, Colden was already comfortably ensconced in City Hall, where he served as both mayor and chief magistrate. Combining this new post with his continued promotion of the Monopoly's steamboat affairs, and it was clear for all to see that Cadwallader D. Colden had become the most influential person in all of Gotham.

Cadwallader D. Colden.

The two defendants, John Kelly and Simeon Burradge, were brought before the bench on an "Indictment for forging and uttering." This meant they stood accused of counterfeiting the check from Pott & McKinne, and representing to the bank employees that it was real. The prosecuting attorney called forth a witness from Pott & McKinne, who the clerk recorded as "John P. McKinny." Then, John Stebbins, the First Teller at the Bank of the United States branch, was called to testify.

The prosecution resting, the defendants' attorney called two men and two women to testify on behalf of Kelly and Burradge.

The defense resting, the jury retired to debate the evidence. In due course, they came back with their verdict: "Not guilty."

While there is no record of the reasoning behind the jury's decision, in all likelihood the verdict was based upon something the lawyers call *scienter*. This is a Latin word which means "knowingly." If Kelly and Burradge didn't know they were passing a forged check, then they could not be found guilty. Given all the privately-issued paper currency floating around, scienter was an area of great legal debate at the time. The courts had placed a very high burden upon prosecutors, who had to show that a defendant actually knew the money they were passing was fake.

Without proving scienter, the defendants walked.

* * *

Through the rest of September and into October, the remaining features that would make the steamship *Savannah* capable of sailing just like any other ship were gradually put into place.

The three masts were erected, section by section, until each was comprised of a lower, middle, and top mast. At the front (or *bow*) of the vessel was the *foremast*, rising some 94 feet above the deck. In the middle (or *amidship*) was the *mainmast*, which was the tallest of the three, at about 96 feet. At the rear (or *stern*) was the *mizzenmast*, measuring not quite 80 feet in height. Lashed to each of these masts were three horizontal *yards*.

As the masts and yards were being erected, so too was the rigging. First came the installation of the *standard rigging*, which included the web-like *shrouds*, as well as other heavy ropes used to interconnect and support the masts. Then came the *running rigging*, or the ropes and pulleys used to alter the position of the yards, or allow the sails to be deployed or adjusted.

Once the large rectangular sails were completed, each was attached to its respective yard. The sails on the lowest set of yards were simply named after their respective masts: the *foresail*, the *mainsail*, and the *mizzen sail*. This last one, the mizzen sail, was actually not furled on a yard, but rather against the mast; it would then be deployed in line with the keel, acting as a kind of stern stabilizer.

The middle set of yards carried the *topsails*, and the highest set of yards carried the *topgallant sails*, in each case with the mast name specifying their particular location.

This complement of masts, yards and sails was no different than that for any other American ship of the time—except for one thing.

The lowest section of each mast was unusually tall. This meant that the lowest yards and sails were mounted higher than was normally the case.

In addition, the *Savannah* had poles attached to the back of the fore and mainmasts, at the height of the lowest yards. These were called *gaffs*, and could be used to deploy schooner-type fore-and-aft sails (i.e., in line with the keel). Gaffs were not a normal part of a ship's sailing arrangement. Moses probably wanted them because they would give him and Steve additional flexibility in sail choice, to contend with whatever sea conditions they encountered.

Finally, projecting out the bow of the *Savannah*, some 34 feet beyond the manly figurehead, was the *bowsprit* and its leading extension, the *jib-boom*. In addition to securing some of the standard rigging supporting the foremast, the bowsprit and jib-boom also carried the triangular *jib sails*.

As any onlooker could see, this steamship had exactly the same sailing capabilities as an "ordinary" ship, and then some. If the new mode of power broke down, the *Savannah* could readily revert to the old mode.

But even with this safeguard of sails in place, it still remained to be seen how the *Savannah*'s design could overcome the many risks that mariners saw for a steam-powered vessel traveling out on the ocean.

* * *

As the *Savannah*'s construction progressed through the end of September, the issue of steamboat safety yet again reared its fearsome head.

News reached Gotham that the Monopoly's *Fulton*, while churning through Long Island Sound in the midnight darkness, had suddenly encountered a sailing sloop, dangerously crossing right in front of the steamboat's path. Because the *Fulton* was charging along at a very brisk 8 miles per hour, and the sloop was making 7 miles per hour itself, there was little time to react. The steamboat's bow smashed right into the sloop, ripping away most of the sails and rigging, thereby leaving it a crippled, leaking hulk. The *Fulton*, which suffered only minor damage, subsequently towed the sloop into the port of Saybrook for repairs, leaving bystanders to wonder which vessel should be considered the true offender.

The steamboat safety debate didn't stop there. About 3½ weeks later, on October 19th, the Monopoly-licensed steamboat *Nautilus*, while on her way to Staten Island, encountered Aaron Ogden's Monopoly-licensed *Atalanta*, which was returning from Elizabethtown, New Jersey. The two steamboats, both moving at full speed, mistakenly passed too close to one another. The resulting collision tore away one of the Dod-designed *Atalanta*'s paddlewheels, and also damaged her engine, leaving the steamboat bobbing helplessly in the water.

These two accidents only amplified the worries many people had about the new mode of transport. Sailing vessels sometimes collided with each other, although it normally was not considered news, given the minimal damage that usually resulted. A crash involving steamboats, however, barreling along at unnaturally high speeds, was far more dramatic, and the newspapers duly took notice. The general public's combined fascination with and leeriness of steamboats also meant that they eagerly gobbled up such stories.

Inevitably, these accidents also evoked a series of provocative questions:

Was steam inherently more dangerous than sail?

Were steamer captains getting too big for their britches?

Or was this new technology just suffering from a peculiar form of growing pains?

Invariably, the answers to questions such as these would depend upon the beholder.

* * *

As the cooler days of autumn took hold, the Company shareholders who had been visiting New York felt the draw of home. By then, the hot, sickly season down South was over, and the crop harvests were already under way. Gradually, the shareholders began to depart. On October 20th, the day after the two Monopoly steamboats collided in the Bay, the ship *Ceres* left New York, carrying the Howard brothers, their wives and children back to Savannah. Robert Habersham embarked separately on the brig *Levant*. Archibald Bulloch and his family also set sail for home, only from Philadelphia, which they had just been visiting.

A few, however, were not yet ready to leave. William Scarbrough and brother-in-law Robert Isaac stayed behind. So too did John Bogue. Together with Gideon Pott and Joseph P. McKinne, the Company still had quite a few eyes overseeing the work of Captain Rogers.

By that time, the whole lot of them must have been relieved to learn that the prospect of being first, at least in the attempt to cross the Atlantic, appeared more secure. Follow-up reports from Britain confirmed that Lord Cochrane's steam vessel project had been delayed by boiler problems. Since Cochrane already had been forced to depart for the fight in South America, his vessel's eventual completion date was in great doubt.

Three and a half weeks into October, the *Savannah*'s sailing apparatus was complete. Next would come the installation of her steaming apparatus. Bringing that machinery to New York was not only impractical, but impossible, since most of it had yet to be manufactured. It made far more sense to move the *Savannah* as close as possible to Daniel Dod's workshop, and Stephen Vail's iron works. That way the vessel itself would be available for re-measurement, testing of parts, and eventually the installation.

So on Saturday, October 24th, Moses ordered a skeleton crew aboard the *Savannah* to cast off from the wharf. They slowly sailed her down the East River, and into the Upper Bay. From there, Moses pointed her westward, and into a narrow waterway called the Kill Van Kull, which led to the lower end of Newark Bay.

At the southwestern corner of that Bay was the entrance to a narrow, winding river-like stretch, bordered by swamps on either side. This was Staten Island Sound, which separated Staten Island from the New Jersey mainland. Moses knew these waters well—he had maneuvered the steamboat *Phoenix* through them on her runs from lower Manhattan to New Brunswick, back in 1809. Just after entering the Sound, the *Savannah* reached Elizabethtown Point, the closest a deep-water vessel could get to Elizabethtown without getting stuck in the marshes.

It was there that Moses ordered the *Savannah* tied up. Dod's workshop was some 2½ miles inland, at Elizabethtown, and Vail's Speedwell Iron Works were about 16 miles beyond that, at Morristown. Carting the machinery down to the Point would be a fairly straightforward affair.

Elizabethtown itself was a neatly-built little farming village, which served as a food basket for the region. Poultry, fruits and vegetables from the farms and fields surrounding the town were regularly sent to New York for sale. The area was particularly well-known for its apples and cider, which were often shipped as far away as Charleston, and Savannah, and beyond.

It was in Elizabethtown that former New Jersey Governor Aaron

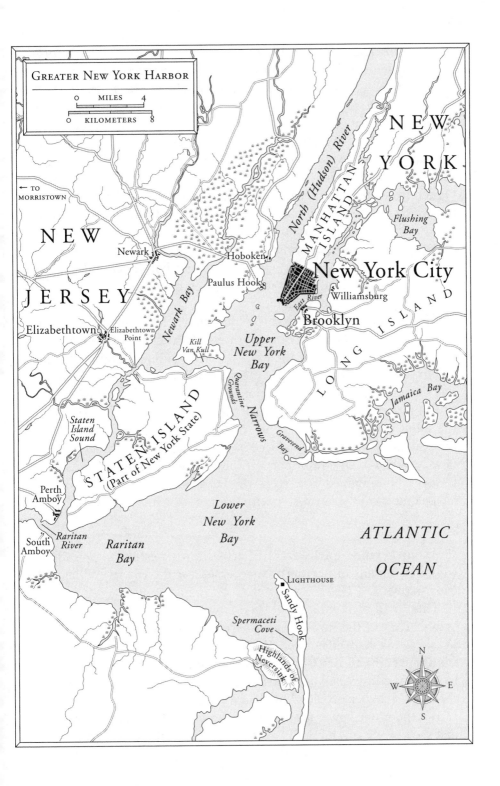

Ogden and Daniel Dod had built their Steam Engine Manufactory. While Ogden supplied most of the money for the enterprise, Dod contributed most of the technical brainpower. Having been trained as a clockmaker, Dod took an early interest in steamboat engines. He built the machinery for Ogden's *Sea Horse* in 1812, which then had been used to challenge the Livingston-Fulton franchise. But that commercial combat had been over for some time. Through a combination of legal maneuverings and olive branches, the Monopoly had managed to turn Ogden from an adversary into an ally, granting him a license in May of 1815 to run his steamboats into New York State waters.

The Steam Engine Manufactory had been quite active for several years, although the costs of managing such a business were formidable. Despite contracts to build steamboat engines both near and far, the debts Ogden and Dod had taken on to keep the business going were beginning to overwhelm them.

Moses, having known Dod for some time, clearly had confidence in his abilities. Daniel Dod counted three U.S. patents to his credit, and was thought to be one of the more creative engine designers in the country. That he could produce the technical drawings for the *Savannah*'s machinery, as Moses envisioned it, was beyond any doubt.

But if there was one aspect of Dod's contract that might have been the subject of some debate, it had to be giving him sanction to build the boilers. The ones to be placed in the *Savannah* were based upon a new design. Given how important they would be to the engine's performance, it remained to be seen whether Dod could actually produce a pair that would pass muster with Captain Rogers.

* * *

About 16 miles northwest of Elizabethtown, nestled in the rolling woods and fields of northern New Jersey, sat the country village of Morristown.

This small community had been anything but quiet a generation before. During the Revolution, the Continental Army under George Washington had encamped there over two winters, acting as a counterweight to British troops occupying New York City. More recently, the town had become a major agricultural depot, thanks to the milling power provided by the rivers and streams in the area.

But the water power around Morristown could support more than just the milling of grains. There was also an iron ore deposit nearby, as well as plenty of forestland. Combined, these resources provided all that was needed to support an iron industry.

So it was that in the year 1808, three men, including a 28-year-old blacksmith named Stephen Vail, purchased a share in an iron-slitting mill situated along the Whippany River. The original purpose of such a mill was the production of iron bars, which were then flattened and "slit" into narrow strips, for the manufacture of such items as nails and barrel hoops. The new owners had bigger plans for the mill, however, and soon began producing more sophisticated products, such as wrought-iron and cast-iron pieces.

Stephen Vail eventually became the dominant partner in the business. His reputation grew, and he became well-known for his precise mathematical calculations. He also kept very detailed accounts of monies owed and paid, which was equally important at a time when sloppy bookkeeping ruined many a business. By 1815, Vail had personally accumulated enough money to buy out the remaining partner in the works, a man named James Canfield.

Like many iron manufacturers, Vail took an interest in steam engines and their newest applications. In time, he gained enough knowledge to begin landing contracts to build them. His more recent work in Savannah on Sheldon C. Dunning's steam-powered saw mill, combined with his growing friendship with Captain Rogers, had helped Vail win the steamship contract. It was, without a doubt, the most publicly-visible work he had ever accepted, making it incumbent upon him to produce the very best parts yet to come out of his Speedwell Iron Works.

The physical operation that Stephen Vail had built was worth little without the human talent that went with it. Beyond the black-smithing and casting skills of Vail himself, the primary work of the foundry was carried out by men with differing skills, working together to make the iron pieces called for in any contract.

One of the most important men at Speedwell was an immigrant from Britain named Samuel Carson. Trained by the famed steam engine makers of Boulton & Watt, Carson had managed to make it to America, despite the best efforts of the British government to prevent such losses of its unrivaled engineering talent. In addition to his own skills as a smith and draftsman, Carson also brought with him a large collection of tables, dimensions and calculations needed for the manufacture of steam engines. For Vail to have acquired such talent was no small feat. The charge for Samuel Carson's services, at $4 per day, was evidence enough of just how valuable he was to Speedwell.

Next came the foreman, who had gained enough knowledge of the foundry's procedures to run the place when Vail was not around.

Then there were the blacksmiths and workers who did most of the hard, hot physical labor of making the iron pieces. These men ran the gamut, from free men, to indentured servants, to young apprentices, to slaves. While New Jersey already had taken steps to restrict and eventually eliminate any slaveholding within the State, it was still legal in 1818. Vail himself owned a small number of slaves, the most skilled of whom worked in the foundry alongside the others.

While the iron men in the foundry kept themselves busy, the Vail home nearby was kept going by the efforts of Stephen's wife of seventeen years, Bethiah Youngs Vail.

Bethiah Youngs Vail.   *Stephen Vail.*

Having borne six children, Bethiah could content herself that four of them had survived the hazards of early life. Running about the house and garden were two daughters, Harriet and Sarah, and two sons, Alfred and George, ranging in age from seven to sixteen. As was common for many children living out in the country, their view of the world had yet to stretch much beyond the rolling hills and leafy woods of their native New Jersey.

That, however, would soon change, when their father returned home from New York with a very unusual visitor.

* * *

Once Moses had brought the *Savannah* to Elizabethtown Point, work on the machinery began in earnest.

At Speedwell, a second attempt would have to be made at boring the cylinder. The solid-iron air pump cast by Allaire, recently carted to Speedwell, would have to be bored, as well. Then the workers could begin making the other parts of the engine.

But first, they needed Vail. He had been in New York for some time, probably to coordinate and confirm the work he was to do on the engine.

Having completed his tasks in Gotham, Vail hopped aboard the Monopoly's Cortland Street steamboat ferry. Accompanying him was a well-dressed man in his early forties, whose greatly receded hairline was countered by prodigious side-whiskers, and a mane of thick, wavy hair on the back half of his head.

The steam ferry carried them across the North River to Paulus Hook. There, Vail and the stranger transferred to a stagecoach, which took them west, through Elizabethtown, and then on to Morristown. By the time they reached Speedwell, it was dark, and the evening had grown both chilly and wet.

As they approached, the stranger could not help but notice that Speedwell's foundry was still active at that hour, and it made him reminisce:

> *The gushing of the river, the hammer's monotonous blow, and the sparks which flew from the forge recalled to my mind scenes at our Swedish ironworks. This pleasant illusion carried me back for a moment to the beloved home of my fathers....*

Their day's journey at an end, Vail ushered the stranger directly into his home. There, they were immediately greeted by Bethiah Vail and the couple's 16-year-old daughter, Harriet. Stephen in turn introduced his family to their new and very extraordinary guest: Baron Axel Leonhard Klinkowström, Lieutenant Colonel of the Swedish Navy.

* * *

When news of Robert Fulton's steamboat triumph reached Europe in late 1807, most observers there were incredulous. This was because so many people had tried so many times in so many different ways to propel a vessel by means of steam, and failed. That it was reported to have been accomplished in as wild a place as America only added to their disbelief.

European men of science and "mechanics" doubted this latest version of the steamboat would last, so heavy was the machinery, and so violent was the shaking that resulted from the engine's motion. But when Robert Fulton, John Stevens and then other American entrepreneurs repeatedly ran their steamboats over several seasons, the wall of skepticism in Europe began to crumble.

In 1812, an enterprising Scottish hotel owner named Henry Bell built and ran a steamboat on the Clyde River, in the west of Scotland. This vessel, the *Comet*, became the first commercially successful steamboat in all of Europe.

Soon thereafter, the British caught the same fever as the Americans. Being the home of the brilliant James Watt and his modernized, more efficient steam engine, Britain quickly became the second most active steamboating country in the world, and its able mechanics and engineers began exporting the new technology to the Continent.

One such member of this British diaspora was an Englishman named Samuel Owen. A Boulton & Watt trainee, Owen first traveled to Sweden in 1804, to install several steam engines. By 1809, he had set up his own factory in Stockholm. There, he produced dozens of steam engines, and taught the first generation of Swedish steam mechanics.

The growing realization that steamboats were authentic led Owen to build one himself, for operation on Lake Mälaren, to the west of Stockholm. The experimental runs of his *Stockholmshäxen* (or *Witch of Stockholm*) in 1816 and 1817 opened the eyes of the Swedish government. One official who studied Owen's work closely was Baron Axel Leonhard Klinkowström.

During his 25 years of service in the Swedish Navy, Lieutenant Colonel Klinkowström had developed a detailed knowledge of shipbuilding. This made him a good candidate to assign the task of learning just how these new steamboats might be used. The Baron spent a lot of time with Owen, making him one of the few native Swedes with a working knowledge of both the old and the new modes of transport.

By 1818, Swedish government officials concluded that they needed to learn more—*a lot more*—about these new steamboats. Since it was the Americans who were the first to successfully run them, and they had the most in operation, and they had built the first steam-powered war vessel (the steam battery *Fulton*), the Swedes decided that it made sense to study their methods.

Given his knowledge, Baron Klinkowström seemed the ideal person to send on such a mission. In the summer of 1818, he was ordered to travel to the United States, and gain as much access as he could to both the steamboats in operation and the people who were building them.

In addition, he received explicit instructions from the country's ruling monarch, King Karl XIV Johan: determine whether the Americans had yet applied steam power to sea-going vessels, with the object of crossing the ocean. This particular request was triggered, in all likelihood, by the mid-summer arrival in Sweden of newspapers describing the Savannah Steam Ship Company's formation.

Departing his homeland on August 2nd, Baron Klinkowström endured a grueling, storm-wracked 75-day voyage, before landing at Newport, Rhode Island on October 15th. From there, he had traveled west to New London, Connecticut, where he boarded the Monopoly's steamboat *Fulton*, for New Haven. Arriving at New Haven after dark, he transferred to the steamboat *Connecticut*, under Captain Elihu S. Bunker, and headed for New York.

That night, the sturdiness of American steamboats was impressed upon the Baron, as the vessel originally conceived as the *Emperor of Russia* pushed its way through a tumultuous Long Island Sound. So violent were the waves that the *Connecticut*'s paddlewheels were alternately completely out of the water, or entirely submerged within it. Even so, the steamboat managed to press on, and by morning was easily churning through the dangerous whirlpools of Hellgate, just north of New York City.

Once Klinkowström had disembarked at the bottom of Fulton Street, he sought out Henrik Gahn, the Swedish-born American who served as Sweden's consul general at New York. Gahn did all he could to help the Baron make the necessary contacts, introducing him to the newly-appointed Secretary of the Navy, Smith Thompson, who was a resident of Gotham. In turn, Klinkowström was able to arrange meetings with engine builders James P. Allaire and Robert McQueen.

Within a few days, the Baron also was introduced to Moses Rogers.

Having described the objective of his trip, the Swede expressed great interest in learning more about the steamship under construction. Captain Rogers "kindly helped me in many thoughtful ways," the Baron subsequently wrote in a letter home. This included an introduction to Stephen Vail.

Vail also was willing to help. "He invited me in a very friendly way to accompany him to his factory," Klinkowström recorded. Once there, the Baron would be free to see and sketch the plans for this steamship, and review other engine drawings Vail had in his possession. It was simply too good an opportunity to pass up.

* * *

"The arrival at Mr. Vail's house pleased me greatly," wrote Klinkowström. Perhaps not knowing what to expect, the reaction of Vail's family seemed to put the Baron at ease.

Mrs. Vail and her daughter, a pretty sixteen-year-old girl, welcomed me without constraint; the small children gathered around their father and wanted to know what he had brought them from the city. They all got little gifts and ran happily on their way. A cheerful fire lighted the room, and Mrs. Vail served tea, which was very welcome on a cold and rainy evening...

The Swede quickly settled in with his host, finding the new environment, with one exception, to his liking:

Life in the Vail household is frugal; the food is sufficient and well-prepared. Order prevailed everywhere. The only thing that I found unattractive was my bedroom, for although it was very clean and furnished with a good bed, it lacked a fireplace, had a drafty window, and was extraordinarily cold...

The next morning, Vail set up a workspace for Klinkowström in the tiny drafting room of Speedwell's workshop. There, the Baron could study any drawings he wished, and make copies.

It didn't take long for news to spread that the Vails had a guest. That he was a European, and a titled one at that, and a naval officer on top of that, made Klinkowström all the more unusual for the people of Morristown. Throughout his first full day at Speedwell, the Baron noticed that seemingly every farmer who knew the Vails found some excuse to come visiting; introductions to their guest inevitably followed. Within a few days' time, the Swede found it difficult to work in the evenings, as the drafting room became crowded with neighbors, all wanting to ask him questions about Europe.

While the Baron juggled drafting with diplomacy, Stephen Vail and his men got to work on the *Savannah*'s engine. In the early days of November, forging began for the piston rods of both the cylinder and the air pump.

Given the strain that the rods would take from the engine's motion, casting such parts would have been foolhardy. Cast iron had many impurities in it, like carbon and oxygen, which made it weak.

Wrought iron, on the other hand, was much stronger. This was because the impurities had been literally pounded out of it. By repeatedly heating the metal and striking it with a hammer, a blacksmith slowly worked the carbon and oxygen out of the metal, leaving as pure an iron object as his skill and strength allowed.

Heat, and beat.

Heat, and beat.

Such was the hard, hot work of the men at Speedwell, as they began *turning* the two piston rods, each requiring hundreds of pounds of impure *pig iron* to manufacture.

Then came another attempt at boring the cylinder. Since a cavity 40-inches in diameter had already been made by the first try in August, the second effort would have to be slightly larger. Increasing the intended diameter by ¾ of an inch, a second boring was made five feet into the cylinder.

Fortunately, this second effort was found to be both symmetric and airtight. Then, the more slender air pump received its boring, also set for a depth of five feet.

It was at this point that Vail realized the drawings produced by Daniel Dod contained an error. The piston rods Dod had designed for both the cylinder and the air pump were eight inches too short. Without lengthening them, the steam engine would not be as powerful as the five foot stroke allowed. So the men set to work correcting this mistake, using 98 pounds worth of pig iron to lengthen the cylinder's piston rod, and 30 pounds for extending the air pump's piston rod.

Baron Klinkowström, in the meantime, was pressing on with his study of the *Savannah*'s plans.

The drawings indicated that two large steam boilers were to be placed deep within the hold.

Above them, the steam engine cylinder would be mounted at a 45° angle, which was unusual. Normally, cylinders were installed with their bottom end resting firmly on the ground (or lower deck, if on a vessel). This meant that the cylinder's piston rod motion was vertical—literally an up-stroke, followed by a down-stroke. Under Captain Rogers' design, the rod's motion would be not quite horizontal, but slanted nevertheless.

Furthermore, the paddlewheels shown in the drawings looked well beyond different. They were uniquely designed to be collapsible, so that they could be dismantled whenever conditions warranted.

Regardless of the work before him, the Baron still found himself the continued object of local curiosity. One of the Vails' neighbors—an old farmer named Kennedy—became a particular favorite, reminding Klinkowström of the farmers back home in the Swedish highlands. Kennedy asked the Baron to visit his house often, sometimes expressly coming to the Vails to fetch their guest.

Invariably, whenever the Swede arrived at the Kennedy home, he would find some of the local farmers gathered there. After enjoying the "good apples and delicious cider" that his host offered, Klinkowström would sit before the fire with these neighbors, and the Kennedy daughters, and tell them stories of Europe. Then, the locals would reciprocate, describing to him their farming methods, leading the Baron to conclude that these Americans had a greater theoretical knowledge of agriculture than their Swedish counterparts.

One Sunday after church, Kennedy invited the Baron to come to his home for a spell. What happened on the walk there so touched the Swede that he felt compelled to record it in a letter home:

Kennedy ... showed me a hillside where, during the Revolution, he had met and conversed with General Washington as he accompanied him on a reconnaissance trip in the area. It was moving to hear with what rapture the old man recalled this beloved general. The tears ran down his cheeks when he spoke his name and described his unassuming way of conversing and fraternizing with his compatriots...

Shortly thereafter, having spent three weeks at Speedwell, Baron Klinkowström felt he had done all the studying of plans that he could.

He packed up, and said his goodbyes to "this serene and hospitable people," as he described them—"I leave them with genuine regret." Yet he had to; there was plenty more for him to do back in New York.

As for the *Savannah's* steam engine, progress was being made, but it was slow. A few days before the Baron left, the air pump was carted from Speedwell to Elizabethtown Point. Along for the ride went a cradle (or *pillow*), which would be used to store the pump on the deck of the ship, until it and the cylinder were installed. This couldn't be done until the boilers were in place.

And the boilers could not be installed until Dod and his mechanics at Elizabethtown actually built a pair that worked to satisfaction. That the boilers were the subject of special scrutiny was due not only to their new design, but also Daniel Dod's less-than-perfect reputation.

* * *

Back in 1816, former New Jersey Governor Aaron Ogden had decided to swap steamboats.

The *Sea Horse*, which he had used to challenge and then join the Monopoly, was growing obsolete. Her technology was four years old, and at a mere 71 tons burthen, she was too small for the growing cross-river ferry route between New York and New Jersey.

So Ogden ordered a replacement to be built, and the Steam Engine Manufactory of Elizabethtown, which he jointly owned with Daniel Dod, naturally got the machinery contract. Dod set to work designing a new, more advanced steam engine for the boat, which was duly named *Atalanta*, after the swift huntress of Greek mythology.

By mid-December of 1816, construction on the *Atalanta* had advanced enough to allow trial runs. On one such trip, she took on a number of passengers at New York for the journey back to New Jersey. Among their number were two young boys, the Wait brothers, who were returning to school at Elizabethtown after visiting their parents in Gotham.

In the *Atalanta's* engine room was Daniel Dod himself, overseeing the first tests of his new engine. With him was an engineer named Mr. Orr. Just before casting off, the decision was made to check the steam pressure in the boilers. Since a pressure gauge had not yet been installed, Mr. Orr proceeded to lift the safety valve on one of the boilers. This would allow a small amount of steam to escape from the boiler, and based upon the lever's "feel," Mr. Orr would have an idea of the pressure level inside.

But without a steam gauge, there was no way for Daniel Dod and Mr. Orr to know that the steam pressure in that boiler had already become dangerously high.

The moment Mr. Orr's hand lifted the safety valve to "let off steam," all that pent-up power rushed toward the tiny opening with a force far stronger than the boiler could handle.

In an instant, the near-end of the boiler exploded outward, shooting hot, scalding steam directly into the passenger cabin directly behind it. Daniel Dod, standing away from the blast, was only slightly injured. Mr. Orr and several passengers, situated right in the main path of the explosion, were more severely scalded. But the brunt of the burning was taken by the young Wait brothers. So horrid were their injuries that by late afternoon, both of them had succumbed.

This tragic accident, and the deaths and scaldings that resulted, forced a number of important questions to the fore.

Why was the Atalanta operating without a steam pressure gauge?

Why weren't Mr. Orr and Mr. Dod paying closer attention to the build-up of pressure in the boilers?

And was it possible that the steam apparatus—indeed, the boilers themselves—had not been designed, or built strongly enough, to cope with this very human error?

Even for a steam engine designer as talented and renowned as Daniel Dod, these were questions which might fade with time, but very likely would not be completely forgotten.

*   *   *

As Dod and his mechanics finished constructing a boiler for the *Savannah*, Moses made a point of testing it. Even though each boiler was expected to operate at only 20 pounds per square inch (for safety's sake), it remained critically important that they be able to withstand higher pressures. So when the first attempts at boilermaking failed to meet the standards set by Moses, he rejected them, and Dod's mechanics started over. The delays inherent in such an exercise put the whole engine installation behind schedule.

The distances involved also had an effect. While hiring Vail and Dod to make the steam engine had the advantage of lower costs than New York, it carried the disadvantage of having to transport parts, patterns, and people between Morristown, Elizabethtown, and the *Savannah* herself. These logistics slowed down the construction process, as well.

It appears that on at least one occasion, the situation, if not the whole idea, seemed hopeless to Stephen Vail. A young boy who was a relative of Vail's former partner, James Canfield, came to visit Speedwell at the time, and many years later recalled his experience:

> *I ... there saw an unusual and extensive work going on and upon enquiry was informed by the proprietor, that he was under contract to construct machinery for a ship in process of building to navigate the Ocean by steam, got up, as he expressed it, by some crazy people of Savannah and which he predicted would prove a failure—*

Whatever doubts may have been harbored by other participants, it is unlikely that Moses betrayed any. With the exception of Gideon Pott and Joseph P. McKinne in New York, the remaining shareholders—William Scarbrough, Robert Isaac, and John Bogue—had all departed for Savannah at the end of October. The execution of the construction plan rested on the shoulders of Captain Rogers, and no other. He had been in such demanding situations before in his steamboat career, but this was by far the most challenging. The *Savannah* would only become a steamship if Moses combined his inner experience with the outer confidence needed to complete her.

Finally, Daniel Dod and his mechanics produced a pair of boilers that passed muster, and they were brought down to Elizabethtown Point to be placed on board. Word of their imminent installation reached Baron Klinkowström in New York, who hurried back to observe.

The boilers were big indeed, measuring 24 feet, 10½ inches in length, and 6 feet in diameter, according to the Baron's calculations. Of equal note was the material used: instead of corrosion-resistant copper, the huge kettles had been made with iron.

The rationale for doing this was two-fold.

First, the cost of copper was such that making the boilers out of the red metal would have been incredibly expensive, and well beyond the Company's budget.

Second, the boilers were a new design, intended to address the problem of salt build-up. Precisely how this new design did so was not publicized, but if these boilers worked, it would be a major technical breakthrough. On the other hand, if they did not work, or could be improved upon (as was likely), it made sense to limit their initial cost.

Getting them into the ship's hold proved a very difficult task. They had to be upended, and maneuvered very gingerly down through the existing main hatch in the deck, just behind the foremast. As Klinkow-ström watched, he took note of the amount of strain being put on the iron plates, and the rivets that held them together.

Once in the hold, the boilers were placed on several layers of clay bricks, which partially surrounded the kettles on the bottom and sides. The bricks served the same purpose as in any fireplace: they diffused the heat produced by the boilers, thereby insulating the wooden tim-bers of the hull from potentially dangerous temperatures.

Once the boilers were in place, the rest of the steam engine could be installed. Back at Speedwell, Vail and his men also began working on the iron paddlewheel arms, which was yet another unusual fea-ture—up to that point, most steamboat paddlewheels had been made almost entirely of wood.

As the work progressed into December, and the weather grew decidedly colder, the waters along the Jersey shore eventually began to freeze. The machinery still was not finished, but Moses feared that if he kept the *Savannah* at Elizabethtown Point much longer, she would be frozen in, and there would be no telling for how long.

So on Christmas Day of 1818, Moses gave the order to cast off. Slowly, the *Savannah* moved eastward, back through the Kill Van Kull, and into Upper New York Bay. Then, Moses turned her north, toward the ice-free waters of the East River. Once there, the *Savannah* was tied up to the wharves, and work on her continued.

*   *   *

During those same months that the *Savannah* was docked at Elizabethtown Point, the shareholders down South had been busily working their way through the usual tasks of autumn, that being har-vesting crops, and selling them.

But beyond these chores, the fall of 1818 proved to be anything but routine.

For starters, early October had brought an early frost to Georgia and South Carolina. Because there had been a severe frost the pre-vious April, cotton planters were left with a growing season of only 5½ months. "Such a season, in this State," reported the *Savannah*

Republican, "is not in the memory of the oldest inhabitants." As crop-damage reports came in, some estimated the year's cotton harvest would be cut in half.

Adding to this disappointment were equally disconcerting financial winds from the West.

The difficulties began when the federally-chartered Bank of the United States was pressured by its biggest customer, the U.S. Treasury, to convert piles of privately-issued Ohio banknotes into specie (i.e., gold or silver). The only way the Bank of the U.S. could do so was by returning the Ohio banknotes to the issuing banks, and demand specie in return. This left the Ohio banks with little or no precious metals in their vaults, and forced them to *suspend*, meaning they would no longer redeem their banknotes for specie. With no ability to convert Ohio banknotes into the internationally recognized money of gold or silver, the true value of that paper currency was put into question.

Soon thereafter, banks in neighboring Kentucky felt compelled to follow suit, suspending the redemption of their own paper currency for specie. This in turn left the true value of Kentucky banknotes up in the air.

For that moment, the events out in Ohio and Kentucky looked like a regional problem. Even so, the rest of the country could not help but wonder whether these financial rumblings were merely a peculiarity of the wild West, or if they just might be contagious.

* * *

As the *Savannah* drew nearer to completion, Moses and Steve had to make efforts to raise a full-time crew. But the attitude they encountered amongst the mariners in New York harbor was very discouraging.

The seemingly never-ending reports of steamboat accidents could not have helped matters. Just a few days after the *Savannah* escaped the New Jersey ice, reports reached Gotham that another steamboat, the *Orleans,* had sunk on the Mississippi River, four miles below Baton Rouge.

Yet the reaction of New York's able-bodied seamen to the *Savannah* rested upon more than the sinking of any single steamboat. The Monopoly's aborted 1816 attempt aside, no one had ever asked them to consider something as radical and revolutionary as crossing the Atlantic using the new mode of power.

Signing up to work on a steam boat operating near the shore was one thing.

But joining the crew of this so-called "steam ship," which would attempt to cross the ocean, was an entirely different, more dangerous matter. Bluntly put, it seemed suicidal.

In due course, the mariners of New York effectively responded to the whole idea by giving this floating contraption tied up to the wharves a description of their own—

"Steam *Coffin*."

CHAPTER EIGHT

COMPLETION,
AND COMPETITION

WHILE MOSES HAD been directing the steam engine's installation in New Jersey, the shareholders down in Georgia had sought official recognition for the Savannah Steam Ship Company.

Most businesses operating in the United States in the early 19th century were simple partnerships between two or more people. There was no requirement to formally organize, or register such combinations with the authorities.

Corporations were a different matter. While the idea of organizing businesses around this more formal structure had been in use for centuries, the actual practice usually had been limited to very great, risky undertakings that required lots of money. Britain's industrial revolution accelerated the use of corporations. The amount of capital needed to build large textile mills, for example, meant that a large number of investors would have to be involved, so the organizational structure of the business became more important.

As the technological revolution spread to and grew within the United States, so did the use of the incorporated enterprise. Within a few years of Robert Fulton's success of 1807, steamboat entrepreneurs were among the first to embrace the corporate structure to organize their efforts.

Their reasoning was as logical as the rise of the corporation itself. Building and operating steamboats were complicated undertakings, requiring both technical expertise, which was in limited supply, and practical experience, which was virtually nonexistent. That such ventures were risky was obvious to all.

In addition, these newfangled steamboats were expensive. The smallest versions cost in the range of $12,000 to $15,000, the whole amount of which was literally in danger of sinking at any time. The larger the steamer and the more complex the design, the more it would cost to build. The Monopoly's enormous *Chancellor Livingston* set a new expense standard when it was launched in 1817, costing some $110,000.

Spreading the risk as widely as possible made a lot of sense, so steamboat entrepreneurs quickly began incorporating, and offering shares to the public. If the stock price was found too high to sell or re-sell, companies sometimes created fractional shares, which allowed even more people to participate.

The process for incorporating a business in the early 19th century was a private affair. The organizers determined the company's by-laws and structure on their own, and began operations. There were usually no requirements to register the venture at any level of government, which, for a new country learning to do things in a new way, was hardly surprising.

There were, however, certain instances when receiving official sanction for a newly-incorporated business was sometimes required, or desired.

First, if the new company wanted special powers, then approval from the State legislature was usually necessary. This included businesses that dealt in the creation of money (such as banks) or the protection of assets well beyond their immediate resources (such as insurance companies). It also included enterprises that would have some type of exclusive power, such as companies operating turnpikes, toll bridges, ferries, or in some cases, steamboats. Both the Steam Boat Company of Georgia and the Livingston-Fulton franchise of New York obviously fit into this exclusive-power category.

The second reason for officially incorporating was far more subjective, but equally important to some entrepreneurs: State incorporation bestowed legitimacy. If the organizers had gone to the trouble of seeking an act of incorporation, and the State legislature had honored this effort by approving it, then the new company would be seen by future investors and the public in a different light. After all, not only did such a venture have clearly stated objectives and written rules for achieving them, but the people's representatives had consented to recognize the new concern, as well. In a world where family made the best business partners, and every paper money transaction had to be scrutinized, such an official seal of approval for larger, riskier enterprises was becoming increasingly important.

It was this second line of reasoning that led the Savannah Steam Ship Company to seek the approval of the Georgia Legislature. Like the U.S. Congress, Georgia's deliberators usually convened toward the end of autumn, so December of 1818 was the Company's first opportunity to initiate the process. The place for petitioning was the capital of Milledgeville, a small hamlet on the Oconee River, near the geographic center of the State.

As the largest investor, William Scarbrough probably took the lead in drafting the petition, which soon turned into "a bill to incorporate the Savannah Steam Ship Company." After the required number of readings on the floors of both the Georgia House of Representatives and the Georgia Senate, the bill was subsequently passed. On December 19th, the bill was placed before Governor William Rabun, who signed it into law as "An Act to incorporate '*The Savannah Steam Ship Company.*'"

Considering the unprecedented nature of the effort, the wording of the Act must have received a great deal of attention from the shareholders. More than any other surviving document, it serves as both a reflection of their status within the Company as well as a clear statement of what they hoped to accomplish.

> Whereas Wm. Scarbrough, A. B. Fannin, J. P. McKinne, Samuel Howard, Charles Howard...

It was tradition to list shareholders from largest to smallest, so these first-named individuals were risking the most out of the $50,000 raised. Having William Scarbrough, by then a former president of the Steam Boat Company of Georgia, and the steam-pioneering Howard brothers as prominent investors represented a strong endorsement of the venture.

> ...John Haslett...

The participation of the most prominent shareholder in the Charleston Steam Boat Company was yet another vote of confidence.

> ...Moses Rogers...

His appearance near the top of the list meant that Moses truly put his money where his mouth was.

...A. S. Bullock...

None other than the man serving as the U.S. Collector of Customs at Savannah was also on board.

...Jno. Bogue...

The packet sloop owner who could not beat Captain Rogers and the new mode of transport had decided to join them.

...Andrew Low & Co...

This Liverpool-tied trading firm brought its three partners of Low, Robert Isaac, and James McHenry into the mix, as well.

...Robert Isaac...

Despite having invested already through the Low partnership, Scarbrough's brother-in-law bought in a second time under his own name.

...I. Minis, S. C. Dunning, J. P. Henry, Jno. Speakman, Robert Mitchell, R. and J. Habersham, Jas. S. Bullock, Gideon Pott, W. S. Gillett and Saml. Yates...

These remaining shareholders had the least amount of money invested, but since at least half of them had been in New York the previous summer to witness the construction, they clearly took their participation very seriously.

Anyone who saw this list of investors, and knew the parties involved, must have been impressed. These participants, which included both new mode proponents and active merchants familiar with the dangers of the sea, had both the knowledge and the experience to comprehend the enormity of the task before them.

Furthermore, the size of this list—comprising 23 individuals—belied yet another important point, which was the organizers' intent to spread the risk. Assuming the worst, a total loss of this first steamship should not financially cripple any one of them.

The investors' participation recorded, the Act then cut to the core:

...have, by their petition, represented, that, with the view of making a laudable and meritorious experiment,...

By attempting something never before tried, the organizers were acknowledging, however indirectly, that they might not succeed.

... they have formed themselves into an association, under the style and name of *The Savannah Steam Ship Company*, to attach, either as auxiliary or principal, the propulsion of steam to sea vessels, ...

The craft under construction was only the beginning. It would move by steam or sail, as circumstances allowed. Once the technology and psychology permitted, vessels that used steam as their primary means of motion would be built.

... for the purpose of navigating the Atlantic and other oceans, ...

In time, these steamships would cross any seas rapidly, and predictably, changing the world, and man's place in it, like never before.

... and that they have provided a ship for that purpose, which is now in a sufficient state of forwardness to afford sanguine expectations of the experiment being tested in the course of a short period ...

Whatever the construction problems being encountered up in New York, the shareholders had confidence enough to declare that the vessel would be completed as promised.

... And in order to ensure and establish their said institution in a permanent and effectual manner, so that the attainment of their object may be more facilitated, have prayed the legislature to grant them an act of incorporation ...

With this petition, the shareholders of the Savannah Steam Ship Company had consciously and publicly outlined their goals in the clearest of terms:
—first, they would make an experiment—*an attempt*—to prove that it was possible to use steam power on long-distance ocean voyages;
—then, they would make improvements, and eventually expand, to bring this new technology to wherever it could prove useful.
Perhaps unconsciously, the shareholders also had expressed all the vital thoughts and emotions that were a part of any great endeavor:
—vision, tempered by caution;
—belief, combined with patience;
—and confidence, pressing toward anticipation.
All that remained was for Captain Rogers to deliver.

* * *

As hot as the summers could be in New York, the winters were often just as cold. The shorelines and waterways around the greater harbor usually froze over, bringing the steamboats to a halt, or at least to heel. On land, the order of the day was settling up any business left over from the previous season, preparing for the next, and keeping warm. If frigid temperatures demanded it, some Gothamites did not hesitate to don fur coats, beaver hats, or even buffalo robes before venturing outside, creating a streetscape that seemed to prowl with hairy animals.

For the many artisans and mechanics whose work exposed them to the elements, the best method of keeping warm in winter was to keep moving. So it was for those laboring to finish the machinery on the steamship *Savannah*, as she lay tied up along the East River.

Part of that workforce included men from Speedwell, whom Stephen Vail had sent over to continue where they had left off. Blacksmiths David Shannon and Ira Arnold pounded out whatever iron pieces were still needed, while additional workers took parts arriving from New Jersey and assembled the engine, the paddlewheels, and the smokestack.

As work progressed on the steam apparatus, so too did fitting out the remainder of the vessel, including the passenger cabins. A visiting painter from Liverpool named John Davies managed to land the contract to paint the interior. Ship chandler Francis Nicoll also continued to supply Moses and Steve with whatever they needed, from files, to paint, to saw blades, to cookware.

Meanwhile, the *Savannah*'s most ardent foreign observer, Baron Klinkowström, had determined that it was time to quit the city. The other major centers of steamboating beckoned, in Philadelphia and Baltimore. So too did the nation's capital at Washington, where the Baron hoped to meet as many senior officials in the American government as possible. Early on the cold, damp morning of January 24th, 1819, he left his lodgings, and boarded a steamboat for what was a foggy passage to Staten Island, the first leg of his trip to the south.

The Baron's departure still left numerous domestic observers in New York, some of whom had been agitated by the steamship's launching and ongoing construction.

The first public evidence of this agitation had come in late December,

* * *

As the true outlines of this first-of-a-kind vessel, the *Savannah*, slowly took shape, the mariners of New York remained unconvinced. To them, this so-called "steam ship" was still nothing more than a "steam coffin," and would most assuredly take anyone foolish enough to serve on it to a watery grave.

The failure to raise a crew in Gotham was not for lack of effort. Steve had tried—there simply were no takers.

If a crew could not be mustered in New York, then the most logical place to look for willing mariners was where familiarity might be used to inspire fidelity.

Under the circumstances, there was no better place for Steve to attempt that than in New London. The reputation of the name Rogers —as a seafaring clan going back generations—would carry far more weight there than any other place imaginable.

Even if potential crewmen were unfamiliar with Moses, given his long absence, or the new mode specifically, they very likely would be quite familiar with his immediate family. Father Amos Rogers, as both mariner and lumber and brickyard owner, had been well-known on both sides of the Thames River for a long time. So too were brothers Amos Junior and Gilbert, who had been sailing the sloops *Industry*, *Reaper* and *Gleaner* in and out of New London for years.

There were also plenty of other members of the Rogers clan who were active mariners, including Steve himself. As recently as the previous summer, he had served as a first mate on Gilbert's sloop, the *Gleaner*.

Adding to Steve's know-ability was also a certain credibility, borne of physique and friendliness. Barrel-chested and standing nearly six feet tall, Steve was, by all accounts, strong—*very strong*. This was complemented by a certain affability, which made obeying his commands, in the eyes of those who knew him, all the easier. For any mariner willing to consider signing up for this "steamship" scheme, Steve's powers were a potent combination. So it was he who was sent to New London for the purpose of mustering a crew.

Among those who apparently did sign up was the youngest brother of Moses, 18-year-old Ebenezer Rogers. While it was a natural-enough thing for him to do, Ebenezer's act was just too much for their mother. As the family remembered it many years later, Sarah Rogers took a stand, and refused to budge.

"No, it is enough to have one son risk his life on such a venture," she replied. "You can't go with Moses."

Those men who did follow through upon signing up were a varied lot. Mariners in early 19th century America came from many backgrounds. Some had the sea in their blood; some were farm boys, looking for adventure; others were immigrants from Europe, starting a new life; and still others were running away from something, be it broken hearts, broken laws, or broken chains.

Steve, it is fair to say, did not necessarily care who they were, where they were from, or what color was their skin. After all, he himself had served with many kinds. What mattered most was their skill, their experience, and their willingness.

* * *

Work on the *Savannah* continued well into February, as the rest of the apparatus was put into place. Anyone curious enough to inspect her had to conclude that she truly was different from anything yet built. Every feature of the vessel seemed intent upon addressing not only the skepticism of veteran mariners, but also any apprehensions of the traveling public.

Starting deep down in the hold of the ship, the two large iron boilers—each some 24 feet long and 6 feet in diameter—were designed to deal with the salt problem that resulted from the use of sea water. Precisely how these boilers worked remains a mystery, but they probably relied on one or more of several salt-reducing methods. One possibility was that the temperature of the boiler water was kept below the point at which heavy salt crust was produced; or, perhaps the boilers were designed to be flushed periodically, removing any salt-saturated water in the process; or, maybe the interiors were constructed with a series of salt traps, to protect any vital parts. Regardless of the precise method, the fear of salt build-up clogging the pipes or weakening the boiler walls had been addressed.

Above the boilers, between the fore and mainmasts, was the largest cylinder yet to be placed in a steam vessel, calculated to provide the power of 72 horses. It was not installed vertically on its end, as was usually done, but nearly upon its side, at a 20° angle, and completely below deck.

This arrangement served several purposes.

First, it slightly lowered the *Savannah*'s center of gravity. If the cylinder had been installed vertically, then some of the machinery would have to rise above the deck line. The vessel already had enough weight up there as it was, with all the usual masts and sails and rigging of a ship. By minimizing the amount of weight above the deck, the *Savannah*'s center of gravity was lowered, and her stability improved.

Second, and more importantly, the angled installation afforded the steam engine the protection of the deck. If a storm brought down one of the masts or yards, the machinery was unlikely to be harmed in any way.

Third, and most important psychologically, this installation was intended to reduce one of the more troubling things about the first generation of steamboats, and that was the degree to which they vibrated.

Steam engines could never transfer all of their power to the intended use. Some of that power would be lost, either on the upstroke or downstroke of the piston. When installed on land, a steam engine's power loss was barely noticeable, since it was secured to the ground. But when fastened within a floating wooden vessel, that power loss was transmitted into the surrounding structure, often resulting in a strong vibration. This vibration was all the more pronounced since steamboats usually had their engine cylinders mounted vertically amidship, at the bottom of the hull. The result, when the engine was operating, was a pronounced throbbing of the vessel, which, along with the noisy clanking of moving parts, made more than a few passengers feel very uncomfortable.

The answer to this problem was to install the cylinder and the adjoining air pump at an angle, forward of the paddlewheel axle and well above the hull's bottom. Then the piston motion in either direction was diffused more broadly throughout the vessel, instead of directly into the bottom of the hull itself. This nearly-horizontal arrangement also increased the distance between the cylinder and the passenger cabins at the stern. The result was a reduced sense of vibration throughout the vessel, as well as less noise.

Moses himself knew this was all true. One of his previous commands, the steamboat *New Jersey*, had just such an arrangement. Using a similar layout in the *Savannah* made plenty of sense. The less passengers *felt* like they were on a steamship, the more comfortable they would be, and part of the strategy to achieve that was the installation of a "horizontal" engine.

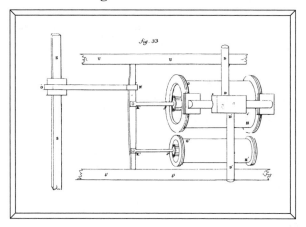

Top-down View of the Savannah's Steam Cylinder and Air Pump.

Next came the paddlewheels, which were an entirely new design. Protruding out of both sides of the hull, about ten feet forward of the mainmast, were iron axles. Bolted to the exposed section of each axle, in identical positions, were two iron arms, an inner (right next to the hull) and an outer (at the axle's tip). Attached to the ends of these arms were wooden paddleboards, clipped at the outer corners and measuring about 4⅔ feet wide by 2¾ feet deep. These arms and boards, permanently fixed in place, served as the spine for each paddlewheel.

The rest of each wheel was not fixed in place. Instead, it consisted of eight removable pairs of iron arms, or spokes, with wooden paddleboards bolted into place at their far ends. When steam power was called for, each set of spokes would be attached to the center of the fixed arms, using especially-strong bolts. Once these spokes and paddleboards were bolted into place, two sets of iron chains that were attached to the paddleboards would be hooked together, thereby holding the arms and boards at equal distances from each other.

When steam power was no longer needed, the movable arms on one-half of the wheel could be unchained, and the four boards and their spokes folded like a fan. Then they could be unbolted, and brought on deck. The paddlewheel could be turned one-half a revolution, and the process repeated for the remaining movable arms. Since there were no wooden housings over the paddlewheels, all that remained protruding from the hull was the axle, the fixed spines, and their paddleboards.

This new design was intended to serve as an antidote to the many concerns about paddlewheels at sea. If the ocean was too rough, most of the paddlewheel structure could be "brought in," avoiding any damage. Furthermore, the steamship's rollover risk would be reduced, since there was little weight left outside the hull, and no paddleboxes to act as "wave traps." Finally, when the *Savannah* was using her sails, no part of the paddlewheels would be dragging in the water, slowing her down.

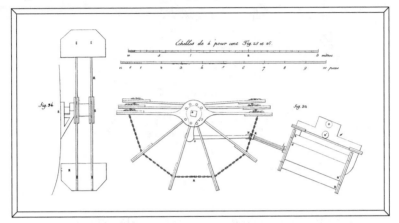

The Savannah's Paddlewheels and Steam Cylinder.

The seemingly fragile appearance of the paddlewheels was, in fact, deceptive. Up to that point, steamboats had wheels made almost entirely of wood. This made them susceptible to both damage and becoming waterlogged. The *Savannah's* wheels, by contrast, made use of so much iron that they were both lighter and stronger than those used by her steamboat cousins.

Lastly, the smokestack, placed between the foremast and mainmast, was unique for a steam vessel. After rising 15 feet above the deck, the stack elbowed backward at an angle for another 7 or 8 feet. The whole of this bent smokestack had been built to swivel from side to side, allowing any smoke, cinders and sparks issuing from it to be directed away from the sails. In combination with the higher-than-normal placement of the lowest set of yards, this swiveling smokestack appeared well-designed to minimize the risk of setting the sails afire.

Taken in full, this steamship creation of Moses Rogers was simply ingenious. Each part of the steam apparatus was intended to address a particular concern of mariners, as well as the fears of the public.

The Steamship Savannah.

Further still, his external conception of the *Savannah* looked as much like the old mode, and as little like the new mode, as was practically possible. The message to any prospective passenger was obvious: travel on this "steamship" is perfectly safe.

Yet the ingenuity Moses displayed could not stop with mechanical innovations and exterior appearances. He also had to consider the other, interior half of the steam passenger puzzle.

* * *

By late February of 1819, the *Savannah*'s completion was finally within sight. While Gotham's attention was distracted temporarily by parades and public dinners for the visiting Hero of New Orleans, General Andrew Jackson, the men from Speedwell finished up their work on board the steamship, and headed back to New Jersey.

Shortly thereafter, their employer, Stephen Vail, finalized his expense accounts for the work done on the *Savannah*. On February 26th, Vail paid a visit to the South Street offices of Pott & McKinne, where he presented a detailed statement of the expenses incurred. The charges spanned from Enos Bonnel's fee for carting the cylinder, back on August 1st, to the blacksmithing of Shannon and Arnold at New York through the winter. The total cost for the work done by Vail and his ironworks came to $3,501.59.

The bill presented, Pott & McKinne had to determine how to pay. Most merchants, regardless of their size, did not keep such large sums of money lying around. Their capital was tied up in numerous transactions with other businesses near and far. Reviewing their accounts, the partnership had to determine at what point monies would be coming in to cover the Speedwell bill, and in return, offer Vail a 3% rate of interest while he waited for final payment.

Based upon this reckoning, Pott & McKinne issued to Stephen Vail promissory notes in the amount of $1,750.80, payable in 60 days, and $1,777.04, payable in 90 days. In return, Vail gave them a receipt, acknowledging that when the notes were paid off, his account with the Savannah Steam Ship Company would be settled.

If Vail wanted the cash before the 60 and 90 day terms of the notes, he probably could sell them, although he would have to accept whatever discount from the face value the buyer demanded. Otherwise, Vail could simply wait the requisite number of days, and return to Pott & McKinne for payment. In the meantime, the steamship *Savannah* would be ready for her trials around the harbor.

* * *

On February 25th, the day before Vail paid his visit to Pott & McKinne, the Company's shareholders gathered for a meeting down in Savannah. Based upon the progress reports coming from Captain Rogers, it was time to formally choose the Company's leadership.

Given his position as the largest shareholder, William Scarbrough was elected "The President of the Savannah Steam Ship Company." For directors, the shareholders chose Scarbrough, Robert Isaac, Sheldon C. Dunning, James S. Bulloch, and Joseph Habersham.

The selection of these five as directors, all based in Savannah, was hardly coincidental. Combined, they had either direct family or close business ties to almost every other shareholder, regardless of their location. If any of the 23 individual investors had a concern, at least one of the directors could serve as their spokesman. It also meant the board could meet quickly, if circumstances, or challenges, required.

* * *

By early March, the *Savannah* surely looked ready to go. The *New-York Gazette* believed as much, running a brief story on the third day of the month:

> The elegant steam-ship Savannah is now on the eve of sailing for Savannah. The superiority of her accommodations, and the probability of the quickness of her passages, must attract general attention.

That the newspaper bothered to note the passenger spaces on board was testament to the thought that went into them. Giving comfort that the steam machinery was safe represented only half of the puzzle for the new mode of transport—the other half was making passengers comfortable, literally. The more at ease a customer was while on board, the less likely he or she would be to worry about the noisy engine and raging boiler fires only a few short steps away. To accomplish this goal, the *Savannah*'s passenger section—which stretched from the mainmast back toward the stern of the ship—had been the object of great attention and expense.

First and foremost, separate main cabins were constructed for the sexes. This was a feature early steamboat entrepreneurs had realized was crucial for attracting female passengers. Such an arrangement was a rarity aboard ocean-crossing merchant ships, making the *Savannah* all the more unusual.

Beyond layout, the cabins' interiors were built out to the highest specifications. Mahogany wood was used throughout, providing a warmth and richness seldom experienced on trans-Atlantic merchant vessels.

Even more unusual were the large mirrors installed along the cabin walls, and inset into support columns. These served to create the illusion of expanse, and counter any sense of claustrophobia while cooped up below deck. This was an especially important tactic to employ given the "steam coffin" nickname the *Savannah* had been given in some quarters.

Determining the number of passenger sleeping berths available depended heavily upon who was doing the counting. In those days, doubling up in one bed or sleeping on a couch were common practices. Applying such subjective measures to the *Savannah* resulted in passenger capacity estimates that ranged from as low as 20 to as high as 60. Under the circumstances, the comfortable number that could be accommodated was probably somewhere in the middle of those two extremes.

The *New-York Gazette*'s article on the *Savannah* was clearly intended as a high compliment. But it would have been impossible for readers not to notice that right below the *Savannah* story, the newspaper also had obligingly provided an update regarding Gotham's own answer to the Georgians:

> We understand that another Steam-Ship is building by Henry Eckford, Esq. It is supposed she is intended as a packet between this port and New Orleans, to touch each way at several of the intermediate ports.

It had been only six weeks since Cadwallader D. Colden and his partners had publicly announced their own oceanic steam effort. Obviously, they were wasting no time.

Key to their speed was founding shareholder Henry Eckford, who was one of the best shipbuilders in the country. He knew precisely how to design sturdy vessels, as evidenced by his official position as the U.S. Naval Constructor at the Brooklyn Navy Yard. He also knew how to build the new mode of transport, as exemplified by his completion of the Monopoly's massive *Chancellor Livingston*. If anyone had the gumption to match the *Savannah*'s design and construction, it was Eckford.

Henry Eckford.

Mayor and Monopoly partner Cadwallader D. Colden's involvement also must have given pause. Rumors the previous autumn that he had been a candidate to become the next Secretary of the Navy made it clear that his star was rising. Carrying both the torch for Fulton and the scars of the cancelled 1816 crossing, Colden—more than any other Gothamite—bore the burden of maintaining the Monopoly's leadership position in this new technology.

Yet right there, within their midst—*in New York City*—lay a cutting-edge steamship, promoted not by Fulton's heirs, but some upstarts from late-to-the-new-mode Georgia, and a Connecticut renegade.

The Monopoly's logical response to this was to revive the failed attempts to start steam packet service to New Orleans. Once that was accomplished, the Monopoly could expand, offering service across the Atlantic.

It was surely noticed by Captain Rogers, William Scarbrough and their fellow shareholders that Colden's rival steamer planned to touch "at several of the intermediate ports" between New York and New Orleans. Since Charleston and Savannah were obvious candidates, it was not difficult to conclude that the New Yorkers intended to compete directly for those markets, if not the glory of introducing long-distance oceanic steaming itself.

* * *

A few days after news of the *Savannah*'s completion and competition hit the papers, Baron Axel Leonhard Klinkowström returned to New York. The Swede had spent much of his time away in Washington, where he managed to meet with many senior officials, including the Navy Commissioners and President Monroe. His sudden reappearance at Gotham was probably due in no small part to the impending test runs of the *Savannah*.

Through the first few weeks of March, Moses took the steamship on very short trial trips up and down the East River. As with Fulton's experiments nearly a dozen years earlier, each time the *Savannah* ventured from her berth, a crowd gathered to watch. "She works to admiration," reported one of the local papers, "and her velocity is such as to give entire satisfaction."

On the afternoon of March 22nd, Moses prepared to take the *Savannah* on her longest test yet. Along for the ride, as he had been for several previous trials, was Baron Klinkowström.

After spending less than one hour getting up steam, Moses ordered the crew to cast off from Fly Market Slip, at the foot of Maiden Lane. Then, at about half past 3 o'clock, he ordered the paddlewheels be put into motion.

With all her sails furled, the *Savannah* steamed southward, past the forest of shipping tied up along the South Street wharves. Then she came into view of the Battery, and the hundreds who had gathered there to watch. One newspaper later reported on "the wonderful celerity with which she is moved through the water." From the vantage point of land, the steamship appeared to work just as intended, as it splashed its way toward Staten Island.

But to the Swedish naval officer standing on the *Savannah*'s deck, the judgments were far more difficult. As Baron Klinkowström bore witness to the steamship's celerity, there was nevertheless a great struggle taking place inside him, and this battle—between the old, the new, and the unknown—was fierce. What emerged from this inner conflict, as he saw it, was a steamship with a number of problems.

First of all, the Baron was worried about the boilers. Captain Rogers had placed the two giant water kettles down in the hold, on a bed of clay bricks. This allowed the bricks to act as both heat insulators and part of the ship's ballast. Baron Klinkowström did not like this arrangement. He thought that while the bricks certainly absorbed the boilers' radiating heat, they simply were not heavy enough to be considered proper ballast for an ocean-going vessel.

A better set-up, he thought, would be to use cast-iron blocks, or *pigs*, molded to fit snugly into the ship's bottom. Not only would they provide the weight necessary for ballast, but the iron pigs could also absorb and dissipate the heat coming from the boilers, just as the bricks did.

Then there was the size of the cylindrical boilers. The Baron thought they took up far too much space in the hold, and combined with the coal used to fuel them, left too little room for cargo.

Further still, he was concerned about spontaneous combustion. Even with the brick insulators partially surrounding them, the boilers gave off heat so strong that the Baron feared for the safety of any cargo in the vicinity. If the ventilation around them was better, he thought, then the heat might dissipate more easily.

Klinkowström also noted the difficulty of getting up sufficient steam. The *Savannah* was under way with a boiler pressure of only one pound per square inch, and the firemen were having difficulty raising it any higher. The genesis for this problem, he thought, had been the boilers' installation, which he had witnessed at Elizabethtown Point. Despite the care taken to maneuver them down the main hatch and into the hold, the boilers still had been subjected to a great deal of stress. The result was loose rivets and hairline cracks along plate seams, all of which became pathways for escaping steam.

Finally, the Baron did not approve of the boilers being made of iron. Given the harsh effects of salt, he believed that they would not last more than two years in operation. Copper, he thought, would have been the better choice.

His second set of concerns related to the installation of the steam cylinder and air pump. The Swede thought their placement—just below the main deck level—was too high, raising the ship's center of gravity. It would have been far better to put them down in the hold with the boilers, thus lowering the center of gravity, and further stabilizing the vessel.

He also did not like the nearly horizontal position of the cylinder. The Baron thought, as did many other new mode proponents, that a cylinder placed at an angle would cause the lower side of the circular piston to wear down over time. This could result in a loss of the tight vacuum seal needed to push the piston up and down. The more advisable installation for the cylinder, he believed, would be vertically, as was typically done.

The third worry came from the motion of the connecting rod and crank. Because a crank mechanism had been used, the paddlewheel axle had to be split into two halves. This in and of itself was not a problem. What did bother the Baron was the overall motion of the rod and crank, which he thought was uneven. The pair of them seemed to move faster once they passed over the far side of the axle. If gearwheels had been used instead, he thought, the connecting rod's motion would have been much smoother. But there wasn't enough room to install such gearing, since the paddlewheel axle had been placed just below the main deck.

The fourth issue was the axle itself. The Baron thought it had been placed too low in the hull. This meant that when the Savannah was buffeted by a breeze, the steamship would tilt slightly, causing the paddlewheel opposite from the prevailing wind to dip too deeply into the water, reducing its efficiency. Rather than installing the axle snugly just *below* the deck, he felt it should have been placed *upon* the deck, thereby raising the paddlewheels accordingly.

Even so, the Baron wondered how the *Savannah*, or any other steam vessel intended for ocean travel, would keep itself at a uniform depth when the progressive use of coals and provisions on a voyage would inevitably raise the floating hull. The paddlewheel blades would seldom dig into the water at the most optimal depth.

His fifth concern was the fixed arms of the paddlewheels. While they clearly were needed to act as the supportive spine for the removable spokes and paddleboards, the Baron thought the fixed arms were too heavy. Even when the detachable parts of the wheels were brought in and laid upon the deck, these fixed arms still represented extra weight outside the hull of the vessel, and could lead to instability in rough weather.

A safer arrangement, he believed, would be to take the extra time necessary to unbolt the fixed arms, and bring them on deck with the rest of the paddlewheels. Then only the axle ends themselves would protrude out of the hull, thereby minimizing the risk of rollover in heavy seas.

His sixth problem lay with the hull design. Klinkowström did not think the *Savannah*'s curved, deep-keeled hull, which was traditional for ocean vessels, was best for a steam-powered craft. Instead, he thought a flat-bottomed hull would be better, since it met with less resistance in the water.

To the Baron's senses, the end result of all these design features was a *Savannah* that was *cranky*. This nautical term meant that a sailing vessel was unstable, or tended to lean to one side. As the steamship churned south toward Staten Island, the light wind pushing on the masts and furled sails was causing it to slightly *heel*, or lean away from the wind. Ideally, a properly balanced sailing ship did not do this. The Baron considered this proof positive of how difficult it might be for a three-masted, fully-rigged vessel to use steam on the open ocean.

The Baron's seventh and final concern was that the *Savannah* was equipped with only one lifeboat. He thought it should have three in total, "light and capacious," with one stowed at the stern, and the other two on either side of the mizzen mast, far away from the engine. Given the many concerns he had with the steamship's design, the Baron clearly wanted to be prepared for the worst.

This dizzying number of criticisms swirling around in Baron

Klinkowström's head betrayed the angst he felt. As a traditional mariner who only recently had become a believer in the new mode, the Swede still had to reconcile his new knowledge with the old ways. Inevitably, the result was a great deal of anxiety, born of fear.

Some of the Baron's ideas made plenty of sense.

Using cast-iron pigs as both ballast and heat absorber was a good one, and a thought which probably came more naturally to someone from a country blessed with abundant iron mines. However, the cost of this alternative was far higher than using clay bricks, which had been the standard from Fulton's first steamboat onward.

Adding gears to the power train also appeared to be a good idea. However, there was no space for them, given the axle's placement just below the deck.

The suggestion that the *Savannah* have three boats for passengers and crew, instead of one, also made sense. The one boat the Baron saw on board probably reflected all that was thought necessary for the trials in port.

The rest of the Baron's critique was based upon controversies yet to be resolved, or conceptions yet to be overturned.

While there was still some debate about the optimal hull for a steam vessel, the Monopoly's *Fulton* and *Connecticut* already had shown that a deep-keeled steamboat traveled straighter than a flat-bottomed one through Long Island Sound.

The boilers aboard the *Savannah* needed to be huge if they were going to generate enough steam to run a cylinder so large.

Because the boilers took up all the space in the hold between the foremast and mainmast, there simply was no room down there for the rest of the engine.

The lack of cargo space on board, completely contrary though it was to the traditional view of commercial vessels, was actually un-important. The *Savannah* was not intended to be a cargo carrier, but rather represented a great leap into the future, where the movement of passengers over the oceans would become a viable business in itself.

Using copper to build the boilers certainly would have been opti-mal, but cost, and the high probability that this new design could be improved, made iron the more logical choice. There was also a counter-intuitive rationale for using the black metal over the red: since iron was so much more susceptible to corrosion, boilers made with it might more readily show whether this new design was effective in dealing with salt build-up.

The extreme heat given off by the boilers was a common problem for all the early steam vessels. There was little that could be done about it, beyond acceptance, and vigilance.

Boiler leaks were also common, and the solution was simple: hot molten lead dribbled around bolts and along plate seams would seal any cracks, making the boilers both water and steam tight.

The nearly horizontal position of the cylinder certainly was a controversial design at the time, but so was the very idea of a steamship. While the Baron *did* recognize the safety benefit of getting all the machinery below deck, what he could not fully appreciate was the psychological benefit from it. But Captain Rogers did. Having spent years dealing with the public's qualms over the new mode of transport, Moses knew that the horizontal set-up would minimize vibration, resulting in a quieter vessel.

And it worked. Even the Baron admitted that the *Savannah*'s engine, properly lubricated with *tallow* (i.e., animal fat), ran "without a lot of noise."

The depth the paddleboards should be immersed to gain maximum power also remained a matter of some debate. While some believed (correctly) that the paddleboards should be only partially submerged to gain the most muscle from the wheels and engine, others thought that a deeper immersion was better. In any event, keeping the paddleboards at the optimal depth, either during heeling or with varying loads on board, was a riddle not easily solved.

The Baron's remaining recommendations, which may have made sense in isolation, nevertheless proved problematic upon closer examination.

While raising the axle above the deck might have satisfied his desire to see the paddleboards' immersion reduced, it also would raise the ship's center of gravity when Klinkowström was trying, by some of his other suggestions, to lower it.

Trying to unfasten the fixed paddlewheel spines at each end of the axle would put those parts, and the crew members unfastening them, at risk of being washed out to sea.

Putting the cylinder down in the hold, or raising the axle above the deck, would have necessitated a longer, more accident-prone connecting rod.

Also, such a long connecting rod would have made the use of motion-smoothing gears even more desirable. But such cogs would have to be installed at deck level, raising the vessel's center of gravity. The gears also would have to be made of weaker cast iron.

On reflection, it was clear that any attempt to change one aspect of the *Savannah's* arrangement had implications for the others. The steam apparatus created by Captain Rogers was a balancing act.

That every moving piece of the steam machinery was designed to operate below deck was testament to just how important Moses thought it was to shield the engine from Nature, as well as the nervous eyes of apprehensive passengers.

That every moving piece of the power train (except the crank) was made of wrought iron also spoke to the importance Moses attached to minimizing the use of cast-iron parts. The stronger the power train, the less likely it was to break; and the simpler the power train mechanism, the easier it might be to fix, if it did break down.

The one aspect of Captain Rogers' design which the Baron admittedly *did* like was the paddlewheels. This new invention of collapsible spokes and boards, he thought, was "an admirable one." Paddlewheels such as these, the Baron later wrote, were "the only ones that can be used aboard steamboats that are intended to be used for crossing major waters or the ocean." Despite the Swede's compliment, Moses nevertheless wanted to take no chances, having ordered Stephen Vail to manufacture ten extra iron spokes, just in case the originals were ever bent, or broke.

One hour and fifteen minutes after leaving Fly Market Slip, the *Savannah* arrived at the Quarantine Grounds, off the eastern shore of Staten Island. Moses immediately ordered her turned about, and pointed back toward Gotham.

In seeing the ease with which the *Savannah* changed course, Baron Klinkowström could not help but acknowledge that she "sails and maneuvers very well." In fact, he would later write, his many criticisms of the steamship's apparatus didn't overthrow the concept at all.

Still, the struggle in the Baron's mind between the old and the new was undeniable. He would continue to hedge his bets, later writing in his official report that this combination of steam and sailing ship "seems to some extent established." It was, under the circumstances, the best he could muster.

Even so, the *Savannah's* potential success made the Baron wonder.

The "mechanical genius" and "spirit of enterprise" these Americans exhibited was inspiring, yet how could his native Swedes be encouraged to act the same, and wholeheartedly adopt this new technology?

Writing to Stockholm later that spring, Klinkowström acknowledged how "old prejudices fight against useful innovations," and how the trial and error of experiments "are of such a kind that they do not always gain people's confidence" in his homeland.

The solution to this problem was to do something dramatic. If only His Majesty, King Karl Johan, would authorize Baron Klinkowström to order a steam vessel built in America, he would gladly stay and oversee its construction. Once completed, the Baron would write, "I will undertake to take it across the sea . . . unless I run into a storm where truly seaworthy ships perish, I shall with the help of the Almighty, bring the boat safely and well across the ocean."

Only Klinkowström wanted such a vessel designed *his* way. There would be no heavy masts and rigging—instead, the vessel would be "supplied with light masts that can be laid down, and be rigged as a light schooner." Further, "the water wheels should be installed in the same way as the steam ship *Savannah*'s," except that it should be possible to bring the entire paddlewheel on deck, in case of a storm. Nothing would hang over the sides of this vessel, save the axle ends.

Also of great importance, the Baron later wrote, would be choosing the safest time to make the crossing. He thought that given construction schedules, and using Allaire and Eckford as his contractors, a new steam vessel could be built and ready no later than June 28th, 1820. This left plenty of time to make a summer voyage.

Finally came consideration of the best route. The Baron's proposal would take no chances. After departing New York through the safety of Long Island Sound, he would pass up through the Nantucket Shoals, go around Cape Cod, and then drop anchor in the Bay of Boston. From there, he would continue northward along the coast, to British Nova Scotia, and put in to Halifax. At that port, he would take on as much coal as the vessel could bear, and "wait for the weather to calm down," around the beginning of August.

Then, the Baron would make the great leap, from Halifax across the Atlantic to the coast of Ireland, which he hoped he could accomplish in 14 days. Skirting along the south coasts of Ireland and Britain, he would maneuver his creation through the English Channel and into the North Sea, avoiding stops in British ports, "except in extreme need."

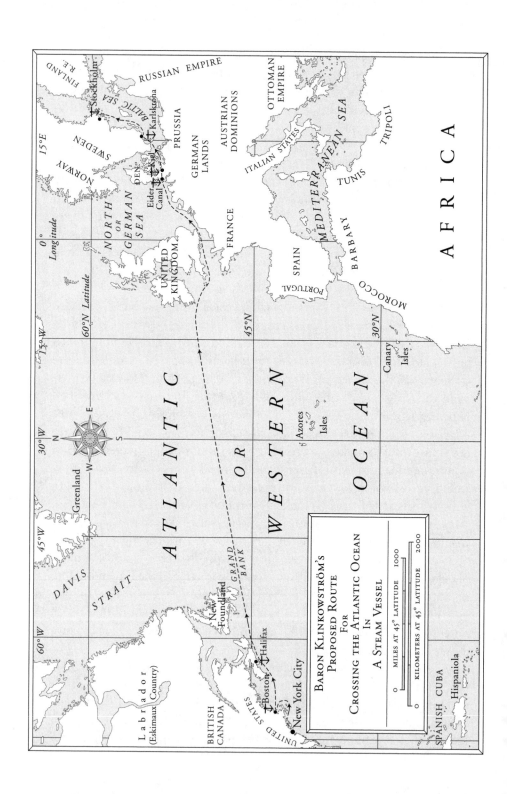

BARON KLINKOWSTRÖM'S
PROPOSED ROUTE
FOR
CROSSING THE ATLANTIC OCEAN
IN
A STEAM VESSEL

MILES AT 45° LATITUDE

KILOMETERS AT 45° LATITUDE

Then, the Baron intended to put in to the Eider River, in the northern German lands. There, he could take his steamer upriver to the Eider Canal, which linked the North Sea with the port of Kiel on the Baltic Sea. This short-cut not only shaved several hundred miles off the trip into the Baltic, but avoided the dangerous waters around the top of Denmark.

Once at Kiel, the Baron could refuel again. He would then take the steamer northeast, through the relative safety of Denmark's many islands, and across the Baltic to the Swedish naval base at Karlskrona. From there, the final leg of the voyage could be made along the Swedish coast to Stockholm.

Such a feat, the Baron would write, surely held the promise of changing everything:

> *... If I were not so convinced of the enterprise's outcome providing one takes all precautions and selects one's season and weather, I should not in all humility dare to suggest to Your Majesty such a plan ... This boat being once on the Stream in Stockholm will allay all the apprehensions and doubts anyone can have against the whole innovation, which will immediately win over the public's confidence ... the introduction of this handsome and useful innovation into Your Majesty's Kingdom will open a new epoch in the annals of Sweden ...*

Yet whether King Karl Johan would ever approve such a scheme was unknown. Even if he did, such a determination was many months away, at the earliest. All Baron Klinkowström could do at that moment, as he stood upon the deck of the *Savannah*, was observe her progress, as she churned back into the East River. The return trip was even faster, taking only 40 minutes.

* * *

With harbor trials complete, Moses made final preparations to take the *Savannah* down to Georgia. While the proposed voyage across the Atlantic could have started from New York, surely most of the shareholders wanted to see the completed result of their venture. Besides, it made sense to test the steamship out on the ocean, but near the coast, before attempting the crossing.

The arrival of the *Savannah* at her home port also would compel the shareholders to bring their vision into focus, and decide upon their next move, whatever that might be. In the three months since the Company's charter had been approved by the Georgia Legislature, plenty had occurred which potentially put the dream in jeopardy.

First, the cost of building the steamship had been more than expected. The money raised easily covered the bill for the ship itself, which Moses later put at $36,000. But the steam apparatus and passenger space fit-out had cost an additional $25,000 to $30,000. This put the *Savannah*'s total construction cost some $10,000 to $15,000 above the $50,000 in capital raised. The solution to this budget overrun was offered by Pott & McKinne, who in effect lent the Savannah Steam Ship Company the funds necessary to complete the vessel.

Second, the country's economic situation since the beginning of the year had grown steadily and disturbingly worse. The refusal of some Western banks to redeem their own currency for gold or silver was no longer an isolated problem. In New York City, notes issued by any banks in Ohio, Kentucky and Tennessee were being accepted at just 80 to 90 cents on the dollar. This creeping instability out West also had begun to affect banks in the South. As a result, Georgia and North Carolina banknotes had dropped in value, and were convertible at New York for 95 to 97 percent of their face amount.

This deflating value of paper money only served to worsen the financial position of the semi-public Bank of the United States. Its largest customer, the federal government, regularly deposited all sorts of monies into the Bank, most of which were privately-issued banknotes. As the value of these banknotes declined, so too did the value of the government's accounts.

Growing suspicions about the Bank of the United States' operations had led Congress to order an investigation into its practices. The report, issued in early 1819, was very unflattering: multiple violations of the Bank's charter had been discovered, including fraud and failure to collect payments for Bank stock already purchased. While Congress didn't want to shut down the Bank of the United States, members knew it had to be cleaned up. So the Bank's president was forced to resign, and in his place came a man with substantial political clout: former Speaker of the House of Representatives Langdon Cheves.

By the time Cheves assumed his duties in early March, rumors were widespread that the Bank of the United States was in such bad shape that it too would have to suspend payments of gold or silver for its own banknotes. If that happened, the effect on the country's entire financial system would be catastrophic.

On top of this, a minor drop in crop prices the previous autumn had turned into a substantial pullback. By mid-March of 1819, Georgia Upland Cotton was being quoted in New York at 23½ to 25 cents per pound. This was 20% below autumn price levels, and more than 25% off the all-time high of 33 cents the previous spring.

All this instability meant pressure for the *Savannah*'s shareholders. Substantially lower crop prices, and a poor harvest brought on by the early frost, meant substantially lower profits. The growing bank crisis meant both borrowers and lenders had to beware.

And finally, the third point of concern was the emergence of the steamship *Savannah*'s competition. The Gothamites had made it clear that they were preparing to challenge the Georgians directly, by putting the passenger trade for Charleston and even Savannah itself into play.

So much disorder in the financial and commodity markets, combined with the appearance of a rival, brought into some question the very objectives of the Savannah Steam Ship Company. If the arrival of Captain Rogers and his revolutionary vessel in Georgia had any purpose at all (beyond an initial sea trial), it would be to force the shareholders to concentrate their minds, for they soon would have some very important decisions to make.

* * *

On Thursday, March 25th, several New York newspapers began running advertisements announcing the *Savannah* as a going commercial packet for the first time:

For SAVANNAH.
The very elegant steam ship SAVANNAH, Moses Rogers, master, will sail the 27th inst. For freight or passage, having spacious accommodations, apply on board at Fly-market wharf, or to
POTT & M'KINNE
56 South Street

But two days later, on the scheduled morning of departure, a revised notice appeared in the newspapers. The *Savannah*, it turned out, would not be leaving until the next day, Sunday, March 28th. This delay gave Moses and Joseph P. McKinne the time they needed to register the steamship at the Custom House, and go over any last minute details.

It also would give the *Savannah* a lot more exposure. All the free newspaper publicity the steamship received over the preceding months had created a sense of anticipation in New York. The public would want to watch the departure, and since Saturdays were work days, the Sabbath was guaranteed to generate a much larger crowd.

One of Gotham's most prominent newspapers, the *Mercantile Advertiser*, took the measure of the moment, and expressed its amazement at what was about to occur:

AGE OF EXPERIMENT

By an advertisement in this day's paper, it will be seen that the new and elegant *Steam Ship* SAVANNAH, is to leave our harbour tomorrow. Who would have had the courage, twenty years ago, to hazard a prediction, that in the year 1819, a ship of 300 tons burden, would be built in the port of New York, to navigate the Atlantic, *propelled by steam?* Such, however, is the fact. With admiring hundreds have we repeatedly viewed this prodigy; and can also bear witness to the wonderful celerity with which she is moved through the water...

Her cabin is finished in an elegant style and is fitted up in the most tasty manner ... For beauty of model, the Savannah has seldom been exceeded. She is commanded by captain Moses Rogers, an experienced engineer, and belongs to a company of enterprising gentlemen in Savannah, who have spared no expence in rendering her an object worthy of public admiration and public patronage...

Recognizing the reluctance of many to entertain travel on such an invention, the paper tried to allay such fears:

... She is so constructed as to be navigable in the usual way, with sails, whenever the weather shall be such as to render the use of her wheels in the least degree dangerous.

This vessel is intended as a "Savannah and Liverpool Packet," and we sincerely hope the liberal-minded proprietors may be abundantly rewarded for their efforts to facilitate the communication between Great Britain and America.

Beyond the public hubbub surrounding the departure, Stevens Rogers had to tend to his own work on board. Besides overseeing the crew, he had the additional responsibility of record-keeping. Federal law dictated that an officer on board any merchant vessel—usually the first mate—needed to keep a logbook.

Such journals could be purchased at any ship chandler or bookseller in the port area. They were usually soft-cover booklets the size of normal writing paper, with pre-printed columns allowing for the notation of time, speed, course, winds, and any general remarks. These flimsy logbooks were easily damaged if they were treated roughly, or got wet. Toss one into the fire, and it would be gone in a matter of seconds, which is probably what happened to many a logbook, so droll and unimportant were the notations in most of them.

But it stood to reason that the logbook for this, the first steamship, should be treated differently.

To that end, Steve got a hold of 24 large sheets of thick paper, capable of withstanding the normal wear and tear of a voyage. He then grabbed a spare piece of duck (probably left over from his sailmaking), and cut it to size. After placing the stack of paper onto the cloth, he then stitched it into place, straight down the middle, creating a book spine. Then he wrapped the edges of the sailcloth around the outermost pages, and stitched them into place. Folding his handiwork closed, Steve had created a 96-page, duck-covered book, measuring about 14 inches by 22 inches. Directly upon the canvas cover, he neatly inscribed in ink the book's title:

STEAM, SHIP.
SAVANNAH,S
LOG, BOOK.

This journal would serve as the official record of whatever happened to the *Savannah*. Her movements and the crew's actions would be recorded there, to the degree specified by law. Hopefully, with a sturdy cover, it also had a chance to survive, as the logbook of such a great experiment deserved.

* * *

On Sunday morning, March 28th, Moses ordered the crew to cast off from Fly Market Wharf. On board for the trip was a harbor pilot, which was obligatory for any large vessel leaving port. He would ride and guide the *Savannah* as far as the lighthouse on Sandy Hook, and the exit to the sea.

Beyond this pilot, there were no passengers on board. There was no cargo, either. Whatever assurances of safety given by Captain Rogers, or by Pott & McKinne, or by the newspapers, no one wanted to risk their life or their property on this "steam coffin."

But many people did want to witness its departure. That morning, as the crowds along the shoreline watched, the steamship's crew got to work deploying sails. There were, it turned out, fresh breezes coming out of the northwest, ideal for pushing any sailing vessel southward to Sandy Hook. The old mode, it appeared, would be used to assist the new.

Only there was no smoke rising from the *Savannah's* bent stack. Her paddlewheels were not deployed, either. As the spectators filling the wharves and Battery stood by and wondered, the steamship steadily, silently sailed past.

The failure of Moses to give the crowds the dramatic display they wanted, and use steam power to depart, was not an oversight. Instead, it was based upon a fear of Gotham's Monopoly.

The *Savannah's* construction had not been taking place in a vacuum. Through the latter months of 1818, the heirs to the Livingston-Fulton steamboat franchise had been locked in legal combat with a feisty southern transplant named Thomas Gibbons.

Having moved up to New Jersey from Savannah some years prior, Gibbons had been one of Aaron Ogden's early steamboating partners. After a falling out between the two men, Gibbons became determined to challenge Ogden's New York steamboat license, as granted to him by the Monopoly.

During the summer of 1818, Gibbons had arranged to build a new steamer, and planned to run it from New Jersey to New York City, in direct opposition to Ogden's steamboat *Atalanta*. Gibbons named his new vessel, appropriately enough, *Bellona*, after the Roman goddess of war. He also hired an aggressive young ferry captain to command her, by the name of Cornelius Vanderbilt.

Beyond personally spiting Ogden, Gibbons made no secret of his ultimate objective, which was to force a federal lawsuit challenging the legality of the Monopoly's entire franchise. Such a State-sponsored grant, Gibbons believed, was contrary to the Constitution, and he made it clear he intended to push his fight all the way to the Supreme Court of the United States.

By late October of 1818 (when the *Savannah* was at Elizabethtown Point), Captain Vanderbilt and the renegade *Bellona* were openly defying the Monopoly. They based the legality of their trips to Gotham upon a federal coasting license, and nothing more.

In response, the Monopoly tried to enforce their franchise by having a warrant served on the *Bellona's* captain.

What followed was a prolonged game of cat-and-mouse. Whenever the authorities tried to serve legal papers on Captain Vanderbilt, he either escaped in the *Bellona* or hid on board, while the law fruitlessly searched for him.

This battle with Gibbons and the *Bellona* had continued into the spring of 1819. Other critics of the Monopoly were also piling on, among them Connecticut interests, who were attacking the unfair advantage the New York-based steamboats enjoyed in Long Island Sound. Despite these challengers all around, the Monopoly was not about to roll over. In fact, it could be argued that like any cornered animal, the Monopoly had become even more dangerous.

All these tribulations had forced Moses to confront the possibility that the Monopoly might interfere with his own steam-powered exit from New York waters. The *Savannah's* trials in the Bay had posed no problem, since at that point, Moses had been operating an unfinished, unregistered vessel. But by the morning of departure, things were different. Not only was the *Savannah* officially registered, but she had advertised for cargo and passengers, as well. There was no denying her new status as a commercial vessel.

If the Monopoly was determined to stop Gibbons and his Bellona, would they also try to stop their ocean-steaming competitor?

If Captain Rogers and his fellow investors later decided that the best ocean route for their steamship included a stop at New York, did it make sense to antagonize the Monopoly at such an early stage?

The dilemma was not a trivial one. Moses already had scraped up against the Monopoly, directly or indirectly, twice before—as captain of the *Phoenix*, back in 1809, and again as captain of the *Eagle*, in 1813. Doing so a third time, when so much was at stake, must have made him wonder. No doubt Moses had talked over the situation with

Gideon Pott and Joseph P. McKinne. In the end, they concluded that discretion was better than confrontation, and a potential seizure of the steamship by the authorities. So the departure would be made with sails only.

At least some of the New York press was sympathetic to the *Savannah's* cause. The *Commercial Advertiser* later opined that "it is questioned . . . whether any peculiar privilege granted to these [steam]boats in our harbor, can exclude Sea Vessels from the use of Steam, either on leaving or entering port. If it does, it surely cannot accord with the intention of the Legislature, and the sooner the law is altered, the better."

Yet such sentiments, expressed after the fact, were of little use to the onlookers packing the Battery that Sunday morning. All they could do was stand and stare, as the steamship silently sailed past them. By noon, the *Savannah* was out of sight, having cleared the Narrows between Staten Island and Brooklyn.

Shortly thereafter, at 1 o'clock, the steamship reached the waters off the northern tip of Sandy Hook. There, the harbor pilot, his job done, disembarked into a nearby boat.

The many months of planning, building, and testing the first steamship in history had finally come to an end. That the *Savannah* worked to satisfaction within the confines of a protected harbor, just like her steamboat relatives, was beyond any reasonable doubt. But what still remained to be seen was whether such a vessel as this could really overcome the multiplied dangers of the deep. There was, of course, only one way to find out.

Under crisp, clear skies and a warm spring sun, Captain Moses Rogers pointed his new command to the southeast, toward the exit from Lower New York Bay. Nearly at his back was a fresh breeze, and directly to his front was the great divide—of light blue, and dark blue. With the direction set, and sails deployed, the steamship *Savannah* and her crew slowly began to push their way forward, ready to challenge the open sea.

CHAPTER NINE

POLITICS, PRESIDENT, POLITICS

WHATEVER TEST TRIPS a new vessel made around its port of birth, such trials could never equal what would be faced once it ventured out onto the ocean. For this reason, the first voyage of a newly-built vessel was of the greatest importance. It would allow the captain to try out every part of his craft, and his crew, to see if they performed as intended. Mariners of the future would refer to this first open-sea test as a *shakedown cruise.*

Such was the practical purpose of the steamship *Savannah's* trip down to Georgia. Whether she would make the journey successfully was unknown. When Steve began his entries in the logbook, he accordingly wrote at the very top of the first page:

A Journal of a voyage from New York towards Savannah on board Steam Ship Savannah Moses Rogers Master

This guarded declaration reflected not any timidity in shaking down a steamship, but rather the obligation to acknowledge the unpredictability of Nature. A sailing ship's crew could only use the ages-old equipment at their disposal to steer them "towards" their intended port. In the end, the winds and the currents would play a large part in determining whether or not their vessel reached its destination. Every mariner knew this instinctively. Despite the *Savannah's* unnatural means of propulsion, Steve must have thought that the use of "towards" in the logbook shouldn't change, either out of tradition, or respect for Nature's power.

Once the *Savannah* sailed outside the protection of New York Bay, at a little past noon on Sunday, March 28th, Steve began a new day in the logbook. This was also tradition, for a very practical reason. When the sun reached high noon (or *meridian*), it was possible to determine a vessel's *latitude*, or distance north or south of the equator. Because knowing their position was so obviously important to mariners, and measuring a vessel's latitude was easily accomplished at high noon, that point in time had come to signify the end of a day at sea.

So when Steve began his first sea day in the *Savannah's* logbook, at noon on the land-day of March 28th, he recorded it as the *beginning* of the sea-day March 29th. When he took his latitude measurement at noon the following day, the sea-day of March 29th would end, and March 30th would begin. In this way, *the sea-day started and ended twelve hours earlier than its land-day counterpart.**

Once the *Savannah* had passed over all the sand bars at the entrance to New York Bay, she was pointed to the south. By 4 o'clock that afternoon, she had made enough progress for Steve to just make out the Neversink Highlands of New Jersey, to the northwest. From this last visible landmark, he officially *took his departure* from the coast. Since there were still favorable winds coming from the west-southwest, Moses decided to let Steve and the crew test the old mode's apparatus through the night. Trying the steam engine could wait.

By Monday morning, the winds had shifted, coming out of the south-southeast. No sailing vessel could advance by heading straight into the wind, so Moses ordered the *Savannah* to change her direction (or *tack*), and sail to the westward. This allowed the sails to catch the southerly winds obliquely, so the ship could make some progress. Off in the distance, Steve saw a brig and a schooner performing the same maneuver—these were probably the brig *Othello* and schooner *Milo*, which had left New York the same day as the steamship, and also were headed for Savannah.

Later that morning, the winds died down, making progress by sail minimal at best. Moses ordered the engine crew to get the steam up, and told Steve to deploy the paddlewheels. But before the machinery could be put into motion, "it come on to blow fresh," as Steve later wrote.

Rather than force a use of the new mode, Moses instead ordered the paddlewheels dismantled, and brought back on deck. This was

---

* Hereafter, logbook references to the *Savannah's* time at sea have been converted to land days.

done in the space of 30 minutes. If the abortive use of steam accomplished anything, at the least it had given the crew practice in deploying and retrieving the wheels under sea conditions. The *Savannah* pressed on, under sail.

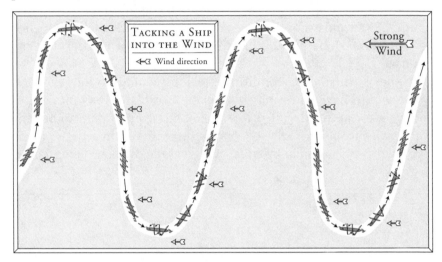

TACKING A SHIP
INTO THE WIND

⟵ Wind direction

Strong Wind

At noon, Steve took his first latitude measurement, and recorded it in the logbook: 39 degrees, 19 minutes north of the equator. This put the *Savannah* somewhere to the east of Cape May, which is on the southern tip of New Jersey.

The steamship's *longitude*—or distance east or west of the imaginary line called Prime Meridian, which runs through Greenwich, England—Steve did not record in the logbook. Once again, he was following tradition.

Measuring *latitude* accurately had been possible for centuries using a *sextant*, or similar device. This made the recording of latitude in a vessel's logbook a long-held, practical exercise.

Measuring *longitude* accurately was different. It required a device called a *chronometer*, which is just another name for a very accurate clock. Many merchant vessels still did not have these costly devices in the early 19th century, so no tradition had developed for recording longitude in the logbook.

Nevertheless, the *Savannah*, like many ocean-*crossing* vessels, did have a chronometer. It was probably kept in the captain's quarters, which Steve, even as first officer, could not enter at will. So the periodic determination of longitude was for Moses to check, whenever he was in his cabin. He then recorded it in a separate logbook, or captain's log.

In any event, at noon that day, the steamship was far enough to the east of New Jersey to make any sighting of the Cape May lighthouse impossible, even with the aid of a spyglass.

By evening, the fresh blow had shifted, coming mostly from the south. The winds soon became so strong that Steve felt compelled to reduce the ship's profile, so he ordered the crew aloft, to furl the mainsail.

Under such adverse conditions, tacking would no longer work. Steve would have to resort to an even more laborious method of sailing into the wind, called *wearing*. This required him to put the *Savannah* through a series of looping maneuvers, in an attempt to make whatever minimal progress was possible, without being forced backward.

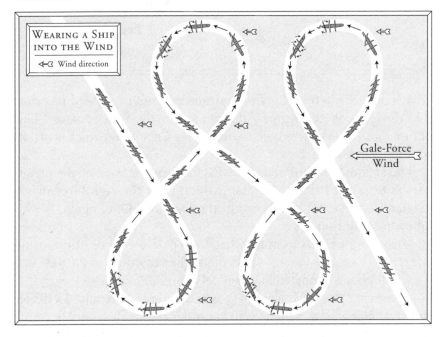

By midnight, the southern gusts had turned into a heavy gale and rain. As the winds grew stronger and the waves higher, it became apparent that the *Savannah* was facing more than just an arduous ocean. Instead, she was plunging directly into a "nor'easter" storm.

Realizing that the sails still deployed could be ripped away at any moment, Steve ordered the crew aloft once again, to furl some of the canvas, either partly, or completely. With only enough sails set to maintain control of the helm, the *Savannah* rode the nor'easter through the night.

For Moses, the storm must have felt like déjà vu. Ten years earlier, these same waters had challenged him in the *Phoenix*, on the first ocean voyage by a steamboat in history. Nature, it appeared, would treat this first ocean voyage by a steamship no differently.

By Tuesday morning, March 30th, Steve thought the storm was even worse. The *Savannah* continued to be rocked by even stronger winds and waves, and pelted with a "hard rain." Progress of any kind was difficult, if not nearly impossible.

Through the rest of Tuesday and into Wednesday morning, Nature's assault on the steamship continued unabated. Steve and the deck hands were kept very busy, adjusting sails or reducing their profile, as the fury demanded.

It wasn't until noon on Wednesday that the worst of the storm had passed, leaving cloudy skies and rough seas in its wake. The *Savannah* and her crew had passed their first test—she could not only sail, but weather a nor'easter, as well.

The waters were still too choppy to try the paddlewheels. But it didn't matter, since the strong winds had shifted dramatically, from southerlies to northerlies, so Steve and the crew took advantage, and set the sails to harness Nature's reward. The *Savannah* was soon barreling over the waves at speeds of 7 to 9 knots, which was nearly as fast as any ship could ever expect to go under canvas.*

By Wednesday evening, the *Savannah* was approaching Cape Hatteras, infamously known to mariners as the Graveyard of the Atlantic. Such a dark description for this area was due in large part to an invisible trap lurking beneath the waves. Stretching from the Cape's point far out into the ocean was an enormous sandbar, which had ended the life of many a vessel, and given a fright to many more a captain.

While sailing well to the east of this sand trap off Cape Hatteras might seem the logical solution, it actually wasn't. This was because just a bit further off the Carolina coast, a powerful ocean current known as the *Gulf Stream* could be found, surging in a northeasterly direction. If a vessel traveling south moved too far to the east trying to avoid the

---

* One knot is one nautical mile per hour. One nautical mile equals ~1.15 statute miles; therefore, one knot equals ~1.15 miles per hour.

sandbar, it risked getting caught by the Gulf Stream. Once within its grasp, a craft could be pulled far to the north before it was able to escape.

So the only way to pass Cape Hatteras going south was to thread the needle. This was done by advancing, carefully, toward the Cape, and regularly checking the water depth and sand colors on the bottom. At the same time, the ocean waters to the east had to be watched for signs of rippling, or foam, or floating "gulf-weed." Evidence of any of these would show that the Gulf Stream was near.

From Wednesday evening through Friday morning, April 2nd, Steve took several soundings for depth. He also pulled up sand samples from the bottom, to check their color and help confirm his location. All the while, Steve maintained a distance from the Cape's lighthouse of at least 5 leagues (or 15 miles), as he slowly sailed the steamship around the great sandbar.

By Friday's meridian, they were safely past the Cape, and the heavy northern winds enjoyed since the nor'easter's passing had withered to a calm. Finally, Nature seemed willing to allow a true test of the unnatural power at the *Savannah's* disposal. Moses ordered the engine crew to get steam up, and by 3 o'clock that afternoon, the paddlewheels were deployed, and put into motion. With all sails furled, the steamship was soon making 4 to 6 knots, as it churned along the South Carolina coast.

By 5 o'clock on Saturday morning, there was enough of a breeze to allow a test of how the *Savannah* would do using both the old and new modes at the same time. So the crew was ordered aloft, to deploy sails on the foremast and mizzenmast. The mainmast sails were left furled, since the black, bent smokestack was still puffing smoke and cinders. The steamship's speed improved, ever so slightly, from 4 knots to 5 knots.

A few hours later, Moses ordered the engine stopped, and the wheels folded up. The machinery had been working for 17 hours straight, its longest run yet.

Steve and the crew then deployed more sails, which pushed the *Savannah* forward until late afternoon, when the winds died down again. Moses ordered the steam engine back into action, and despite renewed breezes from the south, the *Savannah* still made progress steaming into the headwinds.

Since Cape Hatteras, Steve had noted in the logbook having seen quite a few other vessels in the distance. As the steamship passed the lighthouse at the entrance to Charleston harbor, the frequency of sightings increased. Several craft in the vicinity made a point of sailing close enough to gawk at the smoking, splashing *Savannah*, and exchange greetings.

By Sunday morning, the sea had become decidedly rougher. With an additional 15 hours of continuous steaming to its credit, Moses ordered the engine stopped, and then had the wheels folded up, rather than risk any damage. The choppy waves proved to be the precursor of yet another challenge, as dead-ahead, gale-force winds began buffeting the steamship. Steve had no choice but to wear the *Savannah* again, back and forth, to make any headway.

Not until mid-morning on Tuesday, April 6th, did they arrive at the mouth of the Savannah River. Nature, having thrown nearly everything it had at the steamship on this first voyage, settled to a calm once again, thereby conceding the fight, at least for the moment.

The placid waters off Tybee lighthouse provided Moses with the opportunity denied him at New York. Many a sailing vessel successfully made landfall after a voyage only to find no winds along the coastline. This was for many people—passengers and crew alike—the most frustrating part of a long ocean trip: stranded so close to their destination, with no wind to carry them the last few miles into port. The same held true for departures, if there were no breezes in the harbor itself. Such delays in departures or arrivals could last days, or even weeks. For everyone involved, there was no choice but to accept, however grudgingly, this painful, unchangeable fact.

Yet the *Savannah* had the means to overturn it. Moses ordered the engine crew to fire up the boilers once more, while the deck crew deployed the paddlewheels. Soon the steamship was splashing over the submerged sandbar at the river's entrance. Emerging from the river to greet Moses and his men was the steamboat *Charleston*, carrying a complement of passengers on her regular packet trip to the north.

Normally, before a sea vessel crossed over the bar, a local river pilot would come aboard to act as guide. But the *Savannah*'s ability to move in a calm caught the local pilot boat off-guard. Only after the steamship had traversed the bar did the boat come alongside and offer a pilot, who then climbed aboard. Even though Moses knew the river bends well, he was still obliged to accept a pilot for the remaining 12 miles to the city of Savannah.

Upriver, on the Sand Hill itself, the lookout in the Exchange's tower, peering to the southeast, soon beheld the most novel of sights, moving toward him at rapid speed. As word spread through the city that the steamship was approaching, the people of Savannah responded with their feet. By the hundreds, they streamed to the edge of the bluff, and down the sandy ramps which led to the riverfront below. They quickly filled the wharves, as well as the decks of the shipping, and waited to greet this newest contribution to progress which honored their city with its name.

When the *Savannah* reached the southern edges of the port area at mid-afternoon, the people roared to life. As the steamship smoked and churned past them, the crowds packing the piers, shipping and shoreline repeatedly shouted the ages-old salute of approval and encouragement:

Huzzah!

Huzzah!

Huzzah!

Joining the chorus of cheers from shore came still further salutes from the river itself, as the crew of the U.S. Revenue Cutter *Dallas* greeted the steamship with sharp, booming blasts from her deck gun.

The apparition before the people of Savannah—of a three-masted ship, its sails completely furled, a black, bent stack protruding from its deck, belching smoke and cinders, with spinning sidewheels pushing it through the water—made that April 6th, 1819 unlike any day the city had ever seen before. So powerful was the steamship *Savannah*'s display that a local newspaper, *The Georgian*, dared to declare "her appearance inspires instant confidence in her security."

Once the *Savannah* had steamed far enough, Moses ordered the engine stopped in mid-river, and the anchor dropped. It was about 4 o'clock in the afternoon.

As the paddlewheels came to a halt, Moses, Steve and the crew soon found themselves surrounded by boat-loads of well-wishers, as well as information-seekers.

Moses knew that the passage from New York—at 9 days and 6 hours—had taken longer than expected. Evidence to that effect lay tied up to the wharves just a short distance away. The brig *Othello*, under the command of Captain John Mott, had left Gotham the same day as the *Savannah*, but managed to make the trip in only 5 days. The schooner *Milo*, which had reported last seeing the steamship "off the Capes of Delaware," did nearly as well, making the voyage in 6 days.

There were plenty of good reasons why the *Savannah* took longer
to reach port.

First of all, she was a brand new vessel, with mariners aboard who
were working together for the first time. Straightening out the kinks
in craft and crew was a natural part of any shakedown cruise—breaking speed records was not.

Second, she was a revolutionary, experimental vessel, and as such,
was being watched very carefully by a fascinated, yet leery public.
Moses knew full-well that if any accident befell his creation, the psychological impact could be fatal. The key to success was safety, and
having delivered the *Savannah* to her home port without any damage,
he had accomplished his primary mission.

And third, Nature had stubbornly refused to allow many opportunities for using the new mode of power. The first real chance to do
so had not occurred until the steamship was approaching the South
Carolina coast.

Still, the question of passage time remained, so Moses provided an
explanation, which the local newspapers duly reported:

> She had a very boisterous passage. Her commander, captain
> Rogers, was entirely satisfied with her performance.—He attrib-
> utes the length of her passage in some measure to his own
> imperfect knowledge of the coast.

It was a selfless act on his part; as far as the published story went,
Moses publicly blamed no one but himself.

Beyond the question of passage time, the simple news that the
Savannah had arrived safely, and received a hearty welcome for it, represented the overriding sentiment of the press she received. There
was also at least one public compliment from the maritime realm:

> ... Captain Marsh, of the sloop Nimrod, arrived at Georgetown,
> S.C. informs, that on Saturday the 3d instant, off Romain Island,
> he saw the new and elegant steam ship Savannah, performing
> her first trip from New-York for Savannah. Capt. Marsh was at
> a considerable distance from her, but represents her as forming
> the most majestic appearance of any vessel of her tonnage he
> had ever seen, and as making the most astonishing progress.

The pride felt in the steamship's home port was palpable. "It redounds much to the honour of Savannah," declared the local *Republican,* "when it is said, that it was owing to the enterprize of some of her spirited citizens, that the first attempt was made to cross the Atlantic ocean, in a vessel *propelled by steam.*"

* * *

On April 7th, the day after the *Savannah*'s grand arrival in Georgia waters, the New Yorkers responded. Previously put before the State Legislature in Albany was a petition from a group of eleven Gothamites, led by Mayor and Monopoly supporter Cadwallader D. Colden. In the petition, these men...

> ... represented that they are desirous of constructing and employing steam ships in navigating the ocean: That they have a confidence that vessels may be so constructed as to unite all the safety and other advantages of common ships, to the additional velocity to be gained by the application of steam...

Beyond Colden and shipbuilder Henry Eckford, the syndicate included prominent shipping merchants, captains and lawyers within the city. These organizers made it clear that they were thinking for the long term, asking that their "body corporate" have a life stretching all the way to the year 1841.

No less importantly, they were preparing to commit huge sums of money, as proof of their confidence in the future of oceanic steam navigation. The new company would have a minimum capital stock of $250,000, and requested authority to raise as much as $500,000.

Accordingly impressed, the Legislature acquiesced. That April 7th, they passed "an Act for incorporating the Ocean Steam Ship Company."

For the New York Monopoly, there was no turning back.

And for the Savannah Steam Ship Company, there was no turning back, either—the competition had become very real.

* * *

Despite the head-start they enjoyed, Moses Rogers, William Scarbrough and their fellow shareholders were still paying close attention to the rumblings from Gotham. As soon as the *Savannah* had arrived safely at her home port, they felt obliged to respond to their erstwhile competition, using the press as their megaphone. "The *Savannah,* we understand," offered the local *Republican* just three days after her arrival, "will make a trip or two between this and Charleston; and then perhaps, will go to Havana and New-Orleans and immediately return to this place.—She will then proceed to Liverpool, via New-York, unless a sufficiency of passengers should offer direct."

The only explanation for such a seemingly schizophrenic itinerary was the threat posed by the Monopoly.

Going to Charleston made sense, if for no other reason than to test the steamship a bit more.

But going to Havana and New Orleans only made sense if the *Savannah's* owners wanted to beat the Gothamites to their own objectives.

And stopping in New York before attempting the crossing to Liverpool only made sense if the goal was to drum up as much passenger business as possible—and pre-empt the competition in its own market.

Whatever the eventual course of action, it was obvious that the Company's directors were prepared to think flexibly, and could alter their plans to suit whatever opportunities or challenges appeared.

One threat even less welcome than the Monopoly's efforts was the increasingly bad economic news from overseas. Letters arriving from Britain were painting a picture that grew more disturbing by the week. One report from the Scottish city of Glasgow, a major textile center, warned "our markets are quite overloaded with Cotton." The inevitable result was a further weakening in prices. Another Glasgow report stated that there was "a scarcity and pressure for money against speculative houses" which traded in the white fiber. Since virtually all merchants depended upon credit, both giving and accepting it, the firms which played the markets the most aggressively were the ones first to suffer when prices dropped.

In Liverpool, things were no better. "There is a heavy failure here," reported one observer, "and several in Manchester and London, connected more or less in the Cotton trade." The resulting scramble to raise cash to pay off debts also was putting pressure on other commodities. From ashes, to barrel staves, to flour, rice, and tobacco, prices were either stagnant or in retreat.

This left merchants operating on the seaboard of the United States feeling a geo-financial squeeze. To the east, across the Atlantic, their largest trading partners in Britain were so stuffed with American produce that they were becoming sick. From the west, the bank panic that had started in Ohio and Kentucky was steadily creeping across the Appalachian Mountains. Circumstances were so unsettling as to put most merchants into a very defensive frame of mind.

With these worries whirling around them, William Scarbrough and his fellow shareholders had to explore whatever possibilities they could for promoting the steamship, and generating a willing ridership. The opportunity for both soon presented itself in no less a form than the sitting President of the United States, James Monroe.

Soon after his inauguration in 1817, President Monroe, a member of the Democratic-Republican party, had made a journey through the New England States, stronghold of the opposition Federalists, who had bitterly opposed the late war against Britain. The trip's purpose was to make an attempt at healing the deep divisions and anger the conflict had created. This goodwill tour proved to be incredibly successful, with one Federalist newspaper in Boston dubbing it the beginning of an "era of good feeling."

Wishing to be honored in a similar manner, other States began to clamor for a presidential visit. In early 1819, plans were announced for another tour, this time of the South. Once President Monroe's intentions were definite, preparations along his intended route, which included Charleston and Savannah, became very intense, very quickly. The last and only time these cities had ever experienced such a visit was way back in 1791, when President Washington made a point of touring the still-disjointed country.

President Monroe was scheduled to reach Charleston by the middle of April. Since Savannah would be next on the itinerary, some arrangement would have to be made for his travel from one city to the next. This begged an interesting question: why not send the steamship to Charleston, and bring the President to Georgia in the newest of the new mode of transport? This public service would give Captain Rogers another chance to solicit customers, and such a distinguished passenger on the return trip might serve a valuable purpose beyond mere publicity: to wit, the *Savannah* was so safe that even the President himself was comfortable traveling on her.

Before such a voyage to Charleston could be made, however, further preparations were needed, and Stevens Rogers kept track. The day after the steamship's arrival in the Savannah River, he opened the log-book, and started a new page with a new title:

*A Journal on board Steam Ship Savannah
in the harbour of Savannah*

Such an obvious change in the description was not obligatory. American sea law required that a record only be kept during the actual voyage. As a result, most logbook entries stopped once the vessel reached port, only to be started again when it departed. That Steve kept the logbook going reflected just how important he and Moses knew it would be to have a complete record of the *Savannah*'s life.

Reverting to land days while in port, Steve's logbook notations show that an idle crew was considered a wasted resource. Seamen should always be doing something when on board, whether it was moving the ship to a wharf, checking the rigging, drying the sails, or simply being "employed in sundry jobs of ship's duty" (which usually meant cleaning and polishing).

The public's first overt clue that the *Savannah* was preparing for action came six days after her arrival, when the crew was ordered to move her to Steamboat Wharf, so that she could take on more coal. A steward and a cook also came on board the ship, probably in antic-ipation of having passengers to serve.

The following morning, on Tuesday, April 13th, *The Georgian* made the Company's next move its top story:

> We are requested to state, that the Steam Ship Savannah, Cap-tain Rogers, will be in readiness to sail TO-MORROW for *CHARLESTON*, and that the hour of her departure will be designated in the Republican of this afternoon.

In the *Republican* later that day, an advertisement confirmed the next morning's departure, "precisely at 9 o'clock."

Just below it was a notice for the steamboat *Charleston*. Her new master and agents, Captain Horace Utley and the firm of Hall & Hoyt, also were advertising a packet trip to Charleston, but wisely set their steamer's departure for one day later.

They quickly changed their minds. Early the next morning, when *The Georgian* came out, it carried separate advertisements for both the steamship and the steamboat, one right next to the other. Only the *Charleston* was no longer leaving a day later. Instead, she was scheduled to depart that morning, just like the *Savannah*, and at exactly the same time. Whether Captain Utley saw this as just a friendly competition, or an attempt to thwart a potential rival, isn't clear. In any event, passengers heading to the city of Charleston that Wednesday would have a choice to make.

* * *

On the cloud-covered morning of departure, a crowd gathered on Savannah's Steamboat Wharf. Amongst them was a small number of travelers intent on embarking for the sister city to the north. For the first time, they had two steam vessels from which to choose.

On the one hand, there was the steamboat, with which everyone was familiar. It would take the inland route to Charleston, as Captain Utley preferred, with a brief stop in Beaufort. The passage promised to be safe, and predictable.

On the other hand, there was the steamship, brand new and barely tested. It would go by sea, direct to Charleston. Captain Rogers knew well the route "on the outside," having taken the rival steamboat on the same journey many times before. The passage promised to be different, perhaps even something of an adventure.

With these factors weighed, the passengers made their choice.

Onto the steamship *Savannah* came the eminent Stephen Elliott, his wife Esther, and their children. Elliott was one of the most prominent South Carolinians of the time, having helped to establish free public schools in the Palmetto State, as well as the Bank of South Carolina, of which he was president. His wife Esther was part of the extended Habersham family, and the participation of relatives Robert and Joseph in the *Savannah* may have tipped the scales in favor of trying the steamship.

Also coming aboard the *Savannah* was actor Henry James Finn, one of a traveling troupe of thespians managed by a fellow named Charles Gilfert. Finn was one of the more colorful characters in the company, having been born in Australia, raised in New Jersey, and trained in the London and Edinburgh theaters. The rest of his colleagues had already left Georgia for Charleston, where they hoped to perform for President Monroe. Finn had stayed behind temporarily, and needed to catch up as quickly as possible.

Also willing to give the steamship the benefit of any doubts were four other men and one woman, making the total customer count about one dozen, including the Elliott children.

By 10 o'clock, all was ready, so Moses ordered the *Savannah*'s crew to get under way. Once again, the riverbank was packed with spectators, anticipating a race between the two steamers.

But there was no race to be had. The *Charleston*, it turned out, was staying behind, Captain Utley having conceded the day to his competitor.

As the *Savannah* pushed away from the wharf and headed toward the sea, the crowded riverbank cheered her onward. Despite steaming into the wind and against an incoming tide, she nevertheless was reckoned to be making 5 knots. "When you take into consideration the opposing powers of those elements," later wrote one of the passengers, "the difficulties arising from the slower motion of new engines at starting, the weight of the hull, three hundred tons burthen, spars, rigging, machinery, etc., this rapidity appears almost incredible."

By 1 o'clock that afternoon, the steamship had reached Tybee lighthouse, at the mouth of the river. The next step was to simply cross over the great sandbar, and head out to sea.

But the conditions at Tybee gave pause.

"Tempestuous," in the eyes of the passenger-diarist.

"Blowing fresh," in the understated words of Steve.

The pilot thought the waters too rough and the air too thick with fog to proceed any further. Since by law he was responsible for the safe passage of any vessel he guided along the coast, the pilot's will was master. His opinion was reinforced by some of the passengers, who were apprehensive about proceeding, as well.

Under the circumstances, Moses had no choice, so he gave the order to drop anchor just off the lighthouse, and wait. With no improvement in conditions before nightfall, the pilot declared that he had no interest in sleeping on board, and climbed down into a boat, which took him to shore.

Dawn the next morning found the air clear and the sea calm, so Moses ordered the boilers fired up, and told the crew to prepare to get under way. Unfortunately, the land-loving pilot was nowhere to be seen. Departing without a pilot as guide was technically against the law, so once again, Moses had no choice but to wait.

Finally, one hour after sunrise, a boat approached with the pilot.

Moses immediately ordered the anchor pulled up and the steam engine into action. The pilot's tardiness, however, would have ripples far beyond the loss of one hour's daylight.

Once the *Savannah* had steamed over the bar, Moses turned her northward. By 10 o'clock, there were favorable winds that could aid their progress, so the crew climbed high to deploy topgallants (which are the uppermost square-rigged sails), as well as a few smaller studding sails. "A heavy swell and a head sea had been produced by the fresh gale of the preceding night," the passenger-diarist later wrote, "and the ship yawed, as the seamen say, or rolled from one side to the other; this detracted from the velocity with which she would have sailed, because it prevented the wheels acting in concert."

Still, with the power of both wind and steam, the passenger felt as though "we literally flew over the retiring waves." Also novel to his ear was a new kind of order given to the crew whenever the wind changed—

"Funnel there!"

With this command, the deck hands pulled the cables that turned the smokestack, directing the black puffs and orange cinders away from the sails.

By 4 o'clock that afternoon, Charleston lighthouse was spotted to the north by northeast, about 4 leagues (or 12 miles) distant. At that point, the objective was straightforward: get the *Savannah* over the bar at the Bay's entrance before dark.

The going, however, was choppy and rough. By the time the steamship had labored its way to the edge of the Charleston bar, it was early evening, and dark. The chance to cross over had been missed, it was reckoned, by a scant 30 minutes. The pilot's tardiness that morning suddenly took on greater significance. The only thing to do was drop anchor off the bar, and wait for daylight.

The next morning, just after sunrise, the pilot obligingly came out to the ship. Only after the passengers had been served breakfast did Moses order the wheels into motion, at 9 o'clock.

Once the *Savannah* had crossed over the bar and entered the protection of the Bay, any semblance of a wind quickly disappeared. "While other ships were becalmed and lifeless," wrote the passenger-diarist, the steamship was able to press on toward the city as if "before a fair breeze."

The sight of a large, three-masted vessel, its sails furled, puffing smoke and churning rapidly through the tranquil Bay left no doubt as to its identity. The people of Charleston, like their Georgia neighbors, flocked to the waterfront to bear witness and give voice, and the passenger-diarist described the moment:

> ... *we were honored with repeated cheerings from the astonished and delighted crowds that were assembled on the docks and vessels, and they were as cordially returned. We glided quickly and majestically before the city, threading the mazes of our course between the vessels at anchor with the ease and facility of a dolphin...*

Once tied up to the wharves on the Cooper River, the *Savannah's* passengers disembarked, and were quickly replaced by hundreds of Charlestonians, who came aboard to inspect the port's newest visitor. Among this crowd were probably shareholders John Haslett and Samuel Yates, who could take their own measure of the venture they had joined.

The steamship's first passengers, for their part, provided testimony to the local newspapers, speaking highly of the accommodations on board, as well as the "politeness and attention of Capt. Rogers." They also set the record straight on their belated appearance, blaming the pilot's tardy return the prior morning for causing the *Savannah* to miss crossing over the Charleston bar before nightfall.

After registering the steamship's arrival at the Custom House, Moses had to determine the logistics of the impending presidential visit. That, he was better able to determine the next day, Saturday, when the steamboat *Charleston* arrived, bringing Major General Edmund Gaines, his wife Barbara, and three Army aides. These officers served as the President's advance team. Their task was to ensure that the ostensible reason for the Commander-in-Chief's tour—inspecting Charleston's harbor defenses—would go according to plan.

In addition to the steamboat *Charleston*, a number of sailing vessels also made port that weekend. Among them was a two-masted brig, fresh from New York City. While the arrival of such a vessel was not at all out of the ordinary, this particular brig surely must have caught the attention of Stevens Rogers. Her name was *Connecticut*, under the command of Captain James Blin, and Steve knew them well.

* * *

Stevens Rogers had grown up on his father's farm at a place called Goshen Point, which was located just south of New London, at the mouth of the Thames River. The view from the farm was panoramic, and allowed young Steve to watch all manner of sailing craft leaving and entering the port of New London. To the south, out on Long Island Sound, were still more vessels to behold, heading for parts unknown.

This window on the world had a profound effect upon Steve. He declared repeatedly as a boy that he wanted to become a mariner, as had other members of the Rogers clan before him.

His parents, Stevens and Abigail Rogers, had other ideas. Some of those family ancestors who went to sea had never returned. The last thing they wanted was to have their only son become a mariner; it would be far better for him to inherit the farm, and stay safe and sound on land.

To that end, as young Steve grew, his parents insisted on getting him a good education, to prepare him to run the farm and prosper. He attended several schools in the New London area through his teens, until his parents sent him to the prestigious Plainfield Academy, located some 25 miles to the north.

But he didn't stay there long. One day in the summer of 1809, the strapping 20-year-old concluded that he was through with book-learning. Gathering his things, Steve abandoned his studies and headed for home, stopping at the waterfront in downtown New London.

There, along the wharves jutting into the Thames River, the young man began looking for a spot on the crew of any vessel that would have him. He certainly looked the part—given his height and physique, Steve was taller and bigger than most of the men he encountered. His complete lack of experience, however, worked against him.

After repeated rejections, Steve noticed a brig that was tied up to the wharves normally used by smaller sloops and coastal traders. On closer examination, he saw that the brig's name was *Connecticut*. Steve went aboard and found the captain, asking him if he had space for an eager beginner. The captain said he did, and asked the young man's name. Upon hearing whose son stood before him, the captain said he would agree to hire Steve, on the condition that his parents approved.

With this offer in hand, Steve left New London and headed back to the family farm on Goshen Point. His arrival home surprised his parents, who naturally expected him to be at school. After apologizing for leaving his studies, Steve told them that he had made up his mind to go to sea, and that he already had joined the crew of a brig. The only thing that stood in his way was their blessing, which the captain insisted upon.

Who was this captain?

Blin.

Hosea Blin, of the *Connecticut*. Yes, father knew him.

Something in Steve's manner must have told his parents that this time he would not be denied. As if in surrender, father told Steve to gather his things, and accompany him in to New London to see Captain Blin.

Upon reaching the wharves, the two Stevens went aboard the brig, its hold nearly full and ready for departure. Steve's father, after finding Blin and renewing his acquaintance, asked the captain what cargo the *Connecticut* had, and where she was headed.

Barrel staves, baled hay, foodstuffs and livestock was the answer, destined for the British colony of Demerara, on the coast of South America.

Armed with full knowledge of what Steve had gotten himself into, father gave consent for his only son to go.

But that wasn't all. The elder Rogers also qualified his approval, imploring Captain Blin with a very specific request: *work my son hard, and make him as sick of the sea as you possibly can.*

* * *

Whatever notice Moses and Steve gave to their old haunts, the *Charleston* and the *Connecticut*, it paled in comparison to the attention they were receiving for their newest command. On Sunday, Moses opened the *Savannah* to the public. In the logbook, Steve simply recorded that "a large number of people come on board," but given the good weather that day, visitors must have numbered in the thousands. The foot traffic was so heavy that the crew had to spend the next day scraping and re-painting the ship, to bring it back into pristine condition.

While the *Savannah* received a cleaning that Monday, General Gaines and his aides went out to inspect the harbor fortifications. Famed for his defense of Fort Erie during the late war, the General's opinion carried added weight. That evening, Gaines and his entourage made an additional dry-run, attending the theater for a performance by Charles Gilfert's acting troupe.

With the city's preparations for the presidential visit in hand, all that was missing was President Monroe himself. Coming overland from the north, his schedule had been affected by both travel conditions and the eagerness of hosts to cling to their extraordinary guest. The exact date of his arrival was unknown, and the subject of much speculation.

Finally, on Saturday, April 24th, eight days after the *Savannah* tied up at Charleston, the President's nephew, Lieutenant James Monroe, appeared. His uncle's arrival, he reported, was imminent. As the city waited through Sunday, Moses obligingly opened the steamship to visitors once again, who flooded her decks for the day.

The wait finally ended on Monday, when President Monroe landed at the city in a long barge built especially for him. The first chief executive to set foot in Charleston in 28 years, Monroe received a full escort from local militia and cavalry troops, artillery salutes, and wild cheers from the thousands of residents who turned out to greet him.

While the city focused primarily on its distinguished visitor, the purpose of the steamship's extended stay in port also piqued the curiosity of more than a few Charlestonians. Out of politeness, any local views on this subject were probably kept in confidence, at least until the day after the President's arrival, when the *Charleston Courier* let the cat out of the bag:

> It has been intimated that the steam ship *Savannah* would be tendered to take him to the South; but we presume it will not meet his views to proceed by water.

Exactly how President Monroe received an invitation to travel on the steamship isn't clear, but shareholder John Haslett's civic prominence may have given him the clout to help Moses with an audience, or the delivery of a letter.

No matter what their ideals or their ideas, presidents are, at their core, politicians. James Monroe was no different. Somehow he got wind of the local sentiment, and it determined his reply. The President declined the offer, saying that "the people of Charleston did not want him to leave their state in a Georgia conveyance," as Steve would later recall. However, Monroe did promise to visit the steamship during his stay in Savannah.

While the President's answer thwarted the original mission of Moses, he could at least console himself with the prospect of executive attention within a few days. In the meantime, the people of Charleston entertained President Monroe with dinners, tours of their local charities, and a special performance of Shakespeare's *Julius Caesar* (with *Savannah* passenger Henry J. Finn playing Cassius). The Charleston City Council even commissioned a promising young artist named Samuel F. B. Morse to paint the President's portrait, when time allowed.

The business portion of Monroe's visit came on Thursday, April 29th, when Captain Utley had the honor of taking him out in the steamboat *Charleston*, to inspect the harbor defenses. This public service, efficiently carried out, probably gave Moses the idea of how his new command could be of use, once the President reached Savannah.

The following morning, Captain Utley and the steamboat *Charleston* prepared to leave on their normal packet run to Beaufort and Savannah. Perhaps not coincidentally, Moses had delayed his own departure to coincide with Captain Utley's. Only when both vessels had departed without the President would his travel to Beaufort by land be assured.

Climbing aboard the *Savannah* for the voyage home were seven passengers—six men and one young lady—along with a few others who just wanted the opportunity of riding the steamship as far as the bar. Departing with all sails furled and the paddlewheels turning, Moses pointed the *Savannah* south, toward the Bay's entrance, and directly into the wind and against the tide. Crossing over the sandbar in 2½ hours, one passenger calculated the *Savannah* had made 7 knots, despite Nature's impediments.

Once the Bay passengers had disembarked, Moses ordered the steam engine into action again, and steered the *Savannah* down the roily coast, directly into the wind. He seemed intent on beating the *Charleston*, Nature, and the prior passage time in one fell swoop. Captain Utley, for his part, did not join the race, instead taking his steamboat into the protected inland route.

By the next morning, May 1st, Moses had his creation steaming over the bar at Tybee, and by 1 o'clock that afternoon, they had reached the wharves below the Sand Hill, safely depositing their seven passengers.

The trip home had been the *Savannah*'s finest yet. Aside from one very brief spell near the lighthouse, no sails had been used, and despite fighting winds nearly the entire way, the steamship had made the passage in a little over one day.

* * *

With one round-trip coastal packet successfully completed, the Company decided to lay plans for another. Three days after the *Savannah*'s arrival home, the local *Republican* ran the announcement:

Passage to New-York.
The steam-ship SAVANNAH, Captain Rodgers, will make one trip to New-York, previous to her departure for Liverpool, should a sufficient number of passengers offer, and will be ready to proceed in the course of the week or commencement of this next. Apply on board at Taylor's wharf, or to
Scarbrough & M'Kinne.

Such a next-step made plenty of sense, for a number of reasons.

First, it would give Captain Rogers another opportunity to test the ship, the crew and the machinery before attempting the Atlantic crossing. Hopefully, they also could improve on their previous 9-day transit time from New York.

Second, it would give the Company another opportunity to build public confidence in the steamship. The successful transport of nearly a score of customers between Savannah and Charleston surely must have allayed some of the fears over the vessel's safety. By offering passage to a more distant destination, while staying near the coast, Captain Rogers would have another chance to prove—by logical progression—the security of his steamship.

And third, such a packet trip could serve as a testing of the waters, both figuratively and legally, for initiating trans-Atlantic or coastal steamship service, with New York as a port of call.

The need for flexibility was only reinforced by the news and views arriving from Gotham. Of particular interest was a recent issue of New York's *Commercial Advertiser*, which contained a clear pot-shot at the *Savannah*'s performance:

The Steam Ship *Savannah* with a number of passengers, left Savannah on the morning of the 14th inst. and arrived at

Charleston on the 16th. The voyage between those two ports is often performed, by vessels *without steam*, in 18 or 20 hours.

The consequences of the pilot's tardy return to the steamship on the morning of April 15th had rippled far beyond the loss of an hour's steaming time.

Such an attack on the *Savannah* needed rebuttal. Coming to her defense was John Harney, editor of *The Georgian*. Publishing the *Commercial Advertiser*'s swipe at the steamship in his May 6th edition, Harney then noted that despite the delays at each port entrance, the steamship had made the run from Tybee lighthouse to the Charleston bar in the space of only half a day.

In the following morning's edition, *The Georgian* further informed its readers that it had received a detailed description of the steamship's return trip, provided by one of the passengers, and it would publish that letter the next day.

True to his word, Harney printed the passenger's account on Saturday, May 8th, under the title "Plain Facts."

In it, the passenger, after noting the remarks from New York, asserted that when the steamship left the wharf at Charleston, it faced "a strong flood tide and directly contrary wind, rendering the getting to sea perfectly impracticable to any other vessel, several of which were then windbound in Charleston roads." Once out on the ocean, the *Savannah* still had to steam into the wind, yet made the trip, bar to bar, in 17 hours, and from port to port in 26 hours. "And it may not be improper in this place," continued *The Georgian*, "to remark that not a vessel of any description, since the arrival of the steamship, entered this port from the northward till the 4th instant, though so many are expected."

At the same time *The Georgian* was defending the *Savannah*, news of the competition's progress also arrived. The launch date for the Ocean Steam Ship Company's first vessel, reported the New York papers, had been set. While it would take months more to install the machinery, the speed with which the Gothamites were moving was impressive, nevertheless. So too was the size of the adversary they were building to compete with the Georgians—it was reported to be a massive 700 tons burthen, more than twice as large as the *Savannah*, and bigger than any other commercial steam vessel yet constructed.

Nor were the New York rivals limiting themselves to just speed of action and size for advantage. In an effort to give their new steam giant both the honor and the aura of genius and power, they had determined to christen their craft with a name worthy of its ancestry. Plunging into the waters of the East River to challenge the *Savannah* was nothing less than a reincarnation of the creator himself—the Steam Ship *Robert Fulton.*

* * *

While Moses had every reason to be satisfied with the *Savannah's* performance to date, there were some among the crew who found faults of one kind or another. Two days after returning from Charleston, the ship's cook, a man named Joseph, packed his things and left. Three days after that, on Thursday, May 6th, seaman Jacub Leacraft also quit.

Stevens Rogers recorded no specific cause in the logbook for why these men withdrew. Perhaps they had an argument with Moses or Steve or one of their shipmates; maybe they found a better bunk and pay to be had on another vessel; or it could be that as their departure on a much longer voyage drew nearer, these crewmen had fallen victim to second thoughts.

Such apprehensions were understandable. The number of long-distance ocean journeys by steam vessels that turned out as planned could be counted on one hand. That the *Savannah* herself had made one of them probably meant little to these seamen contemplating the width of the Atlantic.

Members of the crew were not the only ones with misgivings. The same day that Jacub Leacraft left the ship, William Scarbrough sat down in his newly-built mansion on West Broad Street, and wrote a rushed letter to his wife Julia. She had taken their ill son, Joseph, up to New York for medical care, and Scarbrough was anxious to know the boy's condition. He also wanted to report on his own doings, including the preparation of their home to receive and host President Monroe, which Scarbrough had volunteered for that purpose:

> *... It was understood the President was not to be here till Monday next; but a Messenger sent to meet him & returned last Evening reports he is to be here tomorrow or Saturday at furthest. I wish for my own Part he was come & gone – as until then all Business*

Arrangements will be broken in upon.—Our House is quite in readiness for him...

Scarbrough then turned to business, which was looking bleaker by the week, and made a plea to Julia to agree to his personal plans for the *Savannah*:

We have advertised the steam ship to make passage to [New] York & to return here ... but from present Appearances, only 3 Passengers having as yet offered, I am afraid she will have to await & I to hurry myself to proceed on in her. – I hope you will not allow any foolish Apprehensions to prevent your going across with me; for in my Mind she is, if any Thing safer than any other Kind of vessel. – But whether she was so or not the Times have become such that I must go & try what I can do with her; as there is too much at Stake as regards myself not to try & speedily do some Thing with her to advantage...

Unfortunately, the Company's best-laid plans had been tossed into the air. With little public appetite for a passage to New York, the ability to build confidence in the *Savannah* by testing various routes was in serious doubt.

This left only one alternative: proceed with the great experiment of steaming across the Atlantic, as soon as conditions allowed. There was no better way to encourage prospective customers to sign up for such a passage than to have the Company's own president and his wife lead the way, by going on the voyage themselves.

But even if William Scarbrough convinced Julia to go, he nevertheless had come to the realization that beyond attempting the crossing, he needed to "do some Thing" with the *Savannah*, and quickly. The economic downturn was getting worse. All possibilities would have to be considered, and his being with the steamship in Europe would put Scarbrough in a better position to determine the Company's next move.

Any final decisions on what to do, however, would have to wait. For the moment, all Savannah eyes were fixed across the river, on the swampy South Carolina shore. It was there that residents would get their first glimpse of the approach of the President of the United States.

CHAPTER TEN

AN OFFER, PREPARATIONS, AND OMENS

WHILE THE Savannah Steam Ship Company's directors wrestled with their shifting plans, the seamen aboard the *Savannah* settled into the predictable routine of "ship's duty." Each new day brought more cleaning, polishing, and whatever "sundry jobs" Moses and Steve thought necessary to keep the steamship in the best condition.

A change of pace for the crew came the day after the departure of shipmate Jacub Leacraft. On Friday, May 7th, a *lighter* (which is a small transport barge) came alongside the steamship with a pile of imported British coal. The crew's task was to haul the coal up onto the *Savannah*'s deck, and down into the fuel bunkers in the hold. At that time, the most efficient way to do this was to form a human line along the route, and pass the coal in buckets. The chore was a tedious one, and required all hands available. Thankfully, the weather cooperated: skies remained clear, and light breezes helped cool off the coaling brigade.

Even so, it would take more than one day to finish the job, so the crew took up the task again on Saturday morning. Once again, gentle breezes and pleasant skies aided the effort.

As the coaling operation neared its end that afternoon, a crowd began to gather on nearby Exchange Wharf. There, a group of city dignitaries piled into an elegant barge. This craft—propelled by ten uniformed rowers—proceeded across the river to the South Carolina shore, landing at a dock used by one of the cross-river ferries. The barge's movement signaled that the long wait was nearly over—President Monroe's arrival was finally at hand.

By late afternoon, the Chief Executive and his entourage emerged from the swampy Carolina lowlands, and came to a halt at the ferry dock, where the receiving committee stood waiting. Once the initial greetings were concluded, President Monroe climbed into the barge, as did the other members of his party, which included Secretary of War John C. Calhoun, General Gaines and his staff, the President's private secretary, Samuel Gouverneur, and finally his nephew, Lieutenant James Monroe.

The people of Savannah were ready for them. The wharves and banks of the river were thick with thousands, ready to welcome the first president to visit their city in 28 years.

As the barge glided across the river, the Georgia shoreline roared to life, and the revenue cutter *Dallas* let loose a 21-gun salute.

Once the presidential party reached Exchange Wharf, the cannons of the locally-mustered Chatham Light Artillery joined in, firing a second salute from high on the bluff. After being welcomed by Mayor James Wayne and the city's aldermen, President Monroe was then escorted up the steep, sandy bank.

At the top of the bluff, the President was directed to the front of the Exchange. Arrayed before him on the wide expanse of Bay Street were all the local militia units, including infantry, cavalry, and artillery, drawn up in a long line paralleling the river. Surrounding the troops at a distance were the people of Savannah, in what was believed to be the largest assemblage in the city's history.

After carefully reviewing each of the military units on foot, the President was invited to proceed to his specially-prepared lodgings. The organizing committee presented him with a choice of transport: a horse, or a fancy carriage called a *barouche*.

President Monroe chose the horse. Mounting up, he proceeded with his militia escort, half in front and half behind, down to the southern end of Bay Street. The column then turned right, onto East Broad Street. Half a dozen blocks later, it turned right again, onto Broughton Street.

From there, the President had the entire city before him. Trotting down the full length of Broughton Street, the fifth freely-elected leader of this new republic was enveloped by throngs of cheering, waving Savannahans, who packed every sidewalk, porch, balcony and window within view.

Once the column reached West Broad Street, and William Scarbrough's new mansion, the escorting militia units came to a halt. Then, in turn, each unit fired off a salute, as the President dismounted, and was escorted inside the mansion.

The welcoming phase, it seemed, came off without a hitch. It was designed not only to celebrate the President's arrival in a memorable way, but to show the city's resources at their best. Yet for all the pageantry of this first ceremony, President Monroe's new hosts were hopeful that they could show him still more impressive things in the days to come.

* * *

Advertisements for the steamship *Savannah*'s departure for New York had continued to run in the local papers up to the day of the President's arrival. But with only a handful of people having offered to go, and a very distinguished guest presently on the scene, the decision was made to cancel the trip. The rationale was simple: better to show the nation's chief executive what the future of ocean travel looked like than make a money-losing voyage. In any event, New York could wait.

The day after the President's arrival was a Sunday. Accordingly, the steamship's crew received the day off, to rest, walk about the city, or attend a church service. Some of them were probably drawn to the activities surrounding President Monroe, the highlight being the dedication of the nearly-completed Independent Presbyterian Church on Bull Street, which had become the tallest structure in the city.

The dedication was followed by a service inside, under the Reverend Henry Kollock. Attending the service along with the President and his suite were city leaders, a sizeable number of Army and Navy officers, and a far larger contingent of Savannah's fairer sex. A good number of the steamship's shareholders were probably there, too, since some of them were church members, and Reverend Kollock had a well-earned reputation for tolerance and inclusion of other denominations and faiths.

Monday saw still more welcoming ceremonies. The morning's event included a gathering at the front of the Exchange of local militia officers, municipal leaders, Army and Navy officers, and prominent citizens. Once organized, they marched from the Exchange over to the front of Scarbrough's house. Upon arrival, they were invited into the mansion to be formally introduced to the President.

Down on the river that same Monday, Steve oversaw the *Savannah*'s crew, as they hauled pine wood aboard, which would serve as fire-starter for the boilers. While taking the President on a tour of the coastal defenses downriver could have been performed by any of the Steam Boat Company of Georgia's vessels, it had been decided that the honor should be given to the *Savannah*.

Once the chore of loading wood was finished, the steamship was ready. The only real interruption to the crew's work occurred later in the day, when a heavy thunder squall came barreling down the river from the northwest, drenching all that stood in its path.

* * *

Tuesday, May 11th dawned clear and pleasant—a perfect day for an open-air excursion. Shortly after sunrise, President Monroe and his entourage made their way down the sandy cliff, surrounded by a mass of spectators. Once they reached Steamboat Wharf, the President was directed to the side of the *Savannah*. Stepping aboard, he was greeted by Captain Rogers.

Following behind was a considerable flock of officials and invited guests, ranging in stature from the national to the local.

Foremost among them was South Carolina native and Secretary of War John C. Calhoun, whose department oversaw all the coastal forts protecting the nation's harbors. Behind Calhoun came the Hero of Fort Erie, General Gaines, as well as other senior officers from military units stationed in Georgia and South Carolina. Most prominent among them was General David Brydie Mitchell, a former governor of Georgia who had become the federal government's agent to the Creek Nation. Also in tow came still more junior officers of the Army, and also a few from the Navy.

Beyond the military, there were a number of prominent civilian guests. Reverend Kollock, who had led the dedication of his new church two days earlier, was on board. So was Chatham County Superior Court Judge John MacPherson Berrien, who, as a *former* Federalist, was the closest thing left of the opposition party in Georgia. Berrien's predecessor on the bench, Thomas U. P. Charlton, was on board, as well. A number of other prominent citizens were also in attendance; although the local papers didn't mention him, it appears William Scarbrough was among them.

By 8 o'clock, the boilers were sufficiently pressurized. Moses ordered the engine into action, and the *Savannah*'s wheels slowly began to push her away from the crowded pier. Since there were light winds blowing downriver, Moses ordered Steve to deploy some of the upper sails. This would not only speed their movement, but show their guests how the steamship could use both modes of power at once.

As the *Savannah* steamed southward, Moses, Steve and the others on board had a chance to take the measure of the unique passenger in their presence. Having just recently celebrated his 61st birthday, James Monroe was considered by most who saw him to be a truly distinguished-looking man. Standing six feet in height with broad shoulders, he certainly looked the part, despite the slight limp in his walk which some people claimed to notice.

His dress and hairstyle were those of someone who had come from another time. President Monroe continued to favor the knee-length breeches and stockings that had begun to fall out of fashion at the turn of the century. And he still favored a little powder in his hair, giving it a grayish tint, a practice which also had been out of vogue for quite awhile.

James Monroe.

Such fashion certainly served to remind anyone who saw him that James Monroe was a part of the Revolutionary generation. As a young lieutenant in the Continental Army, he had crossed the icy Delaware River with General Washington on Christmas night in 1776, surprising the British and Hessian soldiers encamped at Trenton. Monroe still bore the scar from a grievous wound to his left shoulder that he had received during that fight. Had there not been a doctor with his unit, who immediately clamped shut the torn artery in his shoulder, the future fifth president of the United States just might have bled to death on the battlefield.

That finest hour, while still remembered in 1819, was nevertheless more than 42 years in the past. The present era had its own set of challenges, which James Monroe had to confront, and, if possible, address. Overcoming the animosities generated by the late war with Britain still needed more time and effort. There were also smoldering resentments in some quarters—namely, the North and the West— that Monroe was the fourth Virginian out of five presidents so far elected by the Republic.

These kinds of problems were ones that this particular president was well-suited to manage. James Monroe was often described by his contemporaries as an amiable, unassuming man. Such a personal disposition tended to put people around him at ease, and help opposing parties find common ground. Further buttressing this means to an end was the President's undisguised desire that those in his presence behave in a similar manner. The resulting atmosphere enveloping President Monroe—polite and harmonious—was an excellent reflection of his own upbringing in the old school of Virginia manners.

Surely it must have been so on the deck of the *Savannah* that morning, as she smoked and splashed down the river, the many guests aboard inspecting her revolving paddlewheels and humming machinery. Any tensions related to the rough-and-tumble politics of Georgia had to be kept out of the President's sight. Yet under the circumstances, that must have been no easy task, for between two of the generals on board, there was some very bad blood indeed.

* * *

Since the very founding of the United States, people who lived in the State of Georgia had always felt an acute sense of vulnerability. With Spanish colonials directly to their south, in Florida, and Indian tribes that varied from friendly to very hostile to their south and west, settlers in Georgia well-knew that they were living on the wild frontier.

Even by the end of the second war with Britain in 1815, these feelings of insecurity remained. While negotiations with Spain for the acquisition of Florida had begun, friction with the area's Indian tribes, particularly the Seminoles, had intensified. By late 1817, news of continuing attacks on settlers in the Georgia wilderness, and the resulting loss of life, had so terrified the American public as to force the federal government to take more decisive action.

The generals tasked with confronting these Indian raids knew the problem was more complicated than it sounded. Both the Seminoles and the settlers had been subjected to indiscriminate attacks and robbery by roving bands of outlaws, whom the generals called *banditti*. When the banditti attacked the Indians, the latter retaliated against whomever they could find, including settlers. The settlers would then respond in kind, or call out for help. It was these tit-for-tat, hit-and-run raids which compelled a federal response. The use of Spanish Florida as a sanctuary by the Seminoles, and some of their renegade Creek allies, made the crisis all the more delicate and difficult to solve.

Into this foggy morass went General Edmund Gaines, the Hero of Fort Erie, who was one of two brigadiers serving under General Andrew Jackson in the South. General Gaines' orders were clear: protect the settlers, and put an end to the Seminole raids.

On his way to Fort Hawkins, near the Florida border, Gaines passed through the lands of the Creek Indians. There he stopped at the outpost of General David Brydie Mitchell, the former Georgia governor and militia officer who was the U.S. government's official agent to that tribe. General Gaines declared that he expected General Mitchell to help him in organizing the Creeks to fight alongside his own expeditionary force.

But General Mitchell had another view altogether. As the federal government's Indian Agent, he was essentially the U.S. ambassador to the Creek Nation. His primary purpose was to keep the Creeks friendly. His secondary objective was to negotiate a federal purchase of some 1.5 million acres of Creek tribal lands. While Mitchell had obligingly prepared the Creeks to cooperate with the advancing American troops, his assistance, he declared, would stop there. Enlisting the Creeks to fight another tribe, as well as some of their own lawless members, not only ran counter to his primary mission, but might jeopardize the land negotiations, as well.

Having failed to gain any further help from Mitchell, General Gaines nevertheless charged ahead, marching his force into the wilderness of southern Georgia. Soon thereafter, he sent a detachment of his troops to an Indian settlement called Fowltown, with orders to arrest the chief and warriors holed up there. When the Indians forcefully resisted arrest, the American troops returned fire, and quickly overran and destroyed the village.

This action ignited the powder keg that became known as the Seminole War. Hostilities rapidly engulfed all of Georgia's borderlands with Spanish Florida.

When President Monroe learned of one particularly bloody assault on American troops and settlers in December of 1817, he concluded that General Gaines could not handle the job alone. So the President ordered his superior, General Andrew Jackson, to take command in the field, effectively demoting Gaines.

Once on the scene in Georgia, General Jackson wasted no time. He quickly mustered a combined force of federal troops, State militiamen, and Creek warriors, with which he promptly invaded Spanish Florida, and destroyed the Seminole sanctuaries there. The war was over by April of 1818.

In the conflict's wake, Congress wanted explanations. Among those summoned to Washington to field questions surrounding the war's outbreak was the U.S. Agent to the Creek Nation, General David Brydie Mitchell. At the beginning of 1819, Mitchell went before a Senate committee and bluntly offered his own analysis: it was all General Gaines' fault. Gaines' attack on Fowltown destroyed the fragile peace along the border, and led to open warfare.

For the Hero of Fort Erie, this was just too much. General Gaines already had been humiliated once, when the President relieved him of overall command. With Mitchell's testimony, Gaines faced still more embarrassment, this time from an Indian agent whom he thought had been more concerned with negotiating a land treaty with the Creeks than protecting settlers from the Seminoles. Gaines was not about to let things lie as they were, but a formal reply to Mitchell's accusations would have to wait until he had all of the facts organized for his defense.

In the meantime, as the two generals stood on the deck of the *Savannah* that May morning, all they could likely do was glare at each other.

* * *

By half past 10 o'clock that morning, the steamship had reached the waters off Tybee lighthouse. Moses ordered the engine stopped, and the anchor dropped, so that President Monroe could survey the coastal landscape, and the defenses prepared there. Tagging along with the *Savannah* had been the Steam Boat Company of Georgia's *Altamaha*, which was towing two barges full of rowers. If the President wished, the barges could take him ashore, to walk the fortifications.

In the end, that proved unnecessary. After half an hour of visual inspection, Captain Rogers was told to weigh anchor and return to the city. Moses ordered the engine started, and the steamship and her steamboat partner began the trip back upriver.

Soon after beginning her ascent, the *Savannah* came upon Long Island, one of a line of thin, marshy masses which occasionally split the river in two. Anchored near this island was a two-masted brig, flying an unusual flag of wide horizontal stripes, alternating white and blue in color.

This day, the brig's name was *La Fortuna*. But depending upon circumstances, she also could be called *La Union*, or *Le Valient*. The name to be used was ultimately the decision of her commander, Don Williema Wade.

But even this master's name was suspect. In fact, all were *noms de guerre* for Captain William Wade and the brig *Fourth of July*, out of Baltimore. Their bare disguises, and the colors flying from the brig's masthead, clearly marked them as privateers of the United Provinces of South America, fighting for independence from Spain.

As the *Savannah* approached, *La Fortuna*'s crew put their plan into action. Rising up the foremast went the Stars and Stripes, and down came the white-and-blue Patriot flag of Buenos Aires. Once the *Savannah* had nearly reached the privateer, *La Fortuna*'s cannons roared, and her crew quickly followed with three loud cheers, as the President of the United States passed them by on the only steamship in the world.

There was no report in the newspapers as to how President Monroe reacted to this boisterous display of respect. Given his belief in polite manners, he probably acknowledged the privateer's greeting with a wave or a bow, but nothing more. Recognizing this Patriot-sanctioned privateer's very existence in American waters was, in and of itself, contrary to the official position of the United States government, and potentially very risky.

Spain's colonies throughout most of the Americas had been in open revolt for years. The revolutionaries' struggle for independence was a hard one, and they needed all the help they could get.

To that end, the colonial rebels had found hundreds of American seamen, fresh from privateering against the British, who were willing to turn their guns on Spain. While the prospect of plundering Spanish merchantmen was surely uppermost in their minds, these American-crewed privateers also enlisted to fight because they believed in the rebels' cause.

They weren't the only ones. The vast majority of people in the United States agreed with them, seeing the fight of the "South American Patriots" as the righteous continuation of their own American Revolution. The country's newspaper editors also sided with the rebels, and accordingly catered to their readers' thirst for news, filling nearly every issue with reports on the most recent fighting and diplomatic maneuvering.

This positive sentiment toward the South American Patriots extended well into the various branches of the American government. Savannah Customs Collector Archibald S. Bulloch was one of many men in his position who generally chose not to interfere with the Patriot privateers, so long as they kept their noses clean.

Such indirect support for the Patriots' cause led to dangerous friction between the Spanish and American governments. Official U.S. policy was one of neutrality, viewing the many conflicts in Spain's colonies as a form of civil war. But it was hard to maintain this fig leaf when American citizens were not just cheering, but volunteering, and aiding and abetting the Patriots.

The importance of trying to appear neutral, however, was critical. The U.S. Senate had just ratified, three months prior, a treaty for the U.S. acquisition of Spanish Florida. All that remained was the Spanish government's official approval. At a minimum, continuing ill will between the two countries could jeopardize the treaty. At a maximum, if Spain became too antagonized, it might even lash out, and attack the United States.

All privateer captains operating in American waters were well-aware of the tensions created by their presence. This was why they often chose to anchor not in the heart of an American harbor, but on its periphery.

As the *Savannah* steamed past *La Fortuna*, prudence might have suggested that the Patriot brig lie low. But somehow recognizing the democratically-elected leader of their safe haven must have seemed the right and proper thing to do. The result was a traditional mariner's greeting: raising the recipient's colors, followed by a cannon salute, and cheers.

In so doing, *La Fortuna*'s crew may very well have given the President of the United States an idea.

* * *

By the time the *Savannah* had steamed partway back to the city, the outgoing tide had so reduced the river level as to prohibit the steamship from reaching the wharves. So the steamboat *Altamaha* came alongside, as planned, and the inspection party transferred over to her. Moses, Steve and the crew could only stand and watch, as their distinguished passenger continued on without them. Once the *Altamaha* reached the city, 21 booms could be heard echoing down the river, as the revenue cutter *Dallas* fired a salute to the returning President.

It wasn't until early evening that the rising tide allowed the *Savannah* to resume her journey. By that time, everyone within earshot had been treated to yet another round of 21 guns from the *Dallas*, as the President was escorted to a huge public dinner at the south end of Bay Street.

Despite being unable to bring President Monroe all the way back to town, Moses surely must have been pleased that he got the chance to show off his creation. The President certainly enjoyed the excursion, as he had readily told his hosts.

President Monroe also had volunteered another, more tangible compliment. Once the steamship returned from the anticipated voyage across the Atlantic, he suggested that perhaps it could be brought to the nation's capital. The President thought the federal government would have an interest in purchasing the *Savannah*, installing cannons aboard, and putting her to good use.

For what purpose would the government wish to have an armed steamship?

Fighting pirates.

* * *

President Monroe's idea for the *Savannah* made a great deal of sense. *La Fortuna*'s loud salute surely reminded the President that not all South American privateers held such respectful intentions toward the United States.

The reason lay in the Patriot privateers' incredible success in attacking, sinking and capturing Spanish merchantmen throughout the Caribbean, and out into the Atlantic. As the number of enemy targets dwindled, those privateers still hungry for plunder naturally turned to whatever prey they could find. This inevitably led to Patriot-flagged vessels leaving the realm of government-sanctioned privateering, and crossing the line into outright piracy. It mattered not what flag the victim flew when the goal became only financial, and not political.

To make matters worse, the lack of a major presence by any nation's navy in the northern Caribbean and Gulf of Mexico meant that still more free-lance pirates enthusiastically joined in the violent harvest.

Given the proximity of the United States to these waters, and the volume of shipping heading to and from the port of New Orleans, it was only natural that the pirates would pick on American vessels. News of each fresh attack sent shudders through the merchant community, and the brutality of the pirates toward their victims, which ran the gamut, from crucifixion to immolation, horrified the public. Fixing blame on any particular nationality for these outrages was impossible, since survivors described being attacked by pirate crews composed of Spanish loyalists, or rebels, or Americans, or even British and French seamen.

The American authorities, for their part, were trying to fight back with what little they had. The few U.S. revenue cutters available were actively patrolling the coasts, challenging any privateers suspected of piracy. Those pirates who were taken alive and convicted for their crimes were receiving the ultimate punishment, with executions being carried out as far north as Boston.

But these measures were not nearly enough. Taking their cue from the public's outrage, Congress had passed on March 3rd, 1819—their last day in session—"An Act to protect the commerce of the United States, and punish the crime of piracy." In it, the people's representatives made it clear precisely who was being given the power, and the responsibility, to do something:

Be it enacted . . . That the President of the United States be, and hereby is, authorized and requested to employ so many of the public armed vessels, as, in his judgment, the service may require, with suitable instructions to the commanders thereof, in protecting the merchant vessels of the United States and their crews from piratical aggressions and depredations.

With the burden placed squarely upon his shoulders, it was up to President Monroe to determine how best to protect American shipping.

Yet the execution of the law could not be a straightforward exercise, for complex and somewhat contradictory reasons.

On the one hand, the President didn't want to hinder the efforts of any law-abiding privateers, who were contributing to the Patriots' fight for independence. To do so would be contrary to the wishes of the American people, the press, and many public officials.

But on the other hand, these privateers-turned-pirates were attacking not only American vessels, but British, French, Dutch and other European merchantmen, as well. If the pirates were not confronted decisively, there was a very real chance that the European Powers would band together, and send a naval force across the Atlantic to deal with the problem themselves. Having such a multinational fleet thrown into the melee already taking place in and around Central and South America was the last thing the Monroe administration wanted to see.

Under the circumstances, sending in the U.S. Navy to fight the pirates seemed to be an obvious solution. But this was easier said than done, since the Navy's fleet remained fairly small, and already had plenty of tasks to keep it busy, such as patrolling the Atlantic for slave traders, and protecting shipping from still other pirates on the Barbary Coast of North Africa. Sending warships down to Cuban waters, where the worst piracies were being committed, would drain the Navy's already-limited resources. While new vessels were being constructed under the post-war program for "the gradual increase of the Navy," most of them would not be ready for some time.

Under the circumstances, President Monroe must have seen in the *Savannah* an advanced means of fighting the pirates, which also would gain a great deal of attention. A steamship that maneuvered in ways a sailing vessel never could certainly had the potential to force pirate vessels onto the defensive, if not beat them. Furthermore, news that the United States had deployed an armed steamship would surely put the Admiralties of Europe on notice: the Americans were not only addressing the pirate problem, but doing so with the most revolutionary of weapons.

* * *

The day after the President's trip—Wednesday, May 12th—dawned spectacular. Fresh northeasterly breezes throughout the day sent a fleet of puffy, white clouds gliding across the sky. Moses and Steve took advantage accordingly, putting all hands to work loading more wood fuel, in addition to the normal chores of ship's duty.

Every seaman had to use his muscles and his mind as best he could to carry out whatever job lay before him. The only other tool readily at his disposal was a knife. Whether it was needed for cutting a piece of rope, poking a hole in canvas, or doing anything else that seemed possible, having a good knife on hand was a must for any mariner.

In the course of the chores being carried out that beautiful day, one of the knives in use aboard the *Savannah* suddenly slipped, and the air was pierced by a blood-curdling scream. Crewmen quickly rushed over to the side of their shipmate, Daniel Claypit.

If Daniel was like most normal human beings, the immediate look of horror and pain on his face was quickly followed by the massive production of saliva in his mouth. Whatever effort Claypit made to avoid drooling down the front of his shirt was probably overwhelmed by the intent focus he placed upon his left thumb, which he had just cut off.

In short order, the ship's doctor was summoned, along with the ship's medicine chest. Because the *Savannah* was a vessel of size and headed overseas, she was required by law to carry a medicine chest. But the law didn't stipulate that a trained medical doctor be on board—that would have been both too expensive and unachievable, given the scarcity of doctors and the abundance of merchant vessels.

So when it came to assigning responsibility for the medicine chest, practicality ruled the day. The most logical holder of the chest was the one member of the crew who could almost always be found at his unique station, and that was the ship's cook. And since he had control of the medicine chest, the cook also became, by default, the ship's "doctor."

This wasn't as crazy as it might sound. After all, the cook was used to working with all kinds of flesh, and he was also the crewman most likely to have the cleanest hands.

While re-attaching a thumb could be a complicated procedure, if the "doctor" followed the first-aid techniques of the time, he probably approached the situation as though he were repairing a very bad knife cut.

First, a long strip of canvas would be wrapped twice around the middle of Daniel's left arm, and tied in a hard knot. Then, a stick three or four inches long would be inserted between the two canvas turns, and twisted like a screw, until the tightening canvas had arrested the flow of blood into his lower arm.

With the bleeding stopped, the thumb would be put back in place, and held there with wet plaster strips, laid across the cut line. Some lint, or *tow* (which is flax or hemp fiber), would then be applied, to absorb any blood discharge. Finally, a cloth bandage would be rolled around the thumb, to keep everything in place.

As one of the crew applied pressure to the wounded thumb, another shipmate would slowly unwind the tourniquet stick, renewing the flow of blood to the lower arm. If the thumb began to bleed again, the stick could be tightened again, and the procedure repeated until sufficient clotting staunched the flow.

Daniel's thumb would have been watched closely for infection, and the dressings replaced every three or four days. After a week, hopefully, the bandages, lint and plasters could all be removed.

Once the "doctor" had fixed Daniel Claypit's thumb, he soon found that he had another patient to attend to. A crewman—coincidentally named James Monroe—was not feeling well, so the decision was made to bleed him.

This procedure was somewhat controversial at the time, but many physicians continued to swear by it, believing that bleeding could relieve patients suffering from any number of maladies. Merchant crews were well aware of such opinions, and as a result did not shy away from bleeding each other, if they thought it was the best course of action.

The steps for bleeding were fairly simple. First came the tourniquet, with its blood flow-regulating stick. Next came a small incision into a vein, usually in the wrist. Then the arm was placed at a downward angle, to allow the blood to flow out. Once those involved thought enough blood had been discharged, the incision was closed with a bandage, and the patient allowed to rest.

Steve didn't record any other medical events in the logbook for either Daniel Claypit or James Monroe, so both crewmen must have survived their ordeals, and eventually returned to duty.

For fellow seaman John Volien, however, there was no further duty to be done. The day after his shipmates were doctored, Volien left the

Savannah. Once again, Steve did not record the reason for Volien's departure in the logbook, but since the crew spent the day hauling more wood fuel aboard, it must have been obvious that the crossing attempt was imminent. Any chance for any member of the crew to back out would soon be closed.

There certainly was no shortage of reminders as to the dangers they were about to face. Recent reports from out West had detailed the loss of yet another steamboat, the *Franklin*, which had sunk on the Missouri River near St. Genevieve. Probably just as disconcerting was the most recent news from New York: the Monopoly's mighty *Chancellor Livingston* had suffered an engine breakdown while ascending the North River. Fortunately, it had been possible to transfer the *Chancellor's* passengers to a nearby sailing sloop, and coax the crippled steamboat back to Gotham for repairs. A steamship suffering such a mishap in the middle of the ocean might not be so lucky.

*   *   *

After spending Wednesday, Thursday and Friday loading wood under pleasant skies, the crew awoke the following Saturday to rain, and a return to the more mundane tasks of ship's duty. The city and harbor already had returned to normalcy some two days prior, when President Monroe had departed for Augusta.

Yet that Saturday, the 15th of May, would not pass without incident. At about 8 o'clock in the evening, as the crew's workday was winding down, a dark mass of clouds was seen approaching from upriver. Moments later, the wharves and shipping were attacked by a violent gust of wind from the northwest, quickly followed by a thunderburst of rain and lightning.

Before there was time to effectively react, the *Savannah* and other vessels moored nearby were smacked and smashed about. As one of the newspapers later reported, "a dreadful cracking amongst the jibbooms, taffrails, sails, spanker booms, rigging" could be heard all along the riverfront. Three ships broke loose from the wharves, uncontrollably crashing into others nearby.

Within fifteen minutes, the rainsquall had passed, heading further downriver and out to sea. The captains and crews of all the vessels in the harbor began taking stock of the casualties. Two ships, *Antonio* and *Jane*, suffered damage. So did three brigs and a schooner.

So too, unfortunately, did the *Savannah*. She had been torn free of the wharf, and in the mayhem that followed, one of her paddlewheels was damaged. Three wooden paddleboards had been ripped away and set adrift, and some of the removable iron arms were bent. Mysteriously, no other part of the steamship was damaged—not the masts, the sails, or the rigging. Only a part of her new mode of power—the paddlewheel—suffered injury. It was enough to give any superstitious soul the creeps.

At least the planning of Captain Rogers had paid off. He had ordered ten extra iron spokes from Stephen Vail, for just such a circumstance. If the bent ones couldn't be repaired, they were immediately replaced. The damaged paddleboards also could be easily fixed, or rebuilt.

On Sunday, the crew maneuvered the *Savannah* over to the side of the ship *Alexander*, and "made fast." Once the steamship was secured, repairs to the wheel commenced, as did drying out the drenched sails.

Beyond fixing the physical damage, it was also important to address any psychological harm which Nature had inflicted. Two days later, on Tuesday, May 18th, the local *Republican* reported that despite the injury suffered in the squall, the much-anticipated date of departure had been set:

> We are requested to state that, the steam-ship Savannah, captain Rogers, will, without fail, proceed for Liverpool, direct, next Thursday, 20th instant. Passengers, if any offer, can be well accommodated.

The next morning, Wednesday, May 19th, the other two major papers, *The Georgian* and the *Columbian Museum*, obligingly repeated this announcement in their own news sections. The Savannah Steam Ship Company, in turn, took out departure advertisements in all three broadsheets; the one in the *Republican* ran that afternoon, while the other two were slated to run the next morning, on the day of departure.

Like prior advertisements for the *Savannah*, these paid notices were topped by the standard woodcut engraving of a steamboat. The urgency of making a new engraving, with the likeness of a steamship, had been discounted by the Company. It was a minor but perhaps important error. Even if readers knew better, seeing an advertisement depicting a steamboat as the means for crossing the Atlantic was hardly a reassuring message.

That same Wednesday before the scheduled departure, Steve put the crew to work bringing on supplies. Most everything the crew and passengers would eat—from meat, to vegetables, to even bread—was stored in barrels, making the loading a straightforward exercise.

Once that job was done, the steamship had on board everything it would need to begin its great experiment. By law, there had to be "well secured under deck" for every person on board:

—at least sixty gallons of water;

—one hundred pounds of salted flesh meat;

—and one hundred pounds of wholesome ship bread.

These amounts were the bare minimum required. Above and beyond these provisions, Moses and Steve probably procured still other foods that were considered staples on board merchant vessels. Dried peas were a perfect example. They were a favorite, because in addition to being an easily-preserved green vegetable, dried peas filled a barrel with little wasted space. Most likely rounding out the crew's diet were pickled vegetables, an adequate supply of lemon juice, and coffee. For the passengers, an even more varied and appetizing selection of food and drink would have been brought on board.

For the steam engine, there was as much fuel in the bunkers as could be accommodated:

—four cords of pine wood, to be used as kindling in the boilers;

—and one thousand bushels of coal, about all there was available in the city at the time.

This composition, which included so much wood, was intended to give Moses the flexibility to start (and stop) the engine as often as conditions warranted. Since the *Savannah*'s restricted fuel capacity would limit total steaming time to a fraction of the voyage, the ability to steam repeatedly for short periods, whenever circumstances permitted, was important.

Beyond the various foods and fuels, Moses also had ensured there was enough lifeboat capacity on board. Either by previous design or in recognition of Baron Klinkowström's advice, the *Savannah* had been equipped with a twelve-oar long boat and a six-oar jolly boat, giving the crew and passengers means enough to escape should anything go wrong.

There was also one final addition to the crew's complement, made just prior to the steamship's departure. Someone within the Company had seen fit to place on board a group of three orphans, to serve as cabin boys. Ranging in age from ten to fourteen, the names of these youngsters have been lost with the passage of time, but their most likely origin was the Bethesda Home for Boys, an orphanage which had been a Savannah institution since its founding in 1738.

The shareholders in the Savannah Steam Ship Company had more than a passing interest in Bethesda. The Habershams' ancestor, James Habersham, had been one of the founders of the orphanage. Furthermore, no less than 13 of the 23 individuals who had an interest in the steamship were also members of the local Union Society. This multi-denominational organization—founded in Savannah after the Revolution by a Protestant, a Catholic, and a Jew—had made the financial support of Bethesda one of its top priorities.

Putting three orphan boys on a steamship about to embark on a voyage into the unknown might not have seemed to some observers as the most appropriate thing to do. But considering how difficult it was to find a suitable place for any orphan to live and learn a trade, the shareholders must have thought giving these boys such an opportunity was beyond charitable—it was enlightened. The boys would be exposed to a new technology of such great promise that they could grow right with it. Besides, the shareholders believed the *Savannah* to be perfectly safe.

Being the most junior members of the crew, the three boys were put under the charge of Steve as first mate. Just how Moses felt about having these very young men aboard isn't known. On some level, they must have reminded him of his own first forays upon the waters of Long Island Sound with his father; or perhaps his presence at the creation in New York, just a dozen years before.

On another level, though, the orphans' appearance surely reminded Moses of his own children, who were remaining up North with Adelia while he attempted the crossing. The eldest orphan aboard, in particular, may have revived in Moses some heartbreakingly painful memories. That 14-year-old boy was roughly the same age that his first-born son Nathan would have been, were he still alive to witness his father's latest adventure.

* * *

The life that Moses Rogers had led since 1809 was atypical in the extreme. Promoting the first generation of practical steamboats required carefully managing the views of a curious (and suspicious) public, while at the same time innovating constantly. The result was a brand-new profession that epitomized the learn-as-you-go philosophy of work. Add to this the incredible potential of untapped markets, which were full of entrepreneurs anxious to get in on the revolution, and it's easy to see that Moses had been living a vigorous and very novel existence.

But this was only half of Captain Moses Rogers. The other side of this steamboating trailblazer was Moses the husband, and father. For Adelia Rogers, accepting her spouse's unusual career meant keeping the home fires burning, no matter where that might be. From the time Moses assumed his first command of the new mode of transport, those early homes had stretched from New York City, to Bordentown and Trenton in New Jersey, to at least as far south as Baltimore.

Whatever the disruptions encountered in their life together, the family of Moses and Adelia Rogers had continued to grow. Back in late October of 1812, while Moses had been quietly planning his jump from Colonel Stevens' *Phoenix* to the nearly-completed *Eagle*, Adelia gave birth to Daniel Moses Rogers. The newborn was their fourth child, and third son, in the space of 8½ years.

But whatever joy the parents must have felt upon Daniel's birth did not last long. Just a few weeks later, in mid-November, their first-born son, Nathan, tragically lost his life by drowning.

The precise circumstances surrounding Nathan's death faded with the passage of time, and his place was eventually, figuratively taken by a fifth child, Delia Antoinette, in July of 1814. Even so, for a mother and father, this loss of a first son—the namesake of his grandfather, no less—was a memory that could never be forgotten.

* * *

By sunset on Wednesday, May 19th, everything was ready. All the food and fuel was aboard, stowed in the hold. So was some mail, destined for Britain. But beyond that, there was nothing else—the steamship's remaining cargo space, limited though it was, remained empty.

Despite the downturn in business, there was still plenty of cargo being sent across the Atlantic. Indeed, the shareholders themselves had shipments to make, including lots of cotton. But the Company had not actively solicited for any goods to be taken aboard the *Savannah*.

Since Moses had made every one of his steamboat ocean transfers without cargo, it may have been he who suggested nothing be consigned to the hold, save the fuel and ship's stores. The enormous heat put out by the boilers also may have played a role in the decision to forego carrying anything of bulk. No cargo meant one less thing to worry about.

Regardless of the precautions, the outlook for passengers did not look good.

Even William Scarbrough had decided against going across. The economic situation had grown even worse since the steamship had arrived from New York. The value of currency issued by banks out West was by then being quoted as "uncertain," and banknotes from the South also continued to deteriorate, being accepted in New York at 95 cents on the dollar. Lenders of all kinds were nervously asking their borrowers to repay loans, which required not avoidance, but attention. For Scarbrough, the pressure was simply too great—he would have to stay behind, and trust in Captain Rogers.

Nevertheless, Moses would not be alone once he reached the other side. Scarbrough's brother-in-law, shareholder Robert Isaac, had already sailed for Liverpool, and either he or fellow investor Andrew Low would be present there to greet the steamship upon arrival.

As darkness fell that evening, the pleasant weather of earlier in the day gave way to clouds and rain. Since it was their last night in port, at least some of the crew were given liberty to go ashore. It would be their last chance to make merry for some time to come.

The city of Savannah—like any other port in America, or the world, for that matter—had plenty of *grog shops*, which catered to any seaman with a few *shiners* to spend. Once enticed inside, a mariner would be hard-pressed to resist the uniquely American bar-room custom of handing the bottle to the patron, and encouraging him to take as many drinks as he wished.

As the town criers called out midnight, followed by 1 o'clock in the morning on the day of departure, the rain continued to fall. During that darkest spell, around about 2 o'clock, one of the *Savannah's* crew, John Weston, made his way back to the wharf where his vessel, and a dry bunk, lay waiting.

Entry onto the steamship was by means of a typical wooden gangplank. Its width was probably not more than a foot or so, and with all the rain, its surface must have been a bit slippery.

Having reached the side of his ship, John Weston then proceeded to walk the plank. For some reason, either through a loss of faculties or footing, the 25-year-old seaman missed the target in front of him, and plunged into the water below.

The noise of such a fall was enough to be noticed, even at that early hour, and those within earshot quickly set about to find Weston, before it was too late. Given the darkness of the river waters and the well-known, tide-induced undertow, the searchers knew they would have to rescue him quickly.

By the time dawn broke, nearly everyone involved must have long since given up hope of finding John Weston alive. From that point, the crew's rescue effort became a recovery operation.

Using *boat hooks* (which are long wooden poles with an iron hook at one end), Weston's shipmates poked and prodded the muddy bottom in search of his body. The men had to wonder whether they would ever find it. If the powerful currents had not carried Weston away, there was just as much a chance that the alligators had made a meal of him.

Finally, at about 10 o'clock that morning, one of the men caught something on his boat hook. Pulling his catch to the surface revealed the worst, dispelling any thoughts that Weston had somehow survived.

John Weston's body was pulled from the water and brought aboard, where it was placed in a coffin. The authorities immediately convened an inquest, and the jury quickly concluded that his death had been an accident.

One thing no one could quite agree upon was just where Weston was from. The official inquest recorded him as being a native of New Hampshire. But one of the local papers said he was from Portland, in the District of Maine. And Steve wrote in the logbook that he was a native of the Town of Gray, in Massachusetts.

They were all probably right. The Town of Gray was just north of Portland, and the District of Maine was still under the jurisdiction of the Commonwealth of Massachusetts. New Hampshire was most likely Weston's State of birth, taken from his seaman's papers.

In the end, though, it really didn't matter. John Weston was dead, and his shipmates had to ponder what it all meant. Mariners have always been a superstitious lot. The loss of a fellow crewman on the eve of a very dangerous voyage was not a good sign. In combination with the furious rainsquall that damaged nothing of consequence but one of the paddlewheels, the death of Weston must have made more than a few people wonder, both on board and off, whether or not the steamship *Savannah* was doomed.

Yet there was a counterargument to such gloomy thinking. Mariners had long believed the ocean to be such a powerful beast that the only way to satisfy its hunger was to provide it with an offering. While the loss of John Weston was certainly tragic, his death could serve just such a purpose. With the Atlantic waters that churned up and down the Savannah River now sated with a sacrifice, this great experiment, some might have argued, could commence in safety. For men of the sea who knew that their next voyage might be their last, such a rationalization could be the means to a hopeful end—that being survival.

For their captain, however, the far more important thing was to maintain momentum. The newspaper advertisements of the previous two days, and the additional ones appearing while the crew was still searching for Weston's body, had announced loud and clear that the steamship was leaving. Further still, a local merchant periodical, the *Savannah Wholesale Prices Current*, had gone even further in its own edition that morning:

MEMORANDUM.
The Steam Ship Savannah, Capt. Rogers, will sail from this port this day, direct for Liverpool – This is the first vessel that ever attempted to cross the Atlantic by the aid of steam:—May she have a safe and speedy passage to her destined port, and be welcomed by admiring Europeans, as a noble specimen of American ingenuity and enterprise.

Such a sendoff could not be disappointed. True to intent, Moses went to the Custom House before it closed at 1 o'clock that afternoon, and filled out the necessary paperwork for departure. Included among the required forms was an outward foreign manifest, which had to be filed by every vessel heading to a port outside the United States. On it, Moses had to spell out the cargo, item by item, that the *Savannah* was taking.

In the column marked "Packages or Articles in bulk," he simply scrawled "In Balast." This settled the question of cargo—there was none, the coal and wood on board counting as fuel.

What came as more of a surprise to any of the eyes that saw it was what Moses wrote in the blank spaces of the preamble:

Report and Manifest *of the Cargo, laden at the Port of Savannah on board the Steam Ship Savannah of Savannah Moses Rogers Master, bound for St Petersburgh in Russia*

* * *

Above and beyond all the announcements and pronouncements of lofty goals, and despite the obstacles and setbacks overcome during construction, there were still forces at work far more powerful than the dreams and determination of the Savannah Steam Ship Company.

America's adolescent economy had enjoyed a great run since 1815. Foreign appetites for the country's commodities had seemed insatiable. The push to develop the West, as well as inland from the Atlantic coast, had shown tremendous progress, in no small part due to the steamboat.

But by May of 1819, everything seemed to be tumbling down.

Crop prices—the very foundation of the prosperity—had deteriorated still further. Georgia Upland Cotton, by example, had crumpled to 15 cents bid, 17 cents asked, a full 50% below its peak just one year prior.

On top of this, the banking mania of prior years had finally come home to roost. So many new banks had been created, and so much currency printed, and credit extended, that once farm prices began to drop, the financial bubble created began to collapse, and a slow-motion panic ensued. Lenders were pressing over-stretched borrowers for repayment at the same time that trust in the means of repayment—with paper money—was being shaken. Only the true international money—gold and silver—was unquestionably beyond reproach, and people had begun to hoard specie to such a degree that it commanded a premium in trade.

This state of affairs—falling crop prices and uncertain money—left everyone, from banks, to merchants, to brokers of any kind, scrambling to balance their books. The shareholders of the Savannah Steam Ship Company were no different. While some of them had managed their personal finances conservatively, and felt far less need to retrench, there were others who were feeling acute pressure.

Events being what they were, the Company had reached a crossroads. Even if they weren't all individually in difficult straits, the directors still had to make a collective decision for all the shareholders.

After at least several weeks of private discussions, they had concluded that the best course of action was to sell the *Savannah*.

With that hard psychological step taken, the directors then faced a far more difficult question:

Where?

They still wanted to make the crossing attempt. With the *Savannah* presumably safely in European waters, it stood to reason that finding a buyer over there would be easier than finding one in the United States. After all, she would be not just the first steamship that ever crossed the Atlantic, but the first American example of the new mode of transport ever seen by that continent.

Having made this broad geographic decision, the directors then had to consider another, more specific question:

Where in Europe?

There was one obvious candidate, and that was Britain. After the Americans, there was no other nationality in the world that had taken to steamboats like the British. As the home of James Watt, father of the double-acting steam engine, Britain's relatively quick acceptance of the new mode wasn't surprising. Given the importance of ocean commerce to the British Isles, and the shareholders' emotional and financial ties to the Mother Country, it made sense that investors there might be willing to purchase the *Savannah*, or at least take an interest in her.

The one major obstacle to such a transaction was Britain's own economic downturn. The directors were keenly aware of this, thanks to newspaper reports and letters coming across the Atlantic. Shareholder Robert Mitchell, who had just returned from Liverpool a few days prior, could provide still more first-hand knowledge of just how bad things were over there. Under the circumstances, the British appetite for risk did not look particularly favorable at that moment.

The next most likely candidate might be the French, who were far behind the British in adopting steamboats, and making noises about wanting to catch up. Some of the shareholders, most notably Pott & McKinne, had extensive dealings with the cotton-buying port of Havre, so introducing Captain Rogers and the *Savannah* there would be easy.

Beyond the western edges of Europe, there were two other countries that stood out as possible buyers.

One was Sweden. This Scandinavian power had an extensive

coastline that predisposed it to adopting the new mode of transport. The very presence of Baron Klinkowström in America, and the amount of time he had spent studying the *Savannah,* spoke volumes about the interest of Sweden's leadership in steam vessels. Captain Rogers already had in his possession several letters of introduction from the Baron to senior Swedish officials, so a hospitable welcome was assured. Further buttressing this country as a candidate was William Scarbrough's familiarity with the Swedes and their region, thanks to his having just served a year as Sweden's vice-consul at Savannah, and having served as Denmark's for many years prior.

The other potential buyer was Russia. While such a far-off land might seem an odd place to sell such a revolutionary vessel, it actually made a lot of sense. In the eyes of informed Americans at the time, and steamboat entrepreneurs in particular, Russia was, in fact, an inspired (and some might say obvious) choice.

* * *

Throughout the first decades of American independence, people in the United States could not help but take notice of the great powers that still surrounded them.

To the north were their old colonial rulers, in British Canada.

To the west were French colonists in Louisiana, at least until those lands were acquired in 1803.

To the south were the colonies of Spain, stretching from Florida to Mexico.

And finally, to the east, on the Atlantic Ocean and beyond, were warships of the British and French navies, harassing American merchant vessels, impressing their seamen and stealing their cargoes.

It was, for these first generations of independent Americans, a lonely and hostile world.

By 1807, the American desire to reach out to other nations, as well as counter continuing threats from Britain, led the Madison administration to formally establish diplomatic relations with the Russian Empire. Most Americans didn't know much about this huge country on the other side of the world.

But Robert Fulton did. At the least, he knew that Russia was not only enormous, like America, but possessed lots of rivers which would benefit from steamboats. Seeing the opportunity that Russia represented, Fulton had written to American Minister John Quincy Adams in St. Petersburg, asking for a steamboat monopoly in the Russian Empire. After more than a year of long-distance discussions, Russia's emperor, Alexander, had granted just such an exclusive license, subject to Fulton's having a steamboat operating there within 3 years.

That was in December of 1813, just 6 years after Fulton had first run his *North River Steam Boat*, and only one year after Henry Bell began running his *Comet* on the Clyde River in Scotland. At that point, no other countries in the world had steamboats operating successfully. For the leader of Russia, one of the largest, most powerful nations on Earth, to have paid such attention to a new technology—indeed, one that still had a great many doubters—was truly a remarkable thing. It set the Emperor Alexander apart; it made him a *first adopter*.

The Monopoly's plan to activate this imperial grant—by sending their new steamer, the *Emperor of Russia*, across the Atlantic to St. Petersburg in the summer of 1816—was well-known to everyone in the American steamboat industry. So too was the Monopoly's failure.

This had left the Russian market wide open. It was not just the rivers of that empire which held such great promise. Russia also had distant ports on the Arctic Sea, the Baltic Sea, the Black Sea, and the Pacific Ocean. Using the predictable new mode of transport to link these ports to each other, or to major foreign ports, would be enormously beneficial. All that was required to begin this process was for someone to deliver what the Monopoly could not.

* * *

The directors of the Savannah Steam Ship Company, in reviewing all their options, had to consider the basic facts:

—British interest in the *Savannah* would be diminished by the commercial chaos;

—the French were so far behind that the leap to steamships might be too great;

—while the Swedes showed serious interest, their own experience with the new mode of transport also remained quite limited;

—on the other hand, Russia's emperor had shown an early willingness to adopt steamboats. The potential benefits of a steamship operating out of Russian ports were obvious to any true believer thinking forward.

The sum of these parts equaled the whole of the Company's conclusion: send Captain Rogers and the *Savannah* to St. Petersburg, with the goal of selling her to the Imperial Russian government.

As the Company's president and largest investor, William Scarbrough had a substantial say in this decision. He carried the additional clout of having served as Russia's vice-consul at Savannah in 1818, acquainting him in some degree with the ways and means of that giant of a country. Combined with his understanding of the other Baltic powers, Scarbrough could claim a knowledge of Russia far beyond that of his fellow shareholders.

Whether the steamship could make it as far as St. Petersburg, let alone across the Atlantic, was anybody's guess. But given the extraordinarily difficult times the shareholders were facing, they really had little choice but to take the risk.

* * *

Once Moses had filled out the necessary papers at the Custom House, and received clearance to depart, the *Savannah's* eventual destination became public knowledge. As the steamship's newly-disclosed objective slowly spread through the country's newspapers (occasionally with an exclamation point), it surely must have generated some combination of bewilderment and buzz.

Such talk was likely of little interest to Moses. He wanted to get going. Advertisements had already run in two of the city's newspapers that morning, declaring the *Savannah* would leave that day "without fail." Unfortunately, the arrangements for John Weston's inquest, perhaps along with a few other last-minute details, put a departure out of reach.

This made the next day, May 21st, the logical alternative.

Yet no advertisements were run announcing a revised departure. All that readers saw in the papers the next day were reports on the drowning of John Weston, which was explanation enough for why the steamship remained at the wharf.

One likely reason for delaying the departure was the need to bury Weston, which went beyond mere ceremony. Some superstitious mariners believed that so long as a dead crew member remained unburied, his vessel and his shipmates were at risk of experiencing storms at sea. The accepted method for nixing this curse was to ensure that their comrade's remains had been committed to the earth. Only then would it be safe.

But even with Weston properly buried, there was another possible reason for more than a day's delay in the departure: May 21st was a Friday.

The risk of setting sail on Friday was a superstition that had taken hold many centuries before. To do so was considered very unlucky, and there were several reasons to support this line of thinking.

First was the literal meaning of the word "Friday." Some thought it came from the Norse goddess called Frigga, while others believed it was named after another goddess, called Freya. It probably didn't matter to mariners which deity it was—women at sea had been considered unlucky since ancient times, so departing on a day named for a female was to be avoided.

Second, and more importantly for seamen of the Christian faith, Friday was the day that Jesus was crucified. To them, this was the day of redemption. To dare a departure on a Friday was to dare violating "the mysterious character of the day," as some called it, and court disaster at sea. Many Christian mariners at the time held such sentiments, and the last thing Moses needed was a crew in the wrong frame of mind at the beginning of a supernatural voyage.

So Friday, May the 21st came, and went.

The following morning, Saturday, May 22nd, dawned fair and breezy. Wasting as little daylight as possible, Moses ordered the engine crew to start the fires in the boilers at 7 o'clock. In the meantime, Steve oversaw the deck crew's turning of the ship, end for end, and hauling up the anchor.

Along the wharves, early-rising onlookers stood by and watched, as the steamship's crew went through their motions. On board the *Savannah* that morning were some dozen and a half souls. Completely absent from her deck and cabins were passengers of any kind. In the end, this "laudable and meritorious experiment" was to be made by no one but the crew.

By 9 o'clock, steam pressure in the boilers was high enough for Moses to order the engine into action. As dark-black smoke puffed out of the bent stack, the paddlewheels slowly began to move, pushing the *Savannah* forward. After turning downriver, she churned past the long, thick forest of shipping tied up along the waterfront. Shortly thereafter, she steamed past Fort Wayne, on the southern edge of the sandy bluff, and soon disappeared from view.

At noon, the steamship arrived off Tybee lighthouse. The wide-open sea lay dead-ahead. But instead of pressing forward, Moses ordered the engine stopped while the crew let go the anchor, to hold the *Savannah* in place. Then, the jolly boat, which normally hung from the stern, was brought in and lashed to the deck. Some of the spars attached to the masts, which were used to hold smaller maneuvering sails, were also brought down and secured. They wouldn't be needed out on the wide ocean.

By the time these tasks were complete, it was late in the day. With darkness approaching and headwinds blowing from the east, proceeding any further made little sense. While the steam engine could have pushed the *Savannah* onward, Moses wanted to avoid wasting any of his limited fuel supply. It made far more sense to save as much of it as possible for the most dangerous part of the crossing, when they reached landfall on the other side. So rather than force a departure from the coast under less than optimal conditions, Moses decided to wait.

* * *

Upriver, in Savannah itself, each of the local newspapers dutifully reported the steamship's departure. But rather than provide top-of-the-column news stories, as they had always done before, the papers instead offered just brief notes of the *Savannah*'s exit in their shipping sections. Such a subdued reaction to the start of this unprecedented undertaking seemed to betray, in the minds of those left behind, a certain undeniable apprehension.

* * *

Down at Tybee, Sunday found the winds still less than ideal. Again, Moses decided against leaving.

On Monday, May 24th, he waited no longer. Before the sun rose, Moses ordered the steam up, and some of the sails deployed. With clear skies and only light breezes to resist, the *Savannah* steamed over the sandbar by 6 o'clock, bid goodbye to the local pilot, and churned onward. Also taking her departure with the steamship that morning was the Buenos Aires privateer *La Fortuna*, heading for parts unknown.

After several hours of steaming to the northeast, the *Savannah* reached the powerful currents of the Gulf Stream. Still wishing to conserve his fuel, Moses ordered the engine stopped and the wheels taken in, while Steve led the deck crew in making "all sail set to best advantage."

By noon, Steve reckoned they were some 8 leagues (or 24 miles) northeast of the lighthouse. Based upon this last sighting of Tybee, he recorded their official departure time from the coast.

With all preparations and omens behind them, and the Atlantic before them, the *Savannah* and her crew took leave of land. In so doing, they also came face-to-face with the invisible barrier that was arguably as powerful as Nature itself.

CHAPTER ELEVEN

ACROSS

BY THE DAWN of Monday, June 14th, the steamship *Savannah* and her crew found themselves rising and plunging through turbulent seas, while passing rain squalls drenched everyone and everything that stood upon the deck.

Conditions in the North Atlantic had been much the same for the week prior, and under the circumstances, making use of the new mode of power had been difficult. The crew had to hope the sea and sky would improve soon, for they well-knew that the most dangerous part of their voyage was nearly upon them. Based upon their last calculated position, somewhere ahead, to the northeast, lay the coast of Ireland.

Since nearly the start of June, Moses and Steve had set the steamship on a course pointing due east. This was standard procedure for any crossing of the Atlantic from America to the British Isles. Since the power of the Gulf Stream would naturally carry any vessel to the northeast (and right into the west coast of Ireland), it was necessary to sail as far east as possible en route. Ideally, the correct combination of Gulf Stream and wind would allow the vessel to avoid being pushed into Ireland's west coast, and instead skirt along the south coast, ending up in the Irish Sea. Once there, entry into any ports on the eastern coast of Ireland, or the western coast of Britain, could be accomplished with relative ease.

At noon that Monday, Steve measured the steamship's latitude, which he calculated to be 51 degrees, 31 minutes North. This was nearly two degrees further north than the previous day's reading. Both he and Moses knew that if they had not encountered the southern Irish coast at that northerly latitude, it could only mean that the Gulf Stream was pulling the *Savannah* right toward Ireland's west coast. Not wanting to slip any further north, they adjusted course, sailing southeast by east.

Later that same day, they came upon a schooner called the *Ebenezer*, whose crew was grappling with the loss of their main sail's stabilizing pole (or *boom*). The *Savannah* was maneuvered close enough for Moses and Steve to hail the schooner. The *Ebenezer*, they discovered, was ten days out of Liverpool, on a voyage to Newfoundland. Under the circumstances, the schooner's crew must have had a good sense of where to find the Irish coast. Moses and Steve, their intuition confirmed, kept the *Savannah* sailing southeast by east.

Through the night and into Tuesday morning, the *Savannah* appeared to be making little progress. At noon, the overcast sky forced Steve to calculate their latitude by dead reckoning, instead of by direct observation with a sextant. His estimated reading of 51 degrees, 25 minutes North indicated that they had made almost no headway to the south.

By evening, the slight breezes of earlier in the day had withered to a calm. Soon thereafter, the motion of the ocean became quite heavy, and the *Savannah* began to rock and roll, making the helmsman's task of maintaining her course all the more difficult. This was very close to the worst of all worlds for a sailing ship: caught in the Gulf Stream off the southwest coast of Ireland, with all waves and no wind.

But the *Savannah* had other means, and this was precisely the circumstance in which to use them. Moses ordered the engine crew to fire up the boilers, and the deck crew to deploy the paddlewheels.

In short order, the steam engine "set the wheels to going," as Steve later wrote, despite the danger posed to them by the powerful waves. The deck crew, in turn, "took in all sail."

Through the night and into early Wednesday morning, the *Savannah* continued churning through the water under steam power, at a steady 5 knots. A few hours past dawn, Steve and the crew finally spotted land. About 6 leagues (or 18 miles) to the east, they could make out Mizen Head, the southernmost peninsula which jutted out from Ireland's western coast. It was still hardly the ideal place to be, but the new mode of power nevertheless had improved their position since the previous evening.

A light northern breeze obligingly came along soon thereafter. Since this could help keep the steamship away from the treacherous coast, Moses ordered the engine stopped, the wheels brought in, and the sails deployed. Through the rest of what Steve described as a pleasant day, the *Savannah* was blown to the south, eventually rounding Fastnet Rock, a tiny, craggy island to the southeast of Mizen Head.

By the early morning darkness of Thursday, June 17th, the friendly northern winds had died to a calm. While the *Savannah* was in a slightly better position by that time, already having rounded the southwestern-most points of Ireland, the risk to her remained virtually the same as it had been 30 hours earlier. Any sudden appearance of strong southern winds, in combination with the Gulf Stream, could easily slam the vessel against the rocky shore. The best course of action was to move as far along the south coast of Ireland, and into the relative safety of the Irish Sea, as soon as possible.

So once again, Moses ordered the steam up.

* * *

Also in the far southwest corner of Ireland, midway between Fastnet Rock and the mainland, is a small, rough, rocky island by the name of Cape Clear.

Exposed as it is to both the winds and the waves of the Atlantic, Cape Clear Island has always born the brunt of Nature's power. In the early 19th century, no forests of any size could grow there, due to the strength of the storms that the island regularly endured. For Cape Clear's hardy inhabitants, there was no choice but to secure the thatched roofs of their small cottages with straw ropes or old fish netting, to keep them from blowing away. Making a living was just as harsh as the weather, with most residents either laboring to harvest fish from the sea, or barley, flax and potatoes from what little tillable soil they could find on land.

Topographically, the south side of the island is the most dramatic, with enormous rock cliffs steeply descending hundreds of feet to the crashing waves below. On top of those cliffs in 1819, some 480 feet above the ocean, sat a new lighthouse, tall and cylindrical in shape. Next to it was an older, smaller, fort-like stone tower, which had several small windows facing the sea.

Rising from the center of this smaller tower's flat roof was a tall wooden pole. Attached to the top of the pole were two straight wooden arms, which could be pulled into different positions, like the hands of a clock, by means of attached ropes that ran down the pole and into the tower. Whenever the occupants of this little tower wished, they could move the arms into different positions, thereby sending a coded message of letters and numbers, which could be seen far beyond their own isolated position.

Such was the simple yet clever device known as a *semaphore signal station*, one of dozens lining the coasts of Ireland and Britain, used primarily to spot smugglers trying to beat the tariff laws. Cape Clear's signal station, situated as it was off the southwestern tip of Ireland, was among the most remote in the entire system.

When the lookouts on duty there scanned the brightening horizon on the early morning of Thursday, June 17th, 1819, they spotted something unusual out at sea, to the south. In short order, the lookouts "cleared" their signal pole, and sent out a message, to be picked up by the nearest signal station six miles to the eastward, at Kedge Point, on the Irish mainland. The communication was then relayed up the coast, through more than half a dozen signal stations, until it reached the port of Cork.

This was the site of a Royal Navy base, as well as the headquarters of Admiral Sir Josias Rowley, commander of all British government vessels in Ireland.

The base's own semaphore station, having received and decoded the message, immediately sent it up the chain-of-command, for the communication demanded immediate action:

—*Cape Clear was reporting a ship afire out at sea.*

* * *

As the *Savannah* steamed along the southwestern Irish coast that Thursday morning, the crew eventually was able to make out the Old Head of Kinsale, a rocky peninsula projecting out from the mainland.

Shortly thereafter, they also spotted the approach of a small pilot boat. Once its captain had maneuvered his craft close enough, Moses and Steve were able to parlay. The pilot boat's name was *Mary*, and she hailed from the nearby port of Kinsale. Her captain wanted to know the steamship's intentions.

The *Savannah*, in the process of putting much of the most dangerous part of the Irish coast behind her, had nearly depleted her remaining fuel stores. So Moses told the *Mary*'s captain that he was planning to put in to Kinsale for some supplies. (In all likelihood, Moses was thinking "coal.")

This information being worthy of advance notice, the *Mary*'s captain bid farewell, turned north, and sprinted off to Kinsale, bearing news of the steamship's impending arrival.

* * *

Once word had reached the Royal Navy base at Cork that a ship was afire off Cape Clear, the imperative to render aid was obvious. Orders were quickly given to dispatch His Majesty's Revenue Cruiser *Kite*, under the command of Lieutenant John Bowie.

Lieutenant Bowie himself was hardly a neophyte. Having gone to sea at the age of 17, he had served more than six years before receiving his commission as a Royal Navy lieutenant in 1811. Bowie had been on the Irish station since 1817, first commanding the 16-gun revenue cruiser *Minerva*. He was then given charge of the *Kite*, in early 1818. With two years patrolling the Irish coast under his belt, and one year spent commanding the *Kite*, it would be fair to say that Lieutenant Bowie knew his craft, and he knew these waters.

Beyond Bowie was the *Kite* herself. Put into service little more than one year before, this single-masted sloop represented the state-of-the-art for coast guard cruisers. She had a mast that was taller than the length of her sleek black hull, and an uncommonly long bowsprit projecting forward. This arrangement allowed her crew to deploy any number of mainsails and jib-sails, in a variety of positions, to take maximum advantage of whatever winds they might encounter. And unlike the other revenue cruisers stationed around Ireland, which had from 10 to 16 guns weighing and slowing them down, the *Kite* had but one cannon to haul through the water. All of these features for this particular cruiser had been deliberately combined to achieve one overriding goal—in a phrase, the *Kite* was built for speed.

Once the revenue cruiser had angled close enough to her objective that morning, Lieutenant Bowie could see the smoking ship. The absence of any sails deployed on the vessel would have made sense, if the distressed ship's crew thought the canvas might be in danger of combusting. The cruiser bore in to assist.

As the *Kite* drew nearer, there came a moment at which Lieutenant Bowie realized that what he and the Cape Clear signalers thought they had seen was, in fact, false. The victim wasn't afire at all. It was actually a steam vessel, propelling itself through the water without the aid of any sails.

Once he knew what truly lay before him, Lieutenant Bowie justifiably could have called off the rescue mission. But his curiosity must have taken command, and he ordered the *Kite* to give chase.

By 11 o'clock that morning, this steam vessel, rigged like a ship and flying the American flag, had churned well past the Old Head of Kinsale. Despite all best efforts, the *Kite*, slicing through the water at 10 knots, was unable to catch up.

Presumably, Lieutenant Bowie had ordered his crew to hoist the *revenue colors*, which included a long, thin red pennant, signifying that the *Kite* was in pursuit, and wanted the nearest vessel to stop. Whether the steamship misreckoned or mis-regarded such a signal is not at all clear. In any case, Lieutenant Bowie found it necessary to use stronger means to communicate, and ordered the *Kite*'s gun crew into action.

The cruiser fired off a warning shot toward the steamship, but the message from this first blast was not received, as the smoking, splashing vessel pressed onward. Not until several warning shots had been fired did the subject's paddlewheels finally slow down, and come to a halt.

The *Kite* sailed up, and came alongside. Just as the sun reached high noon, Lieutenant Bowie climbed aboard what was the American steamship *Savannah*, from Savannah, and met Captain Moses Rogers.

Lieutenant Bowie enquired as to their destination, and Moses rattled off the ports of call he expected to make:

—Liverpool and London, in Britain;

—then Havre, in France;

—and finally St. Petersburg, Russia.

Moses apparently made no mention to Lieutenant Bowie of making port in Ireland, having changed his mind from earlier that morning.

He simply may have decided not to incur the delay inherent for such a stop. Stormy weather in the mid-Atlantic aside, the voyage had gone well-enough so far. Surely it would be better to press on, and achieve the fastest possible crossing time to Liverpool.

Moses also might have considered the likelihood that putting into an Irish port could be interpreted cynically by steam skeptics. This was especially true after the *Kite* had stopped the steamship, and Moses learned the reason for the cruiser's pursuit. If he then took his creation into port, either at Kinsale or Cork, it wouldn't be difficult for the naysayers to combine the *Kite*'s distress mission with the steamship's port call, and conclude that the *Savannah* really had been in trouble, and was forced to put in. The perceived success of the crossing could be damaged accordingly. So too could the very idea that oceanic steam travel was safe, a judgment the skeptics would gladly welcome.

Whatever his reasons, Moses had changed his mind, and decided to push on to Liverpool.

Once Lieutenant Bowie had finished looking around the steamship, he bid goodbye and disembarked. By that time, the winds had shifted to more advantageous southwesterlies, so Moses ordered Steve to deploy the *Savannah*'s sails "to the best advantage," while the deckhands kept watch of the *Kite*, as she bore away.

* * *

At least a few of the *Savannah*'s crew must have been familiar with the experience of being stopped by a British warship. It was, through much of the United States' early existence, a common event, brought on by a Royal Navy in perpetual search of "deserters."

Such a peremptory trial at sea certainly was not new to Steve. Back in the summer of 1809, when he was on his first cruise in the *Connecticut* with Captain Blin, the brig had been stopped in transit by a British man-o-war. On board the *Connecticut* had come a naval officer, who demanded to see proof that none of Captain Blin's crew had escaped from the Royal Navy.

The means of doing so was for each crewman to produce his *Seaman's Protection Certificate*. This single piece of paper, issued by an American custom house, verified the holder as being a citizen of the United States. Congress had mandated these documents in 1796, for the very purpose of protecting American seamen from being impressed into the Royal Navy.

Each member of the *Connecticut*'s crew provided this evidence of citizenship, except Steve. In the haste of departure from New London, he had overlooked the minor yet important task of getting a certificate issued in his name.

The Royal Navy officer took this lack of credentials as cause to accuse Stevens Rogers of being a runaway from London.

Captain Blin quickly stepped in, asserting that he personally knew Steve's family, and could vouch for the young man's citizenship.

But the British officer refused to buy this claim, and told Steve to get his things together for the return "home."

Captain Blin well-knew that Steve would not go to London. As the one man who had a chance to prevent Rogers' impressment into the Royal Navy, Blin stood his ground, and issued an ultimatum: take the lad, and you'll have to take the *Connecticut*, as well.

This challenge put the boarding officer in a bind. His own story about Steve was obviously a ruse, yet the young seaman didn't have any papers. It made no sense that this Yankee captain would take such a risk with his vessel unless he was certain of his stance. So the officer backed down, leaving empty-handed, and Steve was saved.

Shortly after this close call, Steve sought the help of one of his shipmates. What Steve needed was some way to prove his American citizenship, so this fellow mariner gave him the best substitute for paper credentials available under the circumstances.

Later on that same voyage, the *Connecticut* was stopped again by a British warship, and once again a Royal Navy officer was sent aboard the brig to look for deserters and check papers. When the officer demanded to see everyone's protection certificate, Steve obligingly answered:

"These, Sir, are my credentials."

Pulling up his shirt sleeve, Steve revealed a very distinctive tattoo emblazoned upon his arm, which included his name crowned by an American flag and eagle.

The boldness of Steve's behavior, as well as the permanency of his proof, was enough to prevent a confrontation. Once again, the boarding officer departed empty-handed. While Stevens Rogers had managed to escape impressment for a second time, his encounters with the Royal Navy were far from over.

* * *

With the *Kite* gone and the winds favorable, the steamship *Savannah* proceeded by sail along the south coast of Ireland, heading toward St. George's Channel, which is the entryway to the Irish Sea.

Early the next morning, June 18th, the winds died to a calm yet again. Unfortunately, running the steam engine for any substantial length of time was no longer an option. As Steve noted in the logbook, there was "no Cole to git steam up."

For that Friday, through Saturday and into early Sunday, Steve and the crew made the best of what wind they could find, sailing the *Savannah* in a northeasterly direction, across St. George's Channel and toward the coast of Wales.

At 4 o'clock on Sunday morning, they spotted Holyhead lighthouse, on the northwestern tip of Wales. Once they rounded Holyhead, Moses and Steve set a new course, heading due east, toward Liverpool.

Four hours later, they were close enough to their objective to encounter one of Liverpool's single-masted pilot boats, marked with the number "10" on its sail. In due course, a pilot from the boat climbed aboard the *Savannah*. He would guide her into the River Mersey, and then to the city of Liverpool itself, which lay a couple of miles upriver from the sea.

By 2 o'clock that afternoon, the *Savannah* reached the Mersey's entrance, where a series of channel markers showed the proper route over the sandbar. But the pilot said it wasn't safe to cross—the water level was too low. So Moses ordered the steamship to a halt, and everyone was compelled to wait for the incoming tide.

It wasn't long before the *Savannah* began taking on the properties of a lodestar. As her crew looked on, out from the river and shore came a variety of boats filled with hundreds of people, rowing and sailing their way toward the steamship.

Among the first of this greeting fleet to reach the *Savannah* was a small rowboat full of sailors, which had come from a Royal Navy vessel anchored nearby. Once this boat had pulled alongside the steamship, the officer in command called out to Steve, who was then on deck.

"Where is your master?"

Steve replied with the American answer of the age.

"I have no master, Sir."

To this the officer countered more explicitly:

"Where's your Captain, then?"

"He's below—do you wish to see him?"

"I do, Sir," replied the officer.

In due course, Moses was told of the request, and he came topside.

"Why do you wear that pennant, Sir?" asked the officer.

"That pennant" was the long, thin red-white-and-blue flag flying high from the *Savannah*'s mainmast. It was called a *coachwhip pennant*, and it held a great deal of meaning.

Since the Middle Ages, narrow pennants had been flown from warships to help distinguish them from merchant vessels. In the British Isles, the narrowest of these—coachwhip pennants—had developed an even more elevated status, thanks to a legend born of events a century and a half before.

It was believed that during the First Anglo-Dutch War of 1652, a Dutch admiral had flown a broomstick from his mainmast to warn his British adversary that he was about to be swept from the sea. The Royal Navy admiral had responded by raising an actual coachwhip in retort, signaling that the Dutchman was about to get a whipping. Battle ensued, and the British emerged victorious. True or not, this story stuck, and thereafter, it was said that the Royal Navy had made the flying of a "coachwhip" pennant their symbol for a vessel of war.

In time, whether by long-established tradition or imitation of the British, other nations also adopted the coachwhip pennant as their symbol for government-owned vessels. This naturally included the recently-born United States, which had designed its version of a coachwhip to look like a very long, skinny Stars and Stripes.

That the *Savannah* flew such a pennant—when it normally symbolized warships or other publicly-owned vessels—was due to the earliest efforts of American steamboat operators. Since they considered their paddlewheelers to be for the benefit of everyone, New World promoters of the new mode of transport viewed their steamboats as a form of public vessel. To communicate this fact, they often flew a coachwhip pennant from the steamer's auxiliary mast.

By flying a coachwhip from the *Savannah*'s mainmast, Captain Rogers was simply following this new tradition. Perhaps he also wanted to fly this particular pennant out of simple pride, as a symbol of what the fledgling United States could accomplish.

"Because my country allows me to, Sir," answered Moses.

"My commander thinks it was done to insult him," replied the Royal Navy officer, "and if you don't take it down he will send a force that will do it."

Faced with this ultimatum, Moses ordered the coachwhip pennant hauled down. In its place, he directed the raising of a broad blue pennant covered with stars—this was the flag of a U.S. Navy squadron commander. Then he turned, and called out to the *Savannah*'s crew—

"Get the hot-water engine ready!"

Upon hearing this, the British officer immediately ordered his oarsmen into action. The small boat quickly turned about, and rowed away with all haste.

The officer's misplaced fear, and retreat, was founded in one of the myths of the U.S. Navy's steam battery, the *Fulton*. Among that vessel's many proposed weapons was an apparatus to shoot hot water from the engine's boiler onto the deck of any attacking vessel. While not included in the final construction, news of this novel weaponry had made it across the Atlantic, and into the British perception of what the *Fulton* could do. By implying the *Savannah* had such a feature, Captain Rogers had cleverly played upon that fear, forcing his antagonist's withdrawal, and defusing the confrontation before it escalated any further.

* * *

The verbal jousting which took place over the *Savannah*'s coach-whip pennant was not an isolated incident. Indeed, it was in many ways emblematic of the complex relationship between the United States and the United Kingdom at the time. How Americans viewed their British cousins, and vice versa, was based upon a tangled web of beliefs, emotions and experiences, the bulk of which had been created over the course of little more than one generation.

At the very center of this web were memories of the American Revolution itself, which usually generated very different reactions on either side of the Atlantic.

In the American view, the objectives of that war could be described using the most righteously powerful of words, such as *independence, self-government*, and *liberty*.

From the British perspective, however, the words used to describe that war carried their own force, and a very different meaning: what the Americans had done was commit *treason*, and engage in a *rebellion*.

For all the two countries shared in ancestry, language, political thought and values, the feelings from such a violent family feud—indeed, a kind of civil war—could not help but linger, for years. And for those who had been caught up directly in the struggle, the hard memories could last far longer.

Such was the case for the people of greater New London, Connecticut, once the Revolution reached their doorstep, in September of 1781.

At that point in the struggle, General George Washington had aborted a planned attack on British-occupied New York City, and was marching his combined army of American and French troops to the south. Washington's new objective was the entrapment of a large British force under General Cornwallis, which had landed at Yorktown, on a peninsula in Virginia.

The British, seeking a means of distracting Washington, decided to send a raiding force into Long Island Sound. Their objective was to attack one of the primary havens for American privateers in the area, which was the port of New London. The task of commanding this expedition was given to the most prominent revolutionary-turned-redcoat of the war, General Benedict Arnold.

Early on the morning of September 6th, General Arnold landed his troops on both sides of Connecticut's Thames River. The contingent on the west side of the river, led by Arnold himself, marched north, quickly overrunning Fort Trumbull, and then New London itself, which they promptly put to the torch.

The British force landing on the east side of the river also marched north, and launched several assaults on Fort Griswold, which guarded the Thames River and Groton's port area.

Based upon a mistaken belief that the Americans in Fort Griswold were giving up, the British advanced to accept the surrender, only to be met with musket fire. Incensed by the perceived treachery, the British troops went berserk, charged, breached the fort's walls, and forced the garrison to surrender. The British then proceeded to bayonet to death many of the American wounded, and selectively burn and pillage parts of nearby Groton.

By the time British forces had returned to their ships, much of New London and Groton lay in smoldering ruins. Over 160 buildings of all kinds were destroyed, along with most of the wharves and shipping. Many families, including over a dozen members of the extended Rogers clan, lost property in the fighting and fires.

But it was the loss of life, particularly at Fort Griswold, that cut the deepest. The brutality of the redcoats, commanded by the most reviled of the turncoats, led the surviving kin of those killed in the fort to literally chisel their feelings onto the tombstones of their loved ones.

Moses was only two years old when all of this happened, and Steve was but a twinkle in his mother's eye, but if they had spent any time during their childhoods playing in graveyards, as most boys do, then the words on those memorials to the dead probably left some impression—

"*... fell a sacrifice to british Barbarity...*"

"*... commanded by that most despicable parricide, Benedict Arnold...*"

While the immediacy of the attack on New London, and the Revolution itself, had faded somewhat by the first decade of the 19th century, there were still many participants for whom the feelings remained very strong. Whether they were among the dwindling number of founding fathers, or survivors of Fort Griswold, or old New Jersey farmers named Kennedy, sharing their experiences with the younger generation went beyond mere reminiscence—it was imperative.

Then, with the coming of the second war in 1812, the old animosities felt toward the British, largely kept in-check for so long, were re-ignited.

Even so, American attitudes regarding their former colonial master were hardly universal. While many Americans thought British actions—from impressments of mariners on the high seas, to incitement of the native Indian tribes on the frontier—justified a declaration of war in 1812, a sizeable minority did not. The Congressional vote for war reflected this divided opinion. In the Senate, an amendment calling for hostilities against Britain only at sea was barely defeated, and the final votes for a declaration of war in both houses were about 60% in favor, and 40% against. This split within the country lasted through much of the conflict, leading to deeply-felt patriotism in some, and equally strong doubt and dissension in others.

When it came to active participation in the war effort, individual Americans had a fairly straightforward choice. For those who wanted to serve, the obvious options were volunteering for military service, or signing up with a privateer. For the rest, going about one's business to the greatest degree possible was the order of the day.

So this latter choice was for Captain Moses Rogers, who kept on steamboating out of Philadelphia as best he could, given the Royal Navy blockade of the American coast. Venturing any further toward the sea than Wilmington, Delaware was simply too dangerous. His Majesty's warships could appear almost anywhere, with little or no warning. Adelia's hometown of Stonington learned that reality firsthand, when it was briefly bombarded by the Royal Navy in August of 1814, fortunately with little damage done.

Stevens Rogers, on the other hand, had experiences of a different character altogether. When war was declared in June of 1812, there were plenty of American merchant vessels at sea, and still others which pressed on with planned departures, their owners believing the conflict would be short-lived. These merchantmen became easy prey for the Royal Navy, and on one of their early captures was Steve himself. He was taken to England, but soon freed in a prisoner exchange.

Back home and in need of work by early 1813, Steve signed up to serve as the mate on a schooner, the *Favourite*, under the command of Captain George West. Captain West and his craft, like many other coastal traders during the war, tried to make a living by evading the Royal Navy's imperfect blockade.

On April 5th of that year, the *Favourite* was risking a run from Plymouth, North Carolina to the northward, with a cargo of corn, "pease," hogs lard, hams, tar, and flaxseed. Her destination was Eastport, in the District of Maine, near the frontier with British Canada.

Unfortunately, while skimming over the Atlantic some 50 miles southeast of Long Island, New York, the schooner ran smack into HMS *Valiant*, a 74-gun ship-of-the-line on blockade patrol.

Despite the benefit of fog, the *Favourite*'s attempt to flee proved futile. After a chase of nearly two hours, Captain West accepted the inevitable, and surrendered to the *Valiant*. The warship sent over an officer and four seamen, who directed the schooner's crew to sail to the Royal Navy base at Halifax, Nova Scotia.

For a second time, Steve found himself a prisoner of war. Once more, however, his innate good-humor seems to have put him on the right side of his captors, and he was included in a prisoner exchange a few months later.

Steve tempted capture yet again in December of 1814, when he joined the crew of the ship *Armata* as a third mate. That vessel's captain, Lodowick Leeds, risked sailing from Philadelphia to Amsterdam when rumors of imminent peace were running thick. Luckily, the Christmas eve signing of the Treaty of Ghent, which ended the war, ensured a safe passage across the Atlantic for Steve and the *Armata*, which picked up a cargo from Liverpool for the return trip.

The British perspective during the War of 1812 mirrored the American one. While some had itched for a fight, others despaired over hostilities with a member of the family, and their country's best trading partner. Yet as the conflict dragged on, British animosities had intensified.

The hard feelings didn't end with the war, either. Once peace had been restored in early 1815, both participants and interested observers were able to take stock of the war that had been waged at sea, and the results were nothing less than stunning. While the Royal Navy had captured or destroyed 19 U.S. Navy vessels and over 1,000 enemy merchantmen, the Americans, it turned out, had done even better.

They had managed to sink or capture some 25 Royal Navy vessels, along with over 1,400 British merchantmen.

Since Lord Nelson's momentous victory at Trafalgar in 1805, no country had been able to challenge Britain's Royal Navy. That the United States had been able to fight it to a virtual draw was incomprehensible. Such an outcome felt like victory to the Americans, and to the British it felt like defeat.

Returning to normalcy after the war didn't take long, thanks to the strong economic relationship between Britain and the United States. Commerce was immediately revitalized, as the bounty of American agriculture flowed east across the Atlantic, and in return came shiploads of British manufactured goods. It was really the merchants on both sides of the Anglo-American family who took the lead in mending ties through trade.

But even by the spring of 1819, the bitterness in both countries was difficult to ignore. Among the evidence was recent news of dueling between British and American naval officers at Gibraltar.

Remarkably more dangerous had been the previous year's American incursion into Spanish Florida against the Seminoles. When General Andrew Jackson's troops captured two British subjects during the fighting, the Hero of New Orleans ordered them put on trial in the field, charged with spying and aiding the enemy. Both men were found guilty, and General Jackson immediately had them put to death.

In the United States, reaction to news of the executions ranged from cheers to condemnation.

In Britain, the reaction was fury. Fanned by the island's newspapers, the British public took up the cause of their two dead countrymen, Arbuthnot and Ambrister, turning their names into a rallying cry for reparations, or renewed battle against the Americans.

Only the Cabinet of Lord Liverpool, Britain's prime minister, acted as a brake on calls for retaliation. The Cabinet's position proved to be both prudent and correct. Once more detailed reports were delivered to London, it was clear to Lord Liverpool's ministers that Arbuthnot and Ambrister had been engaged in activities which "deprived them of any claim on their own government for interference."

Nevertheless, it had been a close call. America's minister to London, Richard Rush, would later recount being told by Britain's foreign secretary that:

. . . had the English Cabinet felt and acted otherwise than it did, such was the temper of Parliament, and such the feeling of the country, that he believed WAR MIGHT HAVE BEEN PRODUCED BY HOLDING UP A FINGER; and he even thought that an address to the Crown might have been carried for one, BY NEARLY AN UNANIMOUS VOTE.

The more recent news that Spain had agreed to cede Florida to the United States added to the sense within Britain's hierarchy that the Americans simply wanted all of Europe out of all of the Americas.

And to what end?

Beyond increasing the size of a rapidly expanding United States, it appeared the Americans also wanted to spread the very democratic ideals born out of their revolution, a concept viewed by much of the British establishment as "the most sinister radicalism."

Yet counterbalancing this antagonistic view of the United States held by some in Britain was an entirely different perspective shared by many others. It was based upon the recognition that America was peopled by "our own flesh and blood," as well as the sense that opportunities for trade and investment there had only just begun. And for those who found the cost of land and living too dear in the British Isles, the United States offered the possibility of a new beginning in a New World.

* * *

Such was the state of sentiments between the United States and the United Kingdom in the years that followed the end of their second war. The relationship was arguably the most complex, and conflicted, it had ever been.

But at the mouth of the River Mersey on Sunday afternoon, June 20th, 1819, the strong feelings on both sides must have been largely hidden from view. Bobbing around the American steamship *Savannah* was a small armada of boats, filled with hundreds of British cousins, who had all come out to greet her in recognition of one simple fact: she had made it across.

CHAPTER TWELVE

ALBION, HOSPITALITY, AND RUMORS

B Y LATE AFTERNOON, the tide at the River Mersey's entrance had risen far enough.

At 5 o'clock, Moses ordered the paddlewheels deployed. Once that was done, Steve had the deck crew climb high and furl all the sails.

Down below, Mr. Blackman and his engine crew already had steam up in the boilers. The wood previously used for kindling also would have to serve as the primary fuel, since there was no coal left to run the engine.

With all the sails furled and smoke gently rising from the bent stack, Moses gave the order to proceed. The *Savannah*'s wheels slowly began to turn, pushing her over the massive sandbar and into the river.

* * *

However inconvenient the low tide at the Mersey's entrance had proved to be, it did have one consolation: the three hour wait provided more than enough time for news of the steamship's arrival to travel upriver, to Liverpool.

Up and down the city's waterfront and out into the streets, word of the *Savannah*'s appearance was spread by a thousand tongues or more. By the time a tiny trail of smoke could be seen rising on the western horizon, the people of Liverpool were ready.

* * *

As the *Savannah* proceeded upriver, the view before the crew was expansive. The Mersey itself was deep blue and very wide, measuring some 1½ miles across at the entrance, and narrowing only slightly once it reached Liverpool. In some ways, it felt more like a lake than a river.

Off the right (or *starboard*) side of the steamship, along the Mersey's south bank, lay the county of Cheshire. The shoreline there was largely undeveloped. The only exceptions were at the small villages of Birkenhead and Woodside, where some substantial new construction could be seen, thanks to their being the termini of several cross-river steamboat ferries.

Beyond the shoreline, the landscape of Cheshire rose gently, covered by an irregular checkerboard of light green and dark green fields, bordered by even darker green hedgerows, and speckled with the occasional cottage or barn. This serene scene carried on for about three miles to the southward, until reaching what appeared to be a long ridge.

At the highest point on this ridge, visible from both Liverpool and the sea, was a five-story stone tower, called the Bidston lighthouse. Surrounding this sentinel were dozens of flagpoles, most of which belonged to the various merchant houses in the city. When the Bidston lookouts sighted a vessel approaching from the sea, they would fly a pennant from the owning merchant's flagpole, thereby announcing the craft's arrival.

Off the left (or *larboard*) side of the steamship was the north shore of the River Mersey, and the county of Lancashire. There, the view was quite different. At first, the landscape looked somewhat similar to Cheshire, being farmland and cottages. But this soon gave way, further upriver, to small collections of dwellings and windmills, dotting the landscape right down to the shore. These assemblages eventually turned into a solid mass of buildings, spires and domes that was Liverpool itself.

Separating the city from the river was a long, thin gray line. This was Liverpool's quay, made of huge stone blocks which stretched for over a mile upriver.

Just behind the gray quay was a thicker, uneven line of structures, dullish red in color. This layer was the mass of enormous brick warehouses, five or six stories in height, which spanned most of the waterfront.

Poking up from behind these warehouses were intermittent clusters of masts. Each such concentration marked the location of one of the city's *docks*. These large rectangular pools allowed vessels to enter and leave through gates (or *locks*), which were designed, in the case of "wet" docks, to hold in the water at low tide. Once inside a dock, a vessel, shielded from adverse conditions out on the river, could be moved to any one of its four sides, and loaded or unloaded at will. With 40 acres of these protected docks in operation, and another 11 acres under construction, it was little wonder that Liverpool had become the fastest growing port in Britain, and was second only to London in cargo volume.

As the *Savannah* steamed toward this city of 120,000 people, her crew eventually realized that Liverpool's distant, solid shape was seemingly beginning to shift and move. The closer the steamship got, the more apparent it must have been that the movement was far from imaginary. The massive, long quay was packed with spectators. So were the decks of the shipping moored along the quay. Yet more onlookers bulged out of windows and crowned the roofs of warehouses near the waterfront. And out on the Mersey itself were still others, watching from within a new flotilla of boats that were jockeying into the best viewing positions.

As the smoking, splashing *Savannah* approached, the multitudes crowding the waterfront began to cheer and wave and huzzah, saluting what they knew was the most technologically advanced ocean vessel ever seen on the River Mersey. As soon as the opportunity presented itself, the small boats floating nearby maneuvered up to the steamship's side, and their occupants began climbing aboard the new arrival. One seaman aboard the *Savannah* later recounted that the deck became so packed with people that crewmen had trouble performing their duties as the steamship came to anchor.

For Captain Moses Rogers, it must have been one of the proudest moments of his life. Just one dozen years after being present at the creation, this former sailing sloop master, the son of a lumberyard owner, had done it. He had shown the world that this new mode of transportation was more than a mere provincial curiosity—indeed, it represented the beginning of a global revolution.

* * *

The steamship *Savannah*'s arrival in Albion, the ancient Roman name for Britain, was nothing less than a triumph, given the public's response.

But the tumultuous welcome was deceptive, for it masked a British nation far more unsettled than first appearances would have let on. Throughout much of the United Kingdom of England, Ireland, Scotland and Wales, there was growing and fervent agitation for political reform.

Such calls for change in Britain had come in waves since the American and French revolutions of 1776 and 1789. This most recent movement in Albion was made up of political activists called *Reformers*. While their ranks included people from many walks of life, the bulk of the Reformers were those who worked in the country's factories and fields, especially in the middle and northern counties of England, as well as Scotland.

What the Reformers wanted was simple and straightforward:

—the right to vote for all men;

—the annual election of Parliament, so that members could be replaced quickly if they failed to address the country's problems;

—repeal of the nation's Corn Laws, which gave government the power to limit grain imports, thereby keeping food prices high;

—a cut in taxes, which the Reformers felt they paid disproportionately, as well as a cut in public spending, which they believed was extravagant;

—and at the very least, automatically giving anyone paying taxes the right to vote.

But in the eyes of Britain's existing political establishment of property-owning voters, the need for such reforms was far from obvious:

—giving the vote to *all* men seemed ludicrous, since so many had so little education to call upon in the exercise of such a responsibility;

—a Parliament that was elected every year would be too volatile, and inevitably would change things that were best left alone;

—repeal of the Corn Laws would kill the profitable prices which landed farmers in Britain received for their crops;

—reducing taxes or spending seemed to ignore the fact that the government was struggling already with dramatically reduced finances;

—and "no taxation without representation" was a cry the British establishment had heard a generation before, from the other side of the Atlantic, and they did not want to hear of it again.

The Reformers were hardly satisfied with such reactions to their demands. At the start of 1819, they began to organize on a scale never before seen in Britain. Their efforts were aided by worsening economic conditions, especially a lack of work and affordable food in the manufacturing districts.

Previously, the Reformers' methods had focused upon organizing mass meetings and promoting petitions to the government. But this time around, the reform movement was going to push harder, thanks to a cadre of fanatics within their leadership who pined for change far beyond the goals of the moderates. These *Radicals*, as they were called, wanted nothing less than a revolution in Britain, akin to what had happened in France thirty years earlier.

So instead of just holding meetings and promoting petitions, the Radicals began agitating their followers to make stronger public demonstrations, and take seemingly malevolent measures. Reform meetings held through the winter and spring of 1819 openly discussed the uniting of all the local reform societies throughout Britain into one national organization. Each local society would then elect delegates to represent them within that larger body.

This new effort greatly worried the political establishment. To them, it smacked of a drive to create an illegal *shadow parliament*, intended to challenge the real one.

Adding to the establishment's unease was news that the Radicals had formed something called the Committee of Two Hundred, a council that met secretly in London and coordinated reform activities around the country. It was not difficult for some observers to construe this organ as the potential forerunner to a *shadow government*.

Still more disconcerting were reports that masses of Reformers had begun to drill like soldiers in formation, often under the guidance of military veterans. These exercises, intended to promote better organization at reform rallies, looked to others like the beginnings of a *shadow army*.

As the number of reform meetings spread and the tone of the rhetoric intensified, the government of Lord Liverpool, the Prime Minister, became increasingly worried that this whole reform movement could spin out of control. Lord Liverpool actually had been in Paris in the summer of 1789, when French reformers stormed the Bastille prison to free some of their jailed comrades. Bearing witness to the indecisive response of King Louis XVI's government, he had seen for himself how France's reform movement, so well-intentioned at first, had been allowed to mutate into a violent, multi-headed revolution.

Robert Banks Jenkinson,
also known as
Lord Liverpool.

Thirty years later, with responsibility for his own country's welfare, Lord Liverpool had carefully monitored the progression of Britain's own reform movement. It too had begun with measured calls for change, but it too seemed to be turning more militant, in both its demands and its actions. The resemblance to what had happened in France was both uncanny, and unnerving.

* * *

Upon the *Savannah's* arrival, one of the first issues Liverpool customs officials had to address was the possibility of disease. After all, the steamship had come from a "suspect port," which meant any place where the authorities had reason to believe communicable diseases might exist.

This was no small matter, as the fear of any contagious outbreak was forever on the minds of governments everywhere in the early 19th century. Anyone who needed proof of the risk had only to be reminded of the great yellow fever epidemic of 1804, which reportedly killed 100,000 people in the Spanish city of Cadiz, and one-third of the British colony at Gibraltar. Even if Captain Rogers had a *bill of health* from the Savannah Custom House, stipulating there was no disease on board, it isn't likely the British authorities would have completely relied on it. The rules for issuing such documents were complex enough for a diseased vessel to slip through.

On the positive side, the strictness of British quarantine rules had been under pressure for some time. Many eminent doctors questioned whether the most-feared yellow fever was actually contagious; merchants continually complained about the damage done to perishable cargoes that were subject to long quarantine periods; and passengers often fumed over having to endure still more time on a vessel which had brought them, often very unpleasantly, all the way across the ocean. The many questions and complaints, supported by years without any yellow fever cases in Albion, had led the British government to loosen regulations in 1819. The brand new rules gave local quarantine officers some leeway in judging how much of a risk a new arrival might be.

In the *Savannah*'s case, the crew had been healthy, and there was no cargo aboard that could be infested with disease. Under the new rules, this meant there was no cause to subject the steamship to any kind of quarantine procedure.

The other issue the authorities needed to address was where to put the *Savannah*. She didn't have any cargo to unload, so there was no need to bring her into one of the docks. She would, however, garner a lot of attention, and therefore a lot of visitors.

So the decision was made to moor the *Savannah* off the small village of Tranmere, on the Cheshire side of the river. This might seem like a strange choice, but there was some method to it. First, it got the steamship out of the way—there was no chance the *Savannah*, or her expected visitors, would disrupt the operations of the docks, or the port generally. And second, Tranmere happened to be the terminus of one of the steamboat ferry routes across the Mersey. With several steam ferries keeping up a regular service, it would be easy for them to serve as shuttles to and from the steamship.

While the *Savannah*'s status within the harbor was being set, shareholders Robert Isaac (who had preceded the steamship across) and Andrew Low immediately began to plan for her departure. Since the *Savannah* would be leaving with coal for her own consumption only, it made sense to ask that the usual export duty on it be waived. But honoring such a request was above and beyond the authority of the Liverpool Custom House.

So the day after the steamship's arrival, the firm of Isaac, Low &

Company wrote a letter to the British Treasury in London. In it, they requested the *Savannah* be allowed to ship 100 tons of coal duty-free. They also asked for a waiver of the separate vessel tonnage duty normally charged on any departure from a British port.

With the *Savannah's* public welcome behind her, and regulations and logistics in hand, reaction from the British press came next. *Marwade's Commercial Report* of Liverpool was the first to spread the news:

> Among the arrivals yesterday at this port, we were particularly gratified and astonished by the novel sight of a fine Steam Ship, which came round at half after seven, P.M. without the assistance of a single sheet, in a style which displayed the power and advantage of the application of steam to vessels of the largest size ... She is called the Savannah, Captain Rogers ... Her model is beautiful, and the accommodation for passengers elegant and complete. This is the first ship on this construction that has undertaken a voyage across the Atlantic.

Since *Marwade's* was the first to publish immediately after the *Savannah's* arrival, its complimentary article set the tone for press coverage in Albion. Within days, *Marwade's* story had been reprinted in newspapers and magazines all over the British Isles.

Still other papers coming across from Ireland brought news of the *Savannah's* voyage along its south coast. The *Southern Reporter and Cork Commercial Courier*, which had first spread the news of the pilot boat *Mary's* encounter, was compelled to print a correction two days later:

> On Thursday night [the 17th], after our Paper went to Press, we received a letter from Mr. Gibbons, the agent of Lloyds, at Kinsale, dated at an advanced hour of the day, stating "that the Pilot Hooker Boat, *Mary*, had just come into the harbour and brought information of a Steam Ship from New York, bound for Liverpool, being off and about to put in, wanting some supplies." The contents of this letter were circulated yesterday as the fact of a vessel, worked by Steam across the wide Atlantic, and arriving off our shore, was one which we deemed of much curiosity and interest, and as we were given to understand that she was likely to remain

a day or two in Kinsale, we were anxious to make the circumstances known, in order to give an opportunity to those who may wish to profit of the intelligence by repairing to behold her.

It appears, however, that the *Mary* had been either mistaken, as to the intention of the Steam Ship to put into Kinsale, or that the Capt. of the latter had changed his intention...

This was followed by an account of the chase:

> ... the *Kite*, Revenue Cruiser, Lieut. Bowee, arrived [at Cork] ... after having fallen in with and boarded ... off the harbour, the American Steam Ship "*Savannah*," of and from Savannah, 315 Tons burden, Michael Rogers, Captain and Projector, out 22 days, bound for Liverpool, London, Havre, and St. Petersburgh. The *Kite* chased her during the day, going ten notts, supposing her to be a ship on fire, when at length perceiving the *Kite* in chace, she stopped her engine, till the latter came up...

This news from Cork naturally made its way eastward in steps. Once it reached Dublin, the newspapers of that city largely reprinted the story verbatim. The one exception was *Carrick's Morning Post*, which claimed on June 24th that the *Kite* had been after the steamship "all day." This stretching of the fish was then repeated a day later in Belfast, by *The Belfast News-Letter*.

But the most poignant reaction in Ireland by far came from *The Dublin Journal*:

> We have frequently said that the application of Steam, as a propelling power to vessels, would open a new æra in navigation, and that *Steam Boats* might perform the longest voyages— might cross the Atlantic, or even proceed to the Indian Seas. — The idea, by many, was deemed chimerical, but it has already, in one instance, been realized ...

(Even true believers sometimes had trouble making the transition from "steamboat" to "steamship.")

Cork, Dublin and Liverpool weren't the only port cities with close commercial ties to America that responded positively to the event. So

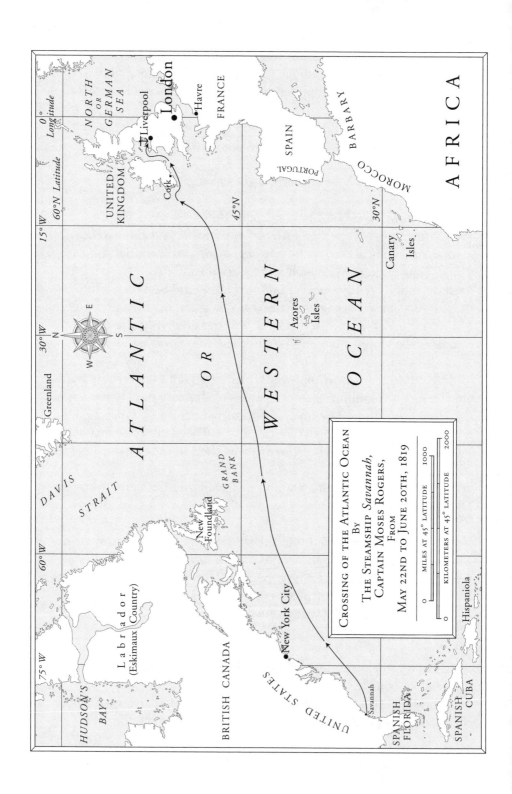

CROSSING OF THE ATLANTIC OCEAN
By
THE STEAMSHIP *Savannah*,
CAPTAIN MOSES ROGERS,
FROM
MAY 22ND TO JUNE 20TH, 1819

MILES AT 45° LATITUDE
0   1000

KILOMETERS AT 45° LATITUDE
0   2000

ATLANTIC

OR

WESTERN

OCEAN

AFRICA

London
Liverpool
Havre
FRANCE
NORTH OR GERMAN SEA
UNITED KINGDOM
Cork
SPAIN
PORTUGAL
MOROCCO
BARBARY
AFRICA
Canary Isles
Azores Isles
Greenland
DAVIS STRAIT
Labrador (Eskimaux Country)
HUDSON'S BAY
BRITISH CANADA
New Foundland
GRAND BANK
New York City
UNITED STATES
Savannah
SPANISH FLORIDA
SPANISH CUBA
Hispaniola

0° Longitude
15° W
30° W
60° W
75° W
60° N Latitude
45° N
30° N

N E S W

too did Bristol. Three of that city's newspapers, in reporting the *Savannah*'s arrival, declared that her crossing by steam "may be considered as an important æra in navigation."

In addition to these reports, Moses provided the newspapers with details of two vessels he had spoken to on the voyage: the ship *Plato*, on June 2nd, at latitude 41° 51′ North, longitude 57° 18′ West, and the ship *Canton*, on June 6th, at latitude 43° 37′ North, longitude 43° 42′ West. Aside from these, the only other unusual sighting noted in the logbook was their passing a massive iceberg at the same latitude as Portland, Maine (or the north coast of Spain).

Thankfully, problems on the voyage had been few. Early on, the boilers suffered from *clinkers*, which were clumps of unburnt coal residue stuck to the grates. These globs interfered with the flow of air around any new coal thrown in, so the grates had to be scraped clean. And the holes on either side of the hull, from which the paddlewheel axle protruded, had proved to be an easy entry point for water in a heavy sea, and it took some effort by the crew to minimize the resulting intake.

Beyond these minor problems, it also had been a turbulent passage. While the first week was relatively pleasant, for nearly every day from June 1st until the 15th, when she reached the coast of Ireland, the *Savannah* had encountered, in Steve's experienced judgment, "rough" or "heavy" seas.

In terms of steam usage, Steve's logbook notations made it a little difficult to calculate the exact number of hours the *Savannah* had been under the artificial power. However, based upon his recordings, it appeared that steam was used on 14 different sea days, for a total of almost 100 hours.

But when it came to reporting this performance, *Marwade's Commercial Report* again set the standard, advising Liverpool readers, and in time the rest of Britain, that the steamship "worked the engine 18 days," not 14 days.

In all likelihood, this higher number came from Moses. How he arrived at it isn't entirely clear, but since there were 4 sea days in which Steve recorded the steam engine being stopped at noon (i.e., the end of a sea day), it could be that Moses, in his own captain's log, recorded the steam engine as running past the end of the given sea day, and into the next. This would have led him to calculate steam usage on 18 different days, rather than the 14 which Steve's notations showed.

Eventually, just like the *Kite*'s chase, the original report on steaming time grew. Some accounts later stated the *Savannah* steamed 18 *entire* days. Whether Moses played any part in suggesting this is uncertain. While he was later reported to have said she had "used her steam full eighteen days," the words don't clarify whether Moses was exaggerating in that particular instance, or simply misinterpreted.

Inflating the steam usage calculation didn't stop with "18 entire days," either. One British publication, *The Imperial Magazine*, went even further, reporting specifically that it was the *first* 18 days of the voyage that were spent steaming exclusively. Still others claimed it was 20 days, with 200 tons of coal consumed, thus calculating a fuel burn rate of ten tons of coal per day—all of it wrong.

That the *Savannah's* success became the object of such inflation is not at all surprising, given the magnitude of what had just been accomplished, combined with the natural human tendency to exaggerate in reaction.

Also of great importance, and subject to its own creative interpretation, was the reporting of the *Savannah's* passage time. The normal method for calculating this was based upon time elapsed, from weighing anchor at the port of departure to dropping anchor in the port of arrival. By this measure, the steamship had taken 29 days and 4 hours to complete the 4,200-mile journey. This was a good passage time, but hardly the fastest. While vessels sailing from Savannah could take as long as 40 days or more to reach Liverpool, it was not unusual for those with very favorable winds and weather to make it in 25 to 30 days.

So the passage time that most British newspapers reported was not 29 days, but 26 days. If the counting began with Steve's taking his point of departure from Tybee Lighthouse and ended with dropping anchor at Liverpool, 26 days was an accurate calculation.

But even this passage time was not out of the ordinary, so another method of measure quickly gained currency. Because steam power promised to overcome the problem of fickle winds near port, perhaps the best gauge of the trip's success was to measure the duration of the actual ocean crossing itself, or "land to land," from America to Ireland. This must have seemed particularly fair since the *Savannah's* coal supply had run out before she reached Liverpool. With improvements in the technology, and more experience in managing the fuel to allow steaming the last few days into port, it could be argued that the land-to-land transit time better illustrated the new mode's potential. This reasoning, or something like it, led some British newspapers and magazines to focus on the *Savannah's* land-to-land voyage time, which was only 21 days.

There was perhaps another reason to promote the land-to-land measurement, and it was tied up to the east side of George's Dock. The ship *Athens*, one of Isaac, Low & Company's own vessels, had, according to the firm's advertisement, "lately arrived from Savannah in 21 days, the shortest passage ever known from that port." Inadvertently, the steamship risked being compared to this "uncommonly fast" sailing ship, regardless of whether they traversed the Atlantic at different times, and under different conditions.

Comparisons with the old mode didn't stop with the *Athens*. There were, it turned out, other sailing ships, such as the *Thalia* of Charleston, which had left the American coast more or less concurrently with the *Savannah*, and arrived at Liverpool in roughly the same amount of time. This left die-hard steam skeptics, and those who felt threatened by the new mode, with some useful ammunition of their own.

Yet while steaming times and passage times and fuel usage could be described, discussed and debated endlessly, nothing could overshadow the most obvious point of all: the *Savannah* had made it safely across the Atlantic. With that important goal fulfilled, the next question which immediately bothered people's minds in Britain was......

Precisely what is this American steamship doing here?

With that issue placed upon the table, the British press went to work.

Some newspapers reported the *Savannah* was on her way to Gothenburg, in Sweden, "for the purpose of making a sale of her to Bernadotte. She put in here for want of fuel, the want of which has occasioned her making a longer passage than she otherwise would have done."

If that is true, then what does the Swedish king intend to do with her?

Even more prevalent were Liverpool news reports that "her destination is said to be St. Petersburgh, as a present to the Emperor Alexander."

If that is the case, then who is the gift-giver?

Since the steamship had been flying a coachwhip pennant upon its arrival, and coachwhips were known to be flown only by publicly-owned vessels, then the source of this great gift must be the American government.

If that is so, then what's the motive?

"The politicians of the day," noted one observer, believed that the "secret views of ambition" of the United States were at play. This the-sis was supported by the common knowledge that the Americans viewed Russia as the only country in a position to check Britain's expanding power. In such a scenario, with the United States and Rus-sia coordinating their actions, Britain could find itself geo-politically surrounded. Therefore, this American gift of a steamship must be intended to further bolster relations with the Emperor Alexander.

Still other reports indirectly supported this rumor of America play-ing the Russia card. A number of Liverpool newspapers claimed that Captain Moses Rogers was, in fact, the brother of Commodore John Rodgers, of the U.S. Navy. Given the liberal spelling methods of the time, it was not difficult for "Rogers" to become "Rodgers," or vice versa. The Commodore's name was well-known to both Royal Navy officers and British merchants alike. During the late war, John Rodgers had set the American record for the most British vessels cap-tured or destroyed—23 in total—and had since become president of the U.S. Navy's Board of Commissioners, making him the most pow-erful American naval official in uniform.

Such a rumor as this probably had its genesis in the coachwhip confrontation. When Moses replaced the American coachwhip pen-nant with that of a U.S. Navy squadron commander, at least some of the people who witnessed it must have combined official pennants with identically-sounding surnames. The result was a presumption of U.S. government ownership of the *Savannah*, brotherhood with Commodore Rodgers, and more. In such ways did the most trivial of incidents ripple through the land of Albion.

Beyond these published reports of the *Savannah*'s purpose, and the speculations swirling around them, there was one additional story regarding her intent that did manage to gain an audience. While the newspapers paid it little if any direct notice, this rumor, this hearsay, was so powerful, and so significant, that it held the potential to cause the greatest anxiety within the British establishment. And the sig-nificance of this particular rumor could be immediately understood at the time simply by uttering one solitary name—

Napoléon.

* * *

There was arguably no other living person who generated a greater range of emotions within the interconnected world of the early 19th century than Napoleon Bonaparte. From 1799, when he grabbed the flailing reins of the French Revolution in a coup d'état, until his defeat by the Allied Powers in 1814, Napoleon had, through incredible guile and determination, turned France into a revolutionary juggernaut.

Those fifteen years in Europe had seen everything: alliances made and broken; mass mobilizations of men and resources; and war, both military and economic, followed by false peace, which inevitably led to more war. The consequences of this long conflict reverberated across oceans, plunging Central and South America into rebellion against the royal rule of Spain, and dragging the progenitor of it all, the United States, into a second war with Britain.

After Napoleon's defeat in 1814, the Allied Powers—Britain, Austria, Prussia and Russia—had to decide what to do with him. To treat the deposed revolutionary Emperor of France too harshly risked creating a backlash, since Napoleon still enjoyed considerable support from within the populations of Europe. The best solution seemed to be placing the man somewhere that physically removed him as a threat, while at the same time giving the appearance of respect for a defeated foe.

The Allied Powers' answer was exile to the tiny Mediterranean island of Elba. There, Napoleon would have sovereign responsibility over the island, as well as command of its small army, made up of his most fanatical followers.

The re-installed Royal French government of King Louis XVIII (whose brother Louis XVI had lost the throne, and his head, in the Revolution of 1789) sought to ensure that Napoleon stayed put. The French Navy was ordered to keep up a constant patrol around Elba. Britain's Royal Navy also maintained a presence, partly to guard against the possibility of assassination, which could have turned the de facto prisoner into a martyr.

This solution, and the European peace that went with it, did not last for long. In February of 1815, less than ten months after his exile began, Napoleon snuck past his guards, and boarded a vessel procured for his escape. After evading the naval patrols around the island, Napoleon landed in the south of France, where he created a sensation. Thousands who still believed Napoleon to be a true son of the Revolution joined his march on Paris. Within days, King Louis XVIII had fled for his life to Belgium, and Napoleon reclaimed the throne of France.

Napoleon Bonaparte.

The reaction of the Allied Powers—who were still debating the shape of a post-Napoleonic Europe at the Congress of Vienna—was shock. They declared Napoleon Bonaparte an outlaw, and prepared for military confrontation. These events, which unfolded so rapidly, sent European financial markets into convulsions, and jolted Americans into wondering if they might be sucked into a renewed war with the British.

True to form, Napoleon did not wait to be attacked. He immediately went on the offensive, moving his forces into Belgium to assault the British and Prussian armies encamped there, before they could be joined by their Austrian and Russian allies. Napoleon's ensuing defeat at the Battle of Waterloo ended his One Hundred Days of rule, and restored Louis XVIII to the French throne.

Immediately after Waterloo, it was Napoleon who had to flee for his own life, to the French port of Rochefort, on the Atlantic coast. There, his followers were arranging his escape by ship to the United States.

But the Royal Navy blocked his departure. Faced with what he thought would be certain death at the hands of the other Allied Powers, Napoleon surrendered to a Royal Navy warship, the HMS *Bellerophon*.

The *Bellerophon* brought Napoleon to the Royal Navy base at Plymouth, on the south coast of England, where they were immediately mobbed. Hundreds upon hundreds of British subjects came out in small boats and surrounded the warship, hoping to get a look at "Boney," as he was more popularly known. For those in Albion who had spent a good part of their lives fighting Napoleon, the reaction of their own countrymen to his presence was undeniably disturbing. The British government, fearing their prisoner might take advantage of legal protections if he were allowed ashore, decided to keep him on the *Bellerophon* until his fate was decided.

Second Secretary of the Admiralty John Barrow proffered what he thought would be the ideal exile for this most dangerous man: the island of St. Helena, located in the middle of the South Atlantic Ocean. Barrow had been there himself, and felt "that little rock at the end of the world" was so isolated that Napoleon could hardly cause any mischief there. This suggestion, duly made and discussed within the British government and amongst the Allied Powers, was agreed to, in July of 1815.

When informed of his fate, Napoleon's reaction was swift and certain:

"Non, non, pour St. Hélène je n'irai pas. Je ne sors pas d'ici. Je n'irai pas à St. Hélène. Je préfère la mort ici."

["No, no, for St. Helena I will not go. I do not leave from here. I will not go to St. Helena. I prefer death here."]

He had no choice. Transferred to HMS *Northumberland,* Napoleon and his small entourage of close aides departed for St. Helena, escorted by four Royal Navy brigs and three troop transports. The entire flotilla arrived at the island in October of 1815.

With Napoleon securely trapped in his new, very isolated prison, Secretary Barrow of the Admiralty felt that "all intrigue would be impossible, and being withdrawn so far from the European world, he would very soon be forgotten."

Such an opinion, it turned out, could not have been further from what became the truth. This was because once the ex-Emperor had landed at St. Helena, the world public's fascination with the personality that was Napoleon Bonaparte quickly manifested itself in hunger for news about him.

Is he in good health?
Has he gained more weight?
What is he saying?
Who is with him?
How are the British treating him?

Newspapers on both sides of the Atlantic were only too willing to oblige their readers' interest. And inevitably, given Napoleon's cunning escape from Elba, the public speculated as to whether he could do it again. As one Philadelphia diarist confidently put it:

> . . . *the British Govt. have finally determined that Buonaparte shall be confined for Life at St. Helena.—if so there is another Chapter to be added to his History, and the troubles of the World probably are not over, tis ten to one he will be in South America in less than a twelve month, where he will find materials for his Business, and fresh fewel to blaze on the Altar of his Ambition . . .*

In the years following Napoleon's arrival at St. Helena, there certainly was plenty of evidence to support such predictions. His youngest brother Jerome, who lived in exile in the German and Austrian lands, was reported to be actively plotting his elder brother's rescue. Brother Lucien, living in Italy, also was implicated in various stories of secret correspondence with Napoleon, and plans for escape. And the oldest of the Bonaparte brothers, Joseph, was understood to be working still other angles from his American exile, on an estate near Bordentown, New Jersey.

It was in anticipation of such scheming that the British had sent so large a force to accompany Napoleon to St. Helena. The responsibility for keeping the prisoner in his place fell upon a lieutenant general of the British Army by the name of Sir Hudson Lowe. Upon the determination of Napoleon's fate, Sir Lowe had been named Governor of the island, which was legally under the control of the East India Company (for use as a supply stop for vessels traveling to the Far East).

Sir Lowe was given ample resources to carry out his task of making the rocky island into a fortress. This included over 2,700 soldiers and officers, organized into three infantry regiments, artillery companies, and a small detachment of cavalry; a system of ten signal towers, built specifically on Napoleon's account, to keep a lookout to seaward; and a Royal Navy squadron of eight or more vessels, commanded by a rear-admiral, which maintained a constant patrol around St. Helena.

In addition, Sir Lowe had the power to regulate the prisoner's life, and did not hesitate to do so. All mail and packages destined for Napoleon's residence, at a place called Longwood, were inspected before being delivered, and he was not allowed to travel beyond a set perimeter around his residence without a British escort. These steps, and still others, were taken amidst growing public rumors, as well as private reports, that parties were planning to effect Napoleon's escape.

The security measures hardly endeared Sir Lowe to the ex-Emperor, who, in one of their few meetings, taunted the Governor:

"I see that you are afraid I will escape—you take useless precautions. . ."

Napoleon and his entourage succeeded in making their displeasure known to the outside world. Through correspondence smuggled off the island, they denounced their treatment at the hands of St. Helena's governor. In time, segments of the British press came to see the jailer in a similar light, and described him accordingly:

Sir Hudson Lowe, Sir Hudson *Low*,
(By name and, ah! By nature so)...

Yet countering the public criticism of "this *kind-hearted* man" were private letters of support, sent to Governor Lowe by leaders of the Allied Powers. One such note came from Count Gneisenau, a Prussian field marshal who had fought Napoleon for years:

Over and over again I have thought of that vast and solitary ocean and that interesting rock on which you are preserving the peace of Europe. Our safety depends on your watchfulness and your strength of character; once you relax your tight guard over the most cunning scoundrel in the world, once you allow your subordinates to grant him favours out of ill-judged pity, our tranquillity will be jeopardised and the honest people of Europe will be abandoned to their former fears.

Such exhortations steeled Sir Lowe to be careful, and remind others of the prisoner's powers:

His mind is tireless, he turns everything to account, tries everything, leaves no stone unturned to attain his purpose, and does nothing unintentionally. I could name several outstanding men who have been his tools without suspecting the fact.

Reports of escape plans and intrigues never seemed to let up. Year after year, the British government had to digest and decide what to do about a broad variety of threats.

There were numerous warnings about fast sailing vessels being equipped in American ports—on the Hudson River, or Philadelphia, or Baltimore, or Charleston—with the intent of reconnoitering St. Helena, or going for an outright rescue.

One letter intercepted at the St. Helena post office, written by a Frenchman in English in the hope that it would avoid detection, described an effort to get Napoleon down a cliff and into a small boat shaped like a barrel, which would be camouflage-painted to look like the sea.

In 1816, there were rumors that an American of French descent was organizing a rescue force of 300 mercenaries, who would land on St. Helena dressed in British Army uniforms, and effect Napoleon's escape.

In late 1817, there were reports of another plot by two exiled French generals and the British political radical Lord Cochrane. They were said to be organizing a rescue expedition comprised of armed vessels and nearly 800 men, which would be used to assault the island prison.

Also in 1817, a "Colonel Latapie" was arrested in Brazil for attempting to use that country as a base to rescue Napoleon. His plot purportedly included outfitting fast-sailing vessels large enough to carry several small steamboats. Upon reaching the vicinity of St. Helena, the steamboats would be deployed, and move in for a rescue under weather conditions that would leave the Royal Navy squadron powerless to stop them.

Still further rumors spoke of French émigrés using Rio de Janeiro as the base to launch some type of submarine vessel to effect Napoleon's escape.

Such seemingly fantastical schemes, in addition to repeated false alarms of successful escape, burdened the government of Lord Liverpool. Their discomfort was only increased by one of Napoleon's entourage, who publicly stated upon his return to Europe in 1818 that various methods of escape had been discussed at Longwood. This same General Gourgaud also claimed that Napoleon had no trouble engaging in secret correspondence with Europe.

News coming across the Atlantic that same year was equally disconcerting. American newspapers reported on exile Joseph Bonaparte's "plan for revolutionising South America," and his purported offer of a $2,000,000 reward for anyone who could rescue his brother from St. Helena.

The British Cabinet, firmly convinced that the threat of escape was real, concluded that the security already in-place for St. Helena was not enough, and felt compelled to consider still more precautionary measures.

In the autumn of 1818, the Allied Powers, meeting at Aix-la-Chapelle, reviewed Napoleon's status on St. Helena, and the steps Britain had taken to keep him there. Given the criticism of Sir Hudson Lowe and the complexities of European politics, stories had circulated prior to the summit that Russia's emperor, Alexander, would press for Napoleon's release.

But on the last day of November 1818, the summit unanimously adopted resolutions making it clear that the Allied Powers had no such intention. In fact, they approved of the security measures taken by the British, recommended even more restrictions, and further declared "that Napoleon Bonaparte has placed himself by his conduct outside the pale of the law of nations."

The Allied Powers' conclusion, while not directly stated, was obvious: the ex-Emperor would never be allowed to leave St. Helena. Such an iron-clad pronouncement was intended to quash any hopes among Napoleon's followers that he would ever lead them again. It also was hoped that the decision would muffle continuing speculation about plots to free him.

But it didn't work. As the year 1819 began, British newspapers continued to publish reports of suspicious vessels lingering around St. Helena, which then fled whenever Royal Navy patrol vessels gave chase. At the same time, American newspapers arriving in Britain brought news that Joseph Bonaparte had recently shipped a diamond —insured for $80,000—from New York City to the French port of Havre, its purpose unknown. And on top of these public reports came private diplomatic dispatches from the British minister to Paris, who relayed intelligence he had received that the South American revolutionaries at Buenos Aires had offered Jerome Bonaparte a leading role in their new government.

The reports seemed endless. When it came to the name "Bonaparte," the *Southern Patriot* of Charleston noted in May of 1819, it appeared as though "we meet with it in the world of politics nearly as often now as when it was the terror of Europe."

Once Napoleon's fate had been determined definitively, the British government did not let its guard down. Instead, it did the opposite. The belief was that the maximum period of danger had arrived. A desperate prisoner, knowing he had no chance of negotiating his way to freedom, might try anything.

Napoleon's behavior certainly was not reassuring. Once news of the Allied Powers' decision reached him in early 1819, the ex-Emperor deliberately made it very difficult for British sentries to catch even a glimpse of him at Longwood.

This conduct led Sir Hudson Lowe to suspect the worst. By June of 1819, the British press was reporting that *all* mail and printed material landed on St. Helena had to be sent directly to the Governor's house for inspection. This included newspapers, on the suspicion that they might contain coded messages for Napoleon. One report even stipulated that editions of *The Morning Chronicle*, a London daily known for its Bonapartist sympathies, were to be especially scrutinized. Another press report stated that Sir Lowe had issued orders forbidding any coastal inhabitants of St. Helena from communicating with or traveling to the interior of the island—where Longwood was located—without a special license. Privately, the Admiralty also had ordered that no Royal Navy personnel in the St. Helena squadron were to have any contact whatsoever with the prisoner, or any member of his entourage, without express permission.

Back in Britain, the infatuation with Napoleon in some quarters continued unabated. A few days before the steamship *Savannah* arrived at Liverpool, Bullock's Museum on the Piccadilly in London auctioned off some of Boney's possessions, captured at the Battle of Waterloo. "A numerous and most fashionable party," according to one newspaper, bid on items ranging from his carriage (which sold for £168), to his snuff box (£166, 19 shillings, 6 pence), to his toothbrush (£3, 13 shillings, 6 pence), to a "Piece of Sponge" (17 shillings, 6 pence).

More ominously, the Radical Reformers continued to express in no uncertain terms their own sympathies for someone they considered a fellow revolutionary. At one of their major rallies, they openly declared:

> ... That this Meeting unequivocally disclaim any share or participation in the disgraceful and cowardly act of the Borough-mongers, in placing the brave Napoleon a prisoner to perish upon a desert Island, shut out from human society, and torn from his only son, whilst he is exposed to the insolence of a hired keeper.

While the Radical Reformers could get away with such public declarations, any open scheming to rescue Napoleon would have been foolish in the extreme. Parliament already had passed a law stipulating that anyone caught doing so—in Britain, or on the high seas—would be arrested and tried as if they were a British subject, regardless of their nationality. The penalty for those found guilty was death.

As if all this agitation over Napoleon weren't enough, there was yet one more ingredient to be stirred into Albion's pot by June of 1819.

The port of Liverpool recently had become the temporary host to several thousand men, all volunteering to fight on behalf of the South American Patriots. Along with thousands more in Dublin, they were awaiting embarkation orders from a General John Devereux, who was an Irish recruiter for the South American independence leader Simón Bolívar. Ironically, many of these recruits were veterans of the British Army; in fact, one brigade of Irish volunteers was said to contain 1,500 veterans from the Battle of Waterloo. All that held them back was the provisioning of vessels for their voyage to South America.

This open activity on behalf of the South American Patriots was putting the British government in a very uncomfortable position. The Spanish Crown complained bitterly about the support the rebels were receiving from a Britain that claimed to be neutral. In response, a law was winding its way through Parliament which would outlaw within Britain the private raising of troops for wars of liberation. Until its passage, however, the South American volunteers loitering in Liverpool and Dublin could do and depart as they pleased, even if it meant eventually sailing right by St. Helena.

This lumpy, acidic, multi-colored stew of factors and fears in the early British summer of 1819 was evidence enough for the wildest of rumors. When it came to deducing the *Savannah*'s true intentions, some observers put the many pieces of the puzzle together, and arrived at a disturbing conclusion: the steamship's *real* mission was to rescue Napoleon Bonaparte from St. Helena.

As outrageous as it might have sounded, such an idea had been broached before. The previous September, in 1818, the London newspapers had been agog with a report about Lord Cochrane's steam vessel, which was then thought to be nearing completion:

> The King's ships at St. Helena lie chiefly at or off James Town, on the leeward side of the island, into which there is good access by the usual way. There is no other access into the island except at the opposite, the windward side, where the entrance from the water by land is easy; but here, there is no anchorage. Off this place two cutters usually cruise. Seafaring men of course speculate on the possibility of BUONAPARTE'S escape; and the most practical chance they think would be, for a strong cutter or two, well appointed with oars, to approach the windward side, beat off the cutters, take and row away with BUONAPARTE,

their prize, to a large ship at some distance, perhaps out of sight of the island, which might convey him to his destination.

A steam-boat can approach the island on every side, its mechanical movement supplying the place of oars, and after taking away BUONAPARTE, being large, and heavily armed, it might beat off any cutters. It might then work up to a large vessel to windward, to deliver its prize, or it might itself convey away BUONAPARTE wholly. The power of going against wind and tide would in those seas be a great protection against the King's ships, and moving as it does without sails, it would not easily be discovered at sea. Experienced nautical men, who have had an opportunity of inspecting the steam-vessel of Lord COCHRANE, have been struck with its remarkable adaptation for navigating upon such a coast as the windward side of St. Helena is represented to be...

As a naval officer, Lord COCHRANE never shewed himself deficient in enterprize, and to his natural ardor is now added the excitement of desperate fortunes. His character has been much mistaken, or there are few things that would gratify him more than to become the liberator of NAPOLEON. The bare attempt, indeed, would seal his future destiny. If he succeeded, his fate would be linked with that of BUONAPARTE; if he failed, he might still become an insurgent admiral. He has nothing to lose in England; every thing to gain out of it. Just such a man—one so completely with the world before him—would be required for the hazardous and daring enterprize. But it is said he is going to Chili. Be it so. It will not be much out of his way to call at St. Helena.

While some of the London press labeled this whole steam-rescue speculation absurd, the number of newspapers which printed the story revealed that many were not prepared to discount the possibility out of hand.

But nine months after these stories had first run, Lord Cochrane's steam vessel remained at the building docks on the Thames River, unfinished and untried. Cochrane's creation had yet to show that a steam-powered craft could even safely navigate across the wide ocean, let alone carry out such a rescue plan. The whole idea, it still could be argued, was preposterous.

But with the arrival of June 20th, 1819, such a claim was no longer true. The steamship *Savannah* was *real*.

* * *

Two days after the *Savannah*'s arrival at Liverpool, it began to rain.

Such weather could not keep away the curious. At about 1 o'clock that afternoon, one of the Mersey River steamboats approached the steamship. Unfortunately, the steamboat's captain either misjudged his speed or the angle of contact, and his steamer rammed into the *Savannah*'s starboard bow, breaking off the anchor.

This minor mishap proved to be the most notable event of the day, according to Steve's continuing entries into the logbook. Otherwise, that Tuesday saw little more of interest, in his opinion, than the river pilot's departure and some wind-swept showers.

Across the Mersey that evening, Liverpool got a lot more than just rain. Between 6 and 9 o'clock, the Dock Police took several people into custody for various offences, and put them in Bridewell Prison, located a few blocks north of George's Dock. This was hardly remarkable in and of itself, except that all of those arrested happened to be members of the city's burgeoning Irish population.

Once news of the jailings had spread, a crowd quickly gathered outside Bridewell Prison. The assemblage loudly began to question the basis for the arrests, and demand that the prisoners, two of whom were women, be released. Within a few hours, the number of people protesting had mushroomed to over 8,000, and scattered amongst them were some of the Irish volunteers for South America. One of the Patriot recruits' officers seemed particularly intent on transforming the crowd into a mob.

He got his wish. In short order, Bridewell's windows were smashed, and the yard door broken down. As the attackers proceeded to pound the prison's main door from its hinges, the jail keeper sent out a call for help. With little ability to resist, and several constables already wounded, Bridewell's keeper decided to let two of the prisoners go. The mob immediately raised the released prisoners upon their shoulders, and triumphantly marched them through the streets.

Soon afterward, the city's mayor, Jonathan Hollinshead, arrived with a contingent of soldiers. Immediately, the huge crowd began to disperse. Several of the ringleaders, including the officer for the South American volunteers, were quickly taken into custody, before they could escape.

The first sketchy reports of the Bridewell riot, which went out before the outcome was known, sent shockwaves throughout the country. It wasn't difficult for people to wonder at first if this was not Britain's Bastille. Once further details of the incident were disseminated, however, that feeling passed, although what transpired immediately thereafter was of little comfort. An attempt by the authorities the next day to round up other agitators amongst the South American volunteers led to another violent confrontation, and retreat by the police. In response, the Liverpool Light Horse cavalry and other military units in the vicinity were called to active duty.

While subsequent days in Liverpool were quiet, and the prison attack wasn't directly tied to the rapidly growing reform movement, the storming of Bridewell nevertheless heightened the public sense of unease. Things were clearly not right in Albion.

* * *

Two days after the Bridewell riot, on Thursday, June 24th, there remained one official guest on board the *Savannah*, and that was an officer from the Liverpool Custom House.

On the surface, his continued presence aboard the steamship—four days after its arrival—made very little if any sense. The *Savannah* had no cargo, and carried nothing across the Atlantic beyond some mail and perhaps a few newspapers.

Below the surface, however, the custom house officer must have had a perfectly good reason for remaining on the steamship for so long. In all likelihood, he was looking for something that captain and crew would never readily admit to having, and that was the writings of William Cobbett.

Cobbett, an Englishman then living in America, was a political radical with a long and controversial history. He had, in the course of his life, served in the British Army in Canada, accused senior officers there of corruption, and then fled to France to avoid retribution. Finding that country in the violent throes of its revolution, Cobbett sailed for America in 1792. Once there, he settled in Philadelphia, and authored pro-British pamphlets under the pen-name of "Peter Porcupine." This last act rehabilitated him, in the eyes of his countrymen, and upon his return to Britain in 1800, he was hailed as a patriotic hero. Cobbett then started a London newspaper, the *Political Register*, and began publishing an unofficial record of Parliament's debates (which eventually became known as *Hansard's*). All the while, he slowly gravitated toward the growing political reform movement.

William Cobbett.

Cobbett's increasingly radical pronouncements against "the system" got him arrested for sedition, and tossed into jail for two years. Upon his release in 1812, Cobbett picked up where he had left off, publishing his radical *Register* as a recurring "pamphlet," to avoid an onerous newspaper tax. The *Register* soon became very popular with the working class, and made Cobbett once more, in the eyes of the British government, a threat.

Fearing arrest, yet again, Cobbett fled, yet again, to the one place he felt he would be safe: the United States. There he took up residence in 1817, at a farm on Long Island, New York.

Even at that distance, the government of Lord Liverpool still feared William Cobbett. No matter that by June of 1819 he was reported to be "still on Long Island, raising turnips and writing books." Regardless of where he lived, or what he claimed to be doing, the British government believed William Cobbett's words made a difference.

So when the Home Office received some disturbing intelligence in mid-June, they took it seriously, and took action. Home Office Undersecretary Henry Hobhouse laid bare the situation in a June 12th letter to Liverpool Customs Collector John Swainson:

Information, which we have received from Lancashire, asserts, as a Fact, that there have arrived from America a large Quantity of printed Papers, written by Cobbett, exciting the people to a general Insurrection, and which are awaiting a favourable Moment for Distribution. If such is the fact, it is not likely that the Importation should have been made into any Port but Liverpool. Lord Sidmouth would therefore be glad to be informed, whether among the recent Entries from the United States, there has been any, which lead you to the knowledge or the Suspicion of the Article imported, being of the nature alluded to.

Such a warning, with all its possible permutations, could not be taken lightly.

What if these writings had yet to arrive?

Even if they had arrived, could more be coming?

And would the couriers openly declare what they had brought?!

Collector John Swainson could hardly be blamed for instituting additional precautions. Less than a week after receiving this letter, into his port had come this American steamship, with a swarm of rumors buzzing around it, and a complete lack of declared cargo. If there was a newly-arrived vessel from the United States which merited special attention, this surely must have been it.

And if the customs officer assigned to the *Savannah* didn't leave her until four days after arrival, it was, in all likelihood, because he had concluded there was nothing on board to be found.

* * *

Two days later, down in London, ministers of Lord Liverpool's government were summoned to the Foreign Office in Downing Street for a meeting. "It is supposed," reported one of the city's newspapers, "that from the required attendance of all the Members, that the object of their meeting was of great importance."

Such Cabinet meetings actually were not that unusual when Parliament was in session. There would have been much to discuss regarding bills and debates before the House of Commons and the House of Lords. The increasing threats and provocative actions of the Radical Reformers, the Bridewell attack, and the South American volunteers were all probably topics of conversation, as well.

It also stands to reason that since news of the steamship *Savannah*'s arrival had been all over the London papers for the past three days, she too had become a part of the discussions at that 3½ hour meeting.

* * *

Roundabout the time the British Cabinet met in London, Stevens Rogers and the *Savannah*'s crew were finishing several days' worth of rituals performed on any vessel after a long voyage, from sail-drying, to paint-scraping.

For his part, Moses received a letter, which made his next move clear:

Captain Rogers

London June 23. 1819.

Dear Sir,

The Newspapers of this City have just announced your safe arrival at Liverpool in the steam ship Savannah, from the United States, upon which event I beg leave to offer you my congratulations.

That a vessel of our country should have been the first one of that description to tempt a boisterous ocean, must, I think, be a source of gratification to the public feelings of every American Citizen. To mine I do assure you that it is. Allow me though a stranger to your person, to add, that in being the first successful navigator of such a ship, you cannot fail to have earned for yourself, an honorable place in fame.

I should esteem it a great favor, if, while you remain in port, you could find the leisure to draw up for me a short account of the exact nature of your machinery, and how it worked on the voyage. But as I can well appreciate the business you must have on hand during your stay, I beg you not to be at this trouble for me should it create any interference with your other engagements.

I am very respectfully
your obt Servt
Richard Rush.

Rush was the American ambassador (or *minister*) to Great Britain, and his indirect invitation to London must have been a very welcome one. By honoring Rush's request, Moses could ask him to provide introductions to people of prominence in the capital, and perhaps elsewhere.

The easiest way to get from Liverpool to London was by stage-coach. The 207-mile trip usually took most of two days, with one overnight stay en route.

Choosing precisely how to go involved a plethora of choices. There were dozens of stagecoach companies operating out of various inns and taverns all over Liverpool. Among those coaches going to London, the first choice to be made was time of departure, either in the early morning or early evening. There was a further choice between the common coaches, which usually carried ten passengers at the least, and mail coaches, which carried only six. The less-crowded mail coaches were more expensive, but many travelers chose to pay up to ride them, in part because an armed guard came along, reducing the risk of highway robbery.

If a passenger wanted a good view of the countryside, however, he was best served by taking one of the common coaches, since four of their ten passengers sat in open seats, behind and above the main cabin. The only risk of these seats was the weather, and the tendency of British stagecoach drivers to make tracks like maniacs, skidding their coaches around corners at high speed. For the uninitiated, it could feel like the whole stage was going to tip over, throwing the topside passengers hard into the ground. Unfortunately, such accidents were not uncommon, but most drivers seemed to know just how hard they could push their horses without upsetting the coach.

Along the way to London, stagecoach passengers trundled through some of the most picturesque scenery in all of England: green farmlands and forests, thatched-roof cottages, long canals filled with horse-drawn boats, and a great many windmills scattered across the landscape. Sometimes passengers found themselves the target audience for local children, who ran alongside and performed tumbles and somersaults, in the hope of receiving a half-penny for their efforts. At other points in the journey, where the road proved to be particularly smooth, the driver would call out to the topside passengers seated behind him to "make a stand," allowing them a chance to stretch their legs, while the coach slowly rolled onward with no time lost.

As the lush English countryside gave way to the outskirts of "the Metropolis," as London was called, the view changed dramatically. The pastoral disappeared, replaced by what one American visitor called "an immense mass of smoky, dark-coloured brick buildings ...

crowded together for many miles, in various directions, with great irregularity in height, and in the various style of fashion."

Britain's capital had just about everything, from what was arguably the largest and finest collection of shops in the world, to a well-regulated fleet of professional hackney coaches, to a vast collection of beautiful squares and parks. But as could be expected for such an enormous city of one million residents, London also had its share of contradictions: great wealth surrounded by grinding poverty; still-novel gas-lit streets that nevertheless remained perpetually muddy; and a well-established tradition of civility that was frequently undermined by the artistry of pickpockets.

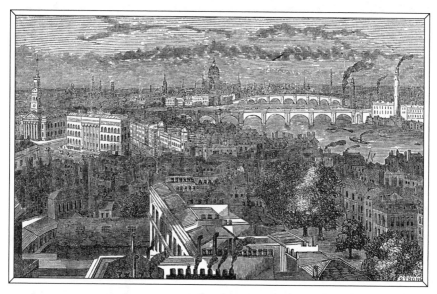

London.

Once Moses had arrived in London, among his first tasks was a visit to Minister Rush, who worked out of 51 Baker Street. This, Moses did on or just before June 30th.

The Richard Rush that Moses met was a thinnish man, not quite 39 years of age. His receding hairline and oval face made him look a lot like his father, the late Dr. Benjamin Rush, a signer of the Declaration of Independence and former Surgeon General of the Continental Army.

This son of a revolutionary had followed in his father's footsteps in many ways. Graduating from the College of New Jersey at Princeton, as his father had, young Richard studied and practiced law in

Philadelphia, and then entered public service, again as his father had before him.

After briefly serving as the Attorney General of Pennsylvania, Rush received an appointment from President Madison in 1811, to serve as Comptroller of the U.S. Treasury at Washington. In 1814, Madison appointed him the U.S. Attorney General.

When James Monroe was elected to the presidency in 1816, Rush stayed on as Attorney General. He also served as interim Secretary of State, until the newly-appointed John Quincy Adams could return from Britain, where he had been serving as the American minister. The vacancy created by Adams' transfer had to be filled, so President Monroe selected Rush to take his place in London.

It was a potentially risky move by Monroe, since Rush had no overseas diplomatic experience whatsoever. But what he did have was a good working knowledge of America's very fragile relationship with Britain. This was largely a result of his time as interim Secretary of State, during which he successfully negotiated the Rush-Bagot Treaty of 1817, which de-militarized the border with British Canada. The signing of this treaty proved that Richard Rush could get along with his British counterparts. Further bolstering his credentials was Rush's intimate familiarity with President Monroe, since the two had served together in Madison's Cabinet.

Richard Rush.

Upon assuming his post in London, Rush had made it a particular point to keep abreast of the Royal Navy's building program, and advances in shipbuilding techniques. He was a firm believer in the need for a strong American Navy, so his interest in the steamship *Savannah* went beyond mere curiosity.

Moses laid out for Rush the basic facts of the trip: the "great ease and safety" with which the *Savannah* had performed the voyage, having "used her steam full eighteen days"; the "extremely unfavorable" weather which had hindered a faster passage; and the exhaustion of their coal supply upon entering the Irish Channel.

Rush, writing a few days later to Secretary of State John Quincy Adams, recounted the steamship's arrival as "having excited equal admiration and astonishment." Rush also admitted that he felt "anxious that this enterprising mariner of our country, who appears to be at once intelligent and patriotic, should have an opportunity while in England of visiting some of the great naval dock yards, and I trust that he will be able to command it."

Next on the agenda were introductions. Rush wrote out for Moses a letter of introduction to America's top diplomat in Sweden, Christopher Hughes. This was followed by another introduction, either by letter or in person, to the Russian minister to Britain, Count Hristofor Lieven, who was just a few blocks away, at 36 Harley Street. In addition, some introduction was made to Sweden's minister to Britain, Baron Gustaf de Stierneld, whose office was also nearby, at 21 Lower Grosvenor Street.

Finally came the matter of the personal future of Captain Moses Rogers himself. With the Atlantic crossing successfully made, and the anticipated sale of the *Savannah* on the horizon, Moses expressed to Rush deep concern about his own options upon returning home. Clearly, business conditions back in America were not good, to put it mildly, and Moses wondered if Rush would write to Washington on his behalf, with the idea of putting his new mode expertise to work for the federal government. This, Richard Rush agreed to do.

While Moses was in London, the city's newspapers continued to publish articles about the *Savannah's* exploits. In particular, the exaggerated story of the revenue cruiser *Kite's* "all day" chase, which had germinated in Ireland, blossomed to the "whole day" in London. *The Star* published this story on June 29th, followed by *The Times* the next day, and *The Public Ledger* the day after that. While such a report surely fascinated some readers, it more than likely disturbed many others—

If a sleek revenue cruiser cannot catch this American steamship, then what could?

By July 2nd, Moses had met with Russia's minister to Britain, Count Lieven. The nobleman obligingly provided him with a letter of introduction to the chief of the Russian Navy.

Beyond business, Moses spent some time taking in the sights and shops of the city. Among the purchases he made was a set of china, which was headed for the cupboards of Bethiah Vail.

The steamboats running along the River Thames also must have attracted his attention. Most of them were a good deal smaller than their American counterparts. The one exception was a recently built 315-ton behemoth called the *London Engineer*, which had the unusual feature of a single large paddlewheel built into the center of the hull. After that came the brand-new 190-ton *Eclipse*, which, just one month prior, had towed the 74-gun HMS *Hastings* down the river, toward the English Channel. The feat was notable in that previous attempts at towing British warships with steamboats had ended in failure. That time, however, it had worked—the *Eclipse* had tugged the *Hastings* all the way to Margate.

* * *

If Moses took the time to look over London's shipbuilding areas, he may have toured Rotherhithe, which is located on the south side of the Thames, about one mile east of the Tower of London. There, in one of the shipyards, sat confirmation that the New York newspaper reports from the previous autumn had been true. Lord Cochrane's steam vessel—designed to cross oceans at will—lay motionless in a dry dock, unassembled and untested.

That Lord Cochrane even thought he could build such a craft was founded in the supreme confidence he had not only in himself, as a decorated naval officer, but also in the revolutionary potential of steam. The result was a willingness to venture into realms where his peers feared to tread.

This also included the realm of politics. Lord Cochrane, unlike most of his contemporaries, believed in the political reform movement, and his outspoken views made him a very visible target. In 1814, Cochrane had been convicted of stock fraud, which he and his supporters claimed was nothing but a clever set-up by his enemies to discredit him. That it certainly had done, leading to Cochrane's expulsion from the House of Commons, and prompting the Royal Navy to dismiss him from service.

Thomas Cochrane,
also known as
Lord Cochrane.

Lord Cochrane had responded by fighting back, winning re-election to the House from another constituency, and continuing to push for reforms. With that colorful, controversial past, the newspapers reveled in publishing stories about Lord Cochrane, making him one of the most talked-about celebrity-warriors of the time.

When news broke in 1818 that he was involved with the construction of a new ocean-going steamer, the British press set about trying to learn its purpose. Since the name *The North Pole* was inscribed on the vessel's stern, it was first claimed that Lord Cochrane's objective was to become the first navigator to reach the top of the world. This would entitle him to a Parliamentary reward of £5,000, and would have been a fitting tweak to the noses of those who previously had forced him from the House of Commons.

But some newspapers smelled deception, including *The Edinburgh Advertiser*, which noted that "his Lordship has a little tendency to stratagem," and explained the basis for their thinking:

> ... The naval success by which he was first distinguished, was obtained by his rendering a cutter so like one of the trading vessels of the *Mediterranean*, that he was alongside of a large *Spanish* xebeck, while the crew were below deck, without the slightest expectation of hostility. His present vessel will never approach the North Seas...

Next came the claim that Lord Cochrane intended to use his steam vessel to explore the River Congo, in Africa. This also turned out to be false, and was very likely Cochrane's way of twisting yet another set of noses, this time at the Admiralty, which had attempted to build a steamboat to explore that river, and failed.

Finally came the report that Lord Cochrane, as the newly-recruited chief of the revolutionary Chilean Navy, had a double-scheme in mind. He intended to arm his ocean-going vessel, the truly-named *Rising Star*, and steam and sail his way across the length of the Atlantic Ocean, to South America. Once there, Cochrane would use it to defeat the Spanish Navy of King Ferdinand VII. It was this third plan that turned out to be the truth.

With the approval of Chile's revolutionary government, the *Rising Star*'s keel was laid near the end of 1817. By the summer of 1818, all that stood in the way of Cochrane's plan was completion of the steam apparatus.

But this final step bothered José Antonio Alvarez Condarco, the Chilean government agent in London who had recruited Lord Cochrane. Building the *Rising Star* was taking longer than anticipated, and Alvarez wanted Cochrane to leave for South America, to assume command of the Chilean Navy.

But Cochrane demurred. He wanted to finish the *Rising Star*, and take it with him to fight the Spanish. He also feared that if he left the steam vessel unfinished, his political enemies would somehow thwart its completion. He further believed the British government was deeply suspicious that he had a plot in mind to rescue Napoleon from St. Helena, and Cochrane was determined to outwit them.

Alvarez, however, was relentless. He continued to pressure Cochrane to go.

By early August of 1818, Lord Cochrane realized that the *Rising Star* would not be finished anytime soon. So he, his wife Kitty and their two sons boarded a fishing boat, and snuck across the English Channel to France. From there, they embarked for South America, leaving the completion of the *Rising Star* in the hands of Alvarez.

The Chilean agent was not at all happy with this new responsibility. He was, by experience, an army officer, not a seaman, sent to London by revolutionary leader Bernardo O'Higgins to find whatever men and materials he could for the fight. With Cochrane gone, Alvarez had no choice but to work directly with an engineer named Alexander Galloway, who was overseeing the *Rising Star*'s machinery installation.

By late September of 1818—about seven weeks after Cochrane's departure, and one week after the London newspapers were filled with the *Rising Star*-Napoleon speculation—things were not going well. Galloway, himself a political radical and friend of Cochrane's, advised Alvarez that the boilers were ready to be installed, but that money was needed to buy a couple of air funnels:

> *I cannot but say, that it is a very great pity that now so much trouble and expense have been incurred in this undertaking, that it should be delayed or stopped for the further expense of only £140.*

Galloway pleaded with Alvarez to come up with the money, "and give the whole experiment that chance of success which its importance deserves."

But Alvarez had no money to give. In reply to Galloway, the Chilean agent expressed his concern over the "delay occasioned by an improper calculation of the time necessary for the construction" of the *Rising Star*. He further complained about how Lord Cochrane had "withdrawn all the interest he had in the operation and left the entire burden on me."

The war vessel's design also worried Alvarez. Like the *London Engineer*, which Galloway had helped build, the *Rising Star* had large paddlewheels installed in the center-bottom of the hull. As with the U.S. Navy's steam battery *Fulton*, this unusual set-up would protect the wheels from cannon shot.

Alvarez, realizing he was ill-equipped to judge the design's merit, decided to seek out the advice of others. On October 21st, 1818 (just days before the *Savannah* was moved to Elizabethtown for her machinery installation), Alvarez was ready to confront Galloway:

My Dear Sir

After serious consultations respecting the machinery of the Rising Star, with skilful persons in this Capital + at the same time being concerned by the force of my own reflections, I have determined at length not to proceed to any further experiments; as I consider those already made sufficient to undeceive all parties, more particularly, when it seems so clear that the said Vessel even when the result should be favourable, <u>it would not move more than three miles an hour it being understood that the obstacle which prevents her from moving onwards when pro- pelled by steam, viz the mass of water lodging in the paddle cases, will always be a material impediment to her sailing by the force of wind, whence it would result that her way at Sea would not be beyond one or two miles per hour, which of course is no object + would always prevent her from being useful</u> on the ocean; for this reason as well as other private ones, I think it best to give up the fruitless project . . .

Having been both ambushed and figuratively yelled at, Galloway immediately fired back:

Dr Sir,

I have received your letter of this day, + I cannot but feel deep regret at your determination respecting the Rising Star. Your reasoning would have been powerful + conclusive against the commencement of the undertaking; <u>but at a period when so much money + time have been already spent upon it, + when so little of both will now be sufficient to try fully the experiment, + put at rest all the conjectures + predictions of both those who have thought well of the project, + those who have</u>

*thought unfavorably of it; I think it would be injudicious under such
circumstances to abandon it ... If it is thus abandoned, a fair + important opportunity will be lost of producing proof where conjecture alone
has hitherto operated; + cannot but throw a damp on the progress of a
Subject so essential to the improvement of Navigation. Shall it be said
that in the year 1818 after spending 4 or £5000 in Machinery, yet
wholly untried, that it was abandoned, because £140 more was requisite
to enable a trial to be made, + by a Gentleman too who had enterprize
to go so far, + yet wanted a small fraction more to finish it?
Every impartial man will proclaim that this project must either have
been taken up unwisely or laid down inconsiderately, – to free the parties from either of these imputations, is one great reason for my solici-
tude to have it completed ... When Lord Cochrane first suggested the
propriety of creating a Steam Vessel to act on the Ocean; I know that
he as a seaman very coolly + Skillfully considered all the impediments
which such a Vessel might offer in sailing under the influence + Agency
of the wind; I know that, all my objections on that heard,
he very satisfactorily removed. A trip under the first fair wind to
Gravesend ... will give you a proof of the sailing capability of the
Rising Star...*

In a series of meetings that followed, Galloway convinced Alvarez
that the *Rising Star* was different from the similarly-built *London
Engineer.* The difficulties "the *Engineer*" had in making headway, with
water being pushed up into the central paddlebox, led many to call it
"the *Mistake.*"

Alvarez eventually agreed to a sailing trial on the Thames, which
was made in early November of 1818. The *Rising Star*, reported Galloway to Lord Cochrane, "passed both up [and] down the River every
vessel large + small." The Chilean agent was "so unexpectedly
delighted" by the results that "he promised that the Machinery should
be completed out of hand."

But two weeks after this sailing trial, no progress had been made,
and Lord Cochrane's friends, as well as the *Rising Star*'s officers, were
asking questions. "They indeed are nearly broken hearted with the
procrastination that regulates her affairs," Galloway told Alvarez.
"Some persons and some interests," Galloway continued, were willing
to denigrate the *Rising Star*'s sailing abilities without even a trial, and
if the vessel had been abandoned without one, ...

... they would have plumed themselves on their prophetic skill and sagacity; and their less confident, but more desirable predictions of the steam Engine Machinery failing would have then been rendered irresistible...

Galloway pleaded with Alvarez to provide the money to continue construction, warning "this delay shakes every body's confidence!"

But the Chilean agent, despite promises, was not budging.

By December of 1818, Galloway told Alvarez "I am quite teazed with applications respecting the *Rising Star*; everybody considers that the whole project is abandoned, and the worst impressions are created."

Yet Alvarez still had no money, and countered that he was both surprised and worried by cost estimates for completing the vessel that seemed to be spiraling out of control.

With progress at a standstill that would continue into the summer of 1819, Galloway could only implore, and vent:

... Great objects cannot be obtained without great hazard and a corresponding energy and power being adopted in the means of obtaining them and I cannot help thinking that if such means had been adopted that the Rising Star would have been half way to Chile by this time...

* * *

In the last days of June 1819, while Captain Rogers was tripping to London, a man by the name of Robert Seppings was busily doing his duty on the Royal Navy base at Plymouth, on the southwest coast of England. Seppings was one of three Surveyors of the Royal Navy, which meant he and his two colleagues were responsible for overseeing the construction and upkeep of all the vessels in the fleet. While based in London, Seppings made periodic visits to the various Navy dockyards to check on things, and at that time, he was inspecting a 120-gun ship-of-the-line, the HMS *St. Vincent.*

For Seppings, being at Plymouth was being at home. Born into a large family in Norfolk in 1767, he was dealt a life-altering blow in his early teens, when his father died. His mother, realizing she couldn't support all of her children, decided to send young Robert to live with her brother, Captain John Milligen, a retired Royal Navy officer living in Plymouth. Uncle John and his wife, having no children of their own, were willing to add yet another to their house full of adopted relatives. Two of Robert's siblings were already there, as were two orphaned cousins.

Shortly after Robert moved into the Milligen household, Uncle John arranged for his nephew to become an apprentice to John Henslow, Master Shipwright at the Plymouth Navy Dockyard. There, Robert learned the craft of shipbuilding, and worked with a variety of materials, including copper, iron, hemp, tar, and oil. But the material he came to understand best of all was wood, cut and shaped in myriad ways to build the warships of the Royal Navy, from the keel on up. Robert's teacher, by chance, was a very good one—eventually, he became Sir John Henslow, Surveyor of the Royal Navy.

Over time, Robert was steadily promoted, showing a purposeful knack for innovation.

His first major invention was a series of specially-designed wooden wedges, which allowed vessels to be raised and lowered in dry dock with far greater ease. What previously had taken the efforts of 500 men could be done with as few as 20 laborers in two-thirds the time. So useful were these wedges that they came to be known as "Seppings blocks."

Robert also pushed his idea of rounding the sterns of warships. With such a design, cannonballs would have a greater chance of glancing off, instead of imbedding and exploding, as they did when hitting traditional flat-sided sterns.

But his most lasting innovation by far was based upon a concept which could be summarized by the use of just one word: *diagonal.*

The worst long-term enemy of a wooden ship is rot. While any such vessel might appear to cope easily enough with the constant water currents swirling around it, the truth was more subtle, and destructive. This was because the endless pushing and pulling on any wooden hull inevitably created cracks in the external timbers. The ensuing seepage of sea water into those cracks, in time, led to the rotting of timbers, both inside and out. Furthermore, too much weight placed at either end of a wooden vessel sometimes led to an arching of the keel. This *hogging* effect, as it was called, greatly weakened the hull, and could result in even more seepage, and more rot.

Robert's solution to these problems sounded deceptively simple: diagonally brace and truss the frame timbers of the hull, thereby creating a far more rigid structure. This would help the hull hold its shape and reduce hogging. It also would keep the external hull boards from moving, and prevent sea water from seeping in.

Robert cited a typical picket gate to illustrate his point. With only supporting horizontal boards at the top and bottom of the gate, the individual wooden pickets initially stayed in place, although eventually, they would weaken, and move. But once a diagonal strip of wood was added, connecting the top and bottom support boards (thereby making the letter "z"), the gate was made dramatically stronger and more durable, pickets and all.

By 1819, Robert's diagonal bracing concept had been adopted by the Royal Navy, and was being noticed by commercial shipbuilders in both Britain and America. In a matter of years, its widespread adoption would lead to dramatic leaps in the size of vessels constructed, and with other advances, usher in a new age of shipbuilding.

Yet for all these successes, there had been setbacks. Four years earlier, in 1815, the Admiralty had determined to build its first steam vessel, which was to be used to explore the Congo River in Africa. The plan was to create a steamboat that could sail its way from Britain to the mouth of the Congo, and then explore upriver using steam power, with plenty of wood fuel to be had along the riverbanks.

A team was assembled to put the plan into action. Boulton, Watt & Company would provide the steam engine; Robert Seppings, by then a Surveyor of the Navy, would be responsible for the hull design; a group of mechanics would effect the installation of the engine and paddlewheels; and Admiral Sir Home Popham would be in charge of trials.

By early 1816, the aptly-named *Congo* was ready to be tested.

Unfortunately, the completed steamboat had some problems. The steam engine turned out to be heavier than expected. As a result, the hull sat too low in the water, leaving the paddlewheels too deeply immersed. This problem was solved by removing some ballast, which lifted the hull and decreased the paddleboards' immersion. But it concurrently raised the vessel's center of gravity in the water. It also came to light that while Robert thought he had been given a *maximum* breadth for the hull, the mechanics' spokesman countered that the breadth they had specified was a *minimum*, and that the hull could be wider.

The end result was a steamboat that managed just 3 knots, and was "very crank," which led to fears about its stability. Since the Admiralty knew American steamboats were achieving 7 to 8 knots on wood fuel, they were forced to conclude that their team was missing some part of the steamboat knowledge being put to use in the New World. Furthermore, the naval officers involved simply did not trust the *Congo*'s seaworthiness with a steam engine in her belly.

So the decision was made to remove the engine, and send the *Congo* to Africa as a sailing vessel. All things considered, it had been a fiasco that probably left a bad taste in the mouths of those involved.

That disappointment, however, was in the past, as Robert oversaw the opening of HMS *St. Vincent*'s hull at the Plymouth dockyard. This 120-gun giant had been fitted with his diagonal bracings, and he wanted to gauge how well its frame timbers were holding up.

What Robert saw pleased him greatly—the *St. Vincent*'s timbers were, as he reported to London, in a "most excellent state of preservation." It was yet more proof positive of the great contributions he was making to the science of shipbuilding. These accomplishments would soon gain the formal recognition they deserved—before the summer was over, Robert would receive his knighthood.

While working at Plymouth, Robert got a letter from Admiral Sir Thomas Byam Martin, who was Comptroller of the Royal Navy. The Admiral advised Seppings that an American ship fitted with a steam engine had arrived recently at Liverpool. It was the decision of the Lords Commissioners of the Admiralty that once he was finished with his duties at Plymouth, Robert Seppings was to proceed directly to Liverpool, with the intent of examining the steamship called *Savannah*.

CHAPTER THIRTEEN

———

HOME FRONT

ONCE THE STEAMSHIP *Savannah* had left the coast of Georgia, any news of her fate depended upon the chance that another vessel might see her, and report the sighting upon arrival in an American port. Then it was up to the newspapers to publish such an account, if they saw fit. This was the only way that Adelia and the children, and Mary Rogers, and the rest of the extended Rogers clan would know that Moses and Steve were alright. The shareholders, too, could do nothing but hope and pray that all was well with their experiment, until they received some confirmation of the fact.

Thankfully, they didn't have to wait very long. On June 3rd, *The New York Evening Post* broke the silence:

Steam ship Savannah.—Capt. Brown, of the schr Union, who arrived this forenoon from Madeira, spoke on the 30th of May, latitude 38, 30, lon 68, steam ship Savannah, bound to Liverpool, with all sail set, and machinery in motion.

The next day, the *Mercantile Advertiser* added that Captain Brown and his crew first thought they were looking at a ship on fire.

This was soon followed by the *Newburyport Herald* of Massachusetts, on June 8th:

Steam Boat at Sea.—Capt. Livingston, of schooner Contract, who here arrived Saturday, saw 29th ult. lat. 27, 30, long 70, a vessel ahead to the Eastward, from which he observed volumes of smoke issuing—judging it to be a vessel on fire stood for her, in order to afford relief "but (observes Capt. L) to our astonishment found she went faster with fire and smoke than we possibly could with all sail set—it was then we discovered that what we supposed a vessel on fire was nothing less than a Steam-boat crossing the Western Ocean, laying his course as we judged for Europe; a proud monument of Yankee skill and enterprize— Success to her."

—(This is undoubtedly the steam-ship Savannah, Capt. Rogers, which sailed from Savannah 22d ult. for Russia.)

For those who received only this latter report, the position recorded by the *Contract* must have given pause. Based upon the coordinates provided, the *Savannah* had been some 500 miles *east of the Bahamas!* This made no sense, and must have sent a chill through anyone who checked the steamship's position on a map. It meant the *Savannah* had gone due southeast after leaving the Georgia coast, and was midway between the Bahamas and Bermuda when sighted. While it was normal for a departing vessel to sail due east, to get as deeply into the Gulf Steam as possible, the stated position implied the *Savannah* had gone right through the Stream, and was way off course. Either this was some kind of mistake, or something had gone very wrong.

The *Savannah*'s status was made all the more confusing when newspapers in New York published the same story, only with the schooner's name being *Peace & Plenty*. It was this account, with the same perplexing position for the contact, which was reprinted the most frequently around the country, including in Charleston and Savannah.

Eventually, it must have become apparent that the *Contract*'s (or *Peace & Plenty*'s) reported latitude of 27 degrees, 30 minutes was incorrect, to the tune of 10 degrees. Those who had the benefit of the schooner *Union*'s account knew *that* vessel had seen the steamship a day later at latitude 38 degrees, 30 minutes. Surely that more northerly reading, which put the *Savannah* solidly within the Gulf Stream some 400 miles due east of Maryland, was the accurate one. At the very least, everyone knew that on May 30th, the steamship was safe.

By mid-June, a clearer, more assured report came out of Baltimore. The captain of a recently-arrived ship, the *Plato*, allowed an extract from his logbook to be published by one of that city's newspapers:

June 2d. clear weather and smooth sea, light winds W. S. W. lat. 42 deg. lon. 59 deg. spoke and passed the elegant steam Ship SAVANNAH,

*out eight days from Savannah, bound to St. Petersburg by way of
Liverpool. She passed us at the rate of nine or ten knots, and the captain informed us that she worked remarkably well, and the greatest
compliment we could bestow, was to give her three cheers, as the happiest effort of mechanical genius that ever appeared on the western
ocean. She returned the compliment.*

Yet the *Plato's* captain could not stop there, and ventured his own
view of the future:

*"Thinks we to ourselves," if America should ever have another war
with any European power (which God forbid), we shall in a short time
have floating steam batteries at sea, as large as Fort M'Henry, when
we shall have a better opportunity of returning shell for shell, than we
had last siege, where many were stationed as targets to be shot at.*

Still more news came a few days later, when the ship *Canton* arrived
at New York from Liverpool. She had passed the *Savannah* on June
6th, and got close enough to receive an "all well" message from the
steamship. The *Canton* reported a latitude reading only, of 42°, 30′
North, which put the steamship somewhere in the Gulf Stream, presumably far to the east of Massachusetts. (In fact, the two vessels had
been southeast of the Grand Bank, about 1,300 miles from Boston.)

As the newspapers from these various eastern ports were trundled,
steamboated and sailed off to neighboring towns and cities, reports
on the steamship's progress steadily spread all over the United States.
Given travel times, people down in Savannah didn't get much of this
news until mid-to-late June.

As the great experiment moved further and further across the
Atlantic, the amount of time it would take for news of additional
sightings to reach any American port naturally increased. So once
the *Canton's* encounter was reported, word of the *Savannah's* fate
dried up—*for weeks.*

It wasn't until August 9th, some 2½ months after the steamship's
departure, that the home front received further news. A British ship,
the *Higson,* arrived at Norfolk, Virginia from Cork, Ireland, carrying
a bundle of English and Irish newspapers, and a local Norfolk correspondent found a story buried within one of them:

I have received no Shipping List by this arrival; but an article of great importance in the <u>Steam World</u>, (if I may use the expression) is contained in the Cork paper of the 19th of June—it is no less than the arrival at Kinsale, in 21 days, of the STEAM-SHIP SAVANNAH, from Savannah, laden with cotton, and passengers—she put in for supplies, would remain a day or two, and then proceed to Liverpool. Previous to her putting in, she was chased by a cutter, under the impression that she was a ship on fire. No further particulars are stated.

This thoroughly garbled, inaccurate report soon reached Charleston, where it was printed by the *City Gazette* on August 17th. Then it was picked up by the Savannah newspapers two days later.

With nothing else to go on, some folks must have wondered why Captain Rogers had decided to stop at such a small port as Kinsale, Ireland. Putting in "for supplies" was awfully cryptic—if anything had given out, it was probably fuel, or perhaps drinking water. In any event, the steamship had made it safely across the open ocean, and the passage time, as stated, appeared to be good.

At the same time newspaper readers down South were pondering the false meaning of Kinsale, newspaper readers up North were absorbing the true meaning of Liverpool. Gotham got the word first, on August 17th, with reprints of *Marwade's* complimentary "without a single sheet" story. Just as in Britain, *Marwade's* became the most widely-published arrival account in the United States. This was soon followed by additional articles describing the *Kite* chase and rumors of the steamship's intentions.

All this largely-true news didn't reach Savannah itself until the end of August. Arriving at the same time was a private letter from an American residing in Liverpool, which was passed on to *The Georgian*, and immediately published:

The steamship Savannah arrived a few days ago, to the great astonishment of the people of this city. She came up without sails, and was much admired. John Bull cannot bear the idea that Jonathan should be the first to sail across the Atlantic by the operation of steam, but it is now too evident to be denied. It will not be like some of our scientific discoveries, the origin of which have been denied to our people, and attempts made by even philosophers to rob us of our infant fame. The report is current here that this ship is commanded by a brother of

Commodore Rogers, and is intended as a present from our government to the Emperor Alexander, and from this wise suggestion the politicians of the day have augured much importance, as 'secret views of ambition' covered hostility to the commerce of Great Britain.

The report of presumed kinship between Moses and Commodore John Rodgers also was reprinted in many American newspapers. This spurred Hezekiah Niles, editor of the widely-read *Niles' Weekly Register*, to go to the trouble of printing a correction, noting that there was "not any relationship between them." Yet another private letter, received at Charleston from Edinburgh, made clear just how welcome the *Savannah*'s arrival had been to the American expatriate community, living as they were in the land of the Royal Navy.

Yet despite the friction evident between the more testy branches of the Anglo-American family, many newspapers in the United States simply chose to ignore the rumors and the jabs. They focused instead upon the accomplishment itself.

The *Richmond Enquirer* went even further, highlighting the significance of what had just occurred, and daring to spell out, with great pride, a thirst for both facts and the future:

The Steam Ship Savannah, Capt. Rogers, is the first steam ship that has crossed the Atlantic.—She sailed, or rather was *steamed* from land to land, from Savannah to Kinsale, in Ireland, in 21 days—during 18 of which she had the use of her machinery. To ascertain the rapidity of her voyage, we must have her log book before us. We must see what kind of weather she had; what *winds*, whether ahead or in her favor; what *course* she took, whether the meanders of the gulf stream, or whether she pointed her head boldly in a straight, unveering line for her destined harbor.
We must know what is the usual length of voyages from Savannah to Kinsale?—What was the duration of those, which were undertaken about the same time by other vessels from the same or other ports? We should wish to know how much nearer is the voyage to Liverpool from N. York, than from Savannah? If five days nearer, then would not the Savannah have traced from New York from land to land in *sixteen days?*
We hope all the facts of this extraordinary enterprize may be given, and the necessary calculations made of the rapidity of the

voyage. For aught that we know, it may form a new era in the art of navigation, almost as important as the discovery of the mariner's compass ... There is no knowing what revolutions it may not produce in the arts of ship building and ship sailing.— The moment, indeed, that the gigantic power of steam was applied successfully to the propulsion of boats, a new direction was given to navigation. Hitherto, we had with difficulty moved our boats by the hand; or they floated with the tide, or had been pushed on by the winds; but now a new impulse was given, a new principle applied; a new power superinduced, which did not depend upon the lazy tides or the capricious winds; but was in a great degree within the control of man, and could be increased at his discretion! The bounds of this augmentation have not yet been discovered. We cannot yet calculate the limits of it. Hitherto, the operation of this new element had been mainly confined to our continent. The Hudson was the first river to witness its triumphs. Then, it was exerted to stem the strong current of the Mississippi. Next, the steam boat was launched upon the bosom of the sea; but still, with the same caution which marked the earlier periods of navigation, ... it went on coasting from port to port ... It had not yet braved all the dangers of the deep, until Captain Rodgers boldly seized the helm, and traversed the Atlantic.—

Thus, steam navigation has successfully advanced from the rivers to the coast, and finally from the coast across the Ocean. The invention was ours; ours was the first steam boat that went against the wind and waves; ours the first steam ship that defies the difficulties of the deep. At every era the triumph belongs to America.

We wish to know all the particulars of this voyage, which relate to the degree of its rapidity or its difficulties. The first experiment is generally the most hazardous and inconvenient. Light breaks in upon us by degrees. The imperfections of machinery, the play of the waves upon the wheels, all those circumstances which distinguish a distant and daring sea navigation, from a coasting voyage, will be gradually disclosed. Old difficulties will be overcome; and new improvements will be introduced. Means, as yet not thought of, will be devised to add wings to its feet. We are yet but in the infancy of steam navigation. The experiment of the Savannah opens a new field of adventure. Not only vessels of passage or of commerce, but of war, are perhaps to experience the effects of it. Changes in the arts of building, of working, and of employing ships of war, dependent upon steam, may yet be in the womb of time, of which the utmost sagacity is unable to form a conception. As America has been the birth place of steam navigation, so will it always find a home here. We have the start of the world; and we will keep it. In a genius for maritime enterprize, we will at least equal any nation, that chooses to cope with us.

Still others saw in the *Savannah*'s triumph the seeds of more localized opportunity. Someone by the pen-name of "PERAMBULATOR" wrote to *Relf's Philadelphia Gazette*, suggesting a solution to that city's challenges:

> *In one of my late rambles through the City and Liberties, I could not help contrasting the situation of journeymen ship-carpenters now, with what it was ten or twelve years ago— Then all were busy either in building or repairing vessels— At this time there are but three vessels building, viz. a schooner in Kensington, a ship of the line at the Navy-Yard, and a steam-boat near thereabout, 93 or 100 feet long— These three vessels afford very inadequate employment for so large a portion of men as the carpenters, caulkers, joiners, blacksmiths, riggers and other persons, who have been accustomed to rely on the building and finishing of ships, for a maintenance.*
> *There must be* <u>*solid*</u> *wealth enough in this city, to spare, without inconvenience to the owners, which would afford employment to a number of these men.— Could not the project of a Steam-ship, to navigate the ocean, as a Packet between this and Charleston, or Liverpool be carried into effect as well here as at Savannah and New York?. . .*

What had seemed outlandish a little more than one year before was suddenly considered not just possible, but repeatable.

For most Americans, though, the *Savannah*'s successful crossing simply reinforced the feeling that they were living in an extraordinary time. There was no better example of this popular sentiment than the toast volunteered at a public dinner in Wiscasset, on the coast of Maine, which paid tribute to their modern era, from the serious to the silly:

> *The Wonders of the Age.—A steam ship—an Iceberg—a Sea Serpent—and a Dandy on a Velocipede!!!*

CHAPTER FOURTEEN

DECISIONS

For as long as the *Savannah* lay anchored in the River Mersey, just off Tranmere, she remained an object of public fascination. Her decks hosted a great many visitors, and it did not escape the notice of some commentators just how many members of the fairer sex made a point of examining the steamship. This latter phenomenon was entirely logical—any invention that promised to reduce the danger, discomfort and duration associated with ocean travel was an innovation that women would want to see.

In turn, the British treated the *Savannah*'s officers, according to Steve's later recollection, with "marked attention." They were invited to tour shipyards, factories and other facilities not normally accessible to the public. Liverpool itself had any number of such installations, from its shipbuilding docks, to a steam-powered rope-making factory, to the well-known Herculaneum potteries.

The huge textile factories for which Britain was particularly renowned were further to the east, in the city of Manchester. It was there, and in other industrial centers, that the political reform movement relentlessly continued to gain momentum during the *Savannah*'s stay.

On June 21st, the day after the steamship's arrival, cotton weavers held an "immense" meeting at St. Peter's Field in Manchester, where they bluntly "resolved to join and exterminate that borough-mongering tyranny that is sweeping us all from off the face of the earth."

Such blistering rhetoric was counterbalanced, somewhat, by more measured yet equally radical pronouncements from a rally of 10,000 Reformers at Hunslett Moor, near the city of Leeds—

"All men are born free;"

"All men are born equal."

By late June, every day's newspaper brought fresh reports of reform meetings being held all around the country.

In Glasgow, a rally of weavers grew so large, with a crowd estimated at 35,000 people, that the local authorities placed a regiment of soldiers and some cavalry on standby, in case there was trouble.

At the town of Blackburn, near Manchester, a "Female Reform Society" was organized, and sent out circulars inviting the wives and daughters of workmen in other towns to form similar societies, and coordinate their actions with other reform groups.

Further accounts indicated that some Reformers were instructing workers in the manufacture of the "revolutionary pike," a long spear that could be used in any armed confrontation.

All this activity, combined with secret reports to the government from a cadre of domestic spies, reinforced the view of Lord Liverpool and his Cabinet that the situation was deteriorating rapidly.

Just as disconcerting was the symbolism creeping into the reform movement. There was no better example of this than what occurred at a huge reform rally held near Manchester, on June 28th (while Moses had been on his way to London). At that gathering, a man named Sir Charles Wolseley, one of the few aristocratic Reformers, gave an incendiary speech, in which he claimed "that his political career commenced in France; that he was one of those who mounted the ramparts of the Bastile at the commencement of the Revolution in that country; and if he did that for France, he should never shrink from attacking the Bastiles of his own country."

Also at that same rally, the *Cap of Liberty* had been called for, which was ceremoniously nailed to the top of a flagstaff. This brimless, loose red hat was a symbol from ancient Rome, worn by slaves who had been given their freedom. Of course, there was no slavery in the British Isles in 1819—in fact, the Royal Navy was actively combating the slave trade on the high seas—but the Cap of Liberty had been adopted by both the Americans and the French during their revolutions as a symbol of the freedom they sought.

Employing such a provocative emblem in Britain had been deliberately avoided by other rally organizers. Its eventual use at Manchester, however, in conjunction with Sir Wolseley's hyperbole, brought the radical reform movement one step closer to what the government could consider treason.

* * *

Back in Liverpool on the 4th of July, the *Savannah*'s crew very likely celebrated their own version of treason and rebellion. If Moses and Steve were prepared, they would have had a new American flag to fly from the steamship, with 21 stars, instead of the 20 used in the previous design. The new star was for the State of Illinois, which, despite having entered the Union the previous December, could not—by a recent law—be recognized on the flag until the first 4th of July following its admission.

Beyond celebrating the Declaration of Independence, the *Savannah*'s crew and all the other Americans in Liverpool had plenty of news from home to mull over. The most recent reports were not at all encouraging. While Britain was experiencing its own commercial chaos, with bankruptcies rising and widespread problems with debt collections, the situation in the United States sounded far worse. A New York City agent for a Yorkshire manufacturer admitted in a published letter that "never before did I witness such distress and embarrassment as every where prevails, on account of the over-stocked markets, and the low price of all descriptions of goods."

Exacerbating the panic in America was the contagious "suspension" by Western banks (refusing to redeem their paper notes for specie), which eventually had spread eastward. By the time it reached Baltimore, the City Bank there, along with thirty commercial houses, had been forced to stop payment.

And the contagion had spread southward, as well. In Charleston, it was reported that an entire street of shops had been forced to close because they were all connected to each other financially. When one shop stopped honoring its debts, the others were compelled to follow suit.

A letter from that same city, published in the London papers in early July, put the state of the American nation in no uncertain terms:

> *However extensive may be the ruin and distress experienced on your side of the water, it cannot, I am confident, be compared with what is felt here—ruin and devastation are pursuing their baleful course in almost every part of the Union, and universal insolvency threatens the whole mercantile community; already many houses, considered hitherto as of the first respectability, (both here, at New York, Philadelphia, Boston, &c.) have sunk within its vortex, and no one can tell who will be solvent on the morrow...*

Such depressing news placed an even greater burden upon Moses. He had to believe that the shareholders were depending on him more than ever to sell the steamship as expeditiously as possible. Whether he, Robert Isaac or Andrew Low tried to interest Liverpool merchants in making an investment in or purchase of the *Savannah* is unknown. In any event, the appetite in Albion for such a venture was probably just about non-existent, given the immediate temper of the times.

The original idea of going to Russia to effect a sale still held the most promise. In planning for the *Savannah*'s departure from Liverpool, Moses had to mull over which route to take to reach the entrance to the Baltic Sea.

He could maneuver the steamship south, around Wales and England, and then through the English Channel to reach the North Sea.

Or, alternately, he could take the *Savannah* northward, rounding the top of Scotland, and thereby enter the North Sea from the opposite direction.

Both routes were about the same distance. Each required its own careful navigation through Britain's coastal waters, which had a well-deserved reputation for being unpredictable and dangerous. But only the southern route offered Moses the option of making his intended ports of call at London and the French port of Havre.

The final decision would have to take all of these circumstances into account, as well as perhaps other extraordinary factors.

* * *

Once news of the *Savannah*'s arrival had spread throughout Albion, she quickly attracted the attention of not only Liverpudlians, but others from further afield.

Among the many who came to Liverpool was an American expatriate from London. Born and raised in northwestern Connecticut, this 38-year-old lawyer had come to Britain back in 1805, to argue his brother's vessel seizure case before the High Court of the Admiralty. Having won substantial damages, he soon found his legal services in high demand with other American merchants who had their own seizure cases to appeal. With his continued success in court, he decided to put down roots in London, becoming his brother's commercial agent, and eventually marrying an English girl, and starting a family.

This expatriate's visit to Liverpool in the early summer of 1819, whether by chance or design, gave him the perfect opportunity to inspect the steamship *Savannah*. Once on board, he carefully examined her machinery, both above and below deck, as well as the rest of the vessel. Then, he took his leave, and returned to London.

Regardless of the immediate impression the *Savannah* may have made upon him, it seems clear that his examination of her planted a seed of some kind in his mind. In time, this seed would grow into a vision of the future that would animate and dominate the life of this American named Junius Smith.

* * *

In the days after July 4th, the *Savannah*'s crew kept up their normal port routine. If they weren't loosening the sails to dry, or scraping the decks, then Steve kept them busy with the usual "sundry jobs of ships duty."

So it was on the cloudy Monday of July 12th. But while the crew labored to keep the steamship pristine for visitors that day, across the river, in Liverpool, another group of men set about the task of showcasing another point of pride all their own. That morning, a collection of about 100 men gathered at the parish church of St. Peter, in the city's center. Once all was ready, the men exited the church and reassembled outside on the street, lining up in formation. Then, those at the front of the company unsheathed their swords, and the whole unit began to march.

As the formation proceeded through the streets of Liverpool, heading toward the Town Hall, onlookers could not help but notice that many of these men were curiously dressed. Some were wearing long robes, others leopard skins, and still others ermine furs. The whole lot of them were kept in step by a small band of musicians amongst their number, including drummers who beat out a regular cadence as they marched. Further complementing their regalia were a series of orange banners and flags, depicting the Lamb, the Ark, and the Bible.

The onlookers soon congealed into a crowd, which began to follow these men as they marched to Town Hall, circled around it, and then continued on, down Dale Street.

At the bottom of Dale, another mass of men waited patiently for the marchers to reach them. Once the two groups came face to face, the die was cast. Melee ensued.

Thrown onto the defensive were the marchers, who were members of the Orange Societies of Liverpool and Manchester. Their ceremonious parading had been in commemoration of the Battle of the Boyne in 1690, in which the Protestant William of Orange had defeated the Catholic James II, thereby ensuring Britain would remain predominantly Protestant.

But the very appearance of Orangemen, never before seen in Liverpool, was too much for the mass of Irish Catholic residents who met them at the bottom of Dale Street. Given the passions involved, the unavoidable result was a full-scale riot.

The Orangemen got the worst of it. Caught off-guard and outnumbered, many suffered injuries, and most of their parade articles were destroyed. Local police quickly moved in, arresting a number of the Irish who had started the fight, and incarcerating them at Bridewell Prison.

Once again, the jail was quickly surrounded by protesters. "The town, during the whole afternoon," reported *Billinge's Liverpool Advertiser*, "was in a state of agitation."

Once more, Liverpool Mayor Jonathan Hollinshead felt compelled to call up local militia units as a precaution. But the crowd massed around the prison showed little interest in fomenting any more trouble, and by evening, most of it had dispersed.

Not surprisingly, news of the attack on the Orangemen quickly spread all over Britain. While the riot had nothing overtly to do with the reform movement, or the restless South American volunteers encamped nearby, or the assault on Bridewell three weeks earlier, it nevertheless added to the sense of instability in Liverpool, at the least. For the country as a whole, it became yet one more indication that— eventually—something was going to happen to tip the country over the edge.

* * *

The day after the Orangemen mayhem, the *Savannah's* crew began taking on supplies, in preparation for their departure. A shore boat came alongside that evening with ten *hogsheads** of drinking water, which were hauled aboard. The next day, July 14th, the crew brought on board four *tierces*** of beef, one barrel of pork, and five barrels of bread.

---

*   A hogshead is equal to 2 barrels.

** A tierce is equal to 1⅓ barrels.

By this time, the questions surrounding the *Savannah*'s export duties had been resolved. Junior Secretary of the Treasury Stephen Lushington, in a letter to Isaac, Low & Company, laid out the terms:

> ... *My Lords see no Sufficient grounds for remitting the Duty on the Coals required for this Vessel but that they will not object to authorizing the Comm.[issioners] on Customs not to insist on the payment of the Tonnage Duty provided no Cargo is shipped on board her beyond the coals necessary for the consumption of the Vessel + the Steam Engine.*

In other words, the general tonnage tax on vessels leaving Britain could be waived. The coals, however, even though acknowledged by the Treasury as not being cargo, would nevertheless be taxed as such!

This decision must have seemed patently unfair to Moses, since merchant ships were already allowed to export duty-free any coal to be used on board, be it in the galley or otherwise. Since all of the *Savannah*'s coal would be used to run the steam engine, and not re-sold, it must have rankled that export duties would still be levied.

If the Lords of the Treasury had any defense for their decision, it was probably the highly irregular if not unprecedented nature of the request. No steam vessel had ever been to Albion asking for such a waiver. At least the Treasury had agreed to forego the general tonnage duty, which the Commissioners of Customs in London duly ordered Liverpool Collector Swainson not to charge the *Savannah*.

The Treasury's decision to charge duty on the coals probably led Moses to limit his purchase of the black fuel at Liverpool. Rather than pay unnecessary taxes, it made sense to buy only as much as he thought necessary to cover the shorter distance to the next port of call. If there was any consolation, it was that with less "cargo" on board, the steamship would ride higher in the water, perhaps marginally improving the paddlewheels' efficiency.

In any event, with food for the crew already procured, food for the boilers came next. On July 16th, a lighter came alongside the steamship at noontime, filled with 36 tons of coal. Steve put all hands to work hauling the fuel into the bunkers. By 7 o'clock that evening, the job was finished—no more coal would be brought on board.

Two days later, Moses ordered the steam engine and paddlewheels be put into motion for a spell, probably to make sure everything was working properly before departure.

Among the *Savannah*'s visitors around this time was a correspondent from the *Cheshire Chronicle*, a newspaper based in the nearby city of Chester. During his time on board, the reporter carefully examined every aspect of the steamship, from the steam engine, to the paddle-wheels, to the passenger accommodations. "We may safely take upon ourselves to say," he later wrote, "that a more handsome specimen of naval architecture never entered a British port ... and the whole is highly creditable to American mechanism and ingenuity."

The correspondent's largely complimentary article, published in the *Cheshire Chronicle* after the *Savannah*'s departure, also addressed the issue of rumors:

> ... We had some conversation with the Capt. (Rogers) who is not remarkable for being communicative; and from the purport of his answers, we are inclined to believe that the rumour of the vessel being a PRESENT to the Emperor Alexander, is totally groundless: but we are nevertheless of [the] opinion that the Czar may PURCHASE it,—if he likes it. The fact is, the Savannah is sent to Europe merely as a specimen of Trans-Atlantic ship architecture, and will become the property of the "highest bidder." A SILENT civility pervades the whole of the crew, from the Captain to the Black Cook, for which the whole inclusive may have private reasons, which it is no business of ours to inquire into.

Precisely why Moses had appeared "not remarkable for being communicative" is unclear.

Maybe he was tired of all the rumors and questions about the *Savannah*'s "true purpose." (Years later, Steve would recount how the British authorities kept a close eye on the steamship during its stay.)

Maybe the speculation on the possibility of a steam-powered rescue of Napoleon from his island jail had led someone to put Moses on notice.

Maybe the continuing bad news from home made the financial burden placed upon him all the heavier, and less talkative as a result.

Or maybe Moses was just anxious to get on with the voyage.

Whatever the reasons, the reporter's emphasized "SILENT civility" of the crew made it obvious to readers that he thought there was *something* about the *Savannah* that captain and crew were not willing to share with him.

On July 19th, the day after the engine and paddlewheels were tested, Moses received a bill of health from the Liverpool Custom House. This document certified that the *Savannah* was disease-free during her time there, and could be useful for future ports of call.

Since the crew had nothing to spread but a little money, they must have had some time ashore at Liverpool. But Steve never noted it in the logbook—except when there was trouble. The same rain-filled day the bill of health came through, a couple of crewmen, James Bruce and John Smith, refused to return to the ship.

Apprised of the situation, Moses told Mr. Blackman to take the jolly boat and go get them.

Despite the second mate's appearance on shore, both men still refused to come. The local watchman on the scene lent a hand, and with some effort finally managed to deposit the pair into the boat.

As they headed back to the ship, John Smith remained unbowed. Determined to resist his unofficial arrest, Smith tried to knock Mr. Blackman overboard, hitting him several times and threatening to kill him. Mr. Blackman held firm, though, and got the cross men out of the jolly boat and onto the *Savannah*.

Still incensed, John Smith "denied his duty."

Any seaman refusing to work had to be dealt with firmly, lest other crew members see leniency as a sign of weakness. So John Smith was promptly taken below deck and put in irons, until he changed his mind.

The next day, July 20th, the Liverpool Custom House cleared the *Savannah* for departure; her eventual destination was listed as St. Petersburg, Russia. She was then free to depart at any time, but Nature was not cooperating. The rain and winds of the previous day had turned into heavy, drenching gales, coming out of the north-northwest.

Rather than attempt a departure under such conditions, Moses bided his time. "All hands" were kept busy with "sundry jobs of ships duty," except for John Smith. He stayed in irons throughout the day.

By first light the following morning, the weather was far better, so Moses made plans to get going. The first order of business was John Smith, and whether he would return to duty. As Smith, his captain and the rest of the crew well-knew, American sea law on this subject was crystal-clear:

... if any seaman or mariner shall absent himself for more than forty-eight hours at one time, he shall forfeit all the wages due to him, and all his goods and chattels which were on board the said ship or vessel...

By refusing to work, John Smith already had "absented himself" from the ship for two days. Steve had made it all official by recording Smith's intransigence in the logbook. In consequence, Captain Rogers had the legal right to dock Smith three days' pay for each day he had "denied his duty."

But anything beyond a 48-hour absence represented the point of no return. John Smith was left with a stark choice: lose six days' pay and go back to work, or risk being fired, losing all of his wages and belongings, and additionally being charged the cost of hiring his replacement.

Such harsh penalties had been approved by Congress at the behest of merchant ship captains, who had plenty of trouble handling their crews. It was imperative that every seaman on board do his job not sometimes, but always. Anything less had the potential to put the vessel, the cargo, and the lives of the crew and passengers at risk.

With his job on the line, John Smith relented. He agreed to do his duty, and the shackles came off.

Immediately thereafter, the crew unmoored the ship. Several hours later, Moses ordered the starboard anchor pulled up. Instead of using either mode of power, he simply allowed the *Savannah* to drift slowly down the Mersey, toward Liverpool.

By mid-day, the "strong breezes" of the morning had strengthened to gale-force winds, still coming from the north. Facing a strong headwind, Moses ordered the left (or *larboard*) anchor dropped, to hold the ship in place.

But this anchor didn't bite into the river bottom. After pulling it up, the crew discovered why: one of the anchor's *flukes*, which is the triangular end of the anchor arm, had broken off. The starboard anchor was then tossed overboard as a replacement. This time, it held.

Putting to sea with a broken anchor was simply out of the question. So Moses made arrangements to get a replacement from shore, but this couldn't be accomplished until well past dark. Departure would have to wait.

* * *

By the time the *Savannah* dropped anchor off Liverpool that evening, the political mood on shore, and throughout Albion, had already reached a new low. The reform rallies had been spreading, and intensifying. Events around the country during the previous ten days had forced the British government to fear, and prepare for, the worst.

On July 12th (the day of the attack on the Orangemen), the Radical Sir Charles Wolseley had been ceremoniously "elected" by 15,000 Reformers at Birmingham to serve as their representative to the House of Commons. This made him the first member of what could become an illegal shadow parliament.

The very next day, Sir Wolseley had been indicted for sedition, based upon his earlier "Bastille" speech. He was soon arrested, and just as soon out on bail.

Further afield, in Montgomeryshire, Wales, a protest over wage cuts in the textile mills had quickly spiraled out of control. The destructive violence of the protesters had forced local officials to swear in extra constables to restore order, as well as mobilize the local cavalry, just in case.

And on July 19th (the same day the *Savannah*'s bill of health was issued), *Billinge's Liverpool Advertiser* reported that based upon orders from the Home Office, "the Liverpool light horse, as well as most of the other corps of volunteer cavalry in the kingdom, have received notice to hold themselves in a state of preparation, on the possibility of their being called out to suppress any domestic disturbance."

The Morning Post of London minced no words in its judgment of what Albion faced:

> ... The most alarming circumstance in the present crisis is the systematic nature of the proceedings, and the extent to which they have been carried. When we find, in various parts of the empire, and at the same time, associations formed, and numerous meetings of the lower orders assembled, all under the same pretext, and professing to act together for the attainment of one and the same object—when that object avowedly is the alteration of the established usages and laws, it is impossible not to think that the State is menaced with serious danger...

The sense of peril was so strong that Lord Sidmouth, the Home Secretary, had vowed not to leave London that summer, as reports of the Reformers' activities continued to pour in.

His anxiety was shared by many others. As one observer from the northern city of Leeds declared:

> *... an important blow will be aimed at the prosperity and peace of the Country, as soon as the parties felt sufficiently strong to undertake their projects with any chance of success. That time I fear is now near at hand...*

* * *

Attracting any passengers for the next leg of the *Savannah*'s voyage would not have been easy. Despite the successful crossing of the Atlantic, and the thousands who came to visit her, nearly everyone remained very reluctant to risk traveling on such a vessel.

Recent news of Britain's own steamboats was hardly reassuring. In early July, the Scottish steamboat *Stirling* had been running on the Firth of Forth, west of Edinburgh, when her boiler exploded. Nine people were scalded, three of them severely. And just as the *Savannah* was preparing for departure, news broke that the Irish Sea steam packet *Talbot*, upon entering Holyhead harbor, had caught fire and partly burned.

The difficulties that the *Talbot* and her fellow steamers were experiencing that summer, as they tried to maintain regular service across the Irish Sea, were obvious to anyone reading the newspapers. The steam packet proprietors felt compelled to advertise how "completely safe" the vessels were, given their "being built of extraordinary strength," with low-risk low-pressure engines. The *Talbot*'s owners had even changed her schedule so that she ran only during daylight, "in compliance with the general wish of their Friends and the Public." But even with these safeguards in place, their sailing packet competitors still did not hesitate to warn passengers about the dangers of steam-powered crossings to Ireland. Under the circumstances, no one needed to be told how perilous a voyage on a revolutionary steamship would be, operating as it did so far from land.

In spite of these discouragements, one person did agree to go in the *Savannah*. On the eve of departure, hobbling onto her deck came a weathered man with a wooden leg. His name was Daniel Barnett.

While he and Elizabeth Barnett were known on land for their confectionary business on Liver Street, Daniel Barnett was also familiar with the sea. He had been, and still considered himself to be, a mariner by profession. Such a man could be quite useful on the voyage ahead. There were many hazards along the coasts of the British Isles. The bodies of water that led into the Baltic Sea—the Skagerrak and the Kattegat—also were known for being difficult and dangerous. Since Moses and Steve had very little if any experience in those waters, Barnett could act as their pathfinder.

The morning after the anchor accident, the Mersey proved to be much calmer. But the winds were still blowing briskly, out of the northwest and directly upriver. Rather than press ahead in less than ideal conditions, Moses held off.

The following morning, July 23rd, justified the delay. Liverpool and the River Mersey were bathed in a beautiful blue sky, dotted with white, puffy "flying clouds."

Once steam was up in the boilers and the paddlewheels deployed, Moses ordered the *Savannah* into motion, at 1 o'clock that afternoon. Bobbing all around her, as Steve noted in the logbook, was "a large fleet of vessels in company." Still more spectators crowded the shoreline, to see the steamship off.

Further complementing the *Savannah*'s departure that afternoon were two other displays of the new mode of transport. Nearby, one of the Mersey steamboats was towing a huge, India-bound merchant ship—the *George Canning*—out to sea. Also splashing down the river was a new steam packet, the *Waterloo*, on her run to Belfast.

As the *Savannah* and the *Waterloo* came alongside one another, the two vessels picked up speed. Whether they were actually trying to race each other to the mouth of the Mersey isn't clear, but that's certainly what it looked like to those watching. The British steamer had a clear advantage in horsepowers generated per ton of burthen. This made all the difference, as the *Waterloo* took the lead, comfortably reaching the exit to the sea well before the *Savannah*.

By 3 o'clock that afternoon, the local pilot had steered the steamship over the sandbar at the mouth of the Mersey. His job done, he transferred to one of the nearby pilot boats, leaving Daniel Barnett as the only guide aboard.

Next came the question of direction: south, around Wales and England, or north, around Scotland?

Moses ordered the *Savannah* to steam due west. With the north coast of Wales visible off the larboard side, the steamship churned onward, through the afternoon, and into the evening.

By midnight, the beacon of Holyhead lighthouse, on the very northwestern tip of Wales, could be seen off the larboard bow, about 3 leagues (or 9 miles) distant. At that point, the full length of the Irish Sea lay before the *Savannah*.

Once past Holyhead, Moses could turn the steamship south, maneuver around Land's End, and head for the English Channel, stopping at whatever ports he wished while en route to St. Petersburg.

Or, he could go north, around Scotland, and into the North Sea.

* * *

One week before the *Savannah*'s departure, members of the Navy Board, the Royal Navy body responsible for maintaining the fleet, sat down in conference at their offices in Somerset House, on the Strand in London. With them was Robert Seppings.

Seppings had been one of the steamship's many visitors in the early part of July. After making his way above and below decks, Robert had found someone with an informed knowledge of the *Savannah*—in all likelihood, one of her officers—to whom he had posed a series of questions. Once finished with his examination, Robert had returned to London.

Sitting before his colleagues, Robert recounted what he had learned about the steamship. It had, he said, "from the best information I could obtain," a 74 horsepower steam engine, and fuel on the crossing of "1,000 bushels of Coals and 4 chord of wood, which were nearly expended on their arrival at Liverpool." As for performance, "they were 26 days on their passage, the Engine was worked 99 hours, and the greatest rate of going, was six miles per hour and proportionally less in a head sea—"

Once he had described the layout of the machinery and make-up of the crew, Robert concluded by giving the assembled experts his professional opinion:

> . . . *It is clear from what has been stated that Vessels fitted on this principle can never be applied to the carrying [of] merchandise, and the little benefit that appears to have been produced, as it respects the shortening the time on the passage, is by no means equal to the many inconveniences of the system. For local passage vessels, no doubt, propelling Apparatus may be, as they are, very advantageously applied, and I think it is very probable that a description of Vessels may be designed*

*and propelled by the power of Steam, to act as local Gun Boats, to pro-
tect any point or Harbour.*

Such an iron-clad conclusion made it abundantly clear that at least
in the mind of Robert Seppings, the barrier remained.

* * *

The evening before the Navy Board heard Robert Seppings' report
on the *Savannah,* one of the London dailies, called *The Statesman*, had
published a long editorial on its front page.

That this particular editorial appeared in that particular newspaper
was noteworthy, in that *The Statesman* was one of the most prominent
Radical newspapers in the capital, and as a daily, could not avoid being
"stamped" (or taxed) accordingly. This made it far more expensive
than the Radical weeklies (like Cobbett's), which avoided the tax, and
therefore skewed *The Statesman's* readership toward those Reformers
who could afford to buy it.

Even more curious was the pen name under which the editorialist
chose to write, which was "Valerius."

It was an unusual and interesting name. Valerius was the *nomen*
of one of the oldest families in ancient Rome, and it came from the
Latin word *valere,* meaning "worthy," or "strong." One of the closest
English words to *valere* is "valor." Among the many ancient Romans
with this name were both emperors and consuls, as well as a poet
named Gaius Valerius Flaccus. His most famous work, coincidentally,
was *Argonautica,* the story of Jason and the Argonauts.

While the precise reasons for selecting *The Statesman* and using
the name "Valerius" were unclear, the point of the editorialist's piece
was not. Its subject was Britain's relationship with a former colony
across the ocean:

*On taking a review of our foreign relations, the United States of
America press themselves more immediately on our attention. The
ambitious projects avowed by America,—that spirit of rivalling us
which points all her designs, and animates all her pursuits,—and the
proximity of her territory to our Trans-Atlantic possessions, combine
to render it more than probable that, at no distant period, her interests
and ours will be brought into hostile collision. When to the above
circumstances are superadded the ardent desire of the Americans to*

*supersede us in the Sovereignty of the Seas, we are seriously apprehen-
sive that, eventually, the term "natural enemies" will be most singularly
applicable by us to that People...*

Valerius then followed with a warning to his countrymen not to
be complacent:

*... Experience has taught us that the means of annoyance which the
Americans possess are far from contemptible; but we recoil from a con-
sideration of the fact, and merge into the comfortable persuasion that
America is a pandemonium...*

* * *

With the Holyhead Lighthouse shining through the midnight
darkness, and the Irish Sea stretched before him, Moses had to choose:
north, or south?

The winds at that moment were "fresh breezes at SW," as Steve
noted in the log. That made it easier to go north, but heading south
by sail and steam was also possible. The new mode was already running, and had been continuously since 1 o'clock that afternoon—it
could simply carry on, pushing them forward in either direction.

Instead, Moses ordered the engine stopped, and the paddlewheels
taken in. Then, he told Steve to "set all sail to the best advantage," as
the *Savannah* slowly made her turn—to the north.

CHAPTER FIFTEEN

———

HELSINGØR

AFTER TURNING NORTH at Holyhead, the *Savannah* spent the next two days smothered in a dense fog. Moses and Steve had to proceed with great caution, lest they run the steamship aground, or into anything else. At several points, visibility was so poor that Steve had the crew take in all the light sails, to slow their progress. At another, they were compelled to *heave to* (i.e., stop), until the fog dissipated enough to allow them to grope their way forward.

Despite the *pea soup*, the *Savannah* was able to reach the North Channel of the Irish Sea by July 25th. At that point, Ireland lay to her west, and Scotland to the east.

The following morning, they broke out of the foggy North Channel and into the clear-aired Atlantic. There, the winds shifted dramatically to dead-ahead northerlies, and after a few hours of slow progress tacking back and forth, Moses decided to get the steam up. With all sails furled and the wheels churning, the steamship plowed forward through choppy seas, heading north by west.

By noon that same day, Mingulay Island was sighted 5 leagues to the north. This tiny landmark was the southernmost in a chain of isles called the Outer Hebrides, which are located off the west coast of Scotland.

From this position, Moses had to choose between two ways forward. He could either go northeast, through the Little Minch, which is the waterway between the mainland-hugging Island of Skye and the Outer Hebrides; or he could go northwest, further out into the Atlantic, passing to the west of the Outer Hebrides. The former was more direct, and afforded some protection from the ocean's power, yet Moses chose the latter. Going out into the Atlantic did give them more room to maneuver, if conditions worsened.

Thankfully, they didn't, as the northerly breezes eventually died to a calm. The *Savannah* steamed onward.

Not until July 28th did renewed winds from the southeast make sailing optimal. Only then did Moses order the switch from the new mode back to the old, ending the longest continuous use yet of the *Savannah*'s machinery. She had steamed for 52 hours straight, overcoming both contrary winds and calm, achieving an average speed of about 6 knots.

Having steamed nearly to the top of the Scottish mainland, Moses had a new choice to make. The shortest route into the North Sea was by way of Pentland Firth, a narrow stretch of water between the mainland and the Orkney Islands. The safer route was further to the north, through the much wider opening between the Orkneys and the distant Shetland Islands. Again, Moses chose the latter, safer course, pointing the *Savannah* northeast, guiding her between tiny Fair Isle and Sumburgh Head, at the southernmost tip of the Shetlands. Along the way, the steamship met several fishing boats, and stopped long enough for the crew to buy a few fish from one of them.

By late morning on July 31st, the *Savannah* was well into the dark-blue waters of the North Sea when the winds died down, and a very strong counter-current slowed progress to 1 or 2 knots.

Once again, Moses ordered the steam up. With sufficient pressure built up in the boilers, the steamship was soon able to charge forward at 6 to 7 knots.

Early the following morning, favorable northeasterlies justified a switch back to sails. A few hours later, the crew sighted the coast of Norway, to the east.

Once the *Savannah* rounded the southwestern corner of Norway, on August 2nd, the crew knew they were nearly upon the first portal to the Baltic Sea, known as the Skagerrak. Further confirmation came from the winds, which suddenly shifted to less-than-welcoming southeasterlies. Through intermittent rain squalls, Steve and the crew tacked northward, and then southward, shortly after which they spotted the lighthouse at the Naze, on the southernmost tip of Norway.

The Skagerrak's eastern winds grew even stronger, and the sea decidedly rougher. Steve and his deck crew continued tacking the *Savannah* back and forth, south and then north, trying to make headway as best they could, as the darkened sky drenched them, then stopped, and then drenched them yet again.

The strength of the easterly headwinds made for slow going. Not until meridian on August 4th had enough progress been made to allow the crew to spot the coast of Denmark. Keeping the shoreline in view, Steve continued making shorter tacks north and south until daylight on August 6th, when the crew spotted Scaw lighthouse, on the very northern tip of Denmark.

At that point, as the *Savannah* rounded the lighthouse, she entered the Kattegat—the body of water that separated Denmark from Sweden, and served as the second portal to the Baltic. This required an overall course change, to the south.

Nature, however, refused to yield. The easterly headwinds of the Skagerrak quickly gave way to southerly headwinds in the Kattegat. Given their strength, and the heavy seas that came with them, using steam continued to be out of the question—the possibility of damage to the wheels was just too great. Under the circumstances, Steve could only shift his tacking, to east, then west, and back again, slowly making headway to the south, as the *Savannah* pitched and rolled through the rain-soaked, thunder-clapping gale.

Not until Sunday, August 8th, did Nature finally give up. By noontime, there were only light winds to resist, so Moses ordered the new mode into action. After a few hours of steaming, the crew caught sight of Kullen lighthouse, on the coast of Sweden. This sentinel marked their entry into the third and final portal to the Baltic, a very slender body of water known as the Sound. Maintaining a southerly course, the *Savannah* steamed onward, cradled by Sweden, immediately to her east, and Denmark, to her west.

By early evening, the steamship had progressed far enough into the Sound to meet a pilot boat from the Danish port of Helsingør*. At this place, it would be necessary to stop and pay a toll before entering the Baltic. Many captains—Americans in particular—did not think this toll was fair, given the principle that the oceans and seas of the world belonged to everyone. But the Danes justified the levy based upon a centuries-old tradition. Besides, they argued, it was a reasonable price to pay for their maintaining buoys, beacons and other safety measures in the Sound.

The local boat volunteered a pilot to guide the *Savannah* into "the Roads," which were the waters off the port where vessels could make

---

* Or "Elsinore" in English.

a safe transit through the Sound. This offer being accepted, a pilot scrambled aboard, and very likely asked Moses a series of questions that went something like this:

Where have you come from in America?

Have you a bill of health from there?

How long have you been from there?

Have you spoken to or been on board of any vessels at Sea or in any port but Liverpool since you left America?

From the Danes' perspective, the import of these questions, and their answers, could not be overstated. In addition to maintaining all of the Sound's safety measures, they also were charged with the responsibility for keeping the Baltic free of any contagious disease. Since the Sound was the only entry point into the "Eastern Sea," it was the most logical place for all vessels to be checked.

The pilot, upon hearing the answers to his questions, instructed Captain Rogers to fly a green flag, which signaled that their voyage had originated in a "suspect port." Then, the pilot guided the *Savannah* through the fading light, as she steamed toward the "neck at the sands" (which is the literal translation of Helsingør). By midnight, they had arrived off the town, and the small bower anchor was tossed into the water, to hold the ship in place until morning.

* * *

At first light, the crew took in the view of their new anchorage. In such calm weather, the Sound's water surface appeared, as one observer once put it, "as still as a millpond." Such stillness in the shallow, transparent waters of the Sound also meant that the light-colored, sandy bottom directly below the steamship was clearly visible for all to see.

To the east, about 3 miles distant, was the coast of Sweden, which appeared steep and rocky, interrupted only by the buildings and church steeples of the small city of Helsingborg. The deepest part of the Sound was actually next to the Swedish coast, but because of the unpredictable currents in that section, the safest place to transit was on the shallower Danish side.

To the west was the coast of Denmark. There, the landscape consisted of low ridges sloping down to the shore, covered with green fields, forests, whitewashed brick cottages, and the intermittent windmill.

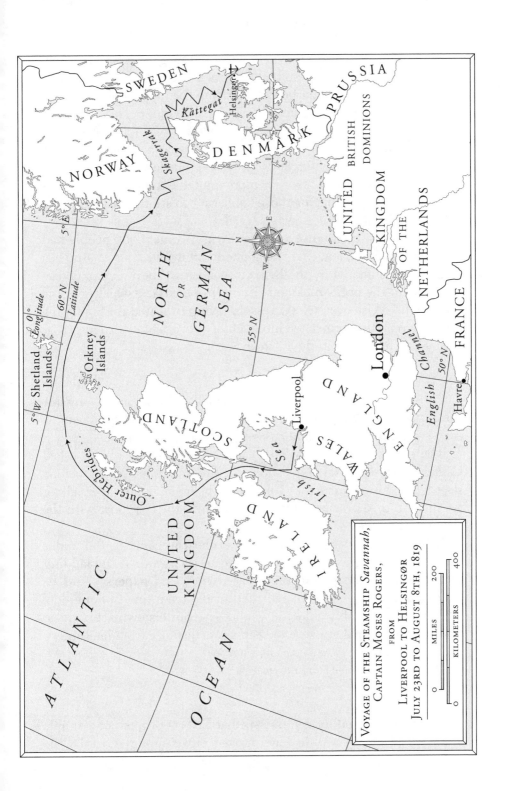

VOYAGE OF THE STEAMSHIP *Savannah*,
CAPTAIN MOSES ROGERS,
FROM
LIVERPOOL TO HELSINGØR
JULY 23RD TO AUGUST 8TH, 1819

MILES   200

KILOMETERS   400

More immediately before them was the town of Helsingør itself, which was built onto a coastal hillside, its brick buildings and houses stretching down to the harbor. Aside from the flat-steeple cathedral in the center of town, the most prominent structure in Helsingør was Kronborg Castle, a square, block-like structure with four corner turrets of unequal size and height. This fortress, armed with scores of cannon, served as the enforcer of the Sound tolls (along with the help of a nearby guard ship). To a far more limited extent, Kronborg was also a tourist attraction, for those hankering to see the castle immortalized by William Shakespeare's *Hamlet*.

For most visitors, however, this town of some 5,000 people had another attraction, and that was a good stiff drink. Since Baltic Sea trade was dominated by the British, their crews' beverage of choice gave rise to the port's nickname in maritime circles, which was the "Gin shop." With over 12,000 vessels having transited the Sound the previous year, that translated into a lot of booze, and made Helsingør the busiest little port in the Eastern Sea.

* * *

Early that morning after arrival, a small sailboat came alongside the *Savannah*. It was one of many ferryboats that did a brisk business carrying captains, crews and passengers to and from shore.

The two men in the ferryboat came aboard and very likely asked Captain Rogers the same questions the pilot had the evening before. Based upon his answers, they told him to bring all of his papers along for the trip to shore. So Moses climbed into the ferryboat with the two men, and they sailed for the harbor.

If Moses experienced what other American captains did under similar circumstances, he was directed to go ashore at the landing place next to the quarantine area. There, his papers could be inspected by a representative of the Royal Quarantine Commission. This person, probably a doctor, would have put his own set of questions to Moses, making sure to keep a safe distance from his subject.

Have you brought your papers on shore?
Where did you come from in America?
What is your destination?
Where is your bill of health?

Inspecting the bill of health issued at Liverpool was not a simple affair. The doctor would have moved close enough to take the document from Moses with a pair of tongs. Then he would have taken it to a nearby table, where he could open the folded paper using the tongs and a stick, being careful not to touch it.

Once the doctor had examined the document, his reply must have elicited a pang of disappointment in Moses: the bill of health from Liverpool would not answer—the *Savannah* would have to be put into quarantine.

The reason why was clear: because Captain Rogers did not have a bill of health issued by a Danish or Russian consul in his original port of departure, his vessel could not be allowed to pass uninterrupted.

The explanation was more complicated: because all countries bordering the Baltic saw the Sound as the natural place to prevent the introduction of any contagious diseases by sea, they looked to the Danes to police the people and cargoes destined for their ports. The result was the Danish Royal Quarantine Commission, which enforced a strict set of rules that determined which vessels could pass into the Baltic freely, and which could not.

The scrutiny didn't stop there. Most of the Baltic countries had agents present at Helsingør, who monitored the Commission's activities, and made sure it was aware of any changes to their own respective quarantine regulations. It was Russia's agent who appears to have been the most hard-nosed of all, probably because of an ukaze which emphasized that he "must personally convince himself" that all aspects of the quarantine regulations at Helsingør were being followed.

For their part, the Danes had done their best to communicate these regulations to the rest of the world. Back in March, while the *Savannah* had been undergoing her final trials in New York, the Danish Consulate General at Philadelphia had issued a public notice regarding Helsingør. Masters of vessels bound for the Baltic were advised to obtain bills of health from the Danish consul resident in their port of departure, or face the consequences:

> ... vessels on their arrival at the Sound without having on board such a Bill of health, will immediately, without regard to any other similar document they may possess, be ordered into a quarantine of observation of at least 4 or 5 days...

This notice was published in all the major American ports, including Savannah. Its one-day run in *The Georgian* and elsewhere must have slipped the notice or remembrance of the shareholders. Considering William Scarbrough previously had served as a diplomat for Denmark, Sweden and Russia, it is especially surprising that he didn't highlight the need for a proper bill of health prior to the voyage.

In the end, though, Moses was the captain of the *Savannah*, and the ultimate responsibility to avoid being quarantined was his. It must have galled him.

Back to the steamship he was ordered, along with the two ferryboat men.

Early that afternoon, a member of the Commission—a man named Möller—was rowed out to the *Savannah*. Given the strictness of the rules, the inspector probably stayed in his own boat alongside the steamship, interviewing Captain Rogers and the crew from a distance. Based on the circumstances, Möller determined that the *Savannah* "is subjected to a Quarantine of observation of four Days, not regarding the Fact that the Crew, 18 in all besides the Captain and the one Passenger taken on board in England, were all healthy and feeling well at the Time of the Examination."

The four days of hurry-up-and-wait commenced at 1:30 P.M. on Monday, August 9th. Steve kept the crew busy with ship's duty, including another round of scraping and painting the *Savannah*. For the extras on board—passenger-guide Daniel Barnett and the Sound pilot—there was nothing to do but bide their time.

The same was true of the two ferryboat men, who had to endure quarantine, as well. This sparked a protest from their employers, the Bakke brothers, who wanted compensation for the time lost. The brothers complained that Captain Rogers was at fault, for failing to provide a correct explanation of the *Savannah*'s particulars when their boatmen came alongside, and then allowing them to come aboard.

The Royal Quarantine Commission was not sympathetic, however, noting that while the captain apparently had erred in explaining his vessel's details, the boatmen had violated the regulations themselves by going aboard a vessel that was flying the green flag. The boatmen had further offended by bringing Captain Rogers ashore. "Compensation they can get least of all, but should be happy to be held in quarantine," concluded one of the Commission members, implying the boatmen's penalty could have been worse.

Finally, after suffering through four days of delay, the *Savannah* was released from quarantine at 2 o'clock on Friday afternoon, August 13th. Moses went on shore to receive his Danish bill of health, and pay the steamship's Sound toll. For a vessel transiting in ballast, the toll was two Riksdollars (equal to two American silver dollars). In the tariff journal, Captain Rogers' destination was listed simply as "the Baltic."

With that business complete, the *Savannah* was ready for departure. The three Danes stuck on board were free to disembark.

So was Daniel Barnett. Having provided guidance through the most unfamiliar and dangerous waters of the voyage, he was free to leave, as well. After saying his goodbyes, Barnett headed for shore, with the intent of looking for passage back to England. The Albion he returned to would be a very different place from the one he had left. Three days after Barnett disembarked from the *Savannah*, an immense crowd of Reformers meeting at St. Peter's Field in Manchester would be attacked by local volunteer cavalrymen, leaving 11 people killed and over 400 wounded. Reformers would call this massacre "Peterloo"—a word play on the Battle of Waterloo—and for months to follow, Britain would be consumed by the political fallout.

One hour after being released from quarantine, the *Savannah* was underway. With winds blowing very favorably from the west-north-west, Moses decided to depart Helsingør under sail. As the steamship glided southward, the crew beheld, off to starboard, the green fields of coastal Denmark, intermittently dotted with cattle and sheep.

By 7 o'clock that evening, the *Savannah* had covered the 20 miles to Copenhagen, the Danish capital. Rather than make a port of call so soon after a detention of four days, Moses decided to press on. The only cause for pause was a brief stop to take on board three hogsheads of drinking water, purchased from a floating purveyor.

As the *Savannah* passed Copenhagen under sail, many eyes fixed upon her unusual outline.

Yet she wasn't the only example of the new mode on view. Further to the south, another steam vessel could be seen splashing its way up the coast. This was the *Caledonia*, the only steamboat operating in Danish waters, making her protected run from the Germanic port of Kiel to Copenhagen.

Among those on the deck of the *Caledonia* were two well-dressed men, who watched with keen interest as the ship with the bent smokestack slowly slid across their bow, far off in the distance. "We passed on our arrival at Copenhagen the great American steam vessel the Savannah," recorded one of them in a letter home. "If she had been a few days later, we should probably have gone in her."

CHAPTER SIXTEEN

―――――――――

LAND OF THE GOTHS
AND VANDALS

I N THE DAYS after leaving Helsingør, the *Savannah* sailed and steamed her way through the western Baltic, as the winds waxed, allowing for good sailing, and waned, giving cause to "get the steam up and set the wheels to going." Along the way, Steve and the deck crew kept a lookout for major landmarks. On Sunday, August 15th, they spotted the island of Bornholm, the easternmost territory of Denmark, and by midnight that same day, they could see the lighthouse on the southern tip of Sweden's Öland Island.

From there, the most direct passage to St. Petersburg was to the east-northeast, into the broadest part of the Baltic. Rather than take that route, Moses ordered the *Savannah* to the north, and into the more slender passage between Öland and Gotland Islands. This was the most direct route to Stockholm. Although Moses made no official indication at either Liverpool or Helsingør, it was clear at this point that he intended to make a port of call at Sweden's capital.

It was in this channel, while the *Savannah* was under sail on the afternoon of August 17th, that powerful northern winds began to buffet the full height of her profile. As the gale strengthened into the evening, Steve and the crew were forced to gradually furl nearly every sail. Steve had no choice but to begin wearing the steamship eastward, and then, well into the night, westward again, to make what little progress he could. The gale became so perilous in the early morning hours that Steve allowed but two sails to be partially set, as the furies roared over the pitching deck and around the bare masts.

The break of day offered no respite. The going remained equally slow and tedious, as the *Savannah* rose and fell into headwinds and heavy seas. By late afternoon, the crew could see a tall sentinel ahead, to the north. This was Landsort lighthouse, on the tiny island of Öja, which formed the southernmost tip of the Stockholm archipelago.

Making any progress toward it proved virtually impossible. Still facing hostile winds and waves, Steve and the crew continued to wear the steamship eastward, and then westward, to little positive effect. Not until the winds had moderated the following morning did Moses feel comfortable ordering the steam engine into operation.

By late afternoon on August 19th, they finally reached the waters off tiny Öja Island. Soon thereafter, the *Savannah* was approached by a small sailboat, which came alongside and offered a pilot. More than any other place yet visited, Moses and Steve needed guidance through the Stockholm archipelago, which consisted of thousands of islands and rocks. Hitting any one of them could lead to disaster.

So the sailboat's offer was readily accepted, and a pilot climbed aboard. Rather than proceed in the fading light, it was decided to drop anchor just off the Landsort lighthouse.

The next day, Friday, the *Savannah* didn't move. Given the shellacking the steamship had just taken from the storm, Moses probably wanted to give crew and craft some time to dry out, and make sure everything presented well.

With that task accomplished by the end of the day, Moses decided to make a very early start. In the soft darkness of 2 o'clock the following morning, he ordered the steam up and the anchor weighed, and the *Savannah* got moving.

After carefully steaming through so many evergreen-covered islands and barren rocks, they reached Dalaro, a small village on an island deep within the archipelago. From there, the run into Stockholm was more or less due northwest. Guidance through this final stretch called for a new pilot, so Moses ordered a brief stop in the waters off the village, while the switch was made. By noon, they were on their way again, steaming into a wide river-like channel that the Swedes call the Saltsjön ("Sált-syohn"), which means "Salt Sea."

As the *Savannah* pushed inland, the crew beheld a misty landscape that must have seemed as if it was from a fairytale. Enveloping them on both sides of the shore were light-green farm fields, in turn surrounded by clusters of dark-green pine trees. Scattered amongst the fields and forests were small, simple cottages, their log sides painted either red or yellow, and their steeply-angled roofs painted black or green. Framing this view were low-lying hills in the distance, nearly every one of them topped by a windmill or two.

Steaming through the Saltsjön at full speed was simply not advisable. The many islands and submerged rocks, combined with natural curves in the waterway, meant that it was a dangerous place for any vessel. Since the *Savannah's* paddlewheels made her extra-wide, the Swedish pilot knew he had to be extra-careful. Just one move too false or too fast could end in a damaged wheel. So the going proved steady, but slow.

By 8 o'clock that evening, they reached a dramatic bend in the Saltsjön. Situated at this bend was the town of Vaxholm, as well as a large fortress with a tall, circular tower, which stood guard against all vessels that approached Stockholm. There, Moses ordered the anchor dropped for the night.

Just after sunrise the next morning, Sunday, August 22nd, Moses ordered the *Savannah's* crew to get under way. Given the predictability afforded by the new mode, it would take only a couple of hours to steam from Vaxholm to the capital city.

Moses, his creation and his crew pressed forward, up the Saltsjön. The serene Sweden that they saw all around them was, in part, deceptive. This largest of Scandinavian countries, like much of Europe, had experienced a great deal of turmoil since the turn of the century. And all of that uproar was the result of events, and machinations, which had taken place both near and far.

* * *

In the last years of the 18th century, Sweden had been a country in uncertain transition.

Her adolescent king, Gustav IV Adolf, had succeeded his assassinated father in 1792, under the supervision, or *regency*, of his uncle Karl. Before the young Gustav Adolf reached the majority age of 18, liberal-minded Karl instituted a number of reforms within Sweden, including freedom of the press. But the shockwaves of the French Revolution proved too much for some of Karl's ministers, who soon began to clamp down on some of these new liberties.

When Gustav Adolf assumed the throne in his own right, in 1796, he dismissed Karl's ministers, and abandoned the liberal policies that his uncle had put into place. The fear of Gustav Adolf was no different from that of any other European monarch—namely, that the ideals of the French and by origin American revolutions could spell the end of his power. So he directed his country's foreign policy to oppose revolutionary France. In 1805, he went even further, committing Sweden to join the Third Coalition of nations allied against Napoleon Bonaparte.

It was this last decision that began the nightmare. In 1807, Napoleon reciprocated, by overrunning and occupying Swedish Pomerania. This province, across the Baltic Sea on the European mainland, had been a part of Sweden for more than 150 years. Its humiliating loss was immediately followed by Russia's invasion and occupation of Finland, a country that had been under Swedish control for more than 500 years. Almost overnight, the Swedish Empire had been reduced to a mere rump state.

Swedish nobles, outraged by Gustav Adolf's despotic rule and disastrous policies, organized a coup d'état against him in 1809. Not only did the nobles drive Gustav Adolf into exile, but they also barred his family line from the crown of Sweden. In his place, they founded a constitutional monarchy, headed by his uncle Karl, who became King Karl XIII. The new monarch quickly negotiated treaties with the belligerents surrounding Sweden, accepting the loss of Finland, while regaining the Pomeranian lands on the Continent.

Having dealt with the threats from without, Karl XIII then turned to address grievances from within. The constitution he signed did much on that score, giving Swedes a new set of liberties, including the return of a free press.

But clear threats to the state remained. There were constant rumors of plotting by his deposed nephew to regain the throne. Further clouding the future was the fact that the childless 61-year-old Karl had no obvious heir.

In response, nobles set out to find a worthy successor for the Swedish throne. While many naturally preferred a native-born candidate, another powerful group of elites and military officers wanted a complete break from Swedish nobility. They sought a proven, natural leader with substantial experience, who was untarnished by the contentious internal politics of the past.

Sweden's interest in—if not infatuation with—all things French led this group to look, somewhat ironically, within Napoleon's realm for a man of stature. Of those identified, one stood out: Jean Baptiste

Bernadotte, one of the original eighteen awarded the rank of Marshal by Napoleon, back in 1804. Marshal Bernadotte had impressed the Swedes with his fair treatment of their prisoners of war during the conflict over Pomerania, and if there was any hope in wresting Finland from the Russians, it would take an experienced general to do it.

Bernadotte was honored by the offer, but wouldn't accept unless Napoleon approved, and Sweden's Diet (or parliament) formally elected him.

Given the Marshal's well-recognized independent streak, Napoleon was dubious of the whole affair, but nevertheless gave his assent.

The renegade Swedish nobleman who had dared make such an offer on behalf of the entire Swedish nation found himself the target of sharp anger on his return home. But he and Bernadotte's other supporters quickly won over the many skeptics. It certainly helped that the royal candidate already had a son to carry on the succession— named, appropriately enough, Oscar.

Soon thereafter, on August 21st, 1810, Jean Baptiste Bernadotte was elected Crown Prince of Sweden. He took the name Karl Johan. With the aging Karl XIII already in declining health, and government ministers squabbling over policy, Crown Prince Karl Johan soon found himself making decisions on behalf of his adopted country.

Jean Baptiste Bernadotte,
also known as
Karl Johan.

Such a radical shift in the leadership of Sweden, undertaken so swiftly, was more than the work of just a clique of nobles and officers. Standing behind them, providing inspirational support, was the power of a great national movement.

The years of unfair, uneven rule under Gustav Adolf, the overrunning of Pomerania, and even more so the loss of Finland, had filled the Swedish people with despair and disgust at the weakness of their government.

Yet this anger proved fertile ground for the seeds of renewal. From deep within Sweden's soul emerged a small group of highly educated and patriotic men, intent upon reversing what they saw as their country's religious, moral and ethical decline. These patriots believed that Gustavian society had become too fat, too self-indulgent, and too focused on form rather than substance. They wanted to remind their fellow countrymen of Sweden's past glory, and exhort them to return to their roots. In time, these men came to be called the *New Romantics*.

The leadership ranks of the New Romantics did not include noblemen, or other members of the Stockholm establishment, but instead men who had grown up in the countryside, and were beginning to make their marks in academia.

Prominent among them was Per Henrik Ling, a doctor and fencing master. Through his thorough knowledge of the human anatomy, Ling developed a rational system of physical training, providing his countrymen with the means to become, and remain, physically fit. In time, Ling's fitness system would be widely adopted throughout Sweden, as well as by schools and armies around the world.

But for most of the New Romantics, the political weapon of choice was not physical fitness. It was, instead, an extremely effective means of communicating ideas in the early 19th century, and that was through poetry. By weaving their messages into what was one of the most common forms of entertainment, especially given Sweden's long winters, these New Romantics were able to reach a very wide audience.

All that was missing from this method was the message itself. This, the New Romantics found in abundance within the old sagas of their Viking ancestors, including the ancient tribes of the Vandals and the Goths. The result was new poems like *Vikingen* ("The Viking"), written by an accomplished history professor at the University of

Uppsala named Erik Gustaf Geijer, and *Song of the Scania Reserves*, by a pastor's son and professor at the University of Lund named Esaias Tegnér.

The values expressed by these poets could not have been any clearer. They unabashedly criticized the Gustavian promotion of pleasure, with its vague internationalism, denigration of religion, and indifference to enterprise. At the same time, these New Romantic poets amplified the ideals and virtues of the Sweden of old—

Belief;

Courage;

Strength;

and *Initiative.*

These were the traits possessed by their Viking ancestors, which, along with hard-nosed common sense and rugged independence, had allowed them to achieve so much.

With the appearance of Crown Prince Karl Johan, the New Romantics found a leader who embodied their ideals. In reaction, they vigorously supported his programs, from strengthening Swedish agriculture, to promoting the Göta Canal and other public works, to encouraging entrepreneurship.

So it was that in this Sweden, upon the death of Karl XIII in 1818, the adopted Jean Baptiste Bernadotte had ascended the throne as Karl XIV Johan, crowned not only King of Sweden and Norway, but also King "of the Goths and of the Vandals."

And so it also was that in this Sweden suddenly appeared, in the year 1819, Captain Moses Rogers and the steamship *Savannah.*

* * *

As the *Savannah* steamed her way up the Saltsjön channel on the approach to Stockholm, the crew first saw a number of small, forested islands. Once past them, the capital city itself came into view, located on a much larger island straddling all the way across the channel.

Straight ahead lay the Slussen, a combination of bridge and lock, which both connected the island city to the southern mainland and held back the fresh waters of Lake Mälaren, located further to the west. To the right of the Slussen—running the whole eastern length of the island city—was the Skars Bron, a long stone quay and promenade. Here the city's merchants had their counting houses, four or five stories in height, with the same high-pitched roofs and brightly-painted facades as the cottages seen in the countryside. Tied up to the quay, and anchored all around the Saltsjön, sat scores of sailing vessels, both Swedish and foreign, which made this capital city of 80,000 the busiest port in the Kingdom, after Göteborg.

As the *Savannah* steamed nearer, her crew eventually came to realize that the decks of all this shipping, as well as the Skars Bron promenade, were packed with people, cheering their approach. Along both shores of the mainland were still more enthusiastic spectators, enveloping the steamship as it churned and smoked its way past them. By Steve's remembrance, the greeting at Stockholm was at least the equal of Liverpool's, if not even more fervent.

Rather than tying up along the Skars Bron quay, Moses was told to take his creation into the Strömmen. This was the "swiftly-flowing water" that separated Stockholm from the northern mainland, and served as another outlet from Lake Mälaren. It was there in the Strömmen—precisely one year to the day after her launch at New York—that the *Savannah* steamed to a halt.

The Strömmen was an unusual place in which to order the steamship to drop anchor. The current there was very strong, due to the constant outflow through the northern locks of Lake Mälaren. The most likely reason it was chosen was because the *Savannah* had no cargo to unload, and thus no immediate need to tie up to the quay. Furthermore, it was Sunday, and it stands to reason that the port authorities wanted the steamship to anchor in mid-stream until its papers, including the Danish bill of health, could be properly reviewed the next day.

But there was one other possible reason for ordering the *Savannah* into the Strömmen. Placing the steamship there meant that it was anchored in the shadow of the Royal Palace, a huge, block-like building that completely dominated the northeastern corner of the island. Situated there, the *Savannah* was in the perfect position to be viewed by King Karl Johan himself.

* * *

The second leg of the *Savannah*'s voyage had taken about 25½ days, not including the more than four days lost at Helsingør. In spite of the fierce weather in the Skagerrak and the Kattegat, and the gale off the Swedish coast, the steamship had actually improved on its prior performance. Total steaming time was 131 hours, or 21% of the

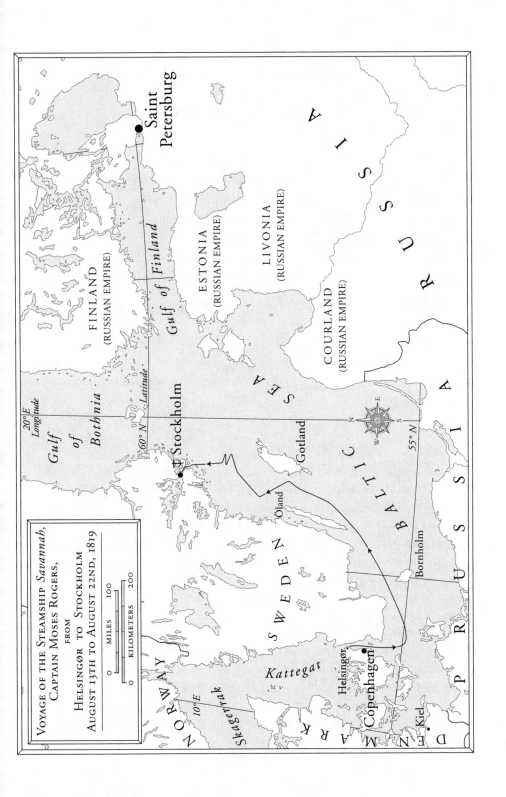

VOICE OF THE STEAMSHIP *Savannah*,
CAPTAIN MOSES ROGERS,
FROM
HELSINGØR TO STOCKHOLM
AUGUST 13TH TO AUGUST 22ND, 1819

MILES   0   100

KILOMETERS   0   100   200

NORWAY

Skagerrak

DENMARK

Kattegat

Helsingør

Copenhagen

Kiel

PRUSSIA

10°E

SWEDEN

Öland

Gotland

Bornholm

BALTIC SEA

Stockholm

20°E
Longitude

Gulf of Bothnia

60°N *Latitude*

Gulf of Finland

FINLAND
(RUSSIAN EMPIRE)

Saint
Petersburg

ESTONIA
(RUSSIAN EMPIRE)

LIVONIA
(RUSSIAN EMPIRE)

COURLAND
(RUSSIAN EMPIRE)

RUSSIA

55°N

Liverpool-to-Stockholm route, as compared with the 99 hours, or 14%, for the Atlantic crossing.

Of equal importance, there had been no problems with the steam engine or the paddlewheels. The voyage, it could be said, was accomplished in complete safety.

On the day after arrival, the first duties for the crew fit the well-worn pattern. Steve put them to work scraping the decks and re-painting the *Savannah's* sides all the way around. At least there was some interesting sightseeing for the men while they worked, for in Stockholm the many water taxis and barges moving about the harbor were rowed almost exclusively by women.

For Moses, the first chore that Monday was to register the steamship's arrival with the authorities, and present his Danish bill of health. That accomplished, one of his next tasks was to visit the top American representative in Sweden, Christopher Hughes.

* * *

Born in Baltimore in 1786, Hughes was the son of an Irish immigrant father who had made good as a merchant and real estate developer in that city.

Just before his 17th birthday, young Christopher had been sent off to study at the College of New Jersey at Princeton, but soon got himself into some sort of trouble, for he was suspended later that year. His father pressed him to return, and after being re-admitted, Hughes went on to receive his degree in 1805, followed by a master's degree in 1809.

Once his formal education was complete, Hughes seemed more interested in play than work. His position as the son of a wealthy Baltimorean gave him far greater leeway to live as he chose, and perhaps think he could tempt fate—Hughes fought four duels in his early years, apparently without serious consequences.

His life's path was settled partially when he went to work for Senator Samuel Smith, a veteran of the Revolution who was one of the most powerful political leaders in Maryland. In short order, Hughes realized that the Senator had something beyond politics which interested him greatly, and that was a daughter named Laura. The Senator did not view young Christopher Hughes as a proper match, and the rest of the Smith family seemed to agree.

The solution for Christopher and Laura was simple enough: they eloped. Married in 1811, the young couple was forced to live with Christopher's twin sister, and hope for an eventual reconciliation with the Smiths.

The following year, the second war against Britain began, and Hughes enlisted in the local militia, becoming a captain of artillery at Fort McHenry. During the summer of 1813, he found himself a guest at President James Madison's Montpelier estate, where he made a favorable impression. Soon thereafter, Hughes began applying for various government posts. In February of 1814, the President nominated him to be the secretary for the newly-formed peace commission, which was being sent to Europe to negotiate directly with the British for an end to hostilities. Hughes eagerly accepted, and before the end of the month was on his way across the Atlantic.

The American peace commissioners who gathered at Ghent (in present-day Belgium) were a substantial lot. They included former Treasury Secretary Albert Gallatin, influential Kentucky Congressman Henry Clay, and the son of a former president, John Quincy Adams, who assumed the role of chief commissioner. In this capacity, Adams took responsibility for instructing Hughes on the discharge of his duties as secretary.

One early lesson came when Adams gave Hughes a draft of a 16-page message to be presented to the British delegation. Hughes went off to make a fair and presentable copy, which he then presented to Adams.

But it wasn't good enough.

"Is this your <u>best</u>, Sir?" replied Adams. "We can't sign such a spot of work as that."

Back Hughes went to create a second copy, which he again presented to Adams.

But it *still* wasn't good enough.

Back to his desk went Hughes for a third time to make another copy, which he presented to Adams yet again.

This time, Adams accepted the letter.

Tough taskmaster that he was, John Quincy Adams came to be something of a father figure to Hughes, and seemed to enjoy the young man's company. In a letter home to his wife Louisa, Adams noted that Hughes was "lively and good-humored, smart at a repartee, and a thorough punster."

When the peace treaty with Britain was signed in December of 1814, Hughes was selected to be one of its messengers. While another copy of the treaty arrived in the U.S. before he did, Hughes still received a lot of attention. Rushing to Washington to provide details of the negotiations, he spent ten days meeting with government officials, including President Madison and Secretary of State James Monroe.

His experience in Ghent convinced Hughes that a career in diplomacy was the future he wished for, and his positive performance also led to a reconciliation with the Smith family. After brief service in the Maryland Legislature and a minor diplomatic assignment, Hughes was appointed in 1816 to serve as chargé d'affaires to Sweden.

Christopher Hughes.

The appointment of Hughes came on the heels of final negotiations over a commercial treaty with the Swedes. With that major agreement complete, it was thought that an American diplomat of minister's rank was no longer necessary in Sweden, so when Hughes arrived at Stockholm in 1817, he became the United States' top representative there. This deliberate reduction in America's presence in Sweden proved to be warranted, for as Christopher Hughes soon discovered, in the wake of the treaty discussions, there really wasn't much for even a chargé d'affaires to do.

* * *

Upon meeting Christopher Hughes, Moses presented him with a letter of introduction:

C. Hughes Junr Esq
     etc etc etc   *London June 30. 1819.*

Dear Sir.

I take great pleasure in affording this letter to our countryman Capt Rogers, the ingenious commander and part owner of the American Steam Ship that has lately crossed the Atlantic. He hopes to have the honor of delivering it to you in Stockholm, and I have ventured to assure him that you will lend him all the kind countenance and advice touching his views in relation to this ship, that you may find in your power...

Believe me my dear Sir yours very sincerely

Richard Rush.

Moses told Christopher Hughes that he had additional letters of introduction. Baron de Stierneld, Sweden's top diplomat in London, had provided two, addressed to the Swedish foreign minister and the chief of the Swedish Navy. Moses also had a letter from Russia's minister to London, Count Lieven, providing an introduction to his country's Minister of Marine.

As Hughes later recounted, Captain Rogers told him that "the circumstances of the company to which the ship belongs, have become very much reduced by the unhappy state of things at home." Their plans to initiate a steam packet service between Savannah, Charleston and New York had been abandoned, by necessity, and the decision made to send the *Savannah* across the Atlantic, and sell her at St. Petersburg. That said, Captain Rogers also stated he was willing to indulge a sale to King Karl Johan, "provided suitable terms could be agreed on."

Whether or not Sweden's adopted king would or could make an offer to buy the steamship remained to be seen. As Moses soon learned, the possibility of such a bid was held captive by the whirlwind of events that had engulfed Bernadotte, and Sweden, in the years after he had become Crown Prince.

* * *

Soon after Jean Baptiste Bernadotte became Crown Prince of Sweden in 1810, relations with his native France deteriorated. Napoleon Bonaparte previously had put an ultimatum to Sweden: either join the

French-inspired Continental System, which forbade any trade with Britain, or expect conflict with France. The choice faced by the Swedes was really between two types of war: the economic kind against Britain, with which Napoleon hoped to ruin its trade-based economy; or the traditional military kind against both France and its ally Denmark, which controlled neighboring Norway.

It was hardly any choice at all. Publicly, the Swedes chose to join the Continental System. But privately, they allowed a great deal of smuggling to take place with Albion, and played down the importance of their choice.

For its part, the British government saw clearly that Sweden and its new Crown Prince had been blackmailed by Napoleon. So rather than view them as an enemy, the British treated the Swedes' lackadaisical adoption of the Continental System with a nod and a wink. This, Bernadotte would never forget.

At the same time Bernadotte was wrangling with his country of birth, he also had to contend with his adopted country's continued obsession with regaining Finland, which had been a part of Sweden for centuries. Such a recovery, Bernadotte realized, was unlikely, if not impossible, given the size of Alexander's Russian Army, which reportedly numbered some one million men.

So Bernadotte developed a new strategy to address the Finnish issue that was simple to describe, yet would be far more difficult to execute. The key to his plan was turning the Swedish nation's gaze away from the loss of Finland in the east, and toward the acquisition of Norway in the west.

But to any informed mind, this sounded as impossible as regaining Finland. After all, Norway had been a part of Denmark for over 400 years, and the Danes had given their Norwegian brothers a great deal of economic freedom, making them largely content with rule from Copenhagen. Furthermore, since Denmark was allied with France, any effort to gain Norway would require Napoleon's approval.

Even so, there was more than a little sense to Bernadotte's idea. The Germanic-speaking Swedes and Norwegians had far more in common than the Swedes had with their Finnic-speaking neighbors to the east. The New Romantics' emphasis on the deeds and virtues of the Vikings—an ancestry which Swedes and Norwegians shared—also served as an important underpinning to Bernadotte's Norway strategy.

Shortly after becoming Crown Prince, Bernadotte suggested to the

French minister at Stockholm that France should convince its Danish ally to give up Norway, with appropriate compensation. Napoleon, however, quickly nixed the idea, believing the Danes would never stand for it. This rejection, as well as Bernadotte's own refusal to join Napoleon in an attack on Russia, deepened the mistrust between these two strong-minded men.

It also set the scene for renewed war in 1812. Not wanting a potential enemy to his rear, Napoleon ordered French troops to overrun the Swedish Pomeranian lands, as they marched east to attack Russia.

Once again, Sweden itself had been invaded.

In reaction, Bernadotte did not dither, like past governments. Instead, he sprang into action. He pushed through the Diet a number of emergency measures, including a draconian law restricting the press. He also raised an expeditionary force, which he would personally lead. Sweden, he declared, would fight alongside the Allies arrayed against Napoleon, for what many thought would be the final struggle.

While the Swedish force that joined the Allies was small, consisting of about 30,000 troops, Bernadotte's intimate knowledge of his old commander's tactics proved to be an indispensable asset. So too was his understanding of what motivated the revolutionary cohorts from all over Europe that marched under Napoleon's banner. Over the course of the campaign, Bernadotte was able to convince some units under French command to either defect, or desert the battlefield.

If there was one criticism the Allies had regarding Sweden's new Crown Prince, it was that he seemed unwilling to commit his troops to any hard fighting.

Yet to Bernadotte, this reticence made perfectly good sense. If his small Swedish force was decimated in battle, he would be in no position to fulfill his goal of gaining Norway from the Danes.

After Napoleon's 1813 defeat at the Battle of Leipzig (in which Bernadotte played a decisive role), the Allies pushed west toward Paris, and victory.

But Sweden's Crown Prince had other plans. Instead of following the Allies into France, Bernadotte turned his divisions northward, to the doorstep of Denmark. With their French ally in full retreat, the Danes were on their own. Confronted by a Swedish army they had no way of repelling, the Danish government was forced to capitulate to Bernadotte. In the subsequent Treaty of Kiel, signed in January of 1814, the Danes agreed to cede Norway to Sweden. In exchange, Sweden would give up the Pomeranian lands, and take on Norway's share of the Danish national debt.

While the post-war handover of territories had been accomplished, the portion of the treaty dealing with the transfer of Norway's debt was another matter. The negotiating and arguing over the precise terms of Sweden's purchase of that debt had dragged on and on.

By the summer of 1819, the talks finally were coming to a head. And Bernadotte, having become the reigning monarch of both Sweden and Norway, soon had to decide whether to pay, or not.

* * *

Along with meeting Christopher Hughes, Moses also presented his other letters of introduction, to the interim Swedish foreign minister, Count Gustaf af Wetterstedt, and the chief of the Swedish Navy, Admiral Count Olof Cederström.

The Admiral was no stranger to the United States. As a young naval officer in 1780, he had been assigned to serve in the French Navy, which was then aiding the Americans in their fight for independence. By September of 1781, Ensign Cederström found himself a part of the French fleet blockading the British forces of Lord Cornwallis, encamped at Yorktown, Virginia.

By the time the *Savannah* arrived at Stockholm, Admiral Cederström very likely had read Baron Klinkowström's letters from America, including the one praising Captain Rogers for his help. Unfortunately, what the Admiral did not have was a report from the Baron on the steamship. Any judgment of this revolutionary vessel would have to be formed independently by those on the scene at Stockholm.

Beyond officially presenting himself to the Swedish government, Moses also must have reviewed the local Stockholm newspapers, to see what kind of impression he and his creation had made.

But there was nothing. Stockholm had four newspapers in 1819, and not one of them ran a story about the steamship during its stay. They also failed to make any mention of its arrival in their shipping sections. This marked the only time in the steamship *Savannah*'s life that she generated no press whatsoever in a port of call.

There could be only one explanation, and that was the restrictive press law instituted in 1812, which was still in place.

While the threat Sweden had faced back then was hopefully gone for good, Bernadotte himself was well-aware that there remained a sizable segment of the Swedish aristocracy that resented his adoption. As insurance, he had determined that control of the press, as well as an observant secret police, would be indispensable tools in helping him retain his position as Sweden's monarch.

With this press power specifically, Bernadotte had the ability to tell editors what they could and could not publish. Any newspaper that dared to print a story deemed contrary to the national interest could be shut down by the government.

The failure of the Stockholm press to carry any mention whatsoever of the *Savannah*'s arrival could mean only one thing: the King of Sweden was very intrigued by this American steamship, and wanted his interest, and its visit, given as little publicity as possible.

While there was nothing to read in the newspapers, Captain Rogers and the *Savannah* were unquestionably making waves in Stockholm society. This was due in part to the efforts of Christopher Hughes, who took Moses around to visit some of his closest friends in the diplomatic community.

One such person was Salomon Dedel, the Dutch minister to Sweden, who, on August 27th, sent a dispatch to his government describing the arrival of this "superb vessel," as well as its particulars. "Captain Rogers has the air of an extremely intelligent man," Dedel wrote, "and I believe one could consult him with benefit" in the application of steam to warships.

The Dutch minister added that the American government had just recently consulted Captain Rogers in the incorporation of a steam engine into a first-class "frigate." (This information surely came from Moses himself, and probably reflected any advice that he had offered to steam engine contractor Robert McQueen & Company, who in turn had incorporated his ideas into their steam battery design, submitted to the U.S. Navy the previous December.)

The Dutchman also informed his government that Captain Rogers intended to sell off the steamship, if possible, to either Karl Johan or Russia's Alexander. According to Dedel, the captain had an asking price of £25,000 (or $111,000), which the diplomat thought was extremely expensive. Regardless of his own opinion, it was clear that despite the silence of the newspapers, there was a lot of discussion within informed circles as to whether or not His Majesty would buy the *Savannah*, and if so, for how much.

The same day Dedel wrote his dispatch, Count Wetterstedt, the acting Swedish foreign minister, also penned a letter to Christopher Hughes. Given the late hour at which it was written, the note didn't reach the Chargé d'Affaires until the next morning.

Count Wetterstedt's letter informed Hughes that the new Crown Prince, Oscar, intended to inspect the *Savannah* that very day, and the Foreign Minister wanted Hughes to be on board to receive the "Prince Royal." The Count also added that the King himself had intended to visit the ship, but the final negotiations over the Norwegian debt, as well as His Majesty's imminent departure on a tour of the interior, "do not leave him a vacant moment."

Hughes made his way down to the harbor later that Saturday morning, to board the steamship and await the royal arrival.

At noon, two barges left the quayside, and headed toward the *Savannah*. In the first long, ornate barge, rowed by 22 oarsmen, came His Highness. Following close behind was another smaller barge, rowed by 6 oarsmen, which carried Oscar's aides and other government officials.

As the two boats made their way across the Strömmen, artillery on shore boomed a salute, in recognition of the water-borne Crown Prince. Once the royal barge reached the side of the steamship, Prince Oscar climbed aboard. Standing by to greet him was Hughes, who later wrote:

> *. . . I received him at the side + presented him to the Captain, who, in our plain way, held out his hand, (which the prince graciously took) + welcomed him. . . .*

Behind came the rest of Oscar's entourage, which included Admiral Count Cederström, and, as Hughes later put it, "ten or twelve Counts + Barons + <u>grandees</u>."

The Crown Prince, with a boyish face, waxed mustache and a head full of curly, jet-black hair, looked not a day older than his 20 years. He quickly had become the focus of much attention upon Bernadotte's adoption back in 1810. While his father had tried in vain to learn the native tongue, young Oscar's agile mind had soaked it up, and by 1819 he was fluent in Swedish, and perfectly able to give a speech in Norwegian, as well. Bernadotte, wanting his son and Sweden's future king to receive the best education possible, had put one of the New Romantics, Erik Gustaf Geijer, in charge of overseeing Oscar's studies. Upon

Bernadotte's accession to the throne, Oscar had become Crown Prince, making him one of the most eligible bachelors in all of Europe.

Captain Rogers and Christopher Hughes took Prince Oscar all over the *Savannah*. "The Prince was much pleased and surprised at the beauty + neatness of the ship," Hughes later wrote, "+ was very curious about the machinery."

As the royal tour made its way into the main cabin below deck, out on the water a small boat approached, with two well-dressed passengers on board. Coming alongside the *Savannah*, the elder of the two men asked the crew on deck if they could come aboard. Since strict orders had been given not to allow anyone on the steamship during the Crown Prince's visit, his request was denied. Undeterred, the older man pulled out a scrap of paper, scribbled a brief note on it, and then asked one of the crew to give it to the captain.

Down below the note was sent, and handed to Moses.

Someone by the name of "Lynedoch" wanted permission to come aboard and inspect the *Savannah*.

Who?

Moses handed the note to Christopher Hughes, who immediately read it.

"Certainly," he replied.

In due course, Prince Oscar bade his hosts goodbye, and climbed back aboard his royal barge. With His Highness safely away, one of the *Savannah*'s mates (either Steve or Mr. Blackman) sauntered up to Christopher Hughes, and couldn't hold back.

"Well, Mr. Hughes, that is a Prince? Is'n't? I <u>guess</u> we have had a much greater man on board."

Hughes asked him what he meant, and the mate recounted President Monroe's visit to the steamship, adding "I guess I had much rather put myself in his hands."

While the mate was judging the Crown Prince by his youthful appearance, he may not have appreciated fully who else had come with Oscar for the inspection. If King Karl Johan could not visit the *Savannah* himself, then he had sent the next best thing—his son's entourage included not only Admiral Count Cederström, but also two generals, Counts Lowenhielm and Skjöldebrand. These three military men were among His Majesty's closest advisors.

With the royal visitor gone, the two fellows waiting in the boat alongside could finally come aboard, to have a look at the steamship.

Bounding onto the deck came a fit and trim man with an oval face, strong straight nose, ruddy cheeks and slightly graying hair, the whole ensemble of which made him appear younger than he actually was. Aside from his being well-dressed, anyone who was especially observant also would have noted that on his left pinky finger he wore a ring.

This newest visitor on the deck of the *Savannah* was General Sir Thomas Graham, a member of the British House of Lords. He was known formally as Lord Lynedoch ("Líne-dock"). With him was the closest thing he had to a son, his younger second cousin, Robert Graham. These native Scots were taking a tour of the Continent on their way to St. Petersburg, where they intended to visit Lord Lynedoch's brother-in-law, who was Britain's minister to Russia. They previously had seen the *Savannah* pass them by as they approached Copenhagen in the steamboat *Caledonia*, and were keen to inspect her firsthand.

It seems that Moses, based upon his reaction to the passed note, had no idea who this Lord Lynedoch was.

But Christopher Hughes clearly did. At nearly 71 years of age, General Sir Thomas Graham already had lived a full and momentous life, and the genesis for much of it could be explained by that ring he was wearing on his left little finger.

* * *

Born in 1748, Thomas Graham's childhood followed the expected path for the son of a prominent Scottish family. Tutored at home, he was sent to study at Oxford when he reached 18, but left two years later without finishing his degree. After spending some time traveling around the Continent, he returned home and ran for Parliament at the age of 24, but lost. Arguably, Thomas Graham's greatest success as a young man occurred on the day after Christmas in 1774, when he married the beautiful Mary Schaw, daughter of the 9th Lord Cathcart.

The couple's early life together was fairly typical for young Scots with means: living in the country, farming, and taking extended vacations to the Continent, much to the good of Mary's uncertain constitution. Thomas himself, in addition to being a gentleman farmer, was well-known at the time for both his horsemanship and marksmanship.

In the spring of 1792, Mary's rapidly deteriorating health dictated another trip to a warmer, drier place. So the Grahams headed south, this time for Provence, on the Mediterranean coast of France.

Mary never made it. Becoming sicker and weaker as the voyage dragged on, she died on board ship in late June, just to the east of Marseilles. The shock of her death was just the beginning for Thomas Graham—the trauma had yet to come.

Rather than risk the delay of a passage back through the Straits of Gibraltar, Graham decided to transport her body home by way of France's famed Canal du Midi, which linked the Mediterranean ports of Agde and Cette with the interior city of Toulouse. At Toulouse, the canal connected with the Garonne River, which flows northwest to the Atlantic Ocean, at the port of Bordeaux. From there, the trip by sea back to Britain would be much shorter.

Graham and a small group of friends made their way with Mary's remains to the port of Agde. Upon landing, French customs officers refused to allow Mary's coffin to enter, unless it was opened. Rather than allow this desecration, Graham journeyed to the nearby port of Cette, where a sympathetic customs official gave him a *bond of caution*, which was a document excusing the coffin from inspection. With his paperwork in order, Graham and his friends placed the coffin in a horse-drawn boat, and commenced the sad journey along the Canal du Midi.

At the city of Toulouse, the party's boat reached the end of the canal. From there, the boat would be dropped down to the Garonne River, for the remainder of the journey to Bordeaux. But before this could be accomplished, a group of National Guards and Volunteers, inebriated with the fervor of the French Revolution, as well as strong drink, came along and denied passage, unless the coffin was opened and examined.

His bond of caution seemingly worthless, Graham raced to the city hall and appealed to the police chief, who refused to act. With no help forthcoming from the local authorities, Graham rushed back to the canal boat to confront the drunken soldiers. His attempts to reason with them proved futile, despite his declarations in favor of liberty, equality, and fraternity. The soldiers, dismissive of the bond of caution issued at Cette, accused Graham of smuggling contraband. They moved in, declaring their intent to break open the lead coffin. As Graham later wrote:

> *... At first I attempted to interfere by advice and entreaties as to the manner of opening it; but this only irritated them to more brutality, and I got as near the other end of the boat as possible and remained almost suffocated with horror and rage...*

The soldiers, having violently broken open the coffin only to find what one would expect, then retired. Later, the police chief arrived, and invited Graham to make an official complaint. Realizing this action would only entail delay and probably no satisfaction, Graham decided that his best option was to get out. "I hope never again to feel such horror," he wrote. "Everything that had passed was so present to my mind that the horrid scene seemed still to be acting before me..."

After replacing the irreparably damaged coffin, Graham and his party, along with the remains of his beloved Mary, quitted Toulouse, and proceeded down the Garonne River toward Bordeaux, and the sea voyage home.

Such a traumatic experience could not but leave a lasting impression upon Graham about the effects of the French Revolution: the rule of law had lost, and the rule of the mob had won.

After returning to Britain and burying his wife, Graham sank into grief. While he couldn't bear to look at her portraits, Graham did determine to carry with him one tangible remembrance of Mary, and that was her wedding ring. He placed it upon the little finger of his left hand, and vowed never to take it off.

Concluding that travel might be the best medicine, Graham left Britain for the Continent. In the summer of 1793, he found himself at Gibraltar just as a Royal Navy fleet was passing into the Mediterranean, on its way to defend the city of Toulon, one of the few enclaves in France resisting the revolutionary juggernaut. Graham volunteered to go along, as an aide to the British general in command.

At Toulon, Graham distinguished himself, repeatedly leading the troops forward, and at one point grabbing the musket of a fallen soldier and taking his place at the front of an attacking column. While the British eventually lost the Battle of Toulon—thanks in part to the efforts of a young French officer named Napoleon Bonaparte—the conduct of Thomas Graham had been noticed, nevertheless. His life soon became a reflection of the long war that was just beginning, and would engulf Europe for two decades.

Returning to Scotland in 1794, Graham immediately raised a battalion of troops, part of the 90th Foot Regiment, and was commissioned a lieutenant-colonel. From then on, his postings and battles epitomized the breadth of the struggle against Napoleon and his revolutionary legions: Gibraltar, the Rhine River, Italy, Gibraltar, Minorca, Sicily, Malta, Egypt, Ireland, the West Indies, Sweden, and

Spain. Along the way, Graham won accolades from his superiors for his counsel and fortitude. Interspersed within this military career, he won elections to Parliament, representing his native Perthshire.

By 1810, Graham was, at 62, a rather old but very experienced major-general at home, recovering from a case of malaria. At that point in the war, Napoleon had conquered almost all of Spain, installing his brother Joseph as king. With General Sir Arthur Wellesley—the Viscount Wellington—regrouping in Portugal, a new commander was needed to lead an Allied garrison still holding out in the Spanish port of Cadiz. Wellington suggested three possible candidates for the command, of which Lord Liverpool, Britain's Secretary of State at the time, chose General Graham.

After bloodying the French troops blockading Cadiz, Graham was ordered to join Wellington in Portugal, where he was made second in command. What soon followed, at the beginning of 1812, was the great Allied offensive that eventually would kick the Bonapartes out of Spain, and turn the Viscount Wellington into the Duke of Wellington. With General Sir Thomas Graham and General Sir Rowland Hill covering his flanks, Wellington pounded the French back, battle by battle, toward Madrid.

The hard campaign wore on General Graham. Most critically, his eyesight deteriorated in the glare of the strong sun and the demands of long nights reading dispatches. In July of 1812, he was compelled to return home to recuperate.

With the renewal of the offensive in the spring of 1813, Wellington needed a replacement for General Graham on his staff. He could have picked any general in the British Army to be at his side for the final push. Yet Wellington chose Graham.

His eyesight having been restored through the British winter, General Graham returned to Portugal. Once again, Wellington marched into Spain, with Graham covering his left flank, and General Hill guarding his right. Together, they forced the enemy back toward the French border along the Pyrenees Mountains. General Graham himself would be the first to break through that barrier, and plant the British flag on French soil.

As the 1813 campaign drew to a close, Graham's eye problem resurfaced, which again forced his return to Britain to recuperate. Even so, his service to his country received the recognition it deserved—Graham was awarded numerous decorations, and received the official thanks of Parliament on three separate occasions. The highest honor came in 1814, when he was raised to the peerage in the House of Lords. From then on, General Sir Thomas Graham became known to all as Baron Lynedoch, of Balgowan.

* * *

Lord Lynedoch still cut a physically fit figure as he walked the decks of the steamship *Savannah.* As his cousin and traveling companion Robert Graham would have told anyone, the nearly 71-year-old General could still ride a horse for as long and as hard as any man a fraction of his age. And the polished yet plain-spoken manner of this titled Scot clearly appealed to his American hosts.

Thomas Graham,
also known as
Lord Lynedoch.

By Robert Graham's lights, the *Savannah* was "a remarkably fine vessel, and beautifully fitted up." He also found Chargé d'Affaires Christopher Hughes to be "uncommonly civil, as was the Captain."

The friendly disposition of Captain Rogers in particular was surprising, Robert later wrote, since "we see by the English papers + heard at Copenhagen that he has not that character generally." Such impressions surely were the result of numerous reprints of the *Cheshire Chronicle's* article, which had described the *Savannah's* master as "not remarkable for being communicative." And if Moses had a reputation in Copenhagen for being cranky, it must have reflected word-of-mouth reports of his reaction to being thrown into quarantine at Helsingør.

For his part, Lord Lynedoch declared that "he was much pleased with the Ship." Captain Rogers returned the favor, offering the two Scotsmen passage on the *Savannah* to St. Petersburg. While no acceptance was made then and there, Robert Graham later wrote "I do not be much surprised if we embark on board of her..."

* * *

The following day was a Sunday, so Moses obligingly opened the steamship for tours by the general public. Precisely how many people visited is unclear, but it was enough to justify Steve dryly noting in the logbook that "a large number of people come on board to see the Ship." Given the *Savannah's* prominent position in the Strömmen, and her nearness to shore, the water taxis would have been able to shuttle thousands of people out to her during the course of the day.

While the steamship was crowded with the curious, a short distance away in the Royal Palace, Sweden's adopted king was busy planning his imminent departure on a tour of the interior. But Karl Johan couldn't begin this tour until the controversy over the Norwegian debt transfer was resolved. The talks had dragged on for years, primarily because Bernadotte did not want to pay. His explanation to the Allies as to why was simple: Danish treachery.

After the Treaty of Kiel (which ceded Norway to Sweden) was signed in early 1814, the Norwegians had seen their chance for independence. Egged on by a Danish prince who claimed the title of King of Norway, they organized a small army to resist any attempt by the Swedes to impose their rule. This forced Bernadotte to march his own army into Norway. After a few brief skirmishes, both sides agreed to negotiate. Bernadotte deftly made a series of concessions regarding self-rule, thereby winning over Norway's leadership, and allowing that country's incorporation into the Swedish realm as a separate kingdom.

But the friction did not end there. Bernadotte accused the Danes of actively encouraging the Norwegians to revolt. This represented a clear violation of the Treaty of Kiel, in which Denmark had agreed to support the transfer of Norway. As far as Bernadotte was concerned, Sweden was no longer liable for assuming the Norwegian portion of Denmark's national debt.

The Four Allied Powers of Austria, Russia, Prussia and Britain had another opinion altogether. After two decades of almost continuous war, they were anxious to maintain the peace. Britain and Russia in particular were determined to find a solution, so that the Baltic Sea would remain a peaceful highway for commerce.

As a result, Bernadotte eventually discovered that his stubborn refusal to assume the Norwegian debt had consequences. Slowly but surely, he was being squeezed. From the west, the British government used its past goodwill, combined with the promise of improved trade, to pressure him into complying. And from the east, Russia, with the Continent's largest standing army, seemed prepared to force Bernadotte's compliance, if necessary.

With Britain's minister to Sweden acting as mediator, all sides entered into protracted negotiations. Not until 1819 was the basis for an agreement hammered out: Sweden was to agree to assume $3 million of Norwegian debt, to be repaid over ten years. As the royal sovereign, Bernadotte would be held personally responsible for paying on schedule, regardless of the state of Sweden's or Norway's finances.

While no one in Europe wanted a confrontation in the summer of 1819, the increased tensions, and pressure on Bernadotte, were obvious. To make sure he got the message, the Four Powers were threatening to break off relations with Sweden if Bernadotte did not agree to the deal. More ominously, European newspapers had reported rumors of Russian Army maneuvers in Finland, and Swedish military countermeasures in reply.

While the terms for an agreement had been negotiated by late August, the necessary papers still had not been signed. The final decision rested with Sweden's adopted king.

* * *

On August 30th, the day after the *Savannah* had been swarmed by the public, Steve put the entire crew to work loading coal, in spite of the occasional rain squall. The coal was needed to fuel a day-excursion which Moses had suggested to Christopher Hughes. The plan was to invite members of the diplomatic community on a short trip down the Saltsjön.

Hughes heartily embraced the idea, and sent out a round of invitations. A number of diplomats readily accepted, provided Captain Rogers would allow each of them to contribute "a Dish or two +

wines" to the on-board buffet. This, Hughes later recorded, Captain Rogers "rather reluctantly agreed to."

While the crew was loading the coal, Lord Lynedoch and Robert Graham paid a visit to Hughes. The two Scots confirmed their intention to accept Captain Rogers' offer of a passage to Russia. Hughes returned the compliment by inviting them to join the day excursion, which was set for Wednesday, September 1st.

His visitors gone, Hughes sat down to write a long dispatch to Secretary of State John Quincy Adams.

> *... We have now in our port the Steam Ship Savannah, of Savannah, Captain Moses Rogers. This proud triumph over what has been considered insurmountable difficulties, as well as over the doubts and sneers of incredulous + envious Europe, has really afforded me a most* impayable *gratification. All classes + sexes of people here have been on board, to witness this wonder of American skill + enterprise. The King has expressed his admiration of it, as well as a strong desire to purchase the ship, which Captain Rogers would indulge H.M. in, provided suitable terms could be agreed on. But the moment is unpropitious! This Government is putting a final close to the Danish + Norwegian negotiations: tomorrow, or next day, the papers will be signed, settling the times + amounts of the different payments of the 3 millions of Hambro Dollars to Denmark for Norway: + his majesty is not in a condition, he says, to disburse money...*

Hughes went on to describe the visits to the *Savannah* by Prince Oscar and Lord Lynedoch. Then he came to a more personal matter, that being the future of Captain Moses Rogers.

> *... He says that he has expended all his earnings in various enterprises + inventions + fears that he may not meet employment at home, for some time, to enable him to maintain his family. That he would be very willing to accept some place in the public service, in some of the Navy yards, where his united abilities, or qualifications, as navigator + engineer, might be useful: that he spoke to Mr. Rush on the subject, who promised to write you, + to request you to bring the subject before the President. He thinks that there may be such a place, as superintendent over some of the steam machinery now constructing at New York: that he wishes to be* useful. *That unless some place, in which he can be* really

useful, can be given to him, to use his own words, "he would rather accept none." He has requested me to mention the subject to you + I now do so, to gratify the wishes of an enterprising, ingenious + patriotic man + not because I consider that my recommendation can be either useful to him; or necessary to you, my dear Sir, to support the fitness of protecting + rewarding a meritorious citizen, who has certainly done a very extraordinary thing, which will add to the reputation of our country for genius + enterprise, + which, by convincing the world of the practicability of applying steam navigation safely to the most distant voyages, may lead to great + important results hereafter...

Hughes then made a pitch to offer Captain Rogers a different kind of recognition:

... if I had the power, I would gratify the first wish of this public spirited + meritorious man's heart, which is, to place his two sons, who are now infants, upon the list, as midshipman.

A *midshipman* is a naval officer in training, and the U.S. Navy's list of midshipman was a coveted honor. If the young Rogers boys, Washington and Daniel, were placed upon this list, it meant that when they came of age, careers as U.S. Navy officers would be open to them.

Hughes then went even further:

If I were a member of Congress, I should not think it unworthy of me, or of the Government, to rise in my place + propose, that, as an evidence of public respect, + as proof that Republics were not negligent in rewarding men of genius + enterprise, the two Sons of Captain Moses Rogers, the intrepid and successful American engineer + navigator, should, from that day, be entered on the list of Midshipman. It seems to me, that it would be an apposite reward, for the extraordinary achievement of this distinguished man: it would be honourable in the Government to take this public notice of him: + it would be giving his children the means of serving themselves + their country in an honourable career. I know that the father would consider it the happiest event of his life, to see his children admitted into the Navy!

Hughes supported his suggestions by pointing out the spirit with which Captain Rogers promoted both his nation and his creation.

He unites in all his thoughts + movements some consideration for the honour + fame of his country: he said to me the other day, "I know Sir, that I am spending + losing money in this expedition: but I have satisfied the world that the thing is practicable: as I am in Europe, I wish to circulate the fame of my ship + of my country as far + as widely as possible, + nothing gives me more pleasure than to show my ship to all people + especially to persons of distinction."

Hughes then recorded a telling swipe that Moses had taken at the Mother Country:

"if I make an exception, it must be with englishmen: for they sneer at us on all occasions, + in many instances were uncivil + insolent to me."

Just what else had happened in Britain—beyond the coachwhip incident—that led Moses to make such a comment is unknown. Positive press and cheering crowds aside, the opinions of those such as Valerius in *The Statesman* more accurately reflected how most of the British political establishment viewed the *Savannah* and her captain. Clearly, any such personal jabs directed at Moses from Albion's elites must have cut him deeply.

In closing, Hughes felt obliged to justify his long dispatch on the *Savannah* and Captain Rogers. It was due in part, he wrote, to knowing the Secretary of State's interest in the "useful arts" (as inventions were commonly called at the time).

Two days later, on September 1st, the diplomats invited on the excursion made their way out to the steamship under cloudy skies. Standing on the *Savannah*'s deck to receive them were Christopher and Laura Hughes, along with Captain Rogers.

Climbing aboard came Austria's minister to Sweden, Count Karl Ludwig von Ficquelmont. An unreconstructed Royalist who had been forced to flee his native France after the Revolution, Count Ficquelmont found a home in the Austrian army and foreign service. The day before, he had written a brief dispatch to his superior, Foreign Minister Klemens Metternich, apprising him of the steamship's arrival and intentions while in Europe.

In addition came Spain's minister, Pantaleon de Moreno y Daoiz, who also had written home the previous day about the *Savannah* and her "gallant captain." Moreno apprised Madrid that he was led to understand Captain Rogers was asking eighteen or twenty thousand pounds sterling (~$80,000–$89,000) for the steamship. This price, he thought, would be difficult to achieve in either Sweden or Russia.

Ministers Salomon Dedel of the Netherlands and the Marquis de Rumigny of France also came aboard. So too did many of the diplomats' wives, and some other legation members. Absent were the Danish and British ministers, as well as Count Wetterstedt, who were all too preoccupied with the Norwegian debt agreement to be drawn away.

The excursion party was rounded out by Lord Lynedoch and Robert Graham. "The day was not favorable for sailing," Robert noted in a letter home, "but served better to show off the steam engine."

That it certainly did, as the *Savannah* got under way at noon, steaming down to Vaxholm fortress and back. "The thing turned out remarkably well," wrote Robert, who figured that they covered the 45-mile round trip in about 5½ or 6 hours. The success of this excursion solidified his and Lord Lynedoch's determination to take passage on the steamship to St. Petersburg.

Soon after their return to Stockholm, the diplomats learned that Bernadotte, in his capacity as King Karl XIV Johan, had signed the papers; the Norwegian debt negotiations finally had been concluded. Sweden had agreed to assume $3 million of debt, to be repaid over ten years, and as the country's sovereign, Bernadotte was personally liable for these payments. Given the economic pressures of the time, and the lack of "hard" money in Sweden and elsewhere, it truly was an "unpropitious" moment for a purchase of the *Savannah*.

* * *

Before Baron Klinkowström had left for the United States the previous summer, Karl Johan had asked him specifically to find out if the Americans were planning to use steam vessels for long-distance ocean voyages. This placed the Swedish monarch in a very small group of visionaries who were willing to consider the possibility of steam navigation on a global scale.

The very appearance of the *Savannah* at Stockholm had proved the point—a new age was dawning. Having asked the question, and seen the answer right outside his palace window, the imperative for King Karl Johan became ... *what to do?*

The dispatches by the Dutch and Spanish ministers at Stockholm made clear that Captain Rogers was willing to name his price for the steamship. And regardless of whether the quoted numbers were accurate or not, it is also clear that Moses was prepared to negotiate. Christopher Hughes said as much in his own dispatch to John Quincy Adams, noting Karl Johan's "strong desire to purchase the ship, which Captain Rogers would indulge H.M. in, provided suitable terms could be agreed on." But it was the imminent signing of the Norwegian debt agreement, with its requirement to pay in specie, that left the Swedish king "not in a condition, he says, to disburse money."

Under the circumstances, if Bernadotte was to make any kind of offer to purchase the *Savannah*, he would have to be creative. With insufficient cash on hand, it appears he may have relied on one of the oldest forms of trade in an attempt to consummate a deal, and that was by suggesting a barter. Based upon an account from one of the *Savannah*'s crewmen printed many years later, the King of Sweden had offered $100,000 worth of hemp and iron, delivered at New York, Philadelphia or Boston, in exchange for the steamship.

That such an offer was hidden from view, only to surface in such an obscure way so long after the fact, seems to reflect not only the style of Bernadotte, but that of sovereigns themselves.

Because Karl Johan never learned Swedish, communications within his government required a laborious procedure. First, documents had to be translated from Swedish into French, before the monarch could read them. Then, the adopted king's response had to be translated from French back into Swedish. The end result could be delay at best, and disarray at worst.

The best way to circumvent this burden was for Bernadotte to receive reports, and give orders, verbally. This he often did, with a small cadre of close aides carrying out his instructions. Given the news blackout in place, and the sensitive nature of the King's finances, it stands to reason that Bernadotte would want any offer to purchase the *Savannah* to be unseen, and untraceable.

In a great many respects, this offer fits the circumstances and people involved. At the time of the *Savannah*'s visit, Sweden only recently had acquired its first commercial steamboat. Bernadotte well-knew that his adopted country's merchants would be unwilling to venture their own capital on something as risky as an ocean-going steam vessel. If he wanted to encourage the new mode of transport, he would have to take action himself. The American steamship represented the most advanced form of this technology to date. The simple fact that it had made the voyage all the way across the Atlantic Ocean to Sweden was proof that this design worked, and could serve as a platform for continued improvements.

With finances tight and economies struggling on both sides of the Atlantic, the best thing to offer, besides cash, was the commodities that America wanted most from Sweden—

Hemp, the best of which came from the Baltic countries;

And *iron*, among which the Swedish ores were considered the purest.

As the sovereign, Bernadotte held a royal prerogative over the country's iron resources, giving him the power to direct how they were used. And hemp could be procured easily enough, if not from his own farmlands, then from others.

The true value of a barter deal is in the eyes of the participants. It would have been very difficult for Bernadotte to sell such large quantities of hemp and iron all at once in the glutted American market. While the nominal value of his bid was said to be $100,000, the immediate market value of these commodities at the time was practically far less.

Just how much less depended upon the judgment of Moses. At New York market prices, $100,000 split equally between the two commodities amounted to about 220 tons of hemp and 475 tons of iron. That would be an enormous amount of material for Pott & McKinne to store, and incredibly hard to sell in the middle of an economic depression. The state of things made the barter's value substantially less than $100,000, and whatever that amount was, Moses couldn't be sure that the other shareholders would agree with his valuation.

This left him with little choice. According to the crewman's account, "the offer was not accepted—the cash being wanted."

* * *

The day after the diplomatic excursion, the *Savannah*'s crew awakened to a steady rain, and the task of loading food and drinking water on board. Before long, the steamship received a visit from the American consul at Stockholm, a Scottish banker named David Erskine.

Like any consul in a port, Erskine's primary job was to deal with matters related to American commerce and crews. The reason for his call stood right next to him, in the form of a man named William Scinnen. While Steve didn't record any details in the logbook, it is very likely that Scinnen was a stranded seaman. American law gave Consul Erskine the power to place him aboard any American vessel for the journey home. Moses could have refused to take Scinnen, but it would have triggered a $100 fine. In any event, Mr. Erskine had no need to impose such a penalty, since Captain Rogers was willing to take Scinnen, despite what this newest crewman may have thought about being sent home in such a craft as a "steamship."

In the greater scheme of things, taking on a stranded mariner was a minor matter, since Moses had a bigger problem to worry about, with shades of Liverpool. He discovered that if the *Savannah* took on more wood or coal than Swedish law allotted for use in a vessel of that size, he would have to pay duty on the fuel as though it was cargo. Repeating the same arguments made to the British authorities, Moses declared that all of the fuel brought on board was for the steam engine, and not for re-sale. But the Swedes refused to budge—the law was the law.

Moses appealed to Christopher Hughes for help, who immediately fired off a letter to Count Wetterstedt, asking that "<u>all duties and imposts whatever</u>" be waived, except for lighthouse and pilot fees.

In a separate private letter, Hughes made a more personal appeal, pointing out that to impose such taxes for "<u>bona-fide</u> fuel" on Captain Rogers would "look like a sort of advantage taken of the form + principles of his ship: He will be obliged to pay as a <u>Trader</u>, when in fact he is not a Trader." Hughes closed by noting that "since he has been in the Port of Stockholm, his Ship has been open to the visits of every one who had any curiosity to see her: + upwards of 20,000 of [His] Majesty's subjects have been on board."

Hughes' visitor count added a great deal of weight to the spirit of his argument. The *Savannah* had been a huge hit with the public.

The Swedish foreign minister wasted no time. He went right to the top, and provided Hughes with an answer later that day:

The King orders me to favor you Sir, to give to Captain Rogers of the American steam ship, who is currently here, all the facilities due to his courageous enterprise. His Majesty grants to him the free export of wood . . . as well as the exemption of all the ordinary port dues. . .

But there was no mention of coal.

While Moses spent the next day ironing out the matter of duties, Steve kept the crew busy preparing for departure, slated for the following day, Saturday, September 4th.

At some point during the course of their work, it was noticed that the jolly boat was missing. So were two of the crew, John Smith and Henry Wanripe.

Unlike their truant shipmates at Liverpool, Smith and Wanripe ended their absence without a fight. They returned from shore in a short time, successfully having gotten drunk. Steve dutifully noted their transgression in the logbook, leaving Smith and Wanripe justifiably liable to any fine or punishment meted out.

For Captain Rogers, the issue of fuel remained far more pressing. With no tax relief on the carrying of coals, Moses decided not to purchase any more. Instead, he would load up on duty-free wood.

This would require more time, so the intended day of departure had to be spent lugging wood aboard—in the rain. Also brought onto the ship was the luggage of Lord Lynedoch and Robert Graham, in preparation for getting under way. Those tasks, and getting the custom house to agree on the final amounts of fuel aboard, took the balance of the day.

Finally, on an overcast Sunday morning—precisely two weeks to the day after the *Savannah*'s arrival—all was ready. At 9 o'clock, the two Grahams embarked. Lord Lynedoch, in addition to carrying diplomatic papers to his brother-in-law in St. Petersburg, also brought along two dozen bottles of Claret, for his and Robert's own consumption. The passenger list was rounded out by Consul Erskine and his wife, who would ride the steamship partway down the Saltsjön.

At 10 o'clock, Moses ordered the steam up and the anchor weighed. To see the *Savannah* off, the Swedes came out in force, as Robert Graham recounted in a letter home:

> *We embarked . . . and about 11 put our wheels in motion with quantities of little boats all round us to see us start— + all the people on the decks of the surrounding ships—which made it a gay looking scene . . .*

Departing Stockholm before the multitudes, the steamship churned eastward, down the Saltsjön. Keeping the steam up proved difficult. The greenness and dampness of the newly-loaded wood, which the firemen had begun to mix with the coal, led to fluctuations in boiler pressure, and forced a couple of brief stops. In time, though, the boilers were got right, and the *Savannah* continued down to Warnholm, where the Erskines went ashore.

Seven hours after leaving Stockholm, the steamship reached

Sandhamn Island, one of the easternmost isles in the archipelago. There, the pilot disembarked, and Moses set the *Savannah* on a course due east, into the Baltic Sea.

* * *

Once the *Savannah* had steamed far enough away from the Swedish mainland, favorable southerly winds appeared, encouraging a switch to sails. Lord Lynedoch watched as one-half of each of the paddlewheels was collapsed, detached, and brought on deck. Then the other halves were turned, so as to be free of the water. This operation, he noted in his little red diary, took only 12 minutes. Finally, the remaining halves were collapsed in place on the fixed arms, so as not to catch any wind.

This procedure completed, the Grahams went below to review their accommodations. Robert noted that they had "a capital collection of stores on board"—salted and fresh meats, plus fresh and dried fruits of all kinds, and a good selection of wines. "I cannot help thinking," he later wrote, "that we can discover the finger of Mr. Hughes the American Chargé d'Affaires at work."

By noon Monday, the *Savannah* cruised past the lighthouse on Finnish-owned Uto Island, in the middle of the upper Baltic.

On Tuesday, the crew spotted Odensholm lighthouse to the south, on the coast of Estonia, which, like Finland, was part of the Russian Empire.

Lord Lynedoch, once he had the benefit of several days' familiarity with Captain Rogers, asked him about the vessel's details, which the General duly recorded in his little red diary. The *Savannah* herself, Moses told him, cost $36,000, with the steam machinery and fit-out accounting for an additional $30,000 in expenditures.

For his part, Robert Graham wrote about the uniqueness of their experience:

> . . . *We have put on our wheels again, + are getting on well in a dead calm—to the great wonder, and annoyance I suppose, of a great bulking Russian vessel . . . which is lying useless in the water, + the stern of which we have just dropped past—We have left far behind us a brig, and a galliotte, which sailed from the Sandhamn lighthouse, (having already got over the troublesome navigation* [through] *the inland), about the time when we left Stockholm . . .*

After 12 hours of steaming, the winds picked up again, around midnight. Moses ordered the engine stopped, and one-half of the wheels brought in. Lord Lynedoch stood at the ready with his watch. This time, the procedure took only 10 minutes. It was after one of these rapid changeovers by the experienced crew that Steve remembered Lord Lynedoch paying his American hosts the ultimate compliment—

"I blame no man born in the United States for being proud of his country, and were I a young man, I'd go there myself."

By that time, the *Savannah* had entered the far narrower Gulf of Finland. The waters there were incredibly transparent, thanks to all the surrounding fresh-water streams and rivers that fed into the Gulf.

These waters were also more dangerous. Compared to the rest of the Baltic, the Gulf of Finland was shallow, and littered with shoals and rocks. By necessity, the crew had to keep a sharp lookout for the many lighthouses dotting the horizon, as well as flags and buoys in the water that marked any hazards. For Robert Graham, the dangers of the Gulf actually offered a kind of untiring entertainment, as he and Lord Lynedoch stood their own watch for the lighthouses, all built to different designs to aid in their identification.

By Wednesday evening, the crew spotted a lighthouse in the distance, to the southeast. Below its glass top were four windows in the tower, stacked one on top of another in a straight line. This was Tolboukin Light, which sat upon a small island in the middle of the still-narrowing Gulf. Just beyond Tolboukin lay another, much larger island. This was called Kotlin Island, and at its far eastern end was the port of Kronstadt, maritime gateway and guardian to the Russian capital of St. Petersburg.

With darkness approaching, it was too late to make it all the way to Kronstadt, given the many hazards. After maneuvering the *Savannah* around to the south of Tolboukin, Moses ordered the crew to furl sails and drop anchor. There, with the lighthouse clearly visible to their north, and a triangular buoy-light marking a coastal shoal to their south, they could easily ascertain if they were drifting from their anchorage during the night.

At sunrise the next morning, Moses ordered signals to be made for a pilot to come aboard, and guide them the remaining 7 miles to Kronstadt. This request went unanswered, so Moses ordered the steam up, and by 7 o'clock they were under way, pilot-less.

The approach to heavily fortified Kronstadt could be a very tricky one. The port was situated on the southeastern end of Kotlin Island, which ran east to west within the narrow Gulf. Proceeding around the north side of the island was very inadvisable, since those waters were shallow, and concealed a number of deliberately unmarked sandbars. Any vessel attempting to mope its way forward that way would probably run aground, or become easy prey for the Russian coastal artillery on the island's north side.

Therefore, the only safe approach, by design, was around the south side. There, the distance between Kotlin Island and the Russian mainland, further to the south, appeared to be about 3½ miles. But this seemingly broad seaway was also deceptive, for beneath its waves was an enormous triangular sandbar, jutting northward from the mainland until it almost touched Kotlin Island. No vessel of size could sail over this sandbar without running aground. This forced all large vessels going to St. Petersburg to pass through the narrow, dredged channel between the northern tip of the sandbar and Kronstadt. The path was easy to find, for upon the triangular sandbar's northern tip was a massive stone battery, rising right out of the water and bristling with cannon. It was called Kronslott. Further guarding this channel were still more fortifications and guns on Kotlin Island itself.

Without a pilot, Moses and Steve had to make sure they avoided not only the great triangular sand trap, but also the shallows along Kotlin Island's south coast. This latter peril was made all the more dangerous that morning by a strong southwesterly wind, which naturally pushed any vessel using the old mode right toward Kotlin's shore. But the *Savannah*, smoking and splashing her way forward, had the means to easily avoid this danger, making her stand out all the more amongst the many sailing vessels that were bobbing meekly at anchor.

As the *Savannah* steamed nearer, those on deck saw dead-ahead the pentagonal granite battery of Kronslott rising directly out of the water, with two tiers of gun ports facing westward. To its left was the narrow channel to St. Petersburg. A little further left (off the larboard bow) was the merchants' harbor of Kronstadt, sheltered from the Gulf by a long granite wall, called a *mole*. In addition to acting as a breakwater to protect the shipping in the harbor, this particular mole served as yet another platform for still more artillery. All of these combined defenses were said to contain some 3,000 guns, making

Kronstadt one of the most heavily fortified bastions in the world.

As the steamship came nearer still, a Russian guardship could be seen anchored in the middle of the channel. Before long, a small boat left the guardship and made its way toward the *Savannah*. Moses ordered the engine to a halt, as the boat came alongside and delivered several Russian officers to the steamship.

Their first order of business was inspecting the ship's papers. Robert Graham himself witnessed just how keen the Russians were to see the Danish bill of health issued at Helsingør.

Their duties complete, the Russians returned to their boat, leaving behind a pilot, who pointed out where the *Savannah* should go to drop anchor. The place selected for the steamship was not within the protected harbor, but rather in the channel itself. This was due to the incredibly strict rules the Russian authorities had regarding fire, which was absolutely forbidden on any vessel within the mole.

Having steamed to her designated safe spot by 9 o'clock, Moses ordered the *Savannah*'s engine to a halt once again, and the anchor dropped. From there, St. Petersburg lay about 20 miles to the east, through open water and then a little way up the Neva River.

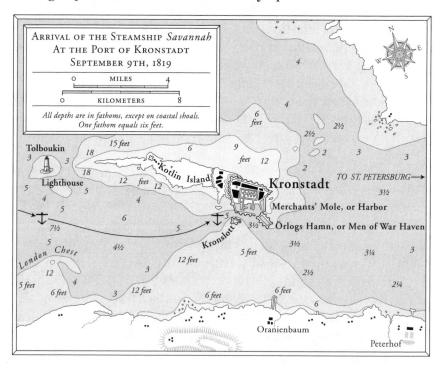

ARRIVAL OF THE STEAMSHIP *Savannah*
AT THE PORT OF KRONSTADT
SEPTEMBER 9TH, 1819

0   MILES   4

0   KILOMETERS   8

All depths are in fathoms, except on coastal shoals.
One fathom equals six feet.

Tolboukin

Lighthouse

Kotlin Island

Kronstadt

TO ST. PETERSBURG→

Merchants' Mole, or Harbor

Kronslott

Orlogs Hamn, or Men of War Haven

London Chest

Oranienbaum

Peterhof

Since it would probably take some time for Captain Rogers to get the necessary clearances to proceed, this was the end of the voyage for Lord Lynedoch and Robert Graham. The trip from Stockholm had taken one hour short of 4 days, which was, as Robert wrote, "reckoned a very fair passage."

Indeed it was, given the vessels left trailing in the *Savannah*'s foam. During the 95 hours of travel, she had used steam to advantage for a total of 24 hours, or a little more than one-quarter of the journey. While this leg of the voyage was significantly shorter than the other two, it still represented an increase in the proportion of steaming time over the Atlantic and North Sea crossings.

Before they disembarked, Lord Lynedoch and Robert Graham sat down to one last breakfast below deck. Yet they could hardly eat it in peace, for as soon as the *Savannah* had dropped anchor, she was immediately swarmed. Rowing out from Kronstadt came hordes of the curious, who quickly climbed aboard the steamship and began crawling all about her decks, including the main cabin where the Grahams were eating.

Once the ship was secure, Moses had to go ashore to officially present himself and his papers. Along for the trip came the two Scots. Climbing aboard the jolly boat with several of the crew, the threesome was rowed over to the port. There, they had to make personal appearances at four different offices, including the custom house (to register their arrival) and the headquarters of Admiral Fyodor Vassilyevich Möller, the island's military governor.

Admiral Möller was delighted to meet Lord Lynedoch, and courteously put his own personal carriage and 14-oar barge at the Scotsman's disposal. With all formalities concluded, the Grahams took the Admiral's barge back to the *Savannah* to collect their baggage, and extend their thanks and goodbyes to her crew. By day's end, they were on their way to St. Petersburg in one of the local steamboats.

As for Moses, the next step was clear, yet uncertain. Admiral Möller surely told him that the Emperor Alexander was on a tour of Finland at that moment, but was expected back any day. Proceeding to St. Petersburg served no purpose in the Emperor's absence. Captain Rogers, his crew, and the *Savannah* herself, could do nothing but wait.

CHAPTER SEVENTEEN

ALL THE RUSSIAS

O NCE THEY HAD arrived at Kronstadt on September 9th, Captain Rogers and his crew bided their time, waiting for news of the Emperor's return. Other than maintenance on the rigging and the busy work of ship's duty, there wasn't much else to do, besides brace themselves against the strong gales that blew in from the west, and endure the occasional thunder squall.

On clearer days, Moses and Steve could use their spyglasses to take in some nearby attractions, as the *Savannah* lay at anchor in "the Roads."

To their south, about 3 miles beyond the massive Kronslott battery, were two long piers jutting out from the shoreline. Directly beyond those piers, on shore, sat a collection of very ornate buildings and gardens. This was Oranienbaum, or "Orange tree," one of the imperial family's summer residences.

Along that same shore, further to the east, was yet another group of buildings, gardens and fountains, along with a T-shaped pier. This was Peterhof, yet another imperial summer residence where the royal family's yachts were kept.

Turning to the north and looking into Kronstadt harbor, the usual forest of masts, rigging and furled sails could be seen. Most of these artificial trees belonged to merchant vessels, which unloaded their cargoes there for transport by smaller craft into St. Petersburg. But some of these sticks belonged to Russian warships, many of which sat in dry docks awaiting repairs, a constant necessity given the harsh winters they endured.

Yet the kind of vessels that surely aroused the most curiosity in Moses were the steamboats which ran on a regular schedule between Kronstadt and St. Petersburg. They were owned by Scottish expatriate Charles Baird, the very man who had beat out Fulton and his entrepreneurial heirs in the contest to see who could deliver a steam vessel first to Russian waters.

Baird had possessed a number of distinct advantages in the competition.

First, he already had been working in Russia for many years, having gained much experience establishing iron foundries and a machine works, and winning government contracts, as well.

Second, he had gained a reputation for not only turning out good products, but doing so efficiently. It led people in St. Petersburg to say for many years to come that if they wanted something to work well, it should operate "like at Baird's works."

And third, he benefited greatly from having seen detailed drawings of one of Robert Fulton's early steamboats.

This was thanks to Pavel Svin'in, the Russian diplomat who had become entranced by steamboats during his two-year posting to America. In the course of his investigations, the Russian had managed to get his hands on a copy of Fulton's drawings. The source, according to Svin'in, was a "Mr. Brown of New York." (This was, in all likelihood, Charles Brownne, who had built Fulton's first ten steamboats.)

Returning home to Russia in late 1813, Svin'in had tried to sabotage Fulton's negotiations with the Emperor for an exclusive steamboat franchise, but failed. Undeterred, he then showed Fulton's steamboat drawings to Charles Baird. While the American's design could not be mimicked exactly, due to the shallow waters in and around St. Petersburg, Baird did benefit in seeing how Fulton laid out the steam engine and paddlewheels.

The result was a specially-designed steamboat, named the *Elizaveta*, in honor of Alexander's wife, the Empress. At only 56 tons, the *Elizaveta* was very light in weight and shallow of draft, allowing her to paddle over the sand bar at the mouth of the Neva River. While not particularly powerful, she still could steam between Kronstadt and St. Petersburg in 2 or 3 hours, which was less than one-half the usual sailing time. Baird subsequently had built several more steamers, for use on the Kronstadt–St. Petersburg run, or as tow-boats. This small fleet represented the only examples of the new mode of transport the people of St. Petersburg had ever seen, until the *Savannah* appeared.

* * *

While Moses, Steve and the crew awaited the return of the Emperor, Lord Lynedoch and Robert Graham were being welcomed into St. Petersburg society.

On the evening of their arrival, Thursday, September 9th, they had landed in the city on one of the steamboats, and had tea with owner Charles Baird and his wife.

On Friday, after meeting Lord Cathcart and delivering to him the Stockholm diplomatic dispatches, the two Grahams were moved to a hotel along the Moika Canal.

On Saturday, they attended the procession of the Blessed Virgin, at the monastery of St. Alexander Nevsky. Much of the nobility was there, including the Empress Elizaveta and the Emperor's brother, Grand Duke Nicholas. Also in attendance was most of the foreign diplomatic corps.

The new face of Lord Lynedoch, standing next to his brother-in-law, Lord Cathcart, could not help but be noticed. Lynedoch's unique means of arrival in Russia made him stand out all the more. This was especially true since Empress Elizaveta herself had been at Oranienbaum on the day of the *Savannah*'s appearance at Kronstadt. The combination of circumstances was simply too powerful to be ignored, and quickly generated an invitation to Lynedoch for a private audience with the Empress.

On Sunday, Lord Lynedoch honored this royal request. He proceeded to the Winter Palace alone, where he was ushered into a richly decorated room for his interview with Elizaveta. As Robert Graham later wrote, after learning the details of his cousin's encounter:

> *. . . The Empress had received him most graciously—very elegant in her manners—asked him a great deal about the Steam ship . . .*

* * *

On Tuesday, September 14th, five days after her arrival, the *Savannah* still sat at Kronstadt. There was nothing for Captain Rogers and the crew to do but keep the steamship in the best condition possible, and weather the gales of wind and rain blowing off the Gulf of Finland. Beyond that was the duty of playing host to the many Russian Navy officers who came on board to inspect the vessel.

Contrary to presumption, many of these naval officers were anything but Russian. Quite a few of them came from elsewhere in Europe.

The presence of these foreigners reflected the imperial view of military and technical ability since Peter the Great: if the expertise didn't exist in Mother Russia, then import it.

This century-long practice had continued into Alexander's reign. While the Russian Army was well-known for being top-heavy with German-born generals, the Russian Navy featured many veterans of Britain's Royal Navy. It was these British-born-and-trained naval officers, armed with letters from friends and colleagues back home in Albion, who went over the *Savannah* from stem to stern.

Despite the presence of many high government officials in St. Petersburg, sanction for the steamship to proceed to the capital city could not be granted. Such permission would only be forthcoming once the Emperor Alexander had returned from his trip through Finland (where his inspection of military units had given rise to the rumors of possible war with Sweden over the Norwegian debt controversy).

Alexander's presence in the capital was vital. While he had a reputation in the United States for being an enlightened monarch, and was well-known for being unpretentious and friendly to strangers, he was still the ultimate leader—the "Emperor of All the Russias." Nothing could happen without his approval.

As a result, Captain Rogers, the *Savannah* and her crew still remained captive to the frigid waters, dull overcast sky, and chilly winds that enveloped them off Kronstadt that late summer evening.

Yet their wait was finally, nearly over. Some 20 miles to the east, in St. Petersburg, all eyes would take note of the message sent by the sudden appearance of an imperial flag flying over the Winter Palace—

The Emperor had returned.

* * *

Sunrise at Kronstadt the following morning revealed an altogether different scene. Gone was the dull grayness overhead. In its place was a warm sun, and fast "flying clouds" which glided across the Gulf sky, toward St. Petersburg. After six days of waiting, the necessary approval finally had come through—the *Savannah* could proceed to the capital city.

At 9 o'clock, a local pilot came aboard. He would guide the steamship through the Bay of St. Petersburg, which lay between Kronstadt and the mouth of the Neva River. Because the sandbar at the river's entrance was so massive, and the waters above it correspondingly so shallow, crossing over the bar, even at high tide, was impossible for a vessel as large as the *Savannah*. So the pilot also would determine precisely where to drop anchor at the mouth of the river.

Moses ordered the engine crew to get the steam up, and the deck crew to deploy the paddlewheels. The sails were left furled.

By 10 o'clock, they were ready to go. The steamship was unmoored, and the wheels put in motion. With strong breezes nearly at their backs, the *Savannah* and her crew soon had the benefit of both wind and steam pushing them through the water. Steve didn't record their speed, but they must have been making more than 10 knots.

Crewmen stationed at the bow kept a close eye on the water depths ahead. As they moved further and further to the east, the Bay's depth gradually diminished, from about 3½ fathoms (or 21 feet) around Kronstadt, to 2½ fathoms at mid-Bay.

The coastline that enveloped the crew on three sides revealed relatively flat and unremarkable terrain. Along the north and south coasts, there were just a few small fishing villages, trees, and in the distance, some scattered hills.

So it looked to the eastward, as well, although everyone aboard knew that the tree-topped shoreline immediately ahead of them masked the city of St. Petersburg, just a few miles beyond. And still further inland lay the vastness of Russia.

It was this sheer size of the place that could not help but influence the Yankee crew's opinion of their new host. The Russian Empire—like the United States—had incredible potential. But beyond recognition of this geographic similarity, and the pioneering spirit that went with it, New World perceptions of Mother Russia in that year of 1819 were largely a result of the opinions many Americans had formed of the solitary man who led her.

* * *

It had been just a dozen years since formal diplomatic relations had been established between the United States and Russia. Yet in that short time, most informed Americans already had gained an impression of Russia's leader, the Emperor Alexander, and they seemed to like what they saw. His simple act of initiating formal relations—at a time when the United States had few friends in the world—was alone sufficient to cause some Americans to think well of him.

But the act that made Alexander a household name, and endeared him to many Americans across the political spectrum, was his offer to mediate an end to the second war with Britain. Given the deep divisions created in the U.S. by the declaration of war, and the failed attempts to stop hostilities before they intensified, Alexander's diplomatic initiative was welcomed by both the no-war and pro-war camps. President James Madison not only accepted Alexander's offer, but sent two peace commissioners to join Minister John Quincy Adams at St. Petersburg to negotiate a truce. That the British subsequently rejected the mediation offer was no fault of Alexander's. His efforts in the name of peace would not be forgotten.

Once the war with Britain ended, Alexander maintained his measured, amicable approach toward the United States. "We have . . . enemies in almost every part of the world and few or no friends anywhere," wrote John Quincy Adams in 1817. "If there be an exception it is in Russia."

The Emperor's efforts to rid the Continent of Napoleon, and promote stability through his Holy Alliance in Europe (which encouraged "Justice, Christian Charity and Peace"), led many Americans to believe that he was a different kind of monarch. In recognition, the Massachusetts Peace Society had sent a gift shipment of books to Alexander, which he gratefully acknowledged. And more recently, the American Academy of Fine Arts in New York had made him an honorary member.

Alexander's domestic policies only reinforced the perception that he was a leader for positive change. Upon becoming Emperor in 1801, he had lifted the bans on foreign travel and the importation of books and periodicals. Then, he had pushed for reform of his country's hospitals and education system. More recently, he had banned the slitting of nostrils as a form of criminal punishment, and sanctioned the founding of a society for prison reform.

Alexander's actions regarding the Russian form of slavery, called *serfdom*, further burnished his image. Soon after ascending the throne, he had signed a law allowing serfs to buy their freedom, as well as land, from their masters. With the final defeat of Napoleon, he had approved the emancipation of serfs in the Baltic regions: Estonia in 1816, Courland in 1817, and most recently Livonia, in early 1819. The next logical step was the elimination of serfdom in all the Russias, and Alexander had recently received proposals from liberal reformers to do just that.

Further afield, the possessions of Poland and Finland had been given their own measures of freedom by Alexander, including elected parliaments, which, like the Russian Senate, exercised the power to govern in conjunction with the Emperor. The Poles also had been allowed a written constitution, and freedom of the press.

With so much already accomplished, Russian liberals wanted more. They were keen for Alexander to set his sights on an even more ambitious target: reform the imperial government itself.

* * *

Once the *Savannah* reached the edge of the sandbar at the mouth of the Neva, the pilot showed Moses and Steve where to drop anchor, near the river's southernmost outlet. The steamship had covered the 14 miles between Kronstadt and the Neva's mouth in about one hour.

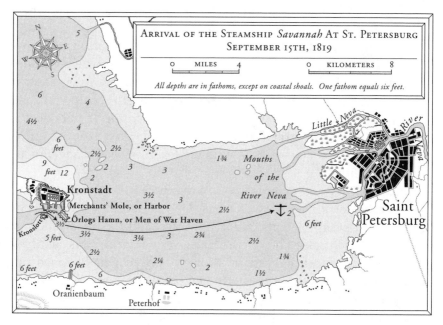

From the deck, the crew could see that this sandbar before them was enormous. Stretching seven miles from north to south, it filled the entire eastern side of the Bay. Further to the east, beyond the sandbar, was a large delta of islands, formed by the splitting of the Neva River further inland. The largest of these islands was called Kammenyi. At the far end of that island, some 6 miles away, lay the center of St. Petersburg, its many steeples and towers visible in the distance.

Within the sandbar itself, there were four channels which provided access into the different branches of the Neva. Since the water depth in these channels was no more than 12 feet, only shallow-draft, flat-bottomed vessels could proceed upriver, all the way to St. Petersburg. The *Savannah*, with a draft of over 14 feet, could go no further.

Around about this time, one of the ferry vessels venturing forth from the Neva came alongside the *Savannah*, and delivered a package addressed to Moses. Enclosed with it was a letter:

St. Petersburg, 15th Sept., 1819.

Dear Sir.—I trust you will do me the favor to receive the small tea-kettle (or coffee-pot) which I take the liberty of sending, as a slight token of my regard, and which may be useful at Mrs. Rodgers' tea table. I beg, too, that you will believe me most sincere in assuring you of the great satisfaction I had in making the passage from Stockholm on board the Savannah.

It gave me the opportunity of coming here in the most agreeable manner possible, and of admiring the successful efforts of your powerful mind.

With best wishes for your future welfare, in which Mr. Graham desires to join, I remain, dear Sir, most truly and obediently yours,

Lyndoch

Capt. Rodgers, of the Savannah.

From out of the package came a small silver tea kettle, standing upon three legs with clawed feet. Underneath the kettle, between the legs, was an inverted dome which could hold a heating element, such as an oil-lamp wick. Arching over the kettle was a silver arm wrapped in a thick wooden handle, and jutting out the front was a long, ornate spout. In Russia, such an appliance was called a *samovar*.

The Samovar presented to Moses Rogers
by Lord Lynedoch.

On the side of the samovar was a remembrance, neatly inscribed:

Presented to Captain Moses Rogers
of the Steam Ship Savannah
(being the first Steam Vessel that had
Crossed the Atlantic)
by Sir Thomas Graham, Lord Lynedoch,
a Passenger from Stockholm to St. Petersburg
September 15th, 1819

* * *

The newspapers of St. Petersburg had been following the *Savannah*'s movements across Northern Europe for some time already. Once she arrived at Kronstadt, the *Savannah* naturally elicited several immediate notices in the city's papers. But it was not until the day after she had anchored off the mouth of the Neva that the most interesting commentary was published. On that day, the *Russian Invalid or Military Journal* gave its readers a sense of what the experts thought of this unique visitor from afar:

> The remarkable steam frigate *Savannah*, the arrival of which into Liverpool from North America was announced in all the public papers and was the worthy object of general curiosity is now in Kronstadt. This vessel is the first steam ship to cross the Atlantic Ocean. It is built of oak wood and is characterized by its strength as well as its beauty and the perfection of the construction of all its parts. Its engines were examined by people qualified in this field in England as well as at home in Kronstadt and are considered worthy of astonishment...

It was a very telling article. Given the large number of Royal Navy officers serving in the Russian Navy, as well as the many British merchants living in St. Petersburg, the *Savannah*'s reputation clearly had preceded her arrival. Furthermore, it was obvious that those "Russians" who went through the steamship at Kronstadt, armed as they were with private opinions from Albion, had concluded the *Savannah* was just as revolutionary as they had been told.

The *Northern Post*, a newspaper with a much broader readership, repeated news of the *Savannah*'s arrival several days later, as well as the high opinions of her machinery in England. The paper further clarified that the steamship could not proceed up the Neva due to its size—if readers wanted to see this novel craft, they need only go down to the mouth of the river to have a look, at the least.

* * *

Because foreigners needed an internal Russian visa to travel from Kronstadt to St. Petersburg, Moses may have been unable to visit the capital city until the *Savannah* was cleared to move across the Bay. Once the steamship was anchored securely off the mouth of the Neva, the trip into St. Petersburg would have taken a couple of hours by oars, and considerably less if Moses was able to hitch a ride on one of the local steamboats.

Once travelers passed over the massive sandbar, they entered the deep-blue waters of the rapidly-flowing Lower Neva River. At various points along the way, the riverbank was interrupted by entryways to the city's canals, which were an inspiration of the city's founder, Peter the Great, who had modeled St. Petersburg after Amsterdam.

Further upriver, one of the first developments seen on the south bank was the great iron and machine works of Charles Baird. Beyond that was the English Quay, a two-mile-long wall of huge granite blocks that rose ten feet above the water's surface. The beautiful stucco houses along the Quay originally had been occupied by British merchants, but by 1819 they were mostly in the hands of the Russian nobility. The foreigners themselves had decamped to newer residential areas on Kammenyi Island, just across the river.

Once in the capital, the first task for any newcomer was to make a visit to the police station. There, the foreigner turned in the visa issued at Kronstadt, enrolled his or her name and profession in a register, and received a "ticket of residence" for St. Petersburg. Keeping each of these documents on one's person at all times was very important; any visitors unable to produce their papers on demand could easily end up in jail.

Once this paperwork was in order, getting one's bearings in St. Petersburg often came next. While any of the many gold and silver

domes, spires and towers breaking the skyline could afford a spectacular view, the best place to gain a sense of the capital at ground level
was by standing on the easternmost point of Kammenyi Island. It
was there, at the split in the Neva River, that a visitor would be treated
to a spectacular panorama of the city.

Directly to the west, on the island itself, was an enormous Greek-
style temple, adorned with tall columns on all sides, and topped by a
slanted, red-tile roof. This was the recently-completed Exchange, the
city's center for trade and commerce, and a symbol of St. Petersburg's
open marketplace.

Turning clockwise to the right, one saw the northern branch of
the Neva, flowing toward the Bay of St. Petersburg. This branch was
crowded with two-masted, flat-bottomed sailing vessels, which hauled
cargoes between Kronstadt and the warehouses on Kammenyi Island.

Further to the right, on the north shore of the mainland, sat a massive, low-lying fortification with gray stone walls. Spiking skyward
from its center was a white tower, topped by a very tall, thin gold-
gilded spire. This imposing stronghold was the Peter and Paul Fortress,
the first structure built in St. Petersburg when it was founded in the
early 18th century. The white tower with the golden spire was the
Peter and Paul Cathedral, tallest building in the city, and final resting
place of Russian royalty going back to Peter the Great himself.

Still further to the right, and due east, was the wide, un-split Neva,
spanned by a pontoon bridge at some distance upriver.

On the south embankment, directly across the river from the Peter
and Paul Fortress, stood a very large, very ornate four-story building,
with hundreds of windows framed by decorative columns. This was
the Winter Palace, the Emperor's official residence in the city.

Further right still, across the southern branch of the Neva, lay
another enormous building, stretching nearly one-quarter of a mile
down the south embankment, with its own gold-gilded spire rising
from its center. This was the Admiralty. In addition to being the headquarters of the Russian Navy, it was also an active shipyard, with a very
large warship sitting in one of its docks, nearly ready to be launched.

Downstream from the Admiralty was another pontoon bridge,
across the Lower Neva. At the bridge's southern end, right next to the
Admiralty, was a plaza which contained a large bronze figure of a man
on a horse. This was the famous statue commemorating the city's
founder, Peter the Great.

Further down the south embankment was the English Quay and its many mansions, stretching for nearly two miles along the Lower Neva. Interspersed throughout the city were dozens of other prominent buildings: museums, churches, academies, government offices, and smaller palaces. Complementing them all were neatly-paved, tree-lined streets noted for their cleanliness.

For well-traveled visitors, it was hard to find enough superlatives to describe Russia's capital in the early 19th century. Many were not shy in categorically stating it to be the most beautiful city in all of Europe, and quite possibly the world. Still others felt such scale and splendor in so remote a place deserved a nickname, and accordingly dubbed St. Petersburg "the Queen of the North."

* * *

St. Petersburg's status as a unique city went well beyond its architecture. As Russia's gateway to the West, its permanent population of 300,000 included many expatriate merchants, further supplemented by visiting businessmen, sea captains, and tourists.

But this collection of guests represented only a part of the population equation. Because the Emperor himself resided in St. Petersburg (as opposed to the old capital of Moscow), all the government ministries, including the armed forces, were obliged to be headquartered there, as well. This added thousands of civil servants, military officers and their families to the city's ranks. And if the imperial family lived in St. Petersburg, then the extensive Russian nobility had to live there too, or at least have a residence handy for occasional visits.

Since many government officials were foreigners imported for their expertise, they added yet another degree of sophistication to the fabric of St. Petersburg. So too did all the diplomatic missions in the city.

All these foreigners running around the capital led to some grumbling among the native Russians. "St. Petersburg is not Russia" was a familiar lament. But as one visitor at the time noted, the city's cosmopolitan composition had its blessings:

One peculiar advantage of the circles in this metropolis is the mixture of persons of all ranks and countries, of all religious denominations, and of the most diversified manners, habits, and humours. It is by no means unusual to see generals, chief officers, decorated personages, merchants, scholars, and artists, together in one company, at the same table;

or to meet in a company of ten or twelve persons, Russians, Germans,
Englishmen, Frenchmen, Spaniards, and Swedes. The first and great
benefit arising from this amalgamation is toleration.

For those who spoke only English, communication was not a great
problem. In addition to the few Americans and far larger numbers of
British living in the city, many Russians in government circles and
the nobility spoke English, as well as French and German. Even on
the streets of St. Petersburg, English could be heard, usually amongst
the multi-lingual entreaties of young boys employed by shopkeepers
to corral new customers. There certainly were plenty of different stores
to be enticed into, from the English Magazine (where Lord Lynedoch
had purchased the samovar), to the many French fashion shops cater-
ing to the nobility.

This sense of hospitality, and security, extended even to sightseeing,
or just walking about the city at nearly any hour—the ever-vigilant
police made sure of that, keeping a close watch on things day and night.

If there was one overtly disquieting aspect to life in St. Petersburg,
it was the people providing much of the manual and menial labor
throughout the city. As one visitor recounted, the men of this class
had a very particular appearance:

They are all clad alike. A long swaddling cloak, either made of sheep-
skin or coarse cloth, is wrapped round their bodies. In hot weather it
is sometimes changed for a coarse shirt and loose trowsers, over which
the shirt usually hangs, and is fastened round the waist by a sash. The
legs are bound round with pieces of sail-cloth, (instead of stockings),
and shoes made of the bark of trees. The hair of the head is cut across,
from one temple to the other, in a line with the eye-brows; from the
temples it hangs perpendicularly down, so as to cover the ears, from
which it is cropped directly across the neck. The hair is often combed
and daily covered with grease. The lower part of the face is concealed
by an hideous and filthy beard.

Men of such description were *serfs*, the Russian version of slaves,
and along with their female counterparts made up over one-half of
the country's population. Their prevalence led many in Russian society to count a free person's wealth based upon how many serfs he or
she owned. The numbers could be staggering: there were quite a few

nobles who each owned more than 10,000 serfs, and one nobleman was purported to control over 100,000 such persons. Even in a world where slavery was still the norm just about everywhere, the Russian version must have seemed, in its scope and practice, as gargantuan as the country itself.

* * *

Once Moses set foot in St. Petersburg, among his first objectives was making calls upon two very important people.

One was the Minister of Marine, that being the official title of the admiral who headed the Russian Navy. This fellow was an import, a Frenchman by the name of the Marquis of Traversé (Trah-ver-sáy). The letter of introduction provided by Count Lieven, the Russian minister to London, served as the key to open this highest door of the Admiralty.

In his letter to the Marquis, Count Lieven described the *Savannah* as being "constructed in an absolutely new way."

Beyond this, however, the Russian diplomat spent far more ink on the seamen than the steamship. Captain Rogers he described as "a person deserving respect due to his personal traits, talents and knowledge," further clarifying that "his particular interest is mechanics and engineering." Referring to Steve, Count Lieven added that "one of his companions is known by his skills in shipbuilding." Given the stir already created by the *Savannah*'s arrival, the Count's letter seemed to set just the right tone for presenting Moses and his creation to the government.

The second person to see was the U.S. minister to Russia, George Washington Campbell. Having arrived in St. Petersburg the previous year with his family, this Tennessee lawyer should have been glad to see a fresh American face in a place where news from home was scarce. The Russian capital was one of the most remote diplomatic outposts maintained by the United States in the early 19th century, and Campbell and his wife Harriot felt that isolation more painfully than most people would ever dare imagine.

* * *

When he was just a little boy, three years of age, George Campbell and his parents left their native Scotland for America, settling in North Carolina in 1772. Family tradition has it that at some point during the Revolution, young George adopted the middle name Washington, in honor of the Continental Army's commander.

As a young man, Campbell went off to study at the College of New Jersey at Princeton, from which he graduated in 1794. After studying law and being admitted to the bar in North Carolina, Campbell felt the call of the West, and moved across the Appalachian Mountains to Knoxville, Tennessee. There, he set up a law practice, and got himself elected to Congress, serving in the House of Representatives from 1803 to 1809. Returning home to serve a spell as a State judge, he was soon elected to represent his adopted Tennessee in the United States Senate.

Arriving in Washington in late 1811, Campbell soon rose to prominence in the Senate, leading the War Hawks in their push for battle against the British. Beyond politics, the Tennesseean also took notice of a young lady from Maryland named Harriot Stoddert, a daughter of the very first Secretary of the Navy, Benjamin Stoddert. In July of 1812, the month after war was declared against Britain, George and Harriot were married at Bladensburg, Maryland.

By 1813, Campbell had become, in the eyes of some observers, the primary advocate of the Madison administration in the Senate. In early 1814, when President Madison was confronted with imploding government finances, he nominated Campbell to serve as Secretary of the Treasury.

It was a thankless appointment. No one else approached had wanted the burden of trying to make sense of spiraling war costs, but Campbell agreed to take on the task.

He didn't last long. After spending just seven months on the job, during which he took a political lambasting from the war's opponents, Campbell resigned due to illness.

After recovering his health, he was elected again to the Senate, and returned to Washington at the very end of 1815.

In early 1818, America's second minister to Russia resigned, leaving his post even before a replacement could be named. This put President James Monroe in a bind—he knew he needed to act quickly to find a suitable candidate.

After considering several possible nominees for the position in Russia, President Monroe thought of Senator Campbell. Such an appointment made sense to the President because Campbell had two important qualifications.

First, the Tennessean's appointment would bring another Westerner into the executive fold. Monroe, as the fourth Virginian of five elected presidents, believed it was very important to geographically balance his Cabinet, as well as all major appointments.

Second, Monroe and Campbell had become close during the war years, when they shared lodgings in the capital. Any American minister to Russia, serving so far from home, would clearly appear more credible if he could claim such a personal friendship with the president himself.

When Secretary of State John Quincy Adams learned of the President's plan to appoint Campbell, he was not at all pleased. Campbell had no diplomatic experience whatsoever. Having been America's first minister to Russia, Adams knew what the post required, and thought there were better men for the job. Yet his pleadings to the President came to nothing.

The opinion of Washington society was even more deadly. "The President is very much and very justly blamed for the appointment of Campbell, a Tennessee Lawyer ingrafted on a Scot," snorted one xenophobic observer, who added "they say it is generally supposed that the President (who is dreadfully in debt) has borrowed money of him."

For himself, Campbell desired "nothing but the hope of being serviceable to the wishes of my government and interest of the state of Tennessee." He accepted the appointment, which paid $9,000 per year, an amount intended to cover not only his salary, but all expenses while he served.

By the summer of 1818, the Campbells, along with their three children (plus a fourth growing within Harriot), were packed and ready. They left Washington for the North, passing through New York (while the *Savannah* was under construction), and proceeding on to Boston. There, they embarked on a Navy frigate, the USS *Guerriere*, for the voyage to St. Petersburg.

The passage was a very difficult one for the parents, especially pregnant Harriot. Campbell recorded both he and his wife being seasick almost continuously across the Atlantic. The children—George, Benjamin, and Elizabeth—seem to have weathered the rocking and swaying of the warship far more comfortably.

Arriving at St. Petersburg in the autumn of 1818, the Campbell family set up house and awaited the return of the Emperor, who was attending the Allied Congress at Aix-la-Chapelle.

Well before then, on October 1st, Harriot gave birth to a third son, who was christened Archibald Monroe Campbell.

Not until January of 1819 did the Emperor return. Only then was Minister Campbell finally able to present his diplomatic credentials to Alexander, and formally begin his duties.

Then, in late March, as the long, hard Russian winter was beginning to give way, the Campbell's eldest son, 5-year-old George Washington, came down with a severe fever. "It did not appear at all alarming in its first stages," wrote his father. But steadily, the fever grew worse.

Campbell's namesake had been battling the illness for over a week when his second boy, 4-year-old Benjamin Stoddert, also came down with his own "violent fever."

Attending to the boys was the Campbell's family physician, British expatriate Sir James Leighton, who was also chief of the Marine Hospital. He administered what medicines he possessed to combat the fevers.

The treatments' positive effects, however, were short-lived. In the early evening of Saturday, April 10th, young Benjamin "died as he lived," wrote Campbell, "like an angel—calm + without a struggle."

At that point, Benjamin's older brother seemed to be doing better, somewhat. "George continues very weak—but has no fever," wrote the father in his diary.

The parents' hopes for his recovery were soon dashed. Just 37 hours later, they lost him, too. Young George's death, in particular, crushed his father, who described his first-born as "possessing sensibility in a degree too tender for this world."

The back-to-back loss of the Campbell boys shook the diplomatic community in St. Petersburg to its core. The next day, April 13th, a funeral service was held for both George and Benjamin at the English Church. The pews were packed with mourners, from foreign ministers and their families, to officials of the Russian government. From there, the boys' bodies were taken to Smolensky Church, where they were put into lead coffins, so that eventually they could be taken home.

"Grief + sorrow like mine are not to be expressed," Campbell wrote the day of the service, but he could not help but do so. Of his first-born, he recorded "perhaps I ought to gather some consolation—(a melancholy one it must be however) from the happiness enjoyed from George's company for five years, seven months, + twelve days."

George W. Campbell.

The raw emotions that George W. Campbell poured into his diary that day deserved to end. But they did not, for 2½ year-old Elizabeth also had become ill. Campbell could not help but notice that her fever "resembles that which carried off her two brothers—with still some shades of difference."

News that a third Campbell child had become ill soon spread to the highest reaches of the imperial government. Rushing to reinforce Dr. Leighton came two more British expatriates: Dr. Henry Galloway, and Sir James Wylie, the Emperor's personal physician. These three men represented the best medical expertise in all the Russias, and they visited the sick child two or even three times every day, holding regular conferences on how best to treat and save their patient.

The day after the boys' funeral, the Campbells received visits from court representatives of both Emperor Alexander and Empress Elizaveta. The royal emissaries asked about the cause of the children's illness, as well as the health of little Elizabeth, and baby Archibald. These imperial inquiries regarding Elizabeth continued day after day, as the team of doctors "attend + apply every remedy," wrote Campbell, "+ use every means in their power of the medical art for her recovery—"

Elizabeth held on until Saturday, April 17th, when, after weakening through the morning, she died at midday. "The grim-messenger of death can now do us little more harm," her father somberly declared. "Our three children are swept away in one dreadful short week—"

Dr. Leighton told Campbell he believed the culprit was typhoid fever, a disease not unique to Russia. It could occur anywhere.

Even so, the loss was too much to bear. Less than a month after Elizabeth's death, Campbell wrote separately to Secretary of State John Quincy Adams and President Monroe, asking that he be recalled.

When Captain Moses Rogers met George W. Campbell, just four months after that, he was looking at a man waiting to hear if he could go home and bury his children. Whatever hurt Moses carried inside over the loss of his own son, Nathan, he must have seen it three-fold in the countenance of America's minister to Russia.

* * *

On Friday, September 17th, two days after the *Savannah* had anchored off St. Petersburg, the Russian Navy was ready to launch the huge warship in the stocks at the Admiralty. Floating such a large, heavy vessel into the shallow Neva River was no small feat. The Russian government, wanting the world to bear witness, sent out invitations to the launch to all the foreign diplomats in St. Petersburg. Moses, it seems, received his own invitation, and took Steve along to watch the ceremony with George W. Campbell.

Unfortunately, the weather that day was not favorable. Dawn brought a heavy gale and downpour from the south. By late morning, the winds had calmed, but the rain continued, leaving those who ventured outside feeling damp, at the least.

Regardless, the launch would go forward. Sitting between the Admiralty building and the river's edge, and ready for birthing, was the massive 110-gun *Tverdyi,* or *"Steadfast."*

Equal to the warship's impressive size was the Russian technique for getting such a huge hull to float on a river only 8 feet deep. The solution was to cradle the vessel in hollow wooden frames, called *camels.* Prior to launching, two of these camels were grappled onto the hull and filled with water. After launching into the river, the whole mass, camels and ship, would rest on the river bottom. Then the water in the camels would be pumped out, creating buoyancy, and causing the vessel to rise in the water. Once floating, the cradled warship could be moved downriver to the Bay, and on to Kronstadt, where the camels would be removed.

At midday, the invited guests began arriving at the Admiralty, where they gathered around the *Tverdyi.* The *corps diplomatique* was given a prominent position on a temporary stand near the vessel's bow, directly opposite the spot designated for the imperial family.

A review of the assembled crowd of Russian dignitaries revealed a number of peculiarities unlikely to be seen anywhere else.

Foremost were the bodies of many of the military officers, which looked almost deformed by a practice called *girding*. This involved the banding of their waists to such a degree that their stomachs looked flat and firm, while their chests bulged outward, so as to appear muscular and robust. Some observers likened the resulting body shape to that of a wasp. This custom carried the risk of great pain, internal injuries, and in a few cases even death, but the Emperor refused to take any action to discourage it, being a devotee of the practice himself.

A more subtle oddity could be seen amongst some of the noble ladies. Whenever these women opened their mouths, they revealed a smile that was "black as coal." This feature they created deliberately by rubbing their teeth with a darkening compound, the result being considered by many in the nobility as a mark of beauty.

Beyond these local eccentricities, Moses and Steve would have seen some familiar faces in the crowd. Within the assembly of diplomats were Lord Lynedoch and Robert Graham, standing next to Lord Cathcart. Also present amongst the government officials was the Minister of Marine, the Marquis de Traversé.

At the appointed time, the Emperor Alexander appeared, escorting the aged Empress Mother, Maria Feodorovna. Directly behind them came the Empress Elizaveta, followed by Grand Duke Nicholas and various ladies of the court.

The man who stood before the assembled crowd as the Emperor of All the Russias presented a tall and slightly plump-looking figure. Not quite 42 years of age, the balding, childless Alexander exuded the aura of a person who was both approachable and amiable. This was, by all accounts, absolutely true. Alexander's disregard for the pomp and ceremony of the imperial court was well-known, as was his informal way of addressing the people around him.

But behind the friendly façade of the Emperor was a very different person—a deeply conflicted man, enduring a constant battle between two alter-egos.

On the one side was Alexander the liberal, enlightened reformer. Such open-minded thinking had been inculcated into him by his Swiss-born tutor, as well as his grandmother, Empress Catherine the Great.

Alexander.

On the other side was Alexander the monarch. This persona was the creation of his father, Emperor Paul I, who taught his son to appreciate the great role he would assume upon ascending the throne, as well as the power, privilege, and prestige that went with it.

Tormenting both Alexanders was the unsettling feeling that someone was out to get them. An attempt to kidnap Alexander on the way to the Allied Congress at Aix-la-Chapelle the previous year had only heightened their fears. Piling on was the memory that their father, the Emperor Paul, had been murdered himself, with his own son's knowledge and tacit approval. These struggles, these torments between the two Alexanders quietly wreaked havoc on the one Alexander visible to the outside world.

Beneath his placid exterior, Alexander was tired—tired of the burdens, tired of the intrigues, and tired of the disappointments. Only a few weeks prior, his fatigue had been laid bare at a private dinner with his brother, Grand Duke Nicholas, whose wife, Princess Charlotte of Prussia, was also present. As Charlotte later remembered:

> *. . . Alexander . . . having sat down between us and talked intimately, suddenly changed the subject and became serious. In pretty well the following words he began to say to us that he had been pleased that morning with the way his brother had acquitted himself of his military command; that he was doubly pleased to see Nicholas carry out his*

duties well because on him would fall one day a heavy weight of
responsibility; and he looked on him as the person who was to replace
him; and that this would happen much sooner than anyone imagined,
since it would occur while he himself was still alive.
We sat there like two statues, open-eyed and dumb.
The Emperor went on: "You seem astonished, but let me tell you that
my brother Constantine, who has never bothered about the throne, is
more than ever determined to renounce it formally and pass on his
rights to his brother Nicholas and his descendants. As for myself,
I have decided to free myself of my functions and to retire from the
world. Never had Europe greater need of young sovereigns in the
plenitude of their energy; as for me I am no longer the man I was, and
I think it is my duty to retire in good time..."
Seeing us on the verge of tears he tried to comfort us and reassure us
by saying that this was not going to happen at once, that some years
must pass before he carried out his plan, then he left us alone, and it
can be imagined in what sort of state of mind we were ... We felt as
if we had been struck down by lightning ... It was an unforgettable
moment in our lives...

Just a few weeks later, this stunning declaration by the Emperor of
All the Russias remained hidden from public view. Instead, all the
immense crowd in front of the Admiralty could see was the Emperor
Alexander, and his brother Grand Duke Nicholas, standing ready to
watch the launching of the *Tverdyi*.

Just as only a tiny, privileged number knew the Emperor's plans
for the future, so too could only a few know the full extent of Alexander's interest in the new mode of transport.

It had begun in 1812, when American Minister John Quincy Adams
had presented Robert Fulton's petition for a steamboat franchise to
the imperial Russian government.

It had continued into 1813, with Alexander's approval of Fulton's
exclusive steamboat right.

It had continued on through 1815, with Scottish expatriate Charles
Baird's early steamboating experiments.

And finally, at the end of 1816, once the New York Monopoly had
failed to deliver a steamboat to Russia, it had culminated in the decision to grant an exclusive steamboat franchise to Baird.

But Alexander's exposure to the new mode's potential had not stopped there. At the close of 1817, the Emperor had begun to receive secret letters from Moses Rogers' old employer, Colonel John Stevens. In them, the Colonel had proposed building a 250- or 300-ton steam vessel in America, and then personally taking it across the Atlantic to Russia, all for two payments totaling $200,000. Colonel Stevens had suggested further that he would stay in Russia, and oversee the construction of additional steam vessels, for payments of $10,000 per year. Such offers from the Colonel had continued arriving in St. Petersburg into the final months of 1818.

For Alexander, it was just too much. Proposals and promises— that's all he had ever heard from these Americans about this new mode of transport.

Yet suddenly, with the appearance of the steamship *Savannah*, the situation had changed dramatically. For the first time, in the Emperor's very presence was an American who delivered.

At half past 1 o'clock, the order was given to release the *Tverdyi*. Slowly, the massive, camel-strapped warship began to slide down the greasy ramp, creaking and smoking as it went, before splashing into the shallow, blue waters of the Neva. The whole experience was, in both Lord Lynedoch's and Robert Graham's words, "very grand."

The ceremony completed, George W. Campbell invited Moses and several other gentlemen back to his home for dinner, which, by the custom of the time, was usually served at mid-afternoon. In all likelihood, Harriot Campbell dined with them, and probably was showing a little by that time—a new baby was due in February.

Dinner surely included a discussion of Captain Rogers' hope to repeat for St. Petersburg what he had done for Stockholm, and that was offer the diplomatic community a short excursion on the *Savannah*. This idea Minister Campbell had accepted, and the trip was set to take place the next day.

It was also probably at this time, or during one of his other meetings with Minister Campbell, that Moses received a more critical view of Russia and its Emperor than was the conventional wisdom back in the United States.

First and foremost was a description of how the Russian government treated information. Diplomatic dispatches aside, no one was allowed to act as the courier of foreign letters into Russia. Such correspondence had to be turned over upon entry, and the Russian government could and did open any mail it wanted, anywhere in the country.

And even though Alexander had lifted the ban on foreign publications long ago, any newspapers or magazines brought into Russia also had to be turned over to the authorities. Articles deemed not in the country's interest were cut out before the periodical was allowed in. The result could be a newspaper that resembled Swiss cheese upon release from the censors, and some publications simply were not allowed into the country at all.

Russia's secret police was as strong as it had ever been. Many prominent families knew they had to guard their words whenever the domestic help was within earshot, since it was believed that many servants were also on the government payroll as spies.

As for Alexander himself, it was clear to Campbell that despite all the talk of reform and liberal ideas, the Emperor had no intention of relinquishing his power over Russia, or his influence in Europe. The proposals for a written constitution and the general emancipation of the serfs were going nowhere. The Russian Senate, despite foreign perceptions, had no real power. Imperial edicts brought before that body were rubber stamped by members beholden to the Emperor for their seats. And Alexander traveled so frequently that the wheels of government often ground to a halt in his absence, out of fear amongst his ministers that they might take a wrong step.

Alexander's actions in support of the established monarchies of Europe also put him at odds with the idea that he was open to any substantial change in the status quo. Stability, it appeared, had become his absolute goal.

Tangible proof of this had come the previous year, when Alexander sold a squadron of warships to King Ferdinand VII of Spain. At the time, it was claimed there was nothing unusual in the transaction. But any knowing observer realized the transfer was intended to bolster the Spanish monarch's navy, as he fought against the rebellions in South America.

Further still, Alexander's support for Napoleon's continued exile on St. Helena only reinforced the perception that the Emperor of All the Russias would take no risks that might upset the established world, at least as he saw it.

* * *

Around the time dinner was finishing at the Campbell's residence, Lord Lynedoch arrived at the Winter Palace with his brothers-in-law,

Lord Cathcart and Frederick Cathcart (who was also visiting St. Petersburg). Their purpose was to gain an audience with the Emperor.

First, Lord Cathcart, who was about to leave his post as Britain's minister to Russia, was ushered into an adjoining room for a long, private meeting with Alexander. Then, Lord Lynedoch and Frederick Cathcart were called in. They came face-to-face with the Emperor, who, instead of keeping his distance like the royalty of old, walked right up and shook hands with each of them.

In the ten-minute conversation that followed, Lord Lynedoch and the Emperor discussed many things: Alexander's admiration for the British infantry; the principles which had guided the Allies in their victory over Napoleon; and the outlook for the royal governments in France and Spain.

But before they could get to any of those great subjects, Lord Lynedoch had to address the very first question put to him by the Emperor—

What did he think of this American steam ship?

* * *

Of all the experiences Stevens Rogers had throughout the voyage of the *Savannah*, the one later remembered as among the most exciting was when he and Moses were introduced to the Emperor Alexander. Precisely when and where this took place is unclear, but it must have been at one of the public events the Emperor attended, or perhaps during a private audience at the Winter Palace.

During their encounter, Alexander suggested to Captain Rogers that he remain in Russian waters with the *Savannah*. They could operate, the monarch offered, under the full protection of the Russian government. Alexander could make such a promise not just because he was Emperor of All the Russias, but due to a specific clause in the exclusive franchise granted to Charles Baird. Any time the imperial government wanted to carve out an exception to Mr. Baird's steamboat monopoly, it had the legal right to do so.

The Emperor's offer was certainly an interesting proposition, even though it didn't fit the objective set by William Scarbrough and the directors. The far better outcome, given the shareholders' immediate needs, remained an outright sale. For that to occur, however, the Russians would have to do more than just inspect the steamship—they also would have to test it.

* * *

By mid-morning on the day after the *Tverdyi's* launch, the *Savannah* was ready. Climbing aboard for the excursion were the foreign ministers of the Netherlands, the Kingdom of Hanover, and other members of St. Petersburg's diplomatic community. There to accompany them was George W. Campbell.

While Minister Campbell and Steve made no record of it in their respective journals, there were others on the steamship besides diplomats that Saturday morning. The Russian government, in all likelihood, had someone representing their interests on board. There was also at least one extra-ordinary passenger along for the ride—an Englishman by the name of John Farey, Esquire.

Farey was a 28-year-old of many talents. He had been a first-class illustrator for British scientific and engineering magazines and encyclopedias since his early teens, winning prestigious awards for his artwork along the way. Farey's many drawing assignments for steam engines had piqued his curiosity, leading him to write a long encyclopedia article on the subject in 1816. This article revealed that he had far more than just artistic talent. A number of engineers encouraged him to write a full treatise on steam engine design. This book, which he would begin writing in 1820, seems to have been the impetus for his visit to St. Petersburg.

During his two months in Russia, Farey managed to gain access to a number of steam engines as part of his research. Clearly, the chance for him to inspect the first steamship to cross an ocean was too good an opportunity to pass up.

By 11 o'clock that morning, steam in the boilers was sufficient to allow the *Savannah* to get under way. As she churned westward, toward Kronstadt, John Farey took note of her operation. "This is a complete ship in all her rigging and upper works," he later wrote. "The building, iron work, and rigging of the vessel are extremely well executed."

However, in observing the engine at work, Farey thought its motion was rather slow; he counted 15 strokes per minute, and estimated its strength at 45 horsepowers. (How he arrived at this number, Farey did not record, but the calculations used to determine horsepower were sometimes the subject of very heated debates amongst engineers at the time.) "The wheels are very judiciously arranged," he nevertheless continued, and turned at 15 revolutions per minute, giving the steamship a speed of 6 miles per hour.

Out to Kronstadt the *Savannah* went, and then back again to the mouth of the Neva, returning by mid-afternoon. For his part, George W. Campbell was pleased with the excursion. "The Savannah is a fine vessel," he later wrote. "Her machinery + wheels work well, + in every respect she fully equaled our expectations."

Yet however satisfied the diplomats were with the steamship, the expectations of others still remained to be met.

* * *

By the end of the diplomatic excursion, the prospects for selling the *Savannah* to the Russian government must have looked good to Moses. After all, the steamship had excited a lot of interest upon its arrival at Kronstadt, as it had everywhere. The St. Petersburg press had provided positive coverage, including descriptions of the *Savannah*'s unique design features. And members of the imperial family were making their own private inquiries regarding the *pyroscaphe*, or fire-vessel, as one Russian newspaper called it. The further success of the diplomats' trip that Saturday certainly reinforced the belief that the best impression was being made.

The next logical step was to get the Russians to begin negotiating a purchase. Such discussions would require the attention of the highest levels within the government.

But whether and how a deal might be struck was thrown into some doubt once the diplomats returned to St. Petersburg from their excursion. The reason why could be readily deduced simply by examining the flagpole atop the Winter Palace. No longer was the imperial flag flying from it, which could mean only one thing—

The Emperor was gone.

* * *

Having spent all of 3½ days in St. Petersburg, Alexander had departed on a trip to Poland. Whether or not the Russian government would offer to purchase the *Savannah* rested upon whatever instructions he had left behind.

For the next two days, Moses, Steve and the crew waited, as gale-force winds buffeted the steamship while it rode at anchor off the Neva bar.

Then, on Tuesday morning, September 21st, Moses ordered the engine crew to fire up the boilers. Once all was ready, he ordered the new mode of power into action. The *Savannah* then proceeded to "run about the harbour four hours," as Steve noted in the logbook.

Whoever else was on board for this seemingly aimless steaming around the Bay of St. Petersburg, Steve did not record. Neither, for that matter, did the local newspapers, which made no mention of the steamship's movements.

Yet aimless excursion it obviously was not, for on board the *Savannah* that hazy day was a group of officials from the Russian government. Those sent to analyze the steamship were most likely from the Ministry of Marine (i.e., the Navy), as well as the Ministry of the Means of Communication, the department responsible for improving transportation throughout the Empire.

And analyze the *Savannah* they certainly did, taking precise notes on all of her particulars and performance.

Some days later, the *Russian Invalid or Military Journal* managed to obtain details of the trials "from a qualified observer." The newspaper, recognizing the degree to which the steamship had "aroused the curiosity of all our readers," dutifully published the observer's account.

The eyewitness praised the *Savannah* as "a vessel marvelously constructed and excellently rigged." He went on to note all of the unusual and unique features of the vessel, from the nearly horizontal cylinder (which generated 60 horsepowers), to the collapsible paddle-wheels (which made 18 revolutions per minute). He also complimented the steamship's "very clever" boiler design (which had required not a single cleaning since leaving America). As for speed, the observer reported that "in calm weather the ship makes per hour 9 versts* which is quite a considerable distance taking into consideration that the ship is large and heavy."

Once the *Savannah* had completed her four hours of trials, the government officials disembarked, and tendered the test results to their respective ministries. With those reports and the Emperor's instructions in hand, it was up to the imperial ministers to take the next step.

Moses didn't have to wait long. The very next day, September 22nd, a well-appointed barge rowed its way through the rain toward the *Savannah*, reaching her side at 1 o'clock that afternoon.

Onto the steamship's deck climbed Ivan Ivanovich, the Marquis de Traversé, "Lord High Admiral" of the Russian Navy.

---

* 9 versts per hour equals about 6 miles per hour.

This old, weathered French sailor, born Jean-Baptiste Prévost de Sansac, had seen and sailed the waters of the Atlantic since before Captain Moses Rogers was even born. That he had managed to attain the highest post within Russia's navy was hardly a fluke—it represented the culmination of decades of loyal service to his adopted country. And that he had been welcomed to Russia in the first place was no coincidence, either—indeed, it was founded upon the Marquis de Traversé's own audacity and bravery in a fight for freedom which had taken place a full generation before.

* * *

Born on the French island colony of Martinique in 1754, Jean-Baptiste Prévost de Sansac committed himself to a life on the ocean from the earliest age. Joining the French Navy as a midshipman in 1765, he spent eight years learning the art of war at sea, before being promoted to *ensign* (or junior officer).

Just a few years after that, Prévost and his generation of young French naval officers were provided with the opportunity of a lifetime. In 1778, their monarch, King Louis XVI, made an alliance with the rebellious Americans in their fight for independence against Britain. Soon thereafter, the French Navy was ordered into action.

Prévost was given his own command, and quickly displayed great skill as a sea-warrior, capturing British merchantmen on both sides of the Atlantic. By 1781, his many victories were recognized by Louis XVI, who bestowed upon him the title of Marquis de Traversé.

With hostilities in America reaching a critical point, the Marquis was given command of the frigate *L'Aigrette**, and ordered to cross the Atlantic to join French naval forces already there. Upon arrival, Traversé and *L'Aigrette* skimmed up and down the American coast, capturing British shipping at a breathtaking rate. At one point, they took four prizes in the space of just a few days.

By early September of 1781, Traversé and *L'Aigrette* had joined the fleet of French Admiral Count de Grasse, which was blockading Lord Cornwallis and his British troops trapped at Yorktown. Since General Washington's Franco-American army made it impossible for Cornwallis to break out by land, a Royal Navy squadron was directed to break through to him by sea. In the ensuing Battle of the Chesapeake,

---

* In English, "aigrette" is a tuft or plume of feathers.

it was the Marquis de Traversé who reportedly first caught sight of the approaching Royal Navy, allowing Admiral de Grasse to deploy his warships to maximum advantage against the attackers. The French naval blockade held, and with the surrender of Lord Cornwallis shortly thereafter, the American Revolution was won.

Returning home with more than a score of captures to his credit, the Marquis de Traversé was considered one of the French Navy's most distinguished captains.

Then came the Revolution of 1789. Anyone feted or favored by Louis XVI became suspect, so Traversé fled to Switzerland. From there he proceeded to Russia, accepting a commission in the Russian Navy offered to him by Catherine the Great. Following the tradition of many expatriates who wanted to be accepted into Russian society, Traversé took on the native forenames Ivan Ivanovich, while keeping his original French title.

Through the decades that followed, the Marquis de Traversé faithfully served his adopted homeland, from the Black Sea to the Baltic Sea. He refused any offers to leave the Russian Navy, and Emperor Alexander rewarded this loyalty with steady promotions, eventually naming him Minister of Marine in 1811.

Once he became chief of the Russian Navy, the aging Traversé displayed an increasing aversion to taking decisive action. Even basic maintenance of the fleet suffered, leading to the slow decay of many vessels under his watch.

This disturbing state of affairs was highlighted by the fate of the eight warships sold the previous year to King Ferdinand VII. These vessels had been in such poor shape that they barely made it to Spain, and were considered unfit for their mission to join the fight in South America. Alexander had been so embarrassed that he felt compelled to send additional, more seaworthy vessels to replace them.

The remaining Baltic Sea fleet at Kronstadt was in no better shape. Anyone going on board these warships could see that they were poorly maintained, and lacked much-needed equipment. Their inability to conduct maneuvers beyond the shallow Bay of St. Petersburg led some to caustically call these waters "the Marquis's puddle."

But the 65-year-old Minister of Marine still had the confidence of the Emperor. This was due in no small part to Traversé's political alliance with a general of the artillery named Arakcheyev. This greatly-feared and widely-despised imperial advisor had so ingratiated himself with Alexander that those in his camp were safe from scrutiny.

The one area of Traversé's administration of the Russian Navy that did show a willingness to accept risks was the field of exploration. With a Navy that always played second fiddle to the much larger Army, the Marquis had to carefully choose where to deploy his limited financial resources. To that end, he usually concentrated his best forces in the Pacific, where distant settlements in the Siberian Far East and Alaska dictated the need for a visible and vibrant presence.

He further supported a number of important expeditions of discovery, two of which had left Kronstadt just a few months before the *Savannah*'s arrival. One was heading for the Pacific, where it would try to emulate the British drive to find a Northwest Passage, only from the opposite direction. The other, headed by a Captain Bellingshausen, planned to sail as close to the South Pole as possible.

Despite the overall condition of the Russian Navy, the Marquis de Traversé's promotion of these far-flung expeditions did speak volumes. It showed that in the name of progress, he was willing to send his finest officers, men, and vessels beyond the bounds of common knowledge.

What remained to be seen was whether the Marquis was actually prepared to acquire something that previously had been beyond the bounds of common belief.

* * *

As the Marquis de Traversé strolled along the decks of the *Savannah* with Captain Rogers, he was shown all the many unique features of this first steamship in the world. His tour naturally included a look at the enormous cylinder, the twin boilers, the collapsible paddle-wheels, and the swiveling funnel.

Once his inspection was complete, the Marquis returned to his barge and headed back to St. Petersburg. He would take what he had learned and infuse it into a special report a few days later. The Marquis de Traversé's resulting official opinion of the steamship *Savannah* proved to be admirably forthright in its particulars:

> *... The ship resembles a frigate and a transport by its outward appearance ... It has elegant and very comfortable cabins ... The wood used for the body ... is rather good and firm ... Rather notable is a rare carefulness with which all the ship, and especially the cabins, was decorated. Art is united with an excellent taste everywhere ... Though*

one cannot praise the riggings in the same way. It seems rather ordinary; masts and spars are too heavy...

The Marquis's entire description of the steam machinery took up all of three scattered sentences within the report. This inattention to that which made the *Savannah* the most revolutionary vessel afloat allowed the Lord High Admiral, and the institution he led, to ignore the possibilities, and fall back upon the old thinking:

> *... One may see from this short description that the Savannah cannot be used as a military or commercial ship, because it does not have enough room either for placing cannons or cargo...*

There would be no offer made to acquire the *Savannah*.

The decision of the Marquis de Traversé to forego a purchase revealed the world as he had known it, and perceived it still to be. While the Americans' unprecedented experiment may have been a success, proving that oceans could be crossed using steam power, Traversé's traditional view still held sway. To the Marquis, a commercial vessel's primary purpose remained carrying cargo, and a frigate's objective in a fight was to blast the enemy out of the water. Those deeply ingrained beliefs overwhelmed any novel propositions about transporting only passengers, or placing greater reliance upon maneuver in battle to win.

* * *

Whatever the Marquis de Traversé had said to Captain Rogers at the end of his inspection, it must have been unequivocal. The very next morning, Moses ordered the crew to fire up the boilers and deploy the wheels, as the chilly winds of early autumn whisked across the damp deck. At 11 o'clock, the anchor was pulled up, and the *Savannah* headed for Kronstadt.

Some advance notice must have been given that the *Savannah* would be moving that morning, because once again there were some temporary passengers on board. Among them was the English engineer John Farey, his interest in the steamship still not satisfied.

As the *Savannah* splashed her way across the Bay, Farey measured her speed yet again. She was going a bit faster than the previous trip, making 6¼ miles per hour. Farey also noted that when one of Baird's steamboats came alongside, it was able to go just a little faster than the *Savannah*, thanks to the Russian vessel's greater horsepower generated per ton of burthen.

At 1 o'clock, the steamship arrived at Kronstadt. There, Moses ordered the anchor dropped, just off the entrance to the merchant's mole. Then he headed ashore, to begin making arrangements.

* * *

While the *Savannah* was steaming westward across the Bay of St. Petersburg that day, far to the south—at the imperial palace of Oranienbaum—an old set of eyes had been looking out at the "fine view of Cronstadt."

Those old eyes belonged to Lord Lynedoch, who was busily stomping about the grounds of the palace, and finding them, by his lights, "a good deal neglected." When he looked out onto the Gulf waters, he surely must have seen the steamship, as it churned and smoked its way toward Kronstadt. Having done so, Lord Lynedoch made a mental note to do something once he got back to St. Petersburg.

* * *

Alexander's invitation to Captain Rogers to stay in Russia with his steamship carried with it a set of calculations for both sides to consider.

From the Emperor's perspective, Russia would gain doubly from such a deal. This American steamship could operate on whatever route its owners and the government chose, to the benefit of Russian commerce and communications. Additionally, the Empire would gain from the presence of one of the most skilled practitioners of the new mode anywhere. True to imperial objectives, Alexander's offer clearly implied that he was interested not only in the machine, but the man.

From Moses Rogers' perspective, accepting such an offer—and the chance to trailblaze yet again—must have been tempting.

But to do so was problematic, to say the least. Despite the opportunity that the Russian market represented, the shareholders needed to sell. Even trying to convince them to take up such a proposition from a distance, before winter set in, was impossible. Moses had his instructions.

Further still, the knowledge of what had happened to the Campbell family must have given pause. Moses had already lost his first-born,

Nathan, seven years earlier. Adelia's reaction to being told she would have to move their four surviving children to a strange foreign land can easily be imagined.

The conclusion Moses had drawn was clear: it was time to go home.

Taking advantage of clear skies over the next several days, Moses and Steve put the crew to work bringing wood and coal on board. Even with the bunkers filled, Moses had no intention of using the fuel unless he had to. The voyage had cost enough already. Steam could be used if circumstances demanded it, but otherwise Moses planned to spend as little fuel and money as possible on the trip home.

With the crew's duties set, Moses once again became preoccupied with his own future. Two days after taking the *Savannah* to Kronstadt, he returned to St. Petersburg to call upon George W. Campbell.

Moses told Minister Campbell that given the uncertainties he expected to encounter back home, he wanted to seek a position working for the U.S. Navy. Moses then asked the Minister if he would be willing to write a letter of recommendation to John Quincy Adams. This, Campbell agreed to do, penning a two-page letter for Moses to hand-deliver to the Secretary of State.

While Moses was busy making arrangements for departure on shore, back on the *Savannah*, the crew continued hauling more wood and coal aboard for the return voyage. It was in the course of these chores that a couple of packages were delivered to the ship, addressed to Steve and Mr. Blackman. Inside the packages, they found two silver snuff boxes. Steve's had a tooled cover, depicting the famous statue of Peter the Great on horseback. Both snuff boxes were gifts from Lord Lynedoch, who had purchased them "for the mates of the *Savannah*" the day after he had been out to visit Oranienbaum.

It was an incredibly thoughtful act. In presenting the samovar to Captain Rogers some days before, the Scotsman already had fulfilled a tradition that was normally the responsibility of an entire shipload of passengers. With these follow-on gifts to the junior officers, Lord Lynedoch had gone above and beyond the call of duty yet again, all because he must have felt he owed the mates of the *Savannah* something beyond a simple thanks.

* * *

By Wednesday, September 29th, the *Savannah* was ready to go. Nature, however, refused to cooperate. Adverse breezes from the southwest made sailing through the channel between Kronslott battery and the mole difficult at best, so Moses ordered the steam up. Under a cloud-covered sky, the *Savannah* slogged straight into the wind, past the guardship, and to a position off the southwest coast of Kotlin Island. Once there, Moses ordered the engine stopped, and the larboard anchor dropped, in about 5 fathoms (or 30 feet) of water.

The *Savannah* and her crew were hardly alone. Anchored all around them were the vessels of many nations, all waiting for their chance to escape before the frigid waters around Kotlin Island turned to ice, trapping them for months to come.

But proceeding any further that day proved to be an impossibility, either by sail or by steam. The "fresh breezes" of the morning gave way to rain and gale-force winds by afternoon. It blew so hard that Steve had the crew take the spars off the masts, and stow them on deck.

The next morning, conditions were even worse. In the Gulf of Finland, such powerful storms during the autumn months were common, and served as Nature's warning that winter was coming.

The roaring winds and sheets of rain barely let up through the day. By late afternoon, the increasing strength of this southwesterly gale was putting great stress upon the single anchor and chain holding the *Savannah* in place.

The problem was the anchor's *scope*, which is the ratio of the anchor cable length in use to the depth of water. In moderate weather, a scope of four times the water depth was usually enough to hold a vessel in place. But in a storm, too little scope can cause an anchor to drag. The solution was a longer length of anchor cable, which would allow the anchor to dig more securely into the bottom.

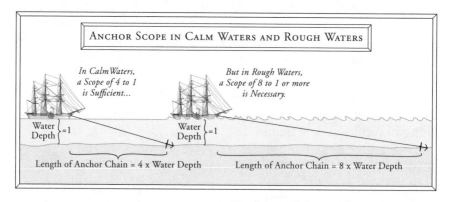

ANCHOR SCOPE IN CALM WATERS AND ROUGH WATERS

In Calm Waters, a Scope of 4 to 1 is Sufficient...

But in Rough Waters, a Scope of 8 to 1 or more is Necessary.

Water Depth } = 1

Water Depth } = 1

Length of Anchor Chain = 4 x Water Depth

Length of Anchor Chain = 8 x Water Depth

So Moses ordered the starboard anchor dropped, along with 50 or 60 fathoms of chain cable. Since the water depth was only 5 fathoms, this newly-deployed anchor would have a scope of 10 to 1, at least. Once the ship was blown downwind far enough to make the cable taught, this anchor dug firmly into place.

Through that evening and into the first minutes of Friday morning, October 1st, ship and crew rode the storm. Even with all her sails furled, the *Savannah*'s masts and rigging still caught a lot of wind.

By half past midnight, the stress on the starboard anchor chain was showing. Moses and Steve felt they had no choice but to order the crew aloft, to reduce the steamship's profile, and hopefully relieve some of the stress on the anchor chain.

As the whole of the *Savannah* continued to rock and sway in the storm, the crewmen took to the fore and aft shrouds, and carefully ascended into the drenching darkness. Once they reached the very top of the fore and mizzen masts, the crew loosened and brought down the topgallant yards. Then they loosened the top sections of those same two masts, and brought them down to the lower mast sections, where they were secured.

But their efforts were too little, too late. Just after the crew had finished this very dangerous task, the starboard anchor chain broke.

The remaining larboard anchor, with its shorter chain, could not possibly hold the ship. The *Savannah* had to be secured quickly, or else she risked being blown right onto Kotlin Island.

So the *kedge* (which is a light anchor) was immediately chucked overboard, along with 100 fathoms of hawser rope. Once the kedge grabbed the bottom at its scope of 20 to 1, the steamship hopefully could ride out the rest of the storm.

But even this didn't work. The powerful gale pushed the *Savannah* so hard that the lightweight kedge failed to gain a grip on the sandy bottom. Within an hour, ship and crew found that they were "arriving on shore."

If Moses and Steve did nothing, the *Savannah* would run aground. It was too late to get the steam up, and probably too dangerous to use the paddlewheels, even if the crew did manage to deploy them safely.

So Moses decided to make a naked run for the haven of Kronstadt mole. The larboard anchor chain was unshackled, and dropped into the surging waters. The kedge was also let go. With howling winds pushing against her bare masts and hull, the anchorless *Savannah* was propelled eastward through the darkness, and away from the rocky shore.

Upon reaching the entrance to the harbor, the steamship was maneuvered through it. Once they entered the calmer waters within the mole, Steve and the crew were able to secure the ship, and wait out the night.

By the light of Friday morning, the worst of the great gale had passed. That the *Savannah* had been in peril, and nearly died just a few hours before, must have been obvious to every member of the crew. Proof positive of this fact dotted the southern coastline of Kotlin Island, where a great many vessels lay beached and battered, their lives at an end.

Getting a replacement anchor was the highest priority. Fortunately, Moses found a Russian Navy brig nearby whose commander was willing to lend one. Moses also decided a local pilot should be brought aboard, to help keep the *Savannah* out of any more trouble.

It wasn't until Saturday that attempting to recover the lost anchors appeared feasible. Moses personally went out in the jolly boat with four of the crew, only to be met by renewed strong winds and rain. Nevertheless, they did manage to retrieve the kedge anchor, only to discover why it hadn't held them during the storm: one of its flukes had broken off, making it useless.

On Sunday, Steve and some of the crew went back out and tried their own luck at anchor-fishing. They managed to pull up the smaller of the two bow anchors, and bring it back to the ship. The larger anchor was beyond recovery, so a new one would have to be procured.

The next several days were spent buying a new large anchor and a new kedge, and returning the borrowed anchor to the Russian brig. Then a third new anchor was brought on board, either because the small bow anchor recovered by Steve exhibited some damage, or Moses wanted insurance in the wake of the *Savannah*'s near-death experience.

Finally, on Wednesday, October 6th, life on board got back to normal. But the autumn winds from the southwest continued unabated, and even strengthened again to gale-force, preventing an immediate departure.

The *Savannah*'s predicament was hardly unique. By that time, the anchorages in and around Kronstadt were filled with dozens of vessels, all waiting for the first favorable weather to depart, before the onset of winter made it impossible.

Like most of the other captains ready to leave, Moses already had cleared his departure with the authorities. While he registered his creation as heading for the United States, he wasn't planning to return to home port. Instead, intriguingly, Captain Rogers had declared that the *Savannah's* destination was Boston, Massachusetts.

Not until dawn on Sunday, October 10th, did the winds shift to friendly northeasterlies. By that time, there were scores of sailing vessels ready to leave. Having kept the steamship under the harbor's protection since the storm, Moses wanted to get back to the waters off the southwest coast of the island, where the rest of the departing fleet was preparing to weigh anchor. So he ordered the engine crew to get steam up.

At 9 o'clock that morning, the wheels were put into motion. The *Savannah* steamed out of Kronstadt and past the Russian guard-ship for the last time. Once she reached the forefront of the multinational fleet just getting under way, Moses ordered the engine stopped, and the wheels taken in.

Then, as Steve later recorded in the logbook, they "set sail in company with about 80 sail of Shiping," and said their goodbyes to all the Russias.

CHAPTER EIGHTEEN

────────

BACK

Four days after departing Kronstadt, the *Savannah* reached the western shores of the Baltic Sea.

Nature had been incredibly kind. Ever since leaving Russian waters, Steve and the crew had taken full advantage of strong easterly winds, which had propelled them under sail at speeds as high as 10 knots. Moses couldn't have asked for better weather—it allowed him to conserve fuel, and minimize costs.

Before they left the Baltic proper, Moses decided to make one last stop, at Copenhagen. He seemed to have two purposes in mind.

First, it would give him another opportunity to show off the steamship, and the capabilities of the new country blossoming on the other side of the Atlantic.

Second, Moses could gauge whether there was any interest in purchasing the *Savannah* in Denmark.

By late morning on October 14th, the steamship had sailed close enough to Copenhagen to encounter one of the local pilot boats. A pilot soon climbed aboard, and guided the *Savannah* into the Outer Roads, just off the city. There, Moses and Steve were told to drop anchor, next to a stone fort rising out of the water called the Tre Kroner Battery, which guarded the approach to the Danish capital.

From their new vantage point, the crew could look due south and see the farms and fields of the Amager Peninsula.

To their west, where the peninsula met the mainland, was Copenhagen itself, split into two parts by a waterway called the Inner Roads, which was filled with shipping. Most of the city proper was on the northern side of this divide, completely surrounded by a collection of earthworks and fortifications, culminating in the star-shaped

Frederick Fortress, which stood guard at the entrance to the Inner Roads. By all appearances, Copenhagen truly was a walled city.

Despite having arrived under sail, the *Savannah*'s distinctive bent smokestack made her identity unmistakable. The curiosity-seekers were soon upon her.

Dagen, one of Copenhagen's main newspapers, later reported that those who went on board the "steam frigate," as it called the *Savannah*, "cannot praise enough her wonderful construction."

The paper went on to declare that the *Savannah* "goes so fast that an English brig off the coast of Scotland . . . with all sails set could not catch up." (This was either a garbled account of the *Kite*'s chase off Ireland, or an inkling of another pursuit of the steamship after it had left Liverpool.)

Dagen also reported that the steamship supposedly was available for purchase, at a price of 60,000 *piasters* (which was another name for Spanish silver dollars). The source of this information was probably Moses himself, and the specification of payment in piasters made it clear that Danish Rix-dollars, or any other paper currency, was not acceptable. Only specie, the true international money, would do.

Moses quickly discovered that the Danes' appetite for something as radical as a steamship was virtually non-existent. The only steam vessel operating in the area was the *Caledonia*, which had just begun running down to Kiel earlier that year. Acquiring an ocean-going steam packet, even if it stayed in the Baltic Sea, would have been a big leap for the Danes.

Furthermore, the merchants at Copenhagen—like nearly everyone else—were in a bad way. The deflation in prices that followed the peace of 1815 had been tough on everyone in Europe dependent upon credit and paper currency. Several hundred Copenhagen merchants already had gone bankrupt since the end of the war, and more would soon follow. Even if there was a party interested in buying the *Savannah* at Copenhagen, the terms of sale—gold or silver only—would have made a transaction next to impossible.

Early on October 17th, after spending several days bobbing in the Outer Roads, Moses ordered Steve and the crew to get under way with sail. Their destination was Helsingør.

Once again, thanks to favorable winds, the *Savannah* was blown straight toward the neck at the sands, which she reached in three hours' time.

Just as vessels had to stop and pay a toll upon entering the Baltic, so too did they have to "heave to" upon exiting, and pay again. So once they reached Helsingør, Moses ordered the *Savannah* to a halt, while he went ashore to clear the ship.

The toll collector, in making his entry for the *Savannah* in the tariff journal, asked what cargo she had. Since all the steamship carried was a few gifts and fuel, Moses told him that he was transiting in ballast.

Port of departure?

"St. Petersburg."

Destination?

"Boston, in America."

Once again, as at Kronstadt, Captain Rogers declared a terminus for his voyage that bore no direct relationship to him or the Savannah Steam Ship Company. There was only one likely explanation: Moses had not given up. He still wanted to try to fulfill the Company's second goal, and initiate the first trans-Atlantic steamship service.

Looking at a map of the Atlantic realm, his choice made plenty of sense. If the port of Savannah was too far, and the port of New York remained legally questionable given the Monopoly's grasp, then the next logical candidate was Boston, Massachusetts.

After all, Boston was the closest major American port to Liverpool. Given the *Savannah*'s limited fuel supply, the best transit time would come from the shortest route. Boston also had long-standing, extensive ties to Albion, and an ocean-crossing steam packet service could make that city the primary transit point for trans-Atlantic travelers. Then the Bostonians would truly gain a competitive leg-up on the Gothamites. What remained to be seen was whether the merchants of that city would bite, and whether the traveling public would, as well.

His toll of two Rix-dollars paid, Moses returned to the ship, and the crew set sail into the Kattegat.

Unlike their previous journey through these waters, this time the transit was swift. Less than a day and a half later, the crew spotted Scaw lighthouse, at the very northern tip of Denmark. Shortly thereafter, the *Savannah* entered the waters of the Skagerrak.

But once they did so, having rounded the top of Denmark, the ideal southeasterly winds, which had pushed them so easily through the Kattegat, disappeared. In their place came strong westerlies, blowing straight over the bow. Within a day, the gusts had grown so strong that Steve felt it necessary to have the crew bring down the topgallant yards. Then, he began tacking the ship back and forth, trying to make headway.

After 2½ days of little progress, Moses decided one final port of call was in order. Perhaps a brief respite would bring better weather. The only question was where to drop anchor.

Along the southeastern coast of Norway, there was one obvious choice: the port of Arendal. Most Americans living in the early 19th century probably had never heard of the place, but among mariners, Arendal had a well-deserved reputation. From its shipyards came some of the best-built vessels in all of Scandinavia.

By the morning of October 22nd, the *Savannah* and her crew had reached the entrance to the fjord that led to Arendal's harbor. A boat soon appeared, which supplied a pilot to guide them in.

They certainly needed one. Upon passing the high cliffs on either side of the fjord's entrance, the *Savannah* had to be maneuvered around many small, rocky islands that peppered the inland waters.

Further inside the fjord lay Arendal itself, situated directly upon a rock-covered peninsula, its irregular houses and barns built right up to the water's edge. The waterfront did not look particularly active, since it was raining and rather windy.

But that soon changed. As the *Savannah* sailed into the harbor, people began flocking to the wharves, and filling the open spaces along the coastline.

After dropping anchor, Moses went ashore. He bought two hogsheads of water from the locals, which the crew dutifully hauled on board. All the while, "a great part of Arendal's inhabitants took the opportunity to view this innovation," reported one of Norway's news-papers, "as a similar ship will probably never again pass these coasts."

In the process of making his way about the town, Moses saw some-thing in one of the boatyards that intrigued him. It was a small, shal-low-bottomed boat, perhaps 18 feet in length, and pointed at both ends. According to the locals, it was designed for either rowing or sailing. It also had one other unusual characteristic: all of its timbers were held together with wooden pegs—no nails whatsoever had been used. The Norwegians called this kind of boat a *sjekte* (syék-tuh).

Moses took a fancy to it.

In due course, he purchased the sjekte, and arranged for it to be brought out to the *Savannah*. The crew hauled it aboard, and lashed it down. To reduce any crowding on the deck, the jolly boat was placed at the ship's stern.

By the next morning, the heavy gales of prior days had given way to friendlier breezes. Moses ordered Steve and the crew to deploy the sails and get under way. Once again, the Norwegians came out to watch. "We have only to regret that we did not see her driven by the steam engine," lamented one of the spectators.

Steering southward, the *Savannah* and her crew reached the fjord's entrance an hour and a half later. Then, with sails set to the best advantage, they headed out onto the open sea.

CHAPTER NINETEEN

TAKING UP THE OFFER

O**N THE LAST DAY** of November 1819, the dawn's early light gradually brought to life the motion of the ocean waves along the American coast.

Off South Carolina and Georgia, the rising of the sun was muted by cloud cover, as well as a fog that hung over the seascape.

For the few souls who were out and about near the entrance to the Savannah River that morning, the eyes strained in search of any vessels that might appear out of the mist, as darkness gave way.

Once the fog began to lift, those with the best of sight near Tybee lighthouse eventually saw the profile of a three-masted, square-rigged vessel—a ship—slowly approaching from the east-northeast. Through the mid-morning hours, its silhouette became clearer and clearer, and eventually proved to be quite unique. The short, bent stick between the foremast and mainmast could belong to only one vessel. The steamship *Savannah* was coming home.

By 9 o'clock, the steamship had sailed over the bar at the entrance to the Savannah River. Then, a local pilot climbed aboard, to guide the *Savannah* up the river on the final leg of her journey.

But the low tide could not be denied. Neither could the still air. So Captain Rogers ordered the crew to drop anchor, until the water level was high enough to allow them to make it all the way upriver to their homeport. In the meantime, he had the engine crew get up steam for the first time since St. Petersburg, while Steve oversaw the furling of the sails, and deployment of the paddlewheels. With no wind to be had, only the new mode could get them into port quickly. The smoke issuing from the stack also would serve as a signal to the Exchange's lookout that the city's namesake had returned.

By afternoon, the tide was high enough to allow them to proceed.

The engine was put into motion, and the *Savannah* began pushing her way upriver.

By early evening, she had made it all the way to the city, arriving, as one observer put it, "in fine style." Once the steamship had reached midstream below the sandy cliff, Moses ordered the engine to a halt, and the anchor dropped. The *Savannah* and her crew were finally home.

* * *

Shortly after their arrival, it surely must have been clear to Moses, Steve and the rest of the crew that the place they had left 6 months and 8 days earlier was not the same. It had changed, and for the worse.

Of all the news that awaited them, among the most shocking was the death of shareholder Charles Howard. His heart, which had bothered him for years, gave out on July 1st. While only 34 years old when he died, the Massachusetts native nevertheless had accomplished much in his brief life. Charles had helped his older brother Samuel introduce the first successful steamboats in Georgia's waters, assisted in the establishment of the first steam packet service between Charleston and Savannah, and played his own part as an investor in the first crossing of the Atlantic by nothing less than a "steamship." Charles seemed to know that his time was coming—he had told his friends and family so—and faced his fate squarely and without fear. Still, his death meant one less proponent for the *Savannah*.

The sad news didn't stop there. Up in Connecticut, Sarah Rogers —sister of Steve, and sister-in-law of Moses—also had died, leaving Amos Junior a widower with six children.

Whatever Moses and Steve felt for these losses, the sobering effects of the economic depression represented a matter far more immediate, and demanding. All the bad news they had heard at Liverpool was not only true, but a pale description of what had transpired while they were away.

* * *

Back in early June, when Moses and his creation were approaching Ireland, newspapers in Charleston and Savannah had been busily reporting on William Scarbrough's efforts to shore up his teetering finances.

A few months prior to that, in March of 1819, the U.S. Revenue Cutter *Dallas*, while patrolling off the Georgia coast, had stopped an incoming British schooner named the *Friendship*, and searched her contents. On board was found John Nystrom, the third partner of the Savannah partnership of Scarbrough & McKinne. Also on board was Nystrom's cargo: 9½ barrels of specie—worth some $111,000— brought from the British island colony of Jamaica.

Dallas Captain John Jackson believed the whole enterprise was in violation of a recent retaliatory law banning British cargoes from the West Indies. He ordered everything seized—schooner, specie, and paperwork—and brought in to Savannah for Customs Collector Archibald S. Bulloch to sort out.

This episode had been largely a private affair, until the newspapers, led by *The Courier* of Charleston, broke the story in June. Only then did the charges start flying.

The Courier published a letter from someone writing under the pen name of "Felix," who accused Captain Jackson of being in cahoots with the specie owners, to land their precious cargo in violation of the law.

His integrity impugned, Captain Jackson quickly counterattacked. Writing to *The Courier*, the Captain stated that based upon the evidence, he believed John Nystrom and a certain someone (whom Jackson refused to name directly) had intentionally tried to circumvent the ban on unloading cargoes from British-flagged vessels out of the West Indies. The *Friendship*, Captain Jackson declared, had been instructed to sail from Jamaica to the Georgia coast, and upon arrival, claim she was in distress. Then the law of the sea would take over, allowing the *Friendship* to make port at Savannah, after which she could quietly unload her barrels of coin.

All these public accusations were just too much for that certain unnamed someone, who was none other than William Scarbrough. In a lengthy letter to the *Savannah Republican*, Scarbrough blasted the "unfounded insinuations" of Felix and the "studied ambiguities" of Captain Jackson. Bringing specie into the country was not illegal, Scarbrough pointed out. In fact, under the difficult circumstances the country faced, it ought to be encouraged!

But getting such a large amount of real money from Jamaica to Savannah required protection, given the very real threat of piracy. Since the Royal Navy squadron commander for the West Indies,

Admiral Sir Home Popham, had refused to provide either transport or escort, partner John Nystrom had to look elsewhere. He settled on a schooner—a *fast* schooner—that could outrun pirates. It just so happened that this vessel—the *Friendship*—was British.

According to Scarbrough, Collector Bulloch had told him that unloading the specie off the coast would be alright, as long as there was no cargo on board the vessel. Yet it was clear from the evidence, Scarbrough declared, that Captain Jackson had seized the *Friendship* in waters beyond his jurisdiction. Scarbrough accused Jackson of wanting to declare the schooner's specie as recovered pirate booty, and receive his share as a reward.

The whole thing had become a very public, very ugly mess. Yet it was only the tip of the iceberg.

While the *Friendship* and the specie were released eventually, there were other forces pressing down upon Scarbrough that very same month. His trading partners in New York, Gideon Pott and Joseph P. McKinne, had been forced to the financial wall. Unable to honor promissory notes they had issued, the firm of Pott & McKinne had *stopped payment*. They simply didn't have enough cash or credit to meet their obligations.

Pott & McKinne's situation had become painfully clear to Scarbrough. Because Scarbrough & McKinne of Savannah had sold so much cotton and other goods to Pott & McKinne of New York, the former held a small mountain of such promissory notes from the latter, which suddenly could not be redeemed.

And there was still more. Scarbrough knew his local partnership with McKinne had multiple debts coming due, including loans from the Planters' Bank, the State Bank of Georgia, the Marine and Fire Insurance Company, and the Bank of the United States. As was the custom at the time, Scarbrough & McKinne had secured *endorsements* for these loans from Andrew Low & Company, and another merchant named William Taylor. This meant that if the original borrower could not repay the loans, then the banks would come after Andrew Low & Company and William Taylor for the funds.

Since it had become obvious that William Scarbrough was in trouble, his endorsers realized that they had to act, just to protect their own interests. With Andrew Low and Robert Isaac away, the task of facing reality and confronting Scarbrough fell upon their third partner, James McHenry. On June 5th, McHenry, Taylor and Scarbrough had all signed a document acknowledging the gravity of the situation. As a consequence, Scarbrough agreed to hand over to his endorsers whatever uncommitted and saleable assets he had: 52 shares of the Steam Boat Company of Georgia, 525 shares of the Marine and Fire Insurance Company of Savannah, 50 shares of the Planters' Bank, 11 shares of the State Bank of Georgia, assorted real estate, and 29 slaves.

The value of the stock shares alone was around $90,000, and yet this would not be enough. Scarbrough felt compelled to take further action. On June 14th, he had walked into State Superior Court in Savannah and filed suit against the New York firm of Pott & McKinne. Presiding over the case was Judge John MacPherson Berrien, who had been one of the guests on the presidential steamship cruise to Tybee. Before Judge Berrien, Scarbrough laid out the bare facts:

> William Scarbrough . . . who being duly sworn on his oath saith, that Gideon Pott and Joseph P. McKinne copartners under the firm of Pott + McKinne are indebted to said firm of Scarbrough + McKinne in the sum of one hundred and twelve thousand + forty eight dollars + forty seven cents...

Just like Scarbrough's imported specie, and the assets surrendered to his endorsers, this debt alone represented an enormous amount of money. Any hope Scarbrough had of collecting it would have to wait until the suit worked its way through the legal process.

In spite of these steps, Scarbrough still found himself on the receiving end of a steady stream of warrants—for overdue tariffs owed to the Custom House, or past-due bank loans, or even debts he still had with Andrew Low & Company.

By August (when Moses and the *Savannah* were in the Baltic), Scarbrough felt compelled to further clarify the status of his relationship with the partner he was then suing. This he did, with a blunt, frank newspaper advertisement:

> Notice.
> The Copartnership heretofore carried on by *W Scarbrough, Joseph M'Kinne & John Nystrom*, under the firm of SCARBROUGH & M'KINNE, is this day dissolved by mutual consent. It is requested that all unsettled accounts may be rendered

in for settlement or liquidation: and that all persons indebted
will forthwith make payment to W. Scarbrough.
WM. SCARBROUGH
J.P. M'KINNE,   *Per Attorney*
JOHN NYSTROM.   *W. Scarbrough.*

Aug 12, 1819

————

The subscriber intending to continue Business in the *Factorage
& Commission Line* alone for his own account, offers his best
services in that Line, to the friends of the former concern and
the public; and to those, disposed to favor him—who may hesitate to do so from his recent embarrassment, a sufficient guarantee will be furnished, under the patronage of friends,
competent to afford it.
WM. SCARBROUGH.

Never before had Scarbrough been in such difficult financial straits.
In spite of it all, his public notice made it clear that he would press on
as best he could. Brother-in-law Robert Isaac, back from Liverpool in
mid-November, surely told him how hard it would be, given the poor
state of the markets in Britain. Both sides of Isaac's own world—Isaac,
Low & Company in Liverpool, and Andrew Low & Company in Savannah—also were having problems collecting and paying off debts.

Despite all these efforts, the pressure on Scarbrough wasn't letting
up. Just prior to the steamship's return, he had been hit with a new lawsuit brought by William Jay, the English architect who had designed
and built his mansion. Jay's bill of $17,484 remained outstanding.

Some of the other shareholders in the Savannah Steam Ship Company were under pressure, too. In total, about one-half of the *Savannah's* owners were feeling the financial pinch to varying degrees.
With Scarbrough at their forefront, it was these investors who were
driving the Company's next move.

* * *

In retrospect, Captain Rogers' decision to forego his planned port
of call at Boston surely must have seemed the right one. Under the
circumstances, selling the vessel remained the best course of action.

Despite all of the missed chances to effect a sale in Europe, the Company still had at least one more promising card to play, and time was of the essence. Given the offer made by President Monroe at the end of the Tybee cruise, the next logical step was to send the steamship to Washington. Once there, Captain Rogers could negotiate a sale of the *Savannah* to the federal government, hopefully recouping the costs of construction. At the same time, the country would gain a unique weapon in the fight against piracy on the high seas.

All the better, Congress was about to reconvene for its usual winter session. Since that body had to approve all government spending, the presence of the House and Senate leadership in Washington could help make for an expeditious sale.

The imperative, then, was to turn the steamship around as quickly as possible, and depart for the nation's capital.

But before this plan could be put into action, there were chores to be done. The gifts received or purchased in Europe had to be unloaded, and arrangements made for their distribution. Some were headed for the homes of the Company's shareholders, while the china Moses had purchased in London was destined for the Vails in New Jersey, and the Norwegian sjekte had to be shipped to Connecticut, as a present to his father.

The crew also needed some attention. On December 1st, the day after their arrival, Moses gave them liberty ashore.

They surely deserved it. Not only had the crew successfully performed the first crossing of an ocean using steam power, but just as importantly, they had conducted the entire voyage in complete safety.

The steamship, too, had performed admirably. As Captain Rogers himself told the *Columbian Museum*, the *Savannah*'s trip home suffered "neither a screw, bolt, or rope-yarn parted, although she experienced very rough weather."

Indeed she had. Soon after leaving Norway, the *Savannah* and her crew had run into a heavy storm in the North Sea. The waters were so violent that a massive wave had ripped the jolly boat from the stern, and carried it away. Fortunately, the sjekte Captain Rogers had purchased at Arendal left them with enough lifeboat capacity on board to proceed.

Sailing north around Scotland, they had found the Atlantic no less forgiving. From Norway to Georgia, the crew had experienced rough, rolling seas and rain for half of the 38-day journey.

While use of the new mode on the return voyage had been limited to departure and arrival, the safe return of the *Savannah* still served a useful purpose in and of itself. By re-crossing the Atlantic, the steamship further dispelled the previous notion that such a vessel could not even make the journey using sails. As a result, the description of the *Savannah's* turbulent trip home without damage was not just reported around the country, but leading news as far away as New York City.

* * *

On the evening of Friday, December 3rd, having spent just 72 hours in port, Moses told the engine crew to get steam up. While the sun had set several hours before, a nearly full moon still illuminated the wharves and shipping to a pale rendition of day.

At 9 o'clock, the ship was unmoored, and the paddlewheels set in motion. As the *Savannah* pushed her way down the moonlit river, her churning wheels and smoking, sparking stack must have offered those who came out to watch a scene that felt like a dream.

The steamship soon left the city far behind, and within a few hours had reached a spot in the river called Five Fathoms Hole, near Salters Island. There, Moses ordered the engine stopped, and the anchor dropped. They would wait until dawn.

The next morning, they quickly got under way. After crossing over the sandbar at Tybee and bidding goodbye to the river pilot, Steve put the deckhands to work setting all sail "to the best advantage." Saving the new mode and its fuel for later, Moses turned his creation to the northeast, and headed toward the nation's capital.

* * *

In the days that followed the *Savannah's* departure, Nature, as if angry at the steamship's success, rose up in challenge once again. While Moses, Steve and the crew skimmed along the Carolina coast, they encountered "smokey" conditions and headwinds, which slowed their progress. This was followed by rough seas, rain squalls, thunder and lightning.

Once they finally rounded the treacherous waters off Cape Hatteras, late on December 8th, it appeared that Nature was spent. The sky turned hazy, and the sea settled down.

But this respite proved to be brief. The following afternoon, Nature "come on to blow a heavy gale," as Steve recorded in the logbook. Climbing up the shrouds went the crew, to close the main topsail, and bring down the fore and aft topgallant yards. While the force of the gale cleared the cloudy sky above, it still beat and battered the *Savannah* for days. The headwinds were so strong that Steve had no choice but to slowly wear the steamship from side to side.

Not until December 13th did Nature finally relent. The following day, the *Savannah* had made enough progress for the crew to spot Cape Henry lighthouse, which marked the entrance to the Chesapeake Bay. Moses ordered the steam up, and the paddlewheels deployed. Soon thereafter, the *Savannah* was splashing into the mouth of the Chesapeake, stopping only briefly to take on a pilot.

Proceeding up-Bay, the steamship passed Norfolk and the entrance to the James River, places that Moses knew well from his days commanding the steamboats *Eagle* and *New Jersey*. A little further north, they steamed past the York River, and the Revolution's decisive battle site at Yorktown.

By evening, the *Savannah* reached the mouth of the Potomac River, where Moses ordered the anchor dropped for the night. Washington, in the District of Columbia, lay some 120 miles upriver.

The next day, the new mode was put back into action, and they steamed one-half the distance to the capital before darkness obliged a stop.

Early the following morning, December 16th, Moses and Steve put the crew to work replenishing their fuel supply with some oak wood. Then they continued their rapid ascent of the wide blue Potomac. Off the starboard side, to the east, the crew saw the wooded shores of Maryland, the trees fully shorn of their leaves and ready for winter; to their west, off the larboard side, were even more bare forests, rising and rolling over the hills of Virginia.

As the river narrowed, the scenery to the west was interrupted eventually by a large country farm, high on a Virginia hill. This was George Washington's Mount Vernon. A little further north appeared the town of Alexandria, which was a part of the District of Columbia. There, the crew could see many large merchant vessels tied up, unloading their cargoes. Fortunately, the Potomac was deep enough to allow the *Savannah* to continue further upriver.

By late afternoon, as the sun was setting and the air grew chilly, the crew saw the nation's capital coming into view. Washington City was built at the convergence of the Eastern and Western Branches of the Potomac. The branches met at Greenleaf's Point, on which sat some minor fortifications for the capital's defense.

By the time the steamship reached the fork in the river, the crew could see a fair distance up the main Western Branch, which continued in a northwesterly direction. About 1½ miles up this branch was a solitary, mile-long pontoon bridge, spanning the breadth of the river. Another one-half mile beyond that, on the north shore, lay a grassy field that stretched due north from the river's edge, gradually rising to the top of a small hill.

At the top of this hill sat a large white mansion. This was the President's House, recently refurbished and whitewashed after its destruction by British troops in the late war. Surrounding it were four brick buildings with white columns. These were the executive office buildings, one each for the Departments of State, Treasury, War and Navy.

Looking up the Eastern Branch, the crew could see the Washington Navy Yard, where some part of the "gradual increase of the Navy" was taking place. The hull of a schooner sat in the stocks, under construction. Nearer still, anchored in the river, lay a brand new, 74-gun ship-of-the-line, the USS *Columbus*, which just recently had been launched from the Yard.

Even though the Western Branch's pontoon bridge was passable (thanks to a raise-able section), proceeding further upriver to the port of Georgetown was not advisable, since the waters there were not particularly deep. The best place for vessels of size to anchor at Washington was right where the two branches met, around Greenleaf's Point.

This is where the river pilot took the *Savannah*. In the rapidly fading light, he steered the steamship into the Eastern Branch, heading for the entrance to the Washington Canal, which was just beyond the Point. There, a long pier stuck out from shore. This was Canal Wharf, where large vessels could tie up.

The steam engine was stopped, and as the ship slowed, the crew made fast to the wharf. By the time all was secure, it was 6 o'clock that evening, and the temperature had dropped to near freezing.

With the journey from Georgia complete, the crew had to wonder what was to become of them.

They had just arrived at the nation's capital.

So too had the cold weather of winter.

It was unlikely they would be departing anytime soon.

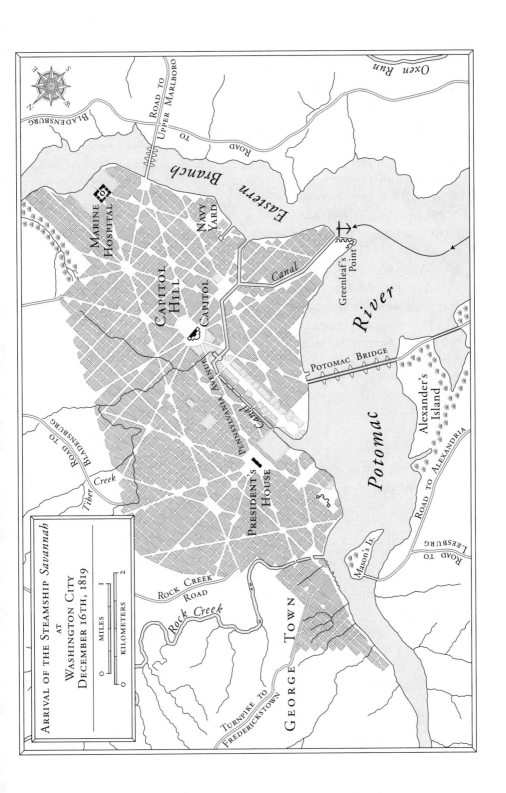

ARRIVAL OF THE STEAMSHIP *Savannah*
AT
WASHINGTON CITY
DECEMBER 16TH, 1819

MILES

KILOMETERS

ROAD TO BLADENSBURG

ROAD TO UPPER MARLBORO

Oxen Run

Eastern Branch

MARINE HOSPITAL

NAVY YARD

CAPITOL HILL

CAPITOL

Canal

Greenleaf's Point

River

ROAD TO BLADENSBURG

Tiber Creek

PENNSYLVANIA AVENUE

Canal

PRESIDENT'S HOUSE

POTOMAC BRIDGE

Potomac

Alexander's Island

ROAD TO ALEXANDRIA

Mason's Is.

ROAD TO LEESBURG

ROCK CREEK ROAD

Rock Creek

GEORGE TOWN

TURNPIKE TO FREDERICKSTOWN

And they still had pay coming.

To top it off, they had been allowed little time ashore since signing up with the *Savannah*. This previously led several of the crew to take matters into their own hands, as they had at Liverpool and Stockholm.

In Washington, it was Frank Smith's turn. Later that evening, around about midnight, Smith appeared on the opposite side of Captain Rogers himself. Just what set Smith off is not entirely clear, but given the late hour and the new locale, it probably had something to do with his interpretation of "sailor's rights."

"Frank Smith damd and swore at the Captain," Steve later recorded in the logbook. Yet this expression of anger proved unfulfilling, so Smith lunged, landing two or three blows on his captain before the crew was able to restrain him.

Assault and battery on a fellow mariner, and the captain no less, was a serious offense. Since the *Savannah* was in an American port, Moses could have summoned the law to take Frank Smith into custody. But since the attack had taken place on board, the captain still had the final say. Given what Moses planned to do the next day, he decided to deal with the situation himself. So Smith was ordered taken below, and clapped in irons.

* * *

The next morning dawned cloudy and cold. The sub-freezing night air slowly gave way to temperatures that reached 50° by noon, providing the crew some relief as they went about the task of performing the usual "sundry jobs on board."

While Steve kept the men occupied, Moses went ashore, and headed to the office of the George Town Importing and Exporting Company. There, he introduced himself to the principal agent for that company, a man by the name of Walter Smith.

Moses presented the agent with a letter. It was written by William Scarbrough, who, in his capacity as the president of the Savannah Steam Ship Company, asked Walter Smith to provide Captain Rogers with a line of credit. This would allow Rogers to cover any costs while the steamship lay at Washington.

Walter Smith duly obliged, in exchange for a 5% commission. Moses asked him to lay out $67.25, so that the river pilot could be paid off. This chore done, Moses took his leave.

He then tromped over to the Georgetown Custom House, to register the *Savannah*'s arrival. Moses had to pay a port entrance fee of $2.50, and a customs duty of 6¢ per ton of burthen, which came to $19.18.

He also asked the customs clerk to tally another charge related to the crew. Every vessel's captain had to pay hospital dues. These monies were used to maintain hospitals for mariners in every port that had a custom house. Paying hospital dues (which were 20¢ per seaman per month served) usually was done only when a captain intended to release his crew.

The clerk calculated the dues back to the *Savannah*'s departure the previous May, coming up with $23.66. After adding on a few other minor costs, the total custom house charges came to $45.68. Moses duly paid with a promissory note from Walter Smith's company, and then left.

The next day, Saturday, December 18th, the *Savannah*'s arrival was announced in the capital's most influential newspaper, the *Daily National Intelligencer*. The paper's information on the steamship was so detailed that it must have come from Moses himself:

> ... She encountered a very heavy gale in the north sea, and two from Savannah to this port ... She also encountered many other gales on her passage out, and has met with no accident excepting the loss of a small boat and anchors. Her machinery has met with no accident...

These words meant a lot. The *National Intelligencer* had been one of the most prominent skeptics of the "bold enterprize" envisioned by the Savannah Steam Ship Company. "There is great doubt," the paper had written nineteen months earlier, "whether steam-boats can safely be employed in crossing the ocean." By reporting so prominently on the *Savannah*'s safe return, the *Intelligencer* was admitting, however indirectly, that it had been mistaken.

That same Saturday, Moses made another visit to the offices of George Town Importing and Exporting, where he withdrew $600 in cash. Returning to the steamship, he began paying off members of the crew through the weekend. And for the first time since March 28th, Steve made no entry into the logbook. The crew's work was done. As they were paid off, they peeled off, to parts unknown.

While Moses was busy tending to logistics on board, he also was preparing for the business of taking up President Monroe's offer. The following Monday, another newspaper, the *National Messenger* of Georgetown, lent a hand:

> The celebrated *Steam Ship Savannah*, has arrived at Washington. This vessel, which presents a satisfactory proof of the practicability of performing the most distant voyages by the aid of steam power, is well worthy of the curiosity of the public.

While Washington readers were absorbing this back-to-back coverage by the *Intelligencer* and the *Messenger*, another far more explicit editorial appeared on Tuesday up in New York City, courtesy of *The National Advocate*:

> The steam ship Savannah has arrived at Washington. She would be a valuable government vessel to carry dispatches and remain in the Mediterranean, or to any part of the world, as she sails without steam uncommonly fast, and with steam, of course, can have greater expedition. We want a vessel of her character.

What prompted *The National Advocate* to express itself so forthrightly isn't precisely known, although the paper was one of the most vocal proponents of a strong Navy. Beyond an editor risking an opinion, Gideon Pott and Joseph P. McKinne were the only New Yorkers with a direct stake in the matter.

That same Tuesday, Moses returned to the offices of George Town Importing and Exporting, taking out another advance, this time for $710. This money he used to finish paying off the crew, and settle a few other minor bills.

Once most of the crewmen had departed, Steve must have taken his own leave. His eventual destination was home to Connecticut, where his betrothed, Mary Rogers, was ready and waiting.

A couple of crew members may have agreed to stay with the *Savannah*, to look after things or escort visitors around the ship. But aside from them, Moses was on his own. The future of the steamship *Savannah*, yet again, rested upon his shoulders.

* * *

Matters on board having been addressed, Moses turned full-heartedly to the task of approaching the federal government regarding a purchase. Help from the other shareholders would have been useful, but at least two of them could not get involved. Archibald S. Bulloch, as the U.S. Collector of Customs, and J. P. Henry, as the newly-appointed U.S. Navy Agent at Savannah, had clear conflicts of interest. Beyond any letters of introduction provided by the shareholders, Moses would have to find his own way around the nation's capital.

The first step was to consider the geography. Washington City was an unusual place, and anything but concentrated. While its streets had been laid out by Pierre L'Enfant several decades earlier, and the roads cut into the earth, much of the city remained green and partly forested. The most significant construction had taken place around certain landmarks within the District, resulting in clusters of development.

A couple of miles to the northwest of the *Savannah*'s berth was the executive area, naturally centered around the President's House and the four executive office buildings. Further assembled around them were still other government offices, as well as the residences of many executive branch employees.

About 1½ miles due north of the steamship was the legislative cluster. This node was anchored by the Capitol building, sitting high on a hill. Surrounding it on three sides were hotels and boardinghouses, where most members of the House and Senate took up residence when Congress was in session.

Just north of the *Savannah*, around Greenleaf's Point, was another small collection of mostly commercial and residential buildings, and further up the Eastern Branch was the fourth and final node, built up around the Navy Yard. Otherwise, aside from the heavily developed Pennsylvania Avenue, much of the District landscape remained pastoral, with cows often left to graze in the open fields. As one foreign observer put it, the impression left was "rather that of a straggling city, than the capital of this vast empire."

Walking around such a dispersed town, especially in December, would be a time-consuming and difficult exercise. The most logical solution was to trust in the availability of hackney carriages, which charged 25¢ for each trip between the clusters (and half as much again after 8 o'clock in the evening). If the carriages were thought to be too inconvenient, or too expensive, then a visitor could always rent a horse. This latter means of transport was available at any number of livery stables, where a good saddle horse could be hired for about $1.50 per day.

Also at issue was where to go.

One obvious destination was the executive branch departments surrounding the President's House.

Another was Congress. As the only acknowledged direct representatives of the people in Washington, their voice would have to be heard. Congress also controlled the federal government's purse strings.

Navigating one's way around the Capitol building at the end of 1819 was not the easiest task. The structure was still being re-built, having been burnt out by the British back in 1814. While the House and Senate chambers had just been re-opened, the center dome remained unfinished, effectively making the Capitol two completed wings separated by a construction site.

The U.S. Capitol in the Early 19th Century.

Even without this hindrance, finding the right members of Congress to talk to presented its own set of challenges, since most of them had no offices in the Capitol building itself. The best way to track down congressmen or senators was to call on them where they lived. Since Congress was in session for only about five months a year, most members took up residence in one of the many boardinghouses that surrounded Capitol Hill.

The advantage of this set-up was more than mere convenience. Since the vast majority of members came to Washington alone, they found the nearby boardinghouses, filled as they usually were with fellow congressmen, to be the optimal home away from home. Not only did it provide them with a temporary political family, but it also made the boardinghouse dinner table one of the best opportunities to gather and discuss the issues (and rumors) of the day.

To the petitioner's advantage, boardinghouse groupings tended to follow State or sectional allegiances. Calling on one congressman at one boardinghouse often could produce introductions to several others from the same State. If petitioners came for a meal, they would gain all the more, being at one of the ideal places not only to give information, but to get it.

Beyond learning how to reach members of Congress was the equally important task of gauging the sentiment of the place. The first session of the 16th Congress had been opened on December 6th, while the *Savannah* and her crew were fighting with Nature off the Carolina coast. Since then, additional members above and beyond the quorum necessary to begin the session had trickled in, and shortly thereafter, their collective sense of priorities was revealed.

On the one hand, the country was suffering through hard times, with government revenues having dropped accordingly. This left legislators in a quandary over what to do. New Hampshire Congressman William Plumer Jr., in a letter to his ex-Senator father, laid bare the choices:

> *All see the necessity of retrenchment, economy, + reform. But every thing is conducted here in so extravagant + wasteful a manner that nothing but absolute want + necessity can bring them to adopt a different course. The probable result will be that Congress will reduce the army, suspend building any more ships, borrow something for a year or two from the sinking fund, + authorize a loan, but all is as yet uncertain...*

Indeed it was, for on the other hand, there were certain pressing issues that needed to be addressed. One of the first to be taken up was a supplemental spending bill for the Navy.

After years of arguing between Federalists, who were pro-Navy, and Democratic-Republicans, who were dismissive of naval power, the debate was over. The Federalists, while practically dead as a political party, had won the argument. Virtually everyone agreed that a strong Navy was imperative to protecting the country's shores and shipping.

The purpose of the supplemental spending bill was to make good on that belief. The Navy had determined that it needed more money to cover past expenditures in 1819, as well as future costs in 1820, particularly for combating the slave trade and piracy.

The general public, and their representatives in Washington, needed no reminders of the latter problem. Since the end of the previous session, the country's newspapers had continued to chronicle the spread of pirate attacks on American shipping. Some sea-borne bandits had actually dared to venture as far north as the Chesapeake Bay. And while dozens of pirates had been captured, put on trial, and some executed, even this did little to stem the bloody tide.

The attacks on merchant ships through 1819 had been so intense that a group of six Boston insurance companies had banded together to write a letter, timed to reach its destination just as Congress reconvened:

Boston, December 1, 1819.

TO James Monroe, President of the United States of America.

The undersigned ask leave to lay before you the annexed statement of facts, relating to piracies and unlawful acts of armed vessels, committed, in many instances near our coast, or in the W. India seas, and some of them, they regret to add, by vessels out of our own ports.

Your memorialists are aware that this subject has already engaged the attention of government, and it is with this view of co-operating with them in checking the progress of this alarming evil, that they have collected this list of piracies, supposing that, from their connection with commerce, more facts of this nature came to their knowledge than to that of the members of government...

Attached to this memorial was a list of 44 piracies committed in the first 11 months of 1819, all assembled from the pages of just one Boston newspaper. While the insurers declared that they would "abstain from offering any comments or opinions" as to the government's course of action, the message to President Monroe was nevertheless unmistakable—

Do something!

* * *

Turning the steamship *Savannah* into a vessel of war would not have been a very difficult task. Her comfortable passenger cabins on the lower deck could be stripped out and used for storage, or as additional bunk space for sailors or a complement of Marines. Her upper deck could be armed with cannon, either fixed on a mount that pivoted (like the revenue cutter *Dallas*), or of the rolling variety, which could be moved about the deck as needed. Such modifications had been made before to countless merchant vessels, turning them into privateers in times of war.

The main vulnerability of the *Savannah* was her paddlewheels. Robert Fulton's steam battery for the Navy, the *Fulton*, and Lord Cochrane's *Rising Star* each tried to address this problem by enclosing their paddlewheels in the center-bottom of the hull, thereby protecting them from cannon fire. The *Savannah* had no such feature, and couldn't without major reconstruction.

What she did have was flexibility. Her paddlewheels were designed as a collection of parts brought together as a whole. If one of them took a hit, then the spare spokes, paddles and chains kept on board could be used for on-the-spot repairs. Besides, if the chance of pirate-shot damaging one of them seemed high, the paddlewheels could be disassembled in a matter of minutes.

Even more impressive were the two things the *Savannah* could provide that all naval officers craved: speed, and maneuverability.

She had already proven herself to be a fast sailer, a testament to the shipbuilding skills of Fickett and Crockett. Add the power of steam at a critical moment, and the *Savannah* would have the speed to catch any pirate vessel afloat.

Yet that was only half of the revolution she promised. Steam power allowed her to maneuver in ways that a wind-borne pirate could only achieve in his dreams. One such example would be steering the *Savannah* under steam into a position called "crossing the T," allowing her broadside cannons to rake the bow or stern of any Jolly Roger.

With artificial speed and maneuverability at her disposal, an armed

Savannah had the potential to strike fear into the pirates, and beat them.

But proposing to arm this first steamship in the world represented an incredibly radical leap of faith.

Up to that point, the federal government's confidence in steam-powered men-of-war had been limited to harbor defense. Once the steam battery *Fulton* had become operational, it was Congress who had pressed for more. Their 1816 law for "the gradual increase of the Navy" had authorized the president to procure steam engines and timbers for the construction of three additional *Fulton*-like batteries.

From the Navy Department's perspective, however, building more steam batteries was a low priority. Of much greater importance was paying off the pile of bills left over from the late war. Then came organizing an expanded construction program for traditional sailing vessels. Only after those tasks were well in-hand did the Navy feel compelled to begin working on the three steam batteries.

By the time they did, in 1818, the Navy soon discovered there was yet another *unspoken* impetus for them to begin building the steam batteries, and that was all of the publicity generated by the *Savannah's* launching. Yet the creation of the first steamship did more than push the Navy to build steam batteries—it also forced them to consider the possibility of steam power at sea.

Pressing the dream upon them had been one of the true believers, New York engine-builder Robert McQueen. After winning the first steam battery engine contract, he had dared to submit to the Navy, in late 1818, a hull design for an ocean-going warship, instead of a harbor-protecting battery.

Publicly, the Board of Navy Commissioners had no reaction to McQueen's proposed design.

Privately, they had ordered Steam Superintendent Francis B. Ogden and Naval Constructor Henry Eckford at New York to come up with a design that was slightly less ambitious. The Navy Board wanted steam batteries that could be transferred safely from port to port, but not necessarily operate at sea for extended periods.

By the autumn of 1819, Eckford had complied, submitting his own design.

Concurrently, the Navy Board had begun pushing forward on procurement, organizing additional contracts for a second steam engine and two sets of live oak frames.

Yet despite all this activity, none of the keels for the three batteries authorized by Congress had been laid, and a finalized design still had not been approved, leaving the funding for a steam Navy both open and fluid.

* * *

In the days just before Christmas, Moses began making the rounds. One of the most logical places for him to go first was the office of the Secretary of State, John Quincy Adams. There were arguably few other people in Washington who would know just how much the *Savannah*'s captain had achieved.

On Thursday, December 23rd, Moses trekked through the crisp winter air, heading toward the brick building with white columns located to the northeast of the President's House. This was the headquarters of the Department of State.

Upon entering the building, Moses climbed the stairs to the second floor, and asked to see Secretary Adams. Making such a call on an official so high in the government was not at all unusual at the time. Besides, Moses had a letter to deliver.

Secretary Adams' office was in the southeast corner of the building, giving him an oblique view, out his southern windows, of the President's House and the Potomac River. Adjacent to his office, in the northeast corner, was an audience chamber where Adams sometimes received larger groups of visitors.

Shortly after New Hampshire Senator John Parrott exited from his own meeting with the Secretary of State, Moses was ushered in.

Before him stood a well-dressed man some 5 feet 7 inches in height, with a round face and a bald crown. What remained of his close-cropped brown hair grew exclusively on the back and sides of his head, ending in side-whiskers which stopped near the bottom of his ears.

At 52 years of age, John Quincy Adams, the son of a revolutionary and former president, had already lived a full and interesting life. He had been the Minister to the Netherlands, Portugal, and Prussia; then a Massachusetts State Senator; and a United States Senator; then the first Minister to Russia; and the commission leader who negotiated the Treaty of Ghent, ending the War of 1812; and then he had served as the Minister to Britain.

At this point in his career, he held one of the most powerful positions in the executive branch. Given the destinies of previous Secretaries of State—Jefferson, Madison, and Monroe—it surely crossed the mind of Moses that he might very well be looking at a future President of the United States.

John Quincy Adams.

From John Quincy Adams' point of view, the reputation and accomplishments of Captain Rogers had preceded him. By that time, Adams had received a dispatch from Richard Rush in London, which described the "equal admiration and astonishment" the steamship had excited in Britain. Adams also had a detailed report from one of his favorite correspondents, Christopher Hughes, describing the *Savannah's* "proud triumph" at Stockholm, and the "impayable gratification" afforded to him by Captain Rogers and his creation. Adams also had a brief dispatch from Consul John Rainals at Copenhagen, relaying the news that the *Savannah* was returning home.

As the two men sat down, Moses pulled out yet another letter to add to the pile, which he handed to Secretary Adams:

St. Petersburg 25th Sept. 1819

Dear Sir,

Captn Rogers of the Steam Ship, the Savannah, who lately arrived here from Stockholm will have the honor to deliver you this. The Savannah has excited much interest as well as the admiration of *all who have seen her here, and particularly of those best qualified to judge of her merits.*

Being the first who crossed the Atlantic or braved the waves of the Baltic in a vessel of this kind, constructed, as I understand, under his own immediate superintendance, Captn Rogers must be intitled to high commendation for the skill + enterprize as well as patriotism displayed on this occasion, + the success with which he has executed so bold an undertaking, which is well calculated to reflect honor on himself + enhance the already high naval character of his country.

He has stated to me his desire to be employed in the naval service of the United States, + indicated a wish that I should communicate the same to you. I know not that any thing I could say would prove useful to him in promoting his views. From the abilities, however, he has shown in his present successful voyage as well as from the long experience he has had, as I understand, in superintending the erection + management of steam vessels, he appears to me well-qualified to render important services to his country in any station in which the government might see proper to place him, and I feel a confidence no efforts would be wanting on his part to perform with fidelity + zeal the duties that might be assigned him.

It is with much satisfaction I embrace this occasion to present Mrs. Campbell's best respects + friendly recollections with mine to Mrs. Adams and you will please accept for yourself renewed assurances of the sincere esteem + very high respect, with which,

I am,

Sir,

Your most obedt.

G. W. Campbell

The Honble
John Q. Adams—
   Secretary of State— +c—

It was, in Adams' own words, "a letter of strong recommendation." Moses then reviewed the details of the voyage, recounting each port of call made (excepting Arendal), and the unsuccessful effort to sell the *Savannah*. Taking up the President's suggestion, Moses told Secretary Adams of the shareholders' intention of offering the steamship to the federal government.

Campbell's letter made it perfectly clear that Moses was thinking about his own future, as well. His interest in a U.S. Navy post, which had been somewhat tentative at Stockholm, had solidified by the end of his time at St. Petersburg. Once he had returned home, and come face-to-face with all the troubles swirling around the country, the Company, and the shareholders, this personal goal became all the more vital.

Moses apparently asked Secretary Adams if he could keep the Campbell letter temporarily, so that he could show it to others. With the promise to return it, he took his leave.

Another important visit for Moses to make was to the office of the *National Intelligencer*, which was located at the northwest corner of Seventh and D Streets. The best time to meet the proprietors of that newspaper was when Congress was not in session. The next day, Friday, December 24th, was just such a moment, since both houses had recessed early for the Christmas weekend.

The owners and editors of the *Intelligencer* were English-born Joseph Gales Jr. and Virginia-born William W. Seaton.

Joseph Gales Jr. had been forced to flee England with his parents, after they had dared to sell political tracts written by the revolutionary Thomas Paine. Finding refuge in America, the Gales family had set up shop in Raleigh, North Carolina, where the elder Joseph began a newspaper. Joseph the younger soon made his way to the nation's capital, where he took a job with the *National Intelligencer*, considered the trumpet of Democratic-Republican administrations since the beginning of Jefferson's presidency. With the retirement of the newspaper's founder, Gales took over, and brought in Seaton to be his partner in 1812.

The two men not only maintained the *Intelligencer's* status as the mouthpiece of Democratic-Republican presidents, but also offered their stenographic skills to the Congress. At a time when journalists were allowed on the floors of the House and Senate to better witness the action, Gales and Seaton made a point of attending every day Congress was in session.

Because of this, Gales was given preferred seating next to the Vice President's chair at the front of the Senate, making it all the easier for him to accurately record the various motions and debates as they unfolded. Seaton received the same privilege in the House, sitting next to Speaker Henry Clay. For the long-term, their extensive note-takings were just beginning to lead to government contracts for publishing the proceedings of Congress. In the short-term, their recordings were printed in the *Daily National Intelligencer*, practically making it the Congressional newspaper of record. Add to this the belief that it served as the Monroe Administration's vocal chords, and it was plain to see that Gales and Seaton's *National Intelligencer* was the newspaper that everyone had to read.

Physically and personally, the two editors could not have been more different.

The 33-year-old Gales stood barely 5 feet 2 inches in height, and possessed a pale face dominated by seemingly black eyes, the whole of which was topped off by a thick gob of hair. Depending upon the judge, his manners were considered either "affable and easy," or rather course and unrefined.

By contrast, Seaton, who was nearly 35, was much taller, with a round face dominated by "penetrating blue eyes." His physique was solid and manly, and he had a personal bearing that exuded both dignity and decisiveness.

Considering it was the *National Intelligencer* that had expressed "great doubt" about the *Savannah*'s great experiment, it stands to reason that Gales and Seaton would want to meet the man who had proved them wrong. Whatever time Moses was given, he made the most of it, describing what he already had done, and what he still hoped to accomplish.

Having presented his case, Moses departed, and made his way through the cold rain to the State Department, where he dropped off the Campbell letter for good.

If there was any doubt about what kind of impression Moses had made on the editors of the *National Intelligencer*, it was soon dispelled. The very next morning, on Christmas Day, Gales and Seaton delivered a gift to Captain Rogers, printed on page three of the newspaper:

> The Steam Ship Savannah is yet in our harbor, and will probably winter here. She is an object worth attention; and, we may add, the enterprize of her projector and commander, entitles him to respect, and deserves reward. We have had an opportunity of seeing some of the letters from Europeans and Americans in Europe, who had an opportunity of seeing and sailing in this vessel. They all speak with admiration of the performance of the vessel, and with praise of the skill and deportment of Captain

Rogers. The National Advocate recommends the employment
of this vessel by the Government as a despatch vessel, combining, in her construction, certainty with celerity. Or, we suggest,
she might be employed as a revenue cutter, for which service she
is well adapted. We understand Capt. R means to offer her to
the Government, and we believe it will find it an advantageous
bargain to purchase her on reasonable terms.

With their editorial, Gales and Seaton planted the seed of yet
another possibility. Fighting pirates in deep water was the Navy's
responsibility. But there were also plenty of bandits operating in the
shallow waters close to shore, particularly along the wild coasts of
Alabama, Mississippi and Louisiana.

Combating such activities along the coast fell squarely on the
nation's small fleet of revenue cutters. Since their primary duty was
enforcing the nation's tariff laws, these vessels had been placed under
the control of that executive body responsible for tax collection, the
Treasury Department.

If the *Savannah* was to be purchased for use as a revenue cutter,
then the Secretary of the Treasury would have to be consulted. By
chance, this man happened to be a native of Georgia by the name of
William Crawford.

But while Crawford's hailing from the same State as the steamship
appeared fortuitous, it remained to be seen whether it would matter
very much. This was because the Secretary of the Treasury's political
priorities of late made the whole revenue cutter suggestion a rather
problematic one.

*　*　*

William H. Crawford was a big, bold, aggressive man.

By the time he was elected to represent Georgia in the U.S. Senate
in 1807, Crawford had already fought two duels, killing one political
opponent, and getting wounded by another. He quickly became one of
the most prominent voices in the Congress. In recognition of his leadership skills, Crawford was elected President pro tempore of the Senate
in 1812. When Vice President George Clinton died in office shortly
thereafter, Crawford took over his duties as Senate President, effectively
making Crawford the acting Vice President of the United States.

With the outbreak of war against Britain that same year, President

Madison asked Crawford to be his Secretary of War, but the Senator declined, instead accepting an offer to become America's minister to France.

Upon his return home in 1815, Crawford was asked again by Madison to be the Secretary of War, and this time he accepted.

Among Crawford's colleagues in the Cabinet was Secretary of State James Monroe. Given the subsequent careers of Secretaries Jefferson and Madison, Monroe looked like a shoe-in to become the next duly-elected president, in 1816. But a group of disgruntled Democratic-Republicans opposed to Monroe decided to offer their party an alternative candidate. The man they chose was William Crawford. The Georgian publicly claimed he didn't want to be considered, but the anti-Monroe forces pushed his candidacy forward, nevertheless.

In the ensuing party caucus vote, the tally was close. Monroe won, with 65 votes, while 54 delegates voted for Crawford. Despite the outcome, the results made it abundantly clear that at some future date, William H. Crawford would be a contender.

William H. Crawford.

In the interests of party unity, President Madison offered Crawford the nomination for Secretary of the Treasury later in 1816, on the understanding that Monroe would keep him there in his own administration. Crawford dutifully accepted.

Beyond his new departmental duties, however, Secretary Crawford quickly focused on the future. Over the next several years, he cultivated allies in Congress, and supported the creation of a newspaper, the *City of Washington Gazette*, which could act as his own political horn, when circumstances required.

For nearly three years, Crawford had carefully bided his time. Then, with the opening of the 16th Congress at the end of 1819, he made his move.

On December 7th, while Moses and the *Savannah* were heading for Washington, President Monroe had sent his annual Message to the newly-installed Congress. In summarizing the nation's finances, he stated that despite the ongoing economic depression, the federal government's expected revenues would cover expenditures for 1819. "For the probable receipts of the next year," the President continued, "I refer you to the statements which will be transmitted from the Treasury, which will enable you to judge whether further provision be necessary."

Three days later, Secretary Crawford sent the Treasury's figures up to Capitol Hill. His report certainly did "enable" the Congress to "judge" whether further taxes would be needed. Crawford's numbers showed a projected deficit for 1820 of nearly $5,000,000! Considering the total budget was $27,000,000, this was an enormous shortfall, and it made President Monroe look like either a smart-aleck or out of touch with reality.

Such a huge discrepancy could not be accidental. Crawford's report clearly seemed intended to embarrass the President, and test the political waters for challenging him for the Democratic-Republican nomination of 1820.

The whole episode, so immediately upon everyone's mind, put Secretary Crawford, and any potential dealings with him, in a much more complicated light.

* * *

The main event on Christmas Day in early 19th century America was dinner. It was a huge affair, replete with every meat and fish that was available, from turkey, roast beef, chicken, hams, herring and oysters, to innumerable side dishes, such as sweet potatoes, squash, celery, pickles, spiced peaches, and a lot more. There would have been plenty to drink, as well.

Precisely where Moses spent that day is unknown, but among the best places in Washington for Christmas dinner was any of the many boardinghouses that dotted the cityscape. Since Congress had recessed until the following Monday, that weekend would have been a good time to go calling.

Georgia had six at-large members in the House, meaning none was tied to representing a specific geographic district in the State. Adding South Carolina's two members who represented the Charleston area, plus the two who covered lower Manhattan, and there were ten congressmen to approach whose constituents had a direct stake in the *Savannah*'s purchase (and a constitutional right to petition their government). Include members from States along the seaboard where Moses had run steamboats, as well as others whose constituents were suffering from piracy, and the result was a very large group of congressmen, and senators, who could be approached with the idea of acquiring the *Savannah.*

Inevitably, in the course of getting the lay of the political land on Capitol Hill, Moses must have heard plenty about what was on the minds of members. Congressman William Plumer Jr. of New Hampshire, writing again to his ex-Senator father, laid out the sentiments that were bubbling just below the public surface:

> *You can have no idea of the complaint + distrust that prevail here. There is not a day passes, in which some abuse is not detected, + some attack made upon the administration. The President has little or no party in the House. It is shrewdly suspected that he begins to be a little superannuated. There is even some talk of opposing his reelection. It is well understood that the ablest men from Virginia are against him. But this will come to nothing, as there is no candidate, on whom they could agree, to oppose him.*

Underlying the Congressman's description was deep discontent over President Monroe's stewardship. At the beginning of the session, Plumer wrote, a group in Congress called the *Radicals* had "charged the Administration with extravagance, profusion in expenditures, + anti republican + aristocratic views + feelings." Such accusations had only been reinforced by the Treasury's deficit announcement, as well as an ongoing social dust-up over the failure of some administration officials to make courtesy calls on members of Congress.

The pulse of the Congress made it clear that getting the government to agree on a purchase of the *Savannah* was going to take leadership. Given the fractious mood on Capitol Hill, and the perceived weakness of the President, there was another person in Washington who had the means to start the ball rolling: the Secretary of the Navy.

The U.S. Navy, forced as it was to defend both the country's shores and its ocean-borne commerce far from home, already had built a reputation as the nation's shield at sea. In recognition of its importance, the Department of the Navy's civilian leader held a seat in the President's Cabinet, and by that measure, was on par with all the other departments, be it War (which ran the Army), or State, or Treasury, or Justice. Further reinforcing the Navy's clout at the Cabinet table were its victories over the Royal Navy during the late conflict, something most of Washington, and the country, duly appreciated.

The Secretary of the Navy at the time was a man by the name of Smith Thompson. Having previously served as Chief Justice of the New York State Supreme Court, Thompson was nominated in 1818 precisely because James Monroe remained very conscious of his own position as the fourth Virginian out of five elected chief executives. In the interest of geographic balance within his Cabinet, the President wanted someone from the North, and having been asked, Smith Thompson accepted.

Smith Thompson.

Secretary Thompson's place in the chain of command was very straightforward. Above him was the President, and below him was the Board of Navy Commissioners, composed of three commodores, the most senior officers in the service.

Through the Secretary's office flowed executive branch memorandums in both directions, as well as letters to and from Congress. Given the public nature of his position, Secretary Thompson also naturally received correspondence from outside the government realm, and right on or just after Christmas Day, he got a very interesting letter:

The Hon^e
Smith Thompson　　　　　　　　　*New York Dec. 21. 1819*
Secy. of Navy

Sir,

I have lately caused to be built at this port a Steam Ship of upwards of 700 tons, with the intention of establishing her as a Packet for the conveyance of Passengers between this port + N. Orleans touching at Charleston + Havana ~. A state of things requiring active operations on the part of the Government in or about the Gulph of Mexico would in great degree defeat the object I have in view. Conceiving that in this event, such a vessel, would materially promote the views of Government + advance the interests of the service, I am induced to place her at your disposal either for sale or charter ~. The character of this vessel is very generally known ~ her engine is of the most approved construction – with a copper boiler which alone cost me near $40,000 – the vessel was built by Mr. Eckford the U.S. naval architect at this station, of the same materials as the national ships of war ~. It is believed that Com. Rogers + Com. Bainbridge have both seen + approved of this vessel, and I am well assured that should the Government have need of a vessel of this description, she would be an ornament to the navy ~
The engine is completely finished + the vessel may be ready for sea in a fortnight.
May I beg that you will honor me with an answer. ~

I have the honor to be
very Respy
yr obt Servt
Jasper Lynch

Whether Captain Moses Rogers realized it or not, the *Savannah's* competition was back.

* * *

Since Captain Rogers had hosted President Monroe on board the steamship the previous May, it stands to reason that he made some attempt to meet with the President in Washington. There were, generally speaking, three ways to do this.

The first and easiest method was to go to one of the President's "drawing rooms," or evening receptions held at the executive mansion. When Congress was in session, these drawing rooms were usually held either weekly or every other week. Just about anyone could attend, from members of the Cabinet, to legislators and their wives, to visiting constituents. Most people got dressed up for the occasion, but it was not uncommon to see country farmers attending in the rough-hewn clothes of those who worked the soil. These receptions, however, were social gatherings, and discussing business was inappropriate.

The second method was to dine with the President. These affairs were usually for just a few dozen guests, but the increased intimacy only seemed to amplify the awkwardness. One congressman at the time described just how stilted the beginning of these presidential dinners could be:

> ... while the Servants were helping us off with our cloaks, Mr. Joseph Jones Monroe, the President's Brother + private secretary, made his <u>Entre</u> from the Drawing room Door ... Mr. Joseph Jones Monroe, with great condescension said he would precede me + introduce me to the president + that he would be obliged if I would introduce the Other Gentlemen – accordingly he set himself in array, and led the van, while we all fell in <u>Indian file</u> and in this order, passed 20 or thirty Gentlemen all sitting in a Row in great + solemn state and mute as fishes, they all it would seem having undergone this grand State Ceremony. Mrs. Monroe was seated at the further end of the room, with Mrs. Hay her Daughter and Miss Gouverneur her niece on each side of her. On our approach she rose and recd us very handsomely, when after being myself presented I introduced the Other Gentlemen – I now Expected to be led up to the President, but turning round, Mr. <u>Joseph Jones Monroe</u> the pilot, was not to be found – accordingly as no One was standing in the room, we all retreated + made the best of our way each One to his respective chair.
>
> I now looked round and Observed the president Sitting very demurely

by the chimney corner, on which I rose + advanced to him, he got up,
shook me by the hand + the Other Gentlemen, following my Example
soon came trooping up, also, and this Grand Ceremony being over all
again was Silence and each One once more resumed his seat. All bore
the appearance of great Solemnity, not a whisper broke on the ear to
interrupt the silence of the place and every One looked as if the next
moment was to be his last.
After a little while the president in a very grave manner began con-
versation with some One who sat next him, and directly Mr. Joseph
Jones Monroe . . . opened the door and ushered in some more victims
who submitted to the same dread ordeal as we had just experienced. . .

That James Monroe did not necessarily possess the gift of gab, and
Elizabeth Monroe did not particularly enjoy her ceremonial duties,
were widely known and lamented facts in Washington society. In any
event, such a social dinner had its limits, too—at most, it could serve
to illuminate one's presence in the city.

The third and most appropriate method was to simply go to the
President's House and request a private audience. If one went in the
company of a member of the Cabinet, or a member of Congress, this
was easily accomplished. Without an escort, entrance would depend
upon familiarity.

Under the circumstances of December 1819, getting President
Monroe to commit to anything in such a meeting would have been
difficult. The budget for 1820 was way out of kilter, the country in
very uncertain times economically, and the President himself was in
a politically weakened state.

Beyond these immediate uncertainties were the more fundamental
features of a president within the American system of government.

First, a chief executive doesn't control the government's purse—
Congress does. Any expenditure above that already sanctioned, or of
a different character, would probably need some kind of approving
nod from the legislative branch.

Second, it is impossible for a president to know everything necessary in order to make a judgment on the many diverse issues which
land upon his desk. That is the whole point of having a Cabinet, and
executive departments.

Even with the piracy problem before him, President Monroe would
have to defer any judgment on a purchase of the *Savannah* to those

best qualified to do so. The ones who could were the three men who made up the Board of Navy Commissioners.

Created by Congress in 1815, the Board's purpose was to concentrate the most experienced naval officers within a body that would manage the Navy's vessels, equipment and personnel in the most efficient manner possible. Previous Secretaries of the Navy had found these many tasks too difficult to juggle alone, especially during the late war. So instead, the day-to-day management would be vested in the Navy Board, staffed by a group of commodores (which was the rank above captain—the rank of "admiral" did not yet exist in the American Navy).

The idea for such a set-up was based upon the Royal Navy's model, which had different boards for different tasks within the service, from the management of dockyards to the "victualling" (or feeding) of sailors. Because the American Navy was so much smaller, the need for multiple boards was thought unnecessary, and all the responsibilities were placed within a single entity, the Board of Navy Commissioners.

Since building and maintaining a naval fleet that could win battles was a very complicated endeavor, the officers nominated for the Board were not only the most senior and experienced, but also, given recent events, the most victorious. Nothing prepared an officer to manage in peacetime like the hard-won lessons of actual combat. The three men who served on the Board at the close of 1819 all fit this mold.

The most junior member was Commodore David Porter, who had fought in the Barbary Wars, and spent two years as a prisoner of Tripoli after his frigate, the USS *Philadelphia*, was captured in 1803. During the War of 1812, he had commanded the USS *Essex* on its marauding mission along the coast of the Americas, sinking and capturing British merchantmen until the Royal Navy caught up with him off Chile.

The second member was Commodore Stephen Decatur, who also had distinguished himself in the Mediterranean Sea against the Barbary pirates. During the late war with Britain, he had attacked and captured the Royal Navy's HMS *Macedonian*, further solidifying his fame. When that conflict ended, he returned to the Mediterranean with a naval squadron, forcing the Barbary Powers to renew their peace treaties with the United States, which they had broken.

The third and senior-most member was Commodore John Rodgers, mistaken as the brother of Moses by the Liverpool newspapers.

While Commodore Rodgers could not claim outright victory over a major Royal Navy warship during the late conflict, he had, nevertheless, inflicted damage that was equally compelling. By the end of hostilities, he had either destroyed or captured 23 British vessels, which was a record, and lost not a single man-of-war under his command. The Commodore's feats at sea were enough to generate a song in his name, "Rodgers and Victory," sung to the tune of "Yankee Doodle." Because he had one of the longest records of service (since 1799), Rodgers had been named the president of the Navy Board immediately upon its creation.

Commodore Rodgers also had something else besides seniority that made him a logical fit for the Board's presidency: he both looked and acted the part. With a sturdy physique, close-cropped dark hair, and a strong face which exuded discipline, the Commodore impressed many with both his natural sense of command and correct deportment as a high official.

John Rodgers.

It didn't take long for such a personality to make his interests known. Once the Navy Board became operational in 1815, Commodore Rodgers reviewed the various laws passed by Congress relating to the service's management, and came to an important conclusion: the civilian Secretary of the Navy was no longer necessary. Since Congress had empowered the new Board to discharge virtually the same duties as the Secretary, the Commodore argued that any remaining powers ought to be transferred to the Board, effectively demoting the civilian Secretary to that of a bystander.

But the Navy Secretary at the time, Benjamin Crowninshield of Massachusetts, would have none of it. He appealed directly to President James Madison, asking him to rule whether "the Board . . . shall control the Secretary, or the Secretary shall control the Board."

Madison decided in favor of continued civilian control. The Secretary of the Navy, acting on the President's directives, would issue the orders. It was then up to the Board of Navy Commissioners to carry them out.

When Secretary Crowninshield announced that he was resigning his post in 1818, the question of a successor weighed greatly upon President James Monroe. The President initially asked Commodore Rodgers if he would accept the position. But the Commodore, upon learning that he would have to resign both the Board presidency and his commission in the Navy in order to serve as a civilian, declined the offer.

Someone else would have to be approached. It was well-understood within government circles that the President wanted "harmony" in the department, so finding a replacement who met the Board's approval was of great importance.

In the end, New York State Supreme Court Chief Justice Smith Thompson was settled upon, in part because President Monroe so valued geographic balance within his sphere of appointments. But beyond being a Northerner, this new Navy Secretary also became the first in a long line of appointees who shared one unusual characteristic: Smith Thompson had no practical experience whatsoever with the sea.

Even so, Thompson was not afraid to remind the Board about who was giving the orders. In June of 1819, some three months after Congress had passed the new act for combating piracy, the Secretary had told Commodore Rodgers point-blank that "you will observe that the execution of the law is under the discretion of the President, so far as respects the employing of our public vessels. Your conduct will therefore be regulated by your instructions. . ."

The procurement of warships, however, was a much more complicated task. Given the technicalities involved, the Board had to take the lead.

With regard to the three steam batteries authorized by Congress, it had done just that. Starting in late 1818, while the *Savannah* was being built, the Board had begun to advance the batteries' construction, maintaining a fairly even tempo through most of the following year.

But on December 7th, 1819, that tempo changed. Appearing in the *City of Washington Gazette* that day was a brief story from Baltimore, where a recently-arrived merchant brig reported that the steamship *Savannah* was headed home from Russia. At the least, this was known; at the most, word had reached Washington that the steamship was already safely back in Georgia.

That same day, the Board of Navy Commissioners got very busy.

With contracts already organized for two steam battery engines and two sets of oak frame timbers, a letter was sent out regarding plans for the third authorized vessel:

> Naval Commissioners Office
> 7 Decr 1819.
>
> Sir,
>
> The Commissioners of the Navy will contract with you for the frame of one steam battery, for which they will allow you one Dollar + forty five cents per cubic foot on delivery at such yard as they may hereafter designate, in the course of the ensuing year.
> If you accept this offer be pleased so to inform the Board by return of mail– + you may proceed immediately to get out the timber. On hearing from you a formal contract will be transmitted to the nearest navy agent for your signature + a set of moulds will be sent by the first opportunity.
> Respectfully
> John Rodgers
>
> Hugh Lindsay esqr
> St. Mary's
> Geo^a

But what about Thomas Vinson? That merchant, from Martha's Vineyard, Massachusetts, had already answered the public advertisement seeking contract bids for the third steam battery's live oak frame. Vinson had offered to deliver the timbers for less, at $1.42½ per cubic foot. And the Navy Board had promptly accepted his offer, on November 12th, and invited him to visit Washington to close the contract "as early as may suit your convenience."

But the Board nixed this previous arrangement on December 7th. Writing to Vinson, Commodore Rodgers stated that "presuming from your silence that you have declined entering into contract" for the third frame, the Board had decided to offer the business to someone else. The Commodore further informed the Massachusetts merchant that "they would have waited a few days longer" to hear from him, but the tree-cutting season down South, where the live oak grew, "was already so far advanced as to forbid" the Board's waiting any longer. That was because the Board wanted the timbers "got out during the present season."

That same December 7th, the Board also sent off a letter to Francis B. Ogden, the superintendent of steam machinery at the Brooklyn Navy Yard. Ogden was informed that he was about to be "punished" with alterations to his and Eckford's previously submitted steam battery design.

The Board also sent off a memorandum to Secretary Thompson, updating him with a list of Navy contracts recently signed. Sandwiched in with agreements to purchase beef, "gun carriage stuff," and other supplies, were the orders for the first two sets of steam battery frames. Those contracts for live oak had been made with a man named Thomas Newell, of Savannah, Georgia.

Two days later, on December 9th, while Moses and the *Savannah* were still en route to Washington, the Board made good on its promise to Francis B. Ogden (who happened to be a nephew of the Monopoly's Aaron Ogden). They sent to him their revised set of hull dimensions for Eckford's new steam battery design. They also fired off a memo to William Doughty, the Naval Constructor at the Washington Navy Yard, instructing him to "estimate in detail" the amount of pine planking and beams that would be needed for the Board's revised design.

By December 13th, Doughty had delivered the new figures. With this information in hand, the Board promptly sent off another letter to Georgia contractor Hugh Lindsay. They offered him yet another contract, this time for the pine planking and beams needed for the steam batteries. The Board further proposed that Lindsay provide this particular timber for not one or two steam batteries, but all three of them. After providing pricing terms, as well as complete specifications for the wood to be delivered, Commodore Rodgers closed with a polite encouragement:

You will be pleased to inform us by return of mail, whether you will accept this offer or not – If you decline we shall immediately contract with some other person – The trees must all be felled this winter.

In the meantime, the Board received a letter from Thomas Vinson of Martha's Vineyard, dated December 2nd. Vinson advised them that, having received their original acceptance letter of November 12th for the third steam battery's frame, he was prepared to follow through:

I had contemplated immediately visiting Washington, but as you have been pleased to state that I may visit your city in order to close the contract "as early as may suit my convenience" I propose making some arrangements relative to that business only, and being at Washington in a few weeks at farthest—say in thirty days—

Given mail delivery times, it was clear that Vinson's December 2nd letter acknowledging the contract and the Board's December 7th letter rescinding it had passed each other in transit. If Thomas Vinson left Martha's Vineyard prior to receiving the Board's follow-on letter, he would show up in Washington with no contract to sign. And if Georgian Hugh Lindsay had not accepted the live oak contract yanked from Vinson by then, the Board would find itself in a very awkward position.

Without a doubt, funding for a steam Navy remained available, and very fluid.

* * *

On the morning after Christmas, the wharves down in Savannah came back to life.

Among the vessels preparing to depart that Sunday was one of the Steam Boat Company of Georgia's packets, making its regular run upriver to the city of Augusta, some 120 miles to the northwest.

Once everything was ready, the crew cast off, and the wheels were set in motion. Slowly, the steamboat pulled away from the wharves, and began its journey up the Savannah River. Along for the trip, besides the usual assortment of cargo and mail, was one extra-ordinary and very unhappy passenger: Stephen Vail, of the Speedwell Iron Works.

At the same time Moses and his creation had been heading north toward Washington, Vail had been sailing south to Savannah. The two had passed each other somewhere below the entrance into the Chesapeake Bay.

Arriving in Savannah on the evening of December 16th (just as the steamship was tying up at Washington), Vail was trapped on board his transport for the night, due to a very hard rainstorm. It was not until 10 o'clock the next morning that he finally was able to go ashore.

Vail immediately went to see Sheldon C. Dunning, whose need for a sawmill steam engine had originally brought him to Savannah, back in late 1817. The purpose of Vail's call was simple. The two promissory notes issued by Pott & McKinne for the work Speedwell had done on the steamship remained unpaid. Vail had not sold them on to anyone else, and when they came due, Pott & McKinne could not deliver payment. Having gotten nowhere with the New York agents of the Savannah Steam Ship Company, Vail decided to approach the other shareholders.

Sheldon Dunning was sympathetic. "He treated Me verry well," wrote Vail to his wife Bethiah, "and promised to do all he can to aid Me in getting My Pay..."

Beyond a promise, though, there was not much Dunning could do. He was, after all, but one shareholder in the Company. Everyone already had paid in their committed capital. The money had been sent to Pott & McKinne, who then paid the bills as the Company's agent. Pott & McKinne had gone belly-up. *They* were the ones responsible. Getting *all* of the shareholders to commit to putting in more money was a tall order when they could justifiably point the finger at their agent.

The prospects for getting paid were clear enough to Vail. "I have My doubts...," he wrote to Bethiah, "but May be mistaken."

On the positive side, Vail did learn that Captain Rogers had taken the steamship to Washington to sell it—if he succeeded, the proceeds could easily pay the outstanding debt. Vail responded to this news by immediately writing to Rogers, explaining the problem.

Vail spent a week trying and failing to get satisfaction from "the Company." So the day after Christmas, he decided to quit Savannah, and go to Augusta. Once there, Vail would catch a stagecoach heading north, and keep on going until he reached the nation's capital.

* * *

On December 27th, the Monday after Christmas, the Board of Navy Commissioners took stock of the situation before them.

On the one hand, the *National Intelligencer*'s Christmas Day editorial—endorsing a government purchase of the *Savannah*—was still fresh in everyone's mind.

On the other hand, the Navy's plan for building the steam batteries remained incomplete, and therefore, uncertain.

With these dynamics in play, the Board went back to work.

Fortunately, prospective contractor Thomas Vinson had not left Martha's Vineyard before receiving the Board's December 7th letter. Nevertheless, their notice that they were canceling his contract for the third steam battery's frame must have sent Vinson through the roof. He had immediately sent a reply, which, for some reason, did not make it into the Commissioners' bound volumes of letters received. No doubt Vinson spit back at the Board their original words on when he should come to close the contract: "as early as may suit your convenience."

The Board tried to explain its actions in a reply that Monday. Their public advertisement for the third battery's frame, they said, had resulted in several proposals from which to choose. The Commissioners told Vinson that they had "entertained hopes at that time that altho' you had offered for two frames you would contract for one." Hearing no reply from Vinson by December 7th, they decided to offer the contract to Mr. Hugh Lindsay, of St. Mary's, Georgia. "Whether he will accept it, is uncertain," Commodore Rodgers explained, and "if he should decline it, we shall then have it in our power to renew the offer to you."

If, however, Mr. Lindsay *did* accept, there were no more steam battery frame contracts available—all three authorized by law would have been spoken for. "It is possible however," continued the Commodore, "that provision may be made this session of Congress for procuring the frames of sloops of war + schooners." If that happened, Rodgers promised Vinson that the Board would be disposed to doing business with him on *those* contracts.

That same Monday, another letter was sent off to Hugh Lindsay, reminding him of the Board's December 7th contract offer for the third frame:

They have as yet received no answer from you – They will wait the return of this mail for an answer, + if they should not then receive one they will proceed to contract with another person.

That fire lit under Lindsay, the Board turned its attention on Tuesday to Thomas Newell of Savannah, who had the contract for the first two steam battery frames. Commodore Rodgers sent him a letter advising that a man from the Navy was on his way to Georgia to oversee the molding of the timbers to the design specifications. Once completed, the frames were to be sent to New York. Left unsaid, but obviously implied, were the Board's previous instructions: cut the trees now, get moving.

For the balance of the week, the Board tied up other loose ends on Newell's contract for the first two frames. They wrote to Navy Agent J. P. Henry in Savannah, advising him to provide funds to the man heading south to oversee the molding of the timbers. They also wrote to the Navy Agent at New York, advising him to accept the frames upon delivery. Finally, on Friday, December 31st, they sent an order to Commodore Thomas Tingey of the Washington Navy Yard, instructing him to ship the timber molds to Savannah "as early as possible."

It had been a very busy December for the Navy Board. A lot of progress had been made on the three steam batteries authorized by Congress. Henry Eckford's design drawings had been modified to the Board's liking. And all of the preparations needed to carry out the contracts on the first two battery frames were in place. Without a doubt, the Board had made far more headway on building the steam batteries in that final month of 1819 than in any other month since Congress had authorized their construction.

Still, there remained much work to be done.

Hugh Lindsay of St. Mary's, Georgia had yet to respond to the offer to contract for the third steam battery's frame, as well as the planking and beams for all three batteries.

Steam superintendent Francis B. Ogden still had to reconcile the Board's new hull design with the engines being built by Robert McQueen & Company.

And on top of all this, as well as the other duties of running a navy of sail, the Board also had to prepare itself for what was an annual ritual in Washington: questions from Congress.

* * *

What Moses Rogers was doing in the days after Christmas, and into the first days of 1820, isn't precisely known. All the publicity and press the steamship *Savannah* and her captain had received over the last year and a half made him close to a household name throughout much of the country. Since the *National Intelligencer* was considered by many to be President Monroe's mouthpiece, their Christmas Day editorial on the *Savannah*'s behalf should have helped to open many a door.

Calling upon the Navy Board should have been easy enough. But first, it would be necessary to get past any gatekeeper. In the Board's case, this consisted of a secretary, who kept the clerks busy and the office running smoothly. The holder of this position at the end of 1819 was a man named James K. Paulding.

He had quite a history when it came to steam.

It was Paulding, along with brothers-in-law William and Washington Irving, who had started the satirical magazine *Salmagundi* in New York City, back in 1807.

It was Paulding, along with the Irvings, who had drawn, quartered and roasted Robert Fulton over and over again, in the months leading up to his creation of the new mode of transport.

And it was Paulding who subsequently landed a job with the Board, and enjoyed, in William Irving's view, "a very happy, independent life among" the "magnificos," as Paulding sometimes called the Navy Commissioners.

In light of Paulding's past, and in view of the Board's accelerating activities on the steam batteries, making any headway with them would have been a very difficult task.

The other option was to go over their heads to their civilian superior, Smith Thompson. This too probably proved fruitless, especially in light of the Navy Secretary's December 28th reply to the offer by Jasper Lynch (and the Ocean Steam Ship Company) to sell their own nearly-completed steam giant:

> ... the government is not in want of such a vessel, as you have described, nor does any authority exist, that would warrant the purchase.

While Secretary Thompson's first reason for rejecting the enormous and untested steamship *Robert Fulton* was debatable, there was no getting around his second reason. The authority to buy a steamship

could come from only one place. If an argument could be made successfully on the *Savannah*'s behalf, it would have to be done in the
halls of Congress.

* * *

Making the rounds in the Capitol building, and the boardinghouses
that surrounded it, would have taken some time. If the intended recipient of a visit was not there, etiquette dictated that a calling card be
left. This obviously served as notice that someone had come calling,
and under the unwritten rules of the American capital, the receiver
was supposed to return the call.

Beyond these simple mechanics for making calls on members of
Congress was the inevitable but necessary prioritizing of visitors that
resulted. Since Congress was only in session from late autumn until
spring, anyone who had business with the federal government—from
contractors, to petitioners, to job applicants, to relief seekers—had to
be in Washington City at the same time. This meant that from the
moment Moses set foot in the District of Columbia, he found himself
to be but one person amongst a multitude trying to get the attention
of some 180-plus representatives and 44 senators.

Besides this, members of Congress had priorities of their own. As
the session entered the new year of 1820, the growing debate over one
important issue seemingly began to overwhelm all others before both
houses. The speeches, jabs and perceived slanders were becoming
more hostile by the day, and when and how they would stop, no one
could be sure.

The battle lines drawn were not between the majority Democratic-
Republicans and the minority Federalists, per se. Instead, the developing schism ran straight across America, dividing the country into North
and South. In the minds of those who lived it, describing this controversy, which was beginning to shake the nation's capital to its very foundation, could be readily achieved by uttering just one simple name—
Missouri.

* * *

By the end of 1819, the United States had come a long way from
its original incarnation, which had taken shape from the Declaration
of Independence in 1776 to the Bill of Rights in 1791. The ideals of
individual liberty and limited, transparent self-government enshrined

in the country's founding documents already had served as a beacon for those who wished to follow, from Europe to South America.

There was, however, one especially glaring contradiction to those ideals, as espoused by the country's founders, and that was the continuing institution of slavery.

This scourge had sullied and scarred the world since the beginning of recorded human history, but starting in the late 18th century, voices in Europe and North America began calling for its abolition.

When America's founding generation debated slavery's place in the proposed Constitution, the need for absolute unity in the face of external threats won out over the desire for absolute ideals. The result was compromise. The new Constitution allowed States that kept slavery to count part of their slave populations toward their census figures. This "three-fifths" rule had the effect of increasing the slave States' representation, and political power, in the House of Representatives and the Electoral College. It was further decreed in the Constitution that no abolition of the slave trade would be allowed for a period of twenty years.

This compromise did not sit well with a small but vocal group of anti-slavery advocates in the North. They organized, grew, and promoted the abolition of slavery at the State level, succeeding in gradually ending the practice wherever they mustered sufficient clout.

In 1807, as soon as the Constitution allowed, Congress passed a law banning the importation of any more slaves. Its provisions were far from flawless, and enforcing the ban against smuggling was difficult, but nevertheless, an important first step had been taken.

Add to it all of the States above the Mason-Dixon line that passed laws gradually emancipating their slaves, and by the year 1815, the shape of the die had been cast. The North was free; and the South was slave.

Once the second war with Britain had ended, the country officially began expanding again. As it did, the perceived balance between free and slave States had to be maintained, at least as far as the pro-slavers were concerned.

Free-State Indiana gained admission in 1816.

Then came slave-State Mississippi in 1817.

Free-State Illinois got the nod in 1818.

Then came slave-State Alabama, just admitted to the Union on December 14th, 1819.

According to petitions before Congress, Maine was next in line, to be admitted as a free State. Then it would be Missouri's turn, as a slave State.

Therein lay the rub. From the anti-slavery perspective, Missouri's admission as a slave State had to be stopped. If it wasn't, then slavery would have spread west of the Mississippi River, which was unacceptable.

The pro-slavery forces countered that Louisiana was on the other side of that great river, and there had been no big fuss when *it* joined the Union as a slave State, back in 1812.

The State of Louisiana was different, replied the anti-slavers, since there was no United States directly to *its* west—that remained Spanish Mexico. But there was plenty of unsettled American land to the west of Missouri, that being the remainder of the Louisiana Purchase. If Missouri became a slave State, then it would be far harder to resist attempts to admit the rest of the Great Plains on the same basis.

When Missouri's bid for admission was put before Congress in early 1819, the bill was amended by the House of Representatives to make Missouri a free State. The Senate, in turn, rejected this modified bill. With adjournment soon thereafter, the 15th Congress left the matter for the next set of legislators.

These first votes over Missouri's admission generated little reaction from either the press or the public, leading many to believe the issue could be readily resolved.

But as the spring planting season came to an end, the true meaning of Missouri became clearer and clearer to those who actively opposed the evil institution. And once the stakes were realized, something incredible happened: anti-slavery forces began to mobilize.

First in New Jersey, and then New York and Pennsylvania, they organized public meetings at which they called for the prohibition of slavery in Missouri. These initial gatherings through the summer of 1819 started a chain reaction of anti-slavery petition drives in the North, and pro-slavery replies over much of the South.

By the time the 16th Congress convened, on December 6th, 1819, the line in the sand had been drawn.

And by the very beginning of 1820, the two sides—having sized up one another—were just taking their first steps up to that line.

* * *

Beyond the increasing acrimony over Missouri's admission, there still remained plenty of other business for the Congress to consider.

One such example was the Navy's supplemental spending bill to cover the costs of ongoing operations, including fighting piracy. It had passed the House on Thursday, December 30th, after which it was immediately sent on to the Senate.

That this bill moved so readily through the Congress—especially after the Treasury Department had projected such a massive budget deficit—spoke volumes about how strongly members felt that more needed to be done to fight piracy. Two days after the Navy's supplemental bill passed the House, the sense of urgency grew further still.

On Saturday, January 1st, 1820, the *National Intelligencer* published the petition that the Boston insurers had sent to President Monroe. This included the entire list of 44 piracies the insurers had attached to their petition, the whole of which took up one and a half columns in the newspaper. Coming as it did precisely one week after the Christmas Day editorial promoting a government purchase of the *Savannah*, this New Year's message was unmistakable. The *National Intelligencer*, pulpit of President James Monroe, believed something dramatic had to be done.

The something that could be done became readily apparent the following Monday, January 3rd, when the Senate received a report from the Navy Board listing all of the contracts the Navy had signed the previous year. Among the several contractors listed for the steam batteries was Thomas Newell of Savannah. But he was only cited for his agreement to provide live oak frames for two of the three authorized steam batteries. A contract for the third frame was nowhere to be seen on the list.

And therein lay the opportunity. The lack of a third timber frame contract left open the possibility that Congress could divert money authorized for the third steam battery to a purchase of the *Savannah*. Rather than waiting a year or more for the completion of a steam battery of limited use, the Navy could have a steamship of proven capability ready for outfitting immediately, and patrolling the sea lanes by springtime.

But according to a newly published booklet, the *Register*, the Navy didn't need a steamship, because it already had one!

The authority of the *Register* was hard to dismiss. Its publisher, Davis & Force of Pennsylvania Avenue, had a government contract to print and deliver this federal information directory by the beginning of the new year. Unfortunately, Davis & Force had run out of typeface, and needed a few extra days to finish the printing. But around the end of the first week of January, their *Register* was printed, and available to members of Congress. (Soon thereafter, a commercial version, called the *National Calendar*, was also printed and available.)

The importance of the *Register* was undeniable, for it was the most comprehensive directory of the federal government available. The *Register* listed all of the members of Congress and their committee assignments. It also listed all of the officials throughout the executive branch, down to the messengers, "the whole prepared from official papers, and information obtained at the proper departments and offices."

In addition to listing government officials, the *Register* further contained a roster of active-duty Navy officers. On page 78, for all to see, was Captain Joseph Bainbridge, who was listed as commander of the great steam-powered harbor-protector, the *Fulton*. But instead of calling this vessel a "Steam Battery," which it was by design, or a "Steam Frigate," which it was sometimes called due to its auxiliary sail rigging, the *Fulton* was suddenly being described as a "Steam Ship."

It had never been called that before. The description was all the more curious since buried further back in the *Register*, the old "Steam Frigate" designation was still used in the section listing junior officers assigned to the *Fulton*. Given the source of the publisher's information, the "Steam Ship" entry on page 78 left little doubt that someone was trying to send a message.

In the meantime, Congress had its own communications to send. On Wednesday, January 5th, Congressman Tunstall Quarles of Kentucky rose in the House to make a motion, which passed on a voice vote:

> Resolved, That the Committee on Naval Affairs be instructed to enquire into the expediency of suspending, for a limited time, so much of the standing appropriation of one million of dollars for the increase of the Navy, as may be consistent with the public service; and also enquire whether any other reduction of the expenses of the Navy can be made, consistent with the public service.

The economic depression and its effect on the government's finances had finally come to action, or at least "enquiries."

This, however, was just the opening shot.

The following Monday, January 10th, Congressman Timothy Fuller rose to speak in the House. He represented the Fourth District of Massachusetts, which included the Boston suburb of Cambridge. Unlike his Federalist colleague, Jonathan Mason, who represented Boston proper, Fuller was a member of the majority Democratic-Republicans.

Given the floor, Fuller offered his own motion, which also passed on a voice vote:

> Resolved, That the Committee on Naval Affairs be instructed to consider the expediency of so modifying the act establishing a Board of Commissioners of the Navy, as to make the Secretary of the Navy, for the time being, the presiding officer of that board: *And, also*, of so limiting the tenor of the commissions of the members thereof, as to secure the accumulating experience and talents of our naval commanders in that department, by a periodical rotation in office.

The underlying meaning of Fuller's motion, and its approval, was obvious to any informed observer: the Massachusetts Congressman and his fellow members thought the three commodores who made up the Navy Board—Rodgers, Decatur, and Porter—had too much leverage.

It was an eyebrow-arching turn of events. Within the short space of six days, the Board of Navy Commissioners suddenly found its power the target of a two-pronged political assault from that body closest to the people: the House of Representatives of the United States.

CHAPTER TWENTY

THE VISE TIGHTENS

WHILE NO ONE knew precisely *how* the fire started, there was no argument over *where* it started.

In the early morning hours of Tuesday, January 11th, 1820, the first flickerings came to life in Mr. Boon's livery stable, which was just behind Mrs. Platt's boardinghouse, on Jefferson Street. If the smell— or the sight of lights dancing in the shadows—did not alert those who were charged with keeping watch, then the ensuing screams of the horses surely did.

The sentries on duty raised the alarm in the usual way, ringing their bells and calling out the location of the fire. Since the men who served in the various fire and axe companies came from all parts of Savannah's populace, it was vitally important that the call to action be spread quickly throughout the city. Under the circumstances, it would have been hard to sleep through all the noise, especially as the roar of the fire, and the urgency of the cries, grew louder.

By the time the half-dozen or so fire companies had organized, strong and steady winds from the west-northwest had already pushed the fire beyond its starting point, and toward the Public Market at Ellis Square. Orange-hot cinders were being blown even further away, landing on top of wood-shingle roofs that had been parched by years of Southern sun. The nearly complete lack of rain through the autumn made every wooden structure even drier still, turning the city of Savannah into a virtual tinderbox.

The fire companies quickly pulled their wagons into Ellis Square, and began pumping water onto the blaze. Reinforcing them were scores more, who formed bucket lines leading from water source to target. Despite the pandemonium, the concentration of forces against the leading edges of the enemy seemed to work. The fire soon appeared to be on the verge of containment.

Then, suddenly, the whole of Ellis Square was rocked by an enormous explosion. One of the burning buildings fronting on the Square immediately disintegrated into a ball of sparks and splinters. The blast sent an earth-shaking shock wave pulsing through the city, causing both firefighters and bystanders to rear back in horror.

Before there was time to recover, a second blast shattered the air, sending still more glowing debris and cinders aloft. There was only one thing which could cause such explosions, and that was gunpowder, stored illegally in the city's center.

These massive eruptions immediately wiped out whatever progress the firefighters had made in containing the blaze. So they fell back, demoralized, taking some barrels of unexploded gunpowder with them, which were dumped down a well in nearby St. James Square.

Throughout the rest of Savannah, the explosions transformed people's emotions in an instant, from concern to shock, quickly followed by fear. The force of the gunpowder blasts shattered windows all over town, the glass shards falling thick onto those standing nearby. Residents some distance from the main disaster began unhinging all their shutters, and placing buckets of water at each window, to douse any falling cinders that might endanger their homes.

For those much closer to the oncoming storm, there seemed but one salvation: the Squares.

Hundreds of people living on Johnson Square and Reynolds Square frantically began hauling every imaginable possession out of their homes, and placing them within the little parks. As the conflagration spread south toward Broughton Street, those who lived in the apparent fire-track also took to the nearby Squares, piling their belongings up into great heaps as fast as they could.

The tremendous noise of the gunpowder blasts did have one small consolation, which was to alert the mariners dozing aboard their vessels along the river that this was no ordinary emergency. Scores of seamen soon began streaming up the sandy cliff to stiffen the resistance. A defensive line was formed along Broughton Street, to keep the main blaze from spreading further south, and hundreds of others set about trying to save several prominent buildings in the fire's path.

Through the rest of the night and into the light hours of morning, the inhabitants labored to smother the flames and slowly bring the destruction to a halt. By early Tuesday afternoon, some 12 hours after the alarm had been raised, the last of the fires was out.

For those who witnessed it, the resulting scene looked like a nightmare. From the eastern edge of Franklin Square, through Ellis and Johnson Squares, and continuing to the edge of Reynolds Square, the city had been burnt to the ground. The only intact structures of note in this stretch were Washington Hall, the Episcopal Church, and the State and Planters' Banks, all saved thanks to the combined exertions of seamen and firemen.

Nearly five blocks of merchant offices, stores and warehouses fronting on the Bay were gone, and scattered throughout the city were individual houses that had been destroyed or damaged by floating cinders. In all, 321 wooden buildings had been consumed, and 35 brick buildings had been burned through, their contents left in ashes. Because many houses in Savannah were double tenements, the total number of households destroyed was even higher. Some 463 residences were reckoned to have been ruined, leaving hundreds upon hundreds of people homeless.

By some minor miracle, the whole of the catastrophe had killed only two people, plus nearly a dozen horses that had been trapped at Boon's stable. But it was the enormous material damage that shook people the most. Many of the city's largest merchants had suffered enormous losses.

This included some of the steamship *Savannah*'s shareholders. Andrew Low & Company's brick store had burned, even though it was thought to be fireproof. Sheldon C. Dunning's store also was destroyed, and Isaac Minis lost property, as well. William Gillett's company and several Habersham enterprises also lost either buildings or merchandise.

In the days immediately following the fire, the Savannah City Council met repeatedly, to receive reports of the damage and determine what actions to take. The disaster left them with a variety of problems which had to be addressed, no matter how uncomfortable the circumstances.

One of the Council's first actions was to order a search of all buildings and shipping for stolen goods, which soon led to a jail bulging with the accused.

Then the violators of the gunpowder ordinance had to be confronted.

A committee had to be formed to come up with a plan for temporary buildings.

And the Public Market at Ellis Square, which was completely destroyed, had to be moved eight blocks inland, to the intersection of South Broad and Bull Streets.

With each of these steps, the Council sought to achieve a return to normalcy as swiftly as possible, despite the devastation.

Private citizens also pitched in to help, opening their homes to friends and neighbors who had lost everything. A transplanted New York baker, Philip Brasch, offered bread free of charge to anyone burnt out by the fire who was unable to afford it. A number of local planters also pitched in, donating corn, rice and beef, to be distributed to those in need.

Businesses improvised, and re-opened as best they could. *The Georgian*, like the other newspapers, lost its establishment to the flames, so editor John Harney had to stitch his operations back together: a new office at Mrs. Gribbin's boardinghouse on the corner of Bay and Lincoln, a letter box at the Exchange, and a printing press set up on the outskirts of the city. Andrew Low & Company opened a temporary office in partner James McHenry's home on Wright Square, and moved what surviving merchandise they had to an undamaged brick store opposite their own.

While these private and public efforts formed the beginnings of recovery, it was obvious that Savannah could not cope with this catastrophe alone. The devastation was just too much to handle. The isolation of the city—from the rest of Georgia, and the country at large—only heightened the Council's belief that they had to seek assistance.

So they approved a petition to the Governor, asking him to call a special session of the State Legislature, at which, they hoped, steps would be taken to aid the sufferers and promote the construction of fire-proof buildings. The Council also accepted an offer by a local merchant, Dr. Joshua E. White, to travel the country and solicit donations for the sufferers.

But within a few days, sentiment on Dr. White's proposal changed. The idea that someone was to be sent out panhandling for money did not sit right with a lot of the public, and the Council withdrew their approval.

Instead, the people of Savannah chose to put their trust in their new mayor, Thomas U. P. Charlton. Two days after the fire, he wrote an open letter, entitled an "Address to the Mayors & Intendants of the United States." In this address, Mayor Charlton informed the nation of the city's tragedy, estimating the total loss at over $4,000,000, making it the most destructive city fire the United States had ever seen. He also asked his fellow Americans for help.

This letter was soon on its way, by land and by sea, to the far reaches of the country. In the days that immediately followed, the people of Savannah could do little more than cope as best they could, and hope that their mayor's plea might eventually elicit some kind of response.

* * *

Some 550 miles to the north, in Washington, Congress was still grappling with the projected budget shortfall for 1820, and figuring out ways to address it.

As far as cuts in the Navy budget were concerned, the service's supporters were beginning to come to the rescue. "We view with feelings of regret and astonishment," opined Baltimore's *Federal Republican*, "any advances made in Congress for the impeding or paralyzing the progress of our little fleet." More such editorials in defense of the Navy soon followed.

With this underpinning of support, the Board of Navy Commissioners offered their own reply to the House resolution asking whether budget cuts could be made "without detriment to the public service." In a letter dated January 17th, Commodore John Rodgers pointed out that "all the live oak necessary for the frames and other parts required for the completion of the ships authorized by law, has been contracted for." So had the greater part of the white oak and pine timber needed for construction. Furthermore, that timber not yet delivered was already in the process of being cut. If all this wood was not used quickly, the Board knew "from past experience" that most of it would quickly rot and warp, as it lay exposed to the elements.

The only solution to this last problem would be to build storehouses to preserve any unused timber. And if the construction of vessels in the stocks was halted, then shelters would have to be built over them, too. This would require additional time, money, and personnel. Under the circumstances, Commodore Rodgers' conclusion was not surprising:

The commissioners are induced to believe that, on the score of economy alone, the building of the ships should not be suspended; in which case, the sum appropriated will be necessary, and will not bear to be diminished.

Navy Secretary Smith Thompson, in passing the Board's reply along to the House Committee on Naval Affairs, attached his own letter, promising to do everything in his power to see that "the best mode of economy" was practiced by his department.

Within the Navy Board's offices, organizing construction for the third steam battery was still not settled, but some of the pieces were beginning to fall into place.

Thomas Vinson of Martha's Vineyard had written back regarding his cancelled contract for the frame, telling the Board that "if Mr. Lindsay does not accept your offer, I will rely on you again offering it to me." Otherwise, Vinson wrote, he would settle for furnishing the timber for other vessels of war, as the Board had suggested.

Fortunately, Hugh Lindsay of Georgia finally had replied to the December 7th offer to provide the third steam battery's frame. The Board's proposal of $1.45 per cubic foot was accepted. Still, Lindsay's letter made no mention of the additional contract offered for the planking and beams for all three batteries. His reply to that proposal, either yea or nay, was presumably still in the mail.

Despite the Board's private actions, and their public reply to the House enquiry, the intrusive skepticism emanating from Capitol Hill failed to dissipate. Upon receiving the Navy's warnings about warping timbers if appropriations were cut, the House took a different tack. Replacing the permanently-established Naval Affairs Committee as inquisitor was a temporarily-formed Select Committee, tasked with addressing "the navy, naval depots, and the protection of our commerce upon the ocean."

The chairman of this Select Committee was Congressman Nathaniel Silsbee of Massachusetts. A Democratic-Republican, Silsbee represented the Second District of the Bay State, which stretched from just north of Federalist-held Boston to the ports of Salem and Gloucester. Like many of his constituents, Silsbee was a mariner, ship owner and merchant, and accordingly would be very concerned about "the protection of our commerce upon the ocean."

The introduction of Nathaniel Silsbee to the debate, together with neighboring legislator Timothy Fuller's prior resolution challenging the Navy Board's structure, exposed a subtle yet unmistakable fact: the strength of the assault on the Board's power was coming from Massachusetts. And the majority-party members leading the charge from within that State's delegation surrounded the port of Boston, and the insurers who were pleading for help against the pirates.

Chairman Silsbee wasted no time. On the same day his committee received the Navy's response to cost-cutting, he sent a counter-reply. In it, the Congressman asked a lot of very specific questions about the status of the Navy's shipbuilding program and overall budget. From queries about material and labor costs for sailing ships under construction, to the monies spent for transportation and recruiting, Silsbee's letter made it quite clear that, as far as he was concerned, every expenditure was on the table.

Having laid out all of his questions regarding the old Navy, Congressman Silsbee then finished with one final probe regarding the new Navy:

Query 11th: What expenses have been incurred in procuring steam engines, and the imperishable materials necessary for building and equipping three steam batteries?

* * *

Down in Savannah, as the local government and private citizens tried to contend with the effects of the great fire, they gradually began receiving responses to Mayor Charlton's call for help.

Especially heartening was the reaction from their commercial rival some 90 miles to the north. The city of Charleston, upon receiving news of the disaster, quickly set to work getting organized. On Saturday, January 15th, the Charleston City Council held a public meeting, at which it was resolved to raise $10,000 for the Savannah sufferers. Private groups, such as the officers of the local naval station, also pitched in, taking up their own collections and sending the monies on. The Charleston Theatre did one better, putting on a benefit concert which raised $330 for the victims. Further up the coast, the port of Georgetown, South Carolina gathered $1,017 more in donations.

Fellow Georgians also answered the call. Augusta's inhabitants quickly gathered $6,885 for the sufferers. Governor John Clark, presiding over a State budget wounded by the depression, decided not to call a special session of the Legislature, but instead sent $10,000 in emergency government funds. Citizens of the State capital, Milledgeville, added still more, contributing $1,794, plus twenty barrels of flour. Many other small towns all over Georgia also answered Mayor Charlton's call, by gathering what money they could and sending it along. Among the many individuals who helped was Henry J. Finn, the actor who had traveled on the steamship *Savannah*—he personally sent $50 from Augusta, where his theater troupe was playing.

As donations began arriving, Savannah's Council had to decide how to divvy them up. On the same day Mayor Charlton had written his appeal to the nation, the Council had passed a resolution clarifying their intention that any donations "be exclusively applied to the assistance, relief and comfort, of those most in want of the aid." Any victims with other means need not apply.

The aid that flowed in from Georgia and neighboring South Carolina was gratefully acknowledged by Mayor Charlton, but it was a mere trifle compared to the damage done. More help was needed. Whether it would be forthcoming from elsewhere in the Union remained an unknown in the days after the great fire. All the people of Savannah could do was wait, and hope.

* * *

Up in Washington, the mood was decidedly different. Congress found itself increasingly consumed by anger and ill-will.

"No two people seem to care a single straw for one another," wrote Congressman John Randolph of Virginia, "+ all fearing the 'effeck' of any 'movement' they may make."

Despite the pressures brought on by the depression, the primary source for the rancor was clear. "Missouri is the only word ever repeated here by the politician," averred Congressman John Tyler, also from Virginia. Speaker of the House Henry Clay had to agree, writing to a friend that "the Missouri subject monopolizes all our conversation, all our thoughts and for three weeks at least to come will all our time. No body seems to think or care about any thing else."

From the Senate's perspective, this question over Missouri's status—free or slave—meant that Maine's impending admittance as a free State was in jeopardy. After all, Maine was actually next in line for Statehood.

So by a bare majority, the Senate declared that if the free-slave, back-and-forth formula was to be maintained, then Maine could *only* enter the Union as a free State *if* Missouri was approved as a slave State. In other words, the slavers wanted to hold Maine a hostage until their opponents capitulated over Missouri.

The resulting atmosphere on Capitol Hill was mind-altering. "The appearance of the Senate to-day," declared North Carolina's Nathaniel Macon on January 13th, "is different from anything I have seen since I have been a member of it. It is the greatness of the question which has produced it."

Virtually everyone else in Washington seemed to feel the same way. Day after day, the visitor galleries of both chambers of Congress were packed. Among the spectators were government officials, foreign diplomats, their wives, as well as people of color, all of them listening intently to the impassioned speeches on the floor, and wondering how it would all turn out.

* * *

On January 24th, the *National Intelligencer* of Washington provided their readers with the most detailed account yet available on the great Savannah fire. Reprinted from a copy of the *Savannah Republican*, the description would have sent a chill down the spine of any merchant who read it.

> ... The flames have prostrated all the buildings which were the pride of our city! Thus was the emporium of our state, which was promising a considerable figure among the commercial cities of our sister states, almost destroyed in *twelve* hours! The commercial part of the town is a heap of ruins! There is but one solitary dry-good store remaining. All, all are gone!

While the account was somewhat exaggerated, there was no denying that this was the worst urban fire the country had ever seen.

Walter Smith of the George Town Importing and Exporting Company did not need any more convincing. He went and got a lawyer, and that same day walked into the U.S. Circuit Court in Washington and filed suit against "The President of the Savannah Steam Ship Company." George Town Importing was owed $1,508.58 plus interest, based upon the advances made to Captain Rogers, and Smith wanted to be paid.

Once his deposition was taken, Smith's lawsuit triggered a standard operating procedure within the Court.

First, a warrant was issued for the defendant's arrest. Actually going out and looking for William Scarbrough would have been a waste of time, especially since Walter Smith had told the Court that the defendant didn't live in the District. So the U.S. Marshal, Tench Ringgold, simply wrote "Non Est" on the warrant (which was shorthand for the Latin phrase *Non Est Inventus*, meaning "Not Found").

Then came the issuance of an *attachment* for any assets belonging to "The President of the Savannah Steam Ship Company." This meant that any property of his in the District would be seized by the Court, until the defendant, or his attorney, showed up to answer the charges. In this particular case, the defendant did have something in the District which could be "attached" to the lawsuit, and that was the steamship *Savannah*.

This attachment in turn triggered an appraisal of the property seized. Four men assigned to the task determined that the "Steam~~boat~~ Ship Savannah with her tackle apparel + furniture" was worth $10,000. This was far below the vessel's actual worth, but given the amount of money George Town Importing was trying to recover, there was really no need to stretch and assign a higher value.

Walter Smith's action was, at a minimum, a nuisance for Moses. Trying to petition the government to purchase the *Savannah* was challenging enough; having the steamship seized by the U.S. Marshal only made it more complicated, if not embarrassing.

On the positive side, the local newspapers made no mention of the case, which was not unusual—someone suing to recover a debt in an age of promissory notes was hardly out of the ordinary. Furthermore, the warrant named only Scarbrough as the defendant, since he was the one who had promised to pay. The U.S. Marshal had no cause to bother the *Savannah*'s captain, leaving Moses free to move about the capital.

Nevertheless, Walter Smith's lawsuit made it abundantly clear that until his bill was paid, the steamship *Savannah* wasn't going anywhere.

* * *

As news of the great Savannah fire spread, and the plea for help from Mayor Charlton was read, citizens all over the United States sprang into action. Up and down the East Coast, mass meetings were called to organize help for the victims. From Portland, in the District of Maine, all the way to New Orleans, cities large and small collected cash contributions, which were sent to the Savannah Council for disbursement.

Given the uncertain value of paper currency at the time, some people didn't have much cash to spare, so they donated what they thought the sufferers would need. Blankets, shoes, clothing, barrels of nails, flour—and even books—were collected to be shipped.

Communities far to the inland also tried to help. The tiny town of Jonesborough, Tennessee collected $700 worth of bacon and assorted merchandise, piled it onto wagons, and paid for it to be driven all the way over the Appalachian Mountains to Augusta.

While donations came from all over the country, it is not surprising that the most active efforts to help came from those cities that had strong commercial and cultural ties to Savannah.

Foremost among them was New York City. Upon receiving the call for help on January 24th, Gotham's leaders immediately called a public meeting, held at the City Hotel on Broadway.

At that meeting, a committee was formed to organize a donation drive. Many of the city's most prominent new mode proponents volunteered to serve. Mayor (and lead promoter of the Ocean Steam Ship Company) Cadwallader D. Colden was named the committee chairman, and his fellow shareholders Henry Eckford and Preserved Fish offered to solicit contributions. The steamship *Savannah*'s Joseph P. McKinne was named the committee secretary, and he along with steam cylinder caster James P. Allaire signed up to canvass the Corlear's Hook ward for donations. McKinne also offered Pott & McKinne's store on South Street as a collection point for any donated goods.

The zeal of these New Yorkers did not go unnoticed. Both the *National Intelligencer* and the *Boston Patriot* lauded their efforts on behalf of the fire victims.

No matter what the amount of aid being collected, however, those Savannah merchants who had suffered the most damage from the fire knew they would have to bear their own burdens.

For Andrew Low & Company, the loss of their supposedly fire-proof brick store was staggering. While resident partners Robert Isaac and James McHenry had been able to save some of their merchandise, the flames nevertheless had consumed $154,056 of inventory, all of it uninsured.

But the financial pain didn't stop there.

By law, the federal government allowed merchants a grace period before they had to pay the duty on imported goods. This gave businesses time to sell some of their merchandise to pay the duties, and in the process helped increase the amount of trade effected (and taxes collected).

The system worked to the benefit of both importer and government, except when business was slow and the goods could not be sold. Then the merchant had to ask the Custom House for an extension on the time allowed to pay the duties. This is precisely what Archibald S. Bulloch and his peers in other ports had been forced to do, over and over again, as the economy had worsened through late 1819.

Andrew Low & Company's problem went beyond that. The goods in their store were gone, burnt to ashes before they could be sold. They already had paid $14,000 in taxes on those goods, and the balance of $21,000 would soon be due and payable. It didn't seem fair that the partners would still be obliged to pay total duties of some $35,000 on imported products that had been destroyed in a fire.

The solution to this problem was a petition, asking that the duties owed be forgiven. But Customs Collector Archibald S. Bulloch had no authority to grant such a request. The only entity that did was Congress.

So partners Robert Isaac and James McHenry drafted a petition to Congress on January 24th, in which they recounted the size and style of their importing business. Since 1816, Andrew Low & Company had been liable for a gargantuan $358,000 in duties, and all had been punctually paid, according to an affidavit provided by Collector Bulloch. After using detailed financial statements to describe their precise losses, Andrew Low & Company asked for relief. Isaac and McHenry requested any unpaid duties on the destroyed goods be cancelled, and suggested the already-paid taxes be used to cover their importation of replacement merchandise. Considering the economic state of things, their proposal seemed intent upon combining fairness for the present with confidence in the future.

The Low partners weren't the only ones asking for relief. Other merchants who had the same problem also sent memorials to Congress, along with testimonials in support, signed by many of their fellow merchants.

In the meantime, the liability for duties on their destroyed goods remained on the books of the Savannah Custom House. All Collector

Bulloch could do was grant the merchants additional extensions, while all of them waited for Congress to answer.

* * *

By early February, it must have become increasingly clear that the opportunity for selling the *Savannah* to the federal government was not open-ended. Instead, it was a window, and it was closing.

The Board of Navy Commissioners had wasted little time in answering Congressman Nathaniel Silsbee's list of queries, including the final one on expenditures for the steam batteries. In a detailed reply dated January 31st, the Board listed all of the contracts made to date for their construction:

```
2 complete engines  . . . . . . . . . . . . . . . . . . . . . . . . . . . . . 43,000
Making boilers, 164,000 lbs. copper, at 10 cents . . . . . . . 16,400
82,000 lbs. copper, castings, &c.        33  . . . . . . . . . . . 27,060
82,000       do.     do.                 31  . . . . . . . . . . . 25,420
3 live oak frames, 36,000 feet      1    45  . . . . . . . . . . . 52,200
90,000 cubic feet yellow pine timber . . . . . . . . . . . . . . . 34,025
                                                            _____
                                                            $223,525
```

Any further enquiry would have confirmed that all three live oak frames were coming from Georgia. So was the yellow pine (for planking and beams), Hugh Lindsay of St. Mary's having finally accepted that contract offered to him. With so much money already committed to building all three steam batteries, finding room for a Navy purchase of the *Savannah* must have appeared difficult by that time.

Yet no matter what their eventual design, the massive steam batteries were ill-suited for fighting pirates. There remained one other possibility for the *Savannah*.

This time, the Senate took the lead. On February 16th, some two weeks after the House had received the Navy Board's report on steam battery contracts, Senator Henry Johnson of Louisiana rose to address his colleagues on the floor, and make a motion:

Resolved, that the Committee on Naval Affairs be instructed to enquire into the expediency of providing, by law, for the purchase of a sufficient number of fit vessels to protect the commerce of the United States in the Gulf of Mexico, and to prevent smuggling on the coast of Louisiana.

After further discussion the following day, the motion was passed.

Based upon the resolution's language, it was clear who the Senate was asking to deal with the piracy problem. The tag-on clause at the end was definitive. Preventing smuggling was the primary purpose of the Treasury Department's revenue cutters. By increasing the number of cutters patrolling in the Gulf of Mexico, not only would smuggling be reduced, but American shipping undoubtedly would be better protected from piracy.

Once the resolution was formally communicated to the Treasury Department, on February 18th, the Senate Naval Affairs Committee stood by, awaiting an answer from Secretary William H. Crawford.

*   *   *

In the weeks following the great fire, the people of Savannah began putting their lives back together. Most of the merchants who had lost their stores and offices moved to temporary quarters, and tried to create some semblance of an ongoing business. Aid was arriving from all around the country, including money, material, and even shiploads of skilled men, looking to take part in the rebuilding effort. And the saw mills in the area, including Sheldon C. Dunning's steam-powered facility, were particularly busy, cranking out loads of lumber for reconstruction. After the initial shock of the fire's destruction, and the hardship that followed, the citizens of Savannah had pulled together, knowing that the country was united behind them in the goal of recovery, and renewal.

Then, the New York money arrived.

Sailing up the Savannah River on February 27th came the brig *Othello*, under the command of Captain John Mott. The *Othello* brought from Gotham a cargo that included clothing and cash for the fire victims. Attached to these donations was a letter from New York Mayor Cadwallader D. Colden, addressed to Savannah Mayor Charlton. This memorial Charlton immediately placed before the city's Council, for review and consideration.

Mayor Colden, writing in his capacity as the chairman of New York City's relief committee, reported that the $10,238.29 included with the letter "disappointed the wishes and expectations of many of our citizens." The lower than hoped-for donations were due, in part, to the burdens already placed upon New York's charitable resources by the economic depression. Further reducing the total collections, the Mayor explained, had been poor timing, since Gotham had just finished raising money for the victims of a large fire in Schenectady, New York.

"It is my duty," Colden continued, "to call your attention to the sub-joined copy of a resolution" passed by the New York relief committee. It was the wish of the committee, he wrote, that the contributions be limited to the "indigent and distressed sufferers by the late fire," and not those who were capable of repairing their own losses. This attached resolution of the New Yorkers was then laid before the Savannah Council:

> Resolved, That it is the wish of the general committee that the money and goods to be remitted to Savannah be applied exclu-sively to the relief of all indigent persons, without distinction of color, who are dependent on their own industry for support, and who have been sufferers by the late fire at that place.

Embedded within this request was a phrase that caused the mem-bers of Savannah's Council to sit up, and take notice: "without distinc-tion of color."

No other contribution coming from anywhere else in the Union contained such language. What was the point behind the New York-ers' use of such a phrase?

Given the stories which had been roiling the country's newspapers for weeks, the Council concluded that the real reason for that partic-ular language could be summed up in one word—*Missouri*.

They had more than the New Yorkers' resolution to support their belief. Perceptions in the North were changing. There was no better evidence than a recently-published letter from a Philadelphia insur-ance company, which informed a Savannah client that it was declining to issue new policies "in any of the slave states." Gotham itself increasingly had become a major source of anti-slavery sentiment. And it probably was not lost upon the Savannah aldermen that their correspondent, Cadwallader D. Colden, in addition to being a lawyer, steamboat entrepreneur, and city mayor, was also the president of the New York Society for Promoting the Manumission of Slaves.

Rather than let the matter pass, the Savannah Council unanimously agreed to instruct Mayor Charlton to write a reply, and send it to Mayor Colden.

* * *

As the debate over Missouri raged on in the House and Senate, other business before the Congress was not forgotten. The tariff relief petitions of Andrew Low & Company and other Savannah merchants, presented to the Senate by Georgia's own legislators, had been referred to the Committee on Finance for consideration. On February 21st, that Committee's chairman, Nathan Sanford of New York, presented its findings to the full Senate.

First, Senator Sanford reviewed the cases made by the various merchants, including Andrew Low & Company's proposal to import a like-amount of goods duty-free, to cover the tariffs already paid.

Then, Senator Sanford chronicled the government's response to previous requests for remitting unpaid duties when calamitous fires had destroyed the merchandise. Sometimes Congress had agreed to cancel the duties, and in other cases it had extended the time allowed to pay them, depending upon circumstances.

Having finished the overview, the New Yorker then presented the Committee's extended conclusion:

> ... the Government is not a party to the private dispositions of the owner, and it bears no share of his hazards ... he holds them as he holds any other goods; and whether they are lost by accident, or sold with profit, the loss or the gain belongs to him alone... The public is never invited to partake of his profits. Is it more reasonable that the public should participate [in] his losses?

The question rhetorically asked, Senator Sanford then gave his final answer:

> ... general relief in such cases is impossible, and partial relief would be unjust.
> The following resolution is proposed:
> Resolved, That it is inexpedient to grant relief...

Not so fast, countered Senator John Elliott of Georgia. He offered his own resolution: Sanford's report should be re-committed to the Finance Committee, with instructions to present a bill offering a partial cancellation of the duties, as well as giving the merchants two extra years to pay off the remainder. This, the Senate agreed to.

Separately, the Senate Naval Affairs Committee received a reply from the Treasury Department regarding the need for more vessels to fight pirates, and combat smuggling. Secretary Crawford had taken one week to respond, providing his answer on February 25th.

In his reply, Crawford focused on the activity over which his department had clear jurisdiction, which was enforcing the tariff laws. He noted that the two revenue cutters then employed in the Gulf were small, at 56 tons burthen, and had very shallow drafts. This allowed them to cruise very close to shore, and maneuver effectively amongst the sandbars and shoals. For the work of suppressing smugglers, that type of vessel was considered the "most fit."

Crawford barely mentioned piracy in his response. Apparently, as far as the Secretary was concerned, the Treasury would combat piracy in the Gulf only to the extent it coincided with smuggling, and not the other way around.

The Treasury Department's position could not have been much more obvious—it was in no need of a vessel as large as the steamship *Savannah* to enforce the tariff laws, no matter what her capabilities. In conjunction with the unwillingness of the Navy to deviate from its own building program, finding a way to consummate President Monroe's offer had reached a dead end.

Precisely when Moses gave up his effort to sell the steamship isn't clear, but by the last week of February, all Congressional exertions had been exhausted. The shareholders down in Savannah must have sensed it too, since the Navy Board already had sent instructions to J. P. Henry, in his capacity as Navy Agent, to make payments on the steam battery timber contracts.

With nowhere else to turn, Moses quit Washington and headed north. He left the capital completely empty-handed. No government sale. No Navy appointment. No entry of his sons onto the list of Navy Midshipmen. Considering the highs of the previous 18 months —the launch at New York, and the triumphant welcomes at Savannah, Charleston, Liverpool, Stockholm, and St. Petersburg—his feelings in February of 1820 must have been very low indeed.

After spending some time in Philadelphia, Moses continued north to New York, where he stopped again for a few days. On March 1st, in that city's *Mercantile Advertiser*, came the inevitable notice:

FOR SALE,
The well known steam ship SAVANNAH, lying at Washington city with her machinery, burthen 319 tons, copper fastened, coppered to the bends with very heavy copper—the fitting of this ship is said to be superior to any other ship that ever sailed out of New York. Inventory to be seen and terms made known at our office. J. & C. BOLTON, 58 Broadway,
N.B. It will cost about $200 to take out her machinery, when she would be the same as any other ship, or her spars and rigging taken off, she would be rendered an elegant steam vessel.

Beyond this unhappy business, there was at least one happy event back in Connecticut for Moses and the extended Rogers family to celebrate. On March 2nd, the day after the *Savannah*'s "for sale" notice began running in New York, Mary Rogers exchanged vows with Steve. The wedding took place in Groton, and given the practice at the time, probably was held at the home of the bride's parents.

The marriage of Steve and Mary became the final link between these two distant branches of the Rogers family tree in greater New London. Stevens was the third sibling, after his sisters Abigail and dearly departed Sarah, to marry into the house of Amos Rogers Senior and his wife Sarah. Moses and Steve, having been related but distantly, and then by affinity, had finally become brothers-in-law directly.

While the extended Rogers clan celebrated this new union in Connecticut, and took the measure of the Norwegian sjekte which Moses had gifted to his father, down in New York, the steamship *Savannah*'s "for sale" advertisement appeared for a second day in the *Mercantile Advertiser*. The only difference was that the newspaper ran the ad on the front page, instead of page two, as originally had been done.

But that was not the only change in the newspaper from the day before. On page two, where the *Savannah*'s "for sale" notice originally had been placed, there appeared another unusual advertisement:

Passage for Charleston, Havana & New Orleans.

The elegant steam ship ROBERT FULTON, ——, master, burthen 750 tons, built in this city entirely of live oak, locust, cedar and Georgia pine, coppered with heavy copper, copper fastened and rigged with lug sails; will leave New York for New-Orleans on the 10th day of April next, touching at Charleston and Havana. This ship is intended as a regular packet, is fitted up exclusively for passengers, in the most commodious and elegant manner, with state rooms. Persons desirous of taking passage for either of the above ports, are invited to apply on board, or to

DAVID DUNHAM & CO, 154 Pearl st.

This advertisement, which also began appearing in several other newspapers, was a little odd in several respects. First of all, announcing the departure of the Ocean Steam Ship Company's brand new, untested vessel more than one month in advance certainly did give the public plenty of notice. But even more peculiar was the lack of a captain's name—this was hardly a way to promote confidence in this newest "steam ship." It implied a lack of preparedness, and unsettled plans.

The underlying purpose of this announcement became clearer in the days to come.

On March 3rd, the steamship *Savannah*'s "for sale" notice appeared again in the *Mercantile Advertiser*, in the third column of page one. The steamship *Robert Fulton*'s departure notice, however, was no longer on page two. It had been moved to page one, in the second column. Anyone reading that newspaper's front page would have seen the two advertisements almost next to each other.

The shifting didn't stop there. On March 4th, the *Savannah*'s "for sale" notice retreated to page three. So too did the *Robert Fulton*'s departure advertisement, which was placed just above the *Savannah*'s in the same column. There the two notices stayed, through March 7th.

This dance and final pairing of the two advertisements could hardly have been a coincidence. The eventual victor in the rivalry was there for all to see: the Ocean Steam Ship Company's reincarnation, the *Robert Fulton*, was ready for business, while the Savannah Steam Ship Company's original creation, the *Savannah*, was aching to be sold.

* * *

While Stevens and Mary Rogers celebrated their wedding day in Connecticut, down in Washington, the Congress faced judgment day. The melee over Missouri had raged through January and February, with exchanges between the two sides reaching new extremes.

Emblematic of the emotions brought to the fore were the words of Senator Rufus King of New York, one of the leading opponents of slavery. "I have yet to learn that one man can make a slave of another," he declared; "if one man cannot do so, no number of individuals can have any better right to do it."

In ferocious reply came warnings, such as those from Senator Walker Freeman of Georgia, who predicted that if the anti-slavery forces didn't back off, the country could see "the father armed against the son, and the son against the father . . . a brother's sword crimsoned with a brother's blood . . . our houses wrapt in flames."

For Speaker of the House Henry Clay, the animosity had gone far enough. "The words, civil war, and disunion," he wrote, "are uttered almost without emotion." That was extremely dangerous.

After the Senate had linked Maine's admission as a free State to Missouri's admission as a slave State, the House had refused to go along, and instead passed its own anti-slavery legislation for Missouri. The conflicting bills were sent to a joint House-Senate committee to be reconciled. The resulting negotiations led the Senate to agree to break down its own bill into parts.

This was the kind of compromise Speaker Clay could work with. He proceeded to place each section of the Senate bill before the House, and force a vote.

The decisive moment arrived late in the day on March 2nd, when the House, exhausted by the acrimony, considered a motion to *remove* an anti-slavery clause added to the Missouri section of the bill. By a vote of 90–87, the motion passed, and the anti-slavery language was taken out.

With each part of the Senate's Maine and Missouri legislation separately approved, Speaker Clay figuratively cobbled them together, and pronounced the entire bill confirmed by the House. Neither side was entirely happy with the result. Subsequent attempts to reconsider the bill were scuttled by the Speaker, who used procedural rules to declare these motions "out of order." The delay gave Clay enough time to shuttle the pieced-together bill off to the Senate, which quickly approved it.

The resulting compromise allowed Maine to enter as a free State and Missouri as a slave State, in exchange for a prohibition of slavery in federal lands north of latitude 36 degrees 30 minutes. This meant that the rest of the Louisiana Purchase, excluding the newly-conceived Arkansas Territory, would enter the Union as free.

The great crisis was seemingly past, but passions on both sides still smoldered, and left many with a sense of foreboding. The whole ordeal had been, as the aged Thomas Jefferson wrote, "like a fire bell in the night."

* * *

Just as the dueling steamship advertisements were playing out in New York's *Mercantile Advertiser*, Savannah Mayor Charlton's reply to Mayor Colden's fire donation note arrived at Gotham. In a long letter, Mayor Charlton offered his thanks for the New York committee's efforts on behalf of the Savannah fire victims. But he also expressed great offense at the terms under which the funds had been provided, and as a result, informed Colden that the Savannah Council had decided to return the fire relief donations.

This reaction by the Savannah Council to one simple phrase— "without distinction of color"—ignited a firestorm. Charlton's letter was printed in full throughout the New York press, from which it spread all over the country.

Mayor Colden felt obliged to reply in turn, stating that the New York committee's resolution language had been insisted upon, but that no offense was intended. The Gothamites just wanted to make sure that the funds went to the sufferers most in need, and not those with other means. Colden further explained that the recent mishandling of relief monies to fire victims at Schenectady had played a role in the resolution's wording.

Most perplexed of all by the Savannah Council's reaction must have been Joseph P. McKinne. As a transplanted son of the South, he had knocked on doors soliciting help, and as the committee's secretary, had collected and sent the donations, paperwork and all, down to Savannah on Captain Mott's *Othello*.

Coming right on the heels of the decisive votes in Congress over Missouri, national reaction to the donation controversy was fierce. A number of towns in the North which had yet to send their monies decided to disburse them locally instead. The Pennsylvania Legislature, which had voted money out of the State's budget for relief, nearly overturned the decision. And one of the donors from Jonesborough, Tennessee wrote that he would not have given, if he had known of the Savannah Council's reaction to the New York donations.

Yet for the many voices of outrage, there were others on both sides who thought the whole controversy had been blown out of proportion. Most prominent among them were plenty of people in Savannah itself, who thought their mayor and council had overreacted to the language in the New Yorkers' resolution.

The damage, however, was done. While some of Gotham's contributors sent their money back to Savannah without conditions, most of the returned donations were kept. The relief effort had become just one more point of friction between North and South, and New York City and Savannah in particular, in the early months of 1820.

* * *

While the controversy over fire relief raged on through the month of March, the steamship *Savannah* remained tied up to the wharves in Washington. Even though she had neither a business nor a buyer, the *Savannah* still gained some welcome attention when she received a visit from a Frenchman by the name of Jean Baptiste Marestier. He made a point of inspecting the *Savannah* from bow to stern, and top to bottom.

Marestier's interest was hardly casual. The French government had concluded the previous summer that since the Americans and the British were barreling ahead with this new mode of transport, it was imperative for them to catch up. In an effort to do so, they had sent Marestier—one of their best naval constructors—to the United States to study steamboats, wherever he could find them. Inspecting the only operational steamship in existence would have been a high priority.

In fact, the desire to understand what the Americans were doing with the new mode of transport went well beyond France. Back in the first week of January 1820, the Navy Board had felt compelled to inform Secretary Thompson of this new phenomenon:

> The Board of Navy Commissioners have the honor to represent to you that in various instances the Ministers of France Russia and Denmark have applied to them for information relatively to scientific military and other improvements made in the naval

service of this country: and that an officer of science high in rank in the Swedish Navy was sent over by his Sovereign for the same object...

Judging from Marestier's later description of the *Savannah*'s voyage, he must have met or corresponded with Captain Rogers at some point while the steamship was docked at the capital. Marestier also made drawings of the *Savannah*'s profile. He drew her paddlewheels, showing how they folded like a fan, as well as a layout of the engine cylinder and air pump. These schematics, made as they were by a highly-trained naval architect, would become the basis for the world's collective memory of what the first steamship actually looked like.

The *Savannah* also received some additional, unwelcome attention. On March 22nd, the U.S. Circuit Court in Washington registered another lawsuit against her. This time, the plaintiff was New York ship chandler Francis H. Nicoll & Company. Having provided all sorts of items to fit out the *Savannah*, Nicoll was owed some $5,000, and Pott & McKinne had failed to pay the bill.

The suit was specifically made against the "Savannah Steam Ship Company," as opposed to any particular individual, which meant that there was no one for U.S. Marshal Tench Ringgold to arrest. Instead, the steamship was "seized" yet again, until the defendant showed up to argue its side of the case.

It turned out that engine designer Daniel Dod faced the same problem as Nicoll. He also had not received payment for the $7,000 of work he had done on the steam engine and boilers. But rather than go to Washington to bring his suit, Dod did it in New York.

Furthermore, instead of taking action against some amorphous corporate entity, Dod's lawyer filed suit against each of the individual shareholders. This was possible because American law had yet to settle the issue of personal liability within a corporate structure—each shareholder still could be held individually liable for the actions of the corporation.

It also meant that Thomas Morris, the U.S. Marshal at New York, could go out and look for real defendants to serve with warrants. This included Gideon Pott, Joseph P. McKinne and Moses Rogers, all described in Dod's complaint as "citizens of the State of New York." If any of the Southerners came north for their seasonal visits, then they could be snagged, as well.

So contemplated, Dod's strategy was put into effect. Supreme Court Chief Justice John Marshall, fulfilling his temporary duty as a federal circuit judge in New York, issued a warrant on April 1st for all 23 individual shareholders of the Savannah Steam Ship Company.

Stephen Vail, on the other hand, chose to stay with the asset itself. Having arrived in Washington overland from Augusta, he found he had little choice but to pile on. Vail filed suit on April 14th, for failure to pay $3,723.75.

The steamship had been seized twice already, so either for good measure or to honor a specific request, U.S. Marshal Tench Ringgold went aboard the *Savannah* and took possession of all the sails, pulleys, cables and chains he could separate from the vessel. He even removed the large anchor, and one of the small bower anchors. Marshal Ringgold then ordered all this "rigging" taken to George Sanford's store, which was located at Coomb's Wharf, on the Potomac's Eastern Branch. There, it was put into storage.

The court was required to value this equipment, which it did in the amount of $4,510, comfortably more than Vail's unpaid bill. Adding a new, slightly more realistic appraisal for the stripped steamship of $15,000, and the total seized value of the *Savannah* was estimated at $19,510.

Given all the suits that had been filed—by Smith, Nicoll, Dod and Vail—the Savannah Steam Ship Company had outstanding debts totaling roughly $17,200. Excluding Walter Smith's account, the sum of unpaid contractor bills was over $15,800. It is no coincidence that this amount was nearly identical to the difference between the cost of the *Savannah*—$66,000, as Moses had told Lord Lynedoch—and the $50,000 in capital originally raised by the Company.

The extra money to complete the *Savannah* had to come from somewhere. The source was Pott & McKinne, who simply extended credit to the Company once the original $50,000 had been spent.

In any case, the precise origin of the extra funds really didn't matter by the early spring of 1820. The Savannah Steam Ship Company had debts to pay in the middle of an economic depression, and the only means of doing so sat tied up to a wharf at the nation's capital.

CHAPTER TWENTY-ONE

THE END, AND RE-BIRTH

BY APRIL OF 1820, nearly everyone—from merchants, to farmers, to mechanics—was feeling the impact of the depression. While the violence of plummeting crop prices and failing banks had passed, the financial carnage left in their wake still had to bandaged, and hopefully healed.

Down South, many of the steamship *Savannah*'s backers were riding out the double storm of economic depression and cataclysmic fire reasonably well. About half of them, though, including some of the largest investors, were in serious trouble.

Isaac Minis had lost property in the fire, and was saddled with too much debt.

Sheldon C. Dunning lost his own store to the flames. Adding to his misfortune was the complete destruction of his steam-powered lumber mill by an arsonist, in early March.

The partners of Andrew Low & Company had to contend with both their fire losses as well as any residual fallout from loans and guarantees made under their name.

And William Scarbrough had never been in so much trouble in his life. His defunct Scarbrough & McKinne partnership was being pressured or pursued by lenders large and small, to whom it owed tens of thousands of dollars. In turn, Scarbrough was pressing forward with his own lawsuit against Pott & McKinne, for money that firm owed to his dissolved partnership. While the outcome of this financial pushing and pulling was far from clear at that point, one thing was certain beyond any reasonable doubt: William Scarbrough's virtually unblemished reputation as one of Savannah's leading merchants had been shredded into tatters.

* * *

For his part, Joseph P. McKinne of New York had problems far bigger and more immediate than angry ex-partners down South. The anemic price of commodities, the burden of the steamship *Savannah*'s disposition, and the chore of distributing the returned fire relief money all paled in comparison to what stared him in the face.

McKinne and his primary business partner, Gideon Pott, were insolvent, with creditors circling around them.

McKinne and another associate had been served with warrants by the U.S. Marshal, for overdue tariffs owed to the New York Custom House.

And even more unsettling, McKinne and his wife Anna faced additional creditors who were preparing to take legal action against their home on Liberty Street.

Gideon Pott was in no better shape. With the squeeze for money on, he had felt compelled to sell his shares in the Tontine Coffee House back in December, netting him a grand total of $350. Such a small sum was hardly noticeable given the debts hanging over him, but evidence enough that anyone caught in the trap of falling prices was forced to scrape together whatever cash they could.

* * *

For Pott & McKinne's rivals at the Ocean Steam Ship Company, April of 1820 was a month not of pressure, but of promise. The *Robert Fulton* finally had been completed—a full year after launching—and his backers were getting ready for the inaugural voyage.

In preparation, the rival company had continued to run advertisements promoting the *Robert Fulton*'s coming departure for Charleston, Havana, and New Orleans.

In addition, the company's president, Cadwallader D. Colden, also had set in motion an effort to give their new ocean steamer an official seal of approval which the *Savannah* had never enjoyed. Colden described it all in a petition to Congress:

> ... your Memorialists have lately by an Act of the Legislature of the State of New York been constituted a Body politic and Corporate under the name and Style of The Ocean Steam Ship Company with a Capital of five hundred thousand Dollars; that their Object is fully to test the experiment of Navigating the Ocean with Steam Vessels (properly so called) and to bring

the same to great practical utility by establishing a certain and rapid intercourse between the United States and Europe, as well as between the extremities of our Atlantic Sea Coast...

The dig at the steamship *Savannah* delivered, Colden proceeded to ask Congress to take action on several fronts.

First, the law that required a vessel to get a new federal registration for every change in ownership was a burden. "From the great number of Stockholders and the frequent transfers of Stock usual in all incorporated Companies it is conceived almost impracticable rigidly to comply," wrote Colden. (Left unsaid, but clearly implied, was that shares in this rival company had become, at least in part, a vehicle for speculation on the dream.) To solve this registration problem, Colden asked that instead of being forced to list every individual shareholder, they be allowed to register their vessels in just the corporate name. This request was a first, and one of many steps that the country had yet to take to make it easier to do business as a corporation.

Second, since the "Steam Vessels in Contemplation" were intended primarily for passengers, letters and public dispatches, it stood to reason that they be considered a form of public vessel. If Congress were to designate the Ocean Steam Ship Company's vessels as being official mail-carriers, then these craft would be eligible for reduced foreign port fees. This reduction in operating expenses would make it easier for the company to turn a profit, and expand service to other ports. The country would benefit accordingly, from not only more rapid travel and communications, but a new means for the fast, dependable delivery of government dispatches.

Not content with his previous allusion to the *Savannah*, Colden then bore in yet deeper:

> ... Your Memorialists, well aware of the great difficulties and disappointments attending a first experiment, and of the vast expenditure required to bring it to the extent contemplated have yet great confidence themselves in the ultimate success of the Enterprize, although they have strong fears that it will be long e'er they shall reap any Emolument from it. But they are sorry to say that confidence is confined to themselves, as the general belief in the practicability of the Scheme, and the public ardor to adventure has been much diminished and checked by the

<u>partial</u> success which attended a late <u>slender effort</u>; inasmuch as no material advantage or rapidity of passage was proven to be derived from it...

The wound inflicted, Colden asked for more.

Third, since the engine on board the *Robert Fulton* required foreign coal in order to run efficiently, fairness dictated that the government exempt such an ocean-going public vessel from paying the normal import duties on the fuel. Plus, since these "Steam Packets" were primarily for passengers, the company also wanted the large amount of sea stores—expended during the voyage for their customers' comfort—to be excluded from any tariff charges.

Then, Colden acknowledged the reality of hard times, and, indirectly, what had just happened to the tariff relief petitions submitted by the merchants of Savannah:

> ... Your Memorialists are sensible of a very proper jealousy, that is always and particularly at the present juncture aroused on any application that may have a tendency to lessen the Revenue of the Country; that it is usually thought inadmissible and rejected as soon as heard, but they hope the Importance of this Subject will entitle it to the serious Consideration of Congress...

Fourth and finally, he presented a small carrot, offering to carry all public dispatches free of charge, while also asking that the U.S. Post Office be authorized to contract with the company for the carriage of mail to foreign ports.

It was quite a wish list, but as Colden pointed out, the cost of not only building but operating such revolutionary inventions was huge. Each request granted would serve to lessen the company's ongoing costs, and make eventual success more likely. The purpose of all these official encouragements, Colden wrote, was to assist in the achievement of the worthiest of goals:

> ... Suffice it to say the expectations of Your Memorialists will not be exceeded if the United States and Great Britain are approximated within a certain and safe passage of fifteen days and the distant points on our extensive Atlantic Sea Coast connected by a proportionate celerity...

This substantial petition, with its many proposals and promises, had been laid before the Senate on March 14th by New York's own Nathan Sanford. On Sanford's motion, the petition was referred to the Committee on Commerce and Manufactures, which the Senator himself chaired.

With that chore in process down in Washington, the Ocean Steam Ship Company set to work finding a captain for its vessel. When the dueling newspaper notices with the *Savannah* ended in early March, the *Robert Fulton* still didn't have a master, and finding the right man was an important part of this inaugural voyage. Having knowledge of the steam technology, while helpful, was not essential, since there would be several engineers on board to manage the machinery. What would be most important, given the intended route and ports of call, was a detailed knowledge of the coast. If the public was going to accept the *Robert Fulton* as a safe means of travel, then they had to have complete confidence in his captain.

In the end, the company decided to hire a man named Robert Inott, who previously had captained the ship *Annisquam* on runs between Gotham and New Orleans.

By mid-April, the *Robert Fulton* and his new master were nearly ready. To ensure that everything on board worked to satisfaction, the new ocean steamer was sent out on a brief trial run. Leaving its East River berth, the vessel pushed south into Upper New York Bay, passed through the Narrows, and then proceeded to Gravesend Bay, before returning to the city. With the successful testing of the engine and paddlewheels, the inaugural voyage was confirmed for Thursday, April 20th.

Unfortunately, the newspapers that morning of departure carried a disappointing notice: the *Robert Fulton* would be "unavoidably detained." The new departure date was set for Sunday, April 23rd, and furthermore, the stop at Charleston had been eliminated.

No public explanation was given for the changes. If there was any positive reason for the delay, it must have been the prospect of departing on a Sunday. This would guarantee plenty of spectators to bear witness, just as the *Robert Fulton*'s competitor had enjoyed when she left Gotham.

Yet even this more ideal departure date could not be delivered. Not until Tuesday, April 25th, was the *Robert Fulton* finally ready to take on passengers.

For the crowds that gathered along the East River to watch, this newest ocean steamer tied up to the wharf certainly was an awesome-looking advancement of the dream. Many of the *Robert Fulton's* features made it clear that designer Henry Eckford had taken Moses Rogers' solutions to the fears of professionals and public, and either done them one better, or audaciously ignored them.

First of all, the vessel was huge. It measured 159 feet in length on the deck, and more than 33 feet in breadth. The burthen of 702 tons made it substantially larger than most merchant vessels afloat. The inherent message was unmistakable: the *Robert Fulton* could handle anything that Nature threw at him.

Second, the hull was rock-solid, thanks to the installation of three *keelsons.* These additional parallel timbers were attached directly to the keel, serving to make the entire collection of keel, ribs and planking both stiff and strong.

Third, the permanent paddlewheel housings, while bulging somewhat from the sides, were built largely flush with the rest of the hull, making the whole combination look more stable, and less susceptible to rolling in heavy seas.

Fourth, this largest steam vessel yet built had an engine to match. Its single cylinder, cast by James P. Allaire, was slightly larger than the *Savannah's*, making it the biggest ever placed on a steamer to date. The massive boilers were also record-breaking in size.

Fifth, the greatest fear—of fire—had been boxed, literally. The entire engine room was encased in lead, and caulked at the seams. Not only did this provide a sound barrier to lessen engine noise in the passenger cabin, but it also prevented any wooden timbers from being directly exposed to the intense heat. Still more cleverly, in the event of fire, this design allowed the engine room to be flooded deliberately, thereby extinguishing the flames, yet without sinking the vessel.

And sixth, the claustrophobic apprehension of traveling on a newer version of the "steam coffin" was countered by unusually large passenger quarters. Skylights running the entire length of the main cabin created an environment which one observer described as "high and airy."

Beyond these innovations, though, the *Robert Fulton* possessed other characteristics with which Eckford seemed to be flouting the conventional wisdom.

First, the steam engine cylinder and apparatus, while impressive, were installed vertically within the hull, which meant that the piston rod and crossbeam towered far above the deck, just behind twin smokestacks. This exposed the engine to the elements, and put a lot of weight above the deck-line.

Second, the vessel did have masts, but there were no yards on them to carry the larger canvas of a square-rigged, ocean-sailing vessel. Instead, the masts were configured to carry less flexible, triangular lug sails.

Third, the twin smokestacks were vertical and straight, and not bent or designed to swivel.

Fourth, the paddlewheels were half-covered by traditional wooden paddleboxes, the whole of which was fixed permanently in place.

With each of these features, Henry Eckford, the experienced shipbuilder, appeared to be ignoring the worries of steam skeptics in a way that Moses Rogers, the experienced steamboat captain, never did. Yet on reflection, even these defiant components of the *Robert Fulton* had their own logic, filling out the missing pieces of the overall design puzzle.

That part of the engine protruding above the deck line would not make the vessel unstable, since it really was not substantial in relation to the enormous hull. Besides, there were no heavy masts or sails that could collapse onto it.

And because there were no square-rigged sails to be used, the need to guide any smokestack sparks and cinders in a particular direction was unnecessary. Therefore, the smokestacks could be built straight up.

Finally, and crucially, the rationale for no substantial sailing apparatus, as well as box-covered paddlewheels that were fixed in place, was based upon a simple, straightforward proposition: Cadwallader D. Colden, Henry Eckford and their partners believed they could deliver a long-distance ocean voyage continuously under steam, without a breakdown. It was a bold promise, and a worthy follow-on to the *Savannah's* unprecedented experiment.

Beyond design, the projectors also took heed of the need for representation on the maiden voyage. As a symbol of the owners' confidence in the *Robert Fulton*, embarking on this trip to New Orleans was one of the Monopoly's acolytes, Jasper Lynch. He had bought into the venture after its formation, helped with construction, and also quietly offered the vessel to the Navy the previous December. Joining Lynch on board that morning for a bon voyage party were hundreds of others, including company president Cadwallader D. Colden.

Casting off from the wharf at a little past 9 o'clock, the *Robert Fulton* was joined by the steamboat *Connecticut*, under Captain Elihu S. Bunker. Such an escort was fitting, since it had been Bunker and the *Connecticut* (originally built as the *Emperor of Russia*) which the Monopoly had hoped to send on the first steam-powered crossing of the Atlantic, back in 1816.

The two steamers churned southward, past thousands of cheering spectators packing the Battery. From there, they proceeded into Upper New York Bay, and after passing through the Narrows, continued on into Lower New York Bay.

Just inside Sandy Hook, Colden and the party-goers transferred over to the *Connecticut*, for the return trip to Gotham. Left behind on the *Robert Fulton* were Captain Inott and his crew, plus Jasper Lynch and an undisclosed number of passengers. Once the transfer was complete, the *Robert Fulton* then steamed out to sea.

On board the *Connecticut*, Colden and his guests held a meeting. They passed a series of resolutions, thanking everyone involved, offering assurances that the new vessel was perfectly safe, and encouraging the public's patronage. Gotham's newspapers dutifully reprinted these resolutions in full.

Throughout all of the published departure notices, as well as these resolutions, the projectors repeatedly referred to the *Robert Fulton* as a "steam ship." Despite their own declaration in the petition to Congress regarding oceanic "steam vessels," and the actual sailing apparatus installed on their own "experiment," this description of their craft betrayed a continuing need, it seems, to compete with the *Savannah*.

She had been a steam *ship*.

So too would he.

She had been built by a steam *ship* company.

So was he.

She, with all the machinery, masts, yards and sails which defined this new name—*steam ship*—had proved that steaming across the wide ocean was possible.

He, without all the old mode equipment necessary for the name, would dare to break the rules, prove that he could do it better, and thereby change the very meaning of the word *ship*.

* * *

At the same time the *Robert Fulton* was steaming out into the Atlantic, Moses Rogers remained land-bound. He confronted problems which were not quite as dire as those faced by the other *Savannah* shareholders, but humbling nevertheless.

His savings were in his creation, and the likelihood of getting more than a fraction of the investment back looked doubtful.

Furthermore, Moses was jobless. Not since 1807, when he abruptly left the schooner *Experiment*, had Moses been caught so flat-footed.

What he did have was free time, something which had been in short supply for the past 2½ years. Adelia and the children were the most obvious beneficiaries.

But beyond reconnecting with his family, Moses still had to re-establish himself. He concluded that the best place to start over was somewhere he knew quite well, and that was Philadelphia. The next step, after setting his sights on the City of Brotherly Love, was to try to find new work, in the middle of what was the worst depression the country had ever seen.

* * *

Down in Washington, the Navy Board must have been pleased. After being the target of two flanking attacks from the House of Representatives just four months earlier, the Board had managed to preserve both its power and its purpose.

The first assault, on the Navy's budget, had been thwarted. The Board's argument that cutting appropriations would actually increase costs, due to the need to preserve construction in progress, had worked. Newspaper editorials in support of maintaining the $1,000,000 annual appropriation also had helped. "The best interests of the nation," concluded the House committee, "are opposed to a suspension."

The second attack, on the Board's make-up and structure, also had been effectively deflected. The idea of making the Navy's civilian leader the presiding officer of the Board was unnecessary, the commodores had argued, because the three-member panel was already "attached to the office of the Secretary." Furthermore, "as it would be often inconvenient, and sometimes impracticable, for the Secretary of the Navy to meet the Board of Commissioners, as their presiding officer, without neglecting other and more important duties," the already-established oversight was all that was needed.

The additional suggestion by the House—that fresh blood be

brought into the Navy Board by periodically rotating its members—was also sunk. What the Board needed, the commodores had countered, was the most experienced officers available, versed in the complexities of contracting, shipbuilding, and maintenance. If any change to the Board's composition was necessary, the President could make it whenever he chose.

Despite this failed effort at reform, Congress did manage to take one positive step with regard to the Navy, if only by the skin of its teeth. On the last day of the session, May 15th, it appropriated $60,000 for the building of "small vessels of war," based upon the Navy's recommendations for combating piracy near the Mississippi River's entrance. Congress also approved "an Act to continue in force" the anti-piracy law already passed back in March of 1819, adding some new punishment provisions.

Beyond receiving new authority to construct small sailing vessels to protect the Gulf coast, the Navy continued building large warships, as previously authorized. This included both 74-gun ships-of-the-line and 44-gun frigates, which formed the backbone of the fleet.

The steam batteries were another matter. Once Congress left town in mid-May, the Navy Board's activities on the new mode slowed down.

The Board told Hugh Lindsay, who had the pine planking contract for all three batteries, that he could deliver pine logs instead of planks, provided he reduced his price accordingly.

The other Georgia contractor who was providing two battery frames, Thomas Newell, was informed that he could take until the end of the year to deliver all the timber required.

And while the Board wasn't happy about the expense involved, it approved the erection of a building at the Brooklyn Navy Yard, to store one of the steam engines already delivered by Robert McQueen's Columbian Foundry.

There was also one additional change which threw the steam batteries' construction timeline into doubt: Henry Eckford, who had submitted the plans for their sea-going design, resigned his position as the U.S. Naval Constructor at New York.

Eckford had his reasons. He and the other naval constructors had recently asked for a pay raise, to $3,000 a year, but were rebuffed. The Board also had been quite strict in demanding its way with regard to vessel design—the widening and lengthening of Eckford's own steam battery submission was but one example. With such insults inflicted, the private sector beckoned.

It was a great loss for the Navy. As the builder of the steamboat *Chancellor Livingston* and the steamship *Robert Fulton*, Henry Eckford was one of the most talented designers in the world for this new mode of transport. Whoever replaced him as Naval Constructor at New York would have big shoes to fill, if the steam batteries were to be completed expeditiously.

* * *

Further south, in Savannah, William Scarbrough was struggling to stay financially afloat, as an assortment of creditors circled around him. Everything he owned was at risk.

On May 13th, an unpaid debt to Andrew Low & Company had forced his West Broad Street mansion onto the public auction block. Fortunately for Scarbrough, his brother-in-law (and Low partner) Robert Isaac was the high bidder at the auction, paying £20,000 (or $88,800) for the house and all of its contents. It was a clever but perfectly legal maneuver: having won the auction, Isaac paid money to extinguish a debt owed to him and his partners, took ownership of the house—thereby shielding it from other creditors—and the Scarbrough family got to stay put.

His home secured, William Scarbrough then had to contend with problems far larger. In late May, the local Planters' Bank won a judgment of nearly $5,000 against his defunct partnership with Joseph P. McKinne, and several merchants received verdicts for lesser amounts.

But these debts were quite minor, compared to multiple lawsuits from the Bank of the United States for over $50,000 in defaulted loans, and the U.S. Custom House for tens of thousands of dollars more in overdue tariffs.

Overwhelming even these was the personal lawsuit of Andrew Low. By the Scotsman's calculation, Scarbrough owed him, man-to-man, a grand total of $175,069 for past-due loans.

On the opposite side of the ledger, Scarbrough had his own lawsuits to prosecute. At the very least, he wanted the record to show who owed him money, and who was the cause of his financial troubles. On June 6th, in Chatham County Superior Court, the case of *Scarbrough & McKinne vs. Pott & McKinne* was decided. The jury found for the plaintiff, calculating that the New York partnership owed the

Savannah firm a grand total of $98,936.03. Whether that money could ever be collected was another matter altogether.

* * *

One of the most time-consuming aspects of lawsuits is interviewing (or *deposing*) all the parties involved. In the early 19th century, the process was far simpler than it later became. At that time, deposing one or two witnesses as to the circumstances behind the lawsuit was often all it took to prepare for the trial stage.

Such was the case in the legal actions taken in Washington against the Savannah Steam Ship Company. The key witnesses to be deposed were those who could verify that a transaction had taken place, and a debt was owed. In the Nicoll lawsuit, the men with this knowledge were Henry Patton, clerk for the ship chandler, and Henry Cooke, the clerk in the counting room of Pott & McKinne.

On May 15th, both men appeared before a magistrate in New York and gave their depositions. Each confirmed the basic facts of the case: Pott & McKinne had been the agents for the Savannah Steam Ship Company; Nicoll's ship chandlery had sold items for the vessel, as reflected in the accounts provided; and Pott & McKinne had failed to honor their promissory notes paying for the merchandise.

While Patton and Cooke's depositions were not out of the ordinary, the particular judge chosen to take them certainly was: New York Mayor and Ocean Steam Ship Company president Cadwallader D. Colden. As the city's chief magistrate, Colden took plenty of depositions, but it seems beyond coincidental that he, of all people, was selected to hear and record the charges against his rival.

Stephen Vail, on the other hand, was kinder. Two days later, he arranged for Henry Cooke to give his deposition in the Speedwell lawsuit to steam engine builder Robert McQueen, who also served as a judge in the Court of Common Pleas.

Once given, these depositions were sent down to the Federal Circuit Court in Washington, where they were added to the case papers already filed. With the evidence submitted, it was then up to one of the plaintiffs to push for action.

* * *

On the evening of June 14th, New Yorkers enjoying the fresh air along the Battery couldn't help but notice a large vessel coming toward them, through the Narrows, puffing smoke. In time, they saw it was the *Robert Fulton*, returning from his maiden voyage.

This newest ocean steamer had successfully made its first round trip—to New Orleans via Havana, and back via Havana and Charleston. The entire voyage had taken 60 days, ports of call included. Counting only time at sea, the *Robert Fulton* had made the voyage from New Orleans in 10 days, virtually all of it under steam, thanks to re-fueling stops. To complete this same 2,000-mile trip, sailing vessels usually took from 2 to 3 weeks, or even longer, making the steamship's certain passage in 1½ weeks look impressive.

The only mechanical mishap experienced on the voyage was the loosening of paddleboards on one of the wheels, which then got fouled up in the housing and forced the steamship to a halt. After some quick repair work, the *Robert Fulton* had been able to resume steaming.

Captain Inott himself suffered the only human injury on the journey, having taken a fall, badly hurting his leg. (The two accidents were combined into one by some observers, but the "Captain Inott fell into the paddlewheel" story was quickly debunked.)

In any event, Inott's injury was serious enough to preclude his continued captainship. Lacking an immediate replacement, the *Robert Fulton*'s proprietors felt forced, for the second time, to run departure advertisements showing their steamship to be without a master. It was hardly a comforting message.

Beyond these minor troubles was the more significant issue of ridership. The *Robert Fulton* had carried around 60 to 70 passengers on the return voyage. While this was a sizeable group, it represented only about one-third of the vessel's carrying capacity. The patronage would have to be larger than that to make the service a success.

The *Robert Fulton*'s disembarking customers provided the much-needed boost. They submitted a long, detailed memorial to *The New-York Evening Post*, which was published the day after their arrival:

> We, the undersigned passengers on board the steam ship Robert Fulton ... unanimously join in recommending her to the attention and patronage of the public.
>
> Having experienced on our passage, several heavy blows, we have had good opportunities to judge whether any good cause existed for the apprehension at first entertained as to her safety in rough weather, and do not hesitate to declare them groundless...

Knowing how much the public are enclined to consider all improvements as useless innovations, until time renders [their] advantages manifest, we have deemed it incumbent upon us to offer this public testimony of our approbation, and to do all in our power, to remove the obstacles which ignorance and prejudice may have thrown in the way of an undertaking, which does honor to the city of New-York...

Ascribing their names to this public testimonial were 31 passengers, including one of the Livingston clan, the actor Henry J. Finn, and most prominently, Lieutenant Commander Isaac McKeever of the U.S. Navy.

By the very wording of the passengers' statement, it was clear that the Ocean Steam Ship Company needed all the help it could get. This was because beyond booking new passengers for the next voyage, there was little else to depend upon. Generating revenues as an official mail carrier was no longer a possibility, since the House of Representatives had failed to vote on the Senate's bill granting that and other privileges. The company couldn't depend upon significant cargo business, either. Everything rode on their ability to attract passengers.

While Cadwallader D. Colden and his fellow investors probably didn't want to admit it, the *Savannah*'s safety record very likely induced at least some of the *Robert Fulton*'s customers to risk booking passage on that first voyage. It also helped that this newest ocean steamer never ventured very far from the coast, making the prospect of an emergency rescue believable.

In any event, with their first trip to New Orleans a success, the Ocean Steam Ship Company immediately faced a new imperative: do it again, just as safely.

* * *

One week after the *Robert Fulton* returned to Gotham, legal proceedings against the rival *Savannah* moved forward in Washington. First before the bench was the suit of Walter Smith and the George Town Importing and Exporting Company. On June 21st, Smith's attorney, Augustus Taney, asked the Federal Court to order the *Savannah* condemned, which meant she would be put up for public auction to pay Smith's bill. Since there was no one present to represent the Savannah Steam Ship Company, Judge William Cranch agreed.

Some 2½ weeks later, on July 7th, the Nicoll suit came before Judge Cranch's court. The attorneys for the ship chandler, having submitted the depositions given by the two clerks in New York, also asked for a judgment of condemnation against the *Savannah*. If it was granted, and Stephen Vail's lawyer did the same, all the suits in Washington would have reached the same conclusion: a forced auction of the steamship was the only way to satisfy the Company's outstanding debts.

This solution was far from ideal for all of the parties involved, but especially the *Savannah*'s owners. The unpredictability of a public auction in the middle of a depression could mean that the steamship might sell for a lot less than its true value. If that happened, and the sale price did not cover the outstanding bills, then the Company still would have unpaid debts. Once their only asset was gone, finding a way to get more than 20 investors to agree to put up more money to satisfy any remaining liabilities would be close to impossible.

What's more, under this scenario, Walter Smith was at risk, too. Even though he had filed his lawsuit first, he would get reimbursed last from the auction proceeds. That's how the law worked: debtors had precedence, meaning the oldest debts got paid off first.

So when Nicoll's lawyers stood before Judge Cranch on July 7th and asked for a judgment of condemnation, they discovered that the Savannah Steam Ship Company suddenly had a representative in the courtroom. That man was none other than Augustus Taney, the same lawyer who had represented Walter Smith of George Town Importing just sixteen days earlier.

In his new capacity as the Savannah Steam Ship Company's counsel, Taney refused to make a case against Nicoll's motion for condemnation. He also said he would not provide any immediate defense against the outstanding debt. Instead, Taney told Judge Cranch that his "mere appearance" in court on behalf of the defendant was enough to justify dissolving the plaintiff's attachment against the *Savannah*. After all, the seizure of the steamship was intended to compel the defendant to appear before the court. The defendant's legal counsel had done so; therefore, any assets seized should be released, and the trial between plaintiff and defendant allowed to continue.

Nicoll's attorneys objected, and for good reason: it was the last day of the Court's term. Any delay in the resolution of their case would push it to the next term, which wouldn't begin until October. So they urged the Court to proceed with the judgment of condemnation, unless Taney was willing to plead his case then and there.

Faced with arguing lawyers, Judge Cranch applied the law. He refused to proceed with a second ruling of condemnation. Further, and most importantly, he ordered that Nicoll's attachment of the *Savannah* be dissolved, based upon the "mere appearance" of the steamship's attorney in court. The Nicoll suit, Judge Cranch directed, could continue "under the ordinary rules," which meant there would be no final judgment until October at the earliest.

The same decision was applied to Stephen Vail's case, as well. This left Augustus Taney's original client, George Town Importing, as the only debtor with an attachment to the *Savannah* itself, and the condemnation to go with it. Taney's scheme succeeded in pushing Walter Smith to the front of the debtors' line—he would be repaid first, if the steamship was sold at auction.

Whatever the merits or demerits of this legal jockeying, the resulting danger to the *Savannah* from the Court's rulings was indisputable: with the condemnation of the steamship for Smith's debt still in place, time was running out.

* * *

Just a few days before the Taney maneuver, on July 2nd, the *Savannah*'s rival, the *Robert Fulton*, was ready to begin a second voyage, to show that he could do it again.

In the wake of Captain Inott's injury on the first voyage, the issue of who would serve as the steamship's new master had remained an open question for ten days after its return. Not until June 24th had the *Robert Fulton*'s owners announced his replacement: Captain John Mott.

This was, by coincidence or not, the same John Mott who previously had sailed his brig *Othello* from New York to Savannah faster than the steamship *Savannah*.

And it was the same John Mott who had transported New York's fire relief donations to Savannah, only to have them rejected by the Council.

After his return to Gotham from the fire donation run, Mott had left the *Othello* in early April. Having no maritime experience past the coast of Georgia, he had taken command of a new vessel, the ship *Commodore Rodgers*. Then Mott had made one trip with the *Rodgers* to New Orleans, and arrived back in New York just before the *Robert Fulton's* return. With his freshly-acquired knowledge of the Gulf Coast, Mott had been hired as the new master of this newest steamship.

As Captain Mott prepared his new command for departure on July 2nd, he could not help but notice that despite all the publicity, endorsements and success surrounding the inaugural voyage, the *Robert Fulton's* decks were far from crowded. In fact, a number of those on board had not booked passage at all, but were only testing the steamship as far as Sandy Hook.

Once the *Robert Fulton* had steamed off and reached the Hook, the temporary guests transferred to the local revenue cutter, which took them back to Gotham. This left "but a few passengers," declared the *Mercantile Advertiser*, as the steamship proceeded out to sea. So disappointing was the passenger count that the *Advertiser* tried to lend a helping hand, declaring that it believed the *Robert Fulton* was well-positioned to deliver on the promise of oceanic steam travel, since "the experiment may be considered as fairly tested."

Speed was now the key. The primary question in the minds of the steamship's projectors must have been whether or not the voyage could be made faster than before.

The answer they received—three weeks later—turned out to be a most unwelcome one. Limping into New York came the *Robert Fulton*, with his paddlewheels motionless, and the only means of progress coming from the natural power of the lug sails. Once the steamship finally made it to the wharves, anyone looking at the engine structure that rose above the deck could tell what had gone wrong.

Midway into the voyage to New Orleans, the *Robert Fulton* had been steaming past the Florida Keys at a very rapid 9 miles per hour, when one of the cast-iron flywheels (which smoothed out the piston rod's motion) suddenly fractured. The engineer on duty quickly shut down the engine, but this abrupt stoppage further broke the balance wheel shaft, as well as the crosshead beam. With no ability to transmit power from the cylinder to the paddlewheel axle, the entire apparatus was crippled in an instant.

Havana had been only 90 miles away at the time, but Captain Mott knew that the Cuban port did not have the facilities for repairing the engine. Neither did New Orleans, for that matter. His only choice was to order the lug sails set, and head back to New York.

That the *Robert Fulton* made it home safely was a relief, of course, and some consolation, given the worst fears many had about using steam at sea. But there could be little room for denial among the shareholders: the sight of this newest steamship, crippled and hobbling into the East River under sail, was nothing short of a public relations disaster.

* * *

On the same day the *Robert Fulton* arrived at New York from his aborted voyage, the Federal Court down in Washington was trying, once again, to resolve the Savannah Steam Ship Company's debts. Walter Smith's lawsuit—having already forced a judgment of condemnation against the *Savannah*—still required some additional paperwork. William Ridgely, the clerk for George Town Importing, provided the Court's clerk with a detailed accounting of the monies lent to "The President of the Savannah Steam Ship Company." Ridgely further confirmed that his employer's commission of 5% was an amount "usually allowed for such agency."

With a judgment of condemnation already made one month prior, a detailed accounting of the debt owed finally submitted, and no defendant appearing (since Taney was back representing his original client), the exercise of the Court's power was only a matter of logistics.

Sometime around the middle of August, the auction of the first steamship in history took place. While its precise details have disappeared with the passage of time, the circumstances of the moment give a sense of the sale price.

On the one hand, given her newness and swiftness, as a sailing ship alone the *Savannah* was easily worth $20,000 to $25,000.

On the other hand, the auction was taking place in the minor port of Washington, while Congress was out of session and the city deserted, in the heat of August, in the middle of an economic depression. With all those factors working against her, it appears that on auction day, the *Savannah* went for a song.

The winning bidder and new owner of the steamship was a man named Nathan H. Holdridge. A native of Mystic, Connecticut, he had commanded a sailing sloop out of nearby Groton back in 1807. This made Holdridge a contemporary of Moses Rogers right when the latter caught steamboat fever. The two surely knew each other.

The familiarity didn't stop there. Holdridge had later moved to

New York, and gone to work for Pott & McKinne, serving as the captain of one of their ships, the *Rubicon*. In that capacity, he had hauled the partnership's cargos to the French port of Havre on a regular basis after the war, and also made periodic trips to Savannah.

As the depression squeezed Pott & McKinne, they had been forced to sell the *Rubicon*, and Holdridge went with her. The ship's new owner, Gotham merchant Henry Thomas, put Holdridge and the *Rubicon* to work on the New York–Savannah route. That set-up had lasted only until January of 1820, when captain and ship were driven ashore on the south coast of Long Island. Having lost the *Rubicon*, Nathan Holdridge needed a new vessel to command.

With his purchase of the *Savannah* successfully made, Holdridge went into the Georgetown Custom House on August 25th, to register himself as both owner and master.

For the Savannah Steam Ship Company, and Moses Rogers, this was the end. Their "laudable and meritorious experiment"—to show the world that steam travel across the oceans was possible—had succeeded. Yet their second goal—of extending that triumph with a regular steam packet service, or a second generation of steamships—was beyond their reach.

Once Captain Holdridge had successfully gained ownership of both vessel and equipment, he had to decide how to bring the two together. Since the *Savannah*'s sails and etceteras were still in storage at George Sanford's lumberyard store, it appears that Holdridge thought it would be easier to bring the stripped steamship to them, rather than the other way around. So the vessel was moved up the Eastern Branch of the Potomac, to Sanford's store at Coomb's Wharf, right next to the Navy Yard. Once there, Holdridge set to work having all of this stored gear re-installed on the *Savannah*.

* * *

While Captain Holdridge and his newly-mustered crew were preparing the *Savannah* for departure in the last days of August, up in New York, resident U.S. Marshal Thomas Morris received word that a person of interest was within his reach.

With paper in hand, Marshal Morris pounced. On August 30th, he served a warrant upon Abraham B. Fannin, as one of the 23 defendants in the case brought against the *Savannah*'s shareholders by Daniel Dod.

But Marshal Morris did more than just serve the defendant with papers—he arrested Fannin, and threw him in jail. Such was the procedure at the time. Debtors could be imprisoned until they paid up, although there was, in the wake of so many bankruptcies, a powerful backlash growing against this practice.

But Abraham Fannin had not been found guilty of anything yet, and was able to post bail, get out of jail, and seek help. He hired local attorney George W. Strong, who, upon learning the particulars of the case, immediately marched into the just-convened Federal Circuit Court, and asked Associate Supreme Court Justice Brockholst Livingston, presiding, for relief.

Justice Livingston did not like what he heard, and acted accordingly:

Let the Plaintiff in this cause appear before me at my Office situate Number Thirty seven in Broadway in the City of New York on Tuesday next being the fifth day of September Instant at ten of the Clock in the forenoon of that day and then and there shew cause why the Capias ad respondendum issued in the above cause should not be quashed as to the above named Abraham B. Fannin and of the Defendants . . .

* * *

On the same day Justice Livingston issued his order to Daniel Dod, down in Washington, Captain Nathan Holdridge told the *Savannah's* new crew to cast off from Coomb's Wharf. With the boilers cold and the paddlewheels folded upon the deck, the men began deploying her sails, as she drifted down the Eastern Branch, and into the undivided Potomac.

From there, Captain Holdridge pointed the steamship downriver, toward the Chesapeake Bay and the sea. His destination was New York.

* * *

On the morning of September 5th, the attorneys in the case of *Daniel Dod vs. Abraham B. Fannin,* "impleaded with others," met in the chambers of Justice Brockholst Livingston. At issue was whether Mr. Fannin could be served with a federal warrant (or *Capias ad respondendum*) for a case filed in the Southern District of New York.

For his part, Abraham Fannin clarified his status:

. . . that he is a Citizen and Inhabitant of the State of Georgia and not of the State of New York, and that he is now and was at the said time

of his arrest in the above cause temporarily in the City of New York for the benefit of his health and expects as soon as the sickly season is over to return to Savannah...

Having heard enough, Justice Livingston ordered both sides to retire, and shifted his activities from chambers to the courtroom itself. Once two other cases on the docket had been addressed, the clerk called the parties in *Dod vs. Fannin* before the bench.

On the motion of defendant Abraham Fannin's counsel, with no objection coming from Daniel Dod's counsel, Justice Livingston issued his ruling:

It is ordered, That the said writ be quashed as to the above defendant, and that the bail-bond, executed by the said defendant, be delivered up to him, or his attorney, to be cancelled.

Justice Livingston's rationale was straightforward: if Daniel Dod wanted to sue Abraham Fannin in federal court, he would have to file the lawsuit where Fannin resided, that being in the District of Georgia, at Savannah. By extension, the same would hold true for the other shareholders who lived outside New York.

Justice Livingston's decision left Daniel Dod with several options—

He could sue the corporate entity, the Savannah Steam Ship Company, although he had decided against that course of action once before.

Or he could try to file lawsuits in the appropriate federal court districts where each of the shareholders lived, as Justice Livingston's ruling suggested.

Or he could go after those shareholders who definitely lived within the Southern District of New York, namely Gideon Pott and Joseph P. McKinne.

* * *

By the time Nathan Holdridge and the *Savannah* were sailing toward Gotham, the *Robert Fulton* was repaired and ready to go.

In mid-August, when the *Robert Fulton* was still laid up, word had circulated that an excursion around Long Island might be in the offing. The purpose of making such a trip was twofold: first, it would allow the repaired engine to be tested; and second, it might serve to allay public concerns about safety.

The Ocean Steam Ship Company's management wasn't particularly keen on the idea, perhaps because it might imply that their craft had a perception problem. Besides, the approach of autumn meant rougher seas off Long Island, and stories about steaming difficulties in poor weather, or sea-sick passengers, could easily make matters worse.

Colden and company nevertheless decided to let the excursion go forward, provided enough tickets could be sold. Advertisements were run in several of the major newspapers, setting the *Robert Fulton*'s circumnavigation of Long Island for Wednesday, September 13th.

But two days before the scheduled departure, things changed. The *Robert Fulton*'s owners didn't think enough tickets had been sold, so they announced the trip's cancellation.

It was just as well, since sailing into the East River that same day came Captain Holdridge and the steamship *Savannah*. With the appearance of his rival, it made far more sense to return the *Robert Fulton* to his primary objective, as a permanent ocean-steaming packet.

In short order, the Ocean Steam Ship Company laid plans to advertise for another departure to New Orleans. Once that was set in motion, the *Robert Fulton*'s owners could only wait and wonder—in the wake of a broken paddlewheel and a busted engine—whether anyone would be willing to go.

* * *

Just a short distance away from the steamship *Robert Fulton* sat the steamship *Savannah*. The plans Captain Holdridge had for his new command required a lay-up of several weeks. In that time, the *Savannah*'s masts and sails would stay; the steam apparatus would not.

While the paddlewheels, axle and smokestack were probably of little use, some parts of the steam engine might be applied elsewhere. James P. Allaire decided he could use the cylinder, which remained one of the largest ever installed in a steam vessel. Purchasing it from Holdridge, he had the cylinder hauled right back to where it had been cast, at the ironworks on Cherry Street. There, it was set up as a blowing cylinder in the foundry.

Once all of the engine parts had been removed, the axle openings in the hull were closed up, and the lower deck and hold cleaned up. Given what Holdridge had in mind for her, there was no need for a name change. The vessel, re-born, would simply be known as the ship *Savannah.*

* * *

While his creation was being torn apart in New York, Moses Rogers was moving on, and rebuilding, in Philadelphia. The immediate object of his attention there was a dwelling at the northeast corner of Market and Water Streets, which he was fitting out for use as a hotel or boarding house.

Philadelphia was a logical place for Moses to put down roots. He knew the city very well, having run steamboats out of it for half a dozen years. It was also a familiar place for Adelia and the children, and not too far from relatives in Connecticut.

But beyond familiarity, the City of Brotherly Love also had something else: it was one of the most vibrant centers for the new mode anywhere, actively exporting engines and even complete steamboats to markets yet untapped. For that reason, Philadelphia offered Moses the best bet to achieve the one thing that he desperately sought: a chance to get back in the game.

* * *

On Thursday, September 21st, while the steamship *Savannah*'s machinery was being dismantled in her port of birth, Amos Rogers Senior ambled down to the docks near his home at Poquonnock Bridge, in Groton, Connecticut.

The patriarch of the family had achieved much in his 66 years. Like many ancestors before him, Amos Senior had mastered the ocean, primarily as a sloop captain. Then he had opened a successful brick and lumber yard, which served much of Groton and the surrounding countryside. He had fathered seven children, and seen each of his five sons learn how to sail. With the union of Mary and Stevens Rogers, both of his daughters had married men linked in some way to the maritime trades. And finally, his youngest child, Ebenezer, had just turned 20, and was out making his own living as a mariner. Without question, Amos the elder could rightly say that his family was both mature and married to the sea.

That Thursday, father Amos intended to take the gift from his eldest son, Moses, out for a short trip. The Norwegian sjekte, given its small size, could be handled easily enough by one person.

Climbing aboard, Amos cast off, and set sail for the open waters of Long Island Sound. In time, he reached the mouth of the Thames River, which he knew better than any other body of water in the world.

Even so, as father Amos and the sjekte pushed on through the waves, the unpredictability of Long Island Sound soon came to the fore. A violent wind squall suddenly appeared, and quickly began rocking the little boat. In an instant, the sjekte capsized, throwing father into the cold water.

The mishap, occurring in full view at the mouth of New London harbor, immediately sparked a rescue effort. By the time those nearest had arrived to help, it was too late. The sjekte had sunk, and Amos Rogers was lifeless.

His body was quickly recovered, and brought to shore. As the law required, an inquest was organized that same day to determine a cause of death. The jury of 12 men balanced the victim's great experience as a mariner with the unpredictable power of Nature, and concluded that Amos Rogers "came to his death by mischance and accident."

The very next day, the funeral of Amos Rogers was held at his home. His wife Sarah was there, along with many others, and the house soon became packed with mourners. Baptist Elder Roswell Burrows gave the eulogy, in which he recited a passage out of the Bible, from Peter's second letter:

> For so an entrance shall be ministered unto you abundantly, into the everlasting kingdom of our Lord...

The huge turnout for the funeral was hardly a surprise. Father Amos was part of an extended clan that was scattered all over New London County. His local business and active involvement in the Baptist Church made him a prominent member of the community. His seafaring days touched people even further away, and newspapers stretching from Boston to New York City reprinted his obituary.

As shocking as the accident was to the many mourners, some family members were not entirely surprised by what had transpired. The clues had been there. Most prominent among them had been the words of Amos Rogers himself, uttered repeatedly a few days before the tragedy: "I have a desire to depart and be with Christ."

* * *

In the same month that saw his creation, the steamship *Savannah*, stripped bare of its innovations, Moses Rogers also lost his father. It must have been especially painful to learn that his gift—the sjekte— had become, in part, the instrument of his father's death. Yet there was little that Moses could do beyond moving on, and getting on.

Given the depression, finding work was not easy. In the cities, thousands of carpenters, mechanics and other skilled laborers had been thrown out of work. Tens of thousands more in the countryside had lost their farms, and were forced to start over. Even the steam-boat building business had flattened out, as entrepreneurs held off on new construction, waiting for signs of better times.

Under the circumstances, going back into the steam*ship* quest at that point was not a realistic option. If Moses was going to get back on his feet, he would need to find another steam*boat* command.

In considering the possibilities, the already-proven markets for steamboating were simply unappealing. The Monopoly still con-trolled all the New York waters. The other major rivers in the East, including the Delaware, were being serviced already, and most had a surplus of competitors. The Mississippi and Ohio Rivers were no dif-ferent; they had scores of steamboats in operation.

Moses likely would not settle for running just any steamboat— that would have been out of character. Ever since he had caught the fever back in 1807, Moses had been a trailblazer. The most appealing position would be one that allowed him to start a new route, and open a new market. While the West had many such opportunities, it was territory Moses did not know at all, and would have required him to be far away from Adelia and the children, who would stay in Philadel-phia. Better would be a steamboat command somewhere in the East.

By the autumn of 1820, Moses finally found an opportunity that fit. His new charge was a little steamboat called the *Pee Dee*.

Completed at Charleston in November of 1819, with a steam engine imported from Philadelphia, the *Pee Dee* had been put under the com-mand of Captain Charles Vanderford, the former master of the ill-fated steamboat *Massachusetts*. From Charleston, Vanderford had taken the *Pee Dee* up the coast, to Georgetown, South Carolina. From there, in January of 1820, they had ventured up the Great Pee Dee River. With some difficulty, Vanderford and the *Pee Dee* made it all the way to their intended destination, a frontier outpost called Cheraw, near the North Carolina border. A few additional trips were made during the spring, but nothing like a regular service had yet been established.

The reasons why were obvious. The Great Pee Dee River was a challenge, to say the least. Winding like a serpent through the South Carolina upcountry, the river was full of surprises, from dozens of horseshoe turns, to sandbars, and snags. While the upper reaches had been largely cleared of obstructions during the latter months of 1819, the lower stretches near the coast were still littered with dangers that only a skilled captain could avoid.

Not only was the going dangerous, but incredibly tedious. The direct distance between Georgetown and Cheraw was about 100 miles, but on the twisting river it was more like 220 miles. Whoever tried to run a steamboat on the Great Pee Dee would need both patience and stamina.

And alertness. The steep, slippery riverbanks were covered with trees, some of which leaned precipitously out over the water. In time, these trees would succumb to the inevitable, and fall in, creating an ever-changing collection of sawyers, part of which would be invisible, thanks to the mud-brown river water.

With all due respect to the upcountry folks who lived there, assuming command of the *Pee Dee* surely must have seemed an off-key note in the career of one of the first steamboat captains in the world.

The Delaware River, Chesapeake Bay and Carolina sea coast were the kind of challenges Moses Rogers had taken on with the new mode of transport, and succeeded.

The Atlantic Ocean, North Sea and Baltic Sea he had all conquered with his own creation, the first steamship in history.

Yet with all of those triumphs behind him, the immediate goal of Captain Moses Rogers in the autumn of 1820 became running a little 111-ton steamer on a minor, muddy river in the wilds of South Carolina.

It truly was a new beginning.

CHAPTER TWENTY-TWO

CARRYING ON

B Y THE EARLY autumn of 1820, the *Robert Fulton* was fully repaired, and ready to make a third attempt at reaching New Orleans.

But the Ocean Steam Ship Company soon discovered that it had a new obstacle to overcome, by the name of "Yellow Jack." Along with the cancellation of the Long Island excursion had come news that New Orleans was being hit by an outbreak of yellow fever.

The idea of inviting customers to trust in a newly repaired steamship, which would then deliver them into the midst of one of the deadliest diseases of their time, was just too much to ask. New Orleans was out of the question. Instead, the *Robert Fulton* would head for Charleston only, on October 5th.

Before the steamship could depart, however, Yellow Jack appeared in Charleston, as well, and those who had booked passage asked that the voyage be delayed. Failing to heed this request would have been foolish, since forcing a departure surely would lead to a raft of cancelled bookings. So the proprietors agreed to wait.

Finally, on October 10th, the *Robert Fulton* left New York. On board were thirty-some passengers, including former *Savannah* shareholder Samuel Howard, his wife Rebecca and their children.

Back in New York, the Ocean Steam Ship Company knew they had to regain the initiative, in the wake of so many mishaps, delays, and then a shortened trip only to Charleston. So immediately upon the *Robert Fulton*'s departure, the steamship's agent, David Dunham & Company, began advertising for the next voyage to New Orleans, which was scheduled for October 29th.

The *Robert Fulton*'s trip down to Charleston proved to be quick, and dangerous. The vessel steamed right into a near-hurricane, and despite punishing headwinds and perilous waves, still managed to make port in 5 days.

Upon their arrival at Charleston, Samuel Howard and the other passengers felt obliged to offer a memorial to the newspapers, endorsing the *Robert Fulton*'s safety, and thanking Captain Mott for his attention to them during the rough passage.

Kind words aside, Captain Mott realized he had a problem. In the course of rocking and rolling its way through the storm, the steamship had burnt far more coal than Mott had expected. The supply loaded at New York, calculated to cover the entire round-trip, was nearly gone. Finding no coal for sale at Charleston, Mott had no choice but to fill the fuel bunkers with less efficient wood. He also wrote back to headquarters, telling them what had happened.

Once Captain Mott's letter arrived at New York, the Ocean Steam Ship Company decided to delay the already-scheduled voyage to New Orleans. Changes to the *Robert Fulton*, they announced, were going to be made.

On the steamship's return trip, the supply of coal and wood quickly gave out, forcing Captain Mott to rely on the lug sails, slowly working his way northward. The winds off New Jersey proved to be so unfriendly, and the sails so inadequate, that the *Robert Fulton* spent three long days within sight of Sandy Hook lighthouse, before finally making it into New York harbor.

This fresh embarrassment only reinforced the imperative to make changes. So shortly after the *Robert Fulton*'s arrival in the East River, he was moved up to the shipyards at Corlear's Hook. There, a crash-construction program was begun. The small, collapsible poles for the lug-sails were removed, and in their place rose three sturdy masts, stepped and lashed together in the normal fashion. Then came the horizontal yards—three per mast—for mainsails, topsails, and top-gallants. To the fore and main masts were attached Spencer masts, in line with the keel. Finally came the remaining rigging, and sails.

By the beginning of November, the re-fitting was finished. What observers saw tied up to the wharves was a very different-looking vessel. It still had the enormous steam engine and paddlewheels of the new mode, but it also had the three-masted, square-rigged sailing apparatus of a true ship. With the Spencer masts and staysails placed aboard, it could also be configured to sail like a schooner, if necessary.

The end result of this makeover was a *Robert Fulton* that truly had become a "steam ship," capable of both steaming and sailing upon the sea.

The end result was also a *Robert Fulton* that looked remarkably like his former rival, the very first steamship, named *Savannah*.

* * *

On October 28th, just as the *Robert Fulton* was about to be moved up to Corlear's Hook for a make-over, Colonel John Stevens took to his desk at his Hoboken estate. At 71 years of age, Moses Rogers' former employer showed few signs of slowing down. In addition to retaining ownership with his sons in a number of Delaware River steamboats, John Stevens also was trying to convince anyone who would listen that the power of steam could be harnessed to pull wagons on iron tracks, or "railroads."

With pen in hand, Colonel Stevens began writing a letter to the President of the United States. The objective of his missive was to resurrect an idea from several years before: rather than spend what he thought would be $600,000 for three Navy steam batteries, why not try a completely different approach?

The government, he suggested, should purchase steam engines "of various powers," to be stored at ports along the eastern seaboard. At the outbreak of war, the engines could be fitted onto any "readily procured" vessels—"ships, tugs, schooners, and sloops"—thereby creating an instant fleet of steam-powered men-of-war. Their machinery would be protected by specially-built shields, and their maneuverability would allow this steam fleet to concentrate firepower upon a single enemy vessel, overwhelming it.

Such a plan as this provided far more flexibility than the Navy's current program for steam batteries, which could protect, at best, only three harbors. Furthermore, these batteries, or "arks," as the Colonel called them, were so enormous they would take far too long to finish.

His idea fully described, Colonel Stevens then presented his proposal: suspend the Navy's program for steam batteries, and have Congress appropriate $40,000 to $50,000 for equipping a vessel of 150 to 300 tons with his steam-and-shield design. If the experiment worked, then the government could determine how to put the plan into effect on a larger scale.

Colonel Stevens' proposal was a creative and interesting counter to the Navy's existing program. While he had made a similar suggestion to President Monroe back in 1817, the Colonel hadn't really pushed the idea until he composed this letter. What had changed in the interim John Stevens did not say specifically, but given the outline of his plan, the recent exploits of his ex-employee were probably not far from his mind.

* * *

With alterations complete, the *Robert Fulton* left New York on November 5th. It was the steamship's fourth voyage, and third attempt to reach New Orleans. While the steam engine was still the primary means of power, Captain Mott also made use of the brand new complement of sails, whenever the winds allowed. The additional speed could only improve the transit time.

Unfortunately, the old mode of power also could make things worse. On the first leg of the journey, toward Charleston, the *Robert Fulton* was hit again by strong winds. The lowest set of yards on all three masts strained under the pressure. Before the crew could make any adjustments, the fore and main yards snapped, and were carried away by the gale.

Captain Mott ordered the steamship onward. After arriving safely at Charleston, Mott determined to make repairs there, and continue the voyage. Thankfully, the rest of the trip to Havana and New Orleans was uneventful, but the damage had already been done. One of the passengers on the first leg to Charleston drove the point home, telling a newspaper that the *Robert Fulton*'s yards were "too slender ... I would recommend to the owners of the Fulton to remedy this in future."

The *Robert Fulton* managed to make it back to New York just before the end of the year, on December 30th. It was a fitting time to take stock. In a little more than seven months of operation, the steamship had made two full trips to New Orleans, one abbreviated trip to Charleston, and one aborted trip to nowhere. One of the paddle-wheels had suffered damage, the steam engine had broken down, and the sailing rig had partially failed. Even worse, each of these mishaps was news, and not just in the ports of call, but all over the country. For the Ocean Steam Ship Company, advancing the dream was proving to be a very difficult task.

* * *

The last months of 1820 were much kinder to the re-born ship *Savannah*. Captain Holdridge began running her as a sailing packet between New York and Savannah, and quickly showed just how fast she could go using the old mode. On his first try at the end of October, Holdridge managed the trip to Georgia in just 90 hours, a little more than one-half the time it usually took.

This quick passage, and a second voyage in December, had the desired effect. Two well-established Savannah merchants, Oliver Sturges and Benjamin Burroughs, agreed to buy in to the ship. By the end of the year, they became part owners along with Holdridge, and began using the *Savannah* as the primary cargo carrier for their partnership of Sturges & Burroughs.

The *Savannah* was still a young ship. Her speed and sturdy construction held the promise of many years of sailing to come. In short order, mentions of her arrival or departure in the shipping section of the newspapers became commonplace. But initially, at least, there were editors who would recall for their readers what the *Savannah* had once been, seeming to betray, at least in the minds of some, a long and kind remembrance.

* * *

As the winter of 1820–21 approached, the nation's capital at Washington City got ready for yet another round of legislating. The Second Session of the 16th Congress convened in mid-November, and soon found itself confronting many of the same issues left over from the previous spring.

For the Navy, another rush of enquiries from the House about expenses had to be answered. In a long reply to one of these queries, Commodore John Rodgers informed the Naval Affairs Committee on December 9th that no new contracts had been signed to advance the building of the steam batteries. The outstanding costs to date of $223,555 remained the same as had been reported the previous January.

Within the Navy Board's office, the loss of momentum on the batteries was just as noticeable. Newly-appointed Naval Constructor John Floyd—despite having been Henry Eckford's assistant—couldn't begin to fill the steam-powered void left by Eckford's departure. Further still, when New York Steam Superintendent Francis B. Ogden had requested permission to build yet another warehouse—this time to

store one of the newly-delivered copper boilers for the batteries—the
Board had agreed. Rather than pushing to assemble the steam battery
components already purchased, the Navy seemed to be sliding back
into the comfortable, knowable status quo.

But this course of action, or inaction, did not prove to be quite that
easy. Stirring things up was Colonel John Stevens' idea for a small
fleet of fighting steamers, which soon spread far beyond President
Monroe.

The Colonel had seen to that personally, taking the time to study
the Navy Board's public reports on steam battery expenditures, as well
as the appropriation by Congress for the construction of small vessels
of war to fight pirates.

Then, the Colonel had written to several members of Congress
about his plan.

To Congressman Thomas Cobb of Georgia, he suggested that the
small vessels authorized in the last session to fight pirates should be
fitted with steam engines.

And to the new Speaker of the House, John Taylor of New York,
he sent a formal petition requesting that his idea be put to a practical
test. Colonel Stevens did not mince words in explaining the rationale
for his petition. If his experiment was successful—

> ... *Such results would naturally excite alarm and jealousy not only
> among the Com[modores] of the Navy Board, but among all grades
> of naval officers. From this view of the subject there cannot be the most
> distant prospect of this business being ever brought forward by the
> Department itself. If ever it should be carried through, it must of neces-
> sity originate with Congress* ...

Speaker Taylor laid the petition before the House on December
20th, where it was promptly referred to the Naval Affairs Committee.
The Committee, in turn, forwarded Colonel Stevens' proposal to the
Board of Navy Commissioners, and asked for a response.

* * *

Some 400 miles further south, in upcountry South Carolina, Captain Moses Rogers was making the most of his new position.

The *Pee Dee* was unlike any other steamboat he had commanded.
At only 111 tons burthen, she was small. Accommodations on board

were quite limited. For that matter, so was the cargo space. To make the run upriver from Georgetown to Cheraw work, the little steamboat had to pull a transport barge behind it. No longer was Moses primarily a passenger captain; instead, for the first time in his steamboat career, he was a cargo hauler.

Towing a barge made the trips up and down the Great Pee Dee River that much more of a challenge. Dodging snags and shallows along the muddy 220-mile course was a near-constant necessity. Under the circumstances, steaming at night was simply out of the question.

Even so, Moses carried on. He plunged into the tasks before him: learning the river, noting the danger spots, securing the best firewood supplies available along the way, and improving on his transit times.

Within a few months, his efforts began to change the very relationship between the tiny town of Cheraw and the Carolina coast. Flatboats filled with produce normally took 20 to 25 days to make the tortuous trip downriver to Georgetown. Yet by January of 1821, Moses and the *Pee Dee* could make the trip in as little as 2 days.

Trade quickly skyrocketed. Farmers and plantation owners all around Cheraw sent whatever they had to sell downriver with the steamboat, including corn, peas, flax-seed, bees-wax, bacon, and lard. But most of all, they sent cotton. Heaping loads of it. The barge that the little *Pee Dee* towed was usually stacked with around 500 bales of the white fiber, as much as safety allowed. Even at the depressed prices of the time, this rapid transport of cargo downriver gave the people in and around Cheraw something they had never really had before, and that was purchasing power.

Moses could satisfy that side of the equation, too. While bushwhacking a flatboat up 220 miles of winding river was possible, few dared to try it. On the other hand, Moses and his steamboat could make the trip upriver in 4 to 5 days. From Georgetown, the *Pee Dee* brought all sorts of things, from the bare necessities of salt, sugar, and coffee, to luxuries such as cheese, brandy, and imported manufactures.

It was little wonder that whenever the *Pee Dee* came splashing up to Cheraw, a crowd quickly gathered down by the riverbank to greet the steamboat, as well as the man that locals called its "active and enterprising commander."

* * *

By the latter days of January 1821, the Ocean Steam Ship Company of New York was pressing forward as aggressively as circumstances allowed. Once the *Robert Fulton* had returned from the fourth voyage at the end of December, his promoters began running a new advertisement, this time for a February 11th departure.

Even so, the difficulties of carrying on were clearly showing.

On the positive side, the new departure notice featured a brand-new, wood-cut engraving of the vessel. It showed the *Robert Fulton* to be not the typical mast-less river steamboat of the initial advertisements, but rather as the fully-equipped "steamship" he had become. This was a distinct improvement—the image finally matched the reality.

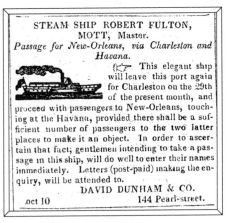

*Steamship Robert Fulton's
Initial Advertisements...*

... and Revised Advertisements.

Yet, on the negative side, the wording of this newest departure notice was hardly comforting. All it could muster was a statement that "several passengers are already engaged" for the next voyage, and this for a vessel that could carry 200 or more. Just as disconcerting was the further advisory that anyone wishing to apply for passage directly on board the steamship could not do so at the commercial wharves along South Street. Instead, they would have to travel up to Corlear's Hook, because that's where the *Robert Fulton* had been taken, once again, for repairs.

* * *

While the *Robert Fulton* was seeking more passengers, Colonel John Stevens, ensconced at his estate at Hoboken, received a letter from Speaker of the House John Taylor. Enclosed in the correspondence was a copy of the report by the Naval Affairs Committee on the Colonel's plan for "Defence of the Seacoast," using a fleet of *Savannah*-like steam vessels.

The bulk of the report consisted of the Navy Board's response to Colonel Stevens' petition. Commodore John Rodgers, on behalf of the commissioners, laid out their position, point-by-point.

First, the Commodore defended the Board's work on the steam batteries to date, which he thought the Colonel "would appear to impeach." He went on to declare that the Board would "do nothing which would jeopardize the public interests by vain projects and visionary schemes." The Navy, Commodore Rodgers pointed out, was already actively preparing to construct a new kind of steam vessel, based upon the design submitted by the very builder of the steamship running between New York and New Orleans.

Second, the Board had already introduced every innovation suggested by Stevens that appeared "advantageous."

Third, it was "impracticable to place engines on board vessels not prepared for them."

Fourth, the Colonel offered "no plan for the protection of the machinery" on his steamers.

Fifth, Rodgers stated that "the Board confidently believe that one of the Steam Batteries which are contemplated to be built by the Board would destroy the whole fleet" of Colonel Stevens' steam-powered vessels.

Sixth, and most pointedly, Commodore Rodgers noted that the Colonel's son, Robert Stevens, had recently visited the Navy Board. When informed of his father's "schemes," the younger Stevens expressed "mortification and regret," and assured the Board that "he had no concern in a project so wild, and offered the infirmities of age as an apology for his father."

For all these reasons, the Commodore concluded, "the Board conceive it unnecessary to proceed into a further investigation" of the Colonel's plan for a steam-and-sail fleet.

Given this official reply by the Navy, the full House of Representatives, in turn, resolved that the Colonel's original petition should be withdrawn.

For John Stevens, this outcome was beyond disappointing. It was humiliating. The Navy Board, and Commodore Rodgers in particular, had made him look like a fool. For a man who had been one of the first inventors of practical steamboats, such treatment was too much to bear in silence. So the Colonel organized his papers, and counter-attacked.

He made copies of every significant piece of correspondence related to his steam fleet plan, and sent them to Hezekiah Niles, owner and editor of the most widely-read newspaper in the country, *Niles' Weekly Register* of Baltimore.

To these papers Colonel Stevens added something more: he challenged Commodore Rodgers to a steam duel, with money to be wagered on the outcome. The Colonel wanted the steamship *Robert Fulton*—upon which the Navy Board claimed its new batteries were being modeled—and his own steamboat *Philadelphia* to both undergo speed tests. The winner of these tests would collect the wagers, deposited with the Bank of the United States.

Colonel Stevens had the utmost confidence in his "Old Sal," as the *Philadelphia* was nicknamed, and very little confidence in the *Robert Fulton*. "It is a notorious fact," he stated in his challenge, that this newest steamship had been unable to work its engines "for some days" on the last voyage to New Orleans. He didn't think it could exceed 7 miles per hour in speed, while the *Philadelphia* certainly did. Besides, this *Robert Fulton*, supposed model of a steamship, "wallowed" in heavy seas, declared the Colonel, and had "by no means proved to be a good and safe sea-vessel."

The successive waves of correspondence from Colonel Stevens must have intimidated Hezekiah Niles, for he published none of it.

John Stevens then tried to enlist the Senate, writing to Senators Rufus King of New York and Mahlon Dickerson of New Jersey. But as Senator King pointed out in his reply, it was already late in the session, and there remained a lot of other unfinished business before the Congress.

With all avenues for his proposal closed, John Stevens realized there was nothing more he could do. The brawl between himself and Commodore Rodgers—fought partly in public, and partly in private—slowly, quietly dissipated. And with the Navy Board refusing to budge, the idea of a steam-powered fleet, fast and nimble, was once again, in Colonel Stevens' own words, "committed to the Tomb of the Capulets."

* * *

Far removed from the ongoing struggle for the dream, Captain Moses Rogers and the steamboat *Pee Dee* continued their runs into the South Carolina upcountry. While there were surely more prominent commands to be had, making the new mode work on the Great Pee Dee River would be no small accomplishment, given the many obstacles. It also would be yet another first for Moses.

As the winter of 1821 gave way to spring, Moses kept running the *Pee Dee* faster and faster. Turnaround time was the key. While he was towing one freight boat up or down the river, another one was being loaded at his destination. Upon arrival at Cheraw, for example, Moses would deliver the towed boat full of cargo. After spending perhaps a day re-fueling and finishing any paperwork, he then would tie the *Pee Dee* to the other freight boat filled with cotton and foodstuffs, and quickly depart downriver.

Within a few months, Moses was able to make the roundtrip passage between Georgetown and Cheraw in about 8 days. Such a rapid transit time was a tiny fraction of what it had taken previously, using flatboats.

The frequency of the trips Moses and the *Pee Dee* made, and the volume of goods they transported, was far beyond anything the people of Cheraw had ever seen before. The frontier outpost's exports of cotton alone during the 1820–21 season reached some 9,500 bales. This was nearly triple the amount that got out during the previous season, with no steamboat running. In turn, Cheraw was able to use these expanded export profits to import goods on an unprecedented scale. Some $200,000 worth of merchandise was brought upriver that same 1820–21 season, virtually all of it by Captain Rogers and the *Pee Dee*. The consequences of this burgeoning trade were readily apparent all over Cheraw, as residents began construction on dozens of new homes, stores and warehouses.

Shareholders in the Pee Dee Steam-Boat Company had reason to be pleased, as well. Captain Rogers' performance allowed them to receive a 12% dividend on their stock, a respectable return considering the risks.

As the spring of 1821 drew to a close, so too did the seasonal rains which kept the Great Pee Dee River flowing deep, and relatively safe. With the hot, sickly summer about to begin, and the upper sections of the river becoming impassable, Moses tied up the *Pee Dee* at Cheraw, and declared the end of his first steamboating season into the Carolina upcountry. He would start up again in the autumn, once the rains had returned.

Until then, his family beckoned. Moses departed for Philadelphia, to spend the summer with Adelia and the children.

As he headed north, Moses surely must have reflected upon the change in his circumstances. In June of 1820, he had been without work, and his steamship creation had been trapped at the nation's capital, snarled in lawsuits. Yet one year later, in June of 1821, not only was Moses back on his feet, but he could justifiably say that he had helped turn the little outpost of Cheraw, South Carolina into a boomtown.

CHAPTER TWENTY-THREE

CLOSURE

B Y THE SUMMER of 1821, the *Robert Fulton* had managed to complete a total of five voyages between New York and New Orleans.

Most dramatically, in late March of that year, the steamship had been confronted by a "piratical schooner" while en route home. Captain Mott refused to stop, so the pirates fired on the *Robert Fulton*, and gave chase.

The ocean bandits really didn't stand a chance. The steamship easily outran the schooner, proving what no one should have doubted: a vessel using steam power could go faster, and maneuver better, than any pirates using sails.

Considering the mishaps of the previous year, the pirate episode was a welcome one. The Ocean Steam Ship Company then tried to build upon it. For subsequent trips, booking agent David Dunham & Company dared to declare not just the day of the steamship's departure, but also the precise date of its arrival at New Orleans.

This was a bold step. Steamboats had been able to make such predictions on short, protected routes for little more than a dozen years. The Black Ball Line of sailing packets, starting in 1818, had declared when they would leave on an ocean voyage, but could never predict when they would arrive.

Yet on the *Robert Fulton*'s third voyage of 1821, this steamship delivered on the promise, arriving at the Crescent City on July 1st, the very date targeted by the owners prior to departure from New York.

It was a startling achievement. For that brief moment, a window on the future had opened. The promise of predictability for long-distance ocean travel, using artificial means, was no longer chimerical— it was *real*.

* * *

By summer's end, as the heat dissipated in the South Carolina upcountry, the frontier town of Cheraw slowly began to awaken. The people there had much for which to be thankful.

For starters, the sickly months had been relatively mild. The local *Pee Dee Gazette* estimated that fewer than 1 person in 100 had come down with a severe case of fever, regardless of the variety.

Further still, the coming harvest in both Carolinas looked like it would be the best in years. Merchants expected trade with the coast to equal the previous season's boom, if not substantially exceed it.

But getting the hoped-for bounty to market would only come to pass if the steamboat *Pee Dee*, tied up at Cheraw since late spring, was running once again. This made the anticipated return of Captain Moses Rogers from Philadelphia the most important event in the Carolina upcountry. Initial reports said he was expected to put the steamboat back into operation by early October, though the final factor in determining that would be the river level.

Beyond Captain Rogers' impending return, the other big news along the Great Pee Dee River was what else he and his steamboat had set in motion. The prosperity they delivered to the upcountry the prior season had convinced a merchant from nearby Fayetteville, North Carolina to order another steamboat built for the river. Constructed at Philadelphia while Captain Rogers was there over the summer, this new steamer, the *Commerce*, was to be coaxed down the coast by his brother, Captain Amos Rogers Junior, as soon as it was ready. Once two steamboats were operating on the Great Pee Dee, little Cheraw would become an even bigger magnet for upcountry trade.

As bales of cotton and other produce began piling up at Cheraw, the locals were naturally anxious for any news on Captain Rogers' whereabouts. The *Pee Dee Gazette* obliged, informing its readers on October 1st that he was expected by the 10th. Once Captain Rogers had returned, the *Gazette* assured its readers, the steamboat would soon be back in operation.

Not until the end of October did Moses finally arrive on the scene. The news soon spread downriver to Georgetown, where the local *Winyaw Intelligencer* enthusiastically announced the appearance at Cheraw of the *Pee Dee*'s "skilful and indefatigable commander."

Once the steamboat was loaded with fuel, and one of the tow boats loaded with freight, all was ready for the commencement of a second season. Unfortunately, Moses judged the water level to be too low to proceed. So he and the people of Cheraw bided their time, and waited for more rain.

* * *

Some 500 miles to the north, off the coast of northern New Jersey, it was coming down in torrents. Gale-force winds and sheets of rain from the east-northeast were pounding every vessel unlucky enough to be at sea.

The strong gusts coming off the Atlantic made sailing for the sanctuary of New York Bay extremely tricky. Misjudging the approach could force a vessel onto the Jersey shore. Attempting such a maneuver at night, without the benefit of moon or stars to reckon by, was all the more risky.

It was a chance that Captain Nathan Holdridge of the ship *Savannah* was willing to take. In the early morning hours of Monday, November 5th, he and his crew carefully felt their way through the roaring storm.

Given the power of the gale, Holdridge knew his first priority was to keep his distance from the Jersey coast. The best strategy was to sail directly into the winds, toward the east-northeast. Once the *Savannah* was far enough to the north and east, she could be turned about, and pointed west—the storm would then blow her straight through the entrance to New York Bay, just above Sandy Hook lighthouse.

To get far enough north and east, Captain Holdridge had to tack the ship back and forth into the gale. Alternating between a northerly and a southerly tack, he and the crew slowly forced the *Savannah* through the drenching darkness, as she rose and fell over thundering swells.

As one of the northerly tacks was being made, ship and crew suddenly encountered the gravest of perils. With no lighthouses nearby, and the shores of Long Island seemingly distant, it would have been hard to make out in a storm. But it was certainly there, nevertheless: a dim, long line of danger, just above the waves, looming straight ahead, and extending far off to both larboard and starboard. It was the Sands.

Paralleling most of the southern coast of Long Island, the Beach of Sands and Stones was a series of very long, thin islands that offered both a haven and a hazard to mariners. If a vessel's draft was shallow enough, it could be maneuvered through one of the many openings in the Sands, and into what was called South Bay. There, with Long Island proper to the north and the Beach of Sands and Stones to the south, small craft found protection from the powerful ocean.

For larger vessels, however, the inlets weren't deep enough to cross. The only thing the Beach of Sands and Stones meant for them was mortality.

Before Captain Holdridge and his crew could point the *Savannah* back out to sea, the ship lurched forward and suddenly jerked to a halt. Surveys on all sides revealed what looked like plenty of water. The only possible explanation was the keel had cut right into a sandbar. The time was 3 o'clock in the morning.

Luckily, the *Savannah* remained "upright and tight," meaning she had sliced straight into the sand and wasn't leaning to one side, and there were no leaks. Trying to force the ship free, with storm waves crashing toward the Beach, was a virtual impossibility. Dropping anchors off the stern—to keep from being driven further onto the sandbank—was the most obvious thing to do, until the weather improved.

Beyond securing his ship, Captain Holdridge's first priority was the passengers. There were only three on this trip, including former steamship shareholder Isaac Minis and his 16-year-old son, Philip. They were all fine, as was the crew.

Next came a cargo check. The 250 bales of cotton on board were still dry, and salvageable.

The situation known, the next step was to make a plan. The passengers would need transporting to shore. Then getting the cotton off—to reduce the weight of the ship pressing down into the sand— would be next. With luck, the *Savannah* could be got off before she settled any deeper.

Once daylight illuminated the surroundings, the reason for the *Savannah*'s grounding became clearer. Due north of her position lay the Old Inlet. This was one of the larger passages through the Beach of Sands and Stones, which led into South Bay. Further north, on Long Island proper, was the outlet for a stream called the Connecticut River. The power of this stream's outflow had not only carved the Old Inlet through the Beach, but also deposited plenty of sediment just beyond it. The result was a series of sandbar traps. The *Savannah* had run aground on one of these, just off a part of the Beach known as Fire Place (which would later provide the Beach's modern name, Fire Island).

Captain Holdridge determined to go ashore for help. He and two crewmen climbed into the jolly boat, and rowed through the rough surf to the Beach. Once ashore, they encountered some local fisherman. Having apprised them of the situation, Holdridge and his oarsmen pushed off, and headed back to the ship.

Rowing into the waves breaking against the Beach, especially in the wake of a storm, was no easy task. Partway back to the ship, the jollyboat was capsized in an instant, throwing the three mariners into the water.

The two rowers quickly recovered. Captain Holdridge did not. Tumbling in the surf, he struggled to overcome the frigid waters and deadly undertow. The fishermen on the Beach saw the trouble, and charged into the water to help. Grabbing hold of the captain before he went under, the men dragged him to the Beach. In the eyes of those who had seen it, Nathan Holdridge was lucky to have survived.

Once the tide went out, it was easier to reach the ship. First, Isaac and Philip Minis and the other passenger, a Mr. Overstreet, were brought ashore. Then, Captain Holdridge, the crew and some local salvagers set about the task of hauling bales of cotton onto the deck, and ferrying them to shore.

While the *Savannah* still had not *bilged*—meaning sprung a leak in the lowest part of the hold—she was still in trouble. With the advance and retreat of each wave, a grave was being dug. The swirling tide around the hull sucked out the surrounding sand, pressing the hull deeper and deeper into the bar, and pushing it closer and closer toward the Beach. Passenger Overstreet, leaving the scene the next day, reported to the New York papers that hopes of getting the *Savannah* off were fading.

Bringing the cotton ashore was slow, hard work. By week's end, only about 120 bales had been salvaged, and most of them were damaged. As the ship slipped further into the sand, hour by hour, the wooden hull eventually, inevitably, sprang a leak. Once the sea began to seep into the hold, the remaining cotton became waterlogged, turning it into even heavier deadweight.

By Monday, November 12th, one week after the grounding, any hope of rescuing the *Savannah* had vanished. She was locked in place, eight or nine feet into the sand, and the power of the sea continued to press and pull against her timbers, creating more cracks in the hull, and more seepage. With the coming of every tide, the water level in the ship's hold rose higher and higher, and there was no stopping it.

In the days that followed, the work crews retrieved what remaining cotton they thought they could salvage. Then, they began stripping the *Savannah* of everything that made her alive. The sails, the rigging, and all of the hardware were methodically removed and slowly brought to shore, as the *Savannah* creaked and moaned with the coming and going of each and every wave.

* * *

As the *Savannah* lay dying in the sands off Long Island, 600 miles to the south, a large crowd gathered at the burial ground of the Antipedo Baptist Church, in Georgetown, South Carolina. They had come from all over town, as well as the surrounding countryside, to pay their respects to someone, as the local *Winyaw Intelligencer* declared, "whose death they deem a public loss."

Lying before these mourners was the coffin of a man who had brought to them a tireless spirit; a man who, when confronted with a challenge, willingly took it on to prove it could be done; a man who had achieved much in the last dozen years of his life, because he believed not only in his mission, but in himself.

Before them lay the coffin of Captain Moses Rogers.

The shock of his death was all the more difficult given the circumstances. On Tuesday morning, November 6th, just one day after the *Savannah* ran aground, Moses and the steamboat *Pee Dee* finally had been able to depart Cheraw.

That same morning, Moses became ill. Rather than cancel what was the first trip of the season, he ordered the crew to press on to Georgetown.

By the time the *Pee Dee* reached her destination, in the early evening of November the 8th, Moses was much worse. A friend came on board to find him bed-ridden, and "quite sick." The best doctor in Georgetown was summoned. He thought Captain Rogers was suffering from yellow fever, and prescribed a remedy.

Rather than try to move Moses, it was decided to keep him on the steamboat. His friend stayed up with him until 1 o'clock in the morning. At that point, Moses "appeared so much better" that the friend went to bed. Two others stayed behind, tending to their patient for the remainder of the night.

The next morning, Friday, November 9th, the friend returned to the steamboat, and had Moses moved to Mrs. Swainston's boarding-house, which was located nearby. Once comfortably settled, Moses "appeared to be much better," the friend later wrote to Adelia. On Saturday he was better still, and his friend thought Moses to be clearly on the mend.

This was not the first time that Captain Rogers had been laid low down South. Back in October of 1817, at the tail end of a yellow fever epidemic in Charleston, he had become very ill. Whatever had ailed Moses left him so incapacitated that it had disrupted his running the steamboat *Charleston* to Sullivan's Island for a time. He quickly recovered, however, resumed his command, and proceeded to take that steamer on its inaugural packet to Savannah less than two months later.

It seemed, four days after this most recent illness came on, that Moses would recover yet again. But on the following Monday, he became "intensely sick," according to his friend. On Tuesday, Moses was better again, and the doctor felt confident that he would recover. Through these days of illness, Moses talked with his friend frequently about the steamboating business, and gave every impression that he believed he would soon be better.

Besides his friend, who was almost always present, and the doctor, Moses had received plenty of attention from others. Aaron Marvin, both a shareholder in the Pee Dee Steam-Boat Company and a prominent member of the Antipedo Baptist Church, had visited him repeatedly.

During one of their conversations, Moses told Aaron Marvin that after his last trip home, he had reflected frequently upon his own situation, compared to that of his family in Connecticut. Moses had described how "all his brothers and the rest of the family" were "professors of religion." In his own case, in spite of all of his accomplishments, something seemed to be missing. Moses told Aaron Marvin that once he fully recovered, "he should for the future lead a different life."

Tuesday night was "very disagreeable" for Moses, and on Wednesday he grew even worse. He repeatedly became delirious, only to regain his senses and tell his friend that he would soon be better. By that time, the doctor thought his patient suffered from more than yellow fever, and the most likely culprit was typhoid fever, or something that looked very much like it.

Moses continued growing even worse into Wednesday night, until, at about 2 o'clock in the morning, "he breathed his last." It was Thursday, November 15th, 1821.

Later that day, the friend wrote a letter to Adelia, describing in detail what had happened, and doing his best to console her. Mr. Marvin, relayed the friend, believed that Moses "had made every exertion to die in peace with his Maker."

Given the suddenness of his death and the distance of relatives, Aaron Marvin made arrangements to bury Moses at the Antipedo Baptist Church cemetery. The local *Winyaw Intelligencer* printed an obituary which ran more than thirty lines, describing Georgetown's grief as "universal." Another local correspondent wrote that the death of Captain Rogers was viewed as a "public calamity," given the great benefits brought by his steamboating efforts. Upriver at Cheraw, the news fell even harder.

Within a few days, word of his death reached Charleston and Savannah, and several days after that, it was announced up North. By early December, newspapers all over the country had printed brief obituaries for Moses Rogers, which was, in and of itself, quite remarkable for the era.

Oftentimes, these obituaries mentioned the most prominent command of his career.

Sometimes, they noted only his most recent.

And other times, the newspapers did not even describe his relation to the new mode of transport at all. They didn't have to—*people knew.*

* * *

With their simultaneous deaths, Captain Moses Rogers and the *Savannah* quietly passed from the scene in the young country by the sea called the United States of America.

Just what Moses had wrought with his creation remained open to debate. By daring to try, he and his partners had fired both imaginations and imitators. By daring to succeed, thereby crossing the Atlantic Ocean in a steamship, he had shown the world that it was possible.

Yet in the wake of this unprecedented voyage, skeptics could still question whether the feat was repeatable, safely, and to practical effect. By the end of 1821, that new challenge had been placed in the hands of those prepared to pick up where Moses Rogers had left off. It was in the hands of those who were prepared to dream more.

APPENDIX

THE BARRIER BROKEN

O NCE MOSES ROGERS and the steamship *Savannah* were gone, fulfilling the dream and the promise of steam-powered travel on the oceans of the world fell upon those who remained. Anyone willing to try still had to face continuing public skepticism, as well as the nagging suspicion among mariners that Nature was simply too strong an opponent.

But in the years immediately following the *Savannah*'s voyage, others began taking the next steps necessary to advance the cause. The decisions made, and the actions taken, were seldom trumpeted publicly by those involved. Nor, for that matter, was their genesis.

* * *

In the United States of the early 1820s, most Americans were focused on one immediate goal, and that was recovery. The effects of the worst economic depression the country had yet seen were still much in evidence, from continuing sheriff sales of foreclosed farms and businesses, to the slower pace of trade. The willingness to take new risks was naturally diminished, as well.

However, there was one bright spot. As soon as it seemed clear that the worst of the depression was over, activity in the new mode of transport took off. Steam vessel construction, which had stalled when the depression first hit, quickly resumed its steep upward trajectory.

The kinds of steamers that were built unsurprisingly reflected the immediate needs of the country. The admittance of six new States in six years, culminating with Missouri in 1821, gave Americans plenty of new lands to settle and farm. Since four of those new members of the Union—Indiana, Illinois, Mississippi, and Missouri—bordered the Mississippi and Ohio Rivers, improving the moving of goods and people on those waterways was of the greatest importance. Minor rivers in the East, like the Great Pee Dee in South Carolina, also got plenty of attention, since they had the potential to open up frontier lands in the older States. With such a strong demand for getting harvested crops to ports along the seaboard, the river-running steamboat solidified its place as the vessel of choice amongst progressive entrepreneurs.

As for oceanic steaming, the American die was cast by the events of 1819. The steamship *Savannah's* successful completion, and voyage, sparked what became the first ocean steamer construction boom in history.

The year 1820 saw, in the *Savannah's* port of birth, not only the appearance of the steamship *Robert Fulton*, but also the completion of the steam schooner *Quiroga* and the steam brig *Braganza*. The *Quiroga* was transferred to Havana to serve as a coastal steam packet on the Cuban coast, while the *Braganza* succeeded in voyaging all the way to Brazil, where she was put into service as a steam packet on the Rio de Janeiro.

In 1821, Gotham produced still more, including the steam schooners *Fidelity* and *Mexican*. The *Fidelity* tested a variety of routes, from Norfolk–New York to Norfolk–New Orleans, while the *Mexican* was sent down to the Gulf, and set up as a steam packet between Cuba and Mexico.

In 1822, the port of Norfolk joined the boom, launching the steam brig *New York*, which tried a variety of routes, from the Chesapeake Bay to Boston.

And in 1823, Gotham launched yet more steam schooners, the *Balize* and the *Fanny*, which headed to New Orleans for coastal service.

What made these steam vessels different from their pre-*Savannah* predecessors was not only their purpose—as ocean steamers—but their *characterization* as such. This represented an epochal shift in thinking. No longer was it necessary to describe all examples of the new mode of transport as "steamboats." Instead, it became common to define those intended for ocean service accordingly, combining their new mode of power with the old mode of sail rigging installed. The result was a brand new series of vessels, including *steam sloops, steam schooners*, and *steam brigs*.

These ocean-going descendants of the steamship *Savannah* hardly found the going easy. The sea smashed one of the *Quiroga's* paddle-wheels on her maiden voyage to Havana, forcing the steam schooner into Hampton Roads, Virginia for repairs; the *Fidelity* suffered several boiler failures; the *Fanny*'s paddlewheel housings were ripped apart in a gale on her trip south, leaving the crew frantically manning the pumps to keep her afloat; and the brig *New York* eventually caught fire, burned, and sank off the coast of Maine. While each accident set the cause back a step, the very existence of such vessels nevertheless pushed the dream of steam power at sea further and further ahead.

Even so, these steam schooners and steam brigs were designed for relatively short voyages. For long-range trips, it was the Ocean Steam Ship Company, and its successors at David Dunham & Company, which continued to lead the way. Recovering from the early mishaps, the *Robert Fulton* provided passage between New York and New Orleans until early 1825. The schedule was somewhat sporadic, and the number of trips per year gradually fell with time, but the steamship managed to complete some dozen and a half trips of varying lengths in the five years that it ran.

Beyond the *Robert Fulton*, though, there were no other steamships built by his promoters in the early 1820s, despite plans to do so. Instead, some of the original shareholders focused on the old mode, starting their own ocean-sailing packet services to compete with the Black Ball Line. If they did stay with the new mode, it was often to feed the insatiable appetite for steamboats in the vast American interior.

Aside from these commercial efforts to artificially overcome Nature on the high seas, there was one other phenomenon in early 1820s America that further compelled the advance of steam power on the oceans, and that was the continuing problem of piracy. Despite the efforts of Congress to build smaller naval vessels to patrol near the American coast, the pirate menace was far more widespread than that. Water-borne bandits had been and still were operating all over the Gulf of Mexico and the Caribbean. The only way to suppress them was with a constant armed presence.

The U.S. Navy acknowledged as much by deploying a squadron of five men-of-war to patrol those seas during 1820. In addition, by the end of that year, the Navy required every one of its vessels, from the largest to the smallest, to sail through the West Indies on the way to or returning from their assignments anywhere in the world. Such an order revealed the enormity of the problem: pirates were operating freely in deep waters, as well as along the shallow coasts.

By early 1822, the situation was far worse. "This system of piracy is now spreading itself to a vast extent," declared the House Naval Affairs Committee, "attracting to it the idle, vicious, and desperate of all nations." So frustrated was the Committee by the lack of progress in confronting the menace that it even dared suggest to the Navy which additional warships should be fitted out and deployed for pirate-fighting.

When Congress re-convened in December of 1822, they quickly made it clear that they had had enough. With fresh reports of savagery on the high seas arriving almost daily, the first bill passed and placed before President Monroe for signature was yet another Act authorizing still more naval forces "for the suppression of piracy."

This time, however, there were three noticeable differences from the last such legislation, approved in May of 1820, when the steamship *Savannah* had been tied up at Washington.

First, Congress appropriated $160,000 in funds for more vessels, nearly three times the amount they had approved back in 1820.

Second, instead of specifying that small vessels be built, as they had before, Congress gave the President wide latitude in deciding what kind of men-of-war to employ.

Third, Congress stipulated that rather than order the Navy to build these new vessels, the President had the power to purchase them from the private sector.

The Navy Board got the message. They recommended to Navy Secretary Smith Thompson that "1 Steam Boat" be procured, as part of this newest anti-piracy push.

With the bill's passage imminent, Secretary Thompson in turn "requested" that the Board purchase "one Steam Boat," along with additional sailing schooners and cutters, all of which would serve as part of this new naval force.

On December 20th, the very day the anti-piracy bill was signed into law, Secretary Thompson further appointed Navy Board Commissioner David Porter to serve as commander of this newly-formed West India Squadron.

Selecting Commodore Porter made plenty of sense. Having briefly been in charge of the steam battery *Fulton* shortly after that vessel's completion, Porter stood out in his belief that the new mode had potential. But since the *Fulton* was not designed for sea duty, and the

Navy Board had done nothing to advance construction of the three additional steam batteries authorized, Porter would have to buy an existing steamer and convert it for Navy use.

Within days, the country's newspapers were foaming with reports of Commodore Porter's movements. After purchasing sailing schooners and cutters at Baltimore, Porter proceeded to New York, where he bought a 100-ton commercial steamboat called the *Enterprize*. Porter had the vessel re-named the "U.S. steam ketch *Sea Gull*," and ordered her down the coast to the Norfolk Navy Yard, where she would be outfitted for battle.

The junior naval officers under Porter's command were dubious of the *Sea Gull*. She was, after all, a steam*boat*, designed for river and bay travel. Only after they were completely satisfied that her newly-installed rig of two masts and sails was adequate did they approve her for sea service. At that point, she became the first ocean-going steam vessel in the history of the U.S. Navy.

Upon completion of the refitting, Commodore Porter re-designated the *Sea Gull* a "steam galliot," and made her his flagship.

His actions were more than mere show. The *Sea Gull* promised unprecedented capability to the leader of this newly-assembled flotilla; with the new mode of power at his disposal, Porter theoretically could show up anywhere on the ocean battlefield he chose. The vessel's new description as a "steam galliot" further impressed the point, since *galliots* were a type of ancient Mediterranean galley known for their speed.

Once the *Sea Gull* and the rest of the "Mosquito Fleet" of small sailing vessels were assembled and ready, Commodore Porter ordered them to sea. Departing Norfolk in February of 1823, this new West India Squadron sailed down to the coast of Spanish Cuba. That island had become the pirates' favorite haven, largely due to Spain's weak control over their colony.

With such a force patrolling the area, many of the sea bandits naturally hid. Commodore Porter proceeded to place his men-of-war on patrols and convoy duty, offering protection to vessels of any nation that asked for it. The *Sea Gull* participated, searching coastal coves, towing small sailing barges, or even just resting at anchor at the newly-established base at Key West, Florida, ready to move at a moment's notice.

Over the course of the next three pirate-fighting seasons, the *Sea Gull* did even more, attacking and capturing pirate vessels, and recapturing American merchantmen and their cargoes. Her exploits in those years were more than a mere footnote—they represented the first successful use in battle of a steam-powered man-of-war in history.

* * *

Like the United States, the Russian Empire's primary focus in the early 1820s was inward. Russia also had enormous swaths of land still to be settled, and dozens of rivers that could serve as highways for commerce.

This imperative to expand and grow led the Emperor Alexander to grant a number of steamboat franchises in the years following the *Savannah's* visit. There was also some promotion of steamboats by the Russian government itself, for towing and exploring, but given the enormous distances between the many ports in the Empire, the introduction of oceanic steaming in Russia had to wait for a foreign undertaking.

That came in 1827, when a British steam packet company initiated service between London and St. Petersburg. Its first steamer, *George IV*, had no greater proponent in Russia than Emperor Nicholas, who had succeeded his brother by that time.

When the Russian Navy did decide to embrace the new mode on the ocean (in the late 1830s), it was up to Emperor Nicholas to approve. Thanks in part to the memory of the American steamship of 1819, the decision was made to send a naval delegation to the United States. Once there, the Russian Navy officers eventually signed a contract for the construction of a steam frigate in the same place that the *Savannah* was built—the City of New York.

* * *

In Sweden, by contrast, the effect of Moses Rogers and the steamship *Savannah* was immediate.

King Karl XIV Johan, overwhelmed by the final negotiations over Norway's debt, as well as his upcoming trip to the provinces, had been unable to visit the steamship when it dropped anchor at Stockholm in August of 1819.

Once he returned from his autumn tour of the provinces, however, the French-born monarch wasted no time. On October 27th, 1819, he ordered the Chief Director of the Swedish Post Office, Baron Wilhelm Carpelan, to determine "in all haste the extent to which the postal service between Sweden and the Continent could be speeded up by using steam vessels."

Baron Carpelan and several other officials had suggested just such an idea several years before, but their proposal had fallen upon deaf ears. Yet in the wake of the American steamship's visit, His Majesty's opinion had changed, and he suddenly wanted details.

Baron Carpelan quickly complied. He recommended that steam-powered postal packets be introduced on the route between Ystad, on the southern tip of Sweden, and Stralsund, directly across the Baltic Sea on the north coast of Prussia. The distance between the two ports was some 90 miles. Instead of a passage of 2 or 3 days, as the sailing packets often required, Baron Carpelan thought a steam vessel could make the crossing reliably in 17 or 18 hours.

In due course, King Karl Johan authorized the Swedish Post Office to order a steam vessel, named the *Constitutionen*, which was launched in August of 1822. By the spring of 1823, the *Constitutionen* was making mail runs across the Baltic, and with it, Sweden's adoption of steam power at sea had begun.

* * *

By the time the French government concluded their country was far behind in its adoption of the new mode, the *Savannah* already had made it across the Atlantic. They responded before the summer of 1819 was out, sending two fact-finding missions to the United States. Of these, naval constructor Jean Baptiste Marestier was the most important, simply because he already possessed a technical knowledge of shipbuilding. The secrets of advanced steam propulsion he could learn, and readily did through his inspection of American vessels, including the *Savannah*.

Upon his return home in the middle of 1820, Marestier became one of the most knowledgeable builders of the new mode in France, even though he had little practical experience.

That changed in October of 1822, when the Minister for Colonies ordered a steam vessel built to serve as a coastal packet in French Guiana, between the ports of Mana and Cayenne.

It was a huge undertaking. While the Ministry of Colonies previously had built two steamboats for use overseas (at the colony of Senegal, in Africa), neither one had used steam power at sea during their transfers. Departing France in October of 1819 and March of 1820, these vessels, the *Voyageur* and *Africain*, had skimmed the coasts completely under sail. Their dismantled paddlewheels had been kept safely stowed on deck, only to be assembled upon arrival.

This time it would be different. The newly-ordered steam vessel was to be sent to French Guiana, which was not in Africa, of course, but South America. Delivery would require a crossing of the Atlantic Ocean, so the assignment for designing this craft was given to Jean Baptiste Marestier.

What he created was a two-masted steam schooner in which the paddlewheel axle could be disconnected from the engine. This meant that although the wheels served as a drag on the vessel's ability to sail, at least they could turn freely when not in use, instead of being locked in place.

Marestier's creation, launched in 1823, was named the *Galibi*. Even though she was built to serve as a colonial packet, the government determined that the French Navy should be in charge of any crossing attempt. So in the summer of 1824, once her trials were complete, she was transferred to the Ministry of Marine and re-named the *Caroline*, becoming the first steam vessel in the French Navy.

Later that year, in October of 1824, Marestier's *Caroline* departed from Brest, the westernmost port in France. After a 36-day voyage under sail and steam, she safely arrived at the port of Cayenne, Guiana, becoming the first French steam vessel ever to cross the Atlantic Ocean.

* * *

Of all the countries that witnessed the voyage of the steamship *Savannah*, none was affected more deeply than the United Kingdom. As an island nation with the most extensive empire in the world, Great Britain depended upon the oceans not only as a protective shield against its enemies, but as the vital link to its far-flung colonies. Ever since Lord Nelson's decisive victory at Trafalgar, in 1805, the Royal Navy had been the undisputed lion of the sea. Britain was safe, believed the country's establishment, because no one could challenge its navy, or its technology.

Captain Moses Rogers and the *Savannah* changed all that. Such a feat as crossing the Atlantic in a steamship made it glaringly obvious that Britain had fallen behind. Once Moses and the *Savannah* had left Albion's waters, the British did not forget this Wonder of the Age which had shocked them. Nor did they wring their hands in fear and anguish.

Instead, the British got cracking.

Even with the *Savannah* out of sight, Lord Liverpool's government discovered that the steamship could not be put out of mind. In addition to continuing newspaper reports, Lord Cathcart, in one of his last dispatches as minister to Russia, made a point of noting how quickly the American steamer had brought his brother-in-law, Lord Lynedoch, to St. Petersburg.

Further pressing the point was another British subject by the name of Charles Broderip. In December of 1819, he wrote to the Admiralty from Paris, presenting his own ideas on how to advance the new mode at sea. Getting the Admiralty's attention was easy—Broderip simply began his petition with a summary of where things stood:

> *The success which has attended the Americans in the application of Steam Engines as a moving power of Vessels, leaves no doubt of the utility of this invention for the purposes to which it has been hitherto applied. The recent voyage of the American Steam-Ship, The Savannah, across the Atlantic, demonstrates the practicability of its application to purposes of still higher importance...*

Broderip went on to describe his scheme to create a steam vessel which could be used as a revenue cutter, post office packet, or dispatch vessel. His special design would feature a lighter engine, less vibration, reduced fuel consumption, and unencumbered sailing capability. Such characteristics would allow for safer and longer journeys using steam. The inventor had been studying and experimenting with steam vessels for years, he declared, and spent upwards of £10,000 on his project. If the Admiralty so desired, he would come to London to explain his proposition in more detail, and submit it for review by "competent, scientific persons."

Charles Broderip's petition would have been greatly discounted if it had been presented one year earlier. In the wake of the *Savannah*, however, it was taken seriously. Lord Melville, the First Lord of the Admiralty, read the petition himself, and instructed Second Secretary John Barrow to write a reply, telling Broderip to either come to London or transmit a copy of his plans for review.

The Admiralty already had been moving in Broderip's direction by the time his petition arrived. The prior August, just a few weeks after Moses and his creation departed from Liverpool, a commissioner at the Royal Navy's dockyard at Deptford, on the Thames River, had cracked the ice. In a letter to the Navy Board, the commissioner dared "beg to observe a steam vessel of sixty Horse Power would be a great utility" in towing men-of-war out to sea.

The Admiralty agreed.

But the Navy Board, being responsible for the construction of such a vessel, was not enthusiastic. Memories of the *Congo* fiasco, which had ended in complete failure, were still very fresh.

The Admiralty, however, would not be denied. In early November of 1819 (while the *Savannah* was en route home from St. Petersburg), they ordered the Navy Board to build the service's first steam-powered tugboat.

The Royal Navy weren't the only ones suddenly taking action. So was the Royal Post Office. Their sailing packets between Britain and Ireland were beginning to encounter serious competition from privately-owned steam vessels (struggling though they were to maintain regular service across the Irish Sea). Rather than hire the existing steamers to carry the mail, Post Office Secretary Francis Freeling thought perhaps the government should just build its own steam vessels.

First, however, came the ideas of Charles Broderip, who traveled to London in the spring of 1820 to discuss his steam scheme in more detail. What Broderip wanted was an existing sailing vessel, say one of the Post Office packets already running across the Irish Sea. On it, he would install paddlewheels and a small but powerful steam engine, placed horizontally within the hold to lessen vibration, while keeping all of the original masts, sails and rigging.

Broderip's objective was to show that through a combination of sailing and steaming, voyages with a degree of "certainty and security" could be achieved, "applicable to all seas, all seasons, and every station." Not only would this be possible for short trips, but for "*distant* service," as well. More specifically, Broderip was thinking of a steam packet to Lisbon, Portugal, and ultimately the Mediterranean Sea.

This first step in the plan, stated the promoter, was an "experiment," which would prove the potential of his design.

If Broderip's proposal had been submitted one year earlier, it would have sounded too good, or too crazy, to be true.

Steam and sail on long ocean voyages?

Horizontal engines?

Yet in the wake of the American experiment, the British could not merely dismiss the whole thing. Discussions went all the way up to the second most powerful man in the government, Chancellor of the Exchequer Nicholas Vansittart. In the end, it was agreed that Broderip's ideas would be submitted to a committee of experts for review. Regardless of the outcome, the Post Office was to start contract negotiations for building two steam vessels of its own.

* * *

In the meantime, John Rennie, one of Britain's most prominent engineering geniuses, was at wit's end. The designer of Waterloo Bridge and many other great civil projects, Rennie had taken an interest in steam vessels some years before. It was in part thanks to his prodding that the Royal Navy had even tried using steamboats to tow warships out to sea.

Once the Admiralty ordered a steam-powered tugboat to be built, Rennie had offered to help, submitting his advice in late 1819. But he soon found the Navy Board resisting certain aspects of his proposed design. By the spring of 1820, Rennie was still trying to counter the Board's misgivings. In a May 22nd letter to their superiors at the Admiralty, Rennie did his best to encourage them to push on:

> . . . *Steam vessels may be said to be in their infancy, and it can scarcely be expected that they are arrived at any thing like a State of perfection. Much however will be learnt by experience and unless some risk is run in the early application of Steam to the Navigation of vessels no improvement will be made.*

The Admiralty really didn't need much prodding. The day after Rennie pled his case, they ordered the Navy Board to get started building a steam tug based upon his design.

Nevertheless, the surveyors on the Board continued to drag their feet. John Rennie, writing to James Watt the younger at the end of the month, vented his frustration:

> . . . *unless the Admiralty cram it down the throats of the Navy Board, nothing will be done; for of all the ignorant, obstinate, and stupid boards under the Crown, the Navy Board is the worst. I am so disgusted with them that, could I at the present moment with decency*

relinquish the works under them which I have in hand, I would do so at once.

But to Sir Robert Seppings, recently knighted Surveyor of the Royal Navy, the hesitation to jump wholeheartedly into building a steam tugboat must have seemed perfectly rational. After all, the Navy Board's attempt to construct the steamer *Congo*, in 1816, had been a disaster. Three years later, when Robert was sent to Liverpool to inspect the *Savannah*, he and the Navy Board still did not accept the significance of the new mode.

That failure to appreciate, however, was changing. All of the movement within the British government since the American steamship's visit had sent a strong message. The problem for Sir Seppings was that he and the rest of the Board still did not have the knowledge.

Thankfully, the Royal Post Office provided a chance for rescue. The two steam vessels *they* had proposed would be built by private contractors who *did* have the knowledge. It was a perfect opportunity to learn on someone else's budget.

Sir Seppings approached the Royal Post Office and offered to help. He suggested that in addition to drawing up and negotiating the builder's contract for their first steam vessel, he would also—if the Post Office wished—oversee its construction.

For the Lords of the Mail, this was simply too good an offer to pass up. They quickly accepted. In early July, they further decided that the Post Office would not take delivery of their first steamer until the Surveyors of the Navy had signed off on its completion.

* * *

By the end of July of 1820, Secretary Francis Freeling of the Royal Post Office had every reason to believe that the steam initiative was going exceedingly well. Their first steam packet, to be named the *Lightning*, had just been ordered; the private contractor, a shipbuilder at Rotherhithe, was about to begin construction; famed steam engine manufacturer Boulton, Watt & Company was to build the vessel's engine; and Sir Seppings, one of the most accomplished surveyors in the Royal Navy's history, was to ensure that it was done right. The next step was to complete the contract for a second steamer as expeditiously as possible.

But before this could be done, Secretary Freeling received a note:

the Chancellor of the Exchequer wanted to see him. On Wednesday, August 2nd, Freeling hurried over to Downing Street, where he found Chancellor Nicholas Vansittart sitting with Treasury Secretary Stephen Lushington (the very same official who had fielded Isaac, Low & Company's request for waiving the *Savannah*'s coal duties).

Chancellor Vansittart told Freeling that he wanted him to meet with a diplomat named Mr. Buchanan. This fellow was Britain's vice-consul at New York, and being in London on a visit, Buchanan had been telling the Chancellor about "the infinitely superior qualities of American Steam Vessels to those built in this Country."

"Mr. Vansittart thought if that were the case," Freeling later wrote, "it would be right to introduce one of those Vessels in preference to building another for the Services at Holyhead."

Freeling replied how anxious the Post Office was to have two steam packets built and operating as soon as possible, before the privately-owned steamers snatched away an even greater share of the passenger traffic crossing the Irish Sea.

To this, the Chancellor had a ready reply. Perhaps "a Vessel might be purchased in America + be here as soon if not sooner than the other Steam Vessel could be built."

Secretary Lushington then completed the set-up, telling Freeling that Vice-Consul Buchanan was already scheduled to be at the Treasury on Friday, at 2 o'clock. That would be a good time for Freeling to come by and meet the gentleman.

Alarm bells must have been wailing inside the Postal Secretary's head. Just 15 months prior, the very idea of buying an American steam vessel and bringing it across the Atlantic would have been considered reckless lunacy. No longer.

Furthermore, Freeling was not sitting with a couple of two-bit Treasury bureaucrats, pretending to be important. Secretary Lushington was a sitting member of the House of Commons, with his own constituency.

So, for that matter, was Vansittart. Even more importantly, as Chancellor of the Exchequer under Britain's parliamentary system, Vansittart drafted the government's budget, and presented it to the Prime Minister, Lord Liverpool. Then, he ushered it through Parliament, until it was approved. Then, he oversaw the actual spending of it, as well. In short, Nicholas Vansittart was the man with the money.

Secretary Freeling quickly mounted his best defense. "Possibly the finest Steam Boat in America might not be precisely applicable to the Service between Great Britain + Ireland," he replied. "I recommended to them strongly not to take any steps without consulting Sir R Seppings + the officers of the Navy Board."

This they promised to do, but the Chancellor's enthusiasm for the idea was unmistakable. "Mr. Buchanan had spoken of the possibility," relayed Vansittart, "of a Voyage being effected from New York to England in 10 days!" Such a feat could be accomplished, said the Chancellor, because "in addition to the powers of Steam those of sails were also largely afforded" for a crossing of the Atlantic.

Even so, Vansittart did not stop there. He went on to say "he thought a Vessel on the American principle might be well adapted for a Packet to the Mediterranean." At a minimum, the distance of such a voyage from the south coast of England was some 1,400 miles, and all of that on the open Atlantic.

Secretary Freeling reminded the Chancellor that the Postal Lords had only just approved the establishment of mail steamers on the Irish Sea (where the passage distance was about 60 miles, not 1,400!). He had "strong doubts" that any further introduction of the new mode would be approved under the circumstances.

Freeling left the meeting and reported its particulars to the Postal Lords, who firmly supported the stance he had taken. In so doing, Freeling and his superiors dodged the last major obstacle to their plan. Later that month, a second postal steamer was ordered, to be named the *Meteor*.

Chancellor Vansittart's keen interest in the "American principle" of steam and sails on the ocean had been reinforced by the committee looking into Charles Broderip's own *Savannah*-like scheme. While they had returned a report which was, not surprisingly, unfavorable, the committee members nevertheless did complement Broderip for "considerable ingenuity in many of the details of his arrangements." In fact, they thought "some of his inventions deserve a further investigation by practical Engineers."

While the Post Office Lords got their way on the second steam vessel, Chancellor Vansittart refused to stand down. Two days after the *Meteor* was ordered, he and the Lords of the Treasury made it clear that they wanted the Post Office to submit Broderip's plan to a practical test. By obvious implication, the Treasury would ensure that the money was there to pay for it.

Under the circumstances, the Postal Lords had to respond, and quickly. They suggested that one of the existing sailing packets which plowed between Holyhead, Wales and Howth, Ireland be purchased. Then it could be fitted with Broderip's steam machinery, and put through trials.

On September 12th, 1820, less than 3 weeks after the Post Office had been directed to test Broderip's plan, the Treasury Lords approved £7,000 (or $31,080) to carry out his experiment. Including the two postal steamers just ordered, Chancellor Vansittart and his colleagues had committed the British government to spending more than £26,000 (or $115,440) for oceanic steam travel in the space of just 2 months.

* * *

While the *civil* works on steam powered vessels proceeded apace, the *military* works did not. By November of 1820, the Admiralty was wondering how their order for a steam tugboat was coming along. The Navy Board duly replied, in a letter to First Secretary John W. Croker:

> ... We desire you will be pleased to acquaint their Lordships that we have prepared a draft for building a Vessel accordingly, but at the same time to submit to them as two Steam Vessels are building by the Post Office on a plan which promises some improvement, whether it may not be advisable to defer proceeding with the Vessel in question until they are launched.

* * *

In the span of just 10 months for the *Lightning* and 9 months for the *Meteor*, the two Post Office steamers were not only built, but tested, and ready for service. On May 31st, 1821, they began running between Holyhead in Wales and Howth in Ireland, becoming the first Royal Post Office steam packets in history.

With burthens in the range of 200 tons and rigged something like two-masted schooners, neither of these vessels was technically a "steamship." Yet their sailing apparatus made good sense, since the postal steamers had been built to cross the Irish Sea, and not the Atlantic Ocean.

In short order, they proved their worth. The *Lightning* and *Meteor* quickly drove the two privately-owned steamers off the Holyhead–Howth route. Several months later, in August, the *Lightning* garnered even more publicity, when she hosted newly-crowned King George IV on a trip to Ireland. In honor of this voyage, the vessel was immediately re-named *Royal Sovereign.*

* * *

The success of the two Post Office steamers put pressure on Charles Broderip. The sailing vessel which the government had purchased for his experiment remained up in Glasgow, where it had been taken for the installation of a horizontal steam engine and paddle-wheels. By the time of His Majesty's trip on the *Lightning*, the Postal Lords were getting impatient. They wanted Broderip to get on with it, and ordered him to bring his creation down to Holyhead for tests.

The converted vessel still wasn't completely ready, but the Postal Lords were insistent, so Broderip felt compelled to comply with their request. Against the advice of the engineers working with him, Broderip took his creation, the *Tartar*, down to Holyhead, arriving in November of 1821 (the same month in which Moses and the *Savannah* died). Once there, Broderip was told to put the experimental steamer into actual operation, carrying the mail and passengers across the Irish Sea.

Broderip was not at all happy about trying the *Tartar* on such a short route. The purpose of the project, after all, was to test his version of the "American principle," and show how a steam-powered sailing vessel sent on a long ocean voyage could provide a level of "certainty and security" never before imagined. The 60-mile runs between Wales and Ireland would hardly allow for that.

Adding to the difficulty was the common knowledge amongst mariners at the time that steam vessels simply could not operate safely at sea during the winter season.

As if this weren't enough, in the ensuing months after the *Tartar*'s arrival at Holyhead, Nature spit out storms on the Irish Sea the likes of which had not been seen in years.

Unfazed by the wisdom or the weather, Broderip took the *Tartar* out, pushing through heavy gales, while the other two postal steamers mostly stayed in port. Even though Broderip was proud of his creation's performance, the ability to fully test his steam-and-sail experiment had been out of the question. The winds on the Irish Sea that winter were so strong, in fact, that Broderip was compelled to reduce the rigging to a bare minimum, and forego the use of sails, running the *Tartar*, in his own words, "as a *mere Steam Boat.*"

* * *

The success of the two Post Office steamers also put pressure on the Navy Board. There was no cause for delay any more. Sir Seppings had watched over the private contractors who built the *Lightning* and the *Meteor*. In so doing, he and the Board had finally gained the knowledge.

On November 21st, 1821—some 5 months after the postal steam packets began running, and just as Broderip and the *Tartar* were beginning their Irish Sea tests—the keel was finally laid for the Royal Navy's first steam-powered tugboat. It had taken the Board 2 years and 11 days to begin carrying out the Admiralty's original order. Slated for use on the Thames River, this steam tug was to be named the *Comet* (which was the same name Scotsman Henry Bell had given to Britain's first commercially successful steamboat, back in 1812).

Once the Admiralty's original command had been obeyed, they decided to push even further. A little more than a month after the *Comet's* construction had begun, the Admiralty ordered the Navy Board to build two more steam tugs, for the naval bases at Portsmouth and Plymouth. Yet again, the Board would drag its feet getting started, focusing instead on making sure the *Comet* was built right.

* * *

The last months of 1821 also saw the promise of Lord Cochrane's steam warrior, the *Rising Star*, finally come to fruition. The arguments between all those involved in her construction had lasted well into 1820. The Chilean revolutionary government's agent in Britain, Antonio Alvarez, had refused to pay for any more work on the vessel. Merchant and investor Edward Ellice in turn threatened to force its sale, and Lord Cochrane's brother, William, found himself stuck in the middle, along with engineer Alexander Galloway.

Eventually, Alvarez agreed that his government would purchase the vessel, but only once it was finished and ready for sea. Whoever paid the costs of completion would receive a special license to trade goods with a newly-independent Chile.

Once the *Rising Star's* engine installation was complete, she was re-floated in February of 1821, and underwent trials on the Thames River in June.

In late October, she departed for South America, only to spring a leak off Portugal. Limping back to Cork, Ireland, the *Rising Star* was quickly repaired, and then made a second attempt at crossing.

This time, the vessel succeeded, arriving at Valparaiso, Chile in April of 1822, although the amount of time spent steaming on the long voyage appears to have been very minimal.

In any event, the *Rising Star* arrived too late to see any action in Chile's war for independence. Her crossing of the Atlantic was largely ignored by steam proponents, probably because the virtually complete use of sails on the voyage, as well as the mishap off Portugal, served little to advance the cause of the new mode at sea.

* * *

The year 1822 saw Britain gripped by steam-mania. The two Post Office steamers, in their first year of operation, had cut the Holyhead–Howth transit time to 7½ hours on average (instead of 15 hours for the sailing packets). Furthermore, other privately-owned steam vessels were making great strides in providing service along the coasts of Albion.

All of this activity awakened Parliament, which held extensive hearings through much of the spring. The Select Committee responsible for overseeing mail delivery from London to Dublin heard testimony from all sorts of people involved in the new mode of transport, and asked them a series of particular questions:

What description of vessel, as to tonnage, form, strength of building, masts and sails, in your opinion, is the best for sea navigation? What description of engine, as to power, materials, and general form and arrangement, and what description of boilers and paddles, in your opinion, are the best? In a gale of wind, with a heavy sea, what is the best mode of managing a steam vessel?

Beyond these general queries, the Committee got even more specific—

Is there a method of getting the paddles off the wheels if the engine is not in use?

Should a low pressure or a high pressure steam engine be used?
Should the machinery parts be made of cast iron, or wrought iron?
Should the boilers be made of copper, or iron?
How can the formation of salt in the boilers be reduced?
What is the best way to prevent fires on board?

On and on their questioning went. Many of the issues discussed were the same ones Moses Rogers had contended with four years earlier in creating the steamship *Savannah*. That they were still being debated reveals just how novel and unsettled the very concept of oceanic steaming remained.

But the broader importance of these many questions was not the primary purpose of the "steamboat" hearings. The Committee's mandate, after all, was limited to the improvement of communications across the Irish Sea. Yet despite the fact that Committee members were focused on trips of between 60 and 120 miles, their questions nevertheless energized other subjects of the Crown to dare to concentrate on the bigger picture, by dreaming of steam-powered voyages far longer, and far more audacious.

* * *

In June of 1822, just as the Parliamentary hearings on steam packets were ending, Charles Broderip finally managed to wrest his experimental *Tartar* away from the Irish Sea postal route, and send her back up to the shipyard in Glasgow. There, he and his team set to work itemizing the remaining alterations needed before trying the steamer on a longer ocean voyage.

Of the greatest concern was the vessel's flat bow. Nautical men originally advised Broderip to leave it alone. Given their expertise in such matters, and his lack thereof, Broderip had felt obligated to accept their opinion. Unfortunately, the bow's shape had impeded the *Tartar*'s ability to cut through the water while steaming on the Irish postal run, hurting her crossing times. If the experiment of a long ocean voyage was to have a fair chance to work, the bow would have to be sharpened, so that it could slice through the water just like any other fast sea-going vessel.

So Broderip added rebuilding the bow to the list of necessary alterations. Once all the changes were settled upon, he submitted them to London.

In early August, Broderip got his answer: the Lords of the Treasury agreed to pay for everything, except sharpening the bow.

* * *

That same month, a young Royal Navy lieutenant by the name of James Henry Johnston set foot in his native England once again. Like many of his fellow officers after the war, Lieutenant Johnston had no official assignment, and was on half-pay. With plenty of time on his hands, Johnston had traveled to India, where he had taken command of a merchantman, the *Cambridge*, for the return voyage home.

Disembarking into the ongoing steam-mania of 1822, Johnston attended a meeting in London for the newly-formed General Steam Navigation Company. The intent of this enterprise was to push the new mode beyond British coastal waters, and initiate steam packet routes to the Continent much longer than the Dover-to-Calais runs already in operation.

But in Lieutenant Johnston's view, far more ambitious endeavors were possible. There lay before proponents of the new mode of transport a much greater prize, if only the effort could be organized and carried out. It was a dream which held the promise of real benefit, not just to improved communications, but as a meaningful contribution to Britain's empire, as well.

James Henry Johnston's idea, however, was far simpler for him to state than for people to accept. Yet his vision was so breathtaking that it could not but immediately seize the attention of anyone who heard it—

Steam packets . . . *to India!*

* * *

It wasn't until February of 1823 that the keels were finally laid for the Royal Navy's second and third steam-powered tugboats. The first steam tug, the *Comet*, had been completed seven months earlier, and with the knowledge gained from its construction and trials, the Navy Board was ready to proceed with the others. The two new tugboats would be named *Lightning* and *Meteor* (not coincidentally, the same names originally given to the Post Office steamers).

By the time the Navy Board began building these two new vessels, their superiors at the Admiralty were already thinking well beyond steam tugboats. During that same month of February, Lord Melville wrote a letter to the Comptroller of the Royal Navy, Admiral Sir Thomas Byam Martin. At the top of this letter's first page, Melville most prominently wrote the word "*Secret.*"

The First Lord of the Admiralty then got right to the point. Explaining that while he believed it was "very improbable" that Britain would find itself at war in the near future, he nevertheless wanted to investigate how steam engines could be fitted quickly into existing warships. Based upon a discussion he had recently had with Sir Seppings, Lord Melville thought two-masted ten-gun brigs would be the best suited for such conversions. Beyond talk, the First Lord made it clear that he also wanted action:

> ... *At any rate however it will be proper* <u>now</u> *to provide Steam Engines for at least six Vessels, in addition to those constructing + intended for the use of the Dock Yards, + I have therefore to desire that you will take the necessary steps for that purpose...*

Melville went on to declare that if the Royal Navy needed still more steam-powered men-of-war beyond the six he proposed, he had no doubt that some of the privately-owned steam packets could be procured on short notice, and armed accordingly.

Initially, however, what he wanted was nothing less than a steam-powered squadron, which could be created quickly on the outbreak of war. The idea was a virtual copy of Colonel John Stevens' plan from two years earlier, of which Lord Melville was surely aware, given its very public rejection by the American Navy. That the Colonel's precise idea—of marrying steam engines to sailing warships—had not even been tested really was of little importance; the arrival of the *Savannah* at Liverpool 3½ years earlier had proved it could work.

Within days, Admiral Sir Byam Martin responded, stating that a new class of brigs on the drawing boards might work for the plan, only their hulls did not seem ideal for the insertion of steam engines. He suggested that if the bottoms could be redesigned, then the engines could be placed low enough in the hulls to provide both stability as well as protection from enemy fire.

Admiral Sir Byam Martin went further still. He enclosed a drawing of the brigs as originally designed, but with red lines added to show how the hulls would need to be changed. The Admiral closed his letter to Lord Melville by asking whether or not this alteration should be made.

Just three days later, on March 3rd, 1823, Lord Melville gave his reply:

Do it.

* * *

After being named to a preliminary fact-finding committee, Lieutenant James Henry Johnston quickly discovered that he was virtually alone. The other participants in the proposed General Steam Navigation Company had no interest in trying to start a steam packet service to India.

The reason why was simple: the whole idea sounded absolutely ludicrous. The shortest distance between Britain and Calcutta was over 8,000 miles. Even then, such a journey through the Mediterranean would require disembarking at Egypt, and crossing politically unstable lands to the port of Suez (on the Red Sea). There, a second steam vessel would be needed to complete the trip. The all-ocean route, around Africa's Cape of Good Hope, was even more daunting, the whole distance being over 12,000 miles. That pirates regularly preyed upon shipping in the Indian Ocean only added to the danger.

Despite the unenthusiastic response to his idea, Lieutenant Johnston was undeterred. He withdrew from the General Steam Navigation Company, and approached a number of prominent merchants in the East India trade. Intrigued by the idea of steam packets to the Far East, they agreed to help, provided Johnston could gain the support of their counterparts in Bengal Province.

With these endorsements won from the British side, Johnston gathered up his plans, and embarked on a passage to India.

* * *

It took Charles Broderip all of the winter and most of the spring of 1823 to complete work on the *Tartar* up in Scotland. All that remained was to put the steam-and-sail vessel through some trials. Once that was done, the *Tartar* would be ready for her first long-distance voyage to Lisbon, which was some 850 miles from the south coast of England.

But those funding the experiment had other plans. The Post Office first ordered the *Tartar* to steam down to Bristol, where she was to tow a sailing packet around Land's End to Falmouth. Unfortunately, fierce weather forced the steamer back to port with damage. Once repaired, the *Tartar* was directed to go to Falmouth directly, which she reached in mid-June. Without any trials, the *Tartar* was then ordered to attempt a voyage to the port of Cadiz, on the southwest coast of Spain.

Broderip was not pleased. His creation wasn't designed to carry enough fuel for this more distant destination, which was nearly 1,100 miles from Falmouth. The *Tartar* would have to depend upon sails for that much more of the journey.

Nevertheless, Broderip personally volunteered to go, and on July 4th, he and the *Tartar* departed on the experimental run. Any hope Broderip had of making a re-fueling stop en route to Cadiz was dashed when he discovered that the captain had strict orders prohibiting him from doing so. They still made the trip in 10 days, steaming for over one-half the distance. A lack of coal at Cadiz, and the captain's orders against going elsewhere, forced the *Tartar* to return to England largely under sail.

Broderip believed his steamer could do even better. Since sailing vessels sometimes needed three weeks or more to reach Cadiz, he thought that with better-quality fuel and a shorter route, the *Tartar* could make the trip even faster. After submitting his report to the Lords of the Mail in August, Broderip asked for permission to try again, this time for Lisbon, as originally intended.

His wish was granted. On September 22nd, Broderip and the *Tartar* departed from Falmouth. After steaming at speeds as high as 6 and 7 miles per hour, and sailing at a much slower rate, they arrived at Lisbon in 5½ days. The *Tartar*'s second experiment had been a triumph, in spite of the fact that she lacked a pointed bow, or a smooth coppered bottom, or the optimal complement of sails.

The return trip was plagued again by the poor quality of coal available for refueling, but Broderip still thought he had proven his point. No steam vessels in the United Kingdom, save the Post Office packets *Royal Sovereign* and *Meteor*, had any chance of weathering the ocean like the *Tartar*. Broderip proposed applying his steam-and-sail plans to a line of postal packets running to Lisbon, and eventually, with more improvements in the technology, the Mediterranean Sea. In his years of correspondence with various parts of the British government since 1819, this had been the goal all along.

Circumstances, however, had changed. While Broderip made his official reports to the Post Office, it soon became clear that the Lords of the Treasury would be calling the shots. After all, they were the ones who had to approve any further spending. The Treasury would be assisted, in turn, by the Lords of the Admiralty, who had just recently assumed responsibility for running all of the Falmouth mail packets.

In time, Charles Broderip would come to realize that the government was no longer interested in putting a British version of the *Savannah* into operation on the Atlantic Ocean. While he was frustrated by the experience, Broderip nevertheless had helped his country. In the wake of the shock of 1819, he had prodded his government into exploring the new mode at sea like never before. It just so happened that by the time he had been able to show what his *Tartar* could do, the Post Office steamers were operational, and the Royal Navy had finally acquired the knowledge. If he wanted to pursue his plans any further, Broderip would have to turn elsewhere.

* * *

In November of 1823, as Broderip was filing his final report on the Lisbon experiment, Admiral Sir Thomas Byam Martin sent an update to Lord Melville regarding his secret instructions for the development of steam-powered brigs:

> *... I beg leave to inform your Lordship that no time having been lost in carrying this purpose into effect, two of the Engines in question have now been completed, and the remaining four are in a state of great forwardness.*
> *As it now therefore becomes necessary to take steps for paying the respective Engineers ... I have to request your Lordship's instructions as to the mode to be pursued, namely, whether the requisite payments shall be made by me as for a secret service, or whether the subject may with propriety be brought before the Board, and payments ordered to be made according to the usual official course.*

Lord Melville replied that the need for secrecy was no longer necessary. Since the engines were about to be delivered to the Royal Navy dockyards, their existence and purpose would become common knowledge. Just keep them in good working order, the First Lord instructed, in case they had to be installed on short notice.

The modified ten-gun brigs that would receive the engines had yet to be built—in fact, they would not be ordered officially for another six months. In the interim, the Admiralty would decide that the engines should not sit in storage, collecting dust. Instead, the machinery should be installed directly into the brigs during construction, creating the first class of ocean-going steam-powered men-of-war in history.

The Royal Navy was on its way.

* * *

Half-way around the world in Calcutta, Lieutenant James Henry Johnston and a select group of merchants were making steady progress. At a public meeting in Town Hall on November 5th, 1823, a self-styled "Committee for Establishing a Communication between England and India by Steam Navigation" was formed.

One of the Committee's immediate objectives was to solicit subscriptions to a Steam Fund. The contributions to this account would serve as prize money. Whoever completed the first round-trip steam voyage between England and Calcutta, which averaged not more than 70 days each way, would win the monies in the Steam Fund.

It was a very bold challenge. That British colonials in India would even dare consider such a proposal was a reflection of how they felt about their place in the world, and those feelings could be readily distilled down to one very powerful word—*isolation*.

Sailing ships from Britain usually took from 5 to 8 months to reach Calcutta, which meant weeks could go by without any news or correspondence from home. The longing for contact with the Mother Country was so strong among the British colonials that sometimes the top story in Calcutta's newspapers was the *absence* of any new ship arrivals. Everything depended upon Nature, as it always had.

Steamships promised to change that. Lieutenant Johnston and the other proponents of the new mode, who came to be known locally as *Steamites*, spent much of 1823 trying to drum up support.

Skepticism, not surprisingly, was widespread. Across the subcontinent, in *The Bombay Courier*, one critic couldn't hold back:

> *A great sensation has been produced by the paragraph which appeared in your paper, adverting to the project of a communication between this country and England, by Steam Packets. The hope of so easy a transition of our thoughts, our properties and ourselves is so animating,*

that anxious expectants of every class, feel its cheering influence—the
prudent already calculate its advantages—and invalids spring resus-
citated from the sickly couch ... And shall these hopes fade? or prove
but the airy vision of unreal things? . . .

In spite of such sarcasm, the Steamites pressed on. With the formation of the Steam Committee, they petitioned the East India Company's Governor General of Bengal, Lord Amherst, asking him to
contribute funds to the effort. The initial reply, relayed by his Chief
Secretary, Charles Lushington, was far from encouraging:

> *... His Lordship in Council cannot relinquish the conviction that the*
> *undertaking is fraught with difficulty and danger. It is not unreason-*
> *able to apprehend that in unsuccessful attempts to achieve this most*
> *arduous enterprize many lives may be lost, or if such extensive calamity*
> *should be avoided, the failures may involve severe pecuniary distress*
> *and even tend to the ruin of individuals...*

The Governor General had gone on to say that while he could not
provide any encouragement for the "commencement" of such a venture, rewarding success was a possibility.

Less than one week later, on November 26th, the Steam Committee submitted a detailed response to Lord Amherst's concerns. "The
length of the voyage and the magnitude of the undertaking may be
appalling to the mind until the alarm shall be dissipated by actual
experiment," they declared. The Committee went on to note that the
feasibility of steaming through stormy seas already had been proven.
The Irish Channel and the Baltic Sea were regularly crossed by steam
vessels. Besides that, "the Americans have traversed the Atlantic and
the establishment of Steam Packets between England and Cadiz
proved the fact that no serious danger is apprehended from their use
in the heaviest seas."

While their understanding of Charles Broderip's experiments was
exaggerated, the Committee's mention of the steamship *Savannah's*
unprecedented feat was not. It remained the most well-known long-
distance voyage by the new mode, and one that clearly had not been
forgotten, even on the far side of the planet.

As to failure, the Committee assured His Lordship that only the largest, most well-established merchants would be solicited for funds, thereby spreading the risk. They closed their reply by stating that they held no illusions:

> ... It must be admitted that the first adventures will labor under considerable disadvantage; For time will be required to reconcile many to the use of Steam Vessels...

The overriding earnestness and humility of the letter did the trick: Lord Amherst approved 20,000 rupees (or $10,000) of government money to be contributed to the Steam Fund. He did, however, add some conditions to those already established. The new rules required that the vessel be at least 300 tons burthen, and it had to make two round trips instead of one, all before the end of 1826.

At a public meeting in Calcutta's Town Hall in December, the Steam Committee's complete correspondence with Lord Amherst was read aloud. Additional amendments and rules were adopted, and finally the prize money subscribed to date was announced. With the Bengal government's contribution, more than 62,000 rupees had been collected. Once further subscriptions came in from the interior provinces, including a contribution from the King of Oude, the total prize money eventually reached nearly 70,000 rupees. With the groundwork laid, the organizers closed the meeting by acknowledging all the efforts of Lieutenant Johnston, who rose and expressed his gratitude for the honor.

The Steam Committee's work up to that point had been the easy part. With the goals, rules, and reward properly defined, the burden of attempting such a feat then shifted almost entirely to Lieutenant Johnston, who had to return to England and build a steamship.

* * *

Upon arriving home, James Henry Johnston soon found that news of the prize for steaming to India had preceded him. Others were already trying to garner support for the effort. But given his intimate involvement with the Steamites' activities in Calcutta, Johnston clearly had a competitive advantage.

The group of true believers he joined decided that the best plan was to build just one steam vessel, for the longer passage around the Cape of Good Hope. This would be far easier to carry out than the two-steamer solution needed for the Mediterranean–Red Sea route.

Through the rest of 1824, Johnston and his assembled team worked feverishly to raise money from London merchants, and then begin construction of their vessel, in the hopes of dissuading any potential rivals.

By February of 1825, they were able to launch their hull into the Thames River. Johnston and his supporters made clear that beyond winning the monies held by the Steam Fund, their long-term plan was to initiate regular steam packet service to India. To capture the spirit of this effort, they gave their vessel a name worthy of such ambitious goals, christening their creation "the *Enterprize*."

* * *

Growing publicity for the attempt to steam to India further energized those in Britain who believed in the new mode's potential. The year 1825 saw a number of groups try to organize steaming across the seas.

Charles Broderip was among them. He became part of an effort to create the Foreign and Colonial Navigation Company, which would traverse the oceans "by the combination of the full Power of Sails and Steam." It was only through this marriage of the old and the new, he and his supporters argued, that long distance steam packets could be effective. "With one exception, Boats only have been employed, or Vessels having Sails only in aid of Steam." This new company would "exclusively combine all the sailing properties of the most perfect Frigates, with the addition of powerful Steam Machinery."

Still others in London pushed far more specific plans. The newly-formed American and Colonial Steam Navigation Company, in a printed prospectus, frankly described the basis for their goal:

> The vast importance of obtaining all the advantages of Steam Navigation between Europe and America, has engaged the serious attention of many leading merchants, bankers, and others, in the principal ports on both sides of the Atlantic...

This group believed that the key question was how to make a steam-powered crossing of the Atlantic as short and safe as possible. To them, the answer was a small port in Ireland called Valencia.

Located on an island of the same name off the southwest coast in

County Kerry, Valencia afforded an ideal spot to begin and end a trans-Atlantic steam crossing. All of the dangers of the south coast of Ireland, as well as the fickle winds and foul weather of the Irish Sea, could be avoided. Furthermore, every major city in Britain and Ireland already was linked to Valencia through a highly efficient system of mail stage-coaches and steamboat packets. If the "proposed Steam Ships" left from this westernmost point in Europe, the saved fuel would allow them to steam for a larger portion of the journey across. On the far side, they would make port and refuel at Halifax, Nova Scotia. Then, the "Steam Ships" would continue their journey to New York, and finally the West Indies. Trans-Atlantic travel times would be cut in half, and the passage would be far safer.

Lest anyone doubt the very possibility of such a service, the promoters made sure to point out what already had been accomplished:

> A Steam Ship of 300 tons has crossed the Atlantic. One of the same magnitude made a voyage of 1,200 miles on a sea more dangerous than the Atlantic, viz., from Falmouth to Cadiz. And one of 750 tons has traded regularly, for some years, between New York and New Orleans...

The key to success, this group continued, was to use vessels large enough to both carry sufficient coal and contend with heavy seas. To do this, they proposed building a new class of mammoth steamships, up to 1,000 tons burthen, a size no longer unheard of, thanks in part to Seppings' diagonal braces. Such a fleet of steam packets would require a lot of money, and the promoters projected they would eventually need £600,000 (or over $2.6 million) to put their plan into effect.

News of this venture excited plenty of interest in the United States. American newspapers eagerly awaited more details, and some New World merchants publicly discussed how they might get into the act.

Back in Britain, however, the promise of trans-Atlantic steaming was temporarily overshadowed by the anticipated voyage of the *Enterprize*.

* * *

By early August of 1825, everything was ready.

The completed *Enterprize*, anchored in the Thames, was truly in a class by herself. Measuring over 120 feet in length and 479 tons burthen, the vessel was as large as some of the merchantmen of the East India Company.

Her steam apparatus and overall design were both impressive, and ingenious.

She had a pair of 60-horsepower cylinders, engineered so that if one cylinder broke down, the other could still turn the wheels. And her huge copper boiler was based upon an efficient new design intended to minimize the salt problem. Furthermore, the whole part of the engine was installed below the deck, protecting it from hazard.

The problems of both ballast and paddleboard depth had been solved by the installation of a number of large iron tanks, placed deep within the hull. The tanks would hold coal, their combined weight serving as ballast. As the coal was consumed by the engine, the emptied tanks would be gradually filled with water as replacement ballast, thereby keeping the hull, and paddleboards, at the same optimal depth.

And whenever steam power was not being used, the paddlewheel axle could be disengaged from the engine, allowing the wheels to turn freely.

Even with all her steam machinery below deck, the *Enterprize* was calculated to hold over 300 tons of coal. With at least one re-fueling stop en route (at the Cape), the vessel was projected to steam most of the way to India. When fuel ran out, or conditions warranted, sails could be used.

And it was her sailing apparatus which determined how the *Enterprize* was perceived, or at least described. Her foremast and mainmast had yards for square-rigged sails, just like a ship, but were rigged to carry lug sails, as well. The mizzenmast at the stern apparently had no yards, and instead was rigged to carry only lug sails. This unusual combination of masts, rigging and sails would give Lieutenant Johnston, who would take command, added flexibility in using the old mode as needed. It also meant that the *Enterprize* was technically not a steam *ship*. Instead, this configuration made her something closer to a steam *barque*, with lugger sails. Sailing barques were an unusual configuration as it was—adding lug sails and steam power to the mix made the *Enterprize* all the more difficult to categorize.

In the end, some observers—still struggling to acknowledge what had already transpired—referred to her as a "steamboat."

A few others offered "steamship."

But overwhelmingly, acceptance of a changed world combined with respect for tradition led the vast majority to reject both those descriptions, and refer to the *Enterprize* as a "steam vessel," or "steam packet."

Regardless, no one questioned the importance of what was about to transpire. On August 6th, James Henry Johnston ordered the engine into operation, and the *Enterprize* began churning down the Thames River, in front of cheering thousands. This was, without a doubt, Britain's reply to America's epochal experiment.

The initial destination was the port of Falmouth, on England's south coast. From there, the steamer would officially begin the voyage to India.

Yet some careful observers along the Thames must have wondered if the *Enterprize* would even make it to Falmouth, for as soon as she began to move, it seemed evident that the steamer was not floating correctly. The culprit was the huge amount of coal stuffed into her, which caused the *Enterprize* to move sluggishly down the river. While such a problem could be rectified once the excess coal had been consumed, the real danger of so much fuel on board soon became obvious.

Shortly after departure, a fire broke out over the boiler. The crew had foolishly placed surplus bags of coal there, which had combusted from the tremendous heat. Fortunately, the flames were extinguished before any serious damage was done, and the *Enterprize* proceeded to Falmouth, which she reached without further incident.

Once additional provisions had been loaded at Falmouth, Captain Johnston welcomed aboard 17 adventurous passengers. On August 16th, 1825, they departed for India, setting a course due south, toward the Cape of Good Hope.

Out on the open Atlantic, the *Enterprize* performed well, regularly achieving speeds under steam of 5 to 7 knots. While the machinery operated precisely as intended, either with or without sails, Captain Johnston and his crew nevertheless discovered a design flaw. The firemen found that the small openings in the fuel bunkers made the task of shifting coals an arduous one. The resulting dust and fumes caused some of the men to faint on the spot.

With his crew exhausted from their duty, Captain Johnston decided to make an unscheduled stop at the island of St. Thomas, off the west coast of Africa. There, Johnston and his crew spent three days shifting coals, cleaning the boiler, and taking on drinking water. Once these tasks were complete, they departed St. Thomas and pressed on toward the Cape.

On September 29th, with the coal nearly gone, Captain Johnston ordered the engine stopped, and the canvas unfurled. Except for one day with no wind, the old mode was used for the remainder of the leg to Cape Town, which was reached on October 13th.

After spending eight days taking on a new supply of coal and provisions, the *Enterprize* departed the Cape, steaming or sailing through the Indian Ocean as conditions allowed.

Finally, on December 8th, the steamer arrived at Calcutta.

Unfortunately, it had taken 113 days and 17 hours to travel the 13,700-mile course from England to Bengal. This was not even close to the Steam Fund's 70-day requirement. While participants in the venture were sorely disappointed, there was no denying one very plain fact: the *Enterprize* had made it, and safely.

What's more, with the most advanced technology available, the vessel had steamed for 63 days of the voyage, and cut the transit time from the usual 5–8 months to less than 4 months. In itself, this performance was a testament to the remarkable advances being made in the new mode of transport.

Nevertheless, given how long the journey had taken, the promoters decided not to attempt a return voyage to England. Instead, the Bengal government agreed to purchase the *Enterprize* for use in the waters off India. The £40,000 paid nearly offset the total cost of the venture. Even though the Steam Fund's conditions were not met, in time the Committee would see fit to reward Lieutenant Johnston with one-half of the prize money. The rest of the Steam Fund was left in place, in the hope that it might entice others to try.

* * *

Despite skepticism, setbacks and stalled efforts, the path for oceanic steam travel through the 1820s and beyond was unstoppable. With each passing year, new strides would be made, and inevitably, some of those who witnessed each extension of the new mode at sea would conclude they could do better.

In time, the dream would become reality, and the oceans of the Earth would be traversed by machines so powerful as to have been once considered chimerical in the extreme. Still other technologies would be developed, eventually allowing humans to artificially alter time and place in ways that would have seemed otherworldly to inhabitants of the early 19th century.

But before such advances could be made, individuals had to believe it was possible. In order to believe it was possible, they had to overcome the fear, and the doubt, which comes with trying to do something that others think cannot be done.

As time passed, the feat of Captain Moses Rogers and the steamship *Savannah* would largely fade from the collective memory. While their Atlantic crossing periodically surfaced in the popular dialogue through the 19th and 20th centuries, the scattered evidence of the effort led many to question what Moses and his fellow promoters had actually achieved. The incredible progress of so many other technologies in the modern era made it all the more difficult to judge this Wonder of an Age from so long ago.

What really mattered, though, was what Moses and his creation had done not only by trying, but especially by succeeding. They had proved that this, the first high technology in history—which allowed humans to artificially alter time and place to practical effect—was not just a *provincial* innovation, but a *global* one.

And in the aftermath of their trans-Atlantic triumph, the thoughts and actions of so many others, sometimes hidden from view, make clear what else Moses Rogers and the steamship *Savannah* had accomplished for eternity.

In the year 1819, the psychological barrier was broken.

APPENDIX

LEGACIES

No STORY EVER truly ends. It continues, in the lives of others, and the events of the future. Once Moses Rogers and the steamship *Savannah* were gone, those people, places and movements that affected them, and which they in turn influenced, carried on. In some cases, these "descendents" quietly faded from the scene, supplying only markers in the historical landscape. Yet in others can be found the signposts pointing the way forward, for steam-powered navigation, other high technologies, and greater progress still to come.

The Shareholders:

John Bogue—the Scottish expatriate merchant who had joined the new mode after he couldn't beat it—left Savannah in 1820, and returned to his native Scotland.

Samuel Yates put up for sale his Charleston ship chandlery in June of 1820. He died shortly thereafter.

John Speakman—founder of the trading firm of John Speakman & Company of Savannah—died on St. Simon's Island, Georgia in the autumn of 1821.

Joseph P. McKinne and his wife Anna lost their house on Liberty Street in New York to creditors at the end of 1820. Moving his family to a boarding house, McKinne continued to work for Pott & McKinne's assignees (which included ship chandler Francis H. Nicoll), who had won the legal right to collect any monies owed to the defunct partnership. McKinne's deteriorating health led his doctors to recommend a warmer climate. With his creditors' permission, McKinne traveled south to Augusta, Georgia in January of 1822, where he joined Anna and their one child at his father-in-law's home. McKinne died there six months later.

Samuel Howard—father of the new mode of transport in Georgia—pressed on with expanding his Steam Boat Company's network within the State, while simultaneously contending with defaulted loans taken out by himself and his deceased brother, Charles. Samuel Howard died in 1823.

James McHenry continued as one of the partners of Andrew Low & Company until his death at Lexington, Georgia in 1826.

Robert Isaac also remained a Low partner until his death from yellow fever in 1827. He was buried at the Old Colonial Cemetery in Savannah. His will bequeathed the Scarbrough mansion, purchased at auction in 1820, to his niece, Charlotte Scarbrough.

Andrew Low—the primary partner of the Savannah firm of Andrew Low & Company, and the Liverpool firm of Isaac, Low & Company—managed to ride out the depression. He used Liverpool as his base into the 1830s, and remained close to Robert Isaac's widow, Lucy, who moved there after her husband's death. Low's nephew, also named Andrew, emigrated from Scotland to Savannah in 1829 to join the family trade. Eventually, this nephew carried on with his own successful firm in Savannah, largely eclipsing the memory of his uncle.

William S. Gillett—having lost his Savannah business in the fire of 1820—moved to South Carolina with his family. He died there in 1829, at the age of 35.

Robert Mitchell remained a merchant and resident of Savannah until his death in 1830. He was buried at the Old Colonial Cemetery.

Joseph Habersham continued to operate in partnership with his brother Robert into the 1820s. He died in 1831, at the age of 46.

William Scarbrough, after being swamped by judgments against him for unpaid debts, took a position as the agent for Andrew Low & Company's steam-powered saw and rice mill in Darien, Georgia. He was able to build upon this, gaining a directorship at the local Bank of Darien by the mid-1820s. Nevertheless, Scarbrough could not regain the prominence he once enjoyed, receiving warrants from the U.S. Marshal every year through the 1820s for monies still owed to the Bank of the United States. In 1828, he gained a son-in-law, the English émigré merchant Godfrey Barnsley, who helped Scarbrough financially through his remaining years. Into the 1830s, Scarbrough worked on numerous inventions, including new steam engine designs, and promoted a project to build a canal and turnpike across Georgia, to link the Atlantic Ocean and the Gulf of Mexico. He died in June of 1838, whilst on a visit to New York. Scarbrough's body was returned to Savannah and buried in the Old Colonial Cemetery, next to his brother-in-law Robert Isaac.

John Haslett—promoter of the Charleston Steam Boat Company—faced multiple lawsuits over unpaid debts in the early 1820s. Nevertheless, he managed to recover, and remained an active merchant in Charleston, where he died in 1839. Haslett was buried in the Congregational (or Circular) Church Yard.

J. P. Henry faced legal judgments for tens of thousands of dollars on past-due loans into the early 1820s. He also recovered, and continued to serve as the U.S. Navy Agent at Savannah until his death in 1842.

Gideon Pott remained Joseph P. McKinne's partner until the latter's death in 1822. Pott was compelled to pursue debt collections on behalf of Pott & McKinne's creditors, including Francis H. Nicoll, well into the mid-1820s. In 1823, Pott entered into a new partnership with another St. Andrew's Society member, John Graham (who was a former shareholder of the Ocean Steam Ship Company). This new firm of Graham & Pott continued to operate until 1835, when it was dissolved. Gideon Pott died in 1843.

James S. Bulloch—one of the Savannah Steam Ship Company's directors—remained a merchant and planter until his death in 1849. His daughter Martha would marry a wealthy New Yorker distinguished for his philanthropy. The couple in turn had a son, who, despite suffering from asthma as a young boy, overcame his affliction to devote his life to public service, becoming the 26th President of the United States. This grandson of James S. Bulloch was named Theodore Roosevelt.

Abraham B. Fannin got married to Jane Williamson on the very day Captain Moses Rogers died. Fannin continued to live and trade in Savannah until his death in 1851.

Isaac Minis was devastated by the depression, defaulting on large loans from the Bank of the United States, among others. As a result, he and his wife Dinah lost their house to creditors. In time, Minis was able to rebuild his life as a merchant, and eventually became involved in the second high technology, investing in the Central Railroad and Banking Company of Georgia. He died in 1856, while visiting his daughters in Philadelphia.

Sheldon C. Dunning, former sailing captain and merchant, suffered greatly through the early 1820s. In addition to the loss of his store and steam-powered lumber mill to fires, Dunning also had to fight off creditors pressing for repayment of loans. He too managed to recover, remaining a part of Savannah's business and civic communities for decades. He died in 1858.

Archibald S. Bulloch and his wife Sarah were forced by the depression to gradually sell off substantial amounts of their holdings, including their new mansion, wharf lots, land, and even personal possessions. Bulloch remained the U.S. Collector of Customs at Savannah until 1822, after which he gradually faded from the city's public and commercial life, until he died in 1859.

Robert Habersham continued to trade at Savannah in partnership with his brother Joseph, until bringing his own sons into the business. He remained a very active member of the community, serving on the 1825 committee which organized a visit to Savannah by the Marquis de Lafayette, who was on his 50th anniversary tour of the United States. Habersham also remained committed to the new high technologies, helping to organize and lead the Central Railroad and Banking Company of Georgia in the late 1830s. He died in 1870.

The Builders:

Daniel Dod moved to New York in the early 1820s, and continued to design steam engines for the new mode of transport. Despite having warrants served on Gideon Pott and Joseph P. McKinne, Dod apparently was unable to collect on his *Savannah* bill. In 1823, Dod was testing one of his new high-pressure boiler designs on the steamboat *Patent* when the end of the boiler blew out, seriously scalding him and several crewmen. Dod insisted he had been the victim of sabotage, before dying of his injuries.

Samuel Fickett, William Crockett and their extended families continued building sailing ships in New York through the 1830s. In addition to trans-Atlantic sailing packets, they also became well-known as the leading builders of coastal sailing vessels, most of which served between Gotham and either Savannah or New Orleans.

Francis H. Nicoll, ship chandler of New York, remained one of Pott & McKinne's assignees, meaning any monetary judgments in favor of the defunct firm would go to him. Because his bill to the Savannah

Steam Ship Company remained unpaid, and Pott & McKinne had difficulty collecting its own monies, in September of 1822, Nicoll decided
to bring a federal suit against the remaining shareholders at Savannah.
He very carefully avoided using the Company's name anywhere in his
complaint, lest the court rule he could not sue the individual shareholders. That December, half a dozen of the shareholders appeared
in Federal Circuit Court at Savannah. They argued that since Nicoll's
suit was a "joint action against all of them," and New Yorker Gideon
Pott lived outside the Circuit Court's jurisdiction, the suit should be
dismissed. Nicoll could bring suit against "all of them" in his own
Federal District of Southern New York. The following February, in
1823, Gideon Pott filed his own deposition, claiming that he had not
promised to pay Nicoll's bill (despite the Pott & McKinne promissory
notes issued). Because four of the surviving shareholders lived outside
the District of Georgia and could not be served with warrants, the
Court made an additional attempt to summon them by newspaper
notices. Failing to gain appearances from each shareholder, Nicoll
apparently dropped his "joint action against all of them." Instead, as
one of the assignees of Pott & McKinne, he continued to press Gideon
Pott on the bankrupt firm's uncollected debts. Under the circumstances, it is unlikely the chandler received payment on his bill. Nicoll
remained a prominent New York merchant into the 1830s. In 1841,
he ran as the Loco Foco Democrats' candidate for governor of Connecticut, and lost. Nicoll died in 1842.

James P. Allaire, of the Allaire Iron Works, remained one of the
most prominent steam engine builders in the United States through
the mid-19th century, especially for the new mode of transport. The
Savannah's cylinder, which Allaire had purchased from Nathan
Holdridge in 1820, remained in use at his Cherry Street foundry for
decades. In 1852, Allaire put the cylinder on display at the New York
Exhibition of the Industry of All Nations. This same fair, contained
within the famed Crystal Palace at 42nd Street and Sixth Avenue, also
exhibited the *Savannah*'s logbook. Allaire died in 1858.

Stephen Vail, of the Speedwell Iron Works, also probably did not
receive payment on his bill. However, he was able to leverage his work
on the *Savannah* into additional business for steam engines and other
high technologies, including the beginnings of the railroad industry.
Vail and his son George also partially funded, and his son Alfred
largely carried out, the earliest experiments of Samuel F. B. Morse for

the electro-magnetic telegraph, which became the third high technology in history. Stephen Vail died in 1864.

The Passengers:

Henry James Finn—the Australian-born, New Jersey-raised and British-trained actor who rode the steamships *Savannah* and *Robert Fulton*—tried his hand at journalism, briefly working for *The Georgian* in 1820. He subsequently returned to a life in the theater, as an actor, comedian and playwright, appearing in productions from Boston to Philadelphia, where he retired from the stage in January of 1840. On his way home to Newport, Rhode Island, Finn took passage on the steamboat *Lexington*, out of New York. As the steamer cruised past the port of Norwalk, Connecticut, wooden timbers next to the smokestack caught fire. Sparks from this combustion in turn ignited bales of cotton stacked upon the deck. Attempts to bring the fire under control proved useless, and the engine quickly broke down, leaving the *Lexington* a flaming, crippled deathtrap. The three lifeboats available were swamped by premature deployment, forcing passengers and crew to frantically push boxes and cotton bales overboard, hoping to ride them to safety. Only three survived the fire and frigid waters. Among the more than 150 souls lost was Henry J. Finn.

General Sir Thomas Graham, Lord Lynedoch, returned home to Britain after his European tour of 1819, although he later made repeated trips to the Continent, especially Italy, for health reasons. He remained a well-known farmer and stock-breeder in Scotland, and could still ride a horse until shortly before his death in 1843, at the age of 95. In preparation for Lynedoch's burial, the decision was made to remove the wedding ring of his beloved wife, Mary, from his left little finger. However, since Lynedoch had worn the ring continuously since her death, the flesh on his finger had grown around it to such a degree as to make removal impossible. The ring was left in place, and Lord Lynedoch was buried next to Mary, in Perthshire, Scotland.

Count Karl Ludwig von Ficquelmont—the French-born Austrian minister to Sweden who rode on the *Savannah* at Stockholm—continued to serve his adopted country as a diplomat into the 1840s. At the outbreak of continent-wide revolutions in 1848, Ficquelmont succeeded his long-time supporter, Klemens Metternich, as Austrian foreign minister. Just two weeks later, with Vienna in revolutionary turmoil, the Count was elevated to the post of President of the Ministerial Council of the Habsburg Empire. This promotion was too much for the public, who began raucous demonstrations outside his office, and occupied his residence. After just 45 days in his new position, Ficquelmont resigned, citing "the force of circumstances."

Robert Graham went on to practice law in Scotland, and briefly served as a Lord of the Treasury in 1834. Upon the death of the childless Lord Lynedoch, Graham inherited his cousin's lands and title. He died in 1859.

The Last Owners:

Oliver Sturges and Benjamin Burroughs, the two Savannah merchants who purchased a partial interest in the sailing ship *Savannah* in late 1820, continued their trading partnership of Sturges & Burroughs until the former's death in 1824.

Captain Nathan Holdridge, of the ships *Rubicon* and *Savannah*, continued to command vessels using the old mode of power throughout the rest of his career. This included work for scheduled sailing packets to Havre and Liverpool, the latter service competing directly with the original Black Ball Line. He died at Black Rock, Connecticut in 1844.

The New Mode Proponents:

David Dunham, principal owner (after the Ocean Steam Ship Company) and agent for the steamship *Robert Fulton*, tragically fell off a sloop in the North River in 1823, and drowned. Ownership for the steamship subsequently shifted back and forth between Henry Eckford and David R. Dunham, a relative of the deceased agent. Through the course of these ownership changes, the *Robert Fulton* continued making sporadic ocean runs to seaboard ports, including New Orleans, until early 1825. All the while, using this steamship for still greater purposes was considered. In 1824, it was proposed that the steamship be sent to the Mediterranean to fight for the Greeks, who were struggling for independence from the Ottoman Turks. In 1825, a resolution was offered in Congress to purchase the *Robert Fulton* for pirate-fighting, in light of the *Sea Gull*'s successes off Cuba. Eventually, Henry Eckford converted the steamship to a sailing man-of-war; Francis H. Nicoll purchased it at a marshal's auction; and the "corvette ship *Robert Fulton"* was then sold to the Brazilian Navy in 1827.

Henry Eckford, after resigning his position as the U.S. Naval Constructor at New York, continued to build large sailing vessels, including four 64-gun frigates for the navies of newly-independent Brazil, Colombia, Peru, and Chile. In 1831, he departed in one of his own just-completed vessels for Constantinople, where he sold it to the Ottoman Empire. Sultan Mahmud II induced Eckford to stay and establish a modern navy yard. Unfortunately, after building several vessels there, the shipbuilder died suddenly in 1832. While the public explanation for his death was cholera, people close to Eckford believed he had been poisoned by those jealous of his relationship with the Sultan. Eckford's body was placed in large cask filled with wine, and returned to New York for burial.

Cadwallader D. Colden was removed as Mayor of New York City by political opponents in 1821. He promptly ran for Congress as a Federalist, despite having been a Democratic-Republican. Colden won in a contested election which revolved around supposedly mistaken transcriptions of his name by two county clerks. Once seated in the House of Representatives, he introduced a new bill granting special privileges to the steamship *Robert Fulton* and its new owner, David Dunham & Company. The bill failed to gain passage, and Colden left Congress after one term. He was subsequently elected to the New York State Senate, and promoted internal improvements and judicial reform. In 1825, Colden wrote a brief history of his ally DeWitt Clinton's efforts to build the recently-completed Erie Canal. In this book, Colden predicted that the Canal's efficient link to the West would make Gotham "one of the greatest commercial cities in the world." Colden spent the rest of his life promoting the completion of the Morris Canal in New Jersey. He died at Jersey City in 1834.

Colonel John Stevens, while maintaining ownership with his sons in numerous steamboats, forged ahead to develop the second high technology: railroads. In 1825, after failing to convince skeptics that steam-powered railroads could work, the Colonel built a small circular track at his estate in Hoboken, New Jersey. On it, he ran a miniature train before invited guests, to prove that "steam wagons"—which also were being tested and introduced in Britain—could pull multiple cars, even uphill. John Stevens died in 1838. The Stevens Institute of Technology, in Hoboken, is named in his honor.

Captain Elihu S. Bunker, master of the steam vessel conceived as

Emperor of Russia and christened as *Connecticut,* continued commanding and building steamboats well into the 1830s. After Congress
passed the first steamboat inspection act in 1838 (to address repeated
boiler explosions), Captain Bunker became one of the first federal
steamboat inspectors.

The Family:

Moses Rogers' body did not remain in the Antipedo Baptist Church
burying ground at Georgetown, South Carolina. Instead, civic leaders
at Cheraw arranged to have his body disinterred, transported upriver
to Cheraw, and reburied in the cemetery of St. David's Episcopal
Church. Captain Daniel Elkins, a friend of Moses who took over command of the steamboat *Pee Dee,* is buried next to him.

Adelia Rogers was left in precarious financial circumstances by the
death of Moses. With four children to raise, she was dependent upon
the charity of family and friends for support. At one point in the early
1820s, she spent nearly six months living with Stephen and Bethiah
Vail at Speedwell, New Jersey. Eventually, with her children grown,
Adelia was able to live comfortably in New York City, where she died
in 1859. She was buried at Green-Wood Cemetery in Brooklyn.

George Washington Rogers, the second son of Moses and Adelia,
followed in his father's footsteps, becoming an experienced steam
engineer. Hired to serve as the chief engineer on the ocean steamer
Arctic, he was lost at sea in 1854, when that vessel collided with
another steamship in the Atlantic, and sank.

Stevens Rogers, at the urging of his wife Mary, gave up challenging
the deep sea. Instead, he went into business with his brother-in-law,
Gilbert Rogers, who had taken over the Groton brick and lumber yard
started by father Amos. This partnership included mastering sloops
up the Connecticut River to Hartford. Gilbert and Steve's joint ventures, combined with marriage to each other's siblings, led these two
distant branches of the Rogers clan to become very close. In the
1850s, Steve accepted several government appointments, as inspector
for the New London Custom House, and as a city tax collector, for
which his innate good-nature served him well. Steve also remained
very active in the Freemasons. Because of his size and reputation for
strength, he was often given the task of carrying the enormous Bible
at Masonic funerals. At various times throughout the remainder of

his life, Steve would provide reporters with details of the *Savannah's* epochal voyage. While his recollection of events decades prior was sometimes inaccurate, Steve's careful preservation of the logbook provided indisputable evidence of the achievement. In 1868, after taking several boys on an extended tour of New London's Revolutionary War sites in the heat of August, Stevens Rogers died of heart failure. His funeral was attended by hundreds of fellow Masons and local citizens. Steve was buried at Cedar Grove Cemetery in New London.

Stevens Rogers in the 1860s . . .   *. . . and with a Masonic Bible.*

The Russians:

Alexander I, Emperor of All the Russias, died in 1825 at Taganrog, on the Sea of Azov. For years afterward, rumors persisted that Alexander had fabricated his own death, using the body of an imperial messenger in place of his own, and retiring to live the rest of his life as a religious pilgrim and hermit. His tomb in the Peter and Paul Cathedral has been opened repeatedly by successive generations, only to be found empty.

Empress Elizaveta was with Alexander when he died, and arranged the sealed transport of his remains to St. Petersburg for burial. She died less than six months later, in 1826, and was buried in the Peter and Paul Cathedral, next to the tomb of Alexander.

Grand Duke Nicholas, brother of Alexander, ascended the throne as Emperor in 1825. He took a great interest in promoting the introduction of oceanic steam packets in the late 1820s, as well as the construction of the Russian Navy's first ocean-going steam warships in the 1830s. Nicholas I died in 1855.

Marquis de Traversé, Lord High Admiral of the Russian Navy, retired from his post in 1828. He refused to accept any Russian titles, preferring to keep the rank of Marquis given to him by Louis XVI, in order to remind his descendants of their French roots. He died in 1831, and was buried on his Russian estate, Romanschina. The Traversay Islands, discovered by Captain Bellingshausen's Antarctic expedition, were named in honor of the Marquis.

The Swedes:

Baron Axel Leonhard Klinkowström, after spending nearly two years in the United States, returned to Sweden in late 1820. His written report on American steam vessels, including the steamship *Savannah*, was bound into a large volume of military correspondence and forgotten. By contrast, his 1824 book, *Bref om de Forenta Staterna* (or *Letters from the United States*), became known as one of the more comprehensive early descriptions of the new republic by the sea. Baron Klinkowström died in 1837.

King Karl XIV Johan, born Jean Baptiste Bernadotte, continued to encourage the construction of steam vessels for Sweden's post office and navy, despite his skepticism toward other technologies. He also remained suspicious of his durability as an adopted monarch, and fought vigorously, and successfully, to retain his power over the press. Karl Johan served as Sweden's king until the end, dying at Stockholm in 1844.

Crown Prince Oscar ascended the throne upon his father's death, becoming King Oscar I, and oversaw the continued introduction of steam-powered vessels by the Swedish government. His successful ascension, and reign, effectively eliminated any chance that the Gustavian line of monarchs could ever regain the Swedish throne.

The French:

Napoleon Bonaparte, former Emperor of France, gradually deteriorated in health on his island prison of St. Helena, where he died in

1821. Following his death, rumors persisted that Napoleon had been poisoned by a member of his entourage, with the knowledge and support of his British jailers.

Jean Baptiste Marestier, French naval constructor, eventually published his findings on American steam vessels. The resulting 1824 book and atlas, *Mémoire sur les Bateaux a Vapeur des États-Unis d'Amérique* (or *Memoir of the Steamboats of the United States of America*), includes the only known technical drawings of the steamship *Savannah*. Beyond the ocean steamer *Caroline*, Marestier continued to design steam vessels for the French government until his death at the port of Brest in 1832.

The British:

Charles Broderip tried to interest one of Britain's leading engineers, Marc Isambard Brunel, in his effort to make an experimental steam voyage to the West Indies. Brunel declined to get involved, declaring "my opinion is that steam cannot do for distant navigation." Broderip was so frustrated by the difficulties he faced in protecting his innovations that he petitioned Parliament in 1826 for a reform of British patent laws. He died shortly thereafter.

Francis Freeling, Secretary of the Royal Post Office, was knighted in 1828. His organizational reforms of the Post Office, as well as leadership in adopting steam vessels for the sea-borne delivery of mail, were widely praised for modernizing the institution. Freeling House, home of the British Postal Museum and Archive in London, is named after him.

Lieutenant James Henry Johnston, commander of the ocean steamer *Enterprize*, left continuing efforts to initiate steam packet service to India in the hands of others. He remained in Calcutta for much of the rest of his life, developing steamboat packet lines along the rivers and coasts of India.

Lord Liverpool, Prime Minister of Britain, successfully confronted the rising reform and revolution movement, which reached its rolling apex starting with the Peterloo Massacre in August of 1819, and finished with the Cato Street Conspiracy to murder the British Cabinet in February of 1820. Given his government's multi-pronged effort to adopt the new mode at sea in the wake of the steamship *Savannah*'s voyage, it stands to reason that Lord Liverpool himself was intimately aware and approved of the steps taken. His administration remained in office until 1827, and at nearly 15 years, is one of the longest in modern British history.

Lord Melville continued as First Lord of the Admiralty until 1827, and was brought back again to serve from 1828 to 1830. In addition to his largely hidden promotion of steam-powered vessels, Lord Melville also publicly encouraged British expeditions to the Arctic, in search of the Northwest Passage. Both Melville Sound and Melville Island, Canada are named in his honor.

Sir Robert Seppings remained a Surveyor of the Royal Navy until resigning in 1832. His system of diagonal bracing of hull timbers, which greatly strengthened any vessel that used it, allowed new mode proponents to build larger, more powerful steamers that experienced less vibration. Diagonal bracing remains a fundamental feature of shipbuilding to this day.

Lord Cochrane, upon his arrival in South America in late 1818, put the tiny Chilean Navy on the offensive. His efforts successfully turned the tide of battle against the Spanish at sea, aiding the Patriots of both Chile and Peru. (The *Rising Star*, arriving too late to fight, was subsequently sold to Buenos Aires merchants, and then a Liverpool-based merchant, before being wrecked in 1830.) In 1823, Lord Cochrane shifted to the Brazilian revolutionaries, and helped them defeat their Portuguese rulers. In 1825, the "insurgent admiral" agreed to join the Greek revolutionaries, who were struggling for independence from the Ottoman Empire. To this fight, he proposed to bring six steam-powered men-of-war, designed by himself and engineer Alexander Galloway. However, construction delays and disputes with the Greeks over their cost resulted in only one steamer making it to the Mediterranean. In 1832, after a change in British government, Cochrane was reinstated as an admiral in the Royal Navy. He continued to push for the introduction of steam power until the end of his life in 1860. In recognition of the contributions made to his country, Lord Cochrane was buried at Westminster Abbey in London.

Marc Isambard Brunel, despite his rejection of Charles Broderip's proposition in the mid-1820s, eventually designed and oversaw construction of the ocean-going steamer *Great Western* in the mid-1830s. Brunel's goal was to become the first to cross the Atlantic *continuously* under steam power. He found a rival in the steamer *Sirius*, built by Junius Smith, the American expatriate who had toured the steamship

Savannah at Liverpool in 1819. In early 1838, both vessels raced across the Atlantic toward New York. While the *Sirius* won the contest, it was the *Great Western* which repeated the feat, thereby initiating the first trans-Atlantic steam packet service in history.

The Americans:

President James Monroe, despite dissension within party ranks, ran for re-election in 1820. With the shattered Federalists unwilling to offer an opponent, Monroe won the Electoral College 231–1. (The lone dissenter was elector William Plumer Sr., father of the New Hampshire Congressman, who claimed he wanted to preserve the distinction of an unanimous electoral vote for George Washington.) President Monroe's second term proved increasingly contentious, as Cabinet Secretaries Adams, Calhoun and Crawford prepared to run as his successor, along with Henry Clay and Andrew Jackson. At the end of his term, James Monroe retired with Elizabeth to their plantation in Virginia. He died at New York City on July 4th, 1831, and was eventually interred at Richmond.

William H. Crawford, Secretary of the Treasury, continued to line up allies in preparation for the presidential election of 1824. However, a combination of political attacks followed by a stroke in 1823 left him largely incapacitated. He came in third in the election, and was overrun by his opponents in the decisive House vote. Returning to Georgia, Crawford served as a superior court judge until his death in 1834.

Henry Clay of Kentucky served as Speaker of the House three separate times. His pivotal role in forging the Missouri Compromise preserved a splintering of the country, as well as the perceived balance between free and slave States. No additional States would be admitted to the Union until 1836–37, when slave-State Arkansas was paired with free-State Michigan.

Commodore John Rodgers served as the president of the Board of Navy Commissioners until 1824, when he was ordered to take command of the Mediterranean Squadron. Upon his return in 1827, he was reinstated as the Navy Board's president. In 1835, the Board was ordered to construct one of the three steam batteries originally authorized in 1816—it was named *Fulton the Second*, and proved to be underpowered. Rodgers served as Board president until his retirement in 1837. He died in 1838. The Navy Board itself was abolished by Congress in 1842.

Smith Thompson remained Secretary of the Navy until 1823, when President Monroe nominated him to serve on the U.S. Supreme Court. Confirmed by the Senate, Thompson later ran for New York Governor while still a sitting Justice, but lost. He remained on the Supreme Court until his death in 1843.

Commodore David Porter, while fighting pirates with the steamer *Sea Gull* and his Mosquito Fleet, invaded the Spanish colonial town of Fajardo, Puerto Rico. For having exceeded his orders, Porter was recalled to the United States and court-martialed. Resigning his naval commission, he accepted the post of commander-in-chief of the Mexican Navy in 1826. Porter subsequently returned to the United States, and was eventually appointed the American minister to the Ottoman Empire. He died at Constantinople in 1843.

John Quincy Adams remained Secretary of State throughout both terms of President Monroe's administration. In that post, he is most well-known for his formulation of the Monroe Doctrine, which stipulated that "the American continents . . . are henceforth not to be considered as subjects for future colonization by any European powers." Adams ran for the presidency in 1824, and since no candidate received a majority of the Electoral College, the election was thrown into the House of Representatives. Fourth-place finisher Henry Clay (who was, once again, Speaker of the House) agreed to support second-place Adams, vaulting him over first-place finisher Andrew Jackson. In return, President Adams nominated Clay to be his Secretary of State. This "corrupt bargain," as Jackson and his supporters called it, led the General to plot his revenge in the election of 1828, which he won over Adams. In 1830, a congressional district in his native Massachusetts elected Adams to the U.S. House of Representatives. He served until his collapse on the floor of the House in 1848. Carried to the Speaker's office, Adams died there two days later.

George Washington Campbell, the American minister to Russia, returned home with his wife and children in the summer of 1820. He accepted no other overseas assignments, and spent much of the rest of his life in his adopted Tennessee. He died in 1848, and was buried in Nashville's City Cemetery.

Christopher Hughes remained the American chargé d'affaires to

Sweden until 1825, when he was appointed to serve in the Netherlands. He returned again to his post in Sweden in 1830, remaining until 1841. The following year, he was again commissioned to serve as a diplomat to the Netherlands, where he stayed until 1845. Hughes never rose above the rank of chargé d'affaires, yet he remained one of John Quincy Adams' favorite correspondents. Hughes died at Baltimore in 1849.

Richard Rush, the American minister to Britain, returned to the United States in 1825 to serve as Treasury Secretary in the Adams administration. In 1828, he was President Adams' running mate for re-election. After their loss, Rush's return to private life was interrupted repeatedly by federal appointments. This included service as the special agent charged with pursuing the bequest of Englishman James Smithson for the creation of a national museum (which became the Smithsonian Institution). Rush died at Philadelphia in 1859.

James K. Paulding remained the Navy Board's secretary until 1823. He continued to write poems, short stories and criticism throughout his life, including a second series of *Salmagundi*, which proved a failure. In 1838, he was appointed Secretary of the Navy by President Martin Van Buren. When pressed to build steam-powered men-of-war, Secretary Paulding publicly went along, but privately declared "I will never consent to let our old ships perish, and transform our Navy into a fleet of sea monsters." Paulding died in 1860, and was buried at Green-Wood Cemetery in Brooklyn, New York.

John Marshall, Chief Justice of the U.S. Supreme Court, presided over the steamboat monopoly case of *Gibbons vs. Ogden*, which was decided in 1824. In his majority opinion, Chief Justice Marshall declared that the exclusive right to run steamboats in New York waters, originally granted to Robert Livingston and Robert Fulton by that State, was unconstitutional. With this ruling, the New York Monopoly and all other exclusive State grants to operate steam vessels collapsed. The case is considered a landmark, since it forced the judicial branch to assert for the first time that the Constitution gave the federal government the exclusive power to regulate interstate commerce. In so doing, the first high technology in history directly contributed to legally unifying a disjointed United States.

ACKNOWLEDGMENTS

It is impossible to thank everyone who contributed to the research, writing, design, and production that underlay this book...

This phrase, or some variation of it, has become a staple of the acknowledgment pages within historical, fact-based works for one simple reason: it is absolutely true. For a story which spans the length of the Atlantic Coast of the United States, and stretches across the ocean to the far reaches of Northern Europe, the number of people who have assisted me—from librarians, to archivists, to researchers, to fellow historians—is truly enormous.

Among those many who deserve a particular note of thanks are Paul Britten-Austin and Veronica Ralston in Sweden, Elena Tsvetkova in Russia, Malene Karner Jacobsen in Denmark, Nina Maqami in the Netherlands, Deirdre MacCloskey in Spain, Christine Sommer in Austria, and Odd Røstvig in Norway. Each of these individuals conducted archival research on my behalf, and found new evidence which added important details and understanding to both the subject and the era. Special thanks also are in order for the many archivists at the National Archives and Records Administration of the United States, for their untiring assistance and professionalism.

To those individuals not mentioned above who assisted me in ways great and small, please accept my apology, and assurance that your contributions to this work are not forgotten. Without your help, this story might not possess the same persuasive power that I believe it unquestionably does.

I also would like to thank John S. Huppuch, John Maxtone-Graham, and Iain Alexander Douglas Blair Cochrane, The Earl of Dundonald, for graciously allowing me to review and use ancestral manuscripts and materials in their possession. These privately-owned sources have added considerable depth and detail to particular aspects of the story.

To my wife Robin and brother Peter, who read the manuscript at various stages, and to Professor William H. Flayhart III,

Captain Robert Ayer, and John Steele Gordon, who read the manuscript in its latter stages, I offer heartfelt thanks for their wisdom and private counsel.

To each of mapmaker David Lindroth, cover artist Samuel Conlogue and book designer Carl W. Scarbrough, I owe my thanks for their patience, professionalism and skill in creating the graphic elements which greatly enhance the storytelling within this work. To copy editor Susan Barba and production coordinator Jennifer Most Delaney, I extend kudos for their counsel and guidance through the most critical stages of the publishing process.

With the help of these many people, I have done my utmost to illuminate the truth of the saga of Captain Moses Rogers and the steamship *Savannah*, as clearly and accurately as possible. Inevitably, however, I am just as human as any reader of this book. Any errors of fact or interpretation found within *Steam Coffin* are mine, and mine alone.

Liberty Forever,

JOHN LAURENCE BUSCH

Source Notes

Abbreviations

Denmark:
DNA   Danish National Archives, Copenhagen.
LS   Landsarkivet for Sjælland (State Archive for Sealand), Helsingør.

Russia:
RSAN Russian State Archive of the Navy, St. Petersburg.
RSHA Russian State Historical Archive, St. Petersburg.

Sweden:
KA   Krigsarkivet (Military Archives of Sweden), Stockholm.
RA   Riksarkivet (National Archives of Sweden), Stockholm.

United Kingdom:
BL   British Library, London.
ICE   Institution of Civil Engineers, London.
NAS   National Archives of Scotland, Edinburgh.
NLS   National Library of Scotland, Edinburgh.
NMM National Maritime Museum, Greenwich.
TNA   The National Archives of the United Kingdom, Kew, London.
  ADM Records of the Admiralty, TNA.
  CUST Records of the Boards of Customs, TNA.
  FO   Records of the Foreign Office, TNA.
  HO   Records of the Home Office, TNA.
  POST Records of the Royal Mail Group plc and predecessors, TNA, The Royal Mail Archives, London.
  T   Records of the Treasury, TNA.

United States:
AC   *Annals of Congress.*
ASP   *American State Papers.*
CSL   Connecticut State Library, Hartford, Connecticut.
DU-ML Duke University, Manuscript Library, Durham, North Carolina.
GHS   Georgia Historical Society, Savannah, Georgia.
GSA   Georgia State Archives, Morrow, Georgia.
HSA   Historic Speedwell Archives, Morristown, New Jersey.
HSP   Historical Society of Pennsylvania, Philadelphia, Pennsylvania.
LOC   Library of Congress, Manuscripts Division, Washington, DC.
MHS   Massachusetts Historical Society, Boston, Massachusetts.
MSA   Maryland State Archives, Annapolis, Maryland.
MYS   G. W. Blunt Library, Mystic Seaport, Connecticut.

NARA   National Archives and Records Administration of the United States, College Park, Morrow, New York, Philadelphia, Waltham, Washington.
  RG21   Records of District Courts of the United States, NARA.
  RG26   Records of the United States Coast Guard, NARA.
  RG36   Records of the United States Customs Service, NARA.
  RG41   Records of the Bureau of Marine Inspection and Navigation, NARA.
  RG45   Naval Records Collection of the Office of Naval Records and Library, NARA.
  RG46   Records of the United States Senate, NARA.
  RG59   General Records of the Department of State, NARA.
  RG84   Records of the Foreign Service Posts of the Department of State, NARA.
  RG233 Records of the United States House of Representatives, NARA.
NJHS   New Jersey Historical Society, Newark, New Jersey.
NLCHS New London County Historical Society, New London, Connecticut.
NYHS   New York Historical Society, New York, New York.
NYPL   New York Public Library, Manuscripts Division, New York, New York.
PEM   Peabody Essex Museum, Peabody, Massachusetts.
PUL   Princeton University Library, Department of Rare Books and Special Collections, Princeton, New Jersey.
SAL   *Statutes at Large of the United States of America.*
SCDAH South Carolina Department of Archives & History, Columbia, South Carolina.
SCHS   South Carolina Historical Society, Charleston, South Carolina.
SI   Smithsonian Institution, Manuscripts Collection, Washington, DC.
SSSLB *Steam Ship Savannah Log Book*, Smithsonian Institution.
USCSS *United States Congressional Serial Set.*

Documents:
ICM   Inward Coastwise Manifest.
OCM   Outward Coastwise Manifest.
PE   Permanent Enrollment.
PR   Permanent Registration.
TE   Temporary Enrollment.
TR   Temporary Registration.

CHAPTER ONE—FIRST, YET AGAIN

– investors from Philadelphia had organized: *Charleston Courier*, 6/10/1816.
– plus some experienced workmen: ibid.
– shares allotted for sale at Charleston … immediately taken up: *City Gazette and Commercial Daily Advertiser* (Charleston) (hereafter, *City Gazette*), 6/14/1816.
– construction began … shipyard near Harleston's Green: ibid, 3/3/1817.
– built … by engine-maker Daniel Large: *Charleston Courier*, 6/10/1816.
– carefully stowed in 21 boxes … : NARA, RG36, Port/Philadelphia, Outward Coastwise Manifest (hereafter, "OCM"), ship *Pennsylvania*, 12/16/1816.
– By early March, it was ready to be launched: *The Times* (Charleston), 3/4/1817.
– most of the spring to install the machinery: *Charleston Courier*, 6/7/1817.
– She measured some 98 feet in *length*: NARA, RG41, Permanent Enrollment (hereafter, "PE") #2, Steam Sloop *Charleston*, 1/4/1821. This appears to be the earliest surviving federal document related to the steamboat *Charleston*; it has

been assumed that the basic characteristics described in this 1821 document were accurate in 1817.

– one could see some sort of bird-like figurehead: ibid.
– single wooden sailing mast: ibid.
– at the rear (or *stern*) of the deck was the *tiller*: *Charleston Courier*, 3/16/1818.
– Her hull was made of *live oak*: *Southern Patriot, And Commercial Advertiser* (Charleston) (hereafter, "*Southern Patriot*"), 3/18/1820.
– *Charleston's* exterior was made from cedar: ibid.
– covered with a thin copper plating: ibid.
– yellow pinewood: *Southern Patriot*, 7/3/1817.
– copper *boilers*: *Charleston Courier*, 6/7/1817.
– the *Charleston's* bell rang out: *City Gazette*, 6/25/1817. This was the procedure followed for the *Charleston's* trips to Sullivan's Island. It stands to reason it was continued for the runs to Savannah.
– including a man named Crocker: *Columbian Museum and Savannah Daily Gazette* (hereafter, "*Columbian Museum*"), 12/13/1817.
– Doddridge Crocker: *City Gazette*, 6/23/1817; *Charleston Courier*, 12/3/1817; SCDAH, Charleston County, Court of Common Pleas, Judgment Roll, Item 186A, *Joseph Young vs. John Haslett and others, otherwise called, Charleston Steamboat Co.*, 6/22/1822.
– native of Connecticut: Way, *The New England Society of Charleston...*, p32.
– Haslett, a 43-year-old native of Ireland: Webber, "Inscriptions from the Independent or Congregational (Circular) Church Yard, Charleston, S.C.," *South Carolina Historical and Genealogical Magazine*, Volume XXIX (1928), p313.
– With a residence on the prestigious East Bay: Schenck & Turner, *The Directory and Stranger's Guide for the City of Charleston*, 1816 and 1819.
– a seat on the city council: City of Charleston, *South Carolina, Year Book—1881*, p370.
– total passenger count was one dozen: *Charleston Courier*, 12/11/1817.
– supported by a crew of eight or so: for a steamboat like the *Charleston*, the minimum crew probably included the captain, a pilot (or tillerman), an engineer, two firemen, two deck hands, and a barkeeper. There also might have been a steward.
– At ten minutes past 8 o'clock: *City Gazette*, 12/15/1817.
– ferrying passengers the 4 miles to Sullivan's Island: *Charleston Courier*, 6/14/1817.
– seen fit to hire a new captain: *City Gazette*, 10/22/1817. The *Charleston's* first master was Captain John R. Caswell (see *City Gazette*, 6/25/1817).
– first ocean voyage by a steamboat: NARA, RG36, Port/Philadelphia, Inward Arrivals, 1806–1810 (Vol. 5), Steam Boat *Phenix* [sic], Moses Rogers, 6/24/1809; also Inward Coastwise Manifest (hereafter, "ICM"), Steamboat *Phenix* [sic], Moses Rogers, 6/24/1809.
– taking another steamboat, the *Eagle* ... to the Chesapeake Bay: NARA, RG36, Port/Philadelphia, OCM, Steam Boat *Eagle*, Moses Rogers, 6/12/1815.
– second captain to bring such a vessel into Norfolk: Emmerson, *The Steam-Boat Comes to Norfolk Harbor,* ..., p3.
– maneuvering ... the *New Jersey* ... to the Chesapeake: NARA, RG36, Port/Philadelphia, OCM, Steam Boat *New Jersey*, Moses Rogers, 11/16/1816.
– There, at eight minutes past 2 o'clock ... Block Island: *Charleston Courier*, 12/15/1817; South Carolina Department of Natural Resources, Map of Several Tracts of Land owned by Springfield Realty Company..., May–1928.
– fields of orange and lemon trees: Mills, *Statistics of South Carolina...*, p378.
– Beaufort usually didn't receive waterborne visitors any larger: ibid, p379.
– 15 minutes after tying up, the *Charleston* was on her way: *Charleston Courier*, 12/15/1817.

- "thick weather.": ibid.
- At 5 o'clock, Captain Rogers ordered ... drop anchor: ibid.
- Born in New London, Connecticut back in 1779: Rogers, *James Rogers of New London...*, p166. The exact birth date of Moses is unknown, but given his stated age at death, the year of birth most likely was 1779. His precise birthplace is also unknown, although a local historian, Richard Wall, stated Moses was born at a house on Truman Street in New London (*The Anchor*, Volume V, No. 7, December 1925). His parents' presence in New London around this time is verified by various sources, including Town of Groton, Land Records, Volume 10, p160, "To Amos Rogers of New London," 11/25/1782.
- James Rogers, who had emigrated from England: Rogers, op. cit., p27.
- Father Amos ... opened a brick and lumberyard: ibid, p166.
- sloop called *Two Brothers*: NARA, RG26, Port/New London, Return of the Names of Seamen, sloop *Two Brothers*, 4/14/1802.
- sloop named *Industry*: ibid, PE#12, sloop *Industry*, 4/14/1802.
- from New Bedford, Massachusetts: ibid, OCM, sloop *Industry*, 5/15/1804.
- to New York City: ibid, OCM, sloop *Industry*, 11/8/1804, among others.
- often his younger brother Amos: ibid, Returns of the Names of Seamen, sloop *Industry*, 4/18/1803, 5/14/1805.
- clay: ibid, ICM, sloop *Industry*, 11/17/1804.
- flour, molasses, rum, beef, pork, cheese, potatoes, mast hoops: ibid, ICM, 5/7/1803, and OCM, 5/15/1804, both for sloop *Industry*.
- even a marble tombstone: ibid, OCM, sloop *Industry*, 11/8/1804.
- Adelia was six years younger than Moses: Rogers, op. cit., p245.
- her father, Captain Nathan Smith: it appears that Adelia was one of a number of children that Nathan Smith fathered out of wedlock. James S. Rogers, in his work, does not provide the name of Adelia's mother. In H. Allen Smith's work on the Smith family of New London County (p114), the author states that Captain Nathan Smith was "said to have had thirteen children," and goes on to list eight offspring from Captain Smith's 1788 marriage to Mary Denison. Adelia was born three years prior, in 1785.
- she gave birth to their first child, a son: Rogers, op. cit., p248.
- named after his grandpa Smith: this is an assumption, but it seems a safe one given how often the extended Rogers family followed this tradition.
- joint owners of a 5-year-old sloop named *Liberty*: NARA, RG26, Port/New London, PE#2, sloop *Liberty*, 3/14/1805.
- continued trading with New York City: ibid, OCMs, sloop *Liberty*, 11/23/1805, 12/27/1805.
- to the capital of Hartford: ibid, OCM, sloop *Liberty*, 4/24/1805.
- Moses ... captain of the schooner *Experiment*: ibid, PE#50, schooner *Experiment*, 5/9/1806.
- With a federal fishing license procured: ibid, Abstract of Allowances to Vessels in the Bank and Cod fisheries, schooner *Experiment*, Moses Rogers, 1/1/1806 to 9/30/1806.
- Moses took the new schooner ... off the coast of Newfoundland: CSL, Coddington Billings Collection, RG69:75, Accounts, "1805–1807 Schooner *Experiment*," receipt dated 9/8/1806.
- returned to Stonington in October: NARA, RG26, Port/New London, PE#70, schooner *Experiment*, 10/21/1806; and Changes of Master, schooner *Experiment*, 10/21/1806. Owner William Williams listed himself as master on the *Experiment*'s Permanent Enrollment form this day, while simultaneously changing her master to Moses Rogers in the separate register. This was probably done for

legal purposes—Williams' name as master would remain on the schooner's Permanent Enrollment form, even though Rogers was officially master.
- Moses took the *Experiment* to New York: ibid, PE#13, schooner *Experiment*, 3/19/1807, describing Temporary Enrollment (hereafter, "TE") #497 at Port/ New York dated 11/17/1806; also, advertisement in the *Commercial Advertiser* (NYC), 11/17/1806, in which the *Experiment* was offered "For Sale, Freight or Charter."
- loaded the schooner's hold with coffee, cocoa, and logwood: *The People's Friend & Daily Advertiser*, 2/3/1807.
- back into New York harbor at the beginning of February 1807: ibid.
- Fulton ... his experiments ... had generated only derision: HSP, George C. Berkeley to James Barry, 9/14/1807 is an excellent example (see below).
- ... Though Will has not had the advantage: *Salmagundi*, 1/24/1807. Irving's brother, William, also contributed to the magazine.
- ... Will Wizard was not a little chagrined: ibid, 2/4/1807.
- Astute readers inevitably made the logical comparison: there should be no doubt that readers of *Salmagundi* "got it." One of the best examples of how far this satire traveled is the previously cited letter of George C. Berkeley to James Barry, 9/14/1807. The writer was commander of the Royal Navy base at Halifax, Nova Scotia. After thanking Barry for sending the latest issue of *Salmagundi*, Admiral Sir Berkeley made it quite clear he understood the satirists' intent, recalling Fulton's experiments with sea mines: "I really give great credit to the Author of the Salmagundy for the very wholesome stripes [i.e., lashes] he bestows upon the Folly of Gotham, The Inhabitants (at least the North River Company) seem to be as completely subdued by Ignorance as by Fear. The Author or rather projector [i.e., Fulton] of your Torpedos [i.e., sea mines] tried his hand upon John Bull's credulity, who possess full as much as his Transatlantick Children, and after a very expensive Trial the Scheme was scouted [i.e., rejected] not perhaps so much from its Failure, as from the Baseness of Cowardice of this species of warfare."
- "no more conjectures on the subject.": *Salmagundi*, 2/4/1807.
- ... we pledge ourselves to the public in general: *Salmagundi*, 2/13/1807.
- by mid-February, Moses had unloaded the *Experiment*'s cargo and departed: *The People's Friend & Daily Advertiser*, 2/17/1807.
- *United States vs. Three Bags of Cocoa*: *Connecticut Gazette*, 8/12/1807; NARA, RG21, District of Connecticut, U.S. District Court, Case Files, 9/10/1807, and Final Record Book (Vol. 3), pp56–58, 61.
- owner William Williams gave Moses a *promissory note*: CSL, Coddington Billings Collection, RG69:75, Accounts, "1805–1807 Schooner *Experiment*," 3/9/1807; after Billings paid off this note, Moses disappears from the surviving records of this merchant.
- Williams ... re-register the schooner *Experiment*: NARA, RG26, Port/New London, PE#13, schooner *Experiment*, 3/19/1807.
- Moses ... the captaincy of a sloop named *Lydia*: ibid, PE#20, sloop *Lydia*, 4/15/1807.
- hauling cargo up to Hartford, as well as down to New York: ibid, OCMs, sloop *Lydia*, 7/8/1807, 7/30/1807.
- having filled the *Lydia*'s hold with barrels of sugar: ibid, 7/30/1807.
- they had written of Wizard's uncertain social ways: *Salmagundi*, 3/7/1807.
- "old Cockloft's, where he never fails": *Salmagundi*, 6/27/1807.
- English mechanic ... "had just arrived in an importation": ibid.
- make limited tests of the boilers and paddlewheels: Philip, *Robert Fulton...*, p193.
- By Sunday, August 9th, he was ready to go: since the Custom House was closed on Sundays, Moses must have cleared the *Lydia* on Saturday, August 8th. While

he might have left on Saturday, it seems far more likely that he chose to spend the evening in New York, depart on Sunday, when businesses were closed, and arrive in New London on Monday, August 10th, which he did (see *Connecticut Gazette*, 8/12/1807).

- "I beat all the sloops ... ": Livingston, Edwin Brockholst, *The Livingstons of Livingston Manor...*, p386.
- double the size of the paddleboards: Philip, op. cit., p199.
- Arriving back in New London the day after: *Connecticut Gazette*, 8/12/1807.
- but her hold was not even close to full this time: NARA, RG26, Port/New London, OCM, sloop *Lydia*, 8/14/1807.
- I was not a little perplexed: *Salmagundi*, 8/14/1807.
- "I wonder what can be the matter": ibid.
- It was not until Sunday, August 16th: *Connecticut Gazette*, 8/19/1807.
- on the steamboat's deck ... 40 or so passengers: Sutcliffe, *Robert Fulton...*, p210.
- "heard a number of sarcastic remarks": Robert Fulton to Joel Barlow, as quoted in Colden, *The Life of Robert Fulton*, p176.
- *The moment arrived*: Sutcliffe, op. cit., pp202–203.
- The steamboat slowly moved ... up the wide river: upon reaching Chancellor Livingston's estate at Clermont, the steamboat dropped anchor, and was greeted by the Chancellor himself. According to Sutcliffe (pp211–212), before the steamboat continued on to Albany, the Chancellor declared "that it was not impossible that before the close of the present century, vessels might even be able to make the voyage to Europe without other motive power than steam." In reaction, his brother John R. Livingston was heard to quip, "Bob has had many a bee in his bonnet before now, but this steam folly will prove the worst yet!" John R.'s early skepticism is notable, since he soon became a convert to, and true believer in, the new mode of transport. Far more important is the Chancellor's prediction. Even Robert R. Livingston, one of the original true believers, could not envision the exponential rapidity with which this first high technology would develop. The first crossing to Europe using steam would take place only a dozen years in the future, and the man who would do it was—at the very moment the Chancellor made his end-of-century prediction—walking the streets of New York City. The first crossing of the Atlantic under continuous steam power would take place just 19 years after that, in 1838.
- tying up to the wharf at 4 o'clock: Whittet-Thomson, "Documents: Robert Fulton's *North River Steam Boat*," *The American Neptune*, #32 (1972), pp211–221.
- Arriving in New London on Sunday: *True Republican* (New London), 8/26/1807.
- back to New York just four days later: NARA, RG26, Port/New London, OCM, sloop *Lydia*, 8/27/1807; *Connecticut Gazette*, 9/2/1807.
- "actively and usefully engaged on the North River": *Connecticut Gazette*, 12/5/1821, quoting the *Winyaw Intelligencer* (Georgetown, SC).
- even the engineer, or captain: Braynard, *S.S. Savannah...*, p3, citing Caulkins, *History of New London...*, p653; and Spears, *Story of the American Merchant Marine*, p340.
- Having waited 12½ hours for the fog to dissipate: *Charleston Courier*, 12/15/1817.
- reinforced complement of 25 passengers: *City Gazette*, 12/15/1817.
- pilot ... proved to have an imperfect knowledge of the area: *Charleston Courier*, 12/15/1817.
- many muddy shallows hidden along the banks: Martin, editor, "A New Englander's Impressions of Georgia in 1817–1818...," *Journal of Southern History*, 1946 (12), p249.
- some rice fields tucked in: Harris, *Remarks made during a Tour...*, p69.

- reeds, high grass, and shrubs: Martin, op. cit., p249.
- The only trees to be seen were so far off: ibid.
- sitting some 50 to 70 feet above the water: Melish, *Travels through the United States of America...*, p36.
- Its spire was manned by a lookout: ibid.
- ten minutes before noon: *Charleston Courier*, 12/15/1817.
- 24 hours of that time spent at anchor: *Columbian Museum*, 12/13/1817.
- Howard had managed to gain the exclusive right to run steamboats: *Acts of the General Assembly of the State of Georgia*, "An Act to encourage an improved mode of transporting merchandize upon the waters of the state of Georgia," assented to 11/18/1814; and *Statutes at Large of South Carolina*, "An Act Concerning the Navigation of Broad, Pacolet and Edisto Rivers; and for Other Purposes," passed 12/21/1814.
- Charles... made the *Charleston*'s booking agent: *Columbian Museum*, 12/13/1817.
- We had the pleasure of witnessing: ibid.
- *... She came up to town in very handsome style*: *Charleston Courier*, 12/15/1817.
- Water transport was far and away the cheapest mode of moving cargoes: there is no better illustration of this fact than an 1816 Senate committee report, which stated that for the same charge of $9.00, one ton of goods could be transported 3,000 miles across the Atlantic Ocean, or 30 miles on land (using wagons). In other words, the cost of transport *over the ocean* was as low as 0.3 cents per ton-mile. The cost of *downriver* transport was only 1.3 cents per ton-mile, and *upriver* transport costs were 5.8 cents per ton-mile. By contrast, transport costs *over land* were, at a minimum, 30 cents per ton-mile, and could go as high as 70 cents per ton-mile, if the roads were in poor condition. See Taylor, *The Transportation Revolution...*, pp132–133, and Appendix A, Table 2.
- New construction was everywhere: PEM, Diary of Abiel Abbot, April 1819.
- number of buildings in the city at over one thousand: Melish, op. cit., p36.
- construction with more expensive brick and stone: "Letters from the United States of America," *The Bee* (Liverpool), p486.
- shipping tied up along the river would be below: Martin, op. cit., p250.
- six wide ramps cut straight down: Stouf, *Plan of the City & Harbour of Savannah...*, 1818.
- Hutchinson's Island ... the city had purchased and drained: Harris, op. cit., p69.
- streets ... consisting instead of the bluff's native sand: *The Bee*, p487.
- turkey vultures: ibid, and Faux, *Memorable Days in America...*, p83.
- the city would register a population of 7,523: Gibson, *Population of the 100 Largest Cities...*, Table 5.
- of whom 3,866 were free white residents: Wade, *Slavery in the Cities...*, p327.
- the additional 582 being black citizens who had their liberty: ibid.
- held all sorts of jobs: Johnson, *Black Savannah, 1788–1864*, p185. Johnson's data are for the year 1823.
- some were themselves slave-owners: ibid, p188.
- develop a skewed view ... American version of slavery: Faux, op. cit., pp41–42.
- "every variety of shade" imaginable: *The Bee*, p487.
- The Steam Boat CHARLESTON will start: *Savannah Republican*, 12/12/1817.
- Charleston off at about twenty minutes past 1: *City Gazette*, 12/17/1817.
- miscalculation of the tide: ibid.
- "judicious management": *City Gazette*, 12/15/1817.
- Another expressed confidence that communication: *Charleston Courier*, 12/19/1817.
- just twenty minutes past her appointed departure: ibid.

- LINE OF AMERICAN PACKETS: *New York Evening Post*, starting 10/24/1817.

CHAPTER TWO—NEW PLAN

- sailing schedule ... North Atlantic trade was founded in the seasons: Wright, *The Origins and Early Years of the Trans-Atlantic Packet Lines...*, pp11–12.
- The British mail brigs left Falmouth: ibid, p13.
- made a stop in each direction: ibid.
- About a half-dozen passengers per sailing: ibid.
- With their greater hull size: the four original Black Ball ships had burthens of 381 to 424 tons, putting them at the upper range for ships active in the North Atlantic trade at that time (see Albion, *Square Riggers on Schedule*, p276).
- "hull of a ship intended for a packet to England": *Poulson's American Daily Advertiser* (Philadelphia) (hereafter, *Poulson's American*), 6/14/1816, citing a New York newspaper article.
- This was the ship *James Monroe*: based upon the timing of the article in conjunction with the known builders of these packet ships, the only one that it could be is the *James Monroe*, which was completed by Adam Brown in 1817. The *Pacific* was completed in 1807. The *Amity* was finished in 1816, and the *Courier* in 1817, but neither was built by Brown. See Fairburn, *Merchant Sail*, p1095.
- the Wrights did business with many New York merchants: Fairburn, op. cit., p1093.
- Francis Thompson and his nephew Jeremiah: Wright, op. cit., p24.
- Benjamin Marshall, also originally from Yorkshire: Fairburn, op. cit., p1093.
- ... Each vessel will be required: MYS, Manuscripts Collection 60, Volume 1, Jeremiah Thompson to Cropper Benson & Co. and Rathbone Hodgson & Co., 10/18/1817.
- ... each of the Owners will direct: ibid.
- ... It is our intention that these Ships shall leave: ibid.
- ... with the general circulation of a Knowledge: ibid.
- If things had gone according to plan: they had not—the *Courier* was three days late, not leaving Liverpool until January 4th, 1818. This tardy departure was the exception, and not tolerated subsequently.
- ... *Thou must put thy Ship*: MYS, op. cit., Jeremiah Thompson to Captain Bowne, 10/25/1817.
- eight passengers came aboard: Albion, *Square Riggers on Schedule*, p22.
- a cargo of apples, cranberries, flour: ibid, p307.
- last-minute mail packet, delivered from the nearby Tontine: ibid, p22.
- ... *I hope thou will be exactly punctual*: Thompson to Bowne, 10/25/1817.
- At precisely 10 o'clock: Albion, op. cit., p22.
- ... *after beginning on the New Plan*: Thompson to Bowne, 10/25/1817.
- the canvas ... middle of the foremast: Albion, *The Rise of the New York Port*, p42.
- the signal used ... to denote: Simons, *Stories of Charleston Harbor*, p38.
- Not until 4 o'clock that afternoon: *Commercial Advertiser* (NYC), 1/6/1818.

CHAPTER THREE—NEW THINKING, EVEN THE CHIMERICAL

- Fulton ... suggested ... Colonel Stevens be included: Philip, *Robert Fulton...*, p193.

- Fulton gave Colonel Stevens an open ticket to inspect: ibid.
- the Colonel signed a contract with a shipbuilder: Turnbull, *John Stevens: An American Record*, pp236–237.
- "to promote the Progress of Science ... ": see Article I, Section 8 of the Constitution.
- Livingston believed ... States ... retained the power to grant monopolies: the Chancellor was hardly alone in this belief. Post-ratification of the Constitution, State legislatures granted some form of steamboat monopoly to applicants in New Hampshire, Vermont, Massachusetts, New York, New Jersey, Pennsylvania, North Carolina, South Carolina, Georgia, Tennessee, and Louisiana.
- voyage down to Wilmington, North Carolina: NARA, RG26, Port/New London, OCM, sloop *Lydia*, 1/30/1808.
- Moses made a point of putting in to New York City: ibid, ICM, sloop *Lydia*, 3/14/1808.
- re-named *North River Steam Boat of Clermont*: there has been much confusion regarding the proper name for Fulton's first successful steamboat. In fact, there are multiple names, all of them correct, depending upon the timeframe. For the first season of late 1807, it was officially the *North River Steam Boat*, or more popularly, "the Steam Boat." From the 1808 season onward, it was officially the *North River Steam Boat of Clermont*, or more popularly, "the *North River*," especially after the *Car of Neptune* became operational. However, once Fulton built several more steamboats to make runs to Albany, the name *"North River"* became confusing, so while the official name did not change, the public began referring to Fulton's first steamboat as "the *Clermont*."
- Colonel John Stevens was celebrating the launch: Turnbull, op. cit., p257.
- sold the *Lydia* to a local merchant: NARA, RG41, Port/Perth Amboy, PE#21, sloop *Lydia*, 5/10/1808.
- Moses and the Hope coasted back and forth: *Commercial Advertiser*, 5/10/1808; NARA, RG36, Port/New York, ICM, sloop *Hope*, 6/8/1808.
- Fulton's Folly ... 100 customers per trip was not unusual: *National Intelligencer*, 7/27/1808, among many others.
- the Colonel's steamboat ... more than 5½ miles per hour: Turnbull, op. cit., p260.
- Moses ... assumed command of a larger sloop, the *Lady Washington*: NARA, RG41, Port/Perth Amboy, PE #46, sloop *Lady Washington*, 9/14/1808.
- Colonel Stevens officially enrolled his steamboat: ibid, PE#51, steamboat *Phoenix*, 9/28/1808.
- Stevens ... defy ... running his *Phoenix* from New York City: *New-York Evening Post*, 10/20/1808.
- Fulton contracted to build his second steamboat: Philip, op. cit., p230.
- destination John Livingston publicly chose was New Brunswick: *Republican Watch-Tower*, 11/4/1808.
- Stevens ... announced his proposal for a line of steamboats: *New-York Evening Post*, 10/20/1808.
- Stevens ... 5 feet, 7 inches in height: Turnbull, op. cit., p3.
- John Stevens ... rank of colonel ... he could use as a title for the rest of his life, if he chose: he did not, almost invariably signing his correspondence "John Stevens." His military rank has been used as a descriptor to more easily differentiate him from others.
- placing tools in his son's little hands: Turnbull, op. cit., p86.
- Rogers ... stood stout and tall: the surviving portraits of Moses clearly imply his frame was solid; while there appear to be no surviving records of his height, younger brother Amos Jr. was recorded as being 5 feet, 11 inches (see NARA, RG36, Port/New London, Register of Seamen, #2314, 5/21/1802).

– Colonel Stevens hired Moses Rogers: the precise timing of the hiring isn't known. The earliest surviving evidence of Moses as captain appears to be a receipt for work done on the *Phoenix*, signed by him—see NJHS, Stevens Family Papers (hereafter, "SFP"), Receipt #11, 5/20/1809. Moses also was listed as "master steam boat" in *Longworth's American Almanac...*, 1809, which was compiled in the spring.
– "New Brunswick Steamboat": *American Citizen,* 5/2/1809.
– John R. Livingston, informed Colonel Stevens: Turnbull, op. cit., p271.
– Moses went into the Custom House: NARA, RG36, Port/Philadelphia, ICM, steamboat *Phenix* [sic]. 6/24/1809, cleared New York 6/7/1809.
– At 11 o'clock on the morning of Saturday, June 10th: Turnbull, op. cit., p275. Turnbull reproduced Robert L. Stevens' complete journal of the voyage. The journal is short and somewhat terse. Robert never mentions Moses, but instead repeatedly refers to actions taken in the first person plural (i.e., "we," "our" and "us"). That Moses Rogers was the captain on this voyage can not be disputed. Based upon the Custom House document cited above, Moses cleared the steamboat *Phoenix* on 6/7/1809 at New York, and he presented his coastal manifest at Philadelphia on 6/24/1809, where it was filed. Further, he was listed as the master of the *"Phenix"* in the Inward Arrivals at Philadelphia (see NARA, RG36, Port/Philadelphia, Inward Arrivals 1806–1810, Volume 5, 6/24/1809). Moses Rogers' command of and responsibility for the steamboat *Phoenix* on this historic voyage is beyond any doubt.
– "the gentlemanly conduct of Captain ROGERS": *Poulson's American,* 8/6/1812.
– "merit, and have received applause": ibid.
– "very unsafe": ibid.
– learn the peculiarities of ... the local officials: the appearance of a steamboat on a regular basis led several towns in New Jersey to try to increase their wharf landing fees.
– Adelia ... doing the steamboat's laundry: NJHS, SFP, washing receipts from Adelia or Moses Rogers, dated 9/27/1810, 6/13/1811, 6/13/1812, and 7/28/1812.
– George Washington, Daniel Moses and Delia Antoinette: Rogers, op. cit., p248. Both George (so called by his mother) and Delia were born at Bordentown, in 1810 and 1814 respectively. Daniel was born at Trenton, where the family moved briefly in 1812 (p341, and NJHS, SFP, Moses Rogers to Robert Stevens, 3/11/1812).
– receipts for everything: NJHS, SFP, Receipt for pine wood purchase, 8/23/1809; Receipt for provisions, 7/1/1809, among many others.
– Stevens and Fulton agreed to share patent credit: ibid, Agreement of Robert Fulton and John Stevens, 12/1/1809.
– territory ... carve it up: Philip, op. cit., p245, and Turnbull, op. cit., p284.
– John Stevens' steam domain ... waterways of Connecticut and Rhode Island: in all likelihood, the familiarity of Moses with Long Island Sound led Stevens to negotiate this carve-out of Livingston and Fulton's northern domain.
– opened a boarding house at Bordentown: *Poulson's American,* 5/15/1811.
– victuals from the Philadelphia markets: ibid.
– "it is always better to keep within the month's pay": NJHS, SFP, Francis Stockton to John Stevens, 8/1/1811.
– "really seems to have the good of the Boat": ibid, Francis Stockton to John Stevens, 6/28/1811.
– Captain Rogers had "dreamt ... there was something trouble the matter": ibid, Francis Stockton to John Stevens, 5/17/1811.
– give all of the steamboat's monies to the Colonel's Philadelphia lawyer: ibid, Francis Stockton to John Stevens, 8/1/1811.

– Moses also provided John Stevens with detailed accounts: ibid, Moses Rogers to John Stevens, 11/2/1811, 11/9/1811 and 11/14/1811.
– Moses implored Colonel Stevens to come to Philadelphia: ibid, Moses Rogers to John Stevens, 8/28/1811.
– One passenger from Charleston ... suggested that a steamboat: ibid, Francis B. Stevens to John Stevens, 10/8/1811.
– budding entrepreneurs publicly claimed ... Rogers had endorsed: ibid, Moses Rogers to John Stevens, 10/8/1811.
– a receipt for every expense incurred: ibid, Robert Stevens to John Stevens, 4/23/1812.
– give up responsibility for making out the steamboat's *waybills*: ibid, Robert Stevens to John Stevens, 3/27/1812.
– runs to Wilmington on Sundays: *Poulson's American*, 6/12/1812, among others.
– Moses continued to try to negotiate: NJHS, SFP, Moses Rogers to John Stevens, 1/9/1812.
– "I am sorry I did not see him,": ibid, Robert Stevens to John Stevens, 5/12/1812.
– "Captain rogers was obliged to attend to some business": ibid, Robert Stevens to John Stevens, 6/8/1812.
– Elihu S. Bunker had come to see him: ibid, Robert Stevens to John Stevens, 8/16/1812.
– Moses ... Grice ... negotiating ... 1809: ibid, Joseph Grice to Robert Stevens, 1/1/1810.
– Measuring 108 feet long: NARA, RG36, Port/Philadelphia, PE#66, steamboat *Eagle*, 6/17/1813.
– the *Eagle's* passengers were encouraged: *Poulson's American*, 8/28/1813.
– Colonel Stevens anxiously keeping track: NJHS, SFP, John Stevens to Robert Stevens, 7/18/1813.
– pleased to learn that the *Phoenix* seemed to outperform her rival: ibid, 8/3/1813.
– Cadwallader D. Colden, offered to provide whatever information: ibid, John Stevens to Robert Stevens, 7/18/1813.
– Horace Binney informed the Colonel: ibid, Horace Binney to John Stevens, 8/10/1813.
– the Colonel exhorted his son Robert: ibid, John Stevens to Robert Stevens, 8/24/1813.
– Robert Stevens felt he had no choice but to lay up the *Phoenix*: ibid, Robert Stevens to Col. Stevens, 10/4/1813.
– Robert Stevens laid plans to ambush the *Eagle*: ibid, Robert Stevens to John Stevens, 10/23/1813.
– *Eagle* ... deck ... moving with each stroke: ibid, Robert Stevens to John Stevens, 10/25/1813.
– ... *that the Eagle,*: ibid, John Stevens to Robert Stevens, 10/26/1813.
– several tons of broken cast-iron parts: ibid, Robert Stevens to John Stevens, 11/1/1813.
– Fulton asked Colonel Stevens to drop any lawsuits: ibid, Robert Fulton to John Stevens, 12/14/1813.
– other newly-introduced steamboats ... shook so much or broke down: ibid, Robert Stevens to John Stevens, 11/1/1813.
– the *Eagle*, repaired and refurbished, returned to the fray: *Poulson's American*, 4/29/1814.
– "making out very poorly,": NJHS, SFP, James Stevens to John Stevens, 9/9/1814.
– overcoming Nature in the way these vessels did was just too bizarre: no one should doubt what a deep impression these first successful steamboats had on the early 19th century souls who saw them. Among the evidence was a new theatrical play

put on at New York in early January of 1809. With the *North River Steam Boat of Clermont's* first full season complete, Gothamites could treat themselves to an evening watching *Harlequin Panattahah, or, the Geni of the Algonquins.* In the first act, the "Geni" proposes to send the chief and princess of the Canadian Algonquins to the island of Manhattan, which the tribe once owned. She waves her wand, and "a magnificent car rises, to transport them to the city" (i.e., New York). "The car ascends; the indians appear lost in admiration for an instant, and then break out into loud exclamations and frantic gestures ... The scene now becomes dark; violent thunder and lightning." Then another "Geni" appears onstage, intent on thwarting the trip of the car to New York. The second Geni "conjures up a Fiery Chariot, drawn by dragons ... They fly off in storm, thunder, &c." In the fourth act, during a scene at New York's Battery, "a real boat" appears, "coming down the Hudson, which sails round the stage." In a later scene, set in the future at a wharf on the North River, a "steam boat" is seen taking its departure with the main characters on board. That this play contained several fantastical depictions of steamboats, which appear to be a parody of the imminent fight between Fulton and Stevens, must have been obvious to all. See *The Public Advertiser,* 1/4/1809.

– just-introduced *teamboats*: Captain Moses Rogers has been given credit previously for taking out the first U.S. patent for "propelling boats by animal power," or *teamboats*. This contention is false. This first teamboat patent, of 2/9/1814, as well as a subsequent one dated 3/3/1815, and a projecting dock patent dated 1/7/1817, all belong to Moses Rogers, merchant of New York City. Proof positive comes from copies of the text of these three patents, previously thought lost in the Patent Office fire of 1836. They are contained in the case papers filed for a lawsuit brought by Moses Rogers, the merchant, against two teamboat operators for patent infringement (see NARA, RG21, Southern District of New York, Circuit Court, Old Equity Case Files, *Moses Rogers vs. Rodman Bowne and Samuel Bowne,* filed 5/11/1820). The signature of "Moses Rogers" in the Bill of Complaint does not readily match that of Captain Rogers. Even more telling are the witnesses listed for the original patent applications, including Archibald Rogers (son of Rogers the merchant), Francis B. Winthrop Jr. (son-in-law) and Samuel M. Hopkins (son-in-law). Further support comes from the SFP, in which Colonel Stevens, who designed his own teamboats, approached "Moses Rogers" and proposed a patent-sharing agreement (8/20/1814). Rogers' reply (8/25/1814) was written from "Shippan near Stamford" in Connecticut, which is where the merchant owned a substantial estate and spent his summers.

– in a word, *chimerical*: for examples, see *National Intelligencer,* 7/7/1815: "his [i.e., Chancellor Livingston's] labors received no other notice than the cold contempt and the malicious ridicule which ever await the chimerical projector"; and 9/7/1820: "In the year 1806, I was one of those who considered the contemplated navigation by steam chimerical"; and the *Baltimore Patriot,* 6/26/1819, regarding steamboats operating on Lake Erie: "It is truly gratifying to reflect that the laudable spirit of a few enterprising individuals has enabled us to witness the completion of an undertaking, which a few years since would have appeared chimerical"; and *The Evening Post* (NYC), 6/6/1820, on the towing of U.S. Navy warships by steamboats: "A few years ago, it would have been thought chimerical in any one to say that a line of battleship could be thus easily moved ... "

– Fulton wrote to Svin'in in April: Sutcliffe, *Robert Fulton...,* p295.

– Fulton wrote to Minister Adams: MHS, Adams Family Papers (hereafter, "AFP"), Robert Fulton to John Quincy Adams (hereafter, "JQA"), 4/20/1812. In this letter, Fulton made no mention of having written previously to Adams on the subject of a steamboat franchise; it would have been customary to do so.

– Alexander (the First), was willing to grant an exclusive steamboat charter: ibid,

Nikolai Rumiantsev to JQA, 11/6~18/1812. The first date shown is based upon the Julian calendar, which Russia was still using; the second date is Gregorian.
- Adams wrote back to Fulton in November of 1812: ibid, JQA to Robert Fulton, 11/15~27/1812.
- "combined attacks of prejudice": NJHS, SFP, John Stevens, "Steamboats on the Sound," -/-/1811.
- Fulton ... not be afraid to cross the ocean in it: Philip, op. cit., p292.
- wear black armbands: *The Columbian* and *The Evening Post*, both of 2/25/1815.
- "towering genius": *The Evening Post*, 2/25/1815.
- William Cutting wrote to John Quincy Adams: NYHS, Le Boeuf Collection, JQA to Levett Harris, 7/28/1815.
- Briscoe and Partridge bought out almost all the existing owners: NARA, RG36, Port/Philadelphia, Proof of Ownership, steamboat *Eagle*, 5/29/1815.
- Moses ... cleared the *Eagle* for departure: ibid, OCM, steamboat *Eagle*, 6/12/1815.
- Arriving safely at Norfolk,: Emmerson, *The Steamboat Comes to Norfolk...*, pp1–5.
- Charles Baird ... proposed: Virginskii, *Robert Fulton...*, p180.
- Baird ... ran it on St. Petersburg's Neva River: ibid, p185.
- Levett Harris, immediately protested: ibid, pp185–186.
- terms of the Fulton charter remained in force: ibid, p188.
- virtually identical to ... Long Island steamer: Colden, op. cit., table after p274.
- Tompkins ... padding his official salary: *The Evening Post*, 4/20/1816. While a number of newspapers reported on Tompkins' questionable activities, *The Evening Post* was among the most aggressive.
- exclusive ... in the Russian empire for 25 years: as previously stated, it was really 15 years.
- New York Insurance Company ... $15,000 policy: Minutes of the New York Insurance Company, 8/2/1816, as quoted by T. B. Bleecker in a letter to *The New York Times*, 2/23/1912. Bleecker was serving as a receiver for the NYIC when he wrote the letter, and clearly had access to the company's minute books, as he indicated. See *USCSS*, 1912, House of Representatives, Document No. 294, p2.
- *It was not the Fulton*: Poulson's American, 8/5/1816.
- *Instead, it was to be Captain Frank Ogden*: The Evening Post, 8/2/1816.
- *Captain Samuel Reid*: Daily National Intelligencer, 8/13/1816.
- *Captain Isaac Hull*: The Evening Post, 8/12/1816; Newburyport Herald, 8/27/1816.
- same advertisement for the same excursion was run again: *The Evening Post*, 8/14/1816.
- the 80-mile trip ... "a pleasant one.": *New-York Gazette*, 8/19/1816.
- the *Car* missed her departure time: *New-York Gazette*, 9/5/1816.
- a "Mr. Baird" was already running a steamboat in Russia: *Independent Chronicle* (Boston), 8/29/1816, among many others.
- We understand that the attempt: *City Gazette*, 9/9/1816, quoting *The Courier*.
- Moses went into the Philadelphia Custom House: NARA, RG36, Port/Philadelphia, Proof of Ownership, steamboat *New Jersey*, 11/16/1816, and OCM, steamboat *New Jersey*, 11/16/1816.
- the *New Jersey* ... "safe and sound": *City Gazette*, 12/3/1816, citing *The Norfolk Herald*. Because the *New Jersey's* figurehead was a large golden horse, some mistakenly called her the *Sea Horse* (see Scharf, *History of Baltimore City...*, p301).
- raise money for a New York-to-Charleston service: *Niles' Weekly Register*, 9/30/1815.
- Another attempt for that same route was made six months later: *City Gazette*, 3/9/1816.
- raise $125,000 for an "ocean steam boat": *Niles' Weekly Register*, 10/19/1816.

- *Massachusetts* … towed repeatedly by schooners: Heyl, *Early American Steamers*, pp135–138.
- as Moses was preparing the *Charleston* for her maiden trip: when Moses left the employ of Briscoe & Partridge at Baltimore in the summer of 1817, it appears that a number of parties filed lawsuits against him for unpaid debts. Since the case papers have not survived, it is impossible to know with certainty the identity of defendant "Moses Rogers," or the precise circumstances of the lawsuits. Based upon timing and the minimal information in surviving court dockets, however, the cases appear to involve Captain Rogers. In one case that stretched back to 1816, the plaintiff was a Moses McCubbin, who claimed he was owed £50. Once Moses Rogers had departed, Levi Hollingsworth—a copper merchant and steamboat shareholder—became a party to this suit, which continued until at least 1820. Other suits for debts were filed against Moses in 1817–1818 by three other parties, including the owners of the steamboats, although none appear to have been carried over into succeeding court terms, implying these cases were dropped or the debts paid off. In an age of handwritten promissory notes, such legal disputes were, in and of themselves, not unusual. It is also worth noting that from a business standpoint, Baltimore had a reputation for being a very aggressive city. See MSA, Baltimore County, Court, City Civil Dockets, terms stretching from 9/1816 to 9/1820, *Moses McCubbin vs. Moses Rogers, Andrew Hunter vs. Moses Rogers, Joseph Chapman vs. Moses Rogers, Levi Hollingsworth et al vs. Moses Rogers*.
- Vanderford's plan … longest steamboat ocean transfer yet attempted: *City of Washington Gazette*, 12/27/1817.
- *Massachusetts* ran aground near Little Egg Harbor: Heyl, op. cit., p137.

CHAPTER FOUR—FOUNDATION, AND FORMATION

- At 11:20 on the morning of December 18th: *The Courier* (Charleston), 12/19/1817.
- the pilot … kept getting the steamboat stuck: *Columbian Museum*, 12/23/1817.
- reversing the paddlewheels: the ability to reverse the direction of a steamboat's paddlewheels to propel it backward was one of the earliest improvements made in steamboat design. The *Eagle*, which Moses captained from 1813 to 1816, is documented as having such a feature; it stands to reason that most if not virtually all steamboats could move backward by 1817.
- "will probably be here this evening": *Columbian Museum*, 12/19/1817.
- Howard ran the notice again: ibid, 12/20/1817.
- Howard ran the advertisement again: ibid, 12/22/1817.
- got the *Charleston* to the wharves … 11:30 A.M.: ibid, 12/23/1817.
- regular sailing packets … arriving at Savannah much sooner: ibid, 12/22/1817 and 12/23/1817.
- The passengers in the steam boat *Charleston*: ibid, 12/23/1817.
- sailing packet owners … shifted their departure notices: *Columbian Museum*, various dates in December 1817 and January 1818.
- the *Charleston* back to her home port in 45 hours: *The Courier* (Charleston), 12/27/1817.
- "skill and outgoing conduct": ibid.
- third trip down … made in only 36 hours: *Columbian Museum*, 12/30/1817.
- fourth trip down … 21 passengers: Daily *Savannah Republican*, 1/6/1817.
- Captain Rogers … spied a three-masted craft: *Southern Patriot*, 1/8/1818.
- square white flag adorned with a solid-black circle: ibid; also Blunt, *The American Coast Pilot*, p154.

- Once the *Charleston* had completed a number of round trips: on one of these early trips, the steamboat took eight slaves from Charleston to Savannah, which triggered the filing of a special passenger manifest. This document required both Moses (as the steamboat captain) and the slaveholder to certify that none of the slaves had been "imported or brought into the United States" at any time after 1/1/1808, the date at which it became illegal to import slaves into the country. See NARA, RG36, Port/Savannah, Coastwise Slave Passenger Manifest, steamboat *Charleston*, 1/8/1818.
- "a very rough sea,": *Southern Patriot*, 1/22/1818.
- cut the one-way transit time to as little as 24½ hours: *Savannah Republican*, 1/17/1818.
- advertised to arrive in Savannah every Monday: *Columbian Museum*, 1/26/1818.
- dropped any invitation for freight: ibid, 1/20/1818, 1/27/1818, 2/3/1818.
- he took the Charleston as far as 10 miles from shore: *Richmond Enquirer*, 6/10/1818.
- $15 for passage between Charleston and Savannah: *The Courier*, 2/6/1818.
- small coastal sloop stuck on a sand bar: ibid, 2/5/1818.
- "a very hard blow and high sea": ibid, 3/6/1818.
- "activity and skill": ibid.
- "skill and judicious management": ibid, 1/30/1818.
- "polite and gentlemanly treatment": ibid.
- "went to sea.": ibid, 4/7/1818; *Southern Patriot*, 4/14/1818.
- Minis ... one of the port's Commissioners of Pilotage: Beers, *The Planters' & Merchants' Almanac ... 1818*.
- Sullivan ... right to use steamboats for towing cargoes: provided he first clear the two rivers, the Upper Connecticut and Upper Merrimack, of obstructions.
- Samuel Howard ... unsuccessful steamboat ventures in Savannah: Rahn, *River Highway for Trade: The Savannah*, p19. Samuel Howard had helped William Longstreet, who built several small experimental steamboats in the years just after Fulton's *North River* triumph. One of Longstreet's earliest steamboating efforts dates from 1808 (see *New-York Gazette*, 11/24/1808).
- the Legislature granted Howard: *Acts of the General Assembly of the State of Georgia*, "An Act to encourage an improved mode of transporting merchandize upon the waters of the State of Georgia," assented to 11/18/1814.
- Howard was able to launch the steamboat *Enterprize*: *Savannah Republican*, 1/18/1816.
- he began running the new steamer up to Augusta: *Augusta Chronicle*, 4/26/1816.
- The Georgia Legislature agreed: *Acts of the General Assembly of the State of Georgia*, "An Act for the incorporation of the Steam Boat Company of Georgia," assented to 12/19/1817.
- Samuel had fought a duel: *Commercial Advertiser*, 9/8/1803.
- Samuel ... capture and burning of two French privateers: *New England Palladium*, 12/13/1811, among others.
- Samuel ... on a charge of rioting: GHS, Chatham County Superior Court, Minutes, 1808–1818, Volume 9, p66, 1/8/1813.
- Samuel was arrested for assault and battery: ibid, p157, 1/6/1814.
- Charles ... suffering from heart complaints for some time: *Columbian Museum*, 7/3/1819.
- the Company's president at the time, William Scarbrough: SCDAH, Charleston County, Equity Bills, 1818, No. 12, 4/16/1818.
- Born to South Carolina in 1776: Piechocinski, *The Old Burying Ground: Colonial Park Cemetery...*, p37.

- his father, also William, was a merchant and shipowner: *The Charleston Morning Post*, 3/2/1787 and 6/14/1787, among many others.
- His mother … descendent of Puritan clergyman John Cotton: Hoffman, *Godfrey Barnsley…*, pp39–40.
- William the Younger … spent his childhood … inland plantations: Hartridge (editor), *The Letters of Robert MacKay*, pp253, 296. William the Elder at various times owned plantations in the Barnwell, Beaufort and Orangeburg Districts of South Carolina.
- William … went on to the University of Edinburgh: ibid, p253.
- Danish government … name him as their vice-consul at Savannah: GSA, William Scarbrough Collection, Nomination of William Scarbrough to His Majesty's Vice Consul…, 7/17/1802; *City Gazette*, 10/12/1802.
- In 1805, he married Julia Bernard: Genealogical Committee of Georgia Historical Society (hereafter, "GC/GHS"), Marriages of Chatham County, Georgia, p72.
- Julia's parties … "blowouts," as she called them: Hartridge, op. cit., p272.
- her occasional singing at them the cause of distress: ibid, p66. Robert MacKay, a British expatriate who dubbed Julia Scarbrough "the Countess" in private letters, is the only known critic of her singing. In an 1807 letter to his wife in Britain, advising of Julia's imminent arrival there, MacKay wrote: "for God's sake, don't ask the Countess to sing, or she will frighten the good people of England—"
- Scarbrough … vice-consul positions … Russia and Sweden: Ruddock, *Palladium of Knowledge…*, 1818.
- new trading partnership … "Scarbrough & McKinne.": *Columbian Museum*, 2/5/1818.
- Vail … ordered engine parts from Dod: Braynard, op. cit., p44.
- small diary Stephen Vail kept on his trip: Vail Diary, 12/30/1817 to 4/30/1818, as cited in Braynard, p42–44.
- "Satisfactory and sociable manner": ibid, p42.
- Steam Boat Company … offer $400,000 in stock to the public: *Savannah Republican*, 3/17/1818. The remaining $200,000 in authorized capital was taken by the State of Georgia itself, making it a partner in the monopoly grant to the Steam Boat Company of Georgia.
- Financial statements were made available for inspection: ibid.
- a first dividend on the outstanding shares of 25%: *Columbian Museum*, 4/1/1818.
- Captain Rogers and the *Charleston* having just arrived: *Savannah Republican*, 5/7/1818.
- Savannah River Navigation Company: *Savannah Republican*, 5/6/1818. Both the Building and Insurance Bank of Georgia and the Savannah River Navigation Company advertised their stock offerings in the newspapers for weeks prior. The Savannah Steam Ship Company did not. This likely reflects the organizers' desire to attract only those willing and able to accept the very risky and speculative nature of the venture, as well as the ability to pull the offering with minimal publicity if the capital could not be raised.
- Within an hour of opening the subscription: *Savannah Republican*, 5/7/1818.
- "It was deemed proper to close the books … ": *The Morning Chronicle*, 5/8/1818.
- John Haslett was among his passengers: *The Courier*, 5/11/1818. While no forename is specified, the passenger is believed to have been John, given the prominence and uniqueness of his name in Charleston, and the just-completed SSSC offering.
- The subscribers were: the earliest list of shareholders for the Savannah Steam Ship Company is from the Act of Incorporation passed by the Georgia Legislature in December 1818. It is unlikely there was any change in this list from the

subscription in May until the incorporation in December. In contrast to most other publicly-offered stock-based companies in Savannah, the SSSC's share-price was never quoted in the local newspapers, simply because the Company's shares were not intended for trade on the open market. This reflects the high-risk, unprecedented nature of the venture, which was not for the financially faint-of-heart. Each of the shareholders surely knew this—once they bought in, they stayed in, to see the "experiment" through.

– William Gillett was the nephew of William Scarbrough: GSA, William Scarbrough Collection, William S. Gillett to William Scarbrough, 10/11/1820.

– Some ... members of Christ Church: GHS, *Marriages of Chatham County...*, p139, 182; also Flores, "Archibald Stobo Bulloch," p6.

– were members of the Independent Presbyterian Church: GC/GHS, *Marriages of Chatham County...*, pp138–139, 147; also GHS, Chatham County Superior Court, Minutes, 1808–1818, Volume 9, p217, 4/28/1815; also, Flores, op. cit., p6.

– were both Congregationalists: "Register of the Independent Congregational (Circular) Church of Charleston, S.C.," *South Carolina Historical and Genealogical Magazine*, Volume XXXIII (1932), pp37, 51, 308, 314 and Volume XXXIV (1933), pp49, 163; also, Webber, "Inscriptions from the Independent or Congregational (Circular) Church...," Volume XXIX (1928), pp313–314.

– Scottish-born immigrants: for Robert Isaac and Robert Mitchell, GC/GHS, *Register of Deaths in Savannah, Georgia*, Volume IV, pp210, 249; for Gideon Pott, see MacBean, *Biographical Register of Saint Andrew's Society...*, Vol. 2, pp5–6; for Andrew Low, see NARA, RG46, Records of Congress, SEN 16A-G4, Petitions to Congress, Petition of Andrew Low and others, 1/24/1820; for John Bogue, see footnote in Legacies.

– John Haslett was himself originally from Ireland: Webber, op. cit., pp313–314.

– these investors in the Savannah Steam Ship Company: not surprisingly, under the circumstances, many of the shareholders were also slaveholders. Based upon surviving data from the 1810 and 1820 censuses, in addition to other sources, the following SSSC investors owned slaves: A. S. Bulloch, James S. Bulloch, William S. Gillett, Robert Habersham, Robert Isaac, James McHenry, Isaac Minis, Robert Mitchell, William Scarbrough, and Samuel Yates. Some of the remaining shareholders also may have owned slaves. Shareholders Moses Rogers and John Haslett are shown in the 1820 census as owning no slaves. While Captain Rogers' precise views on slavery are unknown, it is very likely, given his background, that Moses believed it to be wrong. His native Connecticut passed multiple anti-slavery laws throughout his childhood. In a time when most Americans identified strongly with their States, the impression left upon an adolescent by such repeated acts must have been significant. Furthermore, Moses was a mariner, placing him in a profession that was traditionally sympathetic to the plight of slaves. For anti-slavery Americans in the early 19th century, the realization that they were not in a position to eliminate the practice led many to commit to providing whatever aid and comfort they could to those enslaved. For one possible example, see the *New-York Gazette*, 6/19/1816, in which Samuel Hollingsworth of Baltimore advertises a reward for the return of a slave named Charles. This individual, trained as a waiter, had taken passage from Baltimore to Elkton on the steamboat *Eagle*, Rogers, in August of 1815, under the assumed name of Lloyd. He then continued his journey to Philadelphia on the steamboat *Vesta*. Stated Hollingsworth of Charles: "He ... never before materially misbehaved. I therefore believed him to have been enticed away." Other members of the Hollingsworth clan were investors in the steamboats operated by Briscoe & Partridge, and captained by Rogers. Whether Moses personally knew Charles is impossible to say, but that this slave could so readily make use of the *Eagle* and *Vesta* speaks volumes about the potential early steamboats had for hastening a slave's escape.

CHAPTER FIVE — "SPIRITED"

- "spirited": *Savannah Republican,* 5/7/1818.
- "public spirit": *The Morning Chronicle* (Savannah), 5/8/1818, in describing the SSSC.
- incredibly large number of newspapers: in 1828, Daniel Hewett counted 681 newspapers and 119 magazines as being published in the United States.
- *Your losing a man of such consummate skill: The Courier* (Charleston), 6/15/1818, as seen in the *Commercial Advertiser,* 6/22/1818, also, *City Gazette,* 6/16/1818, among others.
- "navigators think the scheme dangerous": *Columbian Centinel,* 5/23/1818.
- A subscription has been opened: *Daily National Intelligencer,* 5/15/1818.
- reprinted only the first, positive part: *Salem Gazette,* 5/22/1818; *Independent Chronicle,* 5/20/1818.
- other port-based newspapers reprinted the original opinion in full: *The National Advocate,* 5/18/1818; *New-York Evening Post,* 5/18/1818; *Westchester Herald,* 5/26/1818; *Providence Patriot and Columbian Phenix,* 5/28/1818.
- A project is on foot in Savannah: *The Genius of Liberty,* 6/2/1818.
- The Steam Boat has hitherto: *Richmond Enquirer,* 5/19/1818.

CHAPTER SIX — CHOICES

- catfish had been drawn into the injection pipe: *Commercial Advertiser,* 4/8/1816, as reported in the *Baltimore Patriot.*
- Captain Howard brought his wife Rebecca: *City Gazette,* 6/24/1816.
- U.S. Navy lieutenant named Thomas Paine: ibid.
- able to complete three scheduled round trips: ibid, 6/29/1816.
- depending upon him to get them back to the city: ibid, 9/17, 9/18/1816; *The Times* (Charleston), 9/16/1816.
- death toll stood at 5: *The Courier,* 9/17/1816; *Baltimore Patriot,* 9/24/1816.
- ample evidence to back up his claim: *City Gazette,* 9/18/1816.
- Howard took the wounded *Enterprize* back: ibid, 10/10/1816.
- rolled copper cost around 34 cents per pound: *New York Shipping and Commercial List,* 8/21/1818.
- per (English long) ton: the English long ton is 2,240 lbs. The American short ton of 2,000 lbs. had not yet been devised.
- traded for about $105 per ton: *New York Shipping and Commercial List,* 6/30/1818. This was the price for high-quality Swedish iron. English iron was around $90 per ton.
- Large … Originally trained at the famed Boulton & Watt: Scranton, *Proprietary Capitalism,* p87.
- Philadelphia's shipyards had launched hardly any ocean-going vessels: *Commercial Advertiser,* 8/7/1818, among others.
- McQueen … won the contract to build a steam engine: *ASP,* Class 6, *Naval Affairs,* Volume 1, p480, John Rodgers to Benjamin Crowninshield, 1/20/1818.

CHAPTER SEVEN—DIFFERENT FROM ANY WE HAVE YET SEEN

- By 1810 ... over 96,000 residents: Gibson, op. cit., Table 4.
- By 1818 ... ballooned to 120,000 residents: ibid, Table 5; based upon the 1820 Census, New York City had 123,706 residents.
- development ... 2½ miles of the island's 12-mile length: Hooker, *Plan of the City of New York*, 1817.
- few wooden buildings ... thanks to past fires: Fearon, *Sketches of America*, pp22–23.
- older structure lifted up ... moved to the suburbs north of Greenwich Village: Palmer, *Journal of Travels in the United States...*, p333.
- the sharpest of stones: *The Bee*, pp1462–1467.
- "like a parrot on a mahogany table": ibid.
- to roam and fatten up on garbage: *Mercantile Advertiser*, 6/4/1818.
- ban the wandering swine: Palmer, op. cit., p6.
- New York's human inhabitants: Gibson and Jung, *Historical Census Statistics On Population Totals by Race...*, Table 33.
- five major public markets in 1818: Holditch, *The Emigrant's Guide...*, p93.
- One profession that seemed especially well-established: Fearon, op. cit., p26.
- boardinghouse ... from $5 to $10 per week: ibid, p44.
- Moses ... last run as captain of the steamboat *Charleston*: *Southern Patriot*, 5/23/1818.
- Also joining Moses was ... Mr. Blackman: Moses would want a familiar and experienced hand to serve as the *Savannah*'s engineer. Since Blackman was reported to be succeeding Rogers in command of the *Charleston*, but never did (the captainship immediately going to Horace Utley), it stands to reason that Mr. Blackman followed Moses to New York, helped build the *Savannah*, and became her engineer and second mate for the crossing, as described in the *SSSLB*.
- report that the French government had offered: *Richmond Enquirer*, 6/10/1818.
- McKinne ... gone into business in 1810: *Commercial Advertiser*, 10/9/1810.
- Pott himself was a Glasgow native: MacBean, op. cit., Vol. 2, p5.
- he registered in court his intention: NARA, RG45, Correspondence Relating to Aliens (War of 1812), Gideon Pott to James Monroe, 3/5/1813.
- Pott married a Gotham girl: MacBean, op. cit., p5.
- asking ... for official approval to arm their brig: NARA, RG59, War of 1812 Papers, Letters Received concerning Letters of Marque 1812–1814, Hamilton, Palmer and McKinne to James Monroe, 10/16/1812.
- asking for permission to stay: NARA, RG45, Correspondence ... Aliens..., Pott to Monroe, 3/5/1813.
- the request was granted: *Longworth's American Almanac...*, 1813 and 1814. Since Pott & McKinne is listed in both years, and Gideon Pott's residence is listed in the 1814 edition, it seems clear that he remained in New York for the duration of the war.
- McKinne ... taking over the Savannah trading business of a relative: *Savannah Republican*, 2/2/1818.
- Pott ... elected one of the managers: MacBean, op. cit, p5.
- McKinne was also a member: ibid, pp24–25.
- Pott ... home for his family at 26 Greenwich Street: *Longworth's American Almanac...*, 1818.
- Pott ... bought shares in ... the Tontine Coffee House: NYHS, Tontine Coffee House Records, Vol. 1, Transfer of Shares, p142 (3/23/1818), and p144 (4/10/1818).

- McKinne ... and his family returned to New York: *Mercantile Advertiser,* 5/26/1818.
- Pott and McKinne ... at 56 South Street: *Longworth's American Almanac...,* 1818.
- schooner Antelope arrived from Savannah: *Commercial Advertiser,* 5/29/1818. It is unknown whether any of this gear was used on the *Savannah.*
- import some coal directly from Liverpool: *New-York Daily Advertiser,* 10/2/1818.
- mercantile house with strong ties to the French market: Albion, *The Rise of New York Port,* p45; Wright, op. cit., p103; NARA, RG46, Records of the Senate, 35th Congress, 1st Session, Petitions to Committee of Claims, Charlotte Taylor Petition (undated), Sworn Statement of Stevens Rogers, 5/2/1856 (hereafter, "Stevens Rogers Statement").
- Fickett ... outgrown his home market: for evidence, see *Eastern Argus,* 5/24/1810; also, Goold, *Portland in the Past...,* p467, and Rowe, *Shipbuilding Days in Casco Bay...,* p35.
- He and Crockett, who were related by marriage: Maine Historical Society, Fickett, *Notes on the Fickett Family.*
- He and Crockett ... had set up their yard on Water Street: *Longworth's American Almanac...,* 1818 edition.
- brig *Amelia,* with Robert Habersham: *New-York Daily Advertiser,* 6/29/1818, citing "R Habersham" as a passenger, in conjunction with Drew University Archives, Gibbons Family Papers, Thomas Gibbons Correspondence, Robert Habersham (in NYC) to Thomas Gibbons, 8/17/1818.
- brig *Tybee* ... carrying William and Julia Scarbrough: *New-York Evening Post,* 7/6/1818.
- steamers *Pike, Telegraph,* and *James Monroe* ... lost: *New-York Columbian,* 6/24/1818; also, *Commercial Advertiser,* 6/26/1818, among others.
- the *Experiment* ... sprung a leak: *Commercial Advertiser,* 6/29/1818; *New-York Daily Advertiser,* 6/30/1818; *New-York Spectator,* 6/30/1818, among others.
- hired himself out to the sail-making shops: while there appears to be no direct surviving evidence Steve did this, it is strongly implied by the fact that he was put in charge of making the sails and rigging for the *Savannah.* Mariners, while in port, regularly hired themselves out to sailmakers. See Hall, *Sailmaking in Connecticut prior to 1860.*
- physical strength set within a solid frame: Stevens Rogers was later described as one of the two strongest men in all of New London during his time; see NLCHS, Richard B. Wall, Records and Papers (hereafter, "Wall Papers"), p202.
- nearly six feet in height: NARA, RG36, Port/New London, Register of Seamen, #4694, 8/2/1809, Stevens Rogers—his height is listed as 5′ 11″.
- an amiable disposition: Wall Papers, pp10–11, 495.
- each sharing as a great-great-great grandfather: Rogers, op. cit., pp201, 245.
- his brother Amos Junior had married Steve's older sister: ibid, p248.
- Gilbert Rogers, married one of Steve's younger sisters: ibid, p249.
- *Progress of Improvements.—*: *Mercantile Advertiser,* 7/11/1818.
- awkward description ... picked up by other newspapers: *Commercial Advertiser,* 7/11/1818; *New-York Spectator,* 7/14/1818.
- referred to the craft as a "Steam-Boat ship": *New York Gazette,* 8/10/1818.
- other papers fell back on ... "steamboat.": *Niles' Weekly Register,* 8/29/1818.
- Allaire received the final go-ahead to cast: this is imputed by the arrival of the most prominent shareholders by mid-July, in conjunction with delivery of the cylinder to Speedwell on August 1st. See NARA, RG21, Records of the U. S. District Court for the District of Columbia, Case Papers, June Term 1820, Civil Appearances: *Stephen Vail vs. The Savannah Steam Ship Company,* Stephen Vail Accounts, (hereafter, "Vail Accounts").

- dimensions of the cylinder ... identical to ... *Chancellor Livingston*: the bore and stroke dimensions of "the *Chancellor*" and the initial bore and eventual stroke dimensions of the *Savannah* were both 40 inches and 5 feet respectively. See Ridgely-Nevitt, *American Steamships on the Atlantic*, p350.
- The process for casting such a piece: the methodology for casting large iron cylinders changed little through the early-to-mid 19th century. This description is based upon Overman, *The Manufacture of Iron, in all its Various Branches...*, and Abbott, "The Novelty Works, ... " in *Harper's New Monthly Magazine*, No. XII, May 1851, Vol. II, pp721–734.
- about 6 feet in height and 3½ feet in diameter: based upon Vail's later recorded maximum borings of 5 feet 5 inches in depth and 40¾ inches in diameter.
- brig *Speedy Peace* ... with Jacob P. Henry: *New-York Evening Post*, 7/20/1818.
- Mitchell and his wife, on the ship *Rising States*: *New York Daily Advertiser*, 7/25/1818.
- J. P. Henry ... related to Harmon Hendricks: Braynard, op. cit., p46.
- Uriah Hendricks ... emigrated from London: Whiteman, *Copper for America; the Hendricks family...*, p4.
- Harmon joined the family trade as a teenager: ibid, p30.
- Even Paul Revere ... purchased: ibid, pp49, 55.
- contracts from the U.S. Navy: ibid, p50.
- the Monopoly's steamboats had Hendricks copper: ibid, p97.
- earned the nickname "Steamboat" Isaacs: ibid, p153.
- Hendricks himself had invested in the Monopoly's steamers: ibid, p113.
- Hendricks sold $1,679.82 worth of copper: NYHS, Hendricks Collection, Waste Book, p86½. This sale on July 29th was listed as being made to "Pott & McKinney Steam Boat Savannah," with the latter three words crossed out. Later purchases by Pott & McKinne (August 17th, 31st and September 23rd, 24th) clearly listed the client as the "Steam Ship Savannah + owner." With the exception of the minor purchase on August 17th, the later purchases were made after the hull had been launched, so that copper must have been used elsewhere in the *Savannah*, probably for steam machinery parts. The only logical purpose for the enormous amount of copper purchased on July 29th would be to sheath the *Savannah*'s hull prior to her launching.
- regularly rising into the 90s: *Mercantile Advertiser*, 7/13/1818; *Weekly Visitor and Ladies Museum*, 7/4/1818 and 7/18/1818.
- *The North Pole*. – It is said that Lord Cochrane: *Westchester Herald*, 5/5/1818 (quoting from a London newspaper), among many others throughout the eastern United States.
- "islands of ice": *New-York Spectator*, 8/11/1818.
- iceberg ... at a latitude of 29 degrees: *New-York Spectator*, 6/16/1818.
- Cochrane's vessel ... "steam boat" ... calling it anything else ... considered absurd: one newspaper that did was *The Morning Chronicle* (Savannah), 5/8/1818, which altered this same Cochrane story to describe his vessel as a "steam-ship," undoubtedly influenced by its reporting the very same day on the successful offering of shares in the "Savannah Steam Ship Company."
- conflicting reports ... his steam vessel ... intended: *New England Palladium*, 6/2/1818.
- "Lord Cochrane is said to have altered his schemes ... ": *New-York Columbian*, 7/17/1818, among others.
- By a gentleman arrived at Norfolk: *The National Advocate*, 7/20/1818, among others.
- *SIR—In reading the account of Lord Cochrane's*: *The National Advocate*, 7/21/1818. As published, "first effective steamboat navigation" was printed in italics. As

delivered to the editor in longhand, these words would have been underlined, as shown.

- *I doubt very much the possibility*: ibid.
- cylinder was picked up by … Enos Bonnel: Vail Accounts.
- Arriving there on August 1st: Vail Accounts. Given Vail's reputation for meticulous bookkeeping, the expense would have been recorded upon payment, and Enos Bonnel logically would want to be paid upon delivery of the cylinder.
- Moses set up an account with Francis H. Nicoll & Company: NARA, RG21, Records of the U. S. District Court for the District of Columbia, Case Papers, June Term 1820, Civil Appearances, Francis H. Nicoll & Co. accounts, "Steam Ship Savannah Capt. Rogers + Owners" (hereafter, "Nicoll Accounts").
- whose store was located on Front Street: *Longworth's American Almanac*, 1818.
- two men walked into the New York branch: *Mercantile Advertiser*, 8/11/1818; *The National Advocate*, 8/12/1818.
- On board the brig *Georgia* came: *New-York Gazette*, 8/12/1818.
- Now we command you, brethren: Webb, *The Freemason's Monitor…*, p154. This book described in detail the many levels and ceremonies of Freemasonry. It was readily available throughout the U.S. in the early 19th century.
- "the Most Excellent degree of Royal Arch Mason": certificate of Royal Arch Mason Stevens Rogers, dated 8/15/1818, and signed by Billings, Law and Green (private collection).
- Freemasons … limited central authority: Tabbert, *American Freemasons…*, p50.
- Wisdom, brotherhood, and charity to all mankind: ibid, p13.
- *I will bring the blind by a way*: Webb, op. cit., p156.
- For the Company's shareholders and their families: Based upon arrival and departure notices in the newspapers, among other sources, it appears that at least one-half of the Company's shareholders were in New York that summer. Since the papers could not possibly list all passenger arrivals, it is likely that other shareholders were also there. Furthermore, it seems likely that at least some members of Moses and Stevens Rogers' families also were present for the launch, as evidenced by the return from New York of the sloop *Swift*, Captain Paul Rogers Jr. (a distant cousin), to New London, arriving August 24th (see *New-York Daily Advertiser*, 8/28/1818).
- The hull would be registered: NARA, RG36, Port/New York, PE#90, "ship" *Savannah*, 3/27/1819.
- musical band … common practice at major launchings: Lincoln, "Naval Ship Launches as Public Spectacle," *The Mariner's Mirror*, Volume 83 No. 4 (November 1997), pp466–472.
- everything down below was ready: A description of the *Savannah's* launching has not survived. The same can be said generally for early 19th century vessel launchings and ceremonies; precise accounts are very difficult to find. What is described represents the most elementary steps required to launch a large vessel.
- When we behold a vessel launched: "The New Launched Ship," as published by the Religious Tract Society of Philadelphia in *The Seaman's Spy-Glass; or, God's Ways and Works Discovered at Sea*. The sermon's original prose has been altered to free-style verse.
- On Saturday, about half past one o'clock: *New-York Gazette*, 8/24/1818.
- the *Gazette* was compelled to re-print the story: *New-York Gazette*, 8/25/1818. That the Dod-designed *Atalanta* also had suffered a boiler explosion provided yet another compelling reason to seek a correction to the story.
- one steady source of employment came from sailmakers: Hall, op. cit, pp83–84.
- a typical set of sails didn't last more than four or five years: ibid, p34.

- the cost of entering the trade was relatively small: ibid, p58.
- The ideal work place was a loft: ibid, p54.
- the extended tools of sailmaking: ibid, p58.
- Nicoll & Company readily provided all that was required: Nicoll Accounts.
- began boring a circular cavity into it: Vail Accounts.
- 40 inches in diameter, and 5 feet, 5 inches deep: ibid.
- "proved bad,": ibid.
- Cochrane's steamer was indeed intended as a man-of-war: *Commercial Advertiser*, 9/26/1818, among others.
- Colden ... half-Tammany, half-Clintonian: Jenkins, *History of Political Parties in the State of New-York...*, p197. There is ample supporting evidence for this in the proceedings of the State Assembly in early 1818.
- Council of Appointment readily approved Colden: ibid, pp199–200. Governor Clinton, while a member of the Council of Appointment, did not control it. The other four Council members, all State Senators, held great influence, including Clintonian Senator Jabez D. Hammond, who suggested Colden's candidacy for Mayor. According to Jenkins, Clinton actually voted against Colden (because he was still a "Tammany Man"), but the nomination was approved, nevertheless. The Council was abolished in 1821.
- John Kelly and Simeon Burradge: New York County Clerk—Division of Old Records, Court of General Sessions of the City of New York, Minute Book, 9/7/1818 to 12/19/1818, p17.
- "John P. McKinny": ibid. There are two likely explanations for this name being recorded: 1) Joseph P. McKinne was the witness, but since the name Joseph was often abbreviated as "Jos" in the early 19th century, and the name John or Jonathan was abbreviated as "Jo," the clerk may have misread "Jos" for "Jo," and recorded his first name as John; or 2) Joseph P. McKinne had a relative active in the cotton trade named John McKinne, who regularly visited New York and may have been sent to court to represent the firm.
- John Stebbins, the First Teller: *New-York Courier*, 12/31/1816; also, see *Longworth's American Almanac* for 1820, showing Stebbins as an accountant. He subsequently returned to banking in 1821, as a cashier for the North River Bank (*Evening Post*, 5/29/1821).
- scienter was an area of great legal debate: for examples, see Rogers, *The New-York City-hall Recorder*, 1818, pp214–215, and 1822, p200.
- the *foremast*, rising some 94 feet above the deck: KA, Generaladjutantens för Flottans arkiv., Ankomna handlingar, 11/5/1819–1/25/1819 (serie E 11:24), Report of Baron Axel Klinkowström, received 11/5/1819 (hereafter, "Klinkowström Report"), in conjunction with Marestier, *Mémoire sur les Bateaux à Vapeur des Etats Unis d'Amérique, ...*, figure 10. Note: these mast heights are estimates based primarily on Marestier's drawings. Klinkowström's measurements for the masts, which confirm Marestier's, appear to have been made from the "top" up. (The "top," or "fighting top," is the small platform erected at the top of the lowest section of the mast. It supports the shrouds both above and below, and could serve as a platform for snipers in battle.)
- projecting out the bow of the *Savannah*, some 34 feet: Klinkowström Report.
- Fulton ... encountered a sailing sloop: *New-York Gazette*, 9/29/1818.
- The two steamboats, both moving at full speed: *New-York Gazette*, 10/21/1818.
- the ship *Ceres* left New York: *Savannah Republican*, 10/27/1818.
- Habersham embarked ... on the brig *Levant*: *Savannah Republican*, 10/26/1818.
- Bulloch and his family also set sail for home: *Savannah Republican*, 10/16/1818.
- Cochrane's steam vessel ... boiler problems: *The Reporter* (Brattleboro), 9/15/1818. This specific description of the problem, if not printed in the New

York papers, could have been readily learned from British newspapers available at any number of Gotham's coffee houses and libraries.
- Cochrane ... forced to depart for the fight in South America: *New-York Evening Post*, 10/7/1818.
- Elizabethtown Point ... the *Savannah* tied up: *Mercantile Advertiser*, 10/26/1818.
- neatly-built little farming village: Harris, *Remarks Made during a Tour...*, p75.
- Ogden and Daniel Dod had built their Steam Engine Manufactory: Thayer, *As We Were: The Story of Old Elizabethtown*, pp228–229.
- Dod ... trained as a clockmaker: ibid, p228.
- contracts to build steamboat engines both near and far: Dodd and Folsom, *Genealogy and History of the Daniel Dod Family...*, p121.
- Vail, purchased a share in an iron-slitting mill: Cavanaugh et al, *At Speedwell...*, p6.
- Trained by the famed steam engine makers of Boulton & Watt: Scott and Klinkowström, *Baron Klinkowström's America...*, p9.
- The charge for Samuel Carson's services, at $4 per day: Vail Accounts.
- These men ran the gamut, from free men: Cavanaugh et al, op. cit., p24.
- Vail himself owned a small number of slaves: ibid, p8. Based upon the detailed accounts Vail kept of his contract on the *Savannah*, the total billable amount of slave labor used to construct the steamship's apparatus appears to be $13.50.
- Having borne six children, Bethiah: ibid, p6.
- air pump cast by Allaire, recently carted to Speedwell: Vail Accounts.
- Vail hopped aboard the Monopoly's Cortland Street steamboat: Scott and Klinkowström, op. cit., p9.
- Vail and the stranger transferred to a stagecoach: ibid.
- *The gushing of the river*: ibid.
- they were immediately greeted by Bethiah: ibid, p10.
- Owen first traveled to Sweden in 1804: Baker, *The Engine-Powered Vessel...*, p26.
- studied Owen's work ... was ... Klinkowström: Klinkowström Report.
- Klinkowström ... received explicit instructions from ... Karl XIV Johan: ibid.
- Departing his homeland on August 2nd: ibid.
- he boarded the Monopoly's steamboat *Fulton*: Scott and Klinkowström, op. cit., p5.
- the *Connecticut's* paddlewheels were alternately completely out of the water: ibid, p6.
- Gahn did all he could to help: ibid, p8.
- introducing him to the newly-appointed Secretary of the Navy: Klinkowström Report.
- Klinkowström ... arrange meetings with engine builders: ibid.
- also was introduced to Moses Rogers: Scott and Klinkowström, op. cit., p8.
- "kindly helped me in many thoughtful ways": ibid, p9.
- "He invited me in a very friendly way": ibid.
- "The arrival at Mr. Vail's house pleased me greatly": ibid.
- *Mrs. Vail and her daughter*: ibid, p10.
- *Life in the Vail household is frugal*: ibid.
- Throughout his first full day at Speedwell, the Baron noticed: ibid.
- the drafting room became crowded with neighbors: ibid.
- forging began for the piston rods: Vail Accounts.
- each requiring hundreds of pounds of impure *pig iron*: ibid.
- Increasing the intended diameter by ¾ of an inch: ibid.
- the more slender air pump received its boring: ibid.
- piston rods ... eight inches too short: ibid.
- 98 pounds worth of pig iron to lengthen: ibid.

- reminding Klinkowström of the farmers back home: Scott and Klinkowström, op. cit., p10.
- "good apples and delicious cider": ibid.
- *Kennedy ... showed me a hillside where, during the Revolution*: ibid, p11.
- "this serene and hospitable people": ibid, p12.
- a cradle, or *pillow*: Vail Accounts.
- the boilers were ... new design: *Russian Invalid or Military Journal*, 10/24/1819.
- the *Atalanta* had advanced enough to allow trial runs: *Commercial Advertiser*, 12/16 and 12/17/1816; *The Evening Post*, 12/16/1816; *The Columbian*, 12/17/1816, among many others.
- This tragic accident ... forced a number of important questions: see U.S. Dept. of Treasury, *Steam Engines: Letter from the Secretary of the Treasury...*, p99. Captain Elihu S. Bunker, master of the steamboat *Connecticut* in 1816, was the source of both information on and criticism of the *Atalanta* accident in this 1838 publication.
- each boiler ... operate at ... 20 pounds per square inch: *Mercantile Advertiser*, 3/27/1819.
- first attempts at boilermaking ... he rejected them: Rogers USN, "Early Atlantic Steam Navigation, and the Cruise of the Savannah," *Ballou's Monthy Magazine*, Vol. 57, #2 (February 1883), p162. The author, who does not appear to be a direct relative of either Moses or Steve, nevertheless had New London Rogers sources for his article. He stated Captain Rogers "personally tested" every part of the *Savannah's* engine, including the boilers, of which Rogers "rejected six" before finally securing acceptable ones. While there appears to be no surviving evidence to corroborate that precise number of rejections, it is clear from the Vail accounts and the timing of the eventual engine installation that it was the boiler work which held up the construction process. The new boiler design, the unprecedented nature of the voyage, and the *Atalanta*'s accident all serve to support the article's contention that Moses paid special attention to the boiler construction.
- *I ... there saw an unusual and extensive work*: NYHS, steamship *Savannah* file, Charles A. Campfield statement, 10/28/1871. Note: the surname of Vail's old partner has been variously spelled Canfield, Camfield and Campfield. This family had extensive roots in the Morristown area, as well as relatives in Savannah at the time. They clearly knew at least some of the *Savannah*'s investors; an "A Camfield & family" traveled with J. P. McKinne and family from Savannah to New York that May (see *Mercantile Advertiser*, 5/26/1818); an "A Camfield" and "J J Camfield" later returned to Savannah with some of the Howard family (see *Savannah Republican*, 11/30/1818).
- the remaining shareholders ... departed for Savannah at the end of October: *Savannah Republican*, 11/11/1818.
- Klinkowström ... hurried back to observe: Klinkowström Report.
- according to the Baron's calculations: ibid.
- the huge kettles had been made with iron: ibid.
- boilers ... new design ... address the problem of salt build-up: *Russian Invalid or Military Journal*, 10/24/1819; also, see Scott, "Swedish Trade with America in 1820...," *Journal of Modern History*, Vol. 25 (1953), #4, p410, in which Klinkowström writes from New York that "a method is believed to have been discovered recently which prevents corrosion from salt in iron turbines." The only known example of such a design for iron boilers at that time is the *Savannah*.
- through the existing main hatch: Klinkowström Report.
- the boilers were placed on several layers of clay bricks: ibid.
- Christmas Day of 1818 ... order to cast off: *Commercial Advertiser*, 12/26/1818; *New-York Gazette*, 12/28/1818.

- early frost to Georgia: *Savannah Republican,* 10/16/1818.
- "Such a season, in this State,": ibid.
- forced them to *suspend: Baltimore Patriot,* 11/20/1818, among many others.
- another steamboat, the *Orleans,* had sunk: *New-York Gazette,* 12/29/1818; *New-York Columbian,* 12/31/1818.
- "Steam *Coffin.*": Rogers USN, op. cit., p162.

CHAPTER EIGHT—COMPLETION, AND COMPETITION

- *Chancellor Livingston* ... costing some $110,000: Klinkowström Report.
- After the required number of readings: *Georgia State Senate Journal,* 1818, 12/14 and 12/16/1818.
- the bill was placed before Governor William Rabun: *Laws of Georgia,* 1818, "An Act to incorporate 'The Savannah Steam Ship Company'," assented to 12/19/1818. Misspellings of shareholder names in the Act have been corrected.
- fur coats, beaver hats, or even buffalo robes: Palmer, op. cit., p329.
- men from Speedwell ... Vail had sent: Vail Accounts.
- visiting painter from Liverpool named John Davies: *Liverpool Mercury,* 6/25/1819.
- from files, to paint, to saw blades: Nicoll Accounts.
- January 24th, 1819, he left his lodgings: Scott and Klinkowström, p13.
- "The model of the vessel they have had prepared": *New-York Spectator,* 12/22/1818.
- C.D. Colden, John Whetten ... : *The Columbian* (NYC), 1/16/1819.
- sailing the sloops *Industry, Reaper* and *Gleaner:* NARA, RG26, Port/New London, ICMs and OCMs, sloops *Industry, Reaper, Gleaner,* various dates from 1805 to 1819; also, see MYS, Connecticut Ship Database.
- Steve ... had served as a first mate on Gilbert's sloop: NARA, RG26, Port/New London, Returns of Seaman, sloop *Gleaner,* 6/26/1818.
- Steve was, by all accounts, strong: Wall Papers, pp10–11, 202. Steve was described as one of the two strongest men in New London during his time.
- a certain affability: ibid, pp10–11, 495.
- Steve ... to New London for the purpose of mustering a crew: Rogers USN, op. cit., p162.
- "No, it is enough to have one son risk his life ... ": Braynard, op. cit., p75, quoting Grace Rogers Knapp, great granddaughter of Ebenezer. This Sarah Rogers quote had been passed down to Knapp by her grandmother (and Ebenezer's daughter), Harriet Rogers. For supporting evidence, see NARA, RG26, Port/New London, Crew Oaths of Citizenship, sloop *Industry,* Rogers, 3/27/1819 to 3/24/1820, and sloop *Gleaner,* Rogers, 6/25/1819 to 7/11/1820. Master of both vessels during this time was brother Gilbert, and among the crew members listed was Ebenezer Rogers.
- Steve ... had served with many kinds: for examples, see NARA, RG26, Port/New London, Crew Lists, brig *Connecticut,* 8/5/1809 and -/-/1810, and ship *Nabby,* 9/30/1816. At a minimum, Steve served with mariners both white and black, American and French.
- boilers ... 24 feet long and 6 feet in diameter: Klinkowström Report.
- between the fore and mainmasts ... cylinder: TNA, ADM 106/2689, Navy Board Meeting Minutes 1819, 7/16/1819 (hereafter, "Seppings Report").
- largest cylinder yet to be placed in a steam vessel: while the casting of the *Savannah*'s cylinder appears to be the same size as that for the *Chancellor Livingston* (and was probably made from the same model or mold), Vail's final boring of 40¾ inches in diameter was slightly larger than the *Chancellor Livingston*'s 40 inches.

Each cylinder had a 5-foot stroke. See Vail Accounts, and Ridgley-Nevitt, op. cit., p350.

– calculated to provide the power of 72 horses: Rush, *The Court of London...*, p96 (Rush's source was Moses himself). Seppings was told 74 horsepower, perhaps the result of a new calculation done at Liverpool.

– nearly upon its side, at a 20° angle: Seppings Report.

– steamboat *New Jersey*, had just such an arrangement: *New Jersey Journal*, 11/26/1816.

– On February 26th, Vail paid a visit: NARA, RG21, Records/U.S. District Court for DC, Case Papers, June term 1820, Case #430–431, Deposition of Henry Cooke.

– Pott & McKinne issued to Stephen Vail promissory notes: ibid, and Vail Accounts.

– Vail gave them a receipt: ibid, Deposition of Henry Cooke.

– Company's shareholders gathered for a meeting: *Columbian Museum*, 3/2/1819.

– Scarbrough was elected "The President": while the *Columbian Museum* does not report this explicitly, all of a company's officers were traditionally elected at one meeting. In the *Savannah*'s federal registration of 3/27/1819, Scarbrough was described as "the President of the steam ship company."

– The elegant steam-ship Savannah is now: *New-York Gazette*, 3/3/1819.

– separate main cabins were constructed for the sexes: *Mercantile Advertiser*, 3/27/1818.

– Mahogany wood was used: *Cheshire Chronicle*, 7/30/1819.

– large mirrors installed along the cabin walls: ibid; Wall Papers, p495.

– passenger capacity estimates ... as low as 20 to as high as 60: *Russian Invalid, or Military Journal*, 10/14/1819 said 22; *Mercantile Advertiser* (NYC), 3/27/1818 said 32; *Northern Post* (St. Petersburg), 10/29/1819 implied 40; *The Imperial Magazine* (London), Vol. 1 No. 4 (p396) said 60.

– Colden ... Rumors ... next Secretary of the Navy: *Commercial Advertiser* (NYC), 10/9/1818.

– Klinkowström returned to New York: Klinkowström Report.

– The Swede ... managed to meet ... the Navy Commissioners and President Monroe: Klinkowström, "In Monroe's Administration; Letters of Baron Axel Klinkowström," *The American-Scandinavian Review*, Volume XIX, No. 7 (July 1931), pp393–395.

– "She works to admiration": *New-York Gazette*, 3/20/1819.

– Along for the ride ... was Baron Klinkowström: Klinkowström Report.

– "the wonderful celerity": *Mercantile Advertiser*, 3/27/1819.

– Klinkowström ... as he saw it ... steamship with a number of problems: Klinkowström Report.

– "without a lot of noise": ibid.

– the importance Moses attached to minimizing the use of cast-iron parts: recall that for the breakdown of the *Eagle* back in 1813, it was the cast-iron parts of the engine that failed so dramatically.

– collapsible spokes and boards ... "an admirable one": Klinkowström Report.

– the *Savannah* ... "sails and maneuvers very well": ibid.

– "seems to some extent established": ibid.

– "mechanical genius" and "spirit of enterprise": ibid.

– "old prejudices fight against useful innovations": ibid.

– "I will undertake to take it across the sea": ibid.

– ... *If I were not so convinced*: ibid.

– bill for the ship itself ... Moses later put at $36,000: NLS, MSS 16096A, Lord Lynedoch diary, 9/7/1819.

– steam apparatus and passenger space fit-out ... $25,000 to $30,000: ibid. Lord

Lynedoch reported Moses told him $30,000. An earlier account put the cost at about $25,000 (see PEM, Diary of Abiel Abbot, 1818–1827, 4/10/1819).

- The solution to this budget overrun: NARA, RG21, District of Georgia, Savannah, U.S. Circuit Court, Mixed Case Files, *Francis H. Nicoll & Co. vs. W. Scarbrough & others,* 9/13/1822. See also Vail Accounts.
- notes issued by any banks in Ohio ... 80 to 90 cents on the dollar: *New York Shipping and Commercial List,* 3/19/1819.
- Growing suspicions about the Bank of the United States: problems at the second B.U.S. were, in fact, quite minor compared to the real causes of the Panic of 1819. Among these were 1) the failure of President Madison to publicly support the charter renewal of the *first* B.U.S. in 1811; which led to 2) a banking mania, in which State-chartered banks were founded with abandon to fill the gap created by the first B.U.S.'s closure; which was quickly followed by 3) reckless lending practices and failure to keep adequate specie reserves by some of the newly-chartered banks; in conjunction with 4) the massive issuance of short-term U.S. Treasury Bills to fund the Second War against Britain, effectively inflating the money supply even further; which led to 5) Congressional demands that the T-Bills be retired as soon as possible after the war, since they were effectively circulating as currency, and also were being treated like *surrogate specie reserves* by the banks; the whole of which was topped off by 6) Treasury Secretary Crawford forcing the second B.U.S. to convert worthless western banknotes held by the Treasury into current money, when he and the B.U.S. knew that those same banks had virtually no specie in their vaults to back up their liabilities (including issued banknotes).
- Bank of the United States was in such bad shape: Catterall, *The Second Bank of the United States,* pp68–70.
- Cotton was being quoted in New York at 23½ to 25 cents: *New York Shipping and Commercial List,* 3/19/1819.
- For SAVANNAH: *New-York Evening Post,* 3/25/1819; *Mercantile Advertiser,* 3/25/1819.
- the time they needed to register the ship: NARA, RG36, Port/New York, PE #90, "ship" *Savannah,* 3/27/1819. The designation of the *Savannah* as only a "ship" makes clear that either 1) the custom house surveyor at New York who filled out the form refused to acknowledge the new reality in front of his own eyes, or 2) McKinne and Rogers wanted to deny the Monopoly any pretext for a potential seizure of the *Savannah.*
- needed to keep a logbook: *SAL,* 1st Congress, 2nd Session, "An Act for the Government and Regulation of Seamen in the Merchants' Service," passed 7/20/1790.
- STEAM, SHIP: SI, *Steam Ship Savannah Log Book* (hereafter, "*SSSLB*").
- cast off from Fly Market Wharf: *Mercantile Advertiser,* 3/27/1819.
- On board for the trip was a harbor pilot: *SSSLB.*
- all the way to the Supreme Court of the United States: Drew University Archives, Gibbons Family Papers, Thomas Gibbons Correspondence, Daniel D. Tompkins to E. P. Livingston, 10/5/1818.
- "it is questioned ... whether ... ": *Commercial Advertiser* (NY), 3/30/1819.
- onlookers packing the Battery: *Mercantile Advertiser,* 3/30/1819.
- the harbor pilot, his job done, disembarked: *SSSLB.*

CHAPTER NINE—POLITICS, PRESIDENT, POLITICS

- Mariners of the future ... first open-sea test ... *shakedown cruise*: the term "shakedown cruise" did not exist in the 19th century. This is because it was invented in the early 20th century, in imitation of a term created for another high technology, heavier-than-air powered aircraft. When the earliest airplanes took off on their maiden flights, it was called a "shakedown flight," since the strong vibrations of flying would cause any loose parts to "shake down" to the ground. The maritime community adopted and adapted this aeronautical term for nautical use.

— she was pointed to the south: *SSSLB*. Hereafter, the source for numerous references to the *Savannah* and her crew during the voyage are from the *SSSLB*, unless otherwise noted.

— probably the brig *Othello* and schooner *Milo*: *New-York Gazette*, 3/29/1819.

— from the Cape's point ... enormous sandbar: Purdy, *Columbian Navigator...*, p85.

— "gulf-weed": ibid, p92.

— *Charleston*, carrying a complement of passengers: *Charleston Courier*, 4/9/1819.

— By the hundreds, they streamed to the edge of the bluff: *The Georgian*, 4/7/1819; *Savannah Republican*, 4/9/1819, as reprinted in the *Charleston Courier*, 4/12/1819.

— *Huzzah!*: *Savannah Republican*, 4/9/1819, as reprinted in the *Charleston Courier*, 4/12/1819.

— *Dallas* greeted the steamship: *The Georgian*, 4/7/1819.

— "her appearance inspires instant confidence in her security": ibid.

— The brig *Othello* ... managed to make the trip in only 5 days: *Savannah Republican*, 4/5/1819.

— "off the Capes of Delaware": ibid.

— She had a very boisterous passage: *Mercantile Advertiser* (NYC), 4/16/1819.

— *Savannah* had arrived safely ... overriding sentiment of the press: *The Times* (Charleston), 4/8/1819, among others.

— ... Captain Marsh, of the sloop Nimrod: *New-York Gazette*, 4/15/1819.

— "It redounds much to the honour of Savannah,": *Savannah Republican*, 4/9/1819.

— ... represented that they are desirous: New York State, *Laws of the State of New-York*, "An Act for incorporating the Ocean Steam Ship Company," passed 4/7/1819.

— "The Savannah, we understand,": *Savannah Republican*, 4/9/1819.

— stopping in New York ... pre-empt the competition in its own market: subsequent reports indicated the Ocean Steam Ship Company had considered attempting the crossing itself, to be followed by regular trans-Atlantic steam packet service. See *New-York Gazette*, 11/19/1819.

— "our markets are quite overloaded with Cotton": *The Georgian*, 4/5/1819.

— "a scarcity and pressure for money against speculative houses": ibid.

— "There is a heavy failure here": *Charleston Courier*, 4/12/1819.

— Onto the steamship ... came the eminent Stephen Elliott: *Southern Patriot*, 4/16/1819.

— Esther was part of the extended Habersham family: Owens, *Georgia's Planting Prelate*, p8.

— actor Henry James Finn: *Southern Patriot*, 4/16/1819.

— Finn was one of the more colorful characters: Stephenson, *The Charleston Theatre...*, p248.

— his colleagues had already left Georgia: Hoole, *The Antebellum Charleston Theatre*, pp16–17.

— Also willing ... four other men and one woman: *Southern Patriot*, 4/16/1819.

— the riverbank was packed with spectators: *Savannah Republican*, 4/14/1819.

— The *Charleston*, it turned out, was staying behind: while it's possible the *Charleston* might have had mechanical difficulties, there is no surviving evidence to support that explanation. In all likelihood, the passengers seeking transport simply chose the *Savannah*, making the *Charleston's* departure unprofitable, and therefore cancelable.

- the *Savannah* ... making 5 knots.: *The Georgian*, 4/20/1819.
- "When you take into consideration": ibid.
- "Tempestuous": ibid.
- The pilot thought the waters too rough: *Columbian Museum*, 4/15/1819.
- some of the passengers ... apprehensive about proceeding: ibid.
- "A heavy swell and a head sea": *The Georgian*, 4/20/1819.
- missed, it was reckoned, by a scant 30 minutes: *Charleston Courier*, 4/17/1819.
- "While other ships were becalmed": *The Georgian*, 4/20/1819.
- ... *we were honored*: ibid.
- quickly replaced by hundreds of Charlestonians: *City Gazette*, 4/17/1819.
- "politeness and attention of Capt. Rogers": *Charleston Courier*, 4/17/1819.
- the steamboat *Charleston* arrived, bringing ... Gaines: *Southern Patriot*, 4/19/1819.
- *Connecticut*, under the command of Captain James Blin: *City Gazette*, 4/19/1819; MYS, Connecticut Ship Database, 1789–1939, *Connecticut* (Brig), Masters. NARA's New London Custom House records are the source for this database.
- Stevens Rogers had grown up on his father's farm: Rogers, op. cit., pp127, 201; Wall Papers, p231.
- sent him to the prestigious Plainfield Academy: Wall Papers, pp4, 123, 231.
- Steve abandoned his studies: ibid.
- the brig's name was *Connecticut*: NARA, RG36, Port/New London, Crew Lists, brig *Connecticut*, 8/5/1809; also Return of Seamen, brig *Connecticut*, 12/7/1809.
- Barrel staves, baled hay: ibid, Outward Foreign Manifest, brig *Connecticut*, 8/5/1809.
- destined for the British colony of Demerara: ibid.
- Gaines and his aides went out to inspect: *City Gazette*, 4/21/1819.
- Lieutenant James Monroe, appeared: *Charleston Courier*, 4/26/1819.
- It has been intimated: *Charleston Courier*, 4/27/1819.
- "the people of Charleston did not want": Stevens Rogers Statement.
- Finn playing Cassius: *Southern Patriot*, 4/28/1819.
- Captain Utley had the honor of taking him out: *Charleston Courier*, 4/30/1819.
- for the voyage home were seven passengers: *Savannah Republican*, 5/1/1819.
- the *Savannah* had made 7 knots: *Charleston Courier*, 5/1/1819.
- Aside from one very brief spell near the lighthouse: *The Georgian*, 5/8/1819.
- The Steam Ship *Savannah* with a number: *Commercial Advertiser*, 4/24/1819.
- launch date ... had been set: *New-York Gazette*, 4/26/1819, among others.
- ... *It was understood the President*: GSA, William Scarbrough Collection, William Scarbrough to Julia Scarbrough, 5/6/1819.

CHAPTER TEN—AN OFFER, PREPARATIONS, AND OMENS

- dignitaries piled into an elegant barge: *Savannah Republican*, 5/8/1819.
- President Monroe climbed into the barge: *Charleston Courier*, 5/13/1819.
- *Dallas* let loose a 21-gun salute: ibid.
- Chatham Light Artillery joined in: ibid.
- welcomed by Mayor James Wayne: *The Ladies Magazine*, 5/15/1819.
- presented him with a choice of transport: *Charleston Courier*, 5/13/1819.
- Attending the service ... Army and Navy officers: *Charleston Courier*, 5/15/1819.
- shareholders ... were church members: GC/GHS, Marriages of Chatham County, Georgia, pp138–139, 147; also, GHS, Chatham County Superior Court Minutes, Volume 9 (1808–1818), p217.
- included a gathering ... Army and Navy officers: *The Ladies Magazine*, 5/15/1819.
- Following behind ... flock of officials: *Columbian Museum*, 5/13/1819.

- also a few from the Navy: Stevens Rogers Statement. While the identities of these Navy officers is unknown, their presence is important. It is likely that they heard President Monroe suggest a government purchase of the *Savannah*, and would have reported this to their superiors on the Board of Navy Commissioners.
- deploy some of the upper sails: *Columbian Museum*, 5/13/1819. Since Steve mentioned "light breezes at NW" in the log, and the *Museum* noted sails were "partly used," it stands to reason that the upper sails were deployed, thereby avoiding any problems with cinders.
- Monroe … six feet in height with broad shoulders: Morgan, *The Life of James Monroe*, p349.
- slight limp in his walk which some people claimed to notice: Hines, *Early Recollections of Washington City*, p15.
- knee-length breeches and stockings: Faux, *Memorable days in America…*, p46.
- a little powder in his hair: ibid.
- just might have bled to death: Fischer, *Washington's Crossing*, p247.
- James Monroe … an amiable, unassuming man: Faux, op. cit., p46; Cunningham, *The Presidency of James Monroe*, p187.
- atmosphere enveloping … polite and harmonious: Ammon, *James Monroe…*, p360.
- the generals called *banditti*: Silver, *Edmund Pendleton Gaines*, pp64–65.
- he expected General Mitchell to help: Rentz, *The Public Life of David B. Mitchell*, p77.
- it was all General Gaines' fault: ibid, p76; Silver, op. cit., p71.
- Gaines was not about to let things lie as they were: he responded to Mitchell's charges in detail on 10/17/1819 (see *ASP*, Class V, *Military Affairs*, Vol. 2, Document #189). Gaines also falsely accused Mitchell of smuggling slaves, a charge which eventually resulted in Mitchell's removal as Creek Agent (see Rentz, op. cit., pp96–97, 111).
- *Altamaha*, which was towing two barges: *Savannah Republican*, 5/12/1819.
- near this island was a two-masted brig: ibid.
- wide horizontal stripes, alternating white and blue in color: Laurie, *Laurie's Collection of the Maritime Flags of All Nations…*, flags #155, 156.
- Rising up the foremast went the Stars and Stripes: *Savannah Republican*, 5/12/1819.
- *Dallas* fired a salute: ibid.
- The President certainly enjoyed the excursion: ibid; also, Stevens Rogers Statement.
- government would have an interest in purchasing: Stevens Rogers Statement.
- attacked by pirate crews composed of: Wheeler, *In Pirate Waters*, pp84–85.
- executions being carried out as far north as Boston: *Boston Patriot*, 2/19/1819.
- Having such a multinational fleet thrown into the melee: Bealer, *The Privateers of Buenos Aires…*, p174.
- a blood-curdling scream: it stands to reason that any normal person would respond accordingly to the shock and pain of cutting off their thumb.
- required by law to carry a medicine chest: "An Act for the Government and Regulation of Seamen in the Merchants' Service," op. cit., passed 7/20/1790.
- the ship's "doctor": regarding Claypit's thumb, Steve literally wrote in the logbook that "the Doctor done it up." Steve's use of "Doctor" without a surname is indicative of common seaman's slang—the "Doctor" was the cook, who was responsible for the medicine chest. There was no need to be more specific; any knowledgeable person at the time reading the logbook would know to whom the first mate was referring. See Bartlett, *Dictionary of Americanisms*, p117; also see Parsons, *Sailor's Physician…*, pp140–141.

- repairing a very bad knife cut: Parsons, op. cit., pp133–134.
- coincidentally named James Monroe: the appearance of this name in the *Savannah's* logbook has led to some speculation as to whether or not Steve was referring to the President. The same could be supposed of Lieutenant James Monroe, the President's nephew. In both cases, it seems extremely unlikely. With all due respect to the steamship's "doctor," why would President Monroe or his nephew return to the *Savannah* to be bled when there were any number of qualified physicians in the city? The name "James Monroe" was not at all unusual in early 19th century America, and can be found in surviving merchant vessel crew lists and city directories. It therefore stands to reason that the James Monroe referred to in the logbook was a member of the *Savannah's* crew.
- many physicians continued to swear ... bleeding could relieve patients suffering: there are certain circumstances in which bleeding might help certain patients, which is one of the reasons why the practice lasted for centuries. Predicting such a beneficial outcome for any given patient is impossible, but to medical doctors in the early 19th century, if a patient was bled and subsequently recovered, then it could be said that the bleeding had been a success.
- Merchant crews ... did not shy away from bleeding each other: Parsons, op. cit., pp140–141. Parsons specifically included instructions for bleeding in his 1820 book because he knew merchant crews were doing it and would continue to do so, despite his reservations.
- the *Franklin*, which had sunk on the Missouri River: *Commercial Advertiser*, 3/2/1819, among others.
- *Chancellor Livingston* had suffered an engine breakdown: *New York Gazette*, 4/15/1819, among others.
- "a dreadful cracking": *Columbian Museum*, 5/17/1819.
- Three ships broke loose from the wharves: ibid and *S.S.S.L.B.*
- Within fifteen minutes, the rainsquall had passed: *Savannah Republican*, 5/17/1819.
- "well secured under deck": "An Act for the Government and Regulation of Seamen in the Merchants' Service," op. cit., passed 7/20/1790.
- Dried peas were a perfect example: Parsons, op. cit., p165.
- pickled vegetables, an adequate supply of lemon juice, and coffee: ibid, p178.
- four cords of pine wood: The Seppings Report says four cords, which may be right, although it begs the question as to why it took the crew parts of three days to load such a relatively small amount of wood just prior to departure. Other sources claim the steamship had as much as 25 cords for the voyage.
- and one thousand bushels of coal: The Seppings Report says this amount. Other sources put the coal stores at 1,500 bushels.
- twelve-oar long boat and a six-oar jolly boat: RSNA, Fond 166, inv. 1, file 3524.
- a group of three orphans: Wall Papers, p495. Wall cites Steve's daughter, Sarah Rogers, as his source for the boys' story. Their existence is confirmed by the Seppings Report, although he listed two boys; the third may have been the steward described by Seppings.
- shareholders ... were also members of the local Union Society: GHS, Minutes of the Union Society, pp58–61.
- Moses ... his own children ... remaining up North: there appears to be no evidence that Adelia and the children came south with Moses during his captainship of the *Savannah*. Under the circumstances, it made far more sense for them to stay in the North, where family was closer and the summer climate healthier.
- Adelia Rogers ... at least as far south as Baltimore: *Baltimore Patriot*, 5/17/1817.
- Adelia gave birth to Daniel Moses Rogers: Rogers, op. cit., p248.

- Nathan, tragically lost his life by drowning: ibid. Rogers provided no particulars beyond the date and cause of death. Gause's work claimed (on p83) that at one point while the *Phoenix* was operating on the Delaware, the captain tried to pass a boy to the wharf as the steamboat was departing; the captain lost his hold, and the boy fell into the water and drowned. Braynard speculated that the drowned boy might have been Nathan Rogers. However, Gause provided no specifics as to the precise time and place of the accident, or the individuals involved. Braynard provided no additional evidence, either. Based upon a search of multiple sources, there appears to be no surviving evidence to support the speculation that Nathan's drowning was related to the *Phoenix*.
- currency issued by banks out West ... quoted as "uncertain,": *New-York Shipping and Commercial List*, 5/21/1819.
- banknotes from the South ... accepted in New York at 95 cents on the dollar: ibid.
- Robert Isaac, had already sailed for Liverpool: his most likely means of transport was the ship *Athens*, owned and captained by the Low family, which cleared Savannah for Liverpool on 5/7/1819. Isaac was not in Savannah on 6/5/1819 (see NARA, RG21, District/Georgia, Savannah, U.S. Circuit Court, Mixed Case Files, *Scarbrough vs. U.S. Bank*, 1821). Isaac returned from Liverpool on the ship *Georgia* (another Low family vessel), arriving at Savannah on 11/10/1819.
- American bar-room custom ... handing the bottle to the patron: Palmer, *Journal of Travels...*, p26.
- one of the *Savannah*'s crew, John Weston: GC/GHS, *Register of Deaths in Savannah, Georgia*, Vol. IV, p12. Also, *Savannah Republican*, 5/21/1819, and *SSSLB*.
- he was from Portland: *Columbian Museum*, 5/21/1819.
- Custom House ... closed at 1 o'clock that afternoon: *Savannah Republican*, 5/11–20/1819.
- "In Balast": NARA, RG36, Port/Savannah, Outward Foreign Manifest, Steam Ship *Savannah*, 5/20/1819.
- Georgia Upland Cotton ... 15 cents bid, 17 cents asked: *New-York Shipping and Commercial List*, 5/21/1819.
- some ... managed ... personal finances conservatively: GHS, Chatham County Superior Court Minutes, Volume 9 (1812–1818), and Volume 10 (1818–1822), and NARA, RG21, District/Georgia, Savannah, U.S. Circuit and District Courts. A review of these sources shows clearly that while some shareholders were overextended, others—as measured by a lack of lawsuits—were in comparatively better financial condition through the depression. The shareholders who show up the most as either plaintiffs or defendants in the Chatham County Superior Court records during this period are Scarbrough & McKinne, Andrew Low & Co., and Isaac Minis, followed by the Howard brothers and Sheldon C. Dunning.
- Robert Mitchell, who had just returned from Liverpool: *Savannah Republican*, 5/17/1819.
- Scarbrough ... served a year as Sweden's vice-consul at Savannah: Ruddock, *Palladium of Knowledge...*, 1818.
- Scarbrough ... served as Russia's vice-consul at Savannah: ibid.
- (occasionally with an exclamation point): *The Democratic Press*, 6/4/1819.
- dead crew member remained unburied ... shipmates were at risk: Bassett, *Legends and Superstitions of the Sea and of Sailors*, p474.
- women at sea had been considered unlucky since ancient times: ibid, p446.
- "the mysterious character of the day,": ibid, pp443–445, quoting Olmstead in 1841.
- Also taking her departure ... Buenos Aires privateer *La Fortuna*: *The Georgian*, 5/25/1819; *Savannah Republican*, 5/28/1819.

CHAPTER ELEVEN — ACROSS

- Conditions in the North Atlantic had been much the same: *SSSLB*.
- no forests of any size could grow there: Brewer, *The Beauties of Ireland...*, Vol. 2, p463.
- straw ropes, or old fish netting: ibid, p462.
- 480 feet above the ocean: Lankford, *Cape Clear Island: Its People and Landscape*, p18.
- new lighthouse: ibid.
- smaller, fort-like stone tower: ibid, pp18, 95.
- the lookouts on duty ... spotted something unusual: *New-London Gazette*, 4/25/1838 (Stevens Rogers is the source for this article), and *SSSLB*.
- nearest signal station six miles to the eastward: Swift, *Historical Maps of Ireland*, pp94-95, and Leet, *A Directory of the Market Towns ... Ireland*, various pages.
- *Cape Clear was reporting a ship afire*: *New-London Gazette*, 4/25/1838.
- The pilot boat's name was *Mary*: *Southern Reporter and Cork Commercial Courier*, 6/19/1819.
- So Moses told the *Mary's* captain: ibid.
- *Kite*, under the command of Lieutenant John Bowie: *The Navy List*, July 1819, p123.
- Bowie ... gone to sea at the age of 17: TNA, ADM 107/43/108266.
- receiving his commission as a Royal Navy lieutenant: ibid.
- first commanding ... *Minerva*: *The Navy List*, December 1817, p122.
- charge of the *Kite*, in early 1818: *The Navy List*, July 1818, p122.
- *Kite* ... into service ... one year before: Lyon, *The Sailing Navy List*, p334, and *The Navy List*, December 1817, p122, and July 1818, p122.
- state-of-the-art for coast guard cruisers: NMM, ZAZ6476.Lines 1816, and ZAZ6429.Midship section 1817; these drawings are believed to be similar to if not the actual plans for revenue cruisers like the *Kite*.
- other revenue cruisers ... had from 10 to 16 guns: *The Navy List*, July 1819, p123.
- *Kite* had but one cannon: while *The Navy List* of July 1819 shows the *Kite* as having no guns, as do subsequent editions, she would have had at least one cannon on board for signaling purposes, or for use against resisting smugglers. For support, see the *Kite's* earliest surviving crew list, from 1825 (TNA, ADM 119/62), which shows one crewman with the rank of gunner.
- By 11 o'clock that morning: *SSSLB*.
- *Kite* ... 10 knots: *Southern Reporter and Cork Commercial Courier*, 6/19/1819.
- *revenue colors*: Chatterton, *King's Cutters...*, p160; and Phillipson, *Smuggling*, p46.
- several warning shots had been fired: *New-London Gazette*, 4/25/1838, and *New York Journal of Commerce*, 8/26/1850. Stevens Rogers is the source for both articles.
- as the sun reached high noon: *SSSLB*.
- ports of call he expected to make: *Southern Reporter and Cork Commercial Courier*, 6/19/1819.
- stopped in transit by a British man-o-war: Rogers, op. cit., p497; Wall Papers, pp.4, 123, 231, 348.
- Congress had mandated these documents: *SAL*, 4th Congress, 1st Session, "An Act for the Relief and Protection of American Seamen," passed 5/28/1796.
- "These, Sir, are my credentials.": Rogers, op. cit., p497; Wall Papers, p4.
- one of ... pilot boats, marked with the number "10": *SSSLB*, and Tibbles, *Illustrated Catalogue of Marine Paintings...*, p155.
- boats filled with hundreds of people: *New London Gazette*, 4/25/1838.

- "Where is your master?": *New-London Gazette*, 4/25/1838. This article, based upon an interview with Steve, is the earliest known source of this dialogue.
- myths of the U.S. Navy's steam battery ... an apparatus to shoot hot water: Canney, *The Old Steam Navy*, Vol. 1, p4.
- news of this novel weaponry had made it ... into the British perception: Colden, *The Life of Robert Fulton*, p231; Gause, *1836 Semi-Centennial Memoir of Harlan & Hollingsworth Co...*, pp36–37; and also into the French perception—see Roberts, *The Introduction of Steam Technology...*, p47; and the Swedish perception—see Klinkowström Report.
- By implying the *Savannah* had such a feature: according to Steve, when it became known in Liverpool that the *Savannah* had no "hot-water engine," the Royal Navy officers who had provoked the coachwhip incident became the target of "hot-water jeers" from their own countrymen.
- Over 160 buildings of all kinds were destroyed: Harris and Allyn, *The Battle of Groton Heights...*, pp27–28.
- members of the extended Rogers clan, lost property: ibid, pp154–155. Amos Rogers Sr. appears to have been among them, claiming a little over £31 in losses. For comparison, Amos Sr. purchased 1 acre of land in Groton in 1782 for £18.
- " ... *fell a sacrifice to british Barbarity* ... ": Caulkins and Gilman, *The Stone Records of Groton*, opposite p80.
- " ... *commanded by that most despicable parricide, Benedict Arnold* ... ": ibid, p76.
- on one of their early captures was Steve: Rogers, op. cit., pp497–498; Wall Papers, pp348, 495. While no confirming archival evidence appears to have survived for this first capture, its description jives with both the early treatment of prisoners of war and Steve's second capture.
- Steve signed up to serve ... the *Favourite*: NYHS, Thomas Barclay Papers, American Prisoners of War, Port of Halifax, p44; Essex Institute, *American Vessels Captured by the British...*, p117.
- benefit of fog: NMM, NM/RUSI/116, HMS *Valiant* logbook.
- The warship sent over an officer and four seamen: ibid.
- Steve ... innate good-humor: Wall Papers, pp495–496.
- included in a prisoner exchange a few months later: Thomas Barclay Papers, op. cit., p44.
- he joined the crew of the ship *Armata* as a third mate: NARA, RG36, Port/Philadelphia, Crew List, ship *Armata*, 12/20/1814.
- Royal Navy had captured or destroyed 19 U.S. Navy vessels: Dudley, *Splintering the Wooden Wall...*, p137.
- the Americans ... managed to sink or capture some 25 Royal Navy vessels: ibid. Dudley's numbers are losses due to enemy action at sea only. They do not include gunboats or losses on the Great Lakes. If natural causes are included, the total results are even more lopsided: 57 Royal Navy vessels lost to 20 American.
- "deprived them of any claim on their own government for interference.": Morison, *The Oxford History of the American People*, p410, quoting Lord Castlereagh.
- ... *had the English Cabinet felt* ... : Rush, *The Court of London...*, p120. Rush went on to note that Britain's foreign secretary, Lord Castlereagh, "was not a man to speak hastily."
- "the most sinister radicalism.": Powell, *Richard Rush: Republican Diplomat...*, p131.
- "our own flesh and blood,": Napier, *Black Charlie: A Life of Admiral Sir Charles Napier...*, p33.

CHAPTER TWELVE—ALBION, HOSPITALITY, AND RUMORS

– At 5 o'clock: *SSSLB.*
– wood ... kindling ... to serve as the primary fuel: see Seppings Report for confirmation.
– 40 acres of these protected docks: Dupin, *Two Excursions to the Ports of England...*, p31; Smithers, *Liverpool, its Commerce...*, p452.
– long quay was packed with spectators: *New-London Gazette*, 4/25/1838; *New York Journal of Commerce*, 8/26/1850.
– crewmen had trouble performing their duties: "History of the First Steamship That Crossed the Atlantic," *Hunt's Merchants' Magazine...*, 12/1850. "A. Thomas," a fireman on board the *Savannah*, was *Hunt's* source. An "Andrew Thomas" was among those listed as having a letter waiting for him at the Savannah Post Office just after the steamship's transatlantic departure (see *The Georgian*, 6/8/1819).
– Committee of Two Hundred: *The New Times*, 7/15/1819, among others.
– Reformers had begun to drill: Turner, *The Age of Unease...*, p160.
– Lord Liverpool actually had been in Paris: Petrie, *Lord Liverpool and his Times*, p11.
– yellow fever epidemic of 1804: Carson, "The Customs Quarantine Service," *The Mariner's Mirror*, Vol. 64, No. 1 (1978), pp66–67.
– doctors questioned whether ... yellow fever was actually contagious: McDonald, "The History of Quarantine in Britain During the 19th Century," *Bulletin of the History of Medicine* (USA), Vol. XXV, No. 1 (Jan-Feb 1951); Maglen, " 'The First Line of Defence': British Quarantine ... 19th Century," *Social History of Medicine* (UK), Vol. 15, No. 3, p413.
– merchants continually complained ... damage done to perishable cargoes: ibid.
– led the British ... loosen regulations: His Majesty's Stationery Office, *Instructions to Officers...*, p10.
– the crew had been healthy: *SSSLB.*
– to moor the *Savannah* off the small village of Tranmere: *Cheshire Chronicle*, 7/2 and 7/30/1819.
– Tranmere happened to be the terminus: Wardle, "Early Steamships on the Mersey...," *Transactions of the Historic Society of Lancashire and Cheshire*, Vol. XCII, p99.
– Isaac, Low ... letter to the British Treasury: TNA, T2/86, No. 12451; also T11/62, p115.
– Among the arrivals yesterday: *Marwade's Commercial Report*, 6/21/1819, as widely re-printed.
– On Thursday night: *Southern Reporter and Cork Commercial Courier*, 6/19/1819.
– the *Kite* had been after the steamship "all day.": *Carrick's Morning Post*, 6/24/1819.
– We have frequently said that the application of Steam ... : *The Dublin Journal*, 6/21/1819.
– "may be considered as an important æra in navigation.": *The Bristol Observer*, 6/24/1819; *The Bristol Gazette*, 6/24/1819; *Felix Farley's Bristol Journal*, 6/26/1819.
– Moses provided ... details of two vessels he had spoken to: *The British Statesman*, 6/23/1819 (likely re-printed from *Marwade's* of 6/21). The inclusion of both latitude and longitude for these vessel contacts indicates there was another record of the *Savannah's* position kept on board, since the surviving logbook only notes latitude (by tradition). One story handed down described Stevens Rogers as having kept a second, more detailed logbook, which may have had longitude recordings. Steve is said to have reluctantly given this other logbook to an English

nobleman, who came to visit him many years after the voyage and specifically asked for it (see Rogers, op. cit., pp498–499). Separately, Moses probably kept his own captain's log, which was a fairly common practice. Ready access to a chronometer in his cabin would account for any longitude recordings.

– the boilers suffered from *clinkers*: *SSSLB*.
– holes on either side of the hull ... entry point for water: Seppings Report.
– steam was used ... almost 100 hours: *SSSLB*; for confirmation, see Seppings Report, in which Robert Seppings states he was told steam was used 99 hours.
– "worked the engine 18 days,": *Marwade's Commercial Report*, 6/21/1819, as widely re-printed. *The Edinburgh Philosophical Journal* (1820, Vol. II, p197) was more precise, stating "the steam engine was in use during eighteen days of the passage."
– Moses, in his own captain's log: see note above on logbooks.
– "used her steam full eighteen days,": Rush, *The Court of London...*, p96.
– *first* 18 days of the voyage that were spent steaming: *The Imperial Magazine* (Liverpool), Vol. 1, No. 4 (1819), p396.
– others claimed it was 20 days: *Surrey, Southwark, Middlesex, Sussex Gazette*, 8/7/1819, among others, quoting *The Hull Advertiser*.
– the steamship had taken 29 days and 4 hours: if a 5-hour time change is included.
– most British newspapers reported ... 26 days: *Gore's General Advertiser*, 6/24/1819; *Liverpool Mercury*, 6/25/1819; *Billinge's Liverpool Advertiser*, 6/28/1819, among others.
– land-to-land voyage time, which was only 21 days: *Edinburgh Star*, 6/25/1819; *Edinburgh Evening Courant*, 6/26/1819; *Imperial Magazine* (Liverpool), Vol. 1, No. 4 (1819), p396; *Edinburgh Philosophical Journal* (1820), Vol. II, p197.
– ship *Athens* ... "lately arrived from Savannah in 21 days": *The Liverpool Courier*, 6/30/1819.
– *Thalia* ... roughly the same amount of time: *The British Statesman*, 6/23/1819.
– "for the purpose of making a sale of her to Bernadotte": *The Edinburgh Star*, 6/25/1819; this rumor was repeated in the *Caledonian Mercury*, 6/26/1819, among others.
– "her destination is said to be St. Petersburgh": *Gore's General Advertiser*, 6/24/1819; repeated in the *Liverpool Mercury*, 6/25/1819, among many others.
– "The politicians of the day,": *The Georgian*, 8/31/1819.
– claimed ... Moses ... brother of Commodore John Rodgers: *Gore's General Advertiser*, 6/24/1819; repeated in the *Liverpool Mercury*, 6/25/1819, among others.
– John Rodgers ... most British vessels captured or destroyed: Schroeder, *Commodore John Rodgers...*, p125.
– John Barrow proffered what he thought: Lloyd, *Mr. Barrow of the Admiralty...*, p90. St. Helena had been considered briefly for Napoleon's first exile in 1814, but was considered too remote at the time.
– "that little rock": ibid.
– "*Non, non, pour St. Hélène*": ibid, p91.
– "all intrigue would be impossible,": ibid, p90.
– ... *the British Govt. have finally determined that Buonaparte*: HSP, Deborah Logan Diary, pp220–221.
– over 2,700 soldiers and officers: Masson, *Napoleon at St. Helena...*, p108.
– a system of ten signal towers: Morriss, *Cockburn and the British Navy...*, p133.
– Royal Navy squadron of eight or more vessels: TNA, ADM2/1692, John Barrow to Rear Admiral Robert Plampin, 12/14/1818. At that time, the St. Helena squadron contained one ship-of-the-line, two post ships and five sloops.
– "*I see that you are afraid*": Martineau, *Napoleon's St. Helena*, page 56.
– Sir Hudson Lowe, Sir Hudson *Low,*: *The News*, 10/5/1818.

- "this *kind-hearted* man": *The British Monitor*, 6/27/1819.
- *Over and over again*: Martineau, op. cit., p20.
- *His mind is tireless*,: ibid, p196.
- warnings about fast sailing vessels ... on the Hudson River: ibid, p202.
- or Philadelphia: Macartney and Dorrance, *The Bonapartes in America*, pp250–251, 254.
- or Baltimore: Rose, *The Life of Napoleon I*, Vol. II, p513.
- or Charleston: Markham, *The Bonapartes*, pp171–172.
- One letter ... written by a Frenchman in English: Morriss, op. cit., p139.
- mercenaries, who would land on St. Helena dressed in British Army uniforms: Rose, op. cit., p513; Hamilton-Williams, *The Fall of Napoleon...*, p329.
- another plot by two exiled French generals: Martineau, op. cit., p204–205.
- "Colonel Latapie" was arrested: Young, *Napoleon in exile...*, Vol. 1, p297.
- submarine vessel: Hamilton-Williams, op. cit., page 329.
- methods of escape had been discussed: Young, op. cit., Vol. 2, p89.
- no trouble engaging in secret correspondence: ibid, p90.
- "plan for revolutionising South America,": *Mercantile Advertiser* (NYC), 7/22/1818.
- Joseph Bonaparte's ... offer of a $2,000,000 reward: *The New-York Columbian*, 1/9/1818.
- the security already in-place for St. Helena was not enough: Masson, op. cit., p212.
- Alexander, would press for Napoleon's release: *The New-York Columbian*, 10/23/1818.
- "that Napoleon Bonaparte has placed himself": Young, op. cit., Vol. 2, p121.
- Joseph Bonaparte had recently shipped a diamond: *The New-York Columbian*, 12/31/1818; *Columbian Museum*, 1/12/1819, among others.
- dispatches from the British minister to Paris: NLS, MS6193, Stuart de Rothsay to Lord Castlereagh, 2/11/1819.
- "we meet with it in the world of politics": *Southern Patriot*, 5/11/1819.
- very difficult for British sentries to catch even a glimpse: Young, op. cit., Vol. 2, p161.
- printed material ... for inspection ... included newspapers: *The British Statesman*, 6/26/1819.
- editions of *The Morning Chronicle* ... especially scrutinized: *The Morning Chronicle*, 6/26/1819.
- forbidding any coastal inhabitants ... communicating with: *Savannah Republican*, 4/1/1819.
- no Royal Navy personnel ... any contact whatsoever with the prisoner: TNA, ADM 2/1692, John Barrow to Rear Admiral Robert Plampin, 12/14/1818.
- Bullock's Museum on the Piccadilly ... auctioned off: *The National Register*, 6/20/1819.
- "A numerous and most fashionable party,": ibid.
- ... That this Meeting unequivocally disclaim: *St. James's Chronicle*, 7/20–7/22/1819, among many others.
- The penalty for those found guilty was death: Masson, op. cit., pp114–115. Parliament passed this law in April 1816.
- Liverpool ... host to several thousand men: *Cheshire Chronicle*, 6/18/1819, 7/2/1819.
- 1,500 veterans from the Battle of Waterloo: *The Leeds Mercury*, 6/26/1819.
- provisioning of vessels: *The British Volunteer*, 6/26/1819.
- outlaw within Britain the private raising of troops: *The British Monitor*, 6/27/1819, reporting the particulars of this Foreign Enlistment Bill, just passed by the House of Commons.

- The King's ships at St. Helena: *The Courier* (London), 9/18/1818, which appears to have been the first to publish.
- whole steam-rescue speculation absurd: *The Morning Chronicle*, 9/21/1818.
- number of newspapers which printed the story: at least six in London alone.
- Mersey River steamboats : *SSSLB*.
- Dock Police took several people into custody: *Billinge's Liverpool Advertiser*, 6/28/1819.
- guest on board ... officer from the Liverpool Custom House: *SSSLB*.
- "still on Long Island, raising turnips": *The Statesman*, 6/30/1819.
- Information, which we have received: TNA, HO 79/3, Henry Hobhouse to John Swainson, 6/12/1819.
- "It is supposed," reported one of the city's newspapers: *The Traveller*, 6/29/1819.
- Such Cabinet meetings actually were not that unusual: Aspinall, *The Cabinet Council...*, pp187–188. No formal minutes were kept of these early Cabinet meetings.
- sail-drying, to paint-scraping: *SSSLB*.
- *The Newspapers of this City*: PUL, Rush Family Papers, Richard Rush letter book, Richard Rush to Captain Rogers, 6/23/1819. Rush signed his name "RR" in this letter copy book.
- Liverpool to London ... 207-mile trip: Baldwin et al, *Crosby's Complete Pocket Atlas...*, 1818, p295.
- common coaches ... passengers ... mail coaches: White, *Letters on England...*, Vol. 1, pp44–45, Vol. 2, p228.
- The less-crowded mail coaches were more expensive: ibid, Vol. 2, p226.
- local children, who ran alongside: MHS, Mary Turner Sargent Torrey diary, p19.
- "an immense mass of smoky": White, op. cit., Vol. 2, p12.
- one million residents: Baldwin et al, op. cit., p303.
- 51 Baker Street: Critchett & Woods, *The Post Office London Directory for 1820*, plxix.
- Rush had no overseas diplomatic experience: Dykstra, *The Richard Rush Ministry...*, p4.
- Rush ... abreast of the Royal Navy's building: ibid, p7.
- firm believer ... need for a strong American Navy: ibid.
- "great ease and safety" ... "used her steam full eighteen days": Rush, op. cit., p96.
- "having excited equal": PUL, op. cit., Richard Rush to JQA, 7/3/1819 (Dispatch No. 76).
- "anxious that this enterprising mariner": ibid.
- to America's top diplomat in Sweden: ibid, Richard Rush to C. Hughes, 6/30/1819.
- to the Russian minister to Britain, Count Hristofor Lieven: RSAN, Fond 166, inventory 1, file 3524, Hristofor Lieven to Marquis de Traversé, 6/20–7/2/1819 (dates are Julian-Gregorian).
- 36 Harley Street: Critchett & Woods, op. cit., plxix.
- introduction was made to Sweden's minister to Britain: NARA, RG59, Despatches from U.S. Ministers to Sweden and Norway, Christopher Hughes Jr. to JQA, 8/30/1819.
- 21 Lower Grosvenor Street: Critchett & Woods, op. cit., plxix.
- Moses wondered if Rush would write: Hughes to JQA, 8/30/1819.
- Moses had met with Russia's minister to Britain: Lieven to Traversé, 7/2/1819.
- set of china: Braynard, op. cit., p229; Cavanaugh et al, op. cit., p18.
- tugged the *Hastings* all the way to Margate: Brown, *Before the Ironclad...*, p46.
- *The North Pole*: *The Edinburgh Advertiser*, 6/12/1818.
- ... The naval success: ibid.

- explore the River Congo: *The New-York Columbian,* 7/17/1818.
- With the approval of Chile's revolutionary government: NAS, GD233/101/83, William Cochrane statement.
- Alvarez wanted ... Cochrane ... to leave for South America: Cubitt, *Lord Cochrane and the Chilean Navy...,* p49.
- He also feared ... his political enemies would somehow thwart: ibid.
- British government was deeply suspicious ... rescue Napoleon: Thomas, *Cochrane,* p243.
- Cochrane ... snuck across the English Channel: ibid, p244.
- Alvarez ... an army officer: Céspedes and Garreaud, *Gran diccionario de Chile,* Vol. 1, p32.
- *I cannot but say*: NAS, GD233/44/XXIII, Alexander Galloway letter book, Alexander Galloway to José Antonio Alvarez, 9/29/1818.
- "and give the whole experiment": ibid.
- "delay occasioned by": ibid, Alvarez to Galloway, 10/1/1818.
- Lord Cochrane had "withdrawn all the interest": ibid.
- *After serious consultations*: ibid, Alvarez to Galloway, 10/21/1818.
- *I have received your letter of this day*: ibid, Galloway to Alvarez, 10/21/1818.
- "the *Engineer*" ... "the *Mistake.*": *The Journal of Trade and Commerce...,* 9/1/1818, p306.
- "passed both up [and] down the River every vessel": Galloway letter book, Galloway to Lord Cochrane, likely early November 1818.
- "They indeed are nearly broken hearted": ibid, Galloway to Alvarez, 11/16/1818.
- ... *they would have plumed themselves*: ibid.
- "this delay shakes every body's confidence!": ibid.
- "I am quite teazed": ibid, Galloway to Alvarez, 12/2/1818.
- ... *Great objects cannot be obtained*: ibid, Galloway to Alvarez, 12/17/1818.
- Seppings ... Born into a large family in Norfolk: Stephen, *The Dictionary of National Biography,* p1187.
- send young Robert to live with her brother: ibid.
- their house full of adopted relatives: NMM, Packard, "Sir Robert Seppings ... His Family Background," p2.
- Uncle John arranged for his nephew to become an apprentice: ibid, pp2–3.
- "Seppings blocks.": Stephen, op. cit., p1187.
- diagonally brace and truss: ibid, p1188.
- Four years earlier, in 1815, the Admiralty: Greenhill, *Steam & Sail...,* p11.
- A team was assembled: Lloyd, op. cit., pp116–117.
- the completed steamboat had some problems: ibid.
- "very crank,": ibid, p116.
- "most excellent state of preservation.": NMM, ADM/BP/39.B., Robert Seppings to Navy Board, 6/29/1819.
- Robert would receive his knighthood: Stephen, op. cit., p1188.
- Robert got a letter from Admiral Sir Thomas Byam Martin: Seppings Report.

CHAPTER THIRTEEN—HOME FRONT

- the schooner's name being *Peace & Plenty*: *Commercial Advertiser,* 6/8/1819, among others.
- *June 2d. clear weather and smooth sea*: *Niles' Weekly Register,* 6/19/1819.
- She had passed the *Savannah* on June 6th: *Mercantile Advertiser,* 6/19/1819.

– *I have received no Shipping List*: *City Gazette*, 8/17/1819. This "Cork paper" must have been one other than the *Southern Reporter*.
– inaccurate report ... picked up by the Savannah newspapers: *The Georgian*, 8/19/1819; *Columbian Museum*, 8/19/1819.
– Gotham got the word first: *Commercial Advertiser*, 8/17/1819.
– *The steamship Savannah arrived a few days ago*: *The Georgian*, 8/31/1819.
– "not any relationship between them": *Niles' Weekly Register*, 8/28/1819.
– another private letter, received at Charleston from Edinburgh: SCHS, William Moubray Letters (43/2076), Christopher and A. Moubray to William Moubray, 7/2/1819.
– friction evident between the more testy branches of the Anglo-American family: there was still more. "It must be gratifying to the pride of every American, to hear of the safe arrival of the steam ship Savannah," opined the *Baltimore Morning Chronicle*, adding "we wonder what those transcendentally important characters, the Edinburg Reviewers, will say to this." As republished in the *Boston Patriot*, 8/25/1819, among others.
– The Steam Ship Savannah, Capt. Rogers: *Richmond Enquirer*, 8/27/1819.
– *In one of my late rambles*: *Relf's Philadelphia Gazette*, 7/23/1819.
– *The Wonders of the Age*: *Commercial Advertiser*, 7/16/1819, among others.

CHAPTER FOURTEEN — DECISIONS

– "marked attention.": *New London Gazette*, 4/25/1838.
– shipyards, factories and other facilities: *New York Journal of Commerce*, 8/26/1850.
– "resolved to join and exterminate": *Liverpool Mercury*, 7/2/1819.
– "All men are born free;": ibid.
– In Glasgow, a rally of weavers grew so large: ibid.
– "Female Reform Society": *The Public Ledger*, 7/1/1819.
– "revolutionary pike,": *The Morning Post* (London), 7/13/1819.
– claimed "that his political career": *The Traveller*, 7/6/1819.
– *Cap of Liberty*: *The Public Ledger*, 7/1/1819.
– avoided by other rally organizers: ibid.
– could not—by a recent law—be recognized on the flag: SAL, 15th Congress, 1st Session, "An Act to Establish the Flag of the United States," passed 4/4/1818.
– bankruptcies rising: Alison, *Lives of Lord Castlereagh and Sir Charles Stewart...*, Vol. 3, p88.
– widespread problems with debt collections: Picton, *Memorials of Liverpool*, Vol. 1. p406.
– "never before did I witness such distress": *The Traveller*, 7/6/1819.
– the City Bank ... thirty commercial houses ... forced to stop payment: *The British Volunteer*, 7/3/1819.
– In Charleston ... an entire street of shops ... forced to close: *Morning Advertiser* (London), 6/23/1819.
– *However extensive may be the ruin*: ibid, 7/7/1819.
– Among the many who came ... was an American expatriate: Smith, "Origin of Atlantic Steam Navigation," *The Merchants' Magazine and Commercial Review* (New York), XVI, February 1847, pp172–177.
– this 38-year-old lawyer had come to Britain: Pond, *Junius Smith...*, pp87–88.
– about 100 men gathered at the parish church of St. Peter: *Billinge's Liverpool Advertiser*, 7/19/1819, among others.

- unsheathed their swords: ibid.
- Some were wearing long robes, others leopard skins: ibid.
- The onlookers … began to follow these men: ibid.
- Orangemen, never before seen in Liverpool: ibid.
- … *My Lords see no Sufficient grounds*: TNA, T 11/62, p 115, Stephen R. Lushington to Isaac Low & Co., 7/2/1819.
- Commissioners of Customs in London duly ordered: TNA, CUST28/35, 7/3/1819.
- a lighter came alongside the steamship: *SSSLB.*
- "We may safely take upon ourselves to say,": *Cheshire Chronicle*, 7/30/1819.
- … We had some conversation: ibid.
- Steve would recount how the British authorities kept a close eye: *New York Journal of Commerce*, 8/26/1850.
- the possibility of a steam-powered rescue of Napoleon: the British government had ample reason to take this threat seriously. By crossing the Atlantic, the *Savannah* had done something many observers previously thought chimerical; she had outrun one of the fastest revenue cruisers in the British fleet; she had a confusing mix of rumors swirling around her, which easily could have been part of a deception; Captain Rogers had stated his intention of going to Havre, where Joseph Bonaparte (a steamboat investor himself) had recently shipped a valuable diamond; the South American volunteers would be departing shortly for the South Atlantic; and the diversionary threat of a domestic uprising in Britain itself appeared imminent. Still more suspicions might have been raised if it had been learned that Captain Rogers was familiar with Bordentown, home of the exiled Joseph, as well as the fact that Napoleonic exiles Marshal Grouchy and General Clausel had ridden on the steamboat *Eagle* while Rogers was her captain (see various Baltimore newspapers, 5/13/1816).
- Moses received a Bill of Health: LS, Helsingør Health/Quarantine Commission, Medical Reports, 1819, Journal #1200, Steamship *Savannah*, 8/9/1819 (hereafter, "Medical Report, Steamship *Savannah*").
- James Bruce and John Smith: *SSSLB.*
- cleared the *Savannah* for departure: *Billinge's Liverpool Advertiser*, 7/26/1819.
- … if any seaman or mariner: "An Act for the Government and Regulation of Seamen in the Merchant's Service," op. cit., passed 7/20/1790.
- legal right to dock Smith three days' pay: ibid.
- Sir Charles Wolseley had been ceremoniously "elected": *Morning Advertiser*, 7/15/1819.
- Sir Wolseley had been indicted for sedition: *The Morning Post*, 7/16/1819.
- Further afield, in Montgomeryshire, Wales, a protest: ibid.
- … The most alarming circumstance: ibid, 7/17/1819.
- … *an important blow will be aimed*: ibid, 7/19/1819.
- Scottish steamboat *Stirling* … boiler exploded: *The Star* (London), 7/12/1819.
- steam packet *Talbot* … had caught fire: *Morning Advertiser*, 7/19/1819.
- steam packet proprietors … advertise how "completely safe": *The Belfast News Letter*, 7/13/1819.
- "in compliance with the general wish": *The Freeman's Journal*, 7/21/1819.
- sailing packet competitors … warn passengers: *The Belfast News Letter*, 8/20/1819.
- His name was Daniel Barnett: see Chapter 15 footnote for supporting evidence.
- their confectionary business on Liver Street: Gore, *Gore's Directory of Liverpool…*, 1818 and 1821.
- "flying clouds.": *SSSLB.*

- Nearby, one of the Mersey steamboats: *Mercantile Advertiser* (New York), 9/10/1819.
- *Waterloo* took the lead: *Cheshire Chronicle*, 7/30/1819.
- Somerset House, on the Strand: Coad, *The Royal Dockyards...*, pp44–45.
- Robert recounted what he had learned: TNA, ADM 106/2689, Navy Board Meeting Minutes, 7/16/1819 ("Seppings Report").
- "1,000 bushels of Coals and 4 chord of wood": ibid. As previously noted, other post-voyage sources claim differing amounts of coal and wood fuel for the transatlantic voyage. Seppings is the only known contemporary source who specifies the amounts of fuel carried by the *Savannah* for the crossing.
- "the greatest rate of going, was six miles per hour": ibid. It is interesting to recall that HMRC *Kite*, sailing at a speed of 10 knots, was reported to have been unable to catch up to the *Savannah*. It is also intriguing to note that for whatever reason, Steve did not record the *Savannah's* steam-powered speed in the logbook on the day of that chase.
- *... It is clear*: Seppings Report. Commas added to improve readability.
- *The Statesman ... could not avoid being* "stamped": Gilmartin, *Print Politics*, p84.
- *On taking a review*: The Statesman, 7/15/1819. "Valerius" went on to describe how France helped the U.S. win its independence, which led to American friendship toward its newfound ally, followed by the toppling of the monarchies in both France and Spain. The underlying message of "Valerius" was unmistakable: the ideals of the United States represented a direct threat to the established order of Europe.

CHAPTER FIFTEEN — HELSINGØR

- smothered in a dense fog: *SSSLB*.
- Many captains—Americans in particular—did not think this toll was fair: Conway, *A Personal Narrative of a Journey...*, p295.
- maintaining buoys, beacons: Thaarup and Martensen, *The latest revis'd Sound-Tariff...*, p39.
- asked Moses a series of questions: NYPL, Logbook of the Brig *Boxer*, 4/21/1818. This American merchant vessel traveled from New York to Hamburg to St. Petersburg in 1818. Her captain, James Copland, kept a detailed record of his experiences, including what transpired at his stop at Helsingør. Pilots and water taxi-men knew what questions to ask regarding quarantine. It stands to reason that given the similarities between the *Boxer* and the *Savannah*, they would have been treated in similar ways.
- instructed Captain Rogers to fly a green flag: Medical Report, Steamship *Savannah*. See also Schultz, *Ordonnance, touchant la quarantaine établie...*, pp12–13.
- "neck at the sands": Pedersen, *Elsinore: a Guide...*, p4.
- "as still as a millpond.": Conway, op. cit., p290.
- shallow, transparent waters of the Sound: Thomson, *Travels in Sweden...*, p303.
- about 3 miles distant ... coast of Sweden: Pinkerton, *A General Collection ... Interesting Voyages...*, p293.
- deepest part of the Sound ... next to the Swedish coast: Thomson, op. cit., p303.
- safest place to transit ... shallower Danish side: Pinkerton, op. cit., p293.
- Kronborg was also a tourist attraction: Conway, op. cit., p295.
- this town of some 5,000 people: Pinkerton, op. cit., p293.
- "Gin shop.": Jones, *Travels in Norway, Sweden, Finland, Russia...*, p56.
- over 12,000 vessels having transited the Sound: Thaarup and Martensen, op. cit., p38.

- a small sailboat came alongside the *Savannah*: LS, Helsingør Health Commission/Quarantine Commission, Letters Received/Misc. Correspondence, 1819, Journal #1143, J. Bakke and Brother to Commission, 8/10/1819.
- If Moses experienced what other American captains did: NYPL, Logbook of the Brig *Boxer*, 4/21/1818. Captain Copland also had a bill of health from a European port—Hamburg—but lacked one from his port of departure, New York. As a result, the *Boxer* was placed in quarantine.
- representative ... probably a doctor: ibid.
- take the document ... with a pair of tongs: ibid.
- not have a bill of health issued by a Danish or Russian consul: ibid.
- Russia's agent ... "must personally convince himself": Rordansz, *European Commerce, or, Complete Mercantile Guide...*, p106.
- ... vessels on their arrival at the Sound: *The Georgian*, 3/16/1819.
- along with the two ferryboat men: J. Bakke and Brother to Commission, 8/10/1819.
- member of the Commission ... named Möller: Medical Report, Steamship *Savannah*.
- *Savannah* "is subjected to a Quarantine": ibid.
- commenced at 1:30: ibid.
- For the extras on board ... the Sound pilot: while the Sound Pilot is not discussed further in the surviving Royal Quarantine Commission manuscripts or the *SSSLB*, it stands to reason that he too fell under the quarantine order for the *Savannah*.
- the Bakke brothers, who wanted compensation for the time lost: J. Bakke and Brother to Commission, 8/10/1819.
- "Compensation they can get least of all": ibid.
- released from quarantine at 2 o'clock on Friday afternoon, August 13th.: *SSSLB*.
- pay the steamship's Sound toll: DNA, Register of Sound Dues, Tariff Journals, #1819–1B–2, entry #671, 8/13/1819.
- free to disembark ... So was Daniel Barnett: that Barnett was the passenger on the *Savannah* from Liverpool to Helsingør is based upon an accumulation of evidence. The *SSSLB* makes no mention of passengers during any of the steamship's voyages, this information not being a normal part of a vessel's log. The evidence rests with a collection of manuscripts, taken together with additional sources:
  1) The *Savannah*'s Medical Report, previously cited, states that upon arrival at Helsingør, she had a crew of "18 in all besides the Captain," making 19 in total, plus "the one Passenger taken on board in England."
  2) Statens Sjöhistoriska Museum, Stockholm Registry of Arrivals, 8/23/1819, reproduced in NARA, RG59, Despatches from U.S. Consuls in Stockholm, American Ships arrived ... Stockholm ... June 1819: the entry for the *Savannah* states she arrived at Stockholm with a crew of 19 (which matches the Helsingør Medical Report) and no passengers. Therefore, the passenger on board from Liverpool to Helsingør had left the steamship before it reached Stockholm.
  3) Moses paid the *Savannah*'s Sound toll on 8/13/1819. No other vessel from Liverpool paid its toll on that day, or 8/14. (One British vessel from Liverpool apparently passed on 8/12, heading for St. Petersburg, but beyond the timing discrepancy, it begs the question as to how likely it was that a British merchantman would need a pilot to get from Liverpool to Helsingør.)
  4) *SSSLB*: Steve recorded the *Savannah* was released from quarantine at 2 P.M. on 8/13/1819. The passenger on board could not leave the steamship until then; this would place him ashore by mid-afternoon.
  5) LS, Helsingør, City Bailiff's Archive, Visa Journal, 1818–1819, #G–194: on

8/14/1819, Daniel Barnett registered his visa with the Helsingør authorities. The visa had been issued by the "waterscout," a person who worked in the harbor organizing crews and dealing with people matters. Barnett's visa journal entry stated that he was English, a pilot, apparently 45 years old with a "peg leg" (*træben*, in Danish), that he had arrived from Liverpool and that his destination was England. There is no other person listed in the Visa Journal as having arrived from Liverpool during the time the *Savannah* was at Helsingør.
6) *Gore's Directory of Liverpool...*, 1818 and 1821: both list Daniel Barnett as mariner and confectioner. In conjunction with the preceding evidence, the probability that this Barnett is the same as the one at Helsingør appears extremely high.
7) Sea captains regularly hired pilots to guide them through unfamiliar waters. This was certainly true for the Skagerrak and Kattegat. Given the care Moses took to ensure a safe passage for the *Savannah*, it stands to reason that Daniel Barnett served as the steamship's guide and "passenger" from Liverpool to Helsingør.
– Reformers ... at St. Peter's Field ... attacked: Turner, *The Age of Unease...*, p161.
– coastal Denmark ... cattle and sheep: Conway, op. cit., p298.
– "We passed on our arrival at Copenhagen": private manuscript, Robert Graham Letters Diary (hereafter, "Robert Graham Diary"), 8/17/1819.

CHAPTER SIXTEEN—LAND OF THE GOTHS AND VANDALS

– "get the steam up and set the wheels to going": *SSSLB* (literally "got the steam up").
– cottages ... painted either red or yellow: James, *Journal of a Tour in ... Sweden, Russia...*, p187.
– New Romantics ... grown up in the countryside: Gustafson, *A History of Swedish Literature*, p154.
– Per Henrik Ling: Stomberg, *A History of Sweden*, pp622–623.
– Gustavian promotion of pleasure: ibid, pp624, 638.
– hard-nosed common sense and rugged independence: Spongberg, *The Philosophy of Erik Gustaf Geijer*, p1.
– New Romantics ... vigorously supported his programs: ibid, p4, and Gustafson, op. cit., p156.
– King "of the Goths and of the Vandals": Palmer, *Bernadotte: Napoleon's Marshall, Sweden's King*, p227.
– Tied up to the quay, and anchored all around the Saltsjön: Thomson, *Travels in Sweden...*, pp89–90.
– Moses was told to take his creation into the Strömmen: Stockholm Stadsarkiv, Journal övfer inkommande Fartyg år 1819, Fartygsjournaler segel och ångfartyg från utrikes ort 1815–1833 d2 AA vol. 1. In all likelihood, King Karl Johan himself instructed the port authorities to anchor the *Savannah* in the Strömmen, so that he could easily see it from the Royal Palace.
– water taxis ... rowed almost exclusively by women: Thomson, op. cit., p90.
– register the steamship's arrival: Journal övfer inkommande Fartyg år 1819, op. cit.; also Stockholm Registry of Arrivals.
– Born in Baltimore in 1786: Dunham, *The Diplomatic Career of Christopher Hughes*, p2.
– Hughes was the son of an Irish immigrant father: ibid, p4.
– Christopher ... study at the College of New Jersey: ibid, p5.
– Hughes ... receive his degree in 1805: ibid, p6.
– Christopher and Laura ... Married in 1811: ibid, p7.

- In February 1814, the President nominated him: ibid, p11.
- Adams took responsibility for instructing Hughes: ibid, p19.
- "Is this your <u>best</u>, Sir?": ibid.
- "lively and good-humored, smart at a repartee": ibid, p16.
- Hughes ... to serve as chargé d'affaires to Sweden: ibid, p40.
- *I take great pleasure in affording this letter*: PUL, Department of Rare Books and Special Collections, Rush Family Papers, Richard Rush to Christopher Hughes, 6/30/1819. In these letter books, Rush signed his name in shorthand as "R.R."
- Moses told ... Hughes that he had additional letters: NARA, RG59, Despatches from U.S. Ministers to Sweden and Norway, 1813–1906, Christopher Hughes to JQA, 8/30/1819.
- "the circumstances of the company": ibid.
- "provided suitable terms could be agreed on": ibid.
- Swedes chose to join the Continental System: Barton, *Bernadotte, Prince and King...*, p12.
- Bernadotte suggested to the French minister: ibid, pp26–27.
- law restricting the press: Vogel-Rödin, *The Bernadottes...*, p226.
- Bernadotte was able to convince some units ... defect, or desert: Palmer, op. cit., p206.
- Moses also presented his other letters of introduction: while these letters do not appear to have survived, it stands to reason, given Christopher Hughes' mention of them in his dispatch, that Moses used them to gain meetings with Counts Wetterstedt and Cederström.
- interim Swedish foreign minister: Sweden's foreign minister at the time was Lars von Engeström, but due to illness, he had been temporarily replaced by Count Wetterstedt, who served as foreign minister *ad interim* while the *Savannah* was at Stockholm.
- Cederström ... assigned to serve in the French Navy: Tornquist, *The Naval Campaigns of Count de Grasse...*, p149.
- Ensign Cederström found himself a part of the French fleet: ibid, and Benson, *Sweden and the American Revolution*, p96.
- what the Admiral did not have was a report from the Baron: see Klinkowström Report, which did not arrive in Sweden until November 1819.
- But there was nothing: *Dagligt Allehanda, Inrikes Tidningar, Stockholms Post-Tidningar* and *Stockholms Posten* contain no references to the *Savannah* for the period she was at Stockholm. The only known article about the *Savannah* in a Stockholm newspaper was published well after she had left, in the *Stockholms Posten* of 11/4/1819, when she was about to exit the Baltic Sea on her way home.
- observant secret police: Palmer, op. cit., pp225–226.
- Any newspaper that dared to print a story: Oakley, *A Short History of Sweden*, p184.
- "superb vessel,": Nationall Archief (Netherlands), Legatie Zweden en Noorwegen 1814–1864, Salomon Dedel dispatch No. 58, 8/27/1819.
- "Captain Rogers has the air": ibid.
- Count Wetterstedt ... penned a letter to Christopher Hughes: NARA, RG84, Records of the Foreign Service Posts of the Department of State, Sweden, Count Wetterstedt to Christopher Hughes, 8/27/1819.
- "do not leave him a vacant moment": ibid, and Hughes to JQA, 8/30/1819.
- rowed by 22 oarsmen: Slottsarkivet (Palace Archives), Oscar I Hovets Stadsräkenskaper 1819 (Court Accounts), entry #1092, service gratuity and receipt. Hughes, in his dispatch to JQA, said there were 20 oarsmen.
- rowed by 6 oarsmen: ibid.

- artillery on shore boomed a salute: ibid, entry #1093, for gratuity payment to the Royal Svea Artillery Regiment. Royal gratuities to oarsmen and artillerymen on such occasions were customary.
- *I received him at the side*: Hughes to JQA, 8/30/1819.
- "ten or twelve Counts": ibid.
- Bernadotte ... put one of the New Romantics ... in charge: Spongberg, op. cit., p4.
- "The Prince was much pleased": Hughes to JQA, 8/30/1819.
- strict orders had been given: ibid.
- "Certainly," he replied: ibid.
- "Well, Mr. Hughes, that is a Prince?": ibid.
- Lowenhielm and Skjöldebrand ... among His Majesty's closest advisors: Barton, op. cit., p174.
- on his left pinky finger he wore a ring: Graham, *Memoir of General Lord Lynedoch*, p190.
- Lord Lynedoch ("Líne-dock"): this is the pronunciation used by his lineal descendants.
- he married the beautiful Mary Schaw: ibid, p5.
- French customs officers refused: Delavoye, *Life of Thomas Graham...*, p29.
- a group of National Guards and Volunteers ... came along: ibid, and Aspinall-Oglander, *Freshly Remembered; the Story of Thomas Graham...*, p36.
- ... *At first I attempted*: Aspinall-Oglander, op. cit., p36.
- "I hope never again": ibid.
- He placed it upon the little finger of his left hand: Graham, op. cit., p190.
- Graham ... grabbing the musket of a fallen soldier: ibid, p39.
- he was compelled to return home: ibid, pp121–122.
- Graham covering his left flank, and General Hill guarding his right: ibid, p128.
- Lynedoch ... clearly appealed to his American hosts: Hughes to JQA, 8/30/1819. Hughes described Lord Lynedoch as "a very interesting, unaffected man."
- *Savannah* ... "a remarkably fine vessel": Robert Graham Diary, 8/28/1819.
- Hughes ... "uncommonly civil, as was the Captain.": ibid.
- "he was much pleased with the Ship.": Hughes to JQA, 8/30/1819.
- "I do not be much surprised": Robert Graham Diary, 8/28/1819.
- threatening to break off relations with Sweden: NARA, RG59, Despatches ... Ministers ... Sweden..., Hughes to JQA, 5/29/1819.
- "a Dish or two + wines": Hughes to JQA, 8/30/1819.
- Lord Lynedoch and Robert Graham paid a visit: ibid, and Robert Graham Diary, 8/30/1819.
- ... We have now in our port: Hughes to JQA, 8/30/1819.
- on the *Savannah*'s deck ... were Christopher and Laura Hughes: *SSSLB*.
- Austria's minister to Sweden: Robert Graham Diary, 9/1/1819.
- Ficquelmont ... had written a brief dispatch: Austrian State Archive, Haus-, Hof-, und Staatsarchiv, 08: Staatenabteilungen, Schweden, report No. 27, 8/31/1819.
- Moreno y Daoiz, who also had written: Archivo Histórico Nacional (Spain), Ministerio de Estado y sus embajadas y consulados, Suecia: legajo 6064 (1818–1820), No. 51, 8/31/1819.
- Absent were the Danish and British ministers: Robert Graham Diary, 9/1/1819.
- as well as Count Wetterstedt: RA, Hovrättsrådet: Clas Göran Palmgrens Samling, Vol. 1, Hughes to Wetterstedt, No. 1030, 9/2/1819.
- "The day was not favorable for sailing": Robert Graham Diary, 9/1/1819.
- offered $100,000 worth of hemp and iron: *Hunt's Merchants' Magazine...*, 12/1850, account of A. Thomas, fireman.
- "the offer was not accepted": ibid.

- it would have triggered a $100 fine: *SAL*, 7th Congress, 2nd Session, "An Act supplementary to the 'act concerning Consuls and Vice-Consuls, and for the further protection of American Seamen'," passed 2/28/1803.
- "all duties and imposts whatever": RA, Hovrättsrådet: Clas Göran Palmgrens Samling, Vol. 1, Hughes to Wetterstedt, No. 1029, 9/2/1819.
- "look like a sort of advantage": ibid, No. 1030, 9/2/1819.
- *The King orders me*: NARA, RG84, Records of the Foreign Service Posts of the Department of State, Sweden, Wetterstedt to Hughes, 9/2/1819.
- brought onto the ship was the luggage: Robert Graham Diary, 9/4/1819.
- two dozen bottles of Claret: NLS, MSS 16096A, Lord Lynedoch Diary (hereafter, "Lord Lynedoch Diary"), 9/5/1819.
- *We embarked*: Robert Graham Diary, 9/6/1819.
- There, the pilot disembarked: *SSSLB*.
- paddlewheels ... detached ... took only 12 minutes: Lord Lynedoch Diary, 9/5/1819.
- "a capital collection of stores": Robert Graham Diary, 9/6/1819.
- ... *We have put on our wheels again*: ibid, 9/7/1819.
- the procedure took only 10 minutes: Lord Lynedoch Diary, 9/7/1819.
- "I blame no man born in the United States for being proud": Stevens Rogers Statement.
- The waters there were incredibly transparent: Johnston, *Travels through part of the Russian Empire...*, p82.
- Tolboukin Light, which sat upon a small island: Whittle and Laurie, *A Chart of the Gulf of Finland...*, 1818.
- This request went unanswered: Robert Graham Diary, 9/9/1819.
- said to contain some 3,000 guns: LOC, Philander Chase, Journal on board the USS *Guerriere* (transcript), p42; and George W. Campbell Papers, Diary – Mission to Russia, 9/17/1818.
- a small boat left the guardship: Robert Graham Diary, 9/9/1819.
- keen the Russians were to see the Danish bill of health: ibid.
- incredibly strict rules the Russian authorities had regarding fire: ibid.
- Yet they could hardly eat it in peace: ibid.
- personal appearances at four different offices: ibid.
- Möller ... put his own personal carriage: ibid.

CHAPTER SEVENTEEN — ALL THE RUSSIAS

- two long piers jutting out ... Oranienbaum: Whittle and Laurie, *A Chart of the Gulf of Finland...*, 1818.
- Peterhof ... the royal family's yachts were kept: Hunter, *Russia: being a Complete Picture...*, p44.
- Baird ... establishing iron foundries and a machine works: Cross, *By the Banks of the Neva*, p260.
- "like at Baird's works.": Bartlett, *Human Capital...*, p179.
- Baird ... seen detailed drawings ... Fulton's early steamboats: White, "A Russian Sketches Philadelphia," *Pennsylvania Magazine of History and Biography*, Vol. 75, No. 1 (Jan. 1951), p19. Others have wondered about the similarity of Baird's steam engine layout to Fulton's—see Svin'in and Yarmolinsky, *Picturesque United States...*, p11.
- Svin'in had tried to sabotage Fulton's negotiations: American Minister Adams, with due discretion (i.e., without directly naming Svin'in), reported the attempt to Fulton in a letter dated 12/31/1813 (see AFP, JQA Papers).

- At only 56 tons ... *Elizaveta*: Gardiner (editor), *The Advent of Steam...*, p13.
- she still could steam ... one-half the usual sailing time: the passage by sail was usually 4–8 hours. See Johnston, *Travels Through Part of the Russian Empire...*, p91; and "Surgeon in the British Navy," *A Voyage to St. Petersburg...*, p35.
- could steam ... in 2 or 3 hours: Jones, *Travels in Norway, Sweden...*, p322.
- had tea with owner Charles Baird: Robert Graham Diary, 9/9/1819.
- Grahams ... to a hotel along the Moika Canal: Lord Lynedoch Diary, 9/10/1819.
- attended the procession of the Blessed Virgin: ibid.
- Empress Elizaveta herself had been at Oranienbaum: Mikhailovich (editor), *L'impératrice Élisabeth, épouse d'Alexandre Ier...*, Vol. III, pp101–102.
- *... The Empress had received him most graciously*: Robert Graham Diary, 9/12/1819.
- sanction for the steamship to proceed: Johnston (op. cit., p90) noted that even vessels arriving at Kronstadt in ballast (as the *Savannah* had) took time to clear the customs process.
- appearance of an imperial flag: this was (and remains) standard procedure when a monarch is in residence. Wrote G.W. Campbell in his diary on 9/15/1819: "The Emperor arrived last night ... at the Palace," implying common knowledge of Alexander's presence was not known until that day.
- "We have ... enemies": Bergquist, *Russian-American Relations...*, p46.
- Massachusetts Peace Society had sent a gift shipment of books: "My endeavors to promote peace and good will among the nations are already known," wrote Alexander in reply, "and the power and influence which Almighty God has committed to me, shall ever be employed, I trust, in striving to secure to the nations the blessings of that peace which they now enjoy." See *Star of Freedom*, 11/5/1817; also, Gibbon, *Memoirs of the Public Character and Life of Alexander the First...*, p185.
- American Academy of Fine Arts ... made him an honorary member: LOC, George W. Campbell Papers, Alexander Robertson to G.W. Campbell, 7/18/1819.
- Alexander ... banned the slitting of nostrils: Saunders, *Russia in the Age of Reaction and Reform...*, p73.
- founding of a society for prison reform: ibid, p74.
- allowing serfs to buy their freedom, as well as land: Gooding, *Rulers and Subjects: Government and People in Russia...*, p30.
- Enclosed with it was a letter: *Scientific American*, Vol. 10, Issue 5, 10/14/1854.
- samovar ... a remembrance, neatly inscribed: According to Lord Lynedoch's little red diary, the kettle cost him 585 rubles, or ~$439, making it an incredibly generous gift.
- The remarkable steam frigate Savannah: *Russian Invalid or Military Journal*, 9/4/1819. This date, as well as others from Russian sources, is based upon the Julian calendar, which Russia still used.
- The *Northern Post* ... repeated news of the *Savannah*'s arrival: *Northern Post*, 9/6/1819.
- the foreigner turned in the visa issued at Kronstadt: "Surgeon...," op. cit., p59.
- unable to produce their papers ... could easily end up in jail: ibid.
- a spectacular panorama of the city: in addition to numerous contemporary written descriptions, there is the *Panorama of Petersburg in 1820*, painted by Angelo Toselli.
- the most beautiful city in ... quite possibly the world: James, *Journal of a Tour...*, p395.
- "the Queen of the North.": "Surgeon...," op. cit., p36.
- "St. Petersburg is not Russia": Granville, *St. Petersburgh...*, Vol. 1, p486.
- *One peculiar advantage of the circles*: Hunter, *Russia: being a Complete Picture...*, p21.
- boys employed by shopkeepers to corral new customers: Johnston, op. cit., pp104–105.

- many French fashion shops: "Surgeon...," op. cit., p41.
- ever-vigilant police: Granville, op. cit., Vol. II, p459.
- *They are all clad alike*: Johnston, op. cit., pp153–154.
- one nobleman was purported to control over 100,000: James, op. cit., p424.
- "constructed in an absolutely new way": RSNA, Fond 166, Inventory 1, file 3524, Dispatch No. 2987, Count Lieven to Marquis de Traversé, 7/2/1819.
- Family tradition has it ... George adopted the middle name Washington: Looney and Woodward, *Princetonians...*, p341.
- primary advocate of the Madison administration: Jordan, *George Washington Campbell of Tennessee...*, p113.
- Campbell resigned due to illness: ibid, p130.
- they shared lodgings in the capital: Saul, *Distant Friends: the United States and Russia...*, pp86–87.
- Adams ... plan to appoint Campbell ... not at all pleased: Jordan, op. cit., p140.
- "The President is very much and very justly blamed": HSP, Deborah Logan Diary, 5/11/1818.
- "nothing but the hope of being serviceable": LOC, Campbell Papers, manuscript page, while serving as Minister to Russia, undated.
- both he and his wife being seasick: ibid, G.W. Campbell Diary, July-September 1818 (hereafter, "GWC Diary").
- Harriot gave birth ... third son: ibid, Campbell family births page.
- present his diplomatic credentials to Alexander: Saul, op. cit., p87.
- "It did not appear at all alarming": GWC Diary, 4/17/1819.
- "violent fever": ibid, 4/10/1819.
- "possessing sensibility in a degree too tender": ibid, 4/12/1819.
- "resembles that which carried off": ibid, 4/14/1819.
- "attend + apply every remedy,": ibid, 4/15/1819.
- "The grim-messenger of death": ibid, 4/17/1819.
- a month after Elizabeth's death, Campbell wrote separately: Jordan, op. cit., p154.
- Dawn brought a heavy gale and downpour from the south: *SSSLB*.
- cradle the vessel in ... *camels*: James, op. cit., p115.
- The *corps diplomatique* was given a prominent position: Robert Graham Diary, 9/17/1819.
- *girding*: LOC, Philander Chase, op. cit., p62.
- noble ladies ... smile that was "black as coal.": Anschel (editor), *The American Image of Russia...*, p68.
- Alexander appeared, escorting the aged Empress Mother: Robert Graham Diary, 9/17/1819.
- ... *Alexander ... having sat down between us*: Alexandra Feodorovna (Pope-Hennessy, translator), *A Czarina's Story...*, pp44–45.
- the Emperor had begun to receive secret letters: NJHS, SFP, John Stevens to Emperor Alexander, 9/12/1817 and 6/18/1818, among other related papers. Stevens also included, within these letters, proposals to build railroads and produce elongated cannon shells in Russia.
- George W. Campbell invited Moses: GWC Diary, 9/5/1819. Campbell wrote "This day Capt Rogers + other gentlemen dined with me—"
- no one was allowed to act as the courier of foreign letters: Skipton and Michalove, *Postal Censorship in Imperial Russia*, p21.
- Russian government could and did open any mail: Robert Graham Diary; he mentions this well-known fact repeatedly during his time in St. Petersburg.
- Articles deemed not in the country's interest were cut out: Skipton and Michalove, op. cit., p141.
- some publications simply were not allowed into the country: ibid.

- prominent families ... guard their words: Johnston, op. cit., p165.
- clear to Campbell that despite all the talk of reform: Saul, op. cit., p151.
- rubber stamped by members beholden to the Emperor: Jones, op. cit., p378.
- intended to bolster the Spanish monarch's navy: Bartley, *Imperial Russia and the Struggle for Latin American Independence...*, p124.
- Lord Lynedoch arrived at the Winter Palace: Lord Lynedoch Diary, 9/16/1819.
- remembered as among the most exciting ... introduced to the Emperor: *New York Journal of Commerce*, 8/26/1850—the source for this article was Stevens Rogers; also Braynard, op. cit., p174, sourcing Amy Rowe Sedgewick Huppuch to Frank Braynard, 5/19/1958—the writer of this letter was the great-grand-daughter of Stevens Rogers, who reported her great-aunt Sarah (Steve's daughter) as having recounted the imperial meeting.
- carve out an exception ... it had the legal right to do so: Haywood, *The Beginnings of Railway Development in Russia...*, p20.
- foreign ministers of the Netherlands, the Kingdom of Hanover: *SSSLB*, and GWC Diary, 9/18/1819.
- Englishman by the name of John Farey: Cleland, *The Rise and Progress of the City of Glasgow...*, pp241–242.
- Farey ... a first-class illustrator: Woolrich, "John Farey Jr. (1791–1851): Engineer and Polymath," *History of Technology*, Vol. 19 (1997), pp111–142.
- "This is a complete ship in all her rigging": Clelend, op. cit., p242.
- "The Savannah is a fine vessel,": GWC Diary, 9/18/1819.
- "aroused the curiosity": *Russian Invalid or Military Journal*, 10/14/1819.
- " ... which is quite a considerable distance": ibid. A *verst* equals about 2/3rds of a mile.
- Traversé, "Lord High Admiral": *SSSLB*.
- Born on the French island colony of Martinique: Taillemite, *Dictionnaire des Marins Français*, p324.
- Joining the French Navy as a midshipman in 1765: ibid.
- Traversé and *L'Aigrette* skimmed up and down: Shea (editor), *The Operations of the French Fleet under the Count de Grasse...*, p154.
- reportedly first caught sight of the approaching Royal Navy: Taillemite, op. cit., p324.
- eight warships sold ... barely made it to Spain: Bartley, op. cit., p124.
- Baltic Sea fleet ... poorly maintained: Barratt, *Russia in Pacific Waters*, p178; also, see GWC Diary, 9/17/1818, among other contemporary accounts.
- planned to sail as close to the South Pole as possible: Captain Bellingshausen is generally credited as the first explorer to definitively sight the continent of Antarctica.
- Marquis ... special report ... *Savannah*: RSNA, Fond 166, Inventory 1, file 3524, dated 9/14/1819.
- There would be no offer made: ibid.
- Among them was the English engineer John Farey: Cleland, op. cit., p242.
- *Savannah* ... 6¼ miles per hour: ibid.
- "fine view of Cronstadt.": Lord Lynedoch Diary, 9/23/1819.
- Oranienbaum ... "a good deal neglected.": ibid.
- Campbell ... penning a two-page letter for Moses: NARA, RG59, Despatches from U.S. Ministers to Russia, 1808–1906, G.W. Campbell to JQA, 9/25/1819.
- packages were delivered to the ship: Lord Lynedoch Diary, 9/24/1819; Stevens Rogers Statement, among other accounts of the snuff-boxes. "Bought two Tooled snuff boxes for the mates of the Savannah," Lynedoch wrote in his diary. Steve's snuffbox contains an inscription, inside the top, stating it was presented to him by Lord Lynedoch on October 10th, 1819. This was impossible, since that

was the day the *Savannah* departed for home, and Lord Lynedoch and Robert Graham already had left St. Petersburg for the Russian interior some two weeks prior. Either Lord Lynedoch picked an arbitrary date to be engraved inside the snuff box, or Steve had the inscription done at a later date. Mr. Blackman's snuff box has never been identified.

– larboard anchor dropped, in about 5 fathoms: *SSSLB*, along with Whittle and Laurie map.
– *Savannah*'s destination was Boston: *St. Petersburg Gazette*, 10/24/1819.

CHAPTER EIGHTEEN—BACK

– the *Savannah* reached the western shores of the Baltic: *SSSLB*.
– drop anchor, next to a stone fort: *Dagen*, 10/21/1819.
– "cannot praise enough her wonderful construction.": ibid.
– Several hundred Copenhagen merchants already had gone bankrupt: Oakley, *A Short History of Denmark*, p167, and Jacobsen, *An Outline History of Denmark*, p93.
– steamship ... transiting in ballast: DNA, Register of Sound Dues, Tariff Journals, #1819–1B–2, 10/17/1819.
– Arendal's ... rocky islands: Butenschøn, *Travellers Discovering Norway...*, p51.
– "a great part of Arendal's inhabitants": *Christiansands Addresse-Contoirs Efterretninger*, 11/3/1819.
– boat ... its timbers ... held together with wooden pegs: Rogers, op. cit., p166. This particular construction feature was characteristic of sjektes built in eastern Norway, where Arendal is located.
– The Norwegians called ... a *sjekte*: no U.S. custom house documents for this boat appear to have survived. This description of a sjekte is based upon information provided by the Aust-Agder Kulturhistoriske Senter in Arendal, Norway.
– sjekte ... The crew hauled it aboard: *SSSLB*.
– "We have only to regret": *Christiansands Addresse-Contoirs Efterretninger*, 11/3/1819.

CHAPTER NINETEEN—TAKING UP THE OFFER

– "in fine style.": *The Courier* (Charleston), 12/3/1819.
– the death of shareholder Charles Howard: *Columbian Museum*, 7/3/1819.
– Sarah Rogers ... also had died: Rogers, op. cit., p248.
– busily reporting on William Scarbrough's efforts: *The Courier*, 6/7/1819; *The Georgian*, 6/15/1819.
– Pott & McKinne had *stopped payment*: GHS, Chatham County Superior Court Records, Case Files, various files, including 4204, 4212, 4283, 4287 and 4374. With one exception (5/31/1819), all the other refusals to pay by Pott & McKinne were in the month of June. There could be any number of reasons why a merchant would refuse to pay off one or even several promissory notes, but once they failed to pay off any notes presented to them, they were considered to have "stopped payment," and gone bankrupt, at least temporarily.
– William Scarbrough ... who being duly sworn: GHS, Chatham County Superior Court Records, Folder 4332, Affidavit of William Scarbrough before Judge John MacPherson Berrien, 6/14/1819.
– The Copartnership heretofore carried on by: *Columbian Museum*, 8/14/1819.
– Robert Isaac, back from Liverpool: *The Georgian*, 11/12/1819.

- Isaac's own world ... having problems collecting and paying off debts: GHS, Chatham County Superior Court, Civil Minutes, Book Vol. 10, 1818–1822, index.
- a new lawsuit brought by William Jay: NARA, RG21, U.S. Circuit Court, District of Georgia, Savannah, Mixed Case Files, *Jay vs. Scarbrough*, 11/1/1819.
- The gifts ... arrangements made for their distribution: besides the china and the sjekte, the only verified item brought back is a set of iron furniture, gifted by the Emperor Alexander (and currently owned by several museums in Savannah). Other gifts were reported to have been given to Moses while the *Savannah* was in Europe, but their whereabouts are unknown.
- "neither a screw, bolt, or rope-yarn parted": *Columbian Museum*, 12/1/1819.
- trip home ... leading news as far away as New York City: *Commercial Advertiser*, 12/9/1819.
- This was the President's House: while there were a number of names for what is known currently as the White House, this appears to have been the most common one in use at that time.
- 6 o'clock that evening ... near freezing: MHS, AFP, JQA Papers, Weather Record, Washington DC, December 1819.
- temperatures that reached 50° by noon: ibid.
- George Town Importing ... Walter Smith: NARA, RG21, Records of the U. S. District Court – District of Columbia, Case Papers, June term 1820, *Walter Smith vs. The President of the Savannah Steam Ship Company* (hereafter, "*Smith vs. P/SSSC*"), 1/24/1820.
- Moses asked him to lay out $67.25: ibid.
- the total custom house charges came to $45.68: ibid.
- Moses duly paid with a promissory note: ibid. Smith's firm recorded this same bill amount a few days later, which represented their paying off the promissory note that Moses had given to the Custom House.
- ... She encountered a very heavy gale: *Daily National Intelligencer*, 12/18/1819.
- Moses made another visit to ... George Town Importing: *Smith vs. P/SSSC*, 1/24/1820.
- Steve made no entry into the logbook: *SSSLB*.
- The celebrated *Steam Ship Savannah*, has arrived: *National Messenger*, 12/20/1819.
- The steam ship Savannah has arrived: *The National Advocate*, 12/21/1819.
- taking out another advance, this time for $710: *Smith vs. P/SSSC*, 1/24/1820.
- J. P. Henry ... newly-appointed U.S. Navy Agent: *Columbian Museum*, 3/15/1819.
- Bulloch ... Henry ... had clear conflicts of interest: in the correspondence of the Navy Board and the Secretary of the Navy, numerous letters from both Bulloch and Henry can be found, and the subject matter is always official business. None of the letters contain any reference to the *Savannah*, implying Bulloch and Henry took very seriously the possible appearance of a conflict of interest.
- the executive area ... centered around the President's House: Young, *The Washington Community...*, pp66–69.
- cows often left to graze in the open fields: Palmer, op. cit., p34.
- "rather that of a straggling city": Howitt, op. cit., p77.
- hackney carriages, which charged 25¢: Delano, *The Washington Directory*, 1822, p112.
- saddle horse could be hired for about $1.50 per day: Warden, op. cit., p102.
- members took up residence ... boardinghouses: Young, op. cit., p87.
- groupings tended to follow State or sectional allegiances: ibid, p98.
- *All see the necessity of retrenchment*: LOC, Papers of William Plumer and William Plumer Jr., William Plumer Jr. to William Plumer, 12/17/1819.
- dozens of pirates had been captured: Allen, *Our Navy and the West Indian Pirates*, p19.
- insurance companies ... banded together to write a letter: *National Intelligencer*,

1/1/1820, *Baltimore Patriot,* 1/3/1820; *Niles' Weekly Register,* 1/8/1820, among others.

– ordered Steam Superintendent Francis B. Ogden: NARA, RG45, Miscellaneous Letters, John Rodgers to Henry Eckford, 3/10/1819.

– Adams' office was in the southeast corner: Force, op. cit., p178.

– Senator John Parrott exited from his own meeting: MHS, AFP, JQA Papers, JQA Diary, 12/23/1819.

– a brief dispatch from Consul John Rainals: NARA, RG59, Despatches From U.S. Consuls in Copenhagen, Denmark, 1792–1906, John Rainals to JQA, 10/18/1819.

– *Captn Rogers of the Steam Ship…*: NARA, RG59, Despatches from U.S. Ministers to Russia, 1808–1906, George W. Campbell to JQA, 9/25/1819.

– "a letter of strong recommendation": JQA Diary, 12/23/1819.

– asked Secretary Adams if he could keep the Campbell letter: JQA, in his diary, records their meeting on 12/23/1819. However, Adams marked the Campbell letter as being received on 12/24. Since the despatch was purely personal and contained no diplomatic information, it seems most likely that Moses wanted to keep it to show to the editors of the *National Intelligencer* the next day. Moses must have returned the letter to the State Department permanently once this task was completed, which is why JQA marked its receipt on 12/24.

– *Intelligencer …* corner of Seventh and D Streets: Delano, op. cit., p38.

– his parents … dared to sell political tracts: Ames, *A History of the National Intelligencer,* p71.

– Joseph the younger … took a job with the *National Intelligencer:* ibid, p62.

– brought in Seaton to be his partner in 1812: ibid, p86.

– Gales was given preferred seating: ibid, p113; Clark, "Joseph Gales Junior, Editor and Mayor," *Records of the Columbia Historical Society,* Volume 23 (1920), p111.

– Seaton received the same privilege: ibid.

– contracts for publishing the proceedings of Congress: Ames, op. cit., p109.

– Gales stood barely 5 feet 2 inches in height: ibid, p68.

– Gales … "affable and easy,": ibid, p68.

– Gales … course and unrefined: ibid, p84.

– Seaton … round face dominated by "penetrating blue eyes.": ibid, p86.

– Moses … through the cold rain: JQA Weather Record.

– The Steam Ship Savannah is yet in our harbor: *National Intelligencer,* 12/25/1819.

– Crawford … publicly claimed he didn't want to be considered: Brant, *James Madison…,* p404.

– "For the probable receipts of the next year": *AC,* Journal of the Senate, 16th Congress, 1st Session, President's Annual Message, dated 12/7/1819, p18.

– a projected deficit for 1820 of nearly $5,000,000: *AC,* Journal of the House, 16th Congress, 1st Session, Report on the Finances, dated 12/10/1819, p723.

– *You can have no idea of the complaint:* LOC, op. cit., William Plumer Jr. to William Plumer, 12/28/1819.

– the *Radicals* … had "charged the Administration with extravagance": ibid.

– the President wanted someone from the North: Coletta, *American Secretaries of the Navy,* Volume I, p123.

– *I have lately caused to be built:* NARA, RG45, Letters Received by the Secretary of the Navy, Miscellaneous Letters, Jasper Lynch to Smith Thompson, 12/21/1819. It is important to note that this letter was stamped "FREE." The only shareholder of the OSSC known to have a franking privilege was U.S. Naval Constructor Henry Eckford. Therefore, it stands to reason that Eckford knew about Lynch's offer to the Navy. It also seems likely that Eckford deliberately mailed the letter using his franking privilege to alert Secretary Thompson that he was aware such an offer was being made. Combined with Lynch's disclosure of Eckford as the builder of the *Robert Fulton*, it would appear that Eckford took every reasonable step to ensure Thompson was aware of the potential conflict of interest.

- ... *while the Servants were helping us*: LOC, The Papers of Thomas H. Hubbard, Thomas Hubbard to Phebe Hubbard, 2/21/1818.
- Rodgers ... destroyed or captured 23 British vessels: Schroeder, *Commodore John Rodgers...*, p125.
- lost not a single man-of-war under his command: ibid, p126.
- a song in his name, "Rodgers and Victory": Wilson, *A National Song-Book...*, p177.
- Commodore Rodgers ... both looked and acted the part: many years later, Senator Thomas Hart Benton wrote: "Commodore Rodgers ... was to me the complete impersonation of my idea of the perfect naval commander—person, mind, and manners" (Benton, *Thirty Years' View*, Vol. II, p144).
- Commodore Rodgers reviewed the various laws: Guttridge and Smith, *The Commodores*, p274.
- "the Board ... shall control the Secretary": NARA, RG45, Office of the Secretary of the Navy, Letters Sent to the President, Benjamin Crowninshield to James Madison, 6/23/1815.
- Madison decided in favor of continued civilian control: in advising the Navy Board of the President's decision, Secretary Crowninshield pointedly wrote: "This moment I have received from the President his answer ... a copy of which I now lay before you, indulging the hope, that it may be perfectly satisfactory to the Gentlemen comprising the Board" (see NARA, RG45, Office of the Secretary of the Navy, Letters to BNC, Crowninshield to BNC, 6/13/1815). Crowninshield's letter to the Board was written less than two months after news of Napoleon's escape from Elba had reached the United States.
- The President initially asked Commodore Rodgers: Coletta, op. cit., Vol. I, p123.
- the President wanted "harmony" in the department: Williams, *The Life of Washington Irving*, Vol. 1, p170.
- "you will observe that the execution of the law": LOC, Rogers Family Papers: Part III: 24, Smith Thompson to John Rodgers, 6/1/1819.
- The Commissioners of the Navy will contract with you: NARA, RG45, BNC, Miscellaneous Letters Sent, John Rodgers to Hugh Lindsay, 12/7/1819.
- "as early as may suit your convenience.": ibid, Stephen Decatur to Thomas Vinson, 11/12/1819.
- "presuming from your silence": ibid, John Rodgers to Thomas Vinson, 12/7/1819.
- about to be "punished" with alterations: ibid, Journal #2, BNC to Francis B. Ogden, 12/7/1819.
- sent off a memorandum to Secretary Thompson: ibid, Letters Sent to Secretary of the Navy, 12/7/1819.
- the Board made good on its promise to Francis B. Ogden: ibid, Miscellaneous Letters Sent, Journal #2, BNC to Francis B. Ogden, 12/9/1819.
- Francis ... nephew of the Monopoly's Aaron Ogden: Wheeler, *Ogden Family in America, Elizabethtown Branch...*, pp132–138, 252.
- instructing him to "estimate in detail": NARA, RG45, BNC, Journal #2, BNC to William Doughty, 12/9/1819.
- another letter to Georgia contractor Hugh Lindsay: ibid, BNC, Miscellaneous Letters Sent, John Rodgers to Hugh Lindsay, 12/13/1819.
- *I had contemplated immediately visiting Washington*: ibid, Miscellaneous Letters Received, Thomas Vinson to Stephen Decatur, 12/2/1819.
- Vail was trapped on board: Stephen Vail to Bethiah Vail, 12/17/1819, as cited in Braynard, op. cit., pp188–189.
- "He treated Me verry well": ibid.

- Vail ... decided to quit Savannah: HSA, Vail Family Papers, Stephen Vail to Bethiah Vail, 12/28/1819.
- did not make it into the Commissioners' bound volumes: NARA, RG45, BNC, Miscellaneous Letters Received, 1819—Vinson's missing letter, dated 12/16/1819, is referred to in BNC, Miscellaneous Letters Sent, John Rodgers to Thomas Vinson, 12/27/1819.
- They have as yet received no answer: ibid, Miscellaneous Letters Sent, John Rodgers to Hugh Lindsay, 12/27/1819.
- Commodore Rodgers sent him a letter: ibid, John Rodgers to Thomas Newell, 12/28/1819.
- They wrote to Navy Agent J. P. Henry: ibid, Journal #2, BNC to J. P. Henry, 12/29–30/1819.
- They also wrote to the Navy Agent at New York: ibid, BNC to Robert Swartwout, 12/29–30/1819.
- they sent an order to Commodore Thomas Tingey: ibid, BNC to Thomas Tingey, 12/31/1819.
- "a very happy, independent life among" the "magnificos,": Williams, op. cit., p171. Paulding used this term, "magnifico," to describe any senior government official.
- ... the government is not in want of such a vessel: NARA, RG45, Miscellaneous Letters Sent by the Secretary of the Navy, Smith Thompson to Jasper Lynch, 12/28/1819.
- some 180-plus representatives: according to the House Office of the Clerk, there were 186 representatives and 4 delegates (from Territories) in the 16th Congress. The precise number of House members in attendance fluctuated constantly during the early Congresses due to rolling election cycles (some States held elections in the spring), absenteeism, and routine resignations (since there was very little careerism).
- Senate received a report from the Navy Board: *ASP*, Class 6, *Naval Affairs*, Volume 1, 16th Congress, 1st Session, No. 174, Contracts for the Year 1819, communicated 1/3/1820.
- Davis & Force had run out of typeface: NARA, RG59, Miscellaneous Letters of the Department of State, Davis & Force to JQA, 1/1/1820.
- the *Fulton* was suddenly being described as a "Steam Ship": Davis & Force, *A Register of Officers and Agents, Civil, Military, and Naval...*, p78; and Peter Force, *A National Calendar, for 1820...*, p78. This description of the steam battery *Fulton* as a "Steam Ship" was kept in the 1821 editions, compiled in September 1820, since the *Savannah* remained tied up at Washington. However, for subsequent editions (i.e., 1822 onward), the *Fulton*'s description reverted to "Steam Frigate."
- further back ... the old "Steam Frigate" designation was still used: Force, *A National Calendar, for 1820...*, pp83–84.
- Tunstall Quarles of Kentucky rose in the House: *AC*, Journal of the House, 16th Congress, 1st Session, 1/5/1820.
- Timothy Fuller ... Fourth District of Massachusetts: Martis, *The Historical Atlas ... Congressional Districts...*, p65.
- Fuller offered his own motion: ibid, 1/10/1820.

CHAPTER TWENTY—THE VISE TIGHTENS

- early morning hours of Tuesday, January 11th: *The Georgian*, 1/17/1820.
- sentries on duty raised the alarm in the usual way: ibid.

- half-dozen or so fire companies: Maguire, *Historical Souvenir: Savannah Fire Department*, p14.
- strong and steady winds from the west-northwest: *Savannah Republican*, 1/14/1820.
- nearly complete lack of rain through the autumn: ibid.
- taking some barrels of unexploded gunpowder: ibid.
- the glass shards falling thick: University of North Carolina–Chapel Hill, Manuscripts Collection, Arnold and Screven Family Papers, M. Richardson to James P. Screven, 1/13/1820.
- began unhinging all their shutters: ibid.
- some 12 hours after the alarm ... the fires were out: *Savannah Republican*, 1/14/1820.
- 321 wooden buildings had been consumed: *The Georgian*, 1/17/1820.
- the catastrophe had killed only two people: *Savannah Republican*, 1/14/1820.
- plus nearly a dozen horses: ibid.
- Low & Company's brick store ... thought to be fireproof: *New York Gazette*, 1/24/1820.
- search of all buildings and shipping for stolen goods: *The Georgian*, 1/17/1820.
- a jail bulging with the accused: Richardson to Screven, 1/13/1820.
- Philip Brasch, offered bread: *New York Daily Advertiser*, 2/3/1820.
- local planters also pitched in, donating corn, rice and beef: Coulter, "The Great Savannah Fire," *The Georgia Historical Quarterly*, Volume XXIII, No. 1 (March 1939), p7.
- editor John Harney had to stitch his operations back together: *The Georgian*, 1/17/1820.
- a temporary office in partner James McHenry's home: *Columbian Museum*, 1/17/1820.
- Dr. White's proposal ... did not sit right with a lot of the public: *Savannah Republican*, 1/23/1820.
- "We view with feelings of regret": *Federal Republican* (Baltimore), as quoted in *New York Gazette*, 1/22/1820.
- "all the live oak necessary for the frames": *ASP*, House of Representatives, 16th Congress, 1st Session, *Naval Affairs*: Vol. 1, John Rodgers to Smith Thompson, 1/17/1820.
- The commissioners are induced to believe: ibid.
- "the best mode of economy": ibid, Smith Thompson to Stevenson Archer, 1/20/1820.
- "if Mr. Lindsay does not accept your offer": NARA, RG45, BNC, Miscellaneous Letters Received, Thomas Vinson to John Rodgers, 1/5/1820.
- Hugh Lindsay of Georgia finally had replied: ibid, Miscellaneous Letters Sent, John Rodgers to Hugh Lindsay, 2/5/1820.
- The chairman of this Select Committee was Congressman Nathaniel Silsbee: *AC*, Journal of the House, 16th Congress, 1st Session, 1/20/1820. This Select Committee had been formed at the beginning of the session to address issues raised by President Monroe's annual message. See Journal of the House, 12/8/1819.
- Silsbee represented the Second District: Martis, op. cit., p65.
- Chairman Silsbee ... sent a counter-reply: NARA, RG45, BNC, Letters from the Secretary of the Navy, Nathaniel Silsbee to Smith Thompson, 1/20/1820.
- Query 11th: *ASP*, House of Representatives, 16th Congress, 1st Session, *Naval Affairs*: Vol. 1, John Rodgers to Smith Thompson, 1/31/1820.
- the Charleston City Council held a public meeting: *City Gazette*, 1/17/1820.
- the officers of the local naval station, also pitched in: *The Courier*, 4/3/1820.

- Charleston Theatre ... putting on a benefit concert: *Savannah Republican*, 1/27/1820.
- Georgetown, South Carolina gathered $1,017: Coulter, op. cit., p13.
- Augusta's inhabitants quickly gathered $6,885: *Savannah Republican*, 2/2/1820.
- Milledgeville ... contributing $1,794, plus twenty barrels of flour: *Savannah Republican*, 2/7/1820.
- Henry J. Finn, the actor ... sent $50: Coulter, op. cit., p11; *Augusta Chronicle*, 2/8/1820.
- "be exclusively applied to the assistance": Coulter, op. cit., p10.
- "No two people seem to care a single straw": LOC, Papers of John Randolph, John Randolph to James M. Garnett, 1/12/1820.
- "Missouri is the only word ever repeated": LOC, Papers of John Tyler, John Tyler to Dr. Henry Curtis, 2/5/1820.
- "the Missouri subject monopolizes": LOC, Papers of John J. Crittenden, Henry Clay to John J. Crittenden, 1/29/1820, as seen in Moore, *The Missouri Controversy*, p90.
- "The appearance of the Senate to-day": *AC*, Senate Journal, 16th Congress, 1st Session, 1/13/1820.
- the visitor galleries of both chambers of Congress were packed: Moore, op. cit., p91.
- filed suit against "The President of the Savannah Steam...": *Smith vs. P/SSSC*, 1/24/1820.
- Walter Smith had told the Court that the defendant didn't live in the District: ibid.
- "Non Est": ibid.
- "Steamboat Ship Savannah": ibid.
- leaving Moses free to move about: while his movements in January 1820 are not precisely known, it stands to reason that Moses remained in Washington for some time after New Year's Day trying to effect a sale. First evidence of his possible departure are letters being held for him at the Georgetown Post Office, circa 2/1/1820 (see *The Metropolitan*, 2/8/1820).
- Jonesborough, Tennessee collected $700 worth of bacon: Coulter, op. cit., p15.
- Gotham's leaders immediately called a public meeting: *New-York Evening Post*, 1/24/1820; *The Columbian*, 1/26/1820.
- McKinne was named the committee secretary: *The Columbian*, 1/26/1820.
- McKinne ... Allaire, signed up to canvass: ibid, 1/28/1820.
- lauded their efforts: *National Intelligencer*, 1/29/1820; *Boston Patriot*, 1/29/1820.
- the flames ... had consumed $154,056 of inventory: NARA, RG46, Records of Congress, SEN 16A-G4, Petitions to Congress, Petition of Andrew Low and others, 1/24/1820.
- what Archibald S. Bulloch ... had been forced to do: NARA, RG41, Port/Savannah, Monthly Schedule of Bonds, 1819–1820.
- the Board listed all of the contracts made: *ASP*, House of Representatives, 16th Congress, 1st Session, *Naval Affairs*: Vol. 1, John Rodgers to Smith Thompson, 1/31/1820. The numbers in this table do not appear to add because the line item for "copper, castings, &c" at 31 cents per pound should be doubled, since it is for 2 of the 3 batteries authorized.
- Hugh Lindsay of St. Mary's having finally accepted: NARA, RG45, BNC, Miscellaneous Letters Sent, John Rodgers to Hugh Lindsay, 2/5/1820.
- Senator Henry Johnson of Louisiana rose: *AC*, Senate Journal, 16th Congress, 1st Session, 2/16/1820.
- shiploads of skilled men ... rebuilding effort: *The Georgian*, 2/5/1820.
- under the command of Captain John Mott: *Savannah Republican*, 3/2/1820. Based

upon news reports and advertisements, Mott held command of the *Othello* from the early autumn of 1818 through early April 1820.

- "disappointed the wishes and expectations": ibid.
- Resolved, That it is the wish of the general committee: ibid.
- "in any of the slave states": ibid.
- the Savannah Council unanimously agreed: ibid. No SSSC shareholders were serving on the Savannah Council at the time of the Great Fire of 1820.
- Sanford ... presented its findings to the full Senate: *ASP*, Senate, 16th Congress, 1st Session, Finance: Volume 3, p492, No. 581, Remission of Duty.
- Sanford's report should be re-committed: *AC*, Senate Journal, 2/24–25/1820.
- "most fit": *USCSS*, Vol. 27, Document #96, William H. Crawford to James Pleasants, 2/25/1820.
- Navy Board already had sent instructions to J. P. Henry: NARA, RG45, BNC, Journal, Volume 2, BNC to J. P. Henry, 12/29–30/1819, 1/20/1820.
- Mary Rogers exchanged vows with Steve: Rogers, op. cit., p201.
- the Norwegian sjekte which Moses had gifted to his father: ibid, p166 (the boat is incorrectly described as coming from Russia; see *SSSLB*). While there appears to be no surviving documentation confirming precisely when the sjekte arrived at Groton, three months was more than sufficient time for it to be delivered.
- "I have yet to learn that one man can make a slave of another,": King, *The Life & Correspondence of Rufus King*, Volume VI, p276.
- "the father armed against the son,": Moore, op. cit., p93.
- "The words, civil war, and disunion,": Henry Clay to Adam Beatty, 1/22/1820, as quoted in Peterson, *The Great Triumvirate*, p60.
- By a vote of 90–87: *AC*, Journal of the House, 16th Congress, 1st Session, pp1586–1587.
- Subsequent attempts to reconsider the bill were scuttled: ibid, pp1588–1590.
- "like a fire bell in the night.": Peterson, op. cit., p66.
- And one of the donors from Jonesborough ... would not have given: Coulter, op. cit., pp21–22.
- people in Savannah ... thought their mayor and council had overreacted: *Commercial Advertiser*, 3/10/1820, 4/8/1820.
- some of Gotham's contributors sent their money back: Coulter, op. cit., p21.
- The Board ... have the honor to represent: NARA, RG45, BNC, Letters to Secretary of the Navy, John Rodgers to Smith Thompson, 1/6/1820.
- what the first steamship actually looked like: Marestier, *Mémoire sur les Bateaux a vapeur des États Unis d'Amérique...*, various, including pp71–74 and atlas drawings.
- the plaintiff was New York ship chandler Francis H. Nicoll: NARA, RG21, Records of the U.S. District Court, District of Columbia, Case Papers, June term 1820, *Francis H. Nicoll + Henry W. Nicoll vs. The Savannah Steam Ship Company* (hereafter, "*Nicoll vs. SSSC*"), 3/22/1820.
- Dod did it in New York: NARA, RG21, U.S. Circuit Court for the Southern District of New York, Writs of Capias, *Daniel Dod vs. Abraham B. Fannin + others*, 4/1/1820; also, Law Case Files, 1790–1846, under Abraham B. Fannin.
- John Marshall ... temporary duty as a federal circuit judge: ibid. Normally, Associate Justice Brockholst Livingston presided over the New York federal circuit court, but Chief Justice Marshall took his place for the spring term of 1820.
- Vail filed suit on April 14th: NARA, RG21, Records of the U.S. District Court – District of Columbia, Case Papers, June term 1820, *Stephen Vail vs. The Savannah Steam Ship Company* (hereafter, "*Vail vs. SSSC*"), 4/13/1820.

- Ringgold ... took possession of all the sails: ibid.
- to George Sanford's store ... at Coomb's Wharf: ibid, and Delano, op. cit., p69.
- value of the *Savannah* was estimated at $19,510: *Vail vs. SSSC*. If Vail specifically asked for a separate attachment of and accounting for the steamship's rigging, it was a very canny move on his part. It meant that he was the only one of the three plaintiffs who had an attachment on the rigging, so if the *Savannah* was sold at auction, he could argue he should be the only one to receive the sale proceeds on that equipment.

CHAPTER TWENTY-ONE — THE END, AND RE-BIRTH

- Minis ... saddled with too much debt: GHS, Chatham County Superior Court, Minutes, Volume 10, numerous citations for Isaac Minis, in the vast majority of which he is the defendant.
- Dunning lost ... his steam-powered lumber mill: *Savannah Republican*, 3/8/1820.
- McKinne ... served with warrants: NARA, RG21, U.S. Southern District of New York, Circuit Court, Bail Register, May 1820 term, pp176–177, Joseph Bates and Joseph P. McKinne; also Writs of Capias, May 1820 term, *U.S.A. vs. Joseph Bates and Joseph P. McKinne*, various dates.
- creditors ... legal action against their home: New York County Clerk, Division of Old Records, New York City Chancery Court, CL 253, pp283–290; Bill to Foreclose, *John Lewis Augustus Lelievre vs. Joseph Pope McKinne and Anna McKinne and John J. Palmer*, 5/22/1820.
- Gideon Pott ... compelled to sell his shares: NYHS, Tontine Coffee House Records, Vol. 1, Transfer of Shares, pp149–150 (12/30/1819).
- Colden described it all in a petition to Congress: NARA, RG46, Records of Congress, SEN 16A-G2.2, Memorial of the Ocean Steam Ship Company of New York, read 3/14/1820.
- petition was referred to the Committee on Commerce: *AC*, Senate Journal, Volume 9, 3/14/1820.
- decided to hire a man named Robert Inott: *The National Advocate*, 4/10/1820; NARA, RG41, Port/New York, PR #96, steamship *Robert Fulton*, 4/22/1820.
- Inott ... previously had captained the ship *Annisquam*: *New-York Daily Advertiser*, 5/1/1818, among others; NARA, RG41, Port/New York, PE #117, ship *Annisquam*, 5/15/1818.
- *Robert Fulton* ... sent out on a brief trial: *Commercial Advertiser*, 4/17/1820.
- the inaugural voyage was confirmed: *Mercantile Advertiser*, 4/10/1820, among others.
- the *Robert Fulton* would be "unavoidably detained.": *Commercial Advertiser*, 4/20/1820.
- Not until Tuesday, April 25th: *The Columbian*, 4/25/1820.
- measured 159 feet in length: PR #96, steamship *Robert Fulton*, 4/22/1820.
- the installation of three *keelsons*: *The Columbian*, 3/22/1820.
- The massive boilers were also record-breaking: *Commercial Advertiser*, 3/22/1820.
- encased in lead, and caulked at the seams: ibid.
- main cabin ... "high and airy": ibid.
- Casting off from the wharf at a little past 9: *The Columbian*, 4/25/1820.
- an undisclosed number of passengers: no newspaper in New York appears to have reported the passenger count on this maiden voyage; the *Louisiana Advertiser* (5/16/1820) reported 10 passengers arrived on the steamship at New Orleans.
- Gotham's newspapers dutifully reprinted these resolutions: *Commercial Advertiser*, 4/26/1820; *The Columbian*, 4/28/1820, among others.

– *Robert Fulton* ... He: purists will insist that all marine vessels, regardless of their name or type, should be referred to as "she." While assigning a gender to vessels has varied somewhat through time and amongst nationalities, the modern maritime tradition in English-speaking countries has been to describe vessels as being feminine. The *Robert Fulton* is referred to in the masculine to avoid confusion.

– "The best interests of the nation,": *ASP*, House of Representatives, 16th Congress, 1st Session, *Naval Affairs*, Volume 1, No. 181, Suspension of the Standing Appropriation for the Gradual Increase of the Navy, 3/7/1820.

– "attached to the office of the Secretary": ibid, No. 188, Modification of the Act Creating the Board of Commissioners of the Navy, 5/1/1820.

– "as it would be often inconvenient": ibid.

– "small vessels of war,": *SAL*, 16th Congress, 1st Session, "An Act authorizing the building of a certain number of small vessels of war," passed 5/15/1820.

– "an Act to continue in force": ibid, "An Act to continue in force 'An act to protect the commerce of the United States...'," passed 5/15/1820.

– deliver pine logs instead of planks: NARA, RG45, BNC, Journal #2, BNC to Hugh Lindsay, 5/26/1820.

– take until the end of the year to deliver all the timber: ibid, BNC to Thomas M. Newell, 5/26/1820.

– it approved the erection of a building: ibid, BNC to Francis B. Ogden, 6/6/1820.

– resigned his position as the U.S. Naval Constructor: ibid, BNC to Henry Eckford, 6/8/1820; also Letters from Naval Constructors, Henry Eckford to BNC, 6/1/1820.

– had recently asked for a pay raise: NARA, RG45, Letters to the Secretary of the Navy, Henry Eckford et al to Smith Thompson, 1/25/1820.

– mansion onto the public auction block: GSA, William Scarbrough Collection, Judgment—transfer of property, 5/13/1820; and Robert Isaac Will, 8/26/1827.

– Planters' Bank won a judgment: GHS, Chatham County Superior Court, Civil Minutes, Book #10, *Planters' Bank vs. Scarbrough & McKennie* [sic], 5/22/1820.

– lawsuits from the Bank of the United States: NARA, RG21, District of Georgia at Savannah, U.S. Circuit Court, Mixed Case Files, *Bank of the U.S. vs. Scarbrough et al*, filed 11/22/1819, and *Bank of the U.S. vs. Scarbrough*, filed 4/6/1820.

– and the U.S. Custom House: ibid, U.S. District Court, Mixed Case Files, *The United States vs. Scarbrough*, various dates in 1819.

– Scarbrough owed him ... $175,069 for past-due loans: ibid, U.S. Circuit Court, *Andrew Low vs. William Scarbrough*, 11/6/1819.

– *Scarbrough & McKinne vs. Pott & McKinne* was decided: GHS, Chatham County Superior Court, Civil Minutes, Book #10, *Scarbrough & McKennie* [sic] *vs. Pott & McKennie* [sic], 6/6/1820.

– both men appeared before a magistrate in New York: *Nicoll vs. SSSC*, Depositions of Henry Cooke and Henry Patton, dated 5/15/1820.

– Vail ... arranged for ... McQueen: *Vail vs. SSSC*, Deposition of Henry Cooke, 5/17/1820.

– *Robert Fulton* ... from New Orleans in 10 days: *New-York Evening Post*, 6/15/1820.

– loosening of paddleboards: *Commercial Advertiser*, 5/25/1820.

– Inott ... having taken a fall, badly hurting his leg: ibid.

– We, the undersigned passengers: *New-York Evening Post*, 6/15/1820, among others. The Livingston family member who signed this memorial was Lewis Livingston (see *Louisiana Advertiser*, 5/30/1820).

– the House ... failed to vote on the Senate's bill: *AC*, House Journal, 16th Congress, 1st Session, 5/15/1820. House members deftly rejected a motion that they be relieved from any further consideration of the drafted bill; nevertheless, the failure to hold a vote on the bill by this last day of the session effectively killed it.

- Taney, asked … order the *Savannah* condemned: NARA, RG21, District of Columbia, U.S. District Court, Docket-Appearances, June 1820 term, Cases 24, 25.
- the Nicoll suit came before Judge Cranch's court: *Nicoll vs. SSSC*, Case of Attachment; also, Docket-Appearances, June 1820 term, Cases 364, 365.
- it was the last day of the Court's term: NARA, RG21, District of Columbia, U.S. Circuit Court, Minutes, 7/7/1820. Note: although the Case Files and Docket are listed as for the District Court, each of these suits against the SSSC was heard in the U.S. Circuit Court, as was the norm.
- same decision was applied to Stephen Vail's case: *Nicoll vs. SSSC*; also, Docket-Appearances, June 1820 term, Cases 430, 431.
- *Robert Fulton*'s owners announced his replacement: *Commercial Advertiser*, 6/24/1820.
- Mott had made one trip … to New Orleans: *Boston Daily Advertiser*, 4/17/1820; *Louisiana Advertiser*, 5/9/1820; *New-York Daily Advertiser*, 6/12/1820.
- "but a few passengers,": *Commercial Advertiser*, 7/3/1820.
- "the experiment may be considered as fairly tested.": ibid.
- Limping into New York came the *Robert Fulton*: *Mercantile Advertiser*, 7/24/1820.
- provided … a detailed accounting of the monies lent: *Smith vs. P/SSSC*, deposition of William Ridgely, 7/21/1820.
- Taney was back representing his original client: when the Court's clerk entered the Nicoll and Vail cases into the Docket-Appearances journal, Taney was initially listed as the defendant's attorney in both the original debt cases and the separate cases of attachment. But once the cases of attachment were dismissed, the clerk was subsequently corrected, and Taney's name was crossed out as defendant's counsel for the remaining Nicoll and Vail debt cases. This left the SSSC with no legal counsel, and Taney back with his original client, Walter Smith.
- a man named Nathan H. Holdridge: Albion, *Square-Riggers on Schedule*, p337.
- commanded a sailing sloop: MYS, Connecticut Ship Database, sloop *Jennette*, Nathan Holdridge, master, 1807–1808.
- Holdridge … captain … *Rubicon*: *New York Evening Post*, 6/17/1816; *Mercantile Advertiser*, 8/10/1818.
- captain and ship were driven ashore: *New York Evening Post*, 1/19/1820.
- Holdridge went into the Georgetown Custom House: NARA, RG21, Port/Georgetown-DC, TR, ship *Savannah*, 8/25/1820.
- the stripped steamship … moved up the Eastern Branch: this conclusion is based upon an accumulation of evidence, namely 1) that the *Savannah* was docked at the deep-water piers off Greenleaf Point upon her arrival at Washington; 2) U.S. Marshal Tench Ringgold stored the steamship's sails and equipment at Sanford's store (see previous footnote); 3) Sanford's lumberyard store was located at Coomb's Wharf, next to the Washington Navy Yard (see Delano, *The Washington Directory … 1822*, pp69, 87); 4) the *City of Washington Gazette* reported (on 9/12/1820) that "the Steam Ship SAVANNAH, has sailed from the Navy Yard, in this city," and 5) there appears to be no surviving evidence in U.S. Navy records at NARA to indicate that the *Savannah* was ever moved directly to the Washington Navy Yard (as some have previously claimed). Instead, the newspaper's report mistook departure from the adjoining Coomb's Wharf for a departure from the Navy Yard.
- On August 30th, he served a warrant: NARA, RG21, Southern District of New York, U.S. Circuit Court, Law Case Files, *Abraham B. Fannin, impleaded etc. vs. Daniel Dod*, filed 9/5/1820.
- *Let the Plaintiff in this cause appear before me*: ibid.

- *Savannah's* new crew ... began deploying her sails: *Commercial Advertiser,* 9/11/1820; *Mercantile Advertiser,* 9/11/1820. There is no evidence to indicate that Holdridge or his crew knew how to use the steam apparatus. In fact, they waited at Hampton Roads for favorable winds before proceeding north to New York (see *The National Advocate,* 9/8/1820).
- met in the chambers of Justice Brockholst Livingston: NARA, RG21, Southern District of New York, U.S. Circuit Court, Engrossed Minutes, 9/5/1820.
- ... *that he is a Citizen and Inhabitant of the State of Georgia:* Fannin vs. Dod, 9/5/1820.
- *It is ordered, That the said writ be quashed:* Engrossed Minutes, 9/5/1820.
- *Robert Fulton ...* excursion around Long Island: *Commercial Advertiser,* 8/12/1820.
- management wasn't particularly keen on the idea: ibid, 8/23/1820.
- *Robert Fulton's* circumnavigation ... September 13th: *New-York Columbian,* 9/8/1820, among others.
- didn't think enough tickets had been sold: *Commercial Advertiser,* 9/11/1820.
- set up as a blowing cylinder in the foundry: SI, Steamship *Savannah* file, F.E. Sickels to J. Elfreth Watkins, 8/11/1892.
- Moses ... fitting out for use as a hotel: *Poulson's American Daily Advertiser,* 10/9/1820.
- A violent wind squall suddenly appeared: Rogers, op. cit., p166.
- The mishap ... at the mouth of New London harbor: *Connecticut Gazette,* 9/27/1820.
- The sjekte had sunk: CSA, New London County Superior Court, Inquests (1711–1870), Amos Rogers, 9/21/1820.
- "came to his death by mischance and accident": ibid.
- the funeral of Amos Rogers was held at his home: *Connecticut Gazette,* 9/27/1820.
- For so an entrance shall be ministered unto you abundantly: ibid.
- newspapers ... Boston to New York City reprinted his obituary: *The Repertory* (Boston), 10/3/1820; *Commercial Advertiser,* 9/30/1820, among others.
- "I have a desire to depart and be with Christ": *Connecticut Gazette,* 9/27/1820, and *Republican Advocate,* 9/27/1820, both of New London.
- *Pee Dee ...* Completed at Charleston in November: *The Courier,* 12/3/1819.
- under the command of Captain Charles Vanderford: while there appear to be no surviving custom house documents for the *Pee Dee,* all evidence points to Charles Vanderford as her first captain. He later settled in Cheraw. See newspaper articles on the *Pee Dee,* including *City Gazette,* 3/8/1821; *The Essex Register,* 4/18/1825; and Jensen, *The Vanderfords...,* pp95–96.
- Vanderford had taken the *Pee Dee* up the coast: *Winyaw Intelligencer,* 12/18/1819.
- they had ventured up the Great Pee Dee River: *New-York Gazette,* 2/16/1820, quoting the *Winyaw Intelligencer,* 2/2/1820.
- A few additional trips were made during the spring: *Winyaw Intelligencer,* 4/8/1820.
- upper reaches ... cleared of obstructions: Kohn et al, *Internal Improvement in South Carolina...,* p6.
- *Pee Dee ...* a little 111-ton steamer: *New-York Gazette,* 2/16/1820.

CHAPTER TWENTY-TWO — CARRYING ON

- *Robert Fulton ...* for Charleston only: *New-York Daily Advertiser,* 9/28/1820.
- asked that the voyage be delayed: *Commercial Advertiser,* 10/7/1820.
- including former *Savannah* shareholder Samuel Howard: *The Columbian,* 10/11/1820; *City Gazette,* 10/17/1820.

- next voyage to New Orleans ... scheduled: *Commercial Advertiser*, 10/10/1820.
- Samuel Howard and the other passengers felt obliged: *City Gazette*, 10/17/1820.
- the steamship had burnt far more coal: *Mercantile Advertiser*, 10/30/1820.
- He also wrote back to headquarters: *Commercial Advertiser*, 10/24/1820, which contains a letter from one of the *Robert Fulton's* passengers at Charleston. It is logical Mott wrote a letter of his own describing the voyage to his employer. This is further supported by the notice run the very next day by the steamship's agent, announcing a delay in the next scheduled run to New Orleans, in order to allow for modifications to the vessel upon its return to New York. See *Commercial Advertiser*, 10/25/1820.
- *Robert Fulton* spent three long days: *The New-York Evening Post*, 10/30/1820.
- At 71 years of age ... John Stevens: Turnbull, op. cit., p28.
- Colonel Stevens began writing a letter to the President: NJHS, SFP, John Stevens to James Monroe, 10/28/1820.
- resurrect an idea from several years before: ibid, John Stevens to James Monroe, 8/17/1817.
- With alterations complete, the *Robert Fulton* left New York: *The Columbian*, 11/6/1820.
- the fore and main yards snapped: *Commercial Advertiser*, 12/8/1820.
- "too slender ... I would recommend to the owners": *Commercial Advertiser*, 11/23/1820.
- *Robert Fulton* managed to make it back: *Commercial Advertiser*, 12/30/1820.
- Holdridge managed the trip to Georgia in just 90 hours: *Commercial Advertiser*, 11/11/1820.
- a second voyage in December: *The National Advocate*, 12/27/1820.
- they became part owners along with Holdridge: NARA, RG36, Port/Savannah, TR #46, ship *Savannah*, 12/27/1820; Port/New York, PE #7, ship *Savannah*, 1/25/1821.
- recall for their readers what the *Savannah* had once been: *Southern Patriot*, 10/31/1820.
- costs to date of $223,555 remained the same: *ASP*, House of Representatives, 16th Congress, 2nd Session, *Naval Affairs*, Volume 1, p680, John Rodgers to Smith Thompson, 12/9/1820. This cost total as printed in *ASP*.
- Ogden had requested permission to build ... the Board had agreed: NARA, RG45, BNC, Journal #2, BNC to Capt. Evans and Francis B. Ogden, 11/27/1820.
- To Congressman Thomas Cobb: NJHS, SFP, John Stevens to Thomas Cobb, 11/15/1820.
- to the new Speaker of the House, John Taylor: ibid, John Stevens to John Taylor, 11/20/1820.
- ... *Such results would naturally excite alarm*: Stevens to Cobb, 11/15/1820.
- Speaker Taylor laid the petition before the House: *AC*, House Journal, Volume 14, 16th Congress, 2nd Session, 12/20/1820.
- steaming at night was simply out of the question: *Carolina Gazette*, 1/27/1821, quoting the *Winyaw Intelligencer*, 1/24/1821.
- *Pee Dee* could make the trip in as little as 2 days: ibid.
- including corn, peas, flax-seed, bees-wax, bacon, and lard: *The Times*, 5/3/1821; Kohn et al, p121, describes substantial exports of many of these items during the 1820–1821 season.
- From Georgetown, the *Pee Dee* brought all sorts of things: *City Gazette*, 2/14/1821.
- "active and enterprising commander": ibid, 1/26/1821.
- *Robert Fulton* ... began running a new advertisement: *Commercial Advertiser*, 1/22/1821.

- "Defence of the Seacoast,": *ASP*, House of Representatives, 16th Congress, 2nd Session, *Naval Affairs*, Volume 1, p685.
- He made copies ... and sent them to Hezekiah Niles: NJHS, SFP, John Stevens to Hezekiah Niles, 1/23/1821.
- he challenged Commodore Rodgers to a steam duel: ibid, John Stevens to Hezekiah Niles, 1/31/1821.
- "It is a notorious fact,": ibid.
- waves of correspondence from Colonel Stevens ... intimidated ... Niles: Stevens wrote to Niles on 1/23, 1/28, 1/31, and twice in early February of 1821.
- writing to Senators Rufus King ... and Mahlon Dickerson: NJHS, SFP, various John Stevens letters to/from King and Dickerson, February 1821.
- "committed to the Tomb of the Capulets": ibid, John Stevens to Thomas Cobb, 12/-/1820.
- reached some 9,500 bales: Kohn et al, op. cit., p121.
- Some $200,000 worth of merchandise was brought upriver: ibid.
- Shareholders ... Pee Dee Steam-Boat ... 12% dividend: *City Gazette*, 3/16/1821.
- Moses departed for Philadelphia, to spend the summer: *Winyaw Intelligencer*, mid-November/1821, as reprinted in Watkins, op. cit., pp624–625.

CHAPTER TWENTY-THREE — CLOSURE

- *Robert Fulton* ... confronted by a "piratical schooner": *New York Daily Advertiser*, 4/10/1821, among others.
- dared to declare ... the precise date of its arrival: *New-York Spectator*, 7/20/1821; and more importantly, *Niles' Weekly Register*, 8/4/1821.
- fewer than 1 person in 100 ... severe case of fever: *The Courier*, 9/19/1821, quoting the *Pee Dee Gazette*.
- expected trade with the coast to equal the previous season's: ibid.
- put the steamboat back into operation by early October: ibid.
- convinced a merchant from nearby Fayetteville: *The Courier*, 11/5/1821.
- by his brother, Captain Amos Rogers Junior: NARA, RG36, Port/Philadelphia, OCM, steamboat *Commerce*, Rogers, 11/3/1821. Amos Jr. did not make the voyage until December (see *City Gazette*, 12/29/1821).
- Captain Rogers ... expected by the 10th: *City Gazette* (Charleston), 10/13/1821, quoting the *Pee Dee Gazette*, 10/1/1821.
- "skilful and indefatigable commander": *The Courier*, 11/5/1821.
- The strong gusts coming off the Atlantic: *The National Advocate*, 11/7/1821.
- The time was 3 o'clock in the morning: ibid.
- "upright and tight,": ibid.
- There were only three on this trip: *Evening Post*, 11/8/1821; Braynard, op. cit., p203.
- just off a part of the Beach known as Fire Place: *The National Advocate*, 11/7/1821.
- He and two crewmen climbed into the jolly boat: ibid.
- the jollyboat was capsized: ibid.
- The fishermen on the Beach saw the trouble: ibid.
- hopes of getting the Savannah off were fading: *Evening Post*, 11/8/1821.
- only about 120 bales had been salvaged: *The Georgian*, 11/23/1821.
- She was locked in place, eight or nine feet into the sand: ibid.
- all of the hardware were methodically removed: ibid.
- a large crowd gathered at the burial ground: *Winyaw Intelligencer*, post-11/15/1821, as re-printed in Watkins, op. cit., pp624–625.
- A friend came on board to find him: SI, Reference file: SS *Savannah*, typed copy of unsigned letter to Mrs. Moses Rogers, 11/15/1821. Much of the account of

Moses Rogers' death is taken from this letter. While typed copies of manuscripts are cause for caution, the letter's contents clearly point to its authenticity. First, the steamboat *Pee Dee*'s departure and arrival dates within the letter match newspaper accounts. Second, Aron Marvin's participation is logical, given his activities with the Pee Dee Steam Boat Company and the Antipedo Baptist Church (see below). Third, the vocabulary and grammar of the letter are consistent with the early 19th century. It was a common courtesy through the 19th and into the early 20th centuries to protect a source's privacy by withholding their name. While the letter's author could have been anyone, one likely candidate is Captain Daniel Elkins, a native of Nantucket who had previously sailed out of New York for a number of years. He and Moses were good friends in South Carolina. Elkins later took command of the steamboat *Pee Dee*, and died in 1823.

– Moses … so incapacitated … disrupted his running the steamboat: *City Gazette*, 10/22/1817.
– Marvin … a shareholder in the Pee Dee Steam-Boat Company: SCDAH, South Carolina House of Representatives, Petition for Incorporation, Pee Dee Steam Boat Company, late 1819; also, see McCord, *Statutes at Large of South Carolina*, Vol. 8, pp307–308.
– Marvin … a prominent member of the Antipedo Baptist Church: ibid, Petition for Incorporation, Antipedo Baptist Church of Georgetown, 11/25/1812; also, see Skinner, *A Brief History of the Baptists of Georgetown, S.C.*
– death of Captain Rogers … viewed as a "public calamity,": *New-York Gazette*, 11/27/1821.
– obituaries mentioned the most prominent command: *The Courier*, 11/19/1821; *Savannah Republican*, 11/21/1821. *The National Advocate*, 11/28/1821; *Poulson's American*, 11/28/1821; *Daily National Intelligencer*, 11/30/1821.
– they noted only his most recent: *Commercial Advertiser*, 11/27/1821; *New-York Gazette*, 11/27/1821.
– did not even describe his relation to the new mode: *City Gazette*, 11/19/1821.

APPENDIX—THE BARRIER BROKEN

– *Quiroga* was transferred to Havana: *Mercantile Advertiser*, 7/27/1820, among others.
– *Braganza* succeeded … to Brazil: *New-York Evening Post*, 5/3/1820. The *Braganza* eventually had her machinery removed in Brazil, and was sold; see *New York Gazette*, 7/31/1822.
– including the steam schooners *Fidelity* and *Mexican*: NARA, RG41, Port/New York, PE#79, "~~Schooner~~ Steamboat" *Fidelity*, 4/25/1821; and PR#108, Steam Schooner *Mexican*, 5/11/1821. In virtually all newspaper citations, the *Fidelity* was described as a "steam schooner."
– and the *Fanny*: ibid, PE#359, Schooner/Steamboat *Fanny*, 10/24/1823. James P. Allaire and Cornelius Vanderbilt were part owners in this vessel, which, like the *Balize*, was referred to in the newspapers as a "steam schooner." As the custom house descriptions of the *Fidelity* and *Fanny* make clear, the maritime community still struggled to accept the new reality of oceanic steam navigation in the early 1820s, while the press did not.
– smashed one of the *Quiroga*'s paddlewheels: *Mercantile Advertiser*, 7/27/1820.
– the *Fidelity* suffered several boiler failures: *New-York Spectator*, 5/16/1821; Norwich Courier, 12/26/1821.
– the *Fanny*'s paddlewheel housings were ripped apart: *Baltimore Patriot*, 10/29/1823.

- the brig *New York* eventually caught fire: *Baltimore Patriot*, 9/2/1826.
- the *Robert Fulton* ... dozen and a half trips: Ridgely-Nevitt, op. cit., p56, and numerous newspaper citations.
- no other steamships built by his promoters ... despite plans to do so: *AC*, Journal of the House, 17th Congress, 2nd Session, 2/3/1823.
- some of the original shareholders focused on the old mode: Albion, *The Rise of the New York Port*, p44. Most prominently, Preserved Fish co-founded the Blue Swallowtail Line of sailing packets.
- deploying a squadron of five men-of-war: *ASP*, House of Representatives, 16th Congress, 2nd Session, *Naval Affairs*, Volume 1, No. 196, "Condition of the Navy and its Expenses."
- Navy required ... its vessels ... to sail through the West Indies: *USCSS*, 16th Congress, 2nd Session, Document 38, Smith Thompson to James Monroe, 12/27/1820.
- "This system of piracy is now spreading itself to a vast extent": *ASP*, House of Representatives, 17th Congress, 1st Session, *Naval Affairs*, Volume 1, No. 207, "Additional Number of Small Vessels to be Employed for the Suppression of Piracy."
- the Committee ... dared suggest to the Navy: ibid.
- the first bill passed and placed before President Monroe: *SAL*, 17th Congress, 2nd Session, "An Act authorizing an additional naval force for the suppression of piracy," passed 12/20/1822.
- that "1 Steam Boat" be procured: *Baltimore Patriot*, 12/14/1822; *Essex Patriot*, 12/21/1822.
- Secretary Thompson in turn "requested": NARA, RG45, BNC, Letters Received from the Secretary of the Navy, Smith Thompson to John Rodgers, 12/17/1822.
- appointed Navy Board Commissioner David Porter: LOC, David D. Porter Family Papers, Smith Thompson to David Porter, 12/20/1822.
- Porter stood out in his belief: Wheeler, *In Pirate Waters*, p111.
- "U.S. steam ketch *Sea Gull*,": *Baltimore Patriot*, 1/17/1823.
- junior naval officers ... were dubious of the *Sea Gull*: Wheeler, op. cit., p111.
- re-designated the *Sea Gull* a "steam galliot,": *Providence Gazette*, 2/1/1823.
- Porter proceeded to place his men-of-war on patrols and convoy duty: wrote one U.S. Navy officer from Havana—"We afford protection to vessels of all nations requesting it of us; in one fleet from this place, we had English, Danish, Hamburg, and Bremen colors mixed with our own." (*Baltimore Patriot*, 5/16/1823.)
- *Sea Gull* ... attacking and capturing pirate vessels: during her service off Cuba, the *Sea Gull* sometimes worked in concert with Royal Navy vessels, also sent to fight piracy. For the latter part of the anti-piracy campaign, the *Sea Gull*'s master was Lieutenant Commander Isaac McKeever, who had traveled on the *Robert Fulton* for the inaugural return voyage in 1820, and signed the passenger endorsement memorial at New York.
- *George IV* ... no greater proponent ... Emperor Nicholas: Granville, op. cit., Vol. 1, pp463–464.
- Thanks in part to the memory of the American steamship of 1819: Saul, *Distant Friends...*, pp132–133. While Saul offers no direct evidence to this effect, his statement is logical under the circumstances.
- "in all haste the extent to which the postal service": RA, Eriksbergs Arkivet, Autograf samlingen, Wilhelm Carpelan to Karl XIV Johan, 11/8/1819.
- Baron Carpelan ... suggested just such an idea: ibid.
- Baron Carpelan quickly complied: ibid.
- Minister for Colonies ordered a steam vessel: Roberts, op. cit., pp72–73.
- Departing France ... *Voyageur* and *Africain*: ibid, pp58–59.

- the *Caroline* ... first steam vessel in the French Navy: ibid, p84.
- After a 36-day voyage under sail and steam: Spratt, op. cit., p22.
- voyage of the steamship *Savannah*, none was affected more deeply than the United Kingdom: that said, there should be no doubt the continental Europeans recognized the significance of the *Savannah's* voyage beyond the evidence already presented. One additional example is the *Almanac de Gotha*, a French-language annual pocket guide printed in Germany, which contained much of the information any European gentleman would need to conduct his affairs (such as the names of every senior diplomat posted to major foreign capitals). Near the end of each edition of the *Almanac de Gotha* was a brief synopsis of the previous year's major news events. Among the four events listed for June 1819 (in the 1820 edition) was the "arrival at Liverpool of the first steamship that crossed from America to Europe."
- Lord Cathcart, in one of his last dispatches: TNA, FO 65/117, Lord Cathcart to Lord Castlereagh, 10/8–9/26/1819.
- *The success which has attended the Americans*: TNA, ADM 1/4385, Charles Broderip to The Lords Commissioners of the Admiralty, 12/14/1819 (original memorial dated 11/18/1819).
- "competent, scientific persons": ibid.
- Lord Melville ... instructed ... John Barrow to write a reply: ibid.
- "beg to observe a steam vessel ... great utility": TNA, ADM 106/3443, C. Robb to Navy Board, 8/6/1819.
- The Admiralty ... ordered ... first steam-powered tugboat: Lyon, *The Sailing Navy List...*, p149.
- Royal Post Office ... encounter serious competition: Bagwell, *The Post Office Steam Packets...*, p5.
- Broderip ... traveled to London in the spring of 1820: Mason, *Brief Statement of Facts...*, p25. It is worth noting that between the departure of Captain Rogers and the steamship *Savannah* in July 1819 and Broderip's arrival in London in the spring of 1820, the United Kingdom was convulsed by the ongoing political reform movement, including the "Peterloo Massacre," the debate and passage of the Six Acts (intended to prohibit many reform activities), and the Cato Street Conspiracy to murder the British Cabinet.
- placed horizontally within the hold to lessen vibration: ibid, p4.
- "certainty and security": ibid, p27.
- Broderip's ideas would be submitted to a committee: among the members were Sir Joseph Banks and Sir William Congreve.
- submitting his advice in late 1819: ICE, John Rennie Reports, Volume II, 11–160, John Rennie to John Croker, 5/22/1820.
- ... *Steam vessels may be said to be in their infancy...*: ibid.
- The Admiralty ... ordered the Navy Board to get started: TNA, ADM 106/20, Navy Board to John Croker, 11/29/1820.
- ... *unless the Admiralty cram it down the throats*: Smiles, op. cit., p268.
- Sir Seppings approached the Royal Post Office: TNA, POST 41/3, Report No. 298, 7/1/1820.
- until the Surveyors of the Navy had signed off: ibid, Report No. 301, 7/13/1820.
- Freeling hurried over to Downing Street: ibid, POST 34/6, Packet Minutes, 8/2/1820.
- "the infinitely superior qualities of American Steam Vessels": ibid.
- "a Vessel might be purchased in America": ibid.
- who firmly supported the stance he had taken: ibid.
- a second postal steamer was ordered: Owen, "The Post Office Packet Service...," *The Mariner's Mirror*, Vol. 88 (2), 2002, p174.

- committee ... returned a report which was, not surprisingly, unfavorable: TNA, POST 34/6, Packet Minutes, 7/14/1820. Broderip reportedly anticipated as much.
- "considerable ingenuity in many of the details": TNA, T 27/80, Treasury (Arbuthnot) to Postmaster General, 8/25/1820.
- "some of his inventions deserve a further investigation": ibid.
- Vansittart ... and the Lords of the Treasury made it clear: ibid.
- the Treasury Lords approved £7,000: ibid, Treasury (Harrison) to Postmaster General, 9/12/1820, and Treasury (Harrison) to T. Telford, 9/12/1820.
- We desire you will be pleased to acquaint their Lordships: TNA, ADM 106/20, Navy Board to John Croker, 11/29/1820.
- On May 31st, 1821, they began running: Bagwell, op. cit., p8.
- the vessel was immediately re-named *Royal Sovereign*: Actually, it was re-named *Royal Sovereign King George the Fourth*; the name was subsequently shortened repeatedly, until it finally became just *Sovereign*. At this time, it was commonly referred to as *Royal Sovereign*.
- the Postal Lords were getting impatient: Mason, op. cit., p27.
- Broderip took his creation, the *Tartar*, down to Holyhead: ibid.
- "as a *mere Steam Boat*.": ibid, p28.
- keel was finally laid ... first steam-powered tugboat: Lyon, op. cit., p149.
- Admiralty ordered the Navy Board to build two more: ibid.
- *Rising Star* ... arguments between all those involved: NAS, GD 233/1/29, various letters, including 7/20/1820 and 7/27/1820.
- Alvarez agreed ... purchase the vessel: NAS, GD 233/101/83, which includes William Cochrane's description of the threatened sale and deal struck.
- she was re-floated in February of 1821: Spratt, op. cit., pp20–21.
- Post Office steamers ... cut the Holyhead-Howth transit time to 7½ hours: Parliamentary Papers, *Fifth Report of the Select Committee...*, ordered to be printed 6/12/1822, p121 and Appendix No. 2.
- Committee ... asked them a series of particular questions: ibid, p206.
- *Tartar* ... send her back up to the shipyard in Glasgow: Mason, op. cit., p28.
- itemizing the remaining alterations needed: ibid, p29.
- Johnston ... had taken command of a merchantman: TNA, ADM 1/2966, James Henry Johnston to Admiralty, 8/4/1822 and 8/15/1822.
- Johnston attended a meeting ... General Steam Navigation Company: Prinsep, *An Account of Steam Vessels ... in British India*, p5.
- keels were finally laid for the Royal Navy's second and third: Lyon, op.cit., p149.
- Melville ... wrote the word *"Secret."*: DU-ML, Robert Sanders Dundas Papers, Lord Melville to Admiral Sir Thomas Byam Martin, 2/22/1823.
- *At any rate however it will be proper now*: ibid.
- Within days, Admiral Sir Byam Martin responded: ibid, Byam Martin to Lord Melville, 2/28/1823.
- Lord Melville gave his reply: ibid, Lord Melville to Byam Martin, 3/3/1823. Further buttressing the importance of this date in Royal Navy history is the fact that the British Cabinet met on this same day. While it is impossible to say whether Melville wrote his order to Byam Martin before or after the meeting, it stands to reason that the First Lord of the Admiralty at least mentioned his decision to the Cabinet.
- *Do it*: of course, Lord Melville did not literally say or write this—given the standards of civil discourse at the time, that would have been considered extremely rude. Instead, he wrote: "I entirely approve your suggestion that six of the 10 gun Brigs lately ordered to be built should be of such a form as to admit of their receiving + being fitted with the Steam Engines described in your letter."

- no interest in trying to start a steam packet service to India: Prinsep, op. cit., pp5–6.
- around Africa's Cape of Good Hope ... being over 12,000 miles: ibid, p8.
- merchants in the East India trade ... agreed to help: ibid, p6.
- Post Office first ordered the *Tartar* ... to Bristol: Mason, op. cit., p30.
- Lords of the Treasury would be calling the shots: ibid, p31.
- Byam Martin sent an update to Lord Melville: DU-ML, Robert Sanders Dundas Papers, Byam Martin to Lord Melville, 11/26/1823.
- the need for secrecy was no longer necessary: ibid, Lord Melville to Byam Martin, 11/28/1823.
- The modified ten-gun brigs ... not be ordered officially for another six months: Lyon, op. cit., p149.
- At a public meeting in Town Hall: *Bengal Hurkaru*, 12/19/1823.
- came to be known locally as *Steamites*: *Bombay Courier*, 12/20/1823.
- *A great sensation has been produced*: *Bombay Courier*, 6/7/1823.
- *His Lordship in Council cannot relinquish the conviction*: BL-Manuscripts, F/4/776, Bengal Board's Collections, 20983, volume 776, C. Lushington to J. H. Harington, 11/20/1823. The two Lushingtons, Charles of the East India Company and Stephen of the Treasury, were not-too-distantly related.
- "The length of the voyage and the magnitude of the undertaking": ibid, J. H. Harington (for the Steam Committee) to Lord Amherst, 11/26/1823.
- It must be admitted that the first adventures will labor: ibid.
- complete correspondence with Lord Amherst was read aloud: *Bengal Hurkaru*, 12/19/1823.
- total prize money ... nearly 70,000 rupees: Prinsep, op. cit., p6.
- acknowledging all the efforts of Lieutenant Johnston: *Bengal Hurkaru*, 12/19/1823.
- Others were already trying to garner support: Prinsep, op. cit., pp6–7. Another group organized the construction of a steam barque, the *Falcon*, which actually departed Britain in 1825, well before the *Enterprize*. While the *Falcon* successfully reached India, she did not meet the Steam Committee's prize conditions, and received little press or recognition for her voyage.
- By February of 1825, they were able to launch their hull: ibid, p7.
- long-term plan ... regular steam packet service to India: Hoskins, *British Routes to India*, pp94–95.
- Broderip ... to create the Foreign and Colonial Navigation Company: Mason, op. cit., pp45–48.
- The vast importance of obtaining all the advantages: *Prospectus of a Joint Stock Company for Steam Navigation, from Europe to America, and the West Indies*, p9.
- A Steam Ship of 300 tons has crossed the Atlantic: ibid, p7.
- *Enterprize* ... over 120 feet in length and 479 tons burthen: Kennedy, *The History of Steam Navigation*, p47.
- large iron tanks, placed deep within the hull: Prinsep, op. cit., p8.
- the *Enterprize* was perceived, or at least described.: ibid, p7 and woodcut.
- referred to her as a "steamboat": *Newport Mercury*, 10/1/1825, quoting the *New-York Evening Post*, among others.
- A few others offered "steamship": *Essex Register*, 4/27/1826, quoting Calcutta newspapers.
- as a "steam vessel," or "steam packet": *Portsmouth Journal*, 4/30/1825, quoting British newspapers; *Newport Mercury*, 9/17/1825, quoting a London newspaper; *Baltimore Patriot*, 4/20/1826, quoting the *Bengal Hurkaru*, among many others.
- the steamer was not floating correctly: Hoskins, op. cit., p95.
- 17 adventurous passengers: ibid.

- it had taken 113 days and 17 hours: Prinsep, op. cit., p9.
- participants in the venture were sorely disappointed: Hoskins, op. cit., p96.
- had steamed for 63 days of the voyage: Prinsep, op. cit., p9.
- reward Lieutenant Johnston with one-half of the prize money: ibid, p12.
- Rogers ... *Savannah* ... surfaced in the popular dialogue: among the future peaks of Rogers-*Savannah* recognition were—the late 1830s, after the *Sirius* and *Great Western* race—1919, on the centennial of the *Savannah's* voyage—the 1930s–1940s, which included the re-discovery of Marestier's drawings (published in *Yachting* magazine, July 1930), as well as the 1933 creation of National Maritime Day on May 22nd (the *Savannah's* departure date) by President Franklin Delano Roosevelt, and the naming of a Liberty ship after Moses Rogers (in 1942), and the U.S. Post Office issuance of a 125th anniversary stamp (in 1944)—and again in the early 1960s, with the completion of the Nuclear Ship *Savannah*, and the publication of Frank Braynard's book.

APPENDIX—LEGACIES

- John Bogue: NARA, RG21, District of Georgia, Savannah, U.S. District Court, Mixed Case Files, *U.S. vs. John Bogue*, Warrant ("not found"), 2/16/1820; also same venue, U.S. Circuit Court, Mixed Case Files, *Francis H. Nicoll & Co. vs. W. Scarbrough & others*, 9/13/1822.
- Samuel Yates: *City Gazette*, 6/8/1820; SCDAH, Charleston County Will Transcripts, Will of Samuel Yates, Volume 34, pp367–368.
- John Speakman: *Evening Post*, 10/15/1821.
- Joseph P. McKinne: New York County Clerk's Office, Division of Old Records, New York City Chancery Court, CL253, p283, Bill to Foreclose, *John Lewis Augustus Lelievre vs. Joseph Pope McKinne and Anna McKinne and John J. Palmer*, 5/22/1820, and p302, Judgments, 12/8/1820; NARA, RG21, District of Georgia, Savannah, U.S. Circuit Court, Mixed Case Files, *Pott & McKinne vs. Dugas & Cormick*, 3/7/1822.
- Samuel Howard: NARA, RG21, District of Georgia, Savannah, U.S. District Court, Mixed Case Files, various cases, including *U.S. vs. Samuel and Charles Howard* in 1818–1819; GC/GHS, *Register of Deaths in Savannah, Georgia*, Volume IV, p156 (hereafter, "*RDS*").
- James McHenry: *Baltimore Patriot*, 10/13/1826.
- Robert Isaac: *RDS*, Volume IV, p210; GSA, William Scarbrough Collection, Robert Isaac Will, date appears to be 8/26/1827. While Robert Isaac legally owned the Scarbrough mansion after May 1820, it appears to have been effectively under the control of Andrew Low & Co. (see "for sale" advertisement, *The Georgian*, 1/13/1821).
- Andrew Low: Ryan and Golson, *Andrew Low and the Sign...*, in manuscript, pp133–134.
- William S. Gillett: NARA, RG21, District of Georgia, Savannah, U.S. Circuit Court, Mixed Case Files, *Bank of the U.S. vs. Gillett & Co.*, Warrant, 4/14/1821; *The Georgian*, 7/21/1829.
- Robert Mitchell: *RDS*, Volume IV, p249.
- Joseph Habersham: *RDS*, Volume IV, p258; *General Index to Wills, Estates, Administrations, Etc. in Chatham County...*, #164.
- William Scarbrough: *The Georgian*, 5/7/1821, and 1/16/1826; NARA, RG21, District of Georgia, Savannah, U.S. Circuit Court, Mixed Case Files, *Bank of the U.S. vs. William Scarbrough*, 11/22/1819, annual warrants through 1829; Hoffman, *Godfrey Barnsley...*, pp47, 74–75; GSA, Scarbrough Collection, various patent

papers, plus a draft of "Act to incorporate the Georgia-Atlantic and Mexican Gulf Intercommunication Co."; Piechocinski, *The Old Burying Ground...*, pp38, 128.

- John Haslett: NARA, RG21, Eastern District of South Carolina, U.S. District and Circuit Court, Index to Civil Judgments, p75; SCDAH, Charleston District, Court of Equity, Judgment Roll, various suits in 1820, including John Haslett as both plaintiff and defendant; Webber, op. cit., p313.
- J. P. Henry: NARA, RG21, District of Georgia, Savannah, U.S. Circuit Court, Mixed Case Files, various cases from 1820, including *Bank of the U.S. vs. Jacob P. Henry* and *Bank of the U.S. vs. Isaac Minis + J.P. Henry*; also, GHS, Chatham County Superior Court, Minutes, Volume 10, 1818–1822, various cases; *AC*, various citations, including Senate Executive Journal, 1837–1841, p374, re-nomination of Henry as U.S. Navy Agent at Savannah, 3/11/1841; *RDS*, Volume V, p172.
- Gideon Pott: NARA, RG21, District of Georgia, Savannah, U.S. Circuit Court, Minute Book, various Pott & McKinne cases, including from 12/27/1823 to 5/8/1826; MacBean, *Biographical Register of the Saint Andrew's Society...*, Vol. 2, entry 753.
- James S. Bulloch: Bulloch, *A History and Genealogy of the Families of Bulloch...*, pp20–21.
- Abraham B. Fannin: GHS, *Marriages of Chatham County*, op. cit., p128; *RDS*, Volume VI, p93.
- Isaac Minis: NARA, RG21, District of Georgia, Savannah, U.S. District Court, Mixed Case Files, various cases, including *U.S. vs. Isaac Minis* in 1819; also, GHS, Chatham County Superior Court, Minutes, Vol. 10, 1818–1822, various cases; and Kole, *The Minis Family of Georgia*, pp54–55.
- Sheldon C. Dunning: NARA, RG21, District of Georgia, Savannah, U.S. Circuit Court, Mixed Case Files, *Bank of the U.S. vs. Sheldon C. Dunning*, 11/23/1821; also, GHS, Chatham County Superior Court Minutes, Vol. 10, various cases; *General Index to Wills, Estates, Administrations, etc. in Chatham County...*, #196.
- Archibald S. Bulloch: Flores, "Archibald Stobo Bulloch," *Savannah Biographies*, pp9–11.
- Robert Habersham: Shelnutt, "Robert Habersham," *Savannah Biographies*, pp24, 38–39.
- Daniel Dod: *Newport Mercury*, 5/17/1823, among many others, and Braynard, op. cit., p209.
- Samuel Fickett, William Crockett: Fairburn, op. cit., pp2791–2792.
- Francis H. Nicoll: NARA, RG21, District of Georgia, Savannah, U.S. Circuit Court, Mixed Case Files, *Francis H. Nicoll & Co. vs. W. Scarbrough & others*, 9/13/1822; also, Minute Books, various suits of Gideon Pott, "for the use of the Assignees of Pott & McKinne," 12/27/1823 to 5/8/1826; *Connecticut Courant*, 2/27/1841, among others; Thompson, *The History of Long Island...*, p396.
- James P. Allaire: SI, *Savannah* File, F.E. Sickels to J. Elfreth Watkins, 8/11/1892; *Official Catalogue of the New-York Exhibition of the Industry of All Nations, 1853*, pp33, 64.
- Stephen Vail: Cavanaugh et al, op. cit., pp23, 37; Silverman, *Lightning Man...*, pp163, 167, 213.
- Henry James Finn: Stephenson, op. cit., p249; *New York Times*, 1/17/1840; *Hudson River Chronicle*, 1/21/1840, among others.
- General Sir Thomas Graham, Lord Lynedoch: Graham, op. cit., pp187–188, 190.
- Count Karl Ludwig von Ficquelmont: Polišenký, *Aristocrats and the Crowd in the Revolutionary Year 1848...*, pp101, 122.
- Robert Graham: Stephen, *The Dictionary of National Biography*, p361.
- Oliver Sturges and Benjamin Burroughs: Blakely, "Oliver Sturges," *Savannah Biographies*, p11.

- Captain Nathan Holdridge: Albion, *Square Riggers...*, p162; *Pittsfield Sun,* 6/6/1844.
- David Dunham: *Pittsfield Sun,* 4/10/1823, among others; *Boston Daily Advertiser,* 6/6/1823; NARA, RG41, Port/New York, steamship *Robert Fulton,* PRs #191 (6/7/1823), #163 (5/26/1824), #151 (5/6/1825), #430 (12/5/1825); *Newburyport Herald,* 3/26/1824; *Newport Mercury,* 7/17/1824; *AC,* 18th Congress, 2nd Session, Senate Proceedings, pp82–83, 105; *Baltimore Patriot,* 1/3/1826; *Providence Patriot...,* 9/16/1826. Note: the Brazilian Navy changed the *Robert Fulton's* name to *Maria Isabel* (see *Baltimore Patriot,* 3/29/1828).
- Henry Eckford: Fairburn, op. cit., p2782; *New Hampshire Patriot...,* 2/25/1833.
- Cadwallader D. Colden: *New-York Evening Post,* 3/9/1821 and 7/18/1821; *Woodstock Observer,* 5/8/1821; U.S. Congress, House Committee on Elections, *Cases of Contested Elections in Congress, from the Year 1789 to 1834, Inclusive,* pp369–371; *AC,* 17th Congress, 1st Session, House Journal, p133; *Encyclopedia of National Biography,* p200; Colden, *Memoir at the Celebration of the Completion of the New York Canals.* It is interesting to note that New York acquired the nickname "The Empire State" starting in the 1820s; Georgia began to be called "The Empire State of the South" in the 1840s. This rivalry had many seeds—among them was the steamship *Savannah* vs. the steamship *Robert Fulton.*
- Colonel John Stevens: Turnbull, op. cit., p477.
- Captain Elihu S. Bunker: the steamboat inspection act of 1838 (or literally, "An Act to provide for the better security of the lives of passengers on board of vessels propelled in whole or in part by steam") is considered the first major federal consumer protection law in U.S. history.
- Moses Rogers' body: *Cheraw Intelligencer...,* 10/30/1823; *Hartford Courant,* 5/20/1935.
- Adelia Rogers: Cavanaugh et al, op. cit., p67; Rogers, op. cit., p245.
- George Washington Rogers: Rogers, op. cit., p248.
- Stevens Rogers: Wall Papers, pp123, 348; MYS, Connecticut Ship Database, sloops *Gleaner, Frederick, Alexander*; Rogers, op. cit., pp495–496, 499.
- Marquis de Traversé: Sinyukov, *Short Information about Marquis de Traversé's Life.*
- King Karl XIV Johan: Palmer, op. cit., pp238–239.
- Jean Baptiste Marestier: Taillemite, *Dictionnaire des marins français,* pp227–228.
- Charles Broderip: Beamish, *Memoir of the Life of Sir Marc Isambard Brunel,* p188; Hansard, *The Parliamentary Debates,* 3/22/1826; Mason, op. cit., p11; *The London Journal of Arts and Sciences,* Vol. VI, Second Series, p201.
- Lord Liverpool: Hilton, "The Political Arts of Lord Liverpool," *Transactions of the Royal Historical Society,* 5th Series, #38 (1988), pp147–170. Hilton provides a deeper understanding of Liverpool's ways and means as Prime Minister. Foremost among Liverpool's tactics: Cabinet meetings were for discussions, not decision-making, which took place largely in private. Also of great importance was the tactic of deception, which Liverpool and his government practiced regularly, through double-speak and camouflaged action. Hilton believes this *modus operandi,* combined with Liverpool's abilities as a confident and brilliant public debater, represent the secret to success of this privately anxious, apprehensive personality who earned the nickname "Grand Figitatis."
- Commodore John Rodgers: the dangers of placing so much power into a single entity such as the Board of Navy Commissioners were evident to keen minds from the beginning. Among the friendships which U.S. Minister Richard Rush fostered while posted to London was that of Jeremy Bentham, one of the leading legal philosophers of the age. On one of his visits to Bentham's "unique, romantic little homestead" in Westminster, Rush got an earful from his host on the subject of government structure. Rush later recorded the exchange with Bentham:

> *"But what is this," he inquired, "called a Board of Navy Commissioners that you have lately set up? I don't understand it." I explained it to him. "I can't say that I like it," he replied; "the simplicity of your public departments has heretofore been one of their recommendations, but <u>boards</u> make <u>skreens</u>; if any thing goes wrong, you don't know where to find the offender; it was the board that did it, not one of the members; always the <u>board</u>, the <u>board</u>!"*

(as quoted in Powell, op. cit., pp100–101.)

– James K. Paulding: Kime, *Advocate for America...*, p238. Paulding's failure to excite readers with the second series of *Salmagundi* (published in 1819–1820) has been attributed to Washington Irving's absence from the venture. Of equal if not greater importance was the knowledge among informed readers that trying to resurrect William Wizard and Christopher Cockloft was foolish, since their real-life models—Fulton and Livingston—were dead. Further still, the original *Salmagundians* had been proven wrong: steam-powered vessels did work! Paulding appears to have acknowledged as much, however indirectly, when, in *Salmagundi* No. VIII, dated December 18th, 1819 (just two days after the *Savannah* had arrived at Washington), he took note of recent "vast improvements in the mechanical arts."

– John Marshall: key to the *Gibbons vs. Ogden* decision was the Supreme Court's definition of the word "among." As used in the Constitution, the Court ruled that commerce "among the several States" meant "intermingled with them." Since commerce "cannot stop at the external boundary line of each State, but may be introduced into the interior," Congress had the power to regulate interstate commerce (including navigation "in any manner") within a State's boundaries.

SELECTED BIBLIOGRAPHY

The breadth and depth of the historical record for the content of this book—in both published and manuscript form—is awesome. The works listed here either have been used directly in the Source Notes or offer some basis for understanding the subjects and the era described within this story.

BOOKS:

Abbott, Charles, *A Treatise of the Law Relative to Merchant Ships and Seamen: in Four Parts*, 1810.

Adams, John Quincy, *John Quincy Adams in Russia, comprising Portions of the Diary of John Quincy Adams from 1809 to 1814*, 1970.

Adams, John Quincy and Nevins, Allan (editor), *Diary of John Quincy Adams, 1794–1845...*, 1928, 1951.

Ahrens, Toni, *Design Makes a Difference: Shipbuilding in Baltimore, 1795–1835*, 1998.

Albion, Robert G., *The Rise of New York Port*, 1939, 1967.

Albion, Robert G., *Square-Riggers on Schedule: the New York Sailing Packets to England, France, and the Cotton Ports*, 1938, 1965.

Alexandra Feodorovna, and Pope-Hennessy, Una (translator), *A Czarina's Story, being an Account of the Early Married Life of the Emperor Nicholas I of Russia*, 1948.

Alison, Sir Archibald, *Lives of Lord Castlereagh and Sir Charles Stewart, the Second and Third Marquesses of Londonderry...*, 1861.

Allen, Gardner W., *Our Navy and the West Indian Pirates*, 1929.

Allgor, Catherine, *Parlor Politics: in which the Ladies of Washington Helped Build a City and a Government*, 2000.

Almedingen, E. M., *The Emperor Alexander I*, 1966.

Ames, William E., *A History of the National Intelligencer*, 1972.

Ammon, Harry, *James Monroe: the Quest for National Identity*, 1971.

Anschel, Eugene (editor), *The American Image of Russia 1775–1917*, 1974.

Aspinall, Arthur, *The Cabinet Council, 1783–1835*, 1952.

Aspinall-Oglander, Cecil F., *Freshly Remembered; the Story of Thomas Graham, Lord Lynedoch*, 1956.

Association for the Exhibition of the Industry of All Nations, *Official Catalogue of the New-York Exhibition of the Industry of All Nations*, 1853.

Aughton, Peter, *Liverpool: a People's History*, 1990.

Baker, William A., *The Engine-Powered Vessel: from Paddle-Steamer to Nuclear Ship*, 1965.

Baldwin, Cradock et al. (printed for), *Crosby's Complete Pocket Gazetteer of England and Wales: or Traveller's Companion...*, 1818.

Barratt, Glynn, *Russia in Pacific Waters, 1715–1825: a Survey...*, 1981.

Bartlett, C. J., *Great Britain and Sea Power, 1815–1853*, 1963.

Bartlett, Irving H., *John C. Calhoun: a biography*, 1993.

Bartlett, John R., *Dictionary of Americanisms...*, 1848.

Bartlett, Roger P., *Human Capital: the Settlement of Foreigners in Russia, 1762–1804*, 1979.

Bartley, Russell H., *Imperial Russia and the Struggle for Latin American Independence, 1808–1828*, 1978.

Barton, Sir D. Plunket, *Bernadotte, Prince and King, 1810–1844*, 1925.

Bashkina, Nina N. and Trask, David F., *The United States and Russia: the Beginning of Relations, 1765–1815*, 1980.

Bassett, Fletcher S., *Legends and Superstitions of the Sea and of Sailors...*, 1885, 1971.

Bauer, K. Jack, *The New American State Papers, Naval Affairs*, 1981.

Beamish, Richard, *Memoir of the Life of Sir Marc Isambard Brunel*, 1862.

Beers, Andrew, *The Planters' & Merchants' Almanac...*, 1818.

Benson, Adolph B., *Sweden and the American Revolution*, 1926.

Benton, Thomas Hart, *Thirty Years' View...*, 1858.

Blunt, E. M., *The American Coast Pilot...*, 1817.

Blunt, E. M., *Blunt's Stranger's Guide to the City of New York...*, 1817.

Bolster, W. Jeffrey, *Black Jacks: African American Seamen in the Age of Sail*, 1997.

Boydell, John et al., *Boydell's Picturesque Scenery of Norway...*, 1820.

Boyman, Boyman, *Steam Navigation, its Rise and Progress...*, 1840.

Brant, Irving, *James Madison, Commander in Chief, 1812–1836*, 1961.

Braynard, Frank O., *S.S. Savannah: The Elegant Steam Ship*, 1963.

Brewer, J. N., *The Beauties of Ireland: being the Original Delineations, Topographical, Historical, and Biographical, of each County*, 1825–1826.

Bridwell, Ronald E., *"That we should have a port": a History of the Port of Georgetown, South Carolina, 1732–1865*, 1982.

Brown, D. K., *Before the Ironclad: Development of Ship Design, Propulsion, and Armament in the Royal Navy, 1815–60*, 1990.

Brown, D. K., *Paddle Warships: the Earliest Steam Powered Fighting Ships, 1815–1850*, 1993.

Brown, Ralph H., *Mirror for Americans; Likeness of the Eastern Seaboard, 1810*, 1943.

Bulloch, Joseph G. B., *A History and Genealogy of the Families of Bulloch and Stobo...*, 1911.

Burgess, Robert H. and Wood, Graham, H., *Steamboats out of Baltimore*, 1968.

Butenschøn, B.A., *Travellers Discovering Norway in the Last Century—An Anthology*, 1968.

Canney, Donald L., *The Old Steam Navy*, 1990–1993.

Cashin, Edward J., *Beloved Bethesda: a History of George Whitefield's Home for Boys, 1740–2000*, 2001.

Catterall, Ralph C. H., *The Second Bank of the United States*, 1902.

Caulkins, Frances M., *History of New London, Connecticut*, 1895.

Caulkins, Frances M. and Gilman, Emily, *The Stone Records of Groton*, 1903.

Cavanaugh, Cam and Hoskins, Barbara and Pingeon, Frances D., *At Speedwell in the Nineteenth Century*, 1981, 2001.

Céspedes, Mario and Garreaud, Lelia, *Gran diccionario de Chile...*, 1988.

Chapelle, Howard I., *The Pioneer Steamship Savannah; a Study for a Scale Model*, 1961.

Chapelle, Howard I., *The Search for Speed under Sail, 1700–1855*, 1967.

Charleston (SC), City of, *Year Book*, 1881.

Chatterton, E. Keble, *King's Cutters and Smugglers 1700–1855*, 1912.

Cleland, James, *The Rise and Progress of the City of Glasgow: comprising an Account of its Public Buildings, Charities, and Other Concerns*, 1820.

Coad, J. G., *The Royal Dockyards, 1690–1850: Architecture and Engineering Works of the Sailing Navy*, 1989.

Coker, P.C., *Charleston's Maritime Heritage, 1670–1865: an Illustrated History*, 1987.

Colden, Cadwallader D., *The Life of Robert Fulton*, 1817.

Colden, Cadwallader D., *Memoir ... at the Celebration of the Completion of the New York Canals*, 1825.

Coletta, Paolo E., *American Secretaries of the Navy*, 1980.

Congress, United States, House Committee on Elections, *Cases of Contested Elections in Congress, from the Year 1789 to 1834, Inclusive*, 1834.

Conway, Derwent, *A Personal Narrative of a Journey through Norway, Part of Sweden, and the Islands and States of Denmark*, 1829.

Cookson, J. E., *Lord Liverpool's Administration: the Crucial Years, 1815–1822*, 1975.

Cooley, E., *A Description of the Etiquette at Washington City, ...*, 1829.

Cornford, Leslie Cope, *A Century of Sea Trading, 1824–1924, the General Steam Navigation Company...*, 1924.

Corry, John and Troughton, Thomas, *The History of Liverpool: from the Earliest Authenticated Period down to the Present Times*, 1810.

Crisman, Kevin J. and Cohn, Arthur B., *When Horses Walked on Water: Horse-Powered Ferries in Nineteenth-Century America*, 1998.

Critchett & Woods, *The Post Office London Directory for 1820*.

Cross, Anthony, *By the Banks of the Neva*, 1997.

Cunningham, Noble E., *The Presidency of James Monroe*, 1996.

Davis & Force, *A Register of Officers and Agents, Civil, Military, and Naval, in the Service of the United States, ...*, 1820–1824.

Dayton, Fred E., *Steamboats Days*, 1925.

Delano, Judah, *The Washington Directory...*, 1822.

Delavoye, Alexander M., *Life of Thomas Graham, Lord Lynedoch*, 1880.

Dodd, Allison and Folsom, Joseph F., *Genealogy and History of the Daniel Dod Family in America, 1646–1940*, 1940.

Dudley, Wade G., *Splintering the Wooden Wall: the British Blockade of the United States, 1812–1815*, 2003.

Dugdale, James, *The New British Traveler, or Modern Panorama of England and Wales*, 1819.

Duncan, John M., *Travels through Part of the United States and Canada in 1818 and 1819*, 1823.

Dupin, Charles, *Two Excursions to the Ports of England, Scotland, and Ireland...*, 1819.

Emmerson, John C. Jr., *The Steamboat Comes to Norfolk Harbor, and the Log of the First Ten Years*, 1949.

Essex Institute, *American Vessels Captured by the British during the Revolution and War of 1812*, 1911.

Fairburn, William Armstrong, *Merchant Sail*, 1945–1955.

Faux, W., *Memorable Days in America: being a Journal of a Tour to the United States, ...*, 1823.

Fearon, Henry B., *Sketches of America; a Narrative of a Journey of Five Thousand Miles through the Eastern and Western States, 1818*, 1969.

Federal Writers' Project, *A Maritime History of New York*, 1941, 1977.

Federal Writers' Project, *Savannah*, 1937.

Fincham, John, *An Introductory Outline of the Practice of Shipbuilding, ...*, 1825.

Fischer, David Hackett, *Washington's Crossing*, 2004.

Force, Peter, *A National Calendar, for...*, 1820–1824.

Fraser, Charles, *Reminiscences of Charleston...*, 1854.

Fry, Michael, *The Dundas Despotism*, 1992.

Gales and Seaton, *American State Papers. Documents, Legislative and Executive, of the Congress of the United States*, 1832–1861.

Gales and Seaton, *Annals of Congress*, various years.

Gamble, Thomas, *A History of the City Government of Savannah, Georgia, from 1790 to 1901*, 1900.

Gamble, Thomas, *Savannah Duels and Duellists, 1733–1877*, 1923.

Gardiner, Robert (editor) and Greenhill, Basil (consultant editor), *The Advent of Steam: the Merchant Steamship before 1900*, 1993.

Gardiner, Robert (editor) and Lambert, Andrew (consultant editor), *Steam, Steel & Shellfire: the Steam Warship, 1815–1905*, 1992.

Garrison, James H. and Merrill, Walter M., *Behold Me Once More; the Confessions of James Holley Garrison, brother of William Lloyd Garrison*, 1954.

Gash, Norman, *Lord Liverpool: the Life and Political Career of Robert Banks Jenkinson, Second Earl of Liverpool, 1770–1828*, 1984.

Gause, Harry T., *1836 Semi-Centennial Memoir of the Harlan & Hollingsworth Company, Wilmington, Delaware, U.S.A.*, 1886.

Georgia Historical Society, *Genealogical Committee of, Marriages of Chatham County, Georgia*, 1993.

Georgia Historical Society, *Genealogical Committee of, Register of Deaths in Savannah, Georgia*, 1983–.

Georgia, State of, *Acts of the General Assembly of the State of Georgia*, various years.

Georgia, State of, *House Journal*, various years.

Georgia, State of, *Laws of Georgia*, various years.

Georgia, State of, *Senate Journal*, various years.

Gibbon, Edward and Allen, Paul, *Memoirs of the Public Character and Life of Alexander the First, Emperor of All the Russias*, 1818.

Gilmartin, Kevin, *Print Politics: the Press and Radical Opposition in Early Nineteenth-Century England*, 1996.

Gooding, John, *Rulers and Subjects: Government and People in Russia, 1801–1991*, 1996.

Goold, William, *Portland in the Past, with Historical Notes of Old Falmouth*, 1886.

Gore, J., *Gore's Directory of Liverpool and its Environs...*, 1818 and 1821.

Graham, John M., *Memoir of General Lord Lynedoch*, 1877.

Granville, A.B., *St. Petersburgh. A Journal of Travels to and from that Capital...*, 1828.

Great Britain-Admiralty, *The Navy List*, various years.

Green, Constance McLaughlin, *Washington: Village and Capital, 1800–1878*, 1962.

Greenhill, Basil, *Steam & Sail: in Britain and North America*, 1973.

Greenhill, Basil and Giffard, Ann, *Steam, Politics and Patronage: the Transformation of the Royal Navy, 1815–54*, 1994.

Gustafson, Alrik, *A History of Swedish Literature*, 1961.

Guttridge, Leonard F. and Smith, Jay D., *The Commodores*, 1969.

Hamilton-Williams, David, *The Fall of Napoleon*, 1994.

Hansard, T. C., *The Parliamentary Debates*, 1826.

Harden, William, *A History of Savannah and South Georgia*, 1913.

Harris, William T., *Remarks Made during a Tour through the United States of America, in the years 1817, 1818, and 1819*, 1821.

Harris, William W. and Allyn, Charles, *The Battle of Groton Heights: a Collection of Narratives...*, 1882.

Hartley, Janet M., *Alexander I*, 1994.

Hasbrouck, Alfred, *Foreign Legionaries in the Liberation of Spanish South America*, 1928.

Haywood, Richard M., *The Beginnings of Railway Development in Russia in the Reign of Nicholas I, 1835–1842*, 1969.

Herdman, William G., *Herdman's Liverpool*, 1968.

Heyl, Erik, *Early American Steamers*, 1953–1969.

Hines, Christian, *Early Recollections of Washington City*, 1866.

Holditch, Robert, *The Emigrant's Guide to the United States of America...*, 1818.

Holly, David C., *Chesapeake Steamboats: Vanished Fleet*, 1994.

Holmes, T. W., *The Semaphore: the Story of the Admiralty-to-Portsmouth Shutter Telegraph and Semaphore Lines, 1796 to 1847*, 1983.

Hoole, W. Stanley, *The Antebellum Charleston Theatre*, 1946.

Hoskins, Halford L., *British Routes to India*, 1966.

Howitt, E., *Selections from Letters Written during a Tour through the United States in the Summer and Autumn of 1819...*, 1820.

Hunter, C. G., *Russia: being a Complete Picture of that Empire...*, 1817.

Hurd, D. Hamilton, *History of New London County, Connecticut, with Biographical Sketches...*, 1882.

Hyde, Charles K., *Copper for America: the United States Copper Industry from Colonial Times to the 1990s*, 1998.

Jacobsen, Helge S., *An Outline History of Denmark*, 2000.

James, John T., *Journal of a Tour in Germany, Sweden, Russia, Poland in 1813–14*, 1819.

Jenkins, John S., *History of Political Parties in the State of New-York...*, 1846.

Jensen, Cheryl L., *The Vanderfords: Early Settlers in America*, 1992.

Johnson, Whittington B., *Black Savannah, 1788–1864*, 1996.

Johnston, Robert, *Travels through Part of the Russian Empire...*, 1815.

Jones, Charles C. and Dutcher, Salem, *Memorial History of Augusta, Georgia*, 1890, 1980.

Jones, George M., *Travels in Norway, Sweden, Finland, Russia and Turkey...*, 1827.

Jones, W. Glyn, *Denmark: a Modern History*, 1986.

Jordan, Weymouth T., *George Washington Campbell of Tennessee, Western Statesman*, 1955.

Kaye, Thomas, *The Stranger in Liverpool; or, an Historical and Descriptive View of the Town of Liverpool and its Environs*, 1823.

Kennedy, John, *The History of Steam Navigation*, 1903.

Kennedy, Nigel W., *Records of the Early British Steamships...*, 1933.

Kennon, Donald R. and Striner, Richard, *Washington Past and Present: a Guide to the Nation's Capital*, 1983.

Kime, Wayne, *Advocate for America: the Life of James Kirke Paulding*, 2003.

King, Irving H., *The Coast Guard under Sail: the U.S. Revenue Cutter Service, 1789–1865*, 1989.

King, Rufus and King, Charles R. (editor), *The Life and Correspondence of Rufus King...*, 1900.

Klimenko, Michael, *Tsar Alexander I: Portrait of an Autocrat*, 2002.

Kohn, David et al, *Internal Improvement in South Carolina, 1817–1828...*, 1938.

Lambert, Andrew D., *The Last Sailing Battlefleet: Maintaining Naval Mastery 1815–1850*, 1991.

Lankford, Éamon, *Cape Clear Island: Its People and Landscape*, 1999.

Larsen, Karen, *A History of Norway*, 1948.

Laurie, R.H., *Laurie's Collection of the Maritime Flags of all Nations, ...*, 1821.

Leet, Ambrose, *A Directory of the Market Towns, ... Ireland*, 1814.

Livingston, Edwin Brockholst, *The Livingstons of Livingston Manor...*, 1910.

Lloyd, Christopher, *Lord Cochrane: Seaman, Radical, Liberator: a Life of Thomas, Lord Cochrane, 10th Earl of Dundonald*, 1947, 1998.

Lloyd, Christopher, *Mr. Barrow of the Admiralty: a Life of Sir John Barrow, 1764–1848*, 1970.

Longworth, David, *Longworth's American Almanac...*, 1809–1825.

Looney, J. Jefferson and Woodward, Ruth L., *Princetonians 1791–1794*, 1991.

Lyon, David, *The Sailing Navy List: All the Ships of the Royal Navy, Built, Purchased and Captured, 1688–1860*, 1993.

Lytle, William M. and Holdcamper, Forrest R., *Merchant Steam Vessels of the United States, 1790–1868: "The Lytle-Holdcamper List,"…*, 1975.

Macartney, Clarence and Dorrance, John, *The Bonapartes in America*, 1939.

MacBean, William M., *Biographical Register of Saint Andrew's Society of the State of New York…*, 1922–1925.

Macfarlane, Robert, *History of Propellers and Steam Navigation with Biographical Sketches of the Early Inventors*, 1851.

MacGregor, David R., *Fast Sailing Ships: their Design and Construction, 1775–1875*, 1988.

Mackay, Robert and Eliza, and Hartridge, Walter (editor), *The Letters of Robert Mackay to his Wife, written from Ports in America and England, 1795–1816*, 1949.

Maffeo, Steven E., *Most Secret and Confidential: Intelligence in the Age of Nelson*, 2000.

Maguire, John E., *Historical Souvenir: Savannah Fire Department*, 1906.

Marestier, Jean Baptiste, *Mémoire sur les Bateaux à Vapeur des États Unis d'Amérique, …*, 1824.

Marestier, Jean Baptiste and Withington, Sidney (translator), *Memoir on Steamboats of the United States of America*, 1957.

Markham, Felix, *The Bonapartes*, 1975.

Martin, Alexander M., *Romantics, Reformers, Reactionaries: Russian Conservative Thought and Politics in the Reign of Alexander I*, 1997.

Martineau, Gilbert, *Napoleon's St. Helena*, 1969.

Martis, Kenneth C. et al, *The Historical Atlas of the United States Congressional Districts, 1789–1983*, 1982.

Mason, William, *Brief Statement of Facts, connected with the Scientific Pursuits of the late Charles Broderip, Esq.…*, 1829.

Masson, Frédéric, *Napoleon at St. Helena, 1815–1821*, 1950.

McConnell, Allen, *Tsar Alexander I: Paternalistic Reformer*, 1987.

McKee, Christopher, *A Gentlemanly and Honorable Profession: the Creation of the U.S. Naval Officer Corps, 1794–1815*, 1991.

Melish, John, *Travels through the United States of America in the years 1806 & 1807, and 1809, 1810 & 1811, …*, 1818, 1970.

Meredith, William G., *Memorials of Charles John, King of Sweden and Norway*, 1829.

Mikhailovich, Nikolai (editor), *L'Impératrice Élisabeth, épouse d'Alexandre Ier…*, 1908–1909.

Mills, Robert, *Statistics of South Carolina…*, 1826.

Moore, Glover, *The Missouri Controversy, 1819–1821*, 1953.

Morgan, George, *The Life of James Monroe*, 1969.

Morison, Samuel Eliot, *The Oxford History of the American People*, 1965.

Morris, Edward, *The Life of Henry Bell…*, 1844.

Morrison, John H., *History of American Steam Navigation*, 1903, 1967.

Morriss, Roger, *Cockburn and the British Navy in Transition: Admiral Sir George Cockburn, 1772–1853*, 1997.

Muir, Ramsay, *A History of Liverpool*, 1907.

Mulvey, Christopher, *Transatlantic Manners: Social Patterns in Nineteenth-Century Anglo-American Travel Literature*, 1990.

Napier, Priscilla H., *Black Charlie: a Life of Admiral Sir Charles Napier KCB, 1787–1860*, 1995.

New York State, *Laws of the State of New-York*, various years.

Noble, John, *Noble's Instructions to Emigrants; an Attempt to give a Correct Account of the United States of America…*, 1819.

Oakley, Stewart P., *A Short History of Sweden*, 1966.

Osborne, Brian D., *The Ingenious Mr. Bell: a Life of Henry Bell…*, 1995.

Overman, Frederick, *The Manufacture of Iron, in all its Various Branches…*, 1851.

Owens, Hubert B., *Georgia's Planting Prelate...*, 1945.

Palmer, Alan, *Alexander I: Tsar of War and Peace*, 1974.

Palmer, Alan, *Bernadotte: Napoleon's Marshal, Sweden's King*, 1990.

Palmer, John, *Journal of Travels in the United States of North America ... performed in the year 1817...*, 1818.

Pappalardo, Bruno, *Royal Navy Lieutenants' Passing Certificates (1691–1902)*, 2001.

Parliamentary Papers, House of Commons, *Fifth Report of the Select Committee on the Roads from London to Holyhead ... STEAM BOATS &c*, 1822.

Parsons, Usher, Surgeon USN, *Sailor's Physician, Exhibiting the Symptoms, Causes and Treatment of Diseases Incident to Seamen and Passengers in Merchant Vessels, ...*, 1820.

Paulding, James Kirke, *A Sketch of Old England*, 1822.

Paullin, Charles O., *Commodore John Rodgers; Captain, Commodore, and Senior Officer of the American Navy, 1773–1838*, 1910, 1967.

Paullin, Charles O., *Paullin's History of Naval Administration, 1775–1911: a Collection of Articles from the U. S. Naval Institute Proceedings*, 1968.

Payzant, Joan M. and Lewis J., *Like a Weaver's Shuttle: a History of the Halifax-Dartmouth Ferries*, 1979.

Pedersen, Laurits, and Sabra and Boisen (translators), *Elsinore: a Guide and a Historical Account with Special Regard to its English Memories*, 1937.

Perry, John, *American Ferryboats*, 1937.

Perthes, Justus, *Almanach de Gotha*, 1820.

Peterson, Merrill D., *The Great Triumvirate: Webster, Clay and Calhoun*, 1987.

Petrie, Sir Charles, *Lord Liverpool and his Times*, 1954.

Philip, Cynthia Owen, *Robert Fulton, a Biography*, 1985.

Phillipson, David, *Smuggling*, 1973.

Picton, Sir James Allanson, *Memorials of Liverpool, Historical and Topographical...*, 1873.

Piechocinski, Elizabeth C., *The Old Burying Ground: Colonial Park Cemetery, Savannah, Georgia, 1750–1853*, 1999.

Pigot, J. & Co., *The Commercial Directory of Scotland, Ireland, and the Four Most Northern Counties of England for 1820–21 & 22...*, 1820.

Pinkerton, John, *A General Collection of the Best and Most Interesting Voyages and Travels in All Parts of the World...*, *Travels in Denmark, by W. Coxe*, 1809.

Polišenký, Josef V., *Aristocrats and the Crowd in the Revolutionary Year 1848...*, 1980.

Pond, E. Leroy, *Junius Smith: a Biography of the Father of the Atlantic Liner*, 1927.

Popperwell, Ronald G., *Norway*, 1972.

Powell, J. H., *Richard Rush, Republican Diplomat, 1780–1859*, 1942.

Preble, George Henry and Lochhead, John Lipton, *A Chronological History of the Origin and Development of Steam Navigation*, 1883.

Preston, Daniel, *A Comprehensive Catalogue of the Correspondence and Papers of James Monroe*, 2001.

Preston, Daniel (editor) and DeLong, Marlena C. (assistant editor), *The Papers of James Monroe*, 2003–.

Prinsep, G. A., *An Account of Steam Vessels and of Proceedings connected with Steam Navigation in British India*, 1830.

Purdy, John, *The Colombian Navigator, or, Sailing Directory for the American Coasts and the West Indies...*, 1819.

Rappaport, Angelo S., *Superstitions of Sailors*, 1928.

Rees, John S., *History of the Liverpool Pilotage Service...*, 1950.

Religious Tract Society of Philadelphia, *The Seaman's Spy-Glass, or, God's Ways and Works Discovered at Sea*, 1819.

Reps, John W., *Washington on View: the Nation's Capital since 1790*, 1991.

Ridgely-Nevitt, Cedric, *American Steamships on the Atlantic*, 1981.

Rogers, Daniel, *The New-York City-Hall Recorder*, 1818 and 1822 editions.

Rogers, James Swift, *James Rogers of New London, Ct., and his Descendants*, 1902.

Rordansz, C. W., *European Commerce, or, Complete Mercantile Guide to the Continent of Europe...*, 1819.

Rose, John H., *The Life of Napoleon I*, 1902.

Rowe, William, *Shipbuilding Days in Casco Bay, 1727–1890...*, 1929.

Ruddock, Samuel, *Palladium of Knowledge, or, The Carolina and Georgia Almanac*, 1818.

Rush, Richard, *The Court of London from 1819 to 1825*, 1873.

Ryan, Jennifer G. and Golson, Hugh S., *Andrew Low and the Sign of the Buck: Trade, Triumph, Tragedy at the House of Low*, 2008.

Sainty, John Christopher and Collinge, J. M., *Office-Holders in Modern Britain*, 1972–.

Saul, Norman E., *Distant Friends: the United States and Russia, 1763–1867*, 1991.

Saunders, David, *Russia in the Age of Reaction and Reform, 1808–1881*, 1992.

Scharf, J. Thomas, *History of Baltimore City and County...*, 1881.

Schenck & Turner, *The Directory and Stranger's Guide for the City of Charleston...*, 1816 and 1819.

Schroeder, John H., *Commodore John Rodgers: Paragon of the Early American Navy*, 2006.

Scott, Franklin D. (editor/translator) and Klinkowström, Axel, *Baron Klinkowström's America, 1818–1820*, 1952.

Scoville, Joseph A., *The Old Merchants of New York City, 1863–1869*, 1968.

Scranton, Philip, *Proprietary Capitalism: The Textile Manufacture at Philadelphia, 1800–1885*, 1983.

Seaton, Josephine, *William Winston Seaton of the "National Intelligencer": A Biographical Sketch*, 1871, 1970.

Shea, John D. G. (editor), *The Operations of the French Fleet under the Count de Grasse...*, 1864.

Silver, James W., *Edmund Pendleton Gaines, Frontier General*, 1949.

Silverman, Kenneth, *Lightning Man*, 2004.

Simons, Katherine D. M., *Stories of Charleston Harbor*, 1930.

Sinclair, Robert C., *Across the Irish Sea: Belfast-Liverpool Shipping since 1819*, 1990.

Skinner, Virginia B., *A Brief History of the Baptists of Georgetown, S.C.*, 1992.

Skipton, David M. and Michalove, Peter A., *Postal Censorship in Imperial Russia*, 1989.

Smiles, Samuel, *Lives of the Engineers*, 1968.

Smith, Graham, *King's Cutters: the Revenue Service and the War against Smuggling*, 1983.

Smith, H. Allen, *A Genealogical History of the Descendants of the Rev. Nehemiah Smith of New London County, Conn., ...*, 1889.

Smithers, Henry, *Liverpool, its Commerce, Statistics, and Institutions; with a History of the Cotton Trade*, 1825.

South Carolina, State of, *Statutes at Large of South Carolina*, various years.

Spears, John R., *Story of the American Merchant Marine*, 1910.

Spongberg, Viola H., *The Philosophy of Erik Gustaf Geijer*, 1945.

Spratt, H. Philip, *Transatlantic Paddle Steamers*, 1967.

Stephen, Sir Leslie et al, *The Dictionary of National Biography ...* (UK), 1921–1922.

Stevenson, D. Alan, *The World's Lighthouses from Ancient Times to 1820*, 1959.

Stockdale, W. (printed for), *The Royal Kalendar, and Court and City Register for England, Scotland, Ireland, and the Colonies, for the year 1819*, 1819.

Stomberg, Andrew Adin, *A History of Sweden*, 1931.

"Surgeon in the British Navy," *A Voyage to St. Petersburg in 1814, with Remarks on the Imperial Russian Navy*, 1822.

Sutcliffe, Alice Crary, *Robert Fulton and the "Clermont"...*, 1909.
Svin'in, Pavel and Yarmolinsky, Avrahm (editor), *Picturesque United States of America, 1811, 1812, 1813...*, 1930.
Svin'in, Pavel, *Traveling across North America, 1812–1813: Watercolors by the Russian Diplomat*, 1992.
Swift, Michael, *Historical Maps of Ireland*, 1999.
Tabbert, Mark, *American Freemasons: Three Centuries of Building Communities*, 2005.
Taillemite, Étienne, *Dictionnaire des marins français*, 1982.
Taylor, George Rogers, *The Transportation Revolution, 1815–1860*, 1951.
Temin, Peter, *Iron and Steel in Nineteenth-Century America, an Economic Inquiry*, 1964.
Thaarup, Frederik and Martensen, Hans Andersen, *The Latest Revis'd Sound-Tariff: a Manual for Merchants and Masters of Vessels...*, 1821.
Thayer, Theodore, *As We Were: the Story of Old Elizabethtown*, 1964.
Thomas, Donald S., *Cochrane: Britannia's Last Sea-King*, 1978.
Thompson, E. P., *The Making of the English Working Class*, 1964.
Thompson, Benjamin F., *The History of Long Island...*, 1843.
Thomson, Thomas, *Travels in Sweden, during the Autumn of 1812*, 1813.
Tibbles, Anthony, *Illustrated Catalog of Marine Paintings in the Merseyside Maritime Museum, Liverpool*, 1999.
Tornquist, Carl Gustaf, *The Naval Campaigns of Count de Grasse during the American Revolution...*, 1942.
Toselli, Angelo, *Panorama Peterburga 1820 goda*, 1991.
Town, Ithiel, *Atlantic Steam-Ships; Some Ideas and Statements, ...*, 1838.
Troyat, Henri, *Alexander of Russia: Napoleon's Conqueror*, 1982.
Tryon, Warren S., *A Mirror for Americans; Life and Manners in the United States, 1790–1870*, 1952.
Tulard, Jean, *Dictionnaire Napoléon*, 1987.
Turnbull, Archibald D., *John Stevens: An American Record*, 1928.
Turner, Michael J., *The Age of Unease: Government and Reform in Britain, 1782–1832*, 2000.
Tyler, David B., *Steam Conquers the Atlantic*, 1939.
United States, *Statutes at Large of the United States of America*, various years.
United States, *United States Congressional Serial Set*, various years.
Van Thal, Herbert Maurice (editor), *The Prime Ministers*, 1974–75.
Villiers, Alan John, *The Way of a Ship; being Some Account of the Ultimate Development of the Ocean-Going Square-Rigged Sailing Vessel...*, 1970.
Virginskii, V. S., *Robert Fulton 1765–1815*, 1976.
Vogel-Rödin, Gösta (editor) and Britten-Austin, Paul (translator), *The Bernadottes: their Political and Cultural Achievements*, 1991.
Wade, Richard C., *Slavery in the Cities; the South, 1820–1860*, 1964.
Warden, David Bailie, *A Chorographical and Statistical Description of the District of Columbia: the Seat of the General Government of the United States*, 1816.
Warden, David Bailie, *A Statistical, Political, and Historical Account of the United States of North America; from the Period of their First Colonization to the Present Day*, 1819.
Way, William, *History of the New England Society of Charleston, South Carolina...*, 1920.
Webb, Thomas, *The Freemason's Monitor; or, Illustrations of masonry, ...*, 1808.
Wheeler, Richard, *In Pirate Waters*, 1969.
Wheeler, William Ogden, *Ogden Family in America, Elizabethtown Branch...*, 1907.
White, Joshua E., *Letters on England: comprising Descriptive Scenes with Remarks...*, 1816.
Whiteman, Maxwell, *Copper for America; the Hendricks Family and a National Industry, 1755–1939*, 1971.

Williams, Stanley T., *The Life of Washington Irving*, 1935.
Wilson, J. H., *Facts connected with the Origin and Progress of Steam Communication between India and England*, 1850.
Wilson, James J. (compiler), *A National Song-Book, being a Collection of Patriotic, Martial, and Naval Songs and Odes, principally of American Composition*, 1813.
Wilson, Timothy, *Flags at Sea: a Guide to the Flags Flown at Sea by Ships of the Major Maritime Nations, …*, 1999.
Young, James S., *The Washington Community, 1800–1828*, 1966.
Young, Norwood, *Napoleon in Exile: St. Helena (1815–1821)*, 1915.
—, *The Visual Encyclopedia of Nautical Terms under Sail*, 1978.

DISSERTATIONS AND OTHER WORKS:

Bealer, Lewis W., *The Privateers of Buenos Aires, 1815–1821: their Activities in the Hispanic American Wars of Independence*, University of California, 1935.
Bergquist, Harold E., *Russian-American Relations: The Diplomacy of Henry Middleton, American Minister at St. Petersburg, 1820–1830*, Boston University, 1970.
Blakely, Mitchell, "Oliver Sturges," *Savannah Biographies*, Volume 15, Armstrong Atlantic State University, 1987.
Coombe, Philip W., *The Life and Times of James P. Allaire: Early Founder and Steam Engine Builder*, New York University, 1991.
Cubitt, D. J., *Lord Cochrane and the Chilean Navy, 1818–1823*, University of Edinburgh, 1974.
DuBois, Roy L., *John Stevens: Transportation Pioneer*, New York University, 1973.
Dunham, Chester G., *The Diplomatic Career of Christopher Hughes*, Ohio State University, 1968.
Dykstra, Douglas, *The Richard Rush Ministry to Great Britain, 1818–1825*, Kent State University, 1972.
Earman, Cynthia D., *Boardinghouses, Parties and the Creation of a Political Society: Washington City, 1800–1830*, Louisiana State University-Baton Rouge, 1992.
Fickett, Linwood P., *Notes on the Fickett Family*, Maine Historical Society.
Flores, Jan, "Archibald Stobo Bulloch," *Savannah Biographies*, Volume 18, Armstrong Atlantic State University, 1990.
Gibson, Campbell, *Population of the 100 Largest Cities and Other Urban Places in the United States: 1790–1990*, U.S. Census Bureau, Population Division W.P. No. 27, 1998.
Gibson, Campbell and Jung, Kay, *Historical Census Statistics On Population Totals by Race, 1790 to 1990, …, For Large Cities and Other Urban Places in the United States*, U.S. Census Bureau, Population Division W.P. No. 76, 2005.
Gregg, Dorothy, *The Exploitation of the Steamboat: the Case of Colonel John Stevens*, Columbia University, 1951.
Hall, Elton W., *Sailmaking in Connecticut prior to 1860*, University of Delaware, 1968.
Hoffman, Nelson M., *Godfrey Barnsley, 1805–1873: British Cotton Factor in the South*, University of Kansas, 1964, 1976.
McCrary, Royce C., *John MacPherson Berrien of Georgia (1781–1856): a Political Biography*, University of Georgia, 1971.
Packard, Brigadier J. J., *Sir Robert Seppings Kt. FRS, Surveyor of the Royal Navy 1813–1832, His Family Background*, held at NMM, 1975.
Rahn, Ruby A., *River Highway for Trade: The Savannah*, The Georgia Salzberger Society, n.d.
Reeves, Jesse Siddall and Hughes, Christopher, *A Diplomat Glimpses Parnassus: excerpts from the Correspondence of Christopher Hughes*, University of Michigan, 1934.

Rentz, Thomas H., *The Public Life of David B. Mitchell*, University of Georgia, 1955.
Roberts, Stephen S., *The Introduction of Steam Technology in the French Navy, 1818–1852*, University of Chicago, 1976.
Shelnutt, Cherri, "Robert Habersham," *Savannah Biographies*, Volume 14, Armstrong Atlantic State University, 1986.
Sinyukov, V., *Short Information about Marquis de Traversé's Life*, 2002.
Smith, Wallace C., *Georgia Gentlemen: the Habershams of Eighteenth-Century Savannah*, University of North Carolina-Chapel Hill, 1971.
Stephenson, Nan Louise, *The Charlestown Theatre Management of Charles Gilfert, 1817 to 1822*, University of Nebraska-Lincoln, 1988.
Wright, Conrad, *The Origins and Early Years of the Trans-Atlantic Packet Lines of New York, 1817–1835*, Harvard University, 1931.

PAMPHLETS:

American and Colonial Steam Navigation Company, *Prospectus of a Joint Stock Company for Steam Navigation, from Europe to America, and the West Indies*, 1825.
Degrand, P.P.F., and Dearborn, H.A.S., *Revenue Laws and Custom-House Regulations...*, 1821.
Fulton, Robert, *Report of the Practicability of Navigating with Steamboats, on the Southern Waters of the United States, ...*, 1813.
His Majesty's Stationary Office, *Instructions to Officers Appointed to Examine the Masters of all Ships and Vessels Arriving from Foreign Ports*, 1819.
Johnson, Captain J. E., *An Address to the Public, on the Advantages of a Steam Navigation to India*, 1824.
MacLean, Charles, *Observations on Quarantine: being the Substance of a Lecture, delivered at the Liverpool Lyceum, in October, 1824...*, 1824.
Philadelphia (PA), *Report of the Joint Committee appointed by the Select and Common Councils on the Subject of Steam Boats*, 1817.
Schultz, J. Frederik, *Ordonnance, touchant la Quarantaine établie pour les royaumes de Dannemarc & de Norvège*, 8 Fevrier 1805.
Treasury, U.S. Department of the, *Steam Engines: Letter from the Secretary of the Treasury...*, 1838.
Tredgold, Thomas, *Remarks on Steam Navigation, and its Protection, Regulation, and Encouragement...*, 1825.
Watkins, J. Elfreth, *The Log of the Savannah*, 1892.

ARTICLES:

Abbott, Jacob, "The Novelty Works, ... " *Harper's New Monthly Magazine*, No. XII, May 1851, Vol. II.
Bagwell, Philip, "The Post Office Steam Packets, 1821–1836, and the Development of Shipping on the Irish Sea," *Maritime History* (by Robert Craig), Vol. 1, 1971.
Bowden, Mary Weatherspoon, "Cocklofts and Slang-whangers: The Historical Sources of Washington Irving's *Salmagundi*," *New York History*, Volume 61, No. 2 (April 1980).
Braynard, Frank O., "Copper for the Savannah of 1818." *Publication of the American Jewish Society*, Volume 48, No. 3 (March 1959).
Carson, E.A., "The Customs Quarantine Service," *The Mariner's Mirror*, Vol. 64, No. 1 (1978).

Clark, Allen C., "Joseph Gales Junior, Editor and Mayor," *Records of the Columbia Historical Society*, volume 23 (1920).

Coulter, E. Merton, "The Great Savannah Fire of 1820." *Georgia Historical Quarterly*, Volume XXIII, No. 1, March 1939.

Gilfillan, S. C., "The First Sea Going Auxiliary," *Yachting*, July 1930.

Hilton, Boyd, "The Political Arts of Lord Liverpool," *Transactions of the Royal Historical Society*, 5th Series, #38 (1988).

Klinkowström, Axel, "In Monroe's Administration; Letters of Baron Axel Klinkowström," *The American-Scandinavian Review*, Volume XIX, No. 7 (July 1931).

Klinkowström, Axel and Scott, Franklin D., "Swedish trade with America in 1820: a letter of advice from Baron Axel Klinkowström." *The Journal of Modern History*, Volume XXV, No. 4, December 1953.

Lincoln, Margaret, "Naval Ship Launches as Public Spectacle," *The Mariner's Mirror*, Volume 83, No. 4 (Nov. 1997).

Maglen, Krista, " 'The First Line of Defence': British Quarantine ... 19th Century," *Social History of Medicine* (UK), Vol. 15, No. 3 (2002).

Martin, Sidney W., editor, "A New Englander's Impressions of Georgia in 1817–1818: Extracts from the diary of Ebenezer Kellogg," *Journal of Southern History*, 1946 (12).

McDonald, J. C., "The History of Quarantine in Britain during the 19th Century," *Bulletin of the History of Medicine* (USA), Vol. XXV, No. 1 (Jan-Feb 1951.)

Owen, J. R., "The Post Office Packet Service 1821–37: Development of a Steam-Powered Fleet," *The Mariner's Mirror*, Vol. 88 (2), 2002.

Rogers, Eustace B., USN, "Early Atlantic Steam Navigation, and the Cruise of the Savannah," *Ballou's Monthy Magazine*, February 1883.

Smith, Junius, "Origin of Atlantic Steam Navigation," *The Merchants' Magazine and Commercial Review* (New York), XVI, February 1847.

Wall, Richard B., "New London's Hall of Fame—Captains Moses Rogers and Stevens Rogers," *The Anchor* (New London), Vol. V, No. 7, December 1925.

Wardle, Arthur C., "Early Steamships on the Mersey, 1815–1820," *Transactions of the Historic Society of Lancashire and Cheshire*, Vol. XCII, 1940.

Webber, Mabel L., "Inscriptions from the Independent or Congregational (Circular) Church Yard, Charleston, S.C.," *South Carolina Historical and Genealogical Magazine*, Volume XXIX (1928).

White, D. Fedotoff, "A Russian Sketches Philadelphia," *Pennsylvania Magazine of History and Biography*, Vol. 75, No. 1 (Jan. 1951).

Whittet-Thomson, David, "Documents: Robert Fulton's *North River Steam Boat*," *The American Neptune*, #32 (1972).

Woolrich, A. P., "John Farey Jr. (1791–1851): Engineer and Polymath," *History of Technology*, Vol. 19 (1997).

—, "Register of the Independent Congregational (Circular) Church of Charleston, S.C.," *South Carolina Historical and Genealogical Magazine*, Volumes XXXIII (1932) and XXXIV (1933).

SELECTED INDIVIDUALS' MANUSCRIPTS:

Abbot, Abiel, *Diary/Journal*, PEM.
Adams, John Quincy, *Papers*, MHS.
Barclay, Thomas, *Papers*, NYHS.
Billings, Coddington, *Collection*, CSL.
Campbell, George Washington, *Papers*, LOC.
Chase, Philander, *Journal on Board the USS Guerriere*, LOC.
Cochrane, Thomas, *Papers*, NAS.
Copland, Captain James, *Logbook of the Brig Boxer*, NYPL.
Dundas, Robert Saunders, *Papers*, DU-ML.
Galloway, Alexander, *Letterbook*, NAS.
Gibbons, Thomas, *Papers*, Drew University Archives.
Graham, Robert, *Letterbook 1819~1820*, privately held.
Graham, Thomas, *Papers*, NLS.
Hendricks, Harmon, *Waste Book*, NYHS.
Hubbard, Thomas H., *Papers*, LOC.
Kellogg, Ebenezer, *Diary 1817–1818*, University of Georgia Archives.
Logan, Deborah, *Diary*, HSP.
Plumer, William and William Jr., *Papers* (microfilm), LOC.
Porter, David, *Papers*, LOC.
Rodgers, John, *Papers*, LOC.
Rush, Richard, *Papers*, PUL.
Scarbrough, William, *Collection*, GSA.
Steamship *Savannah*, *Logbook*, SI.
Stevens, John, *Papers*, NJHS.
Thompson, Jeremiah, *Letter Copybook*, MYS.
Torrey, Mary Turner Sergent, *Travel Diary 1814–1815*, MHS.
Vail, Stephen, *Papers*, HSA.
Wall, Richard, *Papers*, NLCHS.

MAPS:

Carey, Henry C., *District of Columbia*, 1822.
Carpelan, W. M., *Stockholm*, 1817.
Colburn, Henry (publisher), *St. Petersburgh*, 1827.
Creighton, R., *Map of the County Palatine of Lancaster...*, 1818.
Eddy, John H., *Map of the Country Thirty Miles Round the City of New York*, 1812.
Hooker, W., *Plan of the City of New York*, 1817.
King, Robert et al, *A Map of the City of Washington...*, 1818.
Klinkowström, Axel Leonhard and Müller, C., *Plan af Philadelphia*, 1824.
Mills, Robert, *Mills' Atlas of the State of South Carolina*, 1825.
Stouf, I., *Plan of the City & Harbour of Savannah...*, 1818.
Swire, William, *Liverpool and its Environs...*, 1823–1824.
Whittle and Laurie, *A Chart of the Gulf of Finland...*, 1818.
Wilson, John, *A Map of South Carolina*, 1822.

NEWSPAPERS/PERIODICALS:

Denmark:

Dagen (Copenhagen)

India:

Bengal Hurkaru (Calcutta)
Bombay Courier

Ireland:

The Belfast News Letter
Carrick's Morning Post (Dublin)
The Dublin Journal
The Freeman's Journal (Dublin)
The Patriot (Dublin)
The Southern Reporter (Cork)

Norway:

Christiansands Addresse-Contoirs Efter.
Den Norske Rigstidende (Christiania)

Russia (St. Petersburg):

Le Conservateur Impartial
Northern Post
Russian Invalid or Military Journal
St. Petersburg Gazette

Sweden (Stockholm):

Dagligt Allehanda
Inrikes Tidningar
Stockholms Post-Tidningar
Stockholms Posten

United Kingdom:

The Bee (Liverpool)
Billinge's Liverpool Advertiser
The Bristol Gazette
The Bristol Observer
The British Monitor (London)
The British Statesman (London)
The British Volunteer (Manchester)
Caledonian Mercury (Edinburgh)
The Champion (London)
Cheshire Chronicle (Chester)
The Correspondent (London)
The Courier (London)
The Edinburgh Advertiser
The Edinburgh Evening Courant
Edinburgh Philosophical Journal

The Edinburgh Star
Felix Farley's Bristol Journal
Gore's General Advertiser (Liverpool)
The Hull Advertiser
The Imperial Magazine (London)
Journal of Trade and Commerce (London)
The Leeds Mercury
The Liverpool Courier
Liverpool Mercury
The London Journal of Arts and Sciences
The London and Provincial Sunday Gaz.
Marwade's Commercial Report (Liverpool)
Morning Advertiser (London)
The Morning Chronicle (London)
The Morning Post (London)
The National Register (London)
The News (London)
The New Times (London)
Perth Courier
The Public Ledger (London)
St. James's Chronicle (London)
The Star (London)
The Statesman (London)
Surrey, Southwark, Middlesex, Sussex Gaz.
The Times (London)
The Traveller (London)

United States of America:

The American (NYC)
American Citizen (NYC)
Amer. & Comm. Daily Adv. (Baltimore)
Augusta Chronicle
Baltimore Morning Chronicle
Baltimore Patriot
Boston Daily Advertiser
Boston Patriot
Carolina Gazette (Charleston)
Charleston Courier
Charleston Morning Post
Cheraw Intelligencer and Southern Register
City Gazette (Charleston)
City of Washington Gazette
The Columbian (NYC)
Columbian Centinel (Boston)
Columbian Museum (Savannah)
Commercial Advertiser (NYC)
Connecticut Courant (Hartford)
Connecticut Gazette (New London)
The Democratic Press (Philadelphia)
Eastern Argus (Portland)

Essex Patriot (Haverhill)
The Essex Register (Salem)
Federal Gazette & Baltimore Daily Adv.
Federal Republican (Baltimore)
The Genius of Liberty (Leesburg)
The Georgian (Savannah)
Hartford Courant
Hudson River Chronicle (Sing-Sing)
Hunt's Merchants' Magazine (NYC)
Independent Chronicle (Boston)
The Ladies Magazine (Savannah)
Louisiana Advertiser (New Orleans)
Mercantile Advertiser (NYC)
The Merchants' Magazine (NYC)
The Morning Chronicle (Savannah)
The National Advocate (NYC)
National Intelligencer (Washington)
National Messenger (Georgetown)
Newburyport Herald
New England Palladium (Boston)
New Hampshire Patriot & State Gazette
New Jersey Journal (Elizabethtown)
New London Day
New London Gazette
Newport Mercury
New-York Daily Advertiser
New York Evening Post
New-York Gazette & General Advertiser
New-York Journal of Commerce
New-York Shipping and Commercial List
New-York Spectator
New York Times

Niles' Weekly Register (Baltimore)
The Norfolk Herald
Norwich Courier
Pee Dee Gazette (Cheraw, SC)
The People's Friend (NYC)
The People's Journal (NYC)
Pittsfield Sun
Portsmouth Journal
Poulson's American Daily Adv. (Phila.)
The Providence Gazette
Providence Patriot
The Public Advertiser (NYC)
Relf's Philadelphia Gazette
The Repertory (Boston)
The Reporter (Brattleboro, VT)
Republican Advocate (New London)
Republican Watch-Tower (NYC)
Richmond Enquirer
Salem Gazette
Salmagundi (NYC)
Salmagundi, Second Series (Philadelphia)
Savannah Wholesale Prices Current
Savannah Republican
Scientific American (NYC)
Southern Patriot (Charleston)
Star of Freedom (Newton, PA)
The Times (Charleston)
True Republican (New London)
Weekly Visitor and Ladies Museum (NYC)
Westchester Herald (Mt. Pleasant, NY)
Winyaw Intelligencer (Georgetown, SC)
Woodstock Observer (Woodstock, VT)

Note: newspaper titles changed frequently in the early 19th century; some of the names listed above may vary slightly throughout the book.

INDEX

People

Adams, John Quincy (U.S. Secretary of State): 72, 75, 263–264, 317–318, 373, 389–391, 393, 407, 417, 420, 423, 435, 465–468, 610–612.

Adams, Louisa (wife of John Quincy): 373, 467.

Alexander I (Emperor of All the Russias): 72–73, 76, 82, 264, 297–298, 306, 333, 344, 376, 379, 401, 405–408, 418–419, 421–426, 428, 431–432, 434, 569, 606.

Allaire, James P. (NYC steam engine manufacturer): 126, 137, 140–143, 156, 167, 169, 203, 504, 523, 539, 601.

Alvarez Condarco, José Antonio (Chilean Agent to Britain): 321–325, 580.

Ambrister, Lieutenant Robert (Royal Marines): 283.

Amherst, William Pitt, Lord (Governor General of Bengal): 589–590.

Arakcheyev, General Count Aleksei Andreyevich (Russian Army): 431.

Arbuthnot, Alexander (British trader): 283.

Arnold, General Benedict (turncoat): 280.

Arnold, Ira (Speedwell Iron Works blacksmith): 184, 193.

Bagot, Sir Charles (British Minister to the U.S.): 317.

Bainbridge, Captain Joseph (U.S. Navy): 492.

Bainbridge, Commodore William (U.S. Navy): 475.

Baird, Charles (British-Russian steamboat pioneer): 76–77, 81, 402–404, 411, 423, 426, 433.

Bakke brothers (Helsingør ferry service operators): 360.

Barnett, Daniel (mariner, Liverpool confectioner): 348–349, 360–361.

Barnett, Elizabeth (Liverpool confectioner): 348.

Barnsley, Godfrey (Savannah merchant): 598.

Barrow, John (Second Secretary of the Admiralty): 301–302.

Bell, Henry (British steamboat pioneer): 168, 264, 580.

Bellingshausen, Captain Fabian Gottlieb von (Russian Navy): 432, 607.

Bergh, Christian (NYC shipbuilder): 127.

Bernadotte, Marshal Jean Baptiste (also see Karl XIV Johan): 297, 366–367, 369, 375–381, 387–388, 392–394, 607.

Berrien, John MacPherson (Superior Court Judge of Georgia): 241, 449.

Billings, Coddington (Stonington merchant): 15, 21, 149.

Binney, Horace (Philadelphia lawyer): 64, 67–68.

Blackman, Mr. (Second Mate, steamship *Savannah*): 105, 133, 285, 345, 381.

Blin, Captain Hosea (mariner): 230–231, 275–276.

Blin, Captain James (mariner): 229.

Bogue, John (SSSC shareholder): 87, 101–102, 161, 175, 182, 597.

Bolívar y Palacios, General Simón ... (South American revolutionary, President of Venezuela): 308.

Bolton, J. & C. (NYC merchants): 135, 511.

Bonaparte, Jerome (brother of Napoleon): 303.

Vessels

Subjects

About the Portrait of Captain Moses Rogers

The portrait painting reproduced on the back of this book represents but one part of the historical treasure contained within *Steam Coffin*.

The painting was in poor condition when discovered, with multiple horizontal tears across the canvas, some loss of pigment along the tears, and the accumulation of nearly two centuries of dirt and grime.

As is the case with many portraits from so long ago, attribution of both the artist and the sitter are nowhere to be found on the painting itself. However, the portrait does carry with it a substantial body of evidence which clearly points to the identity of the sitter:

1) On the back of the canvas is an ink stamp for an "oil and colourman" named "J. Sherborn," at "321 Oxford Street" in London. Oil and colourmen sold prepared canvases to painters, with a neutral background already painted onto the canvas. This allowed a portrait painter to focus on painting the sitter's portrait, without having to spend time creating the background. Based upon a review of various London directories, "J. Sherborn" was John Sherborn, oil and colourman, who began operating out of 321 Oxford Street at some time between November 1818 and November 1819. Sherborn remained the sole proprietor of this business at this address until circa 1847.

2) Also on the back of the canvas is another ink stamp, depicting a crown with "LINENS" and "393" below it. This is a British export stamp. Its existence means that at some point, this canvas was exported from the United Kingdom, either as a prepared canvas or a finished portrait. Based upon a review of the many export stamps used by British customs collectors, the stamp on the back of the portrait most closely resembles those used in the late 18th to early 19th centuries.

3) The sitter's clothing—especially his neckwear and shirt collar—dates the portrait to the 1810–1820 period.

4) The sitter's coat, in style and color, is suggestive of a nautical uniform, while not being the regulation attire of either the U.S. Navy or the Royal Navy.

5) The sitter's facial features, hair style and color all bear a striking resemblance to the known profile portrait of Captain Moses Rogers.

6) The portrait painting was previously in the possession of a direct descendant of Moses Rogers.

7) This direct descendant also had multiple portraits of Stevens Rogers, as well as other memorabilia of these two distantly-related families which had been drawn together by three marriages to one another.

Based upon this accumulation of interlocking evidence, the individual depicted in the portrait painting is believed to be Captain Moses Rogers, one of the first steamboat captains in history, the creator of the first steamship ever constructed, and the first to command such a vessel across any ocean in our world.

Maps and Illustrations

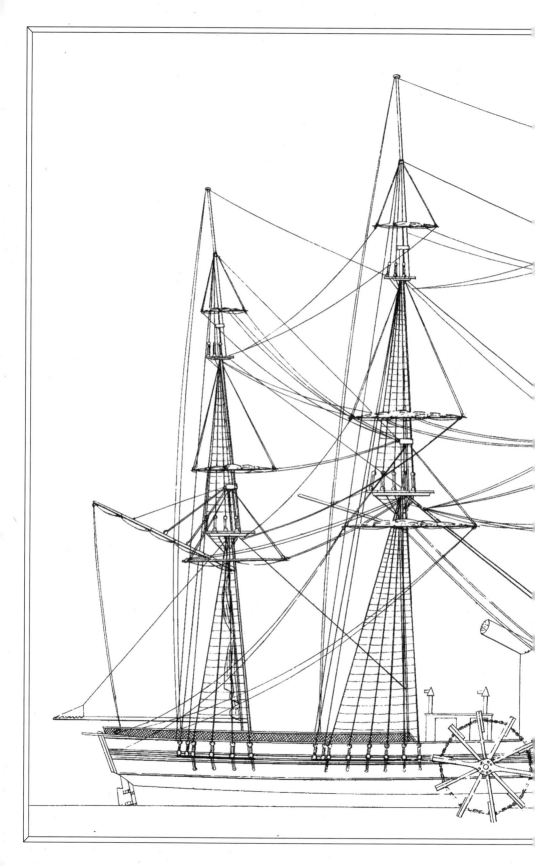